Jan Marsh is best known for her writing on art, literature and gender in the nineteenth century, with acclaimed books including *Pre-Raphaelite Sisterhood*, *The Legend of Elizabeth Siddal* and *Christina Rossetti: A Literary Biography*. She has also written on the Back to the Land movement, and the Bloomsbury artists, as well as editing Christina Rossetti's poetry and stories. Following a pioneering exhibition of the same title, she is co-author of *Pre-Raphaelite Women Artists*, and editor of Dante Gabriel Rossetti's poetry and prose.

By Jan Marsh

Dante Gabriel Rossetti: Painter and Poet
Christina Rossetti: A Literary Biography
The Legend of Elizabeth Siddal
Pre-Raphaelite Sisterhood
Black Victorians: The Black Presence in British Art 1800–1900
William Morris and Red House

Dante Gabriel Rossetti

Painter and Poet

JAN MARSH

PHOENIX

A PHOENIX PAPERBACK

First published in Great Britain in 1999
by Weidenfeld & Nicolson
This paperback edition published in 2005
by Phoenix,
an imprint of Orion Books Ltd,
Orion House, 5 Upper St Martin's Lane,
London WC2H 9EA

1 3 5 7 9 10 8 6 4 2

A CIP catalogue record for this book
is available from the British Library.

ISBN 0 75381 897 3
EAN 9 780753 818978

Printed and bound in Great Britain by
Clays Ltd, St Ives plc

www.orionbooks.co.uk

Contents

Illustrations

Section Two

C. L. Dodgson (Lewis Carroll), photograph of the Rossetti family, Cheyne Walk, 1863[1]

William Downey, photograph of DGR with Algernon Charles Swinburne, Fanny Cornforth and William Rossetti, 1863[1]

William Downey, photograph of DGR, William Bell Scott and John Ruskin, 1863[1]

DGR, woodcut title page for *Goblin Market*, 1862

DGR, *St George and the Dragon*, 1861–2[3]

DGR, '*Miss Rossetti can point to work which could not easily be mended*', 1866[13]

DGR, study of unidentified African-American boy for *The Beloved*, 1865[3]

DGR, study for *Sweet Tooth*, 1863[14]

DGR, study of Kiomi Gray for *The Beloved*, 1865[15]

Jane Morris, 1865[12]

Carte-de-visite photograph of DGR, 1863[16]

DGR, *Proserpine*, 1874[5]

DGR, *The M's at Ems*, 1869[8]

Ford Madox Brown, *DGR as seen August 18, 1879*[17]

DGR, *The Wombat's Death*, 1869[8]

Mary Morris, *Kelmscott Manor*, 1877[12]

Henry T. Dunn, *D. G. Rossetti and Theodore Watts in the Drawing-room at Cheyne Walk*, 1882[1]

DGR, *Self-Portrait sketch*, late 1870s[1]

Frederick J. Shields, *DGR at the Easel*, 1880[18]

DGR, *The Question*, 1875[3]

DGR's tombstone at Birchington-on-Sea, 1998

1 By courtesy of the National Portrait Gallery, London
2 Private collection
3 Sotheby's Picture Library, London
3 Birmingham Museums & Art Gallery
4 Huntington Library, San Marino
5 The Tate Gallery, London
6 Courtesy of the Maas Gallery, London
7 Allingham, William, *The Music Master*, 1855
8 © Copyright The British Museum, London
9 Tullie House Museum & Art Gallery, Carlisle
10 Harry Ransom Humanities Research Center, University of Texas at Austin
11 Fitzwilliam Museum, Cambridge
12 William Morris Gallery, London
13 Wightwick Manor, the National Trust
14 Peter Nahum at the Leicester Galleries, London
15 Victoria & Albert Museum, © V & A Picture Library
16 Popperfoto, London
17 Pierpoint Morgan Library, New York
18 Ashmolean Museum, University of Oxford

Acknowledgements

Thanks are due to all those who in one way or another assisted with or contributed to my research into the life and works of Dante Gabriel Rossetti. They include:

Vivien Allen; Mary Bennett; David Bentley; Florence Boos; Judith Bronkhurst; Sally Brown; Susan Casteras; Julie Codell; Peter Cormack; Gay Daly; Betty Elzea; Jane Ennis; Peter Faulkner; Alicia Faxon; Oliver Garnett; Simon Gatrell; George Brandak; Tim Goad; Alastair Grieve; Halina Graham; Antony H. Harrison; Pam Hirsch; David Horrobin; Julia Ionides; Norman Kelvin; Denis Lanigan; Mark Samuels Lasner; Fiona Lewis; Philippa Lewis; Margaret Macdonald; Dianne Macleod; Peter Marsden and Jenny Ridd; Rupert Maas; Jerome McGann; Tim McGee; Frank Miles, archivist of King's College School; Peter Nahum; Christopher Newall; Pamela Gerrish Nunn; Patricia O'Connor; T. and H. M. O'Conor; Christine Poulson; Nicola Redway; Monty Smith; Virginia Surtees; Angela and John Thirlwell; Nigel Thorp; Teresia van der May; Carolyn Wardle; Ray Watkinson; Stephen Wildman.

Thanks also to the whole community of Pre-Raphaelite scholars and followers, for an ever-increasing body of knowledge and interpretation on which to draw. Sadly, Professor W. E. Fredeman, doyen of this community, died in July 1999, before being able to see his forthcoming ten-volume edition of D. G. Rossetti's correspondence in publication. We all owe an immense debt to his scholarship, which will continue for years to come.

I am grateful to the following institutions for providing access to xerox copies and publications, use of information and in some instances permission to make short quotations from material in their possession:

Arizona State University Library; Ashmolean Museum; Bodleian Library; British Library MS division; Cambridge University Library; Cardiff Central Library; Cecil Higgins Art Gallery, Bedford; Christie's Fine Art; Witt Library, Courtauld Institute; Delaware Art Museum; Durham University Library; Fitzwilliam Museum; Folger Shakespeare Library; Glamorgan County Record Office; Hamilton Kerr Institute,

Cambridge; Harvard University Library; Huntington Library; John Rylands Library, Manchester; Library of Congress, MS division; Llandaff Cathedral; London Library; Mitchell Library, New South Wales; National Art Library; National Museums on Merseyside; New York Public Library; New York University Fales Library; Northwestern University Library; Pennsylvania Historical Society; Princeton University Library; Public Record Office, Kew; Rosenbach Collection, Philadelphia; Shakespeare Centre, Stratford-upon-Avon; Sotheby's; University of Texas at Austin; University of British Columbia; University College Library, London; Whistler Study Centre, University of Glasgow; Wightwick Manor; William Morris Gallery; Working Men's College.

Particular thanks are due to Charles Rossetti for generous permission to quote from family correspondence; to Frank Sharp for many archive items; to Christie Arno, Ruth Brandon, David Elliott, Francis Gotto and David Riding for helpful comments on the text; to copy-editor Jane Birkett; to Christine Slenczka and colleagues for seeing the book through production, and especially to Elsbeth Lindner, for constant encouragement and judicious editing.

Finally, I am grateful for a research fellowship at the Harry Ransom Humanities Research Center, University of Texas at Austin, and for a Writer's Award from the Arts Council of England, based on a chapter of the work while in progress.

Prologue

Of all the notable figures from the world of Victorian art and literature, Dante Gabriel Rossetti is one of the most complex. Heir to a dual Anglo-Italian identity, he was also both painter and poet. Simultaneously escapist and competitive in temperament, he retreated into the past while also leading the avant garde, shunned exhibition while ardently seeking fame, and swung from extreme confidence to despairing self-disgust. His humour was irreverent, his opinions emphatic, his behaviour alternately arrogant and endearing.

His paintings and poetry, fluctuating in popularity and critical esteem, arouse comparably opposing emotions. Currently, his highly coloured iconic images of loose-haired sirens grace countless items of merchandise, liked and loathed in equal measure. Once acclaimed – and attacked for their sensuality – his poems now languish largely unread. Above all, strong reactions are aroused by the dramatic events of his emotional life, now inextricably entwined with responses to his art. Romantically in love with Elizabeth Siddal, he nevertheless postponed marriage and pursued other 'stunners'; buried his poems in Lizzie's coffin and dug them up seven years later; embarked on a culminating affair with Janey, wife of William Morris; collapsed into paranoid delusions following an adverse review.

Oddly, for one who lived intensely in the inner world, Dante Gabriel was not much given to retrospection in correspondence or conversation, and left no autobiographical account. Yet his life was well chronicled and his extensive correspondence is well-preserved. The 'autopsychology' (to use his own term) that emerges from the many sources is vivid, richly detailed and compelling. Born into a cultured yet impoverished family, with a gift for making pictures and. rhymes and indulged as a favoured son, Rossetti was loaded with expectations that he would achieve 'name and fame'. His biography is largely the story of his struggle to do so, holding to Romantic ideals while pursuing material success.

At twenty, his precocious talents made him prime mover of the iconoclastic Pre-Raphaelite Brotherhood or 'PRB' which aimed to break the mould of British art. Politically he was reared as a progressive European liberal until disillusioned by the daunted hopes of 1848. In religion his imagination was shaped by Dantescan themes and Anglo-Catholic imagery, which under pressure from Darwinian theory evolved into oscillating hope and doubt. An industrious artist who aimed to 'achieve something, in some field, each day', he was also given to a Keatsian creative lethargy, commonly construed as idleness.

With a vivid pictorial faculty, his pictures and poems are the record his hand made of his soul's inward experiences. Moving from early poetic realism through medievalist fantasy to sensuous renderings of female beauty and sombre, menacing allegories, his images are symbolic correlatives of thought and emotion. Always, his visions had the quality of intense, waking dreams. 'I do not wrap myself up in my imaginings, it is *they* that envelop *me* from the outer world, whether I will or no,' he once protested.

In demeanour he was the reverse of the dreamy poet. Forthright and imperious, his manner savoured more of the dealing floor than the studio, according to one observer. His language was racy, his wit sharp and unsparing of himself as of others. Bores and fools he could not abide, but he had surprising sympathy for lame ducks and nervous artists. He spent, borrowed and lent freely, yet showed much anxiety over money.

Whatever else he was, Gabriel was loveable, wrote his sister Christina; and indeed he was very generally loved and liked – by his family and friends, by colleagues and students at the Working Men's College and by his models and muses. It was said that there was not a woman he could not have won, and hardly a man who could resist his generous, genuine charm. Laughingly, one friend called him 'the Sultan – for when Rossetti wishes anything done, a dozen fellows fly to serve him'. Warmly sociable, he had many friends in the world of Victorian art and literature: John Millais, Holman Hunt, Robert Browning, John Ruskin, William Morris, Edward Burne-Jones, Algernon Swinburne, James Whistler.

Yet beneath or beside the geniality was another self – perverse, melancholic, subject to baleful moods and scowling outbursts. Idealising women, he also held the 'satanic' powers of evil and envy to be female in origin. A total abstainer until the age of forty, he then became addicted to whisky and chloral. Irascible and intolerant, in the depths of depression he felt himself accursed, surrounded by enemies. So his contrarious character continues to fascinate.

A NOTE ON ILLUSTRATIONS

As this is a biography, and as Rossetti's works are easily and widely
available in art books, calendars and catalogues, the author and publishers
have taken the decision not to reproduce paintings in monochrome, but to
concentrate the space allocated for illustrations on photographs, portrait
drawings and works in black and white. For reference to the full texts from
which quotations of Rossetti's poetry and prose are taken, see the
accompanying volume *Dante Gabriel Rossetti: Collected Writings*,
published simultaneously by J. M. Dent.

CHAPTER ONE

Boyhood

Gabriel Charles Dante Rossetti was born on 12 May 1828, and baptized into the Church of England at All Souls, Langham Place, a fashionable church in central London. Gabriel for his father, as befitted the first-born son of an Italian poet and patriot; Charles for his godfather Charles Lyell, a generous patron to Signor Rossetti; and Dante for Dante Alighieri, the subject of his father's scholarly researches.

'The first associations I have are connected with my father's devoted studies,' Rossetti wrote later; 'in those early days all around me partook of the influence of the great Florentine; till, from viewing it as a natural element, I also, growing older, was drawn within the circle.'[1]

Gabriele Pasquale Giuseppe Rossetti was born in 1783 in the ancient town of Vasto on the Adriatic coast, then within the kingdom of Naples. His mother, born Maria Francesca Pietrocola, was unlettered and his father, Nicolo Rossetti, was a metalworker of reasonable prosperity, for all four sons were educated above artisan level. Gabriele, the youngest, showed skill in literature and art, with poems and carefully preserved Claudian landscapes in sepia. Thanks to the local *marchese*, he was sent to the University of Naples, the first step towards church or court service. But when the installation of Joseph Bonaparte in 1806 removed his patron, he had to shift for himself, writing libretti for the Neapolitan theatre and working in the civic museum, while also pursuing a career as a poetic *improvvisatore*, and failing to gain the university chair of rhetoric. When in 1815 King Ferdinand was restored to power as client of the Austrian empire, Gabriele Rossetti joined the secret society of the Carbonari, dedicated to constitutional government, and the 1820 uprising under General Pepe, when his ode to the new dawn, *'Sei pur bella cogli astri sul crine'* was on everyone's lips. Later, his son's Damozel would inherit those stars in liberty's hair.

With Carbonarism a capital offence, Rossetti went into hiding, his escape after three months organised by the admiral of the British fleet lying off Naples. Young Gabriel knew this history well: as much as Dante, Italian politics dominated the world in which he was raised. He told the story of how, disguised as a British sailor, his father was marched to the harbour by a naval detachment. Shortly afterwards, a summons was received from the government to deliver up the proscribed poet, answered by the message that he was now under the English flag. Ferdinand raged in vain, and on the wings of this dramatic deliverance Gabriele Rossetti left his homeland. In Malta, he was befriended by diplomat and linguist John Hookham Frere, and then sought asylum in Britain, arriving at the beginning of 1824. His political comrades scattered throughout Europe, joining a network of those committed to Italian liberation from Habsburg hegemony.

When Holman Hunt first visited the family in London, he found Signor Rossetti amid a fireside group of foreigners, 'all escaped revolutionists', engrossed in lively argument over current affairs. Each speaker declaimed in turn, 'and while another was taking up the words of mourning and appeal to the too tardy heavens, the predecessor kept up the refrain of sighs and groans'.[2] Gabriel and his brother shrugged; it was always like this. But exciting also: one regular visitor named Sangiovanni had been hunted by the military, and was said to have stabbed a man – a story out of the tales of the *banditti* that enthralled William and Gabriel as boys.

As his father's son, Gabriel would hail the 'sunrise' of 1848, when kings tumbled and they watched 'priests fall together and turn white'. As he grew older, he disengaged himself from politics, whether British or Italian, but retained an ancestral opposition to despotism and a residual commitment to democratic liberalism as it permeated Europe over the next decades.

Born Frances Mary Lavinia Polidori, Gabriel's mother was half-Italian. Her father, Gaetano Polidori, originally from Tuscany, served as Count Alfieri's secretary in Paris until the Revolution when, disliking the Terror, he moved to London, as a teacher and translator. Marrying Englishwoman Anna Mary Pierce, he fathered eight children, the eldest being Dr John Polidori, who attained brief fame as Byron's physician. In Geneva with Shelley, Mary and Claire Clairmont when *Frankenstein* was written, and himself author of *The Vampyre*, John Polidori later showed signs of derangement and committed suicide in London aged twenty-six. To spare the family's feelings – insanity was held to be hereditary – a verdict of 'natural causes' was returned. To Gaetano, the loss of 'this excellent son, on whom I relied for the honour of the English branch of my family' was a supreme misfortune,[3] while for the rest of the family in due course the Byronic connection became a source of mingled pride and tragedy.

Talented and witty, with Romantic yearnings, Frances became a governess, and at twenty-five married the much older Gabriele Rossetti, whose achievements brought a certain renown. With an acknowledged 'passion for intellect', she ardently desired her husband and children to attain distinction. 'I know you are a great keeper of family relics,' Gabriel wrote a quarter of a century later, not doubting that his mother still possessed all their earliest productions.[4] When youthful fervour was extinguished by domestic duties, to her sons and daughters Frances appeared the epitome of calm, self-effacing womanliness, with unfailing moral sense and housewifely competence. To others, she seemed unsympathetic in demeanour and unremarkable in conversation.[5]

After some disappointments, in 1830 Signor Rossetti became professor of Italian at the newly-founded King's College, London, under the patronage of His Majesty William IV. There was no salary, only a proportion of the fees paid by the few students taking Italian, but the position attracted private pupils who provided the main income, so that most days Professor Rossetti went out to give lessons, returning for a delayed siesta in the parlour. In the London of the Reform Acts, he was well connected, counting a number of MPs among his acquaintance.

His other occupation was Dantean scholarship and the explication of archaic texts from early Italian literature. In the evenings the exiles called, for news, gossip and charity. Eminent or indigent, all were welcome, especially if proffering a Masonic handshake. In this circle, 'Don Gabriele' was a man of note. But always an exile, away from his homeland and its occupations, always an alien in England. 'Among my earliest recollections none is stronger than that of my father, standing before the fire, when he came home in the winter evenings and singing to us in his fine voice the patriotic songs familiar to his youth,' wrote his son later; 'tunes which have rung the world's changes since '89; those to which Italy gave birth about the unlucky year '20; and others, harsher and less skilful . . .'[6]

At the same time, his temperament was cheerful and confident. As a father he was warm, intimate, indulgent even while exercising firm paternal authority, apt to quote aphorisms and observe traditions; William recalled him carefully treading round the children as they played on the floor, to avert bad luck. Expressively Southern in word and gesture, like his son after him his opinions were emphatic, whether concerning the Catholic church or the English weather. Once, he declared that if he and a particularly ill-favoured woman were the last couple in creation, the human race would die out.

Bright and handsome with chestnut curls, Gabriele *giovane* or 'our little Dante' was a golden boy, a little prince, with a privileged position as eldest son. He displaced his sister Maria Francesca, his senior by fifteen months, who was sometimes spitefully jealous, and overshadowed his younger brother William Michael. Spirited Christina held her own, as the youngest, though being all so close in age, the four formed a close-knit group. Always 'well brought up', with clear notions of courtesy and deference to their elders, they flourished in an affectionate atmosphere, disciplined without fear. Almost from birth, there was a natural division between the fiery Gabriel and Christina, and the more equable Maria and William. Their father called them 'the storms' and 'the calms' respectively. But Gabriel would also combine with Maria as the elders, or with William versus the girls.

Whatever the permutation, in vehement mood he was sure to impose his will. But the mood passed swiftly, and then Gabriel was the best of brothers; charming, inventive, open-hearted, he inspired lifelong loyalty in them all. Naturally, privilege led to a certain narcissism, and the early experience of domination was formative: Gabriel Rossetti would always be at his best in such a setting. Spoilt, some might say, but also weighted with expectations: the favoured should not fail. After Gabriel's death, William described him without irony as 'the pride and glory of our family', as if he had thus fulfilled his destiny.[7]

The Rossettis lived in a narrow five-storey house at 38 Charlotte Street (later renamed Hallam Street) on the Portland Estate. When Gabriel was eight, they moved to the slightly larger no. 50. Forbidden to play outside like urchins, the children took a daily walk with their mother. One attraction was a large camera obscura on the edge of Regent's Park, another the newly established Zoo. All the children had a passion for animals, the more unusual the better. William had a squirrel in a cage, while Gabriel's pets included a hedgehog whom he once fed with beer, causing the prickly creature to totter unsteadily across the dining table.

In infancy, all four children were taught by Frances, doing their lessons in the family parlour, with additional assistance from their maternal aunts Charlotte and Margaret. They also learnt prayers, Bible stories and moral tales, and on Sundays went dutifully to church, for the Polidori women were devout Anglicans, and this was an Evangelical age. Besides exemplary books, however, there were more entertaining volumes, by Perrault, Grimm and Hoffmann, and an illustrated Shakespeare.

Excursions included visits to family friends, a steamer trip on the Thames or a ride on the newly-built railway. Once a year, singly or in pairs, the children would visit their maternal grandparents in Buckinghamshire, amid orchards and Chiltern woodland. Here too lived aunt Eliza and simple-minded uncle Philip, while uncle Henry, a country solicitor of fussy habit, was not far away. In the large garden, Christina once found a dead mouse, while Gabriel remembered running indoors with some decaying seed-pods, to know what they were, for he was essentially an urban, indoor child, showing no taste for boyish exploration, tree-climbing or ball games. When he was ten, the Polidoris returned to London, and country holidays ceased.

Gabriel's earliest passion was for drawing and colouring. At four-and-a-half, as Maria told their grandmother, he announced 'an *idea* of Drawing'.

Some months later he made a real drawing of such skill that it was proudly preserved among the maternal relics and inspired a family legend. 'Imagine such a baby making a picture!' exclaimed the milkman, seeing him at work in the hallway. Confined to the sofa by an injured foot, he amused himself endlessly by colouring figures from theatrical prints, sold in sheets for toy theatres. Soon after his seventh birthday, he acquired his first colours, telling aunt Eliza that at a fancy fair in Regent's Park he had bought a box of paints, together with a picture of Richard and Richmond fighting, which he gilded and then cut out 'with no white'.

When the prints ran out, he made his own. Two surviving scenes illustrating *The Castle Spectre* show theatrically-costumed characters with capes and rapiers, poised for combat, while the earliest evidence of conscious self-presentation as an artist, around the age of eight, is preserved in a small exercise book containing a few lines announcing the story of Aladdin, authored 'by Gabriel Rossetti, painter of play-pictures'.[8] In compositional terms, this identity would endure in his art, with its many framed scenes of costumed figures. The images, however, came from a vivid visual imagination: as he sat listening to his father sing, he recalled, 'shapes would swarm up in the fire, and change, and run together, and change; faces and figures and all manner of objects, many of them so distinct and clearly perceived that I sometimes took paper and pencil, and tried to fix them before they crumbled ...'[9]

His own earliest original literary work was a drama in large writing on nine small pages called *The Slave*, composed around 1834. No plot was apparent, noted William drily; 'only constant objurgation and fighting'. This was also true of the scenes from Shakespeare that Gabriel had 'the greatest passion' for acting out, the battles and murders in *Richard III* and *Henry VI* being especial favourites. To amuse William when ill he drew the capture of Jack Cade. 'Die, damned wretch!' proclaims Iden. 'Hence will I drag thee headlong by the heels Unto a dunghill which shall be thy grave, And there cut off thy most ungracious head ... leaving thy trunk for crows to feed upon.' The ghost scenes in *Hamlet* were also popular. An illustrated edition of Goethe's *Faust* was devoured. Then came Scott's *Marmion*, Lane's *Arabian Nights* and the works of 'Monk' Lewis.'[10]

The family was virtually bilingual, for though mother, aunts and nursemaids spoke always English, Gabriele Rossetti proudly preserved the language of his nation for his dear 'Dantuccio' and other children. When in summer 1836 Maria was with her mother in the country, her brothers responded with a gleeful duet, in the formal Italian style:

L'amabile Maria
Ringraziata sia

De' due biglietti suoi
Mandati ad ambi noi.

These were the first rhymes Gabriel ever concocted, noted William. *Ambi noi* – us both: figuratively this might stand both for the brothers and for Rossetti's dual identity, as an Italian boy growing up in England.

This year, Gabriel began attending a preparatory school close to home, whither William followed. New lessons included Latin and a formal introduction to outline drawing. At the end-of-term concert, the Rossetti brothers recited the speeches of Mark Antony and Brutus over the body of Caesar. They were clapped to their heart's content, recalled William, for applause was always sweet, and parental pride unbounded.

In 1837, seventeen-year-old Princess Victoria was proclaimed monarch – the first woman for over a century, and a slip of a girl. But if 'God save the Queen' was as yet an unfamiliar phrase, 'Rule Britannia' and 'Lilibulero' were heard on every side. The Napoleonic Wars were still vivid in the national mind and the Duke of Wellington was a living reminder of glory. Economically and politically, Britain was in expansionist mood.

This September, Gabriel proceeded to the junior department of King's College School, located in the basement of the main institution between the Strand and the Thames. Joined by William a few months later, they walked each morning down Regent Street and Haymarket to newly-built Trafalgar Square and then east towards the City, later varying their route, along Oxford Street and through St Giles to Drury Lane. The streets were crowded with carriages, drays, cabs, barrows. Carters manœuvred their horses into alleys and yards. Costermongers sold fruit at street corners; butchers' and grocers' boys delivered to town houses; servants carried messages; rag-and-bone men collected refuse. In the afternoons, ladies and gentlemen paid calls. In these streets, too, were ragged barefoot lads who slept in doorways, and mudlarks who dredged the river shallows for lost and broken items. Waiting for the theatres to open, prostitutes strolled; at KCS, in the early 1840s, the school authorities waged a struggle to exclude whores from the courtyard. Across the road, shops in Holywell Street sold pornographic prints.

This was Gabriel's introduction to the wider world. Later, he would cite the precocious knowledge of 'our learned London children' regarding everything for sale on city streets, including the *filles de nuit*, first identified by an older schoolmate.

The school timetable included much Latin, a little Greek, French and mathematics. In class, pupils sat in ranked order and the emphasis was on information, in Mr Gradgrind's mode: 'In this life, we want nothing but Facts, sir; nothing but Facts!' Enviously, with a lifelong passion for knowledge, Maria tried to compete, borrowing her brothers' Greek grammar. With a natural and cultivated linguistic facility, Rossetti Major held his own tolerably well in the humanities, but absorbed virtually no maths or science, and little systematic learning. He was not top of the class and he won no prizes. William, who fared little better, later blamed peer-group pressure to do as little work as possible, while Gabriel would lament without regretting his boyhood lack of industry. 'I have heard of people being born with silver spoons in their mouths,' he joked. 'I believe at my birth I must have had my hands in my pockets.' Yet it was not laziness, for he could be quickly absorbed in a task of his own choosing. Physically slight, he was timorous rather than tough in the playground; in his own words, he lacked 'courage' and 'hardihood'.[11] Disliking sports, he seldom joined in boisterous games, and refused quarrels, ignoring taunts in an age that measured 'manliness' by literal readiness to square up when challenged. But he suffered no bullying, and once or twice fought tenaciously, as if to prove himself no coward.

One has the sense that the inevitable levelling of school was something of a rude experience for a boy brought up to regard himself as special. Moreover, at home things were predominantly Italian and artistic; at KCS they were English and largely philistine, even though pupils came from the professional classes which admired, if they did not emulate, cultivation. He made no particular friends and despite later fame did not feature in others' recollections. Contemporaries included architect William Burges and painter William Shakespeare Burton. The drawing master was the cele-brated watercolourist John Sell Cotman, who gave out figures of his own to copy; but his one-time pupil left no recollections of this teacher, nor any samples of work under his instruction. Towards the end of his life, Rossetti described himself as somewhat apart from his classmates, enduring rather than enjoying. Perhaps there was some name-calling, in the xenophobic English schoolboy spirit.

At home, his chief passion was for Brigand Tales, forerunners of adventure comics, with titles like *Tales of Chivalry* and *Legends of Terror*. Set in mythical, mountainous regions (often nominally Italian) these were standard boyish stuff, with much gore and a high level of supernatural occurrence; forty years later Gabriel recalled 'a Romance of thrilling interest entitled "Anselmo the Accursed, or the Skeleton Hand!" ' Perhaps in reaction to school studies, any writing 'about devils, spectres, or the supernatural' exerted a strong appeal and all his life Rossetti remained partial to tales of 'bogies' or ghosts, taking a perverse delight in that which science discounted.[12] 'The workday world was not his,' commented

William, and truly Gabriel seems to have lived most vividly in the realm of imagination.

The other children followed his lead, collaborating in 1840 in a plan to produce their 'first four novels' on the same lines, for which Gabriel devised elaborate illustrations in advance of composition. His own story opened in traditional style as a cloaked figure rides towards battlemented towers, 'on a dark and stormy night . . .' His first complete composition was a versified version ('with considerable additions, variations and omissions') of a Border tale from *Legends of Terror*. After a slow start, pirates attack, and gallant Sir Hugh is in the thick of combat:

> 'Strike for the Heron!' was the word,
>   And down upon the foe,
> Foot to foot, and sword to sword,
>   They pressed with blow on blow.
>
> The gallant knight their passage clogs;
>   None could his onset bide;
> 'Down with the sacrilegious dogs!'
>   Resounds on every side . . .

Thereafter the narrative is brisk. Half-written in 1841, it was completed two years later for his grandfather to print in the sequence of booklets with which he amused his retirement. Issuing thus from 'G. Polidori's Private Press at 15 Park Village East, Regent's Park', *Sir Hugh the Heron, a Legendary Tale in Four Parts* offered vigorous if jejune pastiche, with an ending that combined single combat and romantic love in the proper proportions:

> Sir Hugh has made a furious thrust, and grazed his kinsman's arm,
> And from the wound, though small to sight, the blood came spouting warm;
> Then fainter grew the wounded knight, till broken was his sword,
> And from his injured kinsman he received his just reward.
>
> Then stepped the knight to the lady bright, and took her beauteous hand;
> 'I knew thy danger, Beatrice, while yet in a far land:
> And the first sound that I heard, love, when to my halls I came,
> Was thy voice, love, raised in agony, and calling on my name.'

How remarkable, Gabriel commented later, that this puerile attempt showed 'absolutely no promise at all – less than should exist even at twelve. When I wrote it, the *only* English poet I had read was Sir W. Scott, as is plain enough.'[13] But Beatrice is of course the name of Dante's *innamorata*, and although at this date Gabriel tended to drop his third baptismal name, the blend of influences is apparent. He was not far wrong, however, in calling the piece 'absurd trash', for in these days it was Maria and Christina who demonstrated most natural poetic aptitude.

His drawings in this period include a series of twenty-seven enthusiastic but childish illustrations to the *Iliad*, done in February 1840 in response to Maria's passion for Homer, inscribed 'By Gabriel C. Rossetti junr.'; three characters in full medieval fig from Bulwer-Lytton's *Rienzi*, which William accurately called painstaking but wholly derivative; and fifteen scenes for the *Arabian Nights*, including 'The Genie about to kill the Demon' and 'The head of Douban speaking to the King, after it has been cut off'. All are similarly naive, but the resolve to be a professional painter came early. 'I suppose he was barely six or seven when this was definitely regarded, all through the family, as almost a fixed and certain prospect,' wrote William.[14] The exemplary literature of the day gave prominence to citations of early virtue and genius, and child prodigies were celebrated in all fields, so, as if with posterity in mind, by the age of twelve Gabriel was carefully signing and dating his drawings.

His next successes, early in 1842, were a dozen drawings sent to his aunt Charlotte, governess in the Earl of Wicklow's household, for sale in a charity bazaar, with a respectful request for a report on prices obtained. Though he did not receive the proceeds, this may be counted his first commercial endeavour, but sadly there is no record of the results. Taken from Scott and Dickens, nine subjects were copies and three were originals – Quentin Durward, the Highlander and the Dandy. His next achievement, calculated to appeal to his aunt's Royalist sympathies, depicted the hero of Scott's poem *The Cavalier* as a brave gallant in silver armour and red tunic. Proudly signed 'G. Rossetti inv. et del. June 1st 1842', this was, he told Charlotte, 'pronounced by everyone to be the best figure I have ever drawn' and '*entirely original*'. All his subjects came from books or illustrated magazines, one depicting Front-de-Bœuf from *Ivanhoe* perhaps based on a picture of the same scene by Theodor von Holst.[15] Though still derived from theatrical prints, his style was also influenced by the outline illustrations to Shakespeare of the 'universally celebrated' German artist Moritz Retzsch.

Somewhere around this time, Gabriel made his first essay at publication, with *William and Marie*, a ballad half in cod Scots and half in melodramatic verse derived from Felicia Hemans. It came complete with illustration. 'Sir, Should you consider the accompanying ballad not wholly unworthy of a place in your magazine, you would highly oblige me by inserting it,' he wrote. 'PS I have also executed the enclosed sketch, which is intended, if considered sufficiently good, as a headpiece . . .'[16] According to William, the as-yet unidentified editor 'was too sensible to publish either poem or design'. But the double enterprise demonstrates the second of Gabriel's dual identities. He would be a painter, or a poet, or both.

At fourteen, he was the right age to begin professional training. It was agreed he should leave KCS for one of the private art academies that prepared students for the Royal Academy Schools.

The RA dominated the world of art, with its forty Academicians, elected for life and virtually assured of honours and income. The doyen was J. M. W. Turner, now in his late sixties painting impressionistic works of dazzling intensity. In 1839 he had exhibited the acclaimed *Fighting Temeraire tugged to her last berth* and this year he showed a companion pair: *Peace: burial at sea* and *War: the exile and the rock limpet*. 'I am fond of standing by a bright Turner in the Academy,' wrote the young John Ruskin in 1843, 'to listen to the unintentional compliments of the crowd – "What a glaring thing!" "I declare I can't look at it!" "Don't it hurt your eyes?" '[17] Most oil pictures were dark, with carefully graded chiaroscuro. Subjects ranged from scenes from history and literature to landscape and portraiture; animals, flowers, children and idealised images of rural life were popular. Of the current RAs, Edwin Landseer specialised in animals and royal portraits, Daniel Maclise in history and fairies, William Etty in female nudes (then rather out of moral fashion) and Charles Eastlake in Italian scenes featuring romantic brigands. Outside the RA, Clarkson Stanfield specialised in seascapes, Samuel Prout in picturesque topography and Benjamin Robert Haydon in grandiose historical scenes. Star exhibits in 1842, when Gabriel left school, were Landseer's *Sanctuary*, Maclise's *Play Scene from Hamlet*, and *Ophelia* by Richard Redgrave. At the British Institution, Holst showed a striking image of Shelley's tragic heroine Ginevra and Haydon a heroic picture of Wellington revisiting Waterloo, both themes to interest young Gabriel Rossetti.

Professor Rossetti was acquainted with Haydon and Eastlake, and it is likely that the latter was asked for advice on his son's training, for the cultivation of potential patrons was an integral aspect of professional life and Eastlake was secretary of the Fine Art Commission under Prince Albert. The only other family connection with art was Frances Rossetti's cousin Eliza, whose first husband was brother to Thomas Stothard. However it came about, the choice fell upon Sass's art school, close by the British Museum, run by F. S. Cary, whose name it eventually took. Tuition fees were charged and classes consisted of careful copying from prints, studies of drapery and plaster casts of Antique and Renaissance statuary, and the articulation of the human form, learnt through anatomy and *écorché* drawings. The aim was perfect drawing of set items for entrance to the Royal Academy Schools, and Sass's therefore functioned as a kind of foundation course, being particularly recommended by Academicians, whose examiners favoured the 'mechanical precision' of the work that issued from it. As Holman Hunt recalled, shading was represented by 'the most regular cross-hatching' with a dot carefully placed in each square.[18] Virtually all work was in pencil and, as stale bread was used as eraser, the studio was ankle deep in crumbs.

At first, it may be assumed, Gabriel was a diligent attender. By June 1843, he had 'nearly finished studying the bones' and was about to begin drawing an entire skeleton. Study of musculature would follow, for anatomy was the basis of figure painting; while amateur and female artists made anatomical errors through lack of knowledge, a professionally-trained male painter could scarcely do so except by an effort of will.

However, he was often absent with adolescent ailments, being particularly afflicted with boils and skin eruptions. When present, as at KCS he remained somewhat detached; fellow student J. A. Vinter recalled him as 'wayward' and sometimes brusque, a certain lack of approachability alternating with warmth and wit. Once, he exasperated his classmates with a droned rendering of a popular song about a murderess, continuing to hum *sotto voce* when Mr Cary requested silence while showing round a clergyman. On another occasion, Richard Redgrave RA visited the school and observed young Rossetti irreverently making grotesque caricatures of classical figures on the margins of his paper. Such liberties, pronounced the Academician, were inconsistent with the dignity of the Antique.[19] But Gabriel was bored with the Antique, and with perfect copies. He began to haunt print-sellers in Oxford Street and St Giles, spending his (and William's) pocket money on Waverley Novel prints: *The Pass of Aberfoil* (ninepence), C. R. Leslie's *Charles and Lady Bellenden* and *McIvor and his Grey* (1s 6d the pair), John Gilbert's *Richard trampling on the Austrian Flag*. Once he bought *A Shillingsworth of Nonsense*, by the editors of *Punch*, which was 'indeed a shillingsworth of the vilest twaddle', for the sake of forty-eight wood-engravings by Phiz.

In his second year, he joined a student sketching club where members proposed a subject in turn. Typical themes included the death of Marmion (what else?) and the Old Soldier from Goldsmith's *Deserted Village*. Being in a Byronic phase, Gabriel chose 'Minotti firing the train' from the *Siege of Corinth*.

The art event of 1843 was the Westminster Hall exhibition of full-size cartoons by eminent artists for the decoration of the new Houses of Parliament – a display of national pride and state patronage as well as artistic competition, supported by the Queen and her Consort. The subjects were taken from English history, religion and literature, plus 'one or two national allegories'. Eastlake chaired the judging committee, and the results were naturally of interest to aspiring students. Gabriel went on the opening day. 'It is indeed a splendid sight; by far the most interesting exhibition in fact at which I have ever been,' he told his mother. 'The *tout ensemble* on first entrance is most imposing'.[20] Among the prize-winners, his favourite was *Caractacus led captive through the streets of Rome*, by the 26-year-old George Frederic Watts – who, Gabriel added piously, was 'as good as he is talented' and had long been the sole support of his widowed mother.

His letter continued with a disquisition on the state of British art that reads pretentiously from a fifteen-year-old, but reflects current debates on British painting. 'Taken on the whole, this exhibition may be considered as a proof that High Art and high talent are not to be confined to the Continent,' he wrote. Firstly, the common accusation brought against British painters – that they could not depict the figure – was manifestly untrue, since many of the Westminster figures were unclad and uncoloured. Secondly, almost all the competitors were young men, 'thus directly giving the lie to the vile snarling assertion that British Art is slowly but surely falling, never more to rise'. Raised in Britain, Rossetti shared the contemporary nationalism that aspired to outdo France in the fine arts as well as those of warfare and commerce.

He himself had drawn 'some more bones' and was now engaged on an outline of the Farnese Hercules. But, exhilarated by the Westminster cartoons, he was also composing intensively for the sketching club, on the current theme of lovers parting, which he planned 'to treat in several different manners, and to get up in prime style'. Within a month he had six separate compositions, which he confidently claimed would rank as his best sketches to date. When imagination fired, application followed.

His parents, who were in Paris, must have taken heart, for they now had some serious worries. Professor Rossetti had not been well since 1840, when he had completed his magnum opus on the secret lore of Platonic Love in the Middle Ages derived from the Mysteries of Antiquity, in five volumes. Conceived as his life's work, *Amor Platonica* penetrated dense thickets of esoteric knowledge to prove that Dante's writings belonged to a clandestine, anti-Papal alternative to mainstream religion and politics, heavily influenced by gnosticism and freemasonry. Its scholarship was simultaneously arcane, subversive and nonsensical. His patrons Frere and Lyell strongly opposed publication, agreeing to fund the printing only on condition the text was never circulated. Instead, in 1842 the Professor issued a shorter work, asserting that Dante's beloved Beatrice was a purely allegorical figure or cipher, in line with his larger analysis. Reviews mocked the whole enterprise, and by summer 1843 *il professore* was so sick that doctors insisted on rest.

Frances took him to the coast and then to France. In London aunt Margaret kept house during their absence. Indignantly, Gabriel challenged her report that he was reading 'indecent books'; surely his mother understood he wanted to read Shelley's poetry 'solely on account of its splendid versification'. The four children were learning German with genial Dr Adolf Heimann of University College and for their mother compiling a scrapbook of other writings and sketches, for which Gabriel's endeavour was *Sorrentino*, a Faustian tale in which the Devil 'interfered in a very exasperating way' between two lovers. William liked it but Maria declared it 'horrible'. With verbose jocularity, Gabriel told Frances it was 'an unfortunate work, the tribulations whereof have been so many and so great that, if the approbation of others were the only encouragement to an author to continue his literary labours, the romance in question would long since have found its way behind the grate', but which he could not help considering equal to 'very many of the senseless productions which daily issue from the press'.[21] Of course he was joking, and in due course *Sorrentino* did perish in the fire, much to William's regret.

Anxiously, their father inquired when Gabriel would apply to the RA Schools. It was a material matter, for there tuition was free and family finances were now distinctly insecure. 'Remember, my dearly loved son, you have only yourself to rely upon for your welfare,' he would write later. 'Remember that you were born with a marked propensity, and that, from your earliest years, you made us conceive the brightest hopes that you would become a great painter ...'[22]

'You wish me to inform you of my progress in drawing, and of the time at which I hope to become a student of the Academy,' Gabriel replied stiffly. 'Upon the first point I answer that I have finished the outline of the Hercules, and drawn the anatomy-figure. I am now engaged on a finished drawing of the Antinous, which, supposing it to prove good enough, I may perhaps send in to the Academy. The next opportunity for doing so will be at Christmas, when I may probably try, though certainly not unless I feel sure of success, for a rejection is a thing I should by no means relish.' Though his talent was 'undisputably far superior to that of the great majority of his fellow students', fear of failure was acute and enduring.[23] His father's anguish over *Amor Platonica* was a painful example.

The two dates for submitting the required studies of statuary and anatomy fell in June and December, but Gabriel did not have anything ready by Christmas. Instead, he spent two months in Boulogne, at the home of his father's political comrade Giuseppe Maenza, himself a painter, and his wife Clarissa, where he was warmly welcomed; as William often remarked, Gabriel was 'very generally and very greatly liked by persons of extremely diverse character',[24] from street arabs to aristocrats. He returned the affection, acting as an assiduous guide when Signor Maenza visited London twenty years later, and afterwards assisting his widow financially. In Boulogne he and the Maenzas' son Peppino, also an art student, spent much time outdoors, supposedly studying landscape; the local views, he reported, were enough 'to drag out of his bed the greatest sluggard who ever snored'.[25]

Ostensibly for health, it may be that the Boulogne visit was also devised to allay growing friction at home, where his 'laziness' provoked many paternal complaints. For his part, Gabriel had reluctantly to acknowledge his father's failures. In addition to ill-health and critical hostility to his Dantescan theories, private pupils declined as Prince Albert made German rather than Italian the fashionable tongue – a symbolic displacement when gli Tedeschi were ruling most of la bell' Italia. Furthermore, Signor Rossetti's place of honour in the exile community as an ancient Carbonaro was eclipsed by that of Mazzini's militant Young Italy movement, Giovine Italia, with flourishing London activities. On every front, Don Gabriele's reputation crumbled.

Otherwise free of vanity, their father was inordinately eager for recognition, observed William, and could never have been sated by critical applause. Now the hope could no longer be sustained. The next catastrophe fell towards the end of October, while Gabriel was in Boulogne, when Professor Rossetti's sight suddenly failed, almost vanishing in one eye and dimming in the other. Impending blindness threatened to deal the final blow to his career; the family faced penury, until the boys could begin to earn. Perhaps dismissing a certain paternal tendency to melodrama, Gabriel replied only when prompted. 'I cannot imagine that you, who have hitherto enjoyed such excellent sight, are now about to be deprived of it,' he protested. 'I assure you Mamma's letter has made me very dull; it does not contain one single piece of good news . . .'[26] Was this a flat attempt at a joke? He surely knew better than to return a petulant reply to such evidently bad news.

Though he did not go blind, Professor Rossetti remained sick, suffering from a diabetic condition compounded by despondency in which paranoia played a part. In February 1844, Maria, just seventeen, left home to take her first post as governess. Piously, she thanked God for enabling her to help her father, by 'removing the burden of my maintenance which he has borne for so many years'. Soon afterwards, Frances Rossetti resumed the career she had left eighteen years earlier, as daily governess with a banker's family. For the time being, William remained at school, Christina at home, and

Gabriel at Sass's, 'costing something and earning nothing', in his brother's bitter words.

He was now even less diligent, less able to apply himself to cross-hatching. His attendance was irregular and disrespectful. Why were you not here yesterday? inquired Mr Cary. Oh, I had a fit of idleness, replied Rossetti. With hindsight, such behaviour might be ascribed to anxiety, for students often fall behind when troubles occur at home. Moreover, he faced the prospect of having to give up his studies altogether, for it was probably now that an interview was secured for employment as a telegraph operator – a post created by the new technology that revolutionised communications just as the railway transformed transport. Dutifully, he reported to the South Western Railway office in Vauxhall. 'There were two dials like clock faces,' he later told Holman Hunt, who had himself worked as a clerk. The telegraph operator held the handle. 'I laughed to hear the thing going "clock, click, click" and to see the needle moving about in fits.' There, that's all, said the operator; when would he start? Oh, no, it would be quite useless, Gabriel replied; he could not possibly do the job.

If he was to be a famous artist, he could not now turn aside from the chosen path. 'He never doubted of his call to exceptional effort in life,' recalled Hunt.[27]

With the egotism born of inner need, he ignored the domestic downturn. He let his hair grow, and lay in bed late. Often absent from Sass's, he was more likely to be reading, omnivorously and swiftly, with constantly moving tastes. He surged through Shelley, and devoured Coleridge's *Ancient Mariner* and macabre, unfinished *Christabel*, which exerted a lifelong fascination. He read old ballads and the new ones of Elizabeth Barrett, whose 1844 volume contained *The Romaunt of the Page*, *The Lay of the Brown Rosary* and *The Rime of the Duchess May*. He read Victor Hugo, Alfred de Musset, Alexandre Dumas, La Motte Fouqué's *Undine*, Chamisso's *Peter Schlemihl*, Meinhold's *Sidonia* and above all Maturin's 'gloomy and thrilling' romances, *Melmoth the Wanderer*, *Montorio* and *The Wild Irish Boy*. One wholly obscure work that 'seized his soul with spiritual renewal and elevation' was *Vates, or the Philosophy of Madness* by Dr T. G. Hake.

Once more, he could not submit satisfactory drawings to the RA at midsummer, and though some sources record a successful submission, it would appear he failed at the next opportunity also, for in November he went again to Boulogne. Puberty was upon him, and he told William that the market square was full of 'pretty groups of pretty girls' to regale adolescent eyes. Moreover, he was 'gloating' over all the latest French prints, showing vivacious scenes of modern life, and most particularly those by Paul Gavarni of the *vie de bohème* among Parisian painters and students.[28] Then his activities were curtailed and his stay extended by an attack of smallpox, through which he was devotedly nursed by Madame Maenza, to whom he later said he owed his life.

While he was away it was decided that William (who nurtured aspirations to medicine, with no particular aptitude) should leave school. Strings were pulled – many of Professor Rossetti's patrons and friends were anxious to assist – and a clerical position was obtained in the government Excise Department (later Inland Revenue). Here William started on 6 February 1845, aged fifteen, and here he remained for fifty years.

With some lack of feeling, Gabriel wrote that he was delighted at the news and hoped the position would be permanent. He had acquired further covetable prints, including Perrault's Fairy Tales, a 'capital acquisition' for their shared portfolio. And in convalescence he was drawing vigorously, copying Gavarni with a broad well-loaded pen. Two sketches depict a louche couple in an artist's studio; one is inscribed 'No clothes, no money, no wine, no tobacco'. Others show men smoking, dicing and dancing with women.[29] There is no evidence that Gabriel himself indulged in such pursuits, either in Boulogne or London; rather they are borrowed images of life in the *quartier latin*, with all the freedoms that might appeal to a boy of sixteen.

Documented evidence is vague about his activities during the rest of 1845, and it was perhaps now that he learnt to be economical with information. If only to avoid his father's querulous inquiries, he must have been much out of the house, probably in the British Museum, where students gathered to draw classical statuary. The great library there was equally if not more to his taste, with its free access to volumes ancient and modern, in all European languages. Continuing German with Dr Heimann, after a free translation of Bürger's *Lenore* he proceeded ambitiously to tackle the *Nibelungenlied*, reaching as far as the fifth book. 'Let me tell you that 40 cantos (very many more than 800 ballad lines long) are no joke,' he told a friend at the end of the year. There followed *Der Arme Heinrich* by Hartmann von der Auë, a twelfth-century text he rendered into rhyming tetrameters with a Chaucerian flavour as *Henry the Leper*.[30]

He also discovered medieval Italian poetry. Borrowing books from his father and grandfather and making 'continual incursions' into the British Museum, he 'hunted up volumes of the most ancient Italian lyrists', in William's words, and set to translating them, 'glowing from the flame-breath of Dante Alighieri'. He was starting to respond to his namesake. The main sources were two anthologies, *Poeti del primo secolo della Lingua Italiana* (Florence, 1816) and *Raccolta di Rime antiche Toscane* (Palermo,

1817) and though archaic, the language was fresh, lively, occasionally rude.
Preserving the verse forms – sonnet, ballata, canzone, canzonetta –
Rossetti's translations, as later published, follow the *stilnovisti* texts in spirit
rather than letter. Their subjects are love, friendship and poetry, and the
flavour is caught by this rendering from an anonymous author, 'Of true and
false singing':

> A little wild bird sometimes at my ear
>   Sings his own little verses very clear:
> Others sing louder that I do not hear.
>
> For singing loudly is not singing well;
>   But ever by the song that's soft and low
> The master-singer's voice is plain to tell.
>   Few have it, and yet all are masters now,
> And each of them can trill out what he calls
> His ballads, canzonets, and madrigals.
>
> The world with masters is so cover'd o'er,
> There is no room for pupils any more.

'I think that these poems are as yet scarcely at all known in England,' he
wrote a few months later; indeed, they were mostly unfamiliar even to
Italians. While some were too crude to reward either translator or reader, in
his view over a hundred pieces were real gold, imbued with 'tender, noble
and passionate feeling', or simple wisdom, or delicate humour. Dante,
Guido Cavalcanti, Cino da Pistoia, Ciullo d'Alcamo, Jacopo da Lentino,
Guido Guinicelli, Fazio degli Uberti, Cecco Angiolieri, Lapo Gianni: soon,
he had a good deal of material, and the idea of 'collecting all into a book'.
Vinter remembered him pulling sheaves of sonnets from his pockets, when
asked what he had been doing.[31] Many celebrated beautiful *donne*, as in
Uberti's tribute to Angiola:

> I look at the crisp golden-threaded hair
>   Whereof, to thrall my heart, Love twists a net;
> Using at times a string of pearls for bait,
>   And sometimes with a single rose therein ...

Long before Gabriel had any knowledge of women, he had a vocabulary
with which to idealise them. Even more importantly, such idealisation was
the province of art.

Alongside his pictorial studies, Rossetti was thus serving a poetic
apprenticeship through translation, learning the very real discipline of how

verses are filled, motifs developed, rhyme and assonance deployed. He enjoyed the task, and did it well. One might not have expected him to stick at such activity, when he often appeared indolent and easily distracted. Moreover, only a few months before, he had excused himself from writing to his father in Italian, owing to imperfect command of the language. So why did he seek out and devote himself to these early Italian texts?

One reason was that he had time to fill, without a structured timetable to his days, and conscious of still costing rather than contributing to family finances. It may look otherwise, but he was not proud of this dependency. In both British and Italian tradition, financial responsibility was a male prerogative, a marker of masculinity, closely linked to self-esteem. As his later life showed, Gabriel's attitude to money was emphatically not that of Dickens' Harold Skimpole, gaily relying on others to provide. Currently, the earnings of his mother, sister and brother kept the family afloat, at a time made even gloomier by their father's loud lamentations, which William for one found harder to bear than the poverty. In the summer, anxieties were increased when Christina's health also broke down, so that she was sent to the seaside. Doctors, holidays, special diets were all expensive.

Translation therefore helped to demonstrate that he was not the wastrel he sometimes seemed. More importantly, it signalled recognition of his national heritage, personally and politically. By embarking on this project, Gabriel Rossetti junior announced the third generation in lineal descent, paying implicit homage to the literary work of father and grandfather. Since the poems came from the same era as the texts of Professor Rossetti's monumental exegesis, the task obliquely also formed a pendant to those labours, without endorsing the controversial theories there propounded. Moreover, as he acknowledged, many obscure passages would have defeated him without help from his father, so to some degree the project must have been shared, and thus an act of filial support in a difficult time, as he saw his once-heroic parent grow pathetic.

Politically, the translations contributed to the revaluation of Italian culture at a period when nationalisms throughout Europe were celebrating their origins. To show that a refined and courtly literature akin to that of Elizabethan England had flourished in Italy from the twelfth century was to strengthen claims to independence in the present. Gabriel was now of an age to take up his father's cause, and though he did not do so directly, his chosen task identified with Italian history and culture, in quasi-political solidarity.

Earlier in the year he composed what he later described as his first real poem, after the more childish things. The thirtieth anniversary of the Battle of Waterloo – the decisive European event of its day – fell on 18 June 1845. Members of the Bonaparte family occasionally visited the Rossettis. And so in *The End of It* Gabriel plunged dramatically into the psychology of Napoleon's defeat:

> His brows met and his teeth were set
>   And his mouth seemed in pain
> And madness closed and grappled with him
> As they turned the bridle-rein.
> And albeit his eyes went everywhere
>   Yet they saw not anything:
> And he drew the bit tightly, for he thought
> That his horse was stumbling.
>
> There was a great shouting about him
>   And the weight of a great din:
> But what was the battle he had around
>   To the battle he had within?
> A pond in motion to the stress of the ocean
>   A lamp to the furnace-eye
> Or the wind's wild weeping-fits
>   To the voice of Austerlitz
>   When it shook upon the sky . . .

It was not great verse. But perhaps he would be a poet, not a painter. A month later, however, at this year's Westminster Hall exhibition he saw the *Spirit of Justice* by Ford Madox Brown, having previously admired the same artist's *Body of Harold brought before William the Conqueror*. Here was pictorial inspiration once more. And he had a new friend in fellow student Walter Deverell, whose father, after an unsteady career, was currently deputy director of the School of Design. Eldest of eight, Walter was a lad of parts and lively interests to match Gabriel's; at fourteen, his journal shows him keenly absorbed by politics, theatre, racing, landscape, poetry and the arts. After a year in a legal office, he had enrolled at Sass's on the understanding that he had to make his own way in the world, and was also aiming for the RA Schools.

Gabriel Charles Dante Rossetti was finally admitted to the Antique School of the Royal Academy on the north side of Trafalgar Square in December 1845. 'Dear me, sir, you have a fine name!' said Keeper Jones when he heard its full extent.[32] Indeed, his reputation preceded him, according to an eye witness, who had heard him spoken of as a poet and as a clever sketcher of chivalric and satiric subjects. As the freshmen arrived, the other students turned, seeing among the group a slight, dark lad, with loose-curled masses of rich brown hair, strong brows over deep-set dark-ringed eyes and a rather scowling, intense expression. Tossing hair back from his face, both hands in pockets, he displayed 'an *insouciant* air which savoured of defiance, mental pride and thorough self-reliance'[33] but may also have masked insecurity. He dressed with deliberate slovenliness – a none-too-clean collar, unblacked boots, a well-worn coat. Sartorial disregard was customary for art students, but his was marked.

By July 1846, having completed the requisite probation drawings, Gabriel Rossetti had received the full admission ticket, allowing six years' attendance and submission for the medals and prizes awarded to the best students. More drawing from casts and drapery awaited him. The same month, owing to debts and artistic rejection, his father's friend Benjamin Robert Haydon killed himself in his studio, a tragic warning of what failure could mean.

CHAPTER TWO

Studenthood

At the Academy, students were allowed six years in which to graduate from the Antique to the Life class, to draw the human figure, and thence to the Painting class. Transition was by means of accomplished works but, practically speaking, there was little tuition. 'I thought there was no teaching whatsoever,' commented G. F. Watts. The Keeper of the Antique School merely walked round every day, pointing out a defect in the drawing – of the limb of Apollo, for example – 'saying it was too long or too short or too much bent' but never showing how it should be done.[1] The students gained more from each other than from the instructors, added Millais. On a rota basis, Academicians visited to overlook the students' work, and every year the professors gave formal, often repeated lectures on Perspective, Anatomy, Art History. It was an old-fashioned system, aggravated by the unwritten rule that students spend three years before progressing from Antique to Life, by which time they had spent months in front of the same plaster casts.

Rossetti was once observed drawing from the cast of Ghiberti's great bronze doors from the Baptistery in Florence, then one of the less renowned wonders of Italian sculpture but much admired by the current Keeper, who believed Ghiberti to be in advance of his time, and profoundly influential on Raphael, the greatest of all artists. But not surprisingly Gabriel preferred making original designs – knights rescuing ladies, or stirring incidents from the Romantic poets – and in any case daily attendance was not obligatory; indeed, students were encouraged to use other resources such as the adjacent National Gallery with the steadily growing collection of Old Masters, or the sculpture galleries at the British Museum, with the great Parthenon frieze where, as he remarked, the Antique students gathered, irreverently slanging Art and artists over their 'cheese-and-hunch'.

Best of all, perhaps, for one with a distaste for being tied down, was the liberty to be in any of these places, or none, as he pleased. During 1846, at eighteen years of age, Gabriel enjoyed an unusual degree of freedom. He had however practically no money, apart from an occasional gift from aunt Charlotte and what he could cajole from William for the 'joint' purchase of books and prints. Lacking direction also, he coasted contemporary culture, lighting on the alternative and unexpected.

Early in 1847, acknowledging his weakened state, his father resigned from King's College. Now visibly declining, Professor Rossetti sat with a strong lamp and large eye-shade, a shrunken figure composing verses and letters of grief and reproach. He was old, toothless and nearly blind, he told Lyell, and would soon be in his grave.

By contrast, his son had everything before him. In March Gabriel drew a self-portrait – the artist as a young poet in the style of Shelley or Keats, with a 'profusion of elf-locks' as William put it.[2] The steady gaze came from studying his face in reflection, but also mirrored his inner aspect, delineating a serious, sensitive figure, with a Romantic restless soul.

He was reading the works of Leigh Hunt, friend of the Romantic poets and author of *The Story of Rimini* and *Abou ben Adhem* ('May his tribe increase!'), as well as those of Ebenezer Jones, whom he later described as 'the neglected genius of our modern school of poetry'. But his latest literary hero was Robert Browning, who a year earlier had eloped with Miss Barrett and was now living in Italy. Currently, Browning was known for dense, unsuccessful verse dramas. In *Paracelsus*, set in sixteenth-century Würzburg, the eponymous hero is a student possessed of Promethean visions that spoke directly to ambitious youth:

> What fairer seal
> Shall I require to my authentic mission
> Than this fierce energy? – this instinct striving
> Because its nature is to strive?
>
> . . .
>
> How know I else such glorious fate my own
> But in the restless irresistible force
> That works within me?

Gabriel began to mix with other fellows of wayward, whimsical disposition and to cultivate eccentric tastes. Fellow student Tom Doughty, son of the American landscape painter, introduced him to a quick-witted compatriot named Charley Ware, whose 'literary likings' centred on Edgar Allan Poe's macabre tales and spooky, grotesque poems:

> 'Prophet!' said I, 'thing of evil –
> Prophet still, if bird or devil!

By that Heaven that bends above us –
By that God we both adore –
Tell this soul with sorrow laden
If, within the distant Aidenn,
It shall clasp a sainted maiden
  Whom the angels name Lenore ...'
    Quoth the Raven, 'Nevermore.'

Through Alex Munro, a young sculptor from Inverness who entered the Academy Schools in April 1847, the Rossetti brothers came to know a certain Major Campbell, formerly of the Indian army, an 'amusing, chatty talker' who dabbled in literature and once a week offered tea, tobacco (which William alone accepted) and literary conversation spiced with gossip and stories. In comic mode, Rossetti drafted a macabre ballad called *The Dutchman's Wager*, based on the folk-tale of a smoking duel with the Devil, whose ending surely evokes the evenings spent in Campbell's company:

' "Well, well," said the Major, resuming his pipe, whence the vapour issues with a sigh for human incredulity. "You need not believe it, but it has all the elements of belief. For was it not told to someone who told it to me; and have I not now told it to you; and will you not in your turn tell it again?" '[3]

Flatteringly, Campbell predicted great things for Gabriel's future. The occasion may well have been the first version of the poem that would become Rossetti's most famous:

The blessed damsel leaned against
  The silver bar of heaven
Her eyes knew more of rest and shade
  Than a deep water, even.
She had three lilies in her hand,
  And the stars in her hair were seven.

This, he said towards the end of his life, 'I wrote (and have altered little since) when I was 18.' Its immediate inspiration was Lenore, the 'sainted maiden' mourned in *The Raven*. Poe, Rossetti explained, had 'done the utmost it was possible to do with the grief of the lover on earth, and so I determined to reverse the conditions and give utterance to the yearning of the loved one in heaven'.[4]

The Damozel (as she became) inhabits a Dantesque heaven, as might have been expected. Her lover's vision of her state has much in common with that of Beatrice at the close of the *Vita Nuova*, the text of Dante's youthful, concealed passion, which in due course would form the centrepiece of Rossetti's translations from the Italian. Numerous additional literary sources have been cited: Cino da Pistoia, Petrarch, Cavalcanti, Coleridge, Keats, *Queen Mab*, *Faust*. To these names should surely be added those of Felicia Hemans, mourning poet par excellence, Ebenezer Jones and Elizabeth Barrett Browning, whose *Poet's Vow* provided the verse form. But *The Blessed Damozel* is imitative of none of these, nor of the mellifluous pieties poured out by minor poets on grief and heavenly consolation. It has weak passages, and awkward ones, but vivid picturing, with verbal immediacy and archaic language (its 'Gothic manner' as Rossetti put it[5]), give the verse an intense, naive charm that more mature writing could hardly emulate. Subsequent changes to the text underline its importance; in many ways the *Damozel* remained Rossetti's signature piece. It marked his first true accession of poetic power.

> She gazed, and listened, and then said,
>   Less sad of speech than mild:
> 'All this is when he comes.' She ceased;
>   The light thrilled past her, filled
> With Angels, in strong level lapse.
>   Her eyes prayed, and she smiled.
>
> (I saw her smile.) But soon their flight
>   Was vague 'mid the poised spheres.
> And then she cast her arm along
>   The golden barriers,
> And laid her face between her hands,
>   And wept. (I heard her tears.)

Most strikingly, the damsel is amorous, envisaging a holy but surely consummated reunion, as the lovers lie in the shadow of the 'living mystic tree'. Though dead, she is no spirit, but a warm-bosomed woman of chaste but distinctly physical desires. And yet, at the same time she stands for the unrealisable, neo-platonic ideal.

Always taken at face value as one of romantic love, the theme however additionally holds hidden reference to Rossetti's political heritage. The figure with three lilies and seven stars awaiting the arrival of her lover would in this interpretation be Italy longing for liberation – the stars loosely standing for her regions. In *Sei pur bella*, his father had so apostrophised the dawn of freedom in his homeland:

> Lovely art thou, stars within thy hair,
>   Shine as with the living sapphire's ray;

Sweet indeed the fragrance of thy breast,
Rosy-vestured harbinger of day.

With the smile of realised desire
Thou declarest from the neighbouring height
That in all Italia's garden bright
Bondage is for ever done away ...

In thy crown perennial lilies blow ...

A second poem in comparable vein was entitled 'On Mary's Portrait, which I painted six years ago'. Later recast as *The Portrait*, this was a monologue in the voice of a painter who, inspired by the poetry of Keats and Hunt, muses on the picture of his now dead beloved. In imagination he returns to happier days, with the discreet yet palpable eroticism that would become a Rossettian hallmark:

How long we sat there, who shall say?
   There was no Time while we sat there.
But I remember that we found
   Very few words, and then our hair
Had to be untangled when we rose.
The day was burning to its close
   This side and that, like molten walls
   The skies stood round; at intervals
Swept with long weary flights of crows.

This intensely imagined vision was fictional. Gabriel had no beloved, no romantic relationship. 'I loved thee ere I loved a woman, Love,' he wrote later.[6] He had desires, however, and a poetic vocabulary with which to express them. Verse, it would moreover appear, offered the blend of idealism, modernity, romance and daring that he craved, and that the RA Schools did not provide.

Around this time, possibly through Charley Ware, Gabriel also met Philip Bailey, author of *Festus*, who belonged to a group of younger writers whom critics dubbed 'the Spasmodics' since their verse lacked suavity and decorum, and was packed with abrupt, extravagant imagery. Spasmodic poems tended to be obscure, violent and verbose, delineating intense psychological conflict. Protagonists were lonely, unappreciated poets, full of ambition, inner turmoil and Faustian fantasies. In Bailey's poem, the existential hero – one of Paracelsus's fellow students – enters into dialogue with Lucifer, dramatising a long struggle over his soul. Though now deservedly forgotten, *Festus* enjoyed a distinct *réclame*. Comparing it with the Book of Job, *Faust*, *Manfred*, *Prometheus* and *The Excursion*, critic George Gilfillan said it solved 'the grand problem of the reconciliation of the individual to God'. So Gabriel Rossetti was far from alone in declaring it 'sublime'.[7]

'My spirit is on edge,' Festus declares: 'I can enjoy Nought which has not the honeyed sting of sin, That soothing fret which makes the young untried Longing to be beforehand with their nature ...' Charley Ware lived in lodgings, apparently with a woman. Carefully brought up, still sharing a bedroom with his brother, Gabriel was young enough to find glamour in the life thus revealed. The frames began to unfold: liberty, licence; wisdom, worldliness; sin, sophistication; devilment, depravity. With juvenile bravado, he began to flirt with transgression. In his beloved prints, Faust's confrontation with Mephistopheles was thrillingly depicted by Retzsch and Delacroix. In *Sorrentino*, his adolescent excursion into *diablerie*, the Devil had been antagonist, as also in a projected prose tale called *Deuced Odd*, where the Fiend was disguised as an actor; at this age, William recalled, his brother entered fully into the satanic spirit, albeit with ironic, would-be maturity.

From infancy Gabriel had attended church weekly, and participated in domestic prayers. Martin and Westall's dramatic illustrations to the Bible were the earliest influence on his pictorial imagination together with those of Isaac Taylor. He knew the Scriptures and the Litany. 'Good Lord, deliver us from all blindness of heart; from pride, vainglory, and hypocrisy ... and from all the deceits of the world, the flesh, and the devil ...' His first beliefs came from his mother, whose faith sustained her through many troubles, and who had been raised in the Evangelical mode where daily examination of conscience or moral reckoning was a typical practice. Such teaching, traceable in Gabriel's lifelong habit of aiming to accomplish 'something in some branch of work' every day,[8] emphasised personal probity and temperance, with the assurance that good children would go to heaven, bad ones to hell. On the paternal side, too, both *l'inferno* and *il paradiso* were vividly apprehended in the *libri sommamente mistici* that inspired Professor Rossetti's scholarship.

Around the time he started at Sass's, Gabriel stopped going to church. His father, a Catholic politically opposed to the Papacy, did not attend, and though the boys might have been expected to proceed from catechism to confirmation, neither was pressed to do so. William experienced a sudden, absolute perception of the Judaeo-Christian deity as a cruel tyrant, and for ever rejected all revealed religion. Gabriel, by contrast, did not doubt the existence of God, but merely drifted away, as boys do; religion was after all chiefly a female affair. But his disengagement may have been hastened by the Anglo-Catholic fervour that swept into the parish where the family worshipped. In the late 1840s Christ Church, Albany Street became a controversial Tractarian conversion centre, spearheading a new religion of asceticism and self-sacrifice, repentance and redemption. Maria responded with lifelong ardour, followed by Christina, their aunts and mother. Later, William mocked the 'old women in and out of cassocks' who promoted his sisters' excessive piety.

With his liking for strong savours, Gabriel might have been drawn to the Anglo-Catholic blend of rigour and mysticism. Instead, he at first turned away, affecting a rebellious morality. Holman Hunt recalled his claim that 'the fact that so many modern poets had been defiant was enough to justify revolt'. Once, when they shared a studio, Hunt was overcome with despair. Hammering on the locked door, Gabriel demanded who the devil was in there with Hunt. It *was* the devil, Hunt replied with dark humour, as he turned the key. Starting to jolly Holman out of his gloom, Rossetti then asked if he really believed in the devil? Hunt gave the standard reply about opposing powers contending within each individual. Good and evil must therefore be equal, Gabriel countered, and 'equally justified'.[9]

This was not the whole picture, however. As Hunt also discerned, beneath all discordant professions Rossetti 'still cherished the habits of thought he had contracted at his mother's knee, and I do not think he ever altogether cast away the gentle yoke from his oft o'er weighted heart'. He was never a convinced rationalist, much less an atheist. Moreover, as for all his generation, biblical language was a second tongue and thus a means of conceptualisation. Inevitably, his ideas of good and evil, sorrow and joy, bliss and despair were inflected, if not shaped, by scripture.

Job, Ecclesiastes and Revelation were his favourite books. A fellow student recalled him once entering the studio chanting from the first chapter of Job, as if reciting the collect of the day:

> And the Lord saith unto Satan, whence comest thou? Then Satan answered the Lord and said, From going to and fro in the earth, and from walking up and down in it . . .

If he partly identified with Job as one afflicted with sore boils from the sole of his foot unto his crown, he also pondered the meaning of a deity who allowed Satan to assault the virtuous man with manifold disasters. In his lowest moments, Professor Rossetti felt similarly accursed, and there are indications that in these years his son too experienced what is now called depression.

Hunt described his own bleak moods as being visited by 'black angels' under the aegis of the 'Prince of Darkness' – whatever he might symbolise. Gabriel called them variously the 'blue devils', the 'shadowed valley' and the 'Black Visitant', which came he knew not whence.[10] As at other times he was sanguine and insouciant, such figures, like those of Faust and Festus, dramatised psychological contests between his Guardian Angel and the King of Demons, to use imagery with which he was familiar. Satan strove to make Job denounce God for his afflictions, and in time Rossetti's inner demons would cause comparable despair. Yet he does not seem to have believed literally in the devil; indeed, he enjoyed Gothick stories because they were manifestly fanciful. Demons, spirits and spectres however offered resonant personifications of conflicting fears and desires. Youthful diabolism was one way of testing their true power.

And thus, in 1846–7 he adopted 'that great painter' Theodor von Holst as his favourite artist, well aware that this was a deviant, defiant choice. An artist of the 'satanic school' in the footsteps of Fuseli, Holst was known for daemonic and grisly subjects. Later, Rossetti characterised him as 'the Edgar Poe of painting'.[11] Works in Holst's studio sale in 1844 included images of Charon ferrying the Dead, Faust surrounded by apparitions, a Water-witch and the Last Day of a Condemned Man. A little after this, Rossetti sought out a private collection of similar drawings, and in his room pinned in place of honour an illustrated engraving – probably that in which a young man dices against the devil for his soul. One idle evening Charley Ware made a vivid sketch of Gabriel, Tom Doughty and himself playing cards with Satan, which surely echoed this image.

'A fig for Satan, Burgraves! Burgraves, a fig for God!' Rossetti wrote in 1847, translating from Victor Hugo.

> The Devil, hobbling up the stairs,
>   Comes for me with his ugly throng.
>   Love on: who cares?
>   Who cares? Love on.

So he began creating an alternative pantheon, in opposition to the approved model. 'Study therefore the great works of the great masters, for ever,' wrote the great Sir Joshua Reynolds, founder of the Royal Academy, in *Discourses* to the students. 'Consider them as models which you are to imitate, and at the same time as rivals with whom you are to contend.'[12] The same principles were laid down in the lectures given by the Academy's professors that Gabriel attended, while to the young and presumptuous who might be tempted to trust their own talents, Reynolds's *Discourse VI* added a warning, 'against that false opinion, but too prevalent among artists, of the imaginary power of native genius, and its sufficiency in great works'.

Such opinion, in Sir Joshua's view, led either to 'vain confidence, or a sluggish despair, both equally fatal to all proficiency'.

In time Rossetti would experience both. But in his second artistic hero he incidentally discovered a stick to wave defiantly at Reynolds. On the last day of April in 1847, an attendant at the British Museum offered him one of William Blake's notebooks, crammed with almost indecipherable prose, verse and sketches. The price quoted was ten shillings. Blake had died the year before Gabriel was born, a marginal figure in the annals of art, dismissed as half-crazed and pathetic in the eyes of the world. A few of his quaint verses and visionary engravings were familiar: *Songs of Innocence and Experience*, the Book of Job, and the illustrations to Dante, since everything to do with this subject found its way to Charlotte Street. The notebook came from Blake's widow, and Gabriel must have spoken eagerly of the artist before it was offered for sale.

William produced the money. 'Across a confused tangle of false starts, alternative forms and cancellings', Gabriel then copied out the poetry, leaving the prose for his brother. Here, to their delight, they found the most outspoken '(and no doubt, in a sense, the most irrational) epigrams', jeering at Correggio, Titian, Rubens, Rembrandt, Reynolds and Gainsborough. 'The Man who never in his Mind and Thoughts travel'd to Heaven is no Artist,' pronounced Blake, who had not remained in the RA Schools long enough to become a painter. Imagination was paramount, not technical proficiency. Such was balsam to Gabriel's soul, wrote William.[13]

Following Holst, in a Northern Gothic visual tradition that goes back to Hieronymus Bosch, he began to produce his own drawings on supernatural themes. The sequence of extant works includes Mephistopheles and Faust, Chamisso's Shadowless Man, a winged demon, a ghost, two girls with a serpent-entwined cross and above all images from Poe: the Raven, the Sleeper, Ulalume. Typically containing human figures in the company of spirits, all represent moments of intersection between life and death, physical and spiritual, outer and inner. The graphic style gestures towards etching, with etiolated figures, scratchy lines and odd, unbalanced composi-tions. In keeping with the unnatural nature of the scenes, the spectral images are sketched in like fugitive shadows. These are the first of Rossetti's visual works to exhibit his individual sensibility. They are intense, expressive, original. Later, he noted how the depressive demons could be chased away by intense immersion in art or poetry.

In July 1847 the grandfatherly printing press in Park Village brought forth a booklet entitled *Verses*, by Christina G. Rossetti. She was now sixteen, and an inevitable gap had opened between them, owing partly to age, partly to her emphatic, girlish religion, and partly to Gabriel's active life outside home in which she had no share. Poetry, however, had been pouring from Christina's pen for the past two years. One Sunday when all were at home, Maria pronounced one poem so good that Christina would undoubtedly prove 'the poet of the family'.[14] The prediction may have startled Gabriel, who had seen himself as leader in this field; at any rate it struck him, for it was he who afterwards related the incident. The forty-six poems in *Verses* confirmed her talent. Grandpapa presented her with a bouquet and a *canzone* to mark the occasion, the little book was distributed to family and friends, and Gabriel drew a profile portrait of his sister with chignon and ringlets – every inch the young authoress – which was inserted as frontispiece into one precious copy of *Verses*.[15] For the same volume he illustrated four of her poems, including *The Ruined Cross* and *The Dream*:

> Tell me, dost thou remember the old time
> We sat together by that sunny stream,
> And dreamed our happiness was too sublime
> Only to be a dream?

'In poetics my elder brother was my acute and most helpful critic,' wrote Christina later.[16] In return Gabriel paid tribute to her gifts, saying she was the finest living woman poet by a long way. While mocking conceit, all the Rossettis were possessed of unshakeable family solidarity, and through their lives he was a supportive poetic brother, albeit on a sometimes fitful basis. He was also highly competitive, quickly feeling the spur of rivalry, and it may be that Christina's auspicious debut prompted him to look to his laurels.

In September, he responded to a request from a family friend to compose an elegy on the death of a young gentleman, in the tradition of Augustan mourning tributes such as Professor Rossetti might have penned for a noble family in his homeland. Merely conventional threnodies were in order, but *Sacred to the Memory of Algernon R. G. Stanhope* was a more original monologue as if in the voice of the boy's mother, gently disputing standard consolations:

> Pause awhile, cherub, in thy song;
> Let thy curl-shaded face
> Lean to us from thy heavenly seat
> With the old childish grace;
> And tell us, dearest – *is* it then,
> Truly, 'a better place?'

Twenty-one stanzas: feeble stuff, in all candour. And the next item copied into his notebook[17] was a doggerel squib, 'written when Louis Philippe visited England, on being told he was the greatest King in Europe':

> Art thou the greatest King in Europe? Then
> May we have no more of thy brethren!
> 'Twould raise to an immoderate point the hopes
> Of those good folk here who sell microscopes.

He would do better. He had the idea of a blank verse narrative based on the tales of his father's comrades hunted by Austrian soldiers, or that of Sangiovanni, who had knifed a man. And then, one day this autumn, he was at the British Museum when a huge Assyrian sculpture recently excavated by Sir Henry Layard arrived for installation. 'And as I made the last door spin, / And issued, they were hoisting in / A wingèd beast from Nineveh,' he would relate. 'Some colour'd Arab straw-matting, / Half-ripp'd, was still upon the thing ...' Its antiquity made him ponder on the rise and fall of civilisations.

In due course, this became a serious piece; for the moment, he was absorbed in a new conviction, for he had spent the morning laboriously copying *Pauline*, an anonymous effusion of youthful angst and arrogance much in keeping with his own moods, which he believed was the work of Browning. Promptly, he penned a letter, and weeks later gratifying confirmation arrived from Florence. 'Scarcely half a dozen of my friends are aware that such a literary sin is chargeable to me,' wrote Browning, courteously thanking his correspondent for 'the honour and pleasure' of his note.[18]

Gabriel and William liked playing *bouts-rimés*, the literary parlour game in which contestants set each other rhyme words for poems to be composed against the clock. Some of Gabriel's resulting sonnets were naturally very Dantesque; others contained very warm lines: 'her white breasts heaved Like heaving water with their weight of lace', and 'She opened her moist crimson lips to sing And from her throat that is so white and full The notes leaped like a fountain ...'

Poetry did not go down too well at home, however. It hindered his progress in art. A 'sharp, even severe' reprimand followed, as William recalled. But to all such reprehensions Gabriel was 'at all times more than sufficiently stubborn'. There was a confrontation. No exact details are recorded, but Gabriel replied rudely, perhaps even mockingly. His father was outraged and distressed. A painful scene ensued, followed by a stand-off. Then, as Christina recalled, their mother intervened, to 'get the words unsaid'. Gabriel apologised. Henceforth, however, filial deference was largely formal, though long afterwards the incident would return to haunt him. 'My brother, more than our father, was in the wrong,' William noted.[19]

But the rebuke was effective, for Gabriel did not mean to fail. This summer, Deverell had a work accepted for the RA exhibition, the premier showcase, as did James Collinson, a fellow student who worshipped at the Rossettis' church, while the Academy's boy wonder John Millais, younger than Gabriel, was in his second year as exhibitor. It was time to begin in earnest. His chosen subject was both sacred and satanic, depicting a girl and an elderly priest holding a crucifix, with 'the devil slinking behind them baffled' and the title *Retro me Sathana!*[20]

Pious in theme but bold in treatment, this was both diabolic and Catholic. Images of Satan belonged to superstition, while cassocked priests and Latin quotations were read as attacks on the English Church and state in the current atmosphere of controversy over the reintroduction of Catholic bishops in Britain. Yet the image was vividly relevant to Tractarian fervour, offering to those like Maria and Christina a symbolic pictorialisation of their rejection of the devil and all his works by means of devotion to the Cross. Perhaps the young woman in Gabriel's composition was partly inspired by his sisters. The first Anglican sisterhood since the Reformation had recently been established in Christ Church parish and Maria ardently desired to take the veil.

The composition was carefully drawn out, on a canvas of reasonable size. But to paint, Gabriel had to find other premises. Oils and pigments are not compatible with family life, and in any case, as he told Walter Deverell early in 1848, their house was being decorated 'and all my traps have been moved up into an attic, to make room for ladders, whitewash-pails, and suchlike gear'.[21] So he was working in the studio of John Hancock, a young sculptor, just off the Hampstead Road, where he would be 'all day and every day' until the exhibition deadline in March.

Gabriel had met Hancock at Sass's, and sat to him for a profile portrait that is the earliest surviving image of Rossetti in adulthood, emphasising his full lips and tousled hair. In exchange for studio space, Gabriel offered tuition in Italian, for Hancock hoped to study in Rome, the sculptural centre of Europe. To Hancock's young cousin Tom, Rossetti appeared 'joyous, buoyant, defiant, hearty'. As they chatted around the table, he would dash off pen-and-ink sketches, or, picking up on the slang term 'slosh' for anything weak or conventional, he jeered at Sir 'Sloshua' Reynolds. 'How much I owe to listening to his talk at a very impressionable age,' recalled Tom. 'It was from him I first learnt, what scarcely any schoolmaster would have taught at that time, that Shelley and Keats were great poets.'[22]

But though he remembered Gabriel irreverently intoning the words of

Job as he entered the studio – an apt text for the subject on the easel – Tom Hancock recalled nothing of an oil painting. According to William, *Retro me* was worked on for three or four months[23] before being shown to Eastlake, lately Keeper of the National Gallery, for an encouraging word; would this please the RA jury? Eastlake was most *dis*couraging. Quietly, the canvas was put aside, and later destroyed.

Lack of skill was a factor – Rossetti had received no instruction in the use of oils, relying on the power of 'native genius' in defiance of the great Reynolds – but the subject was decidedly objectionable to Eastlake, whose religion was of a most orthodox kind.

'In the lexicon of youth, which fate reserves / For a bright manhood, there is no such word as – *fail*!' wrote Bulwer-Lytton, author of *Rienzi*. Rossetti never spoke of this rebuff, though he may have suffered when Deverell's own picture of Margaret from *Faust* was accepted for the 1848 Academy. With understandable pique he turned back to literature. In March he copied out his Italian translations from the poets of the *dolce stil nuovo* and sent them with some original poems to Leigh Hunt, asking advice as to choice of profession.

Prefacing his letter with fulsome praise of Hunt's own works ('I possess all the old editions of your poems and both the more modern ones ... You have delighted me – strengthened me – instructed me: you do so still') he explained that he had been dedicated to painting since childhood. 'Lately, however,' he went on, 'my mind has been directed also toward another object whose attainment, I confess, has sometimes interfered with my steadier purpose; this object is the power of expressing my thoughts in poetry.' Should he pursue art or literature? Ending with imitative flourish, he declared that 'he whose "heart is faint" should at least endeavour to preserve the outward semblance of boldness, or the "fair lady" will be doubly unattainable. And what lady is fairer than the Muse?'[24]

In reply Leigh Hunt criticised the translations (no doubt to Gabriel's chagrin) as harsh and metrically incorrect, but in the original compositions he saluted 'an unquestionable poet, thoughtful, imaginative and with rare powers of expression. I hailed you as such at once, without any misgiving.' The choice of profession was, however, difficult. 'If you paint as well as you write, you may be a rich man,' he continued. 'But I need hardly tell you that poetry, even the very best – nay, the best – in this respect, is apt to be the worst – is not a thing for a man to live upon while he is in the flesh, however immortal it may render him in spirit.'[25]

It was a reply to die for, and came at an opportune moment, when Gabriel had nothing to show for his weeks in Hancock's studio. 'I have been for some days in a state of considerable exhilaration,' he wrote, forwarding the precious missive to aunt Charlotte. 'Not long since I sent some poems of mine to Leigh Hunt, requesting him to read them and tell me if they were worth anything. His answer is so flattering that I cannot quote any part of it, lest it should look like conceit. Moreover, he requests me, as soon as he has moved into another home (by reason of which removal he is in a state of some bustle and confusion) to give him the pleasure of my acquaintance!!!!'[26]

It was this kind of thing that created Rossetti's youthful reputation. Not yet twenty, with no finished paintings or silver medals to his name, his unpublished verses elicited high commendation from a most eminent poet and critic, who had been friend and editor to Keats, Byron and Shelley.

If Gabriel took up the invitation to call, the experience must have disappointed, or some account would surely survive. But it seems probable that the author of *Jenny kissed me* was the indirect inspiration for Gabriel's next poetic endeavour, the monologue *Jenny*, addressed to a sleeping harlot, with what would become a famous opening:

> Lazy laughing languid Jenny
> Fond of a kiss and fond of a guinea . . .

With an epigraph from Shelley, quoting Goethe: 'What, still here! in this enlightened age', in its original version *Jenny* was a literary production, inspired by the memoirs of a celebrated courtesan.[27] While developing Rossetti's poetic vocabulary, it remained an unachieved piece, mainly in couplets, moralising on notions of progress and Man's unchanging nature:

> Like a toad within a stone
> Seated, while Time crumbleth on;
> Which hath sat there since earth was curst
> When man's seed sinned at the first . . .

as well as the temptations of the flesh:

> Peril of mine, trouble of mine,
> Thine arms are bare and thy shoulders shine,
> And through the kerchief and through the vest
> Strikes the white of each breathing breast,
> And the down is warm on thy velvet cheek
> And the thigh from thy rich side slopes oblique . . .

The erring metres might have displeased Leigh Hunt, but the tone was Keatsian.

After a hundred lines or so, *Jenny* was laid aside. Looking back, Rossetti acknowledged that the subject was 'quite beyond me then'. Lacking sexual experience, he could hardly write on such themes.

So he heeded Leigh Hunt's advice, and returned to painting. Aunt Charlotte made a timely offer to pay for tuition, from an established artist. Graciously, Gabriel accepted. 'The motive which has induced me to lay myself under so great an obligation to you is the knowledge that, unless I obtain by some means the advantage which you have offered me, my artistic career will be incalculably retarded, if not altogether frustrated,' he wrote pompously. He did not of course doubt his ability, but was hampered by 'ignorance of certain apparently insignificant technicalities'.[28] With guidance, such skills would swiftly be acquired.

He had a potential tutor in view. 'Sir, I am a student in the Antique School of the Royal Academy,' he wrote to Ford Madox Brown in March, using the address in the Academy catalogue, and again laying on the flattery. 'Since the first time I ever went to an exhibition (which was several years ago, and when I saw a picture of yours from Byron's *Giaour*) I have always listened with avidity if your name happened to be mentioned ...' He listed the 'glorious works' which had kept him 'standing in the same spot for fabulous lengths of time'. He claimed to be a constant student of *Mary Queen of Scots* and an illustration of the Westminster design *Justice* hung on his wall. Would Mr Brown favour him with 'invaluable assistance' as a teacher?[29]

Mr Brown took a stout stick to call on young Gabriel C. Rossetti and, if necessary, thrash him for impertinence. Such, at any rate, was the story told to Holman Hunt a few weeks later and not denied by Brown.

When Gabriel came downstairs, Brown was so disarmed by the sincerity of his admiration that he offered free instruction. 'My first pupil ... will see what we can make of him', he recorded in his diary,[30] and suggested that aunt Charlotte's money be spent instead on the Dickinsons' life class in Maddox Street, open to all on a subscription basis. Kept at home for a time with a recurrence of the 'old atrocious boils', Gabriel enrolled here on 11 April, and then moved his traps from Hancock's studio to Brown's, in Clipstone Street. On 4 May he began work under new tutelage.

Standard training at this date comprised copying in oils and painting still life, learning in the process how to prepare a canvas, lay a ground, grind and mix colours, set a palette, begin the forms and build up figures, shadows, reflections, highlights, flesh tones. W. P. Frith recalled his first exercise as copying an antique model using only black and white; then came a still life of a brown jar, wicker-covered bottle and old inkstand.[31] Rossetti's equivalents were a copy of Brown's *Seraphs watching the Crown of Thorns*, painted in the style of the 'Early Masters', followed by a still life of pigment phials and pickle jar. At times he struggled. Brown recalled him once 'howling on his belly' in frustration on the studio floor, and reduced to maudlin profanity by folds of drapery.[32] But his efforts were by no means discreditable. Though the drapery is clumsily done, the still life objects have solidity and sit convincingly in their spaces; the glass is transparent and the lights are precise and fine.

Having trained in Antwerp and worked in Paris and Rome, Madox Brown had a deeper knowledge of European art than most British painters, but little success in producing works that pleased the public, for he favoured serious historical pictures rather than pretty scenes. Slow of speech, he was warm and radical in sympathies, open, straightforward, sometimes prickly, prone to comic malapropisms. Gabriel's vivacity lightened his tendency to moroseness, while Brown's seriousness steadied Rossetti. Both shared a stubborn independence and subversive distrust of imposed authority. Both believed in art's high calling, without pomposity. From Brown, it is surmised, Rossetti first heard of the Nazarene painters in Rome, the group of dedicated German artists calling themselves Lukasbrüder after the patron saint of painting, whose pictures paid homage to early Flemish and Italian quattrocento art.

Signor Bruno, *all'Italiano*, was warmly welcomed by the Rossetti family, whose sympathy was roused when they learnt that, at the young age of twenty-seven, he was already a widower, struggling to support a daughter who currently boarded with relatives.

Soon tutor and pupil were on terms of affectionate teasing. Facetiously, Rossetti translated Brown's other names too: *Guado* (ford) *Pazzo* (mad) *Bue* (ox).[33] At other times, they were 'Messer Bruno' and 'Messer Dante'. In these few short weeks, they made friends for life, and like an unsworn vow of brotherhood the relationship proved a keystone of Rossetti's life, never eclipsed or betrayed. Through all – or almost all – vicissitudes, his affection for and reliance on Brown remained a steadfast clasp of true metal.

Meanwhile, he also learnt life-drawing under the instruction of Brown's friend Charles Lucy at the Maddox Street class, open early morning and evening. At first, he went with Deverell at six o'clock in the morning, boasting later in life of breakfasting on coffee from a street-corner stand to avoid troubling the household. Soon, however, he switched to the evening class, between seven and ten. 'He and I used often to walk home together,' recalled fellow painter Henry Wells.[34]

The model sat four nights a week, the pose being set by the artists in turn. Many of the models would have been men, since post-Renaissance art was founded on the heroic male figure, but here Rossetti, who had not hitherto drawn from the nude, also encountered the undraped female figure, and learnt through study how real life differs from the Antique ideal.

Artists' access to undressed women was a sensitive topic. It was alleged to leau to licentiousness, in the privacy of the studio if not the life class. Outside the art world, female nude modelling was universally regarded as at least immodest and usually immoral. Rossetti's stiff handling of the subject in later years suggests he experienced anxieties of this kind, and was never wholly at ease with women's naked bodies as objects of close observation. Certainly, unlike many contemporaries, he did not routinely practise nude drawing in order to perfect his skills, and always appears to have been happier with draped figures.

Politically, it was a stirring spring for those in exile. Through Europe, demands for constitutional reform spread from state to state. In February, insurrection in Paris brought memories of an earlier overthrow. Gavarni drew the Defenders of the Barricade. Louis Philippe fled to England in disguise and a Republic was declared. In March, Milan rose against the occupying Austrian army. 'All 'armi, o l'Italia!' wrote Professor Rossetti. Venice proclaimed itself a republic. In Rome the new Pope created an elected assembly for the Papal States. In Naples King Ferdinand's power tottered; General Pepe invited his old comrade Gabriele Rossetti to return. It was beginning to look like a 'year of revolutions'. Hailing the downfall of priests and despots, young Gabriel wrote lines that seem to speak with his father's voice, entitled *At the Sun-rise in 1848*.[35]

In London, a great demonstration was organised by disenfranchised workers in support of the People's Charter. The authorities prepared for violent confrontation and in the Revenue Office William Rossetti was among those sworn in as special constables. There was no need; their route blocked, the Chartists dispersed. The government, largely responsible for predicting insurrection, claimed a great victory.

Partly sympathetic, partly conscious of a historic event, art students Holman Hunt and John Millais went to watch the marchers assemble in Kennington. Gabriel Rossetti, by contrast, penned a disdainful sheet. Satirically entitled *The English Revolution of 1848*, it carried a subtitle declaring 'No connection with the one over the way' in protest against 'unprincipled persons' who claimed the cause was the same:

> O thou great Spirit of the World! shall not the lofty things
> He saith be borne until all time for noble lessonings?
> Shall not our sons tell to their sons what we could do and dare
> In this great year Forty-eight and in Trafalgar Square?

. . .

> Upon what point of London, say, shall our next vengeance burst?
> Shall the Exchange, or Parliament, be immolated first?
> Which of the Squares shall we burn down? which of the Palaces?
> (*The speaker is nailed by a policeman*)
> Oh please sir, don't! It isn't me. It's him. Oh don't sir, please!

'It may be as well to say that my brother had no real grounded objection to the principles of "The People's Charter",' explained William. 'I dare say he never knew accurately what they were: but he did dislike bluster and blusterers, noise-mongers and noise, and he has here indulged himself in a fling at them.'[36] But the response seems to have stemmed rather from disappointment, since Gabriel's doggerel piece critiques the British demonstrators' cowardice not their cause. In London, there was no heroic uprising, merely a petition. Elsewhere in Europe, by contrast, rousing events profoundly stirred his sympathies, as political causes worthy of sacrifice.

All the talk among the Italian exiles this spring was of tyranny overthrown and triumphal return. Now was the moment for Gabriel's projected poem inspired by the story of Sangiovanni, and so he began *A Last Confession*, a dramatic monologue in the voice of a young Lombardian patriot with a price on his head. 'Italy, the weeping desolate mother, long has claimed Her sons' strong arms to lean on,' he declaims. 'And from her need Had grown the fashion of my whole poor life Which I was proud to yield her, as my father Had yielded his.'

Gabriel said later that 'the first nucleus of the *Confession* was the *very* earliest thing' in his first book of poems, 'the simple and genuine result of my having passed my whole boyhood among people just like the speaker'. The theme, 'if any, was my absolute birth-right', he added, 'and the poem was conceived and in a manner begun long before 1848 (the date afterwards put to it, as characteristic of patriotic struggles) and at a time when Byron and Shelley were about the limits of my modern English poetic studies'.[37]

The idea may be earlier, but emotionally the poem is inspired by the events of 1848. For patriotism's sake the narrator has adopted an orphan girl, whom he comes to love. When she proves inconstant, fearing she will consort with Austrian soldiers, the young outlaw buys her a pearl-handled dagger. She laughs dismissively.

> And then came a fire
> That burnt my hand; and then the fire was blood
> And sea and sky were blood and fire, and all
> The day was one red blindness; till it seemed
> Within the whirling brain's eclipse, that she
> Or I or all things bled or burned to death . . .

The girl is, of course, Italy, which proved unequal to the revolutionary times. Through May 1848 the cause of liberation waned. In the north the Austrian yoke was reimposed. France and Britain declined to intervene. The new Pope was pusillanimous. In the south, Ferdinand reneged on his reforms, and allowed the Neapolitan *lazzaroni* to terrorise the citizenry with riots, looting and murder. The crushing of 'the late insurrection' was headlined in June. The Italian spring was over. 'She wept. (I heard her tears.)'

His idealism betrayed, the young patriot of *A Last Confession* realises that he has killed the faithless girl:

> And then I found her laid against my feet
> And knew that I had stabbed her, and saw still
> Her look in falling. For she took the knife
> Deep in her heart, even as I bade her then,
> And fell . . .

Many years later, arguing over art and politics, Rossetti would protest that he did not think 'the apotheosis' of early Italian poetry more important than its nation's unity – only that he could contribute to the former while powerless in respect of the latter.[38] Had political events in 1848 been different, however, one wonders if young Gabriele Carlo might have accompanied his father home in triumph to Naples. More committed to the ancestral cause than he ever acknowledged, he instead turned his back on politics.

CHAPTER THREE

Brotherhood

In May of this revolutionary 1848, Rossetti was twenty. At the Academy, among all the predictable cattle pieces, seascapes and simpering maidens, one painting caught his attention. Showing the escape of the lovers from Keats's *Eve of St Agnes*, it was by William Holman Hunt, the fellow student who had noted him copying the Ghiberti reliefs. The picture was a stunner, said Gabriel with characteristic hyperbole, and so was Keats. Could he come and see Hunt's other work? 'A few days more and he was in my studio,' recalled Hunt, remembering the impetuous manner. 'I showed him all my pictures, even those I had put aside for the nonce . . .'[1] Inspired by the European uprisings, for his next subject Hunt had chosen the medieval patriot Rienzi vowing to avenge the death of his brother. 'But for that event, the future liberator of Rome might have been but a dreamer, a scholar, a poet . . .' Like Rossetti's juvenile drawings, it came from the novel by Bulwer-Lytton, but was now newly topical.

At the end of the month, Brown was off to Paris, where insurrection simmered. Gabriel was bored with still life, and felt he had learnt the rudiments of painting. Could he work with Hunt instead? This was impractical, for Hunt was already giving studio space to penniless Fred Stephens, stuck in the Antique school, and in any case was mostly out, painting *Rienzi*'s landscape background on Hampstead Heath. But he seized on Gabriel as the appropriate model for his hero, and over the summer they became fast friends.

Hunt saw Gabriel as 'of decidedly Southern breed and aspect' with olive skin. About five feet seven in height, he walked with a slight roll, swinging his hips. His brow was high and rounded, like that of Shakespeare; his deep-set grey eyes surrounded by darker skin that resembled bruising; his nose aquiline in profile and distinctively cleft at the bridge. With his 'pushing stride and careless exclamations', he appeared arrogant, but on acquaintance proved courteous, gentle, winsome and richly interested in others' pursuits, much as he talked of his own.[2]

In Hunt, Rossetti found a kindred spirit, with high ambitions. Generous and good-hearted, with a broad English face like Hogarth's, Holman possessed boisterous energy and a laugh that in Gabriel's words 'answers one's own like a grotto full of echoes'.[3] He worked hard, painting all day and drawing at the Academy life class in the evenings. But he often also stayed up late, talking and smoking, and was usually the one to propose a vigorous row on the midnight river, or a dawn walk to Hampstead.

Hunt's closest friend at this date was John Millais, the Academy's marvellous boy, who had entered the Schools at the age of eleven. Millais had helped Hunt complete *The Eve of St Agnes* as sending-in day approached, but this year his own submission, in the style of Etty, had been rejected. Currently he was painting in the country.

They all knew each other from the sketching clubs. Originally called the HBs (as in pencils) one of these had recently been reconstituted as the Cyclographic Society. Though only fragmentary details survive, some fifteen members are named in various accounts. Each artist contributed a compositional design, circulated for criticism (hence the group's name, wittily adapted from an instrument for drawing circles), with the criticism being removed with the drawing when the portfolio was returned in due course. The club suffered from rivalry and facetiousness, which may not have been cured by the introduction of a printed criticism sheet with a stern rubric asking members to avoid satire and ridicule, 'which ever defeat the true end of criticism, and are more likely to produce unkindly feeling and dissension'.[4] But it was stimulating, and the meetings were companionable. 'I shall see you and the rest of our friends at the Club on Saturday as usual,' Gabriel wrote Deverell in January, promising to drag along Hancock and Munro as well. 'For my part I vote that we organise a press-gang.' Too many of the fellows made excuses.[5]

According to Vinter, the group was drawn together by shared enthusiasm for Keats. The earliest surviving Cyclographic drawing is a study for *Hyperion* by Holman Hunt, inscribed and dated 1847. The first surviving criticism sheet, dated March 1848, is for Rossetti's composition for *La belle dame sans merci*.[6]

'I know it was about this time that when the portfolio was opened at Millais's house, some designs of DGR's attracted our regard,' recalled Hunt.[7] This response was heartening, although criticism was not lacking. 'Girl's drapery scantily composed ... man's left leg badly drawn,' wrote Millais. 'Mouth of the lady too small,' added N. E. Green. 'The dog breaks the line of the male figure with some advantage – but catches the eye too much,' noted William Dennis. The conception, however, was '*excellent* and worth painting' (Millais); 'beautifully designed, good subject ... would paint well' (Hunt); 'most agreeable ... sunny, wild, & like Spenser' (Hancock); 'begin to paint this subject as soon as you can' (Collinson);

'very clever indeed' (J. T. Clifton); 'with the rest I say "paint it".' (J. B. Keene). Though the dog was not in the poem, its instinctive dread of supernatural presence was well conveyed, concluded Richard Burchett.

Rossetti's next submission was the scene from *Faust* in which Margaret is tormented by the Evil Spirit during the Dies Irae. In Millais's view it was '*very clever and original*' and '*beautifully executed*'. Hunt said it gave a better idea of Goethe than any translation, or even Moritz Retzsch's famous illustration. Deverell could 'do nothing but repeat the well deserved eulogies': the Cyclographic members had never been more unanimous. The composition, which is indebted to renderings of the subject by Delacroix and Ary Scheffer, was nevertheless also criticised for failures of perspective and anatomy, and for the melodramatic rendering of Mephistopheles, in Millais's view a commonplace devil with horns poking through his cowl, and in Keene's opinion more like an old granny than a spectre. Countering this, Hunt joked that as Rossetti had never seen the Evil One with his own eyes, the depiction was naturally less convincing.[8]

Hunt's concurrent designs included 'Peace and War' from a poem by Leigh Hunt, and 'One step to the death bed', from Shelley's *Ginevra*. Millais's offerings probably included the design for *Ferdinand and Ariel*. At some stage, however, Rossetti (who 'liked to rule his little kingdom with an absolute sway', in Vinter's words) proposed that everyone illustrate Keats's *Isabella*; among the eight scenes listed for choice were 'The Lovers', 'The Brothers' and 'The Pot of Basil'. Hunt drew Lorenzo as warehouse clerk to Isabella's evil brothers, and here originated Millais's delicate, angular drawing of a couple in late medieval dress now called *Lovers by a Rosebush*, and his preliminary design for *Lorenzo and Isabella*.[9]

Characteristically contrary, Rossetti made no *Isabella* design. Instead he sat up all night working on Coleridge's Genevieve, with an exaggeratedly Gothic feel derived from Retszch. This too returned from the Cyclographic Club with high praise.

Perhaps with Eastlake's censure of *Retro me* in mind, he took neither a Keatsian nor a Faustian theme for his next easel painting. His sister's pious fervour and Brown's *Our Lady of Saturday Night* had given him a new idea. Not a Madonna and child, but the childhood of the Madonna. A sacred subject, emblematic of perfect goodness, *The Girlhood of Mary Virgin* chimed with both Anglo-Catholic symbolism and with contemporary ideals of femininity. Submissive, virtuous, obedient, the Virgin embroiders from a lily. The Holy Dove hovers. Outside St Joachim prunes a vine. On the floor a thorn branch prefigures the Seven Sorrows. Painters like Murillo had treated the subject very inadequately, Gabriel told his godfather confidently; rather than reading, he would show St Anne teaching Mary to sew.[10]

Once the pictorial idea was in place, he was eager to begin, making a colour sketch, and a nude study, presumably at the Maddox Street life class. For the head of St Anne, he planned to use his mother, with Christina for the Virgin: her features and demeanour matched his conception exactly. But then application evaporated; it was seven months to the exhibition deadline.

For once he was in funds. His godfather Charles Lyell had advanced ten pounds for a portrait of Professor Rossetti, with fifteen to follow on completion. Hunt had found a new studio in Cleveland Street. To make room for two easels, Gabriel persuaded Holman to rent a small bedroom as well, he himself continuing to sleep at home.

While the studio was being whitewashed, they made excursions, to Rochester on the river Medway and by steamer to Greenwich. Gabriel was versifying again, translating the sonnets of the *Vita Nuova* and swapping *bouts-rimés* with William and Christina, holidaying *en famille* at Brighton. On the grass of Blackheath, he read from the newly issued *Life and Letters of John Keats*.

'I am certain of nothing but the holiness of the heart's affections and the truth of imagination,' wrote Keats. 'The excellency of every art is its intensity.' His correspondence revealed a congenial anti-scientific temper, and an inspiring commitment to rich Romantic imagery. 'Be more of an artist', Keats told Shelley; 'load every rift of your subject with ore.' He also had much to say to ambitious young men, including: 'I would sooner fail than not be among the greatest.'

On Greenwich pier waiting for the boat back, Gabriel startled a barefoot boy with sonorous declamation. 'Shall the tyrants rule for ever, or the priests of the bloody faith?' he demanded. 'Or shall they roll on the tide of a mighty river, whose waters are ended in death?' The lad stared. An old waterman intervened. 'What's the good of asking the boy sich out of the way questions? Why, you don't know the answers yourself!' Rossetti roared with laughter, as Hunt recalled.[11] But the lines were not merely rhetorical, for in Italy tyrants and priests continued to rule. General Pepe fled from Naples once more and the exiles gave up all hope of return. 'Horrible, horrible!' lamented Gabriel's father, in his histrionic manner.

Chi a venti non sa, mai non saprà, began one of Professor Rossetti's proverbs; 'if you don't know at twenty, you never will know ...' One evening, in the Cleveland Street studio, Rossetti and Hunt drew up a 'manifesto' affirming belief only in 'man's own genius or heroism'. Pinned on the wall, for 'all decent fellows' to sign,[12] it began: 'We, the undersigned, declare that the following list of Immortals constitutes the whole of our

Creed, and that there exists no other Immortality than what is centred in their names and in the names of their contemporaries . . .'

Of course, it was deliberately shocking; the 'creed' had 'already caused considerable horror among our acquaintance'. Avoiding outright blasphemy, however, the list began with Christ, who was awarded four stars, as leading 'Immortal'. Positivist in approach, it also included Isaiah and the author of Job, before continuing with an assortment of 'great men' from Western art and literature. Conspicuously absent are Greek and Latin authors, religious figures and major national heroes like Napoleon or Nelson, though King Alfred, Columbus, Cromwell, Hampden and Newton are listed, together with George Washington, Joan of Arc and the Polish patriot Kosciusko. Of the remaining forty names, half are drawn from literature, including Dante, Boccaccio, Chaucer, Spenser, Shakespeare, Cervantes, Goethe, Byron, Keats, Shelley, Wordsworth, Landor, Hood, Thackeray, Longfellow, Leigh Hunt, Tennyson, and both Brownings.[13]

There is now no way of knowing which artist contributed which names on the list, which also featured 'Early Gothic Architects' and 'Early English Balladists'. Above all, however, the List of Immortals is a declaration of youthful independence. The young painters would choose their own role models.

There were rival Italian opera companies in London, at Covent Garden and Her Majesty's, with the sopranos Jenny Lind and Giulia Grisi. The denunciation in the first act of *Lucretia Borgia* was tremendous, Gabriel told William: 'Grisi screamed continuously for about two minutes and was immense.'[14] With the exception of their father, a compatriot of Donizetti and Rossini who had written *libretti* in his day, none of the Rossettis was musical, and Gabriel, who tended to refer not to music but to 'noise', passed on to the Heimanns complimentary tickets for the incomparable Lind. With James Collinson for company, he preferred the cheap theatres, having a special predilection for really awful melodramas. They mingled with the populace and young gents (owing to whores in the foyers, respectable families did not go to theatres) and left before the end.

Here was his natural element, a modified *vie de bohème*, amongst high-spirited companions with diverse talents. He would make trends, not follow them. Collinson was a stunner, he declared, who would be a great painter. Dumpy, nervous Collinson, son of a bookseller in the East Midlands, was less sure. But Gabriel's confidence was great. Finding James with no design for the Cyclographic, he drew 'an angular saint' to circulate under Collinson's name – for which hoax he expected both would be kicked out. Too bad; none of the members had any imagination. Instead he launched a poetical club, for 'all the nice chaps we know who do anything in the literary line'.[15] Soon John Hancock was sweating over a contribution.

Deverell came, and Hunt, Tommy Woolner and of course William. Gabriel swore all to secrecy. Mistakenly, he assumed Christina would join, forgetting the female proscription on 'showing off', and could not even persuade her to let him read her poems aloud.

Woolner was a sculptor, the son of a postal worker – 'frank, decisive, confident'. One night, amid a good deal of hilarity, he and Hunt composed a poem together, contributing alternate stanzas to a declamation in the 'metaphysico-mysterioso-obscure' manner, as Gabriel jokingly described Hunt's portions.

Under such stimulus, his own poetry flowed. The latest piece was *Vingt-et-un*, inspired by von Holst's picture *The Wish*, where a beautiful woman, richly dressed, 'with a peculiar fixedness of expression' sits in lamp-light, dealing out cards.[16] 'Could you not drink her gaze like wine?' begins the poem. As for the cards of life:

> Her fingers let them swiftly through,
>   Smooth, polished, silent things;
> And each one, as it falls, reflects
>   In swift light-shadowings,
> Crimson and orange, green and blue,
>   The great eyes of her rings.
>
> . . .
>
> We play together, she and we,
>   Within a vain, strange land . . .

When Hunt complained of obscurity, Gabriel joked that it was difficult to describe 'the moment of death, from experience'. More seriously he added that the figure was a personification of intellectual pleasure, since twenty-one was 'the age at which the mind is most liable to be beguiled for a time from its proper purpose'.[17] He was within a year of his own twenty-first birthday. His father fretted anxiously over lack of progress on the portrait for Lyell.

Hunt's account of Rossetti's verse-writing is vivid. 'When he had once sat down and was engaged in the effort to chase his errant thoughts into an orderly road, and the spectral fancies had all to be kept in his mind's eye, his tongue was hushed, he remained fixed and inattentive to all that went on about him,' this began; 'he rocked himself to and fro, and at times he moaned lowly, or hummed for a brief minute, as though telling off some idea. All this while he peered intently before him, looking hungry and eager, and passing by in his regard any who came before him, as if not seen at all. Then he would often get up and walk out of the room without saying a word.'[18]

Temporarily, he might be wrapt and oblivious. Then he could be brusque, offhand, even churlish. A moment passed, and he was genial, imperious, witty, given to terrible puns. The moods swung, unpredictably. Everyone remarked on his habit of tuneless humming when abstracted, and his vehemence if an opinion was challenged. Others noted his 'arbitrary' viewpoints: the same thing would be lauded one day, damned the next.

Collinson was working on a long poem on the childhood of Christ, with incidents emblematical of the 'five sorrowful mysteries' of the Atonement. At Christ Church, he had been conspicuous for piety, and now he had 'gone over' to Rome, a convert to high devotionalism in the footsteps of Cardinal Newman. Under his influence Gabriel's notions became markedly Romanish; in all probability James was the source of the 'symbolic accessories' in *The Girlhood*, such as the pile of books inscribed with the Marian Virtues and the emblematic palm and thorn.

Holman recalled that around this time, a fellow student – presumably Collinson – had endeavoured to convert him to Catholicism, and although Gabriel was not drawn towards formal conversion, being always resistant to dogma, there is no doubt that at this period he was strongly influenced by religious ideas and imagery. High Church doctrines featured promi-nently in his new poem *Mater pulchrae delectionis* (afterwards revised as *Ave*), an avowedly Marian composition which, as William said, expressed belief 'of a strongly Roman Catholic kind':[19]

> Mother of Christ from stall to rood,
> And wife unto the Holy Ghost
>
> . . .
>
> Into our shadow bend thy face,
> Bowing thee from the secret place,
> O Mary Virgin, full of grace!

When he told Lyell he hoped *The Girlhood* would appeal to 'members of a Christian community'[20] – perhaps hoping for a patron among the wealthy worshippers at Christ Church, or maybe the devout Marchioness of Bath, aunt Charlotte's current employer – his motive was not merely venal; nor was his Romanism play-acting. If he employed sacred emblems partly in a spirit of romance, prompted by his liking for things arcane, he also responded to a religion of mystery and symbol, which Dante and his companions had shared. Temperamentally, he preferred faith to facts and doctrines of confession and absolution to rigorous English moralism. His imagination was drawn to extremes, with a Blakean idea of opposites or contraries. *The Blessed Damozel* and *Jenny* offered verbal versions of purity and impurity. Visually, *Faust*'s Margaret was complemented by Mary. And where Margaret's fall is accomplished by Faust in concert with Satan, the Virgin's role is the redemption of mankind from the world and the devil.

So this autumn, when making copies of his poems, he gave them a book-like title, *Songs of the Art-Catholic*, in keeping with the devotional mood. They were sent to William Bell Scott, whose poems had attracted his attention and was also a painter. It was the start of another long friendship.[21]

By calling himself an 'Art-Catholic' Rossetti seems to have meant that just as 'Anglo-Catholics' supported pre-Reformation practices, so in art he endorsed forms and subjects from earlier ages; in William's gloss, this was 'medieval and unmodern', Catholic in sentiment but not doctrine. On the face of it, however, like his Marian poem the appellation was certain to be taken as a declaration of Roman sympathies.

Another of the Art-Catholic's songs was *My Sister's Sleep*, written in September. He hoped it was 'simpler and more like nature'.[22] As it opens, mother and brother are keeping watch over a sick-bed on Christmas Eve:

> Outside, there was a good moon up
>   Whose trailing shadow fell within;
>   The depth of clouds that it was in
> Seemed hollow, like an altar-cup.
>
> I watched it through the lattice work.
>   We had some plants of evergreen
>   Standing upon the sill: just then
> It passed behind, and made them dark.

As midnight strikes, they trust her rest may not be disturbed. But, imperceptibly, the sister dies.

> For my part, I but hid my face,
>   And held my breath, and spoke no word:
>   And there was naught spoken; but I heard
> The silence for a little space.
>
> Our mother bowed herself and wept:
>   And both my arms fell; and I said,
>   'God knows I knew that she was dead!'
> And there, all white, my sister slept.
>
> Then kneeling, upon Christmas morn,
>   A little after twelve o'clock,

We said, as when the last chime struck,
'Christ's blessing on the newly born!'

Later, Gabriel would think this 'rather spoony stuff'. But now, with Major Campbell's encouragement, the poem was forwarded to an old-fashioned 'magazine of literature and fashion', where it was promptly quoted in full in a rapturous article by Elizabeth Youatt, who had previously admired Christina's *Verses*.[23] It was, she declared, a poem 'we sit down to write and linger over, pointing out its beauties and dwelling upon its occasional touches of simple and exquisite pathos'. The most exquisite lines were italicised, and indeed the stanzas were liberally interspersed with Ms Youatt's own exclamations. How beautiful! How touching! Gentle reader, have you ever found yourself a lone watcher by the bed of sickness when the busy household was hushed?

Evidently no Anglo-Catholic, she did not remark on the sacramental symbolism. But she informed readers that the anonymous author was 'very young, humble, and yet ambitious'. Somewhat oddly, the magazine's editor-in-chief added a disclaimer, noting the poem's faulty rhymes – 'calms' and 'arms', 'born' and 'dawn'. Gabriel could only relish this Keatsian touch, later writing of his 'very earliest days of boyish rhyming, when I was rather proud to be as Cockney as Keats *could* be . . .' In time, however, he altered his endings, and at the end of his life took Keats to task for misrhyming.[24]

The young Rossettis were doing well. Aiming higher than Gabriel, William sent a poem to the *Athenaeum*, leading literary weekly, where it was printed on 23 September. Following this triumph, Gabriel persuaded Christina to submit a pair of poems, suitably retitled by himself, which were also accepted. He felt protective towards her, perhaps newly conscious of her restricted choices. Escorting her to the Zoo, a shared pleasure, he made her laugh by inventing comic biographies for the animals, and walking across Regent's Park he declared the sunset was setting fire to the trees and rooftops. When she dreamed of dawn as a multitude of canaries, he said it was a symbolic image, and promised to paint it, with the dreamer clad in yellow and the ground covered with primroses. He promised a poem too, but never produced either; such whimsical gestures were typical. 'He was always like that as far back as I can remember,' she said fondly.[25]

Somewhat to the family's surprise, James Collinson proposed to Christina. Barely acquainted with him, she declined, being a devout Anglican. James reconsidered, and rejoined the Church of England. On this basis and with the prospect of a long engagement, Christina accepted, and proceeded to fall in love. Wittingly or not, Gabriel surely played a part in this. Collinson was lonely in London, and the Rossetti home was welcoming. Christina was a promising poetess who at seventeen badly wished to escape the family vocation of governessing. She had no other suitors, and at the very least Gabriel must have encouraged James's proposal. Probably at the same time, Christina sat to James for a portrait and to Gabriel for the Virgin, displaying a timid demeanour to both. In November William accompanied James and portrait to the Collinson home in Nottinghamshire, signalling approval of the engagement. Meanwhile Gabriel wrote a sonnet for *The Girlhood*, extolling the qualities appropriate to both the Mother of God and the God-fearing Englishwoman:

> Loving she was, with temperate respect:
> A profound simpleness of intellect
> Was hers, and extreme patience; from the knee
> Faithful and hopeful; wise in charity;
> Strong in grave peace; in duty circumspect ...

The litany echoed the limited perspective offered to girls by both church and state, in opposition to those who sought a more active social role for women. This year the first serious school for girls, Queen's College, opened within a few blocks of the Rossettis' home. Though his mother, aunts and sister Maria were all teachers, working professionally, and he himself far from a misogynist, Gabriel always retained a rather traditional view of 'profound simpleness of intellect' as woman's true inheritance.

By contrast, the masculine sphere was one of endeavour, self-improvement, mental and material achievement. In *The Choice*, a sequence of three sonnets drafted around this time, he was rather portentously concerned with life-decisions. 'Eat thou and drink; tomorrow thou shalt die' began the first, on the *carpe diem* theme. 'Watch thou and fear' began the second, in religious vein. 'Think thou and act' was the conclusion, with Romantic-bourgeois optimism. On all sides, young men were exhorted to earnest enterprise.

His portrait of his father was successsfully finished, though to his dismay Professor Rossetti praised it over-effusively. He himself feared the work was a failure, and was happier translating Dante's *Vita Nuova*, paying careful tribute to his godfather's own work on the poet and listing thirteen scenes from the text which he hoped to illustrate, including one showing Dante drawing an angel on the anniversary of Beatrice's death. If a commission was hoped for, none came, and within a short while Charles Lyell was dead.

Gabriel deleted his godfather's name and for the first time brought Dante forward in his signature. Hitherto accustomed to signing himself

'G. C. Rossetti', he now chose 'Gabriel Dante Rossetti', which within a few months would transpose to 'Dante Gabriel Rossetti', and thence attain the familiar signature and monogram 'DGR', by which he would become known to friends and to posterity. Thus on reaching his majority he claimed the ancestral identity his father had chosen for him at birth.

It was a potentially hubristic gesture, as if an English poetaster should rename himself Shakespeare Smith, but it is clear that from around his twentieth year Rossetti found in Dante not just a namesake but a predecessor and role model. Keeping always a respectful distance, he appropriated Alighieri as if his avatar as well as his translator and illustrator. Being young, he adopted the Dante of the *Vita Nuova* – a book, he wrote, 'which only youth could have produced and which must chiefly remain sacred to the young, to each of whom the figure of Beatrice ... will seem a friend of his own heart'.[26] Taking at face value Beatrice's words 'questi *fu* tal nella vita nuova', he believed Dante was shown truly in the text, where the character who emerges is moody, secretive, idealistic and strangely modern – a figure with whom it was easy for a young man of Italian ancestry to identify even across six centuries.

Christina later wrote with feeling of the Dantesque net into which all the family were drawn, recalling how Gabriel immersed himself in the life of the illustrious Florentine. The obsession shaped Rossetti's art and parts of his life, through seeming correspondences with what he called the poet's 'autopsychology' in the *Vita Nuova*. His first image from the text, showing Dante so wrapt in remembrance of Beatrice that he fails to notice visitors, might almost be a depiction of himself, obliviously absorbed in writing or designing.

He had been familiar with Dante's own visage from the age of twelve, when tracings of a supposed portrait by Giotto discovered by the eccentric scholar Seymour Kirkup had been sent to Don Gabriele, together with a death-mask. He knew Lyell's translations of Dante's *Canzoniere*, as well as his father's work. He believed himself to be the first to translate the *Vita Nuova* with full sympathy, placing it also in context by approaching Dante and his contemporaries in a spirit of fellow feeling rather than pedantic scholarship. Indeed, he reconstructed Dante's circle as a fraternal group not unlike the sketching club, circulating sonnets instead of angular drawings. As if to point the parallel, in the redesigned *Dante drawing an Angel* of 1849 the features of his own friends are visible in the visitors' faces.

The *Vita Nuova* is as much about art as about love, and the struggle to realise perfection of expression. Rossetti's diffidence regarding his own work was not affectation. Airily confident, he was rarely satisfied. He had difficulty bringing any work to conclusion, the projected or as it were Platonic work never being matched by the actual product. Achievement always fell below aim. 'Ah, but a man's reach should exceed his grasp', was a Victorian maxim, coined by his hero Robert Browning. But Gabriel was never reconciled to the discrepancy.

He had high hopes of *The Girlhood*, however, envisaging it on the walls of next summer's Royal Academy show. But he was nervous. Calling at the studio to meet his young correspondent, W. B. Scott was astonished to find the oil paint being applied as thinly as watercolour, on a canvas so primed with white that the surface was as smooth as cardboard and every tint transparent. In retrospect he was impressed with the innovation, although in fact Gabriel was simply inexperienced. Seeing the picture years later, he noted how timidly it had been painted.

It was slow work. On 26 November, St Anne acquired a red snood, while alongside Hunt's Rienzi put on a white stocking. Gabriel was more excited by the fact that Browning's *Blot in the 'Scutcheon* was receiving a rare performance at Sadler's Wells. 'Of course I must be there, as the great author may be visible,' he told Woolner, proposing to collect him en route.[27] Woolner's Stanhope Street studio was large and cavernous, filled with pails of clay, plaster moulds, wet shrouds. A looming figure depicted the Present striding purposefully over the prostrate Past. In energy and ambition, Gabriel and Woolner were kindred, or rival, spirits.

Hunt, by his own account, was nurturing views on a revolution in art that would accompany his generation's accession to fame. Together, he and Gabriel formulated a grand design. 'In our scheme, when we attained recognition,' Hunt recalled, 'each of us was to have a set of studios attached to his house, some for working in ourselves in diverse branches of art, some for showing our productions to admirers, who would be attended to by our pupils when we were too busy to be disturbed . . .'[28]

But where were such admirers to come from? Oh, Britain was full of rich men, ready and eager to buy, replied Gabriel, cheerfully. His ideas of patronage owed more to the Renaissance, perhaps, but it was undoubtedly true that Britain was prosperous, and on the verge of a boom in art sales, fuelled by commercial wealth. Press and Parliament were full of talk of a new age, under the young Queen and her husband, patron of art and science.

When John Millais returned to London, he was excited by talk of new departures. One evening the fellows were invited to the studio at his parents' house in Gower Street, where they leafed through Retzsch outlines and Lasinio's engravings of fourteenth-century frescoes in Pisa, smiling a little at the quaintness but also struck by the fresh and simple sweetness.

The mood was right, as William later described with understandable hyperbole. 'The British School of Painting was in 1848 wishy washy to the last degree; nothing imagined finely, nor descried keenly, nor executed puissantly,' he wrote. 'The three young men hated all this. They hated the cant about Raphael and the Great Masters, for utter cant it was in the mouths of such underlings of the brush as they saw all around them; and they determined to make a new start on a new basis.'[29]

Hunt identified this evening in Gower Street as the birth-day of the PRB, insisting that it was his idea to adopt the name 'Pre-Raphaelite' in proud solidarity with the artists of the quattrocento, and Gabriel who proposed a Brotherhood. It was certainly Gabriel who wrote a sonnet, *To the Young Painters of England, in memory of those before Raphael*, which exhorted his companions to emulation:

> because of this
> Stand not ye idle in the market-place.
> Which of ye knoweth *he* is not that last
> Who may be first by faith and will?

They should look forward to the 'lights of the Great Past', he urged, newly lit and 'fair for the Future's track'.

Curiously enough, however, the exact formation of the PRB was neither recorded nor remembered. 'It came into being in 1848, or even 1849,' wrote William in 1886. The notion of a brotherhood doubtless came from the Nazarene Lukasbrüder, that of secrecy from the clandestine Carbonari to which his father had belonged in the dangerous days in Naples. But it also seems that the beginning was altogether more casual, at first more of an idea than a reality. 'What you call the movement was serious enough,' commented Rossetti at the end of his life, 'but the banding together under that title was all a joke.'[30]

The initial meeting, if such it was, took place on 31 December, 'the last day of 1848', when the Brothers made a resolution to meet a year hence and on the last day of every succeeding year.[31] Their identity would be concealed behind the cryptic initials 'PRB', added to each painter's signature on their exhibition pieces.

Twenty years later, Gabriel denied being leader or *chef de l'école Pré-Raphaélite* when so dubbed by a French critic, mortified to see Holman Hunt described as his disciple when, in reality, Hunt was the true Pre-Raphaelite.[32] Hunt, who fought a losing battle on this issue in old age, would have concurred, while William suggested a triumvirate title. 'Rossetti had an abundance of ideas, pictorial and also literary, and was fuller of "notions" than the other two, and had more turn for proselytising and "pronouncements", but he was not at all more resolute in wanting to do something good which should also be something new,' he wrote. 'He was perhaps the most defiant of the three; and undoubtedly a kind of adolescent defiance, along with art-sympathies highly developed in one direction and unduly, or even ignorantly restricted in others, played a part, and no small part in Praeraphaelitism. But Hunt, if less strictly defiant, was still more tough, and Millais was all eagerness for the fray – "longing to be at 'em" and to show his own mettle. The fact is that none of the three could have done as much as an innovator without the other two.'[33]

The fact is that each was looking for a way to make a mark. Millais, who had long mapped out a conventional career crowned with glory, was angry with the Academy, whose favoured student he had been. Hunt, with a certain chip on his shoulder, was determined to distinguish himself from the crowd. Gabriel, by contrast, needed allies, lest his singularity leave him on the margins. Millais's technical brilliance meant that no group with whom he was associated could be easily ignored, while the other two offered the seriousness and imagination that so much contemporary art lacked. It was a good combination.

Thereafter recruitment was rather random. According to Hunt, Gabriel proposed Woolner, Collinson and William, whereupon he countered with Fred Stephens, his protégé, and Millais was dismayed by the prospect of so many untalented novices. This has a ring of truth but leaves questions hanging. Where was Deverell, prime mover in the Cyclographic and Gabriel's close friend? What of Hancock, or Bernhard Smith, Woolner's studio companion? Above all, what of Madox Brown, who would have lent substance to an as-yet lightweight team? Who else might have been considered and was not invited? It is hard to escape the inference that, at least to begin with, the banding together under a self-mocking title with a secret insignia was indeed largely a joke, not meant too seriously. Certainly Madox Brown felt that way. 'You will remember that with all of us, whatever used to be thought of Rossetti's, Hunt's and Millais's talents, the words Pre-Raphaelite Brotherhood or the letters PRB used to be looked upon as the childish or ridiculous part of the business,' he remarked a year or so later.[34]

Once the Brotherhood was in being, however, it became a focus of friendship and excellent company. 'We were really like brothers,' recalled William, 'continuously together, and confiding to one another all experiences bearing upon questions of art and literature, and many affecting us as individuals. We dropped using the term "Esquire" on letters and substituted "PRB" ... There were monthly meetings, at the houses or studios of the various members; occasionally a moonlight walk or a night on the Thames. Beyond this, very few days can have passed in a year when two or more PRB's did not foregather for one purpose or another.'[35]

Socially, the group replicated to some degree the fraternity and high spirits of such a pleasure-loving Sienese *brigata* as depicted in Rossetti's translation of Folgore's *Months*:

> For January I give you vests of skins,
>   And mighty fires in halls and torches lit ...
> Or issuing forth at seasons in the day,
>   Ye'll fling soft handfuls of the fair white snow
> Among the damsels standing round, in play;
>   And when you are all tired and all aglow,
> Indoors again the court shall hold its sway
>   And the free Fellowship continue so.

Of the PRB, Woolner was the loudest and most opinionated, Hunt the most mature, Millais the most gifted, Rossetti the most imaginative. Collinson and Stephens, it may as well be said, were dull spirits, whose smaller wits acted as foils to the others and ballast to their energies.

Why 'Pre-Raphaelite' exactly? Again, no one could precisely recall. At this date, Raphael was regarded as the greatest Master, the summit to which all previous artists were pathways and from which all subsequent art descended. But Western art before Raphael was not then called 'pre-Raphaelite', the usual designation for works from the Florentine and Sienese schools being 'the Italian Primitives'. Latterly, the term 'Early Christian' was also in use. Hunt recalled a conversation in the RA Schools on the merits of such works, when Raphael's *Transfiguration* was criticised. 'Ah,' said a fellow student, 'then you are a "pre-Raphaelite"?'[36] Intended pejoratively, the term was then defiantly adopted, Hunt and Rossetti being additionally delighted to find that Keats too had praised the 'early men'. But in some ways the name was misleading, for many of the artists admired by the PRB were Northern, not Italian. Examples of neither style were numerous in Britain, where the post-Raphael tradition ruled, although the National Gallery now began to acquire earlier works, and critics to describe them. Anna Jameson's two-volume *Memoirs of the Early Italian Painters* in 1845 was followed by Lord Lindsay's three-volume *Sketches of the History of Christian Art* (1847). At some date in 1847, Rossetti saw an early German Annunciation in an auction-house, and in spring 1848 an exhibition of early Italians was held at the British Institution. However casually chosen, the name matched a mood.

'Let us not forget the soul for the hand,' wrote Stephens, arguing that the 'primitive' should not be disdained for lack of technical virtuosity. Giotto, Gozzoli, Ghiberti, Fra Angelico, Masaccio, Orcagna belonged to the youth of art, not to the floridity of its decline. Artists should always remember that 'without the pure heart, nothing can be done worthy of us'; therefore, the new generation should follow their path, 'guided by their light: not so subservient as to lose our own freedom, but in the confidence of equal power and equal destiny; and then rely that we shall obtain the same success and equal or greater power, such as is given to the age in which we live.'[37]

No aesthetic uniformity was intended. Hunt was working on the rhetorical *Rienzi*, Millais on the startling perspective of *Isabella*, Rossetti on the pietistic *Girlhood*. Each PR Brother expected to develop his own subjects and treatment; no collective style would be imposed, let alone an Italian Primitive pastiche. If the group flourished, the association would be of mutual benefit.

Principles therefore emerged gradually. Chief among them was sincerity, a quality involving both form and content. As far as possible, everything should be painted 'from nature' – that is, from actuality rather than ideal forms copied from the existing artistic repertoire. Landscapes should be real places, objects real things. Figures should be drawn from life and faces from models with appropriate expression.

Customarily, such methods were used for genre subjects, of everyday life. The PRB applied them to higher themes, insisting on the sincerity of 'genuine ideas' drawn from scripture, literature, history and imagination, where traditionally idealism reigned. They would bring 'nature' to such subjects, without baseness or sensuality, which were 'a degradation at all times'.

Rossetti had a fount of such ideas, 'deep down and in the recesses of his being', according to Hunt; 'and these were always speaking to him, and he listened as one does to ever-advancing music.' Inwardly, he saw delectable images, and 'trained a cunning hand to give them form for other eyes.'[38] As yet, however, he lacked full skill – unlike Millais, who once his design was completed painted apparently without thought, chatting away the while, secure in the knowledge that all pictorial problems were solved. With difficulty, Gabriel finished his *Girlhood*, continually worried that he would make a 'muff' of some or all of the elements. The child-sized angel was a particular problem, despite four or five models. Aggravating the nervousness of one small girl, he shouted and stamped, causing her to scream with fright. But as Hunt also observed, when absorbed at the easel Gabriel was not distracted. Refusing to go home, he would 'sit through the night, sleeping where he sat for an hour at a time, recommencing his work when he woke. He ate whatever was at hand when hunger suggested, and when time came for bed on the second night he would ask me to leave him; in the morning I would find him still at his engrossing task.'[39]

When the Academy deadline approached in March, he instead sent his picture to the unjuried 'Free Exhibition', where artists paid for wall space. It was inscribed with the date 1849, his name 'Dante Gabriele Rossetti', and the initials 'P. R. B' – although in the event this earliest documented evidence of the Brotherhood's existence went unnoticed.

According to their own testimony, his Brethren were taken aback by this move, having believed all would submit together to the Royal Academy. But this is doutbful, for Millais and Hunt well understood Gabriel's position. It was his exhibition debut. In conventional terms, his picture was quaint, 'out of drawing' in key places, and its paint exceptionally thin. Its subject was provocative, for on the frame he inscribed his sonnet praising the Virgin and in the catalogue printed another explicating the symbolism in a frankly Catholic manner. There was heightened tension in the country at large over the expanding role of the Church of Rome in religious and (as it was feared) political affairs, which made such artistic motifs over a foreign name vulnerable to censure. 'My brother was proud and in his way prudent,' wrote William, 'and he must have contemplated with revulsion the mere possibility of being rejected at the Academy.'[40]

Thankfully, *The Girlhood* was a success. Though less prestigious than the RA show, the Free Exhibition was widely noticed. Like many a fond mother, Frances Rossetti kept the reviews – *Morning Chronicle, Literary Gazette, Observer, Athenaeum*. Singling out the novice work 'from one young in experience, new to fame', the last was fully appreciative of its frame of reference. 'The picture, which is full of allegory, has much of that sacred mysticism inseparable from the work of the early masters, and much of the tone of the poets of the same time,' observed the critic. 'While immature practice is visible in the executive department of the work, every allusion gives evidence of maturity of thought – every detail that might enrich or amplify the subject has found a place in it. Its spiritualized attributes, and the great sensibility with which it is wrought, inspire the expectation that Mr Rossetti will continue to pursue the lofty career which he has so successfully begun.'[41]

A most encouraging success, reported William. Visiting the exhibition a little while later, Gabriel saw the *Art Journal* critic carefully inspecting his work. 'I therefore anticipate on the first of next month to be either praised or regularly cut up,' he told his aunt. 'As the paper is very influential, I hope it will be the former.'[42] It was. Millais's *Isabella* and Hunt's *Rienzi*, hung as planned at the RA, were also well received. Suddenly, the still-secret Brotherhood had taken off. William began keeping a journal on its behalf, intended as an informal record of work in progress. Although, for as yet unexplained reasons, Gabriel later destroyed about 40 of the final 140 pages, it presents a vivid diary of daily events, beginning *in medias res*:

May 1849. *Tuesday 15th*. At Millais's; Hunt, Stephens, Collinson, Gabriel and myself. Gabriel brought with him his design of *Dante Drawing the Figure of an*

Angel on the first anniversary of Beatrice's death, which he completed in the course of the day and intended for Millais. Millais has done some figures of the populace in his design of the Abbey at Caen since last night, and has also continued painting on the beard in the head of Ferdinand listening to Ariel, being that of Stephens. He says he has begun his 'Castle-moat' poem, and is to continue it after we left (1 o'clock). The plan of writing this diary was fixed, and will, I am in hopes, be steadily persevered in. We minutely analyzed such defects as there are in Patmore's 'River' from Gabriel's recitation; who also read his poem (in progress) intended as introductory to the *Vita Nuova*. In the course of conversation, Millais told me that there is a pool suitable for my Patmore subject on Wimbledon Common. Having settled to our unanimous satisfaction Compton's identity in appearance with a Llama, we separated.[43]

Compton was a former RA student who had been involved in the literary club. On Wednesday Gabriel, busy with a new subject inspired by a song in *Pippa Passes*, called on Woolner. On Thursday Millais reported that he had put some fat figures into his Caen drawing, 'finding his general tendency to be towards thin ones'. On Friday Woolner and Bernhard Smith heard Gabriel read his Dante translation. On Saturday all gathered at Woolner's studio, where the talk covered 'the worst pictures in the Academy, swimming, dreams, early recollections and our personal characters'. On Monday evening Millais took Gabriel and Woolner to meet engraver Edward Bateman; 'Gabriel recited lots of Patmore, Browning, Mrs Browning, etc.', and presented Smith with a copy of Browning's poems, adding 'PRB' to Bernhard's name on the flyleaf.[44] This was arbitrary but also indicative. Others were now eager to join. When Hancock asked if he might use the initials, he was told it would have to be put to the vote. From casual beginnings, the Brotherhood began to take on a real shape.

CHAPTER FOUR

Young Painters of England

Potential patrons appeared. A bearded man in black called at Charlotte Street, asking for Mr G. D. Rossetti – as given in the Free Exhibition catalogue – but did not leave his own name; while a former schoolfellow named Nockells Cottingham 'descanted glowingly' on Gabriel's genius, asked the price of *The Girlhood*, promised commissions for Hunt and Woolner, and invited all three to see the medieval carving and stained glass acquired by his father's church restoration firm. Gabriel was elated. When his aunt asked what price he charged for a portrait, he replied boastfully that as it was desirable he should 'come before the public next year as prominently as possible', he was already at work on new subjects, and so his portrait charges would be high (5 guineas in chalks, 8 guineas for oil).[1] But he tempered his tone with due courtesy, which was just as well, for when Cottingham failed to make good his promises, aunt Charlotte persuaded Lady Bath to buy *The Girlhood*, for the high price of £80. The Marchioness was Anglo-Catholic, but the work hung oddly with the ancestral busts, Old Master copies and horseflesh on view at Longleat, the Baths' great country house.

Sensing the mood, Millais's new subject was the childhood of Jesus, Hunt's the conversion of Britain in the days of the Druids. Gabriel by contrast looked to Browning's *Pippa Passes*, designing an elaborate figure composition entitled *Hist! said Kate the Queen*. Returning to the Maddox Street life class, he painted from a model calling herself Mrs de Banks, whose half-finished image he gave to Henry Wells. Having not used the Cleveland Street studio since March, he belatedly withdrew from his share of the rent, causing an abrupt flit that was more awkward for Holman than himself.

Still working on the *Vita Nuova*, he redrew the scene showing Dante drawing an angel in memory of Beatrice, copying medieval garments from Camille Bonnard's *Costumes historiques* and using Millais as model for the poet; inscribed to 'his PR Brother', this was kept by Millais to the end of his life. He was also composing a new poem, about Dante's exile at the court of

Can Grande della Scala in Verona. This was a tribute to his father, a fellow-Italian poet who had found refuge but not honour in a foreign city and who like Dante had kept faith with his ideals. By an easy transposition, the poem's lines could read:

> Shall not his birth's baptismal town
> One last high presage yet fulfil
> And at that font in *Naples* still
> His forehead take the laurel-crown?
> O God! or shall dead souls deny
> The undying soul its prophecy?

As Professor Rossetti lamented, he would now die in exile. A few weeks later, liberal forces were defeated in Hungary as in Italy. 'How long, O Lord, The day of the great reckoning ... ?' protested William, in verse, while Gabriel echoed the allusion to Revelation in one sonnet aligning Austria with Antichrist, and another deploring the lack of international solidarity. When printing the latter twenty years later, he thought of referring explicitly in the title to other instances: 'the Refusal of Aid to Hungary 1849, to Poland 1861, to Crete 1867'. This if nothing else marks him as a child of 1848 and confirms that the collapse of the revolutionary movement – 'the temporary collapse as we now know it to have been', in William's later words – was a harder blow than he could easily admit, causing him to turn away from such affairs.

Literary enthusiasms were diverse and always easily aroused. Learning that the wife of Charles Wells, author of *Joseph and his Brethren* (1824), was trying to get his works republished, Gabriel at once proposed an edition with illustrations by the PRB and an 'elaborate preface' by himself – which would prove the first of many such quixotic endeavours. The next idea was a magazine, for which they would all write and contribute etchings. In discussion on 14 August, the title 'Monthly Thoughts in Literature, Poetry and Art' was agreed, the number of illustrations increased to two per issue and the price from sixpence to a shilling. Although it is true that in all walks of life more projects are proposed than realised, something in Gabriel's temperament gave him a manic edge when floating ideas. In this instance his main abettor was William North, a young literary journalist and political radical who already had a history of launching short-lived magazines.[2]

Rossetti knew he ought to stick to painting, but he had Lady Bath's money, and as soon as Hunt was paid for *Rienzi*, Gabriel settled on their going to France and Belgium together. But first, Hunt had to paint his Druid background, finding suitable landscape in the Lea Valley. Collinson

and William were in the Isle of Wight; Millais was also out of town. Gabriel
and Woolner went to see Grisi in *Les Huguenots*, and wrote several poems
apiece. Inspired by Keats's ode *On Indolence*, Gabriel's *Idle Blessedness*, for
most designedly difficult *bouts-rimés*, contained rueful observations on his
own character. 'I know not how it is, I have the knack / In lazy moods, of
seeking no excuse,' he wrote.

> I give the sack
> To thought, and lounge or shuffle on the track
> Of what employment seems of the least use:
> And in such ways I find a constant sluice
> For drowzy humours ...

Though he confessed to 'wasting' several days in the British Museum,
reading up 'all manner of old romaunts' in search of 'stunning words' (no
doubt including the archaic 'damozel') he was anything but idle. With the
magazine in mind, he began a chivalric romance of his own, a confession of
medieval seduction and shame, cast as a dialogue between sisters named
Amelotte and Hélénon, entitled 'Bride-chamber Talk'. Twelve stanzas were
soon written. He mapped out two more tales for versifying – 'when free of
existing nightmares' – derived from tales in the *Gesta Romanorum*, one to
be called 'The Scrip and Staff', and added new stanzas to *My Sister's Sleep*.
This was destined for the first issue.[3] In addition, there would be
Woolner's *My Beautiful Lady*, illustrated by Hunt, and an article by
Stephens on 'Early Italian Art'. Gratifyingly, Coventry Patmore offered a
poem.

'I believe we have found a publisher for the Magazine – viz., Aylott and
Jones, 8 Paternoster Row,' he wrote late one night to update William. The
partners in the venture numbered nine, if J. R. Herbert was included.
Collinson was being urged to join. Deverell was getting estimates. North
said his printer would charge £13 per issue, including the prospectus, while
Tuppers estimated that for the magazine alone. The etchings were costed at
2s or 2s 6d per hundred, plus paper. As to sales, Gabriel was convinced that
between them they could secure at least 250 prepublication subscribers.

Such was the birth of *The Germ*, the title finally chosen for the magazine
which, with a handful of paintings and a larger number of exquisite
drawings in mannered, linear mode, comprises the actual achievement of the
PRB. In his absence, William was appointed editor. By 24 September, the
prospectus was being printed, by the firm of George Tupper, whose
brother was an artist. Instead of finishing his poem, Gabriel began a prose
tale called *Hand and Soul* about a thirteenth-century Italian painter.
William was writing a poem of modern life, about which Gabriel was

affectionately abusive. The heroine's husband sounded 'a wretched sneak', he wrote.

With the launch scheduled for December, there was plenty of time for the proposed trip to Paris. They ought not to go at all, with so much to do. So of course they went.

It was Hunt's first foreign trip. Since Gabriel had last been in Boulogne nearly five years before, France had undergone its own 1848 revolution, and the atmosphere was still unsettled. Paris was nevertheless the cultural capital of Europe, thanks in part to state patronage. With its outstanding national collections, its annual Salon, its École des Beaux-Arts, its famous *ateliers* run by eminent painters and sculptors, as a fine-art centre Paris was now unrivalled. In Hunt's words, the opportunity of seeing the collections in the Louvre and Luxembourg, then so much finer than London's National Gallery, and of seeing current work by the artists of France, 'so much more favoured than those of England', was of vital importance to 'two students eager to track the way leading to poetic art'.[4] There was, too, more than a small element of competition; both Hunt and Rossetti shared distinctly John Bullish attitudes.

They left London on the afternoon of 27 September, travelling by train, itself still something of a novelty. The wind snatched at the smoke from the engine. Trees and telegraph wires shook as they passed. Walls and hedges ended abruptly. Frowning with concentration, Hunt was reading Alexandre Dumas. Gabriel began a travel diary, in blank verse.

They took the evening boat, and the next morning walked on the cliffs, where Gabriel composed a sonnet, and on the beach, where they waded for starfish. Then they caught the train again, sweeping past haystacks and windmills. Halting at Amiens, the locomotive 'snorts, chafes and bridles like three hundred horse', its smoke like a thick black mane. In Paris they lodged at no. 4 rue Geoffrey Marie, off the rue Montmartre, not far from Notre Dame de Lorette, Gavarni's own district. They met up with fellow artist J. L. Brodie, a friend of Brown's, who introduced 'two very nice French fellows' named Cotourrier and Lavasseur, with whom they breakfasted at a dairy in the *quartier*. At the Place de la Bastille, they paused in honour of history; Hunt and Brodie smoked cigars, while Gabriel extemporised a sonnet. They climbed the towers of Notre Dame, where he composed another, likening the state of France to their ascent. From the darkness of political upheaval, the country would 'step forth on the light in a still sky'.

One morning their French companions were missing from the *laiterie*. The proprietress whispered about police inquiries, consequent on the students' involvement in the recent *événements*. Later in the day Gabriel and Hunt were greeted by one of their new friends, unrecognisably clean-shaven, hurriedly leaving for the provinces.

France and England were still national rivals, Trafalgar and Waterloo still vivid memories. If in cultural matters Britain stood in inferior relation to France, the young visitors were more than ready to criticise things French merely for being French. With the energy of tourists, however, they saw everything, and Gabriel wrote a poem on almost everything: the Louvre, the Luxembourg Gallery, the Beaux-Arts, the Musée de Cluny, the Gobelins tapestry works, the rail trip to Versailles. 'Hunt and I begin to like Paris immensely,' Gabriel told William on 4 October. 'At the Luxembourg there are the following really wonderful pictures – viz., two by Delaroche, two by Robert Fleury, one by Ingres, one by Hesse.' Some by Scheffer, Granet and others were good. The rest, 'with a few mediocre exceptions, we considered trash'.[5]

'We brought with us a double judgement,' wrote Hunt later, 'to decide whether a work interested the eye and the mind beyond it ... and if so, whether and in what degree it was rich in artistic grace and accomplishment.'[6] But they also brought a baggage of prejudice, partly inspired by envy, which manifested itself in front of French painting. To their eyes, war, murder, lust and pride were the common subjects, accompanied by boastfulness of handling underscored by the size of the artist's signature. Courbet's immense *Decadence of Rome* they therefore scouted, though Géricault's *Raft of the Medusa* was too impressive to disdain. They missed much of the newest work; as Hunt later noted, in 1849 they had 'no means of divining the existence' of Millet. They saw nothing by Rosa Bonheur, even though *Labourage nivernais* was a showpiece of the 1849 Salon, the ox team painted with almost Pre-Raphaelite detail, and discerned little impulse in art comparable with their own, regarding 'ideal' or official painting as stilted and stagey and the revolt against it as ugly, untouched by the poetic. The only exceptions were Flandrin's neo-Gothic frescoes in St Germain des Prés, 'the most perfect works, taken *in toto*, that we have seen in our lives', reported Gabriel. 'Wonderful! Wonderful!! Wonderful!!!'

Mostly, however, they devoured the works of the great Past rather than the puny Present. The Louvre was so large they ran through the rooms, dispensing instant judgements. 'A most wonderful copy of a fresco by Fra Angelico' (the first they had ever seen), 'a tremendous Van Eyck, some mighty things by that real stunner Leonardo, some ineffably poetical Mantegnas,' reported Rossetti breathlessly; 'several wonderful early Christians [Italians] whom nobody ever heard of, some tremendous portraits by some Venetian whose name I forget, and a stunning *Francis I* by Titian.'[7]

Both the *Concert Champêtre* attributed to Giorgione and Mantegna's dancing nymphs on Mount Parnassus prompted instant sonnets, as did Ingres's *Ruggiero and Angelica*, where the naked heroine is chained to a rock for sacrifice to a sea-monster:

> Under his lord, the griffin-horse ramps blind
>> With rigid wings and tail. The spear's lithe stem
> Thrills in the roaring of those jaws ...

Rossetti was of an age to respond to sexual imagery and such neo-classical eroticism made a lasting impression.

So too, for contrary reasons, did 'Rubens, Correggio *et hoc genus omne*', whose works provoked a howl of disgust, the 'cry of the PRB', against carked and dimpled flesh, stagnant pools of paint. 'Who that has eyes cannot see that Rubens and Correggio must have been very weak and vulgar fellows,' Blake had written. 'And are we to imitate their execution? This is as if a healthy child should be compelled to walk like a cripple ...'

The bookstalls and print-sellers were an anticipated delight. Gabriel augmented his stock of Gavarni's. But as with Rubens's carnality, their English souls were revolted by the famous cancan at Valentino's, where the high-kicking women wore no undergarments. 'I confess, William, and avow to thee (soft in thine ear)', wrote Gabriel,

> that such sweet female whims
> As nasty backsides out and wriggled limbs
> Nor bitch-squeaks, nor the smell of heated q....s
> Are not a passion of mine naturally.

'So do not let anyone see this letter,' he added; 'or else scratch out this sonnet first.'[8] It was a vulgar production that reveals both susceptibility and shock in one who, despite surface sophistication, retained a virginal puritanism. It was easier to stare at the decomposing flesh of a murdered man in the morgue than at knickerless dancers. With laddish insularity, the travellers declared they had not seen six pretty women since leaving London.

After a fortnight, having spent three-quarters of their funds, they left for Belgium, delayed three days in obtaining visas. 'Curse the big mounds of sand-weed!' wrote Gabriel on the journey. 'Curse every beastly station on the road!' To Hunt, however, Rossetti was 'a perfect travelling companion, ever in the best of temper' and their journey 'overbrimming with delight in the beauties of both nature and art'.[9]

Their first destination, obligatory to all Britons, was Waterloo, 'the name which travels side by side with English life from childhood'. Thirty years before, Gabriel's uncle John had been there with Byron, purchasing a sabre and other military trophies. Now empty, the battlefield was overrun by guides, discoursing on the 'fallen thousands' of three nations. Gabriel wrote an anti-heroic sonnet, half concealing his disappointment. A wayside shrine to the Virgin pleased him more.

Brussels was boring too; offered 'a lot of scientific and industrial silliness' on the sightseeing trail, they sought only the old and quaint. Antwerp was not much better, for here Rubens was 'the God of painters', with 'slosh by miles' in the museum and even the artist's chair in a glass case. They mimed being sick. There was more in the cathedral. 'Let's go,' they said, but

> There is a monument
> We pass. 'Messieurs, you tread upon the grave
> Of the great Rubens.' 'Well, that's one good job!
> What time this evening is the train for Ghent?'

In the margins of Anna Jameson's *Sacred and Legendary Art*, they wrote 'Spit here' beside the reviled name.

In Ghent they admired the elaborate polyptych by Van Eyck in St Bavon's Cathedral, and were intrigued by the Béguinage, where each resident had a house to herself, dedicated to a different saint. 'In some cases where the name was more than usually quaint, we felt disposed to knock at the door and ask if he was in,' Gabriel told Collinson, teasingly, 'but refrained as it was rather late, and we feared he might have gone to bed.'[10]

Bruges was best. 'Dear PRB,' wrote Gabriel to James, '[t]his is a most stunning place, immeasurably the best we have come to. There is a quantity of first-rate architecture, and very little or no Rubens.' They climbed the belfry tower with the carillon sounding, and in museums and churches they devoured the works of Van Eyck and discovered Memling.

There were no works by Memling in London. Here in the Hospital of St John they saw the great altarpiece depicting the beheading of St John the Baptist, the Sacred Conversation or Mystic Marriage of St Catherine, and the Vision of St John in Patmos. 'I assure you that the perfection of character, and even drawing, the astounding finish, the glory of colour and above all the pure religious sentiment and ecstatic poetry of these works, is not to be conceived or described,' reported Gabriel in a rhapsody of applause. 'The mind is at first bewildered by such God-like completeness ... and then finds these feelings so much increased by analysis that the last impression left is mainly one of utter shame at its own inferiority.'

The Sacred Conversation inspired a sonnet. St John's visions, floating in the sky, were 'wonderfully mystical and poetical'. The medium was not oil, he added technically, but 'some vehicle of which brandy and white of egg are the principal components'. The panels were in excellent condition and the colours could hardly have been more brilliant on the day they were painted.[11]

They returned the next day and then purchased presents – 'an extraordinary self-concocting coffee-pot for state occasions of the PRB', and an old book with spells for raising the Devil – which proved remarkably effective, according to one of his biographers, judged by Rossetti's later life. Going home via Ostend and Dover, the first voice they heard was that of a respectful police constable: how unlike those in France.

But was Rossetti genuinely xenophobic? He spoke French, Italian, some German. He grew up in a cosmopolitan community and had carried letters from his father to friends in Paris. He was confident, outgoing, full of charm, well able to negotiate and bargain. His artist's eye had feasted on wonders as well as slosh. Yet he consistently rubbished France and Belgium for being foreign, like any ignorant Briton, and quite unlike his brother who, when he had the means, travelled extensively, with pleasure and assurance. One wonders if the visa delay in Paris indicates a *contretemps* that made Gabriel feel vulnerable on account of his national origin; his father still feared a conspiracy against his life.

More significantly, the art was unsettling. In London, the PRBs could survey the whole artistic scene, keep up with all cultural developments. Paris, by contrast, made them feel provincial. Moreover, both there and in Belgium the art of the past was sobering, making him feel inadequate. Gabriel had seen much (apart from Rubens) to admire, and did so wholeheartedly. But at the same time his confidence was dented. The result was crude nationalism. 'My brother was in many respects an Englishman in grain,' wrote William; '– and even a prejudiced Englishman quite ready – *too* ready, I always thought – to abuse foreigners.'[12]

Back in London, the first task was to find a new studio. On 6 November, Rossetti went with Hunt and Stephens to inspect a large old house by the river at Chelsea, reputedly built on the site of a mansion once occupied by Elizabeth I and therefore known as Queen's or Tudor House. It could accommodate several studios, besides bedrooms, dining room, kitchens and garden. The rent was £70 a year. In the evening they gathered at Woolner's studio. It looked promising. 'Gabriel, Hunt and myself, think of going at once, and Stephens and Collinson would join after April,' recorded William. Deverell would come too. ' "PRB" might be written on the bell and stand for "please ring the bell" to the profane.'[13] The Brotherhood would have a base.

But it was on a long lease, so the expense was prohibitive, and eventually all settled for separate studios. Rossetti took a room at 72 Newman Street, where the ground floor was occupied by a dancing academy or 'hop-shop' not unlike that run by Mr Turveydrop in Dickens's *Bleak House*. It was a neighbourhood of artists, musicians, frame-makers. He continued to sleep at Charlotte Street, but did not always go home at night.

Under the punning title 'St Wagnes' Eve'[14] a typical evening in the studio was described in doggerel to Christina a few weeks later:

> The hop-shop is shut up: the night doth wear.
>   Here, early, Collinson this evening fell
>   'Into the gulfs of sleep'; and Deverell
> Has turned the pivot of his chair
> The whole of this night long; and Hancock there
>   Has laboured to repeat, in accents screechy
>   'Guardami ben, ben son Beatrice';
> And Bernhard Smith still beamed, serene and square.
> By eight, the coffee was all drunk. At nine
>   We gave the cat some milk. Our talk did shelve,
>   Ere ten, to gasps and stupor. Helpless grief
> Made, towards eleven, my inmost spirit pine,
>   Knowing North's hour. And Hancock, hard on twelve,
>   Showed an engraving of his bas-relief.

This bore some relation to reality. Collinson did tend to fall asleep. Hancock, who was sculpting Beatrice, did have a high-pitched voice. North was a man of eccentric habits.

Gabriel himself was notorious for reciting twenty or thirty pages of Browning's *Sordello*, a poetic drama in six dense books, set during the wars of the Guelphs and Ghibellines. Whenever the PRB were gathered, they were likely to hear it again, whether they wished or no. 'But friends / wake up; the ghost's gone and the story ends / I'd fain hope, sweetly ... / Who would has heard Sordello's story told.' The fellows teased him about it. *Sordello* was unreadable, unending. A sonnet went to Woolner, and a careful, well-composed illustration – five medieval figures on the city ramparts – was given to Stephens, 'from his P. R. Brother Dante G. Rossetti'. It might have served for a painting but there were many other contenders, including *Kate the Queen* and *The Laboratory*, also by Browning. Or, most promisingly, a triptych on the life of the Virgin, showing the Holy Family at Passover, flanked by Mary planting a lily and with St John. Or maybe St Luke, patron of painters. Or what about Paolo and Francesca, adulterous lovers from the *Inferno*, also in three panels? On 25 November, he decided on the Annunciation.

'The Virgin is to be in bed, but without any bedclothes on, an arrangement which may be justified in consideration of the hot climate, and the Angel Gabriel will be presenting a lily to her,' noted William in the PRB Journal. 'The picture ... will be almost entirely white.'[15]

There was logic in the choice of subject. Maybe Lady Bath would like a second picture of Mary, as in a sequel; the Annunciation contains the finished stole Mary embroiders in *The Girlhood*. Or it could be half a diptych, tall and narrow. Most importantly, however, it marks the impact of Rossetti's foreign trip on his artistic ideas, for the two pictures are very differently conceived and painted. *The Girlhood* is a self-contained, tableau-like composition, which the viewer observes from a reverent distance. The figures do not look out, or at each other. The *Annunciation* is altogether bolder, in both brushwork and iconography, breaking with tradition by showing the Virgin not at her devotions but suddenly awakened by the Archangelic visitor, who is tall, well-formed, without wings, floating on flames. Primary red, blue and yellow relieve the white drapery and walls. Above all, by means of foreshortening, the viewer is pulled into the picture.

On his travels, Rossetti had seen quite a few Annunciations. They were not numerous in Britain, but he had read Anna Jameson on the subject, including her account of a miniature in the Bibliothèque Nationale, in which the Archangel in crimson robe and white tunic stands 'with a proud commanding air, like a magnificent surly god', while the Virgin, 'sinks back alarmed, almost fainting'. In his own version, several borrowed motifs come together, showing that while the depiction was bold it was also consciously in homage. The curious tree outside the window, for example, carries a traditional reference to Mary's redemptive role between the tree of knowledge and that of the Cross. The tonal values echo those in two grisaille panels of the same subject in the great Van Eyck altarpiece in Ghent, which Rossetti had carefully studied and would visit again; twenty years on, he told a friend that he had seen the work '2 or 3 times and always with the greatest delight'.[16]

Rather like these figures, and those of Van Eyck's 'tremendous' Virgin in the Louvre, Rossetti's figures are too large for the room they occupy. Van Eyck's presentation, however, is traditional, with Angel and Virgin facing each other in profile. Rossetti twists the viewpoint, so that the Virgin is seen frontally, almost as if from over the Angel's shoulder. This recalls Rogier van der Weyden's version in the Louvre, where her foreshortened bed defines the depth of the picture space as she turns towards the Angel, who as in Rossetti's image hovers just off the floor.

In early Northern versions of the scene, derived from a mystical exegesis by Ivo de Chartres that links the Annunciation with Psalm 19 in which God sets 'a tabernacle for the sun, which is as a bridegroom coming out of his chamber', the Virgin herself becomes such a bridal chamber, for the birth of Christ. Similarly, in Rossetti's white picture, set at sunrise, light emanates from the Angel, dimming the earthly lamp above the bed. The chosen viewpoint shrinks the space between the figures, traditionally symbolic of the gap between human and divine, itself rendered by Rossetti as a dividing line along the edge of the curtain and the bed. Across this are placed the dove and the lily stem, instruments of divine conception aimed straight at the Virgin's womb in clear allusion to existing iconography.[17]

Thus, though not immediately recognisable as such, the composition was inspired by the wealth of fifteenth-century work he and Hunt had just seen, and the excitement thereby engendered. Its most striking aspect, however, is its physicality. Shorn of the sacred theme, it shows a virile young man waking a girl, not unlike Madeline's encounter with Porphyro in *The Eve of St Agnes*. Visually, the lily is poised at the same angle as that of Ruggiero's lance thrust into the monster's jaws in Ingres's painting, whose sexual symbolism Rossetti had clearly grasped. Moreover, though the Angel is not a self-portrait, he bears the same name as the artist, and beneath the loose white robe is visibly naked. Gabriel had been sexually unsettled in Paris and seems to have endowed his canvas with something of this erotic feeling.

As befits an important composition, it took some time to realise. On 8 December, he drew the Angel, using the same model as for St Joachim in *The Girlhood*. On 16 December he started painting. But there were obstacles, and other demands on his time, principally *The Germ*, whose publication was imminent. The Keatsian 'Bride-chamber Talk' gained further stanzas. On 13 December *My Sister's Sleep* was shown to Patmore, who liked the sentiment but criticised the scansion. Then Gabriel began designing a picture of Giotto painting Dante, and on 20 December decided to finish his prose story of a thirteenth-century Florentine artist. He stayed up late, and in the morning *Hand and Soul* was done. William made a fair copy for the printer. On Christmas Eve, they corrected proofs, and the first issue was ready. 'Thus then, after many changes and counter changes, will stand the contents,' noted William: 'Woolner's "My Lady" [poem], Ford Brown's "Love of Beauty", Tupper's "Subject in Art" [articles], Patmore's "Seasons" [poem], our Sister's "Dream-land" [poem], Gabriel's "My Sister's Sleep" and "Hand and Soul", my [William's] review of *The Bothie* [*of Toper na fuoisch*, by Clough] and sonnet "Her First Season", Tupper's "Sketch from Nature" and our Sister's "An End".'[18] The etching, flagged on the cover, was Hunt's double illustration to Woolner's poem.

Finally, on New Year's Eve, just before noon, the first fifty copies were delivered. It was something of a triumph.

Hand and Soul, so swiftly completed, is arguably the best thing in *The Germ*, remarkable for imaginative fluency and subtle feeling. It may also stand as the clearest expression of 'the principles in Art of the PRB', on which there had been some talk of preparing a statement, but which no one had the confidence to attempt. Furthermore, it is transposed autobiography, revealing Gabriel's own aspirations in art.

The protagonist is a real, if fictional, pre-Raphaelite, one of the virtually anonymous painters of the *dugento*. Named Chiaro dell'Erma, he is of 'very honourable family in Arezzo'. Discovering art almost for himself, he endeavours like his author to draw from early boyhood, with 'extreme longing after a visible embodiment of his thoughts', which strengthened as his years increased, 'until he would feel faint in sunsets and at the sight of stately persons ...'

Seeking out a renowned master in Pisa, he realises that the work is lifeless and incomplete. So, like young Master Rossetti, he paints alone, with the thought of greatness always before him, 'weak with yearning, like one who gazes upon a path of stars'. At first Chiaro paints for fame, until his name is 'spoken throughout all Tuscany'. But a weight is at his heart, for he dreams of a mystical lady who is 'his own gracious and holy Italian art', with unfathomable eyes, that he aspires to reverence. Moreover, success brings only unrest of the spirit. So he sets a watch on his soul and paints only sacred subjects, forgetful of worldly beauty and passion. 'And the weight was still close to Chiaro's heart: but he held in his breath, never resting (for he was afraid) and would not know it.' When at work, he is wholly absorbed, but when idle his thoughts beat round and round, stealthily, seeking a point for attack; therefore Chiaro fears sloth.

Pisa is riven by factional violence like that between Guelph and Ghibelline. One day there is a violent skirmish, right beside Chiaro's fresco of Peace. 'At once the whole archway was dazzling with the light of confused swords; and they who had left turned back; and they who were still behind made haste to come forth; and there was so much blood cast up the walls on a sudden, that it ran in long streams down Chiaro's paintings.' His allegory of Peace is the site of war. 'May one be a devil and not know it?' Both fame and faith have failed. In despair, Chiaro has a vision: a woman appears in his studio, clad in green and grey raiment:

It seemed that the first thoughts he had ever known were given him as at first from her eyes, and he knew her hair to be the golden veil through which he beheld his dreams. Though her hands were joined, her face was not lifted, but set forward; and though her gaze was austere, yet her mouth was supreme in gentleness ... He was like one who, scaling a great steepness, hears his own voice echoed in some place much higher than he can see ... As the woman stood, her speech was with Chiaro: not, as it were, from her mouth or in his ears; but distinctly between them.

She is the image or embodiment of his soul, a Shelleyan spirit with a Blakean message, who urges him to seek neither fame nor faith but simply to search the conscience of his heart and paint his inner vision. 'Not till thou lean over the water shalt thou see thine image therein: stand erect, and it shall slope from thy feet and be lost. Know that there is but this means whereby thou may'st serve God with man: – Set thine hand and thy soul to serve man with God.'

Later, William summarised this as meaning that 'the proper business of a painter is to "paint his soul" ... if he faithfully follow his own genuine inspirations he will be fulfilling his pictorial duty'.[19] This was of course the task of the Romantic artist, to seek to know and be true to the inner self, rather than follow external precepts, whether worldly or moral. In practice the challenge was more complex. How should an artist know that his inspirations are 'genuine'? How distinguish soul from self, how be sure he is serving both God and man, the earthly and the spiritual realms? What if, as in England, there seemed no customers for such visions? How might one aim for greatness without desiring glory?

The ending of the tale takes place in the present, as the narrator discovers in the Pitti Palace a small panel by an unknown artist, showing a half-finished picture of a woman in green and grey drapery, 'chaste and early in its fashion', like those of the Italian Primitives. Identified as by Chiaro dell'Erma, it is dismissed as quaint and worthless by the other students in the gallery, who are studying Raphael. They laugh at the narrator, saying the English are wrapt by mysticism, as if in their fogs.

'I wrote the tale ... all one night in December 1849,' Gabriel recalled forty years later, describing the experience by visual metaphor. 'In such a case a landscape and sky all unsurmised open gradually in the mind – a sort of spiritual "Turner" among whose hills one ranges and in whose waters one strikes out at unknown liberty.'[20] Afterwards, he added, he fell fast asleep, for like Chiaro, 'he felt weak and haggard; like one just come out of a dusk, hollow country, bewildered with echoes, where he had lost himself ...'

He added an epigraph from one of his Italian translations, which must in part have suggested the story: 'I turn to where I heard That whisper in the night, And there a breath of light Shines like a silver star. The same is mine own soul ...'

We may regret that *Hand and Soul* is the only work of prose fiction Gabriel completed, for though it is a young man's tale, with self-indulgent passages, it is deftly and stylishly composed, with scarcely a false note. Had he wished, Rossetti might have found his métier here. And although Chiaro is a romanticised self-portrait, the story offers an eloquent account of its author at the age of twenty-one, after seeing some of the great works of

Western art for the first time. Gabriel had been encouraged to cultivate lofty ambitions to be both successful and good, to gain fame for the Rossetti name and contribute to the spiritual elevation of society. Inwardly, he was possessed by 'extreme longing' to make visible versions of the pictures he saw in his mind's eye, whether derived from nature or imagination. Inevitably, what he produced fell short of those inner visions – which almost seem, like Blake's, to have had the quality of external images. As in his triple sonnet *The Choice*, there were paths to choose from, but no certain way of combining all goals. The 'ecstatic' pictorial poetry of Memling, Van Eyck, Mantegna and the rest, with all its so-called strangeness, underlined the limitations of his own endeavours even as it nourished them.

The sequel to the resolution of Chiaro's dilemma was, not surprisingly, a renewal of discontent with the *Annunciation*. Two days after his all-night writing session, Gabriel 'again got some idea of painting the subject of Francesca da Rimini, instead of what he is now doing'. On Boxing Day, however, realism prevailed: he went back to painting the Virgin's head.

'Very early in life', as his first biographer noted, 'he formed the resolution that the sun should never set without having witnessed something done by him in some branch of work'.[21]

On 1 January 1850 the PRB held its first formal anniversary meeting, postponed from the previous day and largely devoted to ideas for promoting *The Germ*. The evidence suggests that Gabriel's involvement was slackening, now the project was launched. Certainly he took little part in pushing the magazine to the notice of 'literary men, etc', to make it known. But he did push on with *Bride-chamber Talk*, which would prove a lifelong task, and added to *The Blessed Damozel*. He wrote to Bell Scott, inviting him to contribute, and devised the poetical-sounding pseudonym 'Ellen Alleyn' for Christina, currently with aunt Charlotte at Longleat.

Germ no. 2 appeared on 31 January. It contained Collinson's etching and poem *The Child Jesus*, poems by Patmore, Deverell, Scott, Calder Campbell and all three Rossettis, and Stephens's continued defence of 'pre-Raphaelite' art, with provocative polemic against the 'conventionalism, gaudy colour, false sentiment and poverty of invention' in most contemporary pictures.

The printing bill for no. 1 came to £18, and only around 100 copies had sold. 'This is a kind of experiment that won't bear repetition,' remarked William. Gabriel agreed, seemingly content to let *The Germ* wither in the pod. But the venture had its spin-offs. On 2 February the weekly *Critic* asked if *The Germ* could supply an art reviewer – unpaid, but, as William noted with characteristic double negatives, 'not I think disadvantageous for the PRB, as it would enable us to review the exhibitions in our own feeling'.[22] He therefore volunteered his own services. A few weeks on, he was recruited by the *Spectator*, and nominated Stephens to *The Critic* in his stead. Later, Stephens would work for the *Athenaeum*, whose art critic he remained for forty years.

William's first review was of the British Institution exhibition. Gabriel wrote some of the copy, praising works by Charles Lucy and Henry Mark Anthony, good friends of Brown, and complimenting a visual version of 'Mrs Browning's wondrous "Deserted Garden" [where] 'the white statue appears to listen; there is a peacock still about the place ... the encroachment of moss and grass and green mildew is everywhere.' Scorn was poured on Frank Stone, however, the artist who was also the *Athenaeum's* art critic and therefore author of the favourable remarks on the PRB in 1849. No answering charity informed Gabriel's judgement, boldly inserted over William's initials, on Stone's painting of young women in faded yellow and pink, whose faces were made of wax, hair of Berlin wool-work and hands of scented soap, and had all the liveliness of lay-figures. Madox Brown's advice was to tone down the sarcasm.

Apparently defunct, *The Germ* revived towards the end of February, when George Tupper offered to subsidise two more issues. There had been encouraging notices, and it might become viable. Gabriel was drawn back into literary matters and spent a whole day at home, polishing *Dante in Exile*. Datelined March, the issue was a month behindhand. No etching was ready. They decided to print his poems from Boulogne and Bruges, and he suggested changing the magazine title to *The Artist*. In the end no. 3 appeared as *Art and Poetry, being Thoughts towards Nature. Conducted Principally by Artists*. Its tone was lowered by a comic poem from Jack Tupper, who as brother of the printer had some privileges. In apparent mockery of his style, Rossetti once sent him a poem in verse, beginning 'Dear Jack, Alack!'.

For issue no. 4, he prepared an illustration to *Hand and Soul*, showing Chiaro at his easel with a young woman; both faces are reflected in the mirror and both hands hold the brush as her image is placed on the canvas. Simultaneously, he began work on *St Agnes of Intercession*, another tale in the same mode, about a painter who finds he is a reincarnation of a fifteenth-century Italian artist. This fanciful idea was inspired by Poe, but also suggests Rossetti's inner vision. When wrapt in work, he felt like a painter from an earlier age, or one born in the wrong century; in a previous life, had he perhaps been a real pre-Raphaelite? Millais agreed to design an etching. As for his own *Hand and Soul* illustration, when Rossetti saw the result, he tore up the proof in dismay and scratched the plate, rendering it unusable. Somehow, the original drawing went to Patmore.[23] Deverell came to the rescue, with an illustration to his own poem inspired by *Twelfth Night*.

Years later, annoyed by Rossetti's prominence in the emerging histories of the Pre-Raphaelite movement, Millais complained about the magazine's literary bias. 'We made a great mistake in accepting others to form a brotherhood with us,' he wrote to Hunt. 'We brought out our very precious guineas to start the *Germ*, in which the writers published their poems and articles; and we did etchings in addition. Did they ever do anything for us?'[24] But this was unfair. Had the magazine succeeded, all reputations would have benefited.

Coventry Patmore, one of the rising stars in poetry, was currently writing *The Angel in the House*, a paean to marriage that would be acclaimed, and later excoriated. More thrillingly, he was in contact with Tennyson who, on the death of Wordsworth this year, was appointed Poet Laureate. Tennyson was the big name, and the aspiring *Germ* poets – Gabriel, William, Christina, Woolner and Tupper – were impressed. One evening, there was a large gathering at Newman Street. At midnight, William appeared, triumphantly waving an advance copy of Tennyson's new poem, *In Memoriam*, an extended elegy for his friend Arthur Hallam, 'printed strictly for private perusal'. The little volume was at once passed to Gabriel, who proceeded to read it aloud, entire. Almost simultaneously, Browning's new poem *Christmas Eve and Easter Day* was just published; William hastened a review into issue 4.

The exhibition season was fast approaching. The Virgin's face was not yet painted. Gabriel wanted a model with red hair, but in the end used Christina again, for the face, with a professional model for the hair. Among the last details were the flames licking round the Angel's feet, for which a chemical concoction was ignited. Together with Deverell's *Twelfth Night* it went to the National Institution, into which the Free Exhibition had metamorphosed. The paint must have been still wet in places.

The work was signed 'DGR March 1850'. The Feast of the Annunciation is 25 March, old Lady Day. And to underline the homage to earlier times, it was titled *Ecce Ancilla Domini!*, echoing Mary's words ('Behold the handmaid of the Lord') that are inscribed in gold on Van Eyck's *Annunciation* like a primitive speech bubble. Gabriel was much taken with such 'quaint' features. Further increasing the Gothic references, he painted words on the frame, copied from a brass-rubbing owned by Stephens. Typological in content, they matched the scriptural lines attached to Millais's and Hunt's canvases, and were deliberately provocative. 'My people are beginning to wail over the Popish inscription,' he reported.

Millais's picture, *Christ in the Carpenter's Shop*, which Gabriel saw for the first time on 8 April, complemented his own in showing a biblical scene rendered with both realism and symbol. With this and other works in the new style, he may have felt hopeful, until the first review appeared, in the *Athenaeum*.

Evidently smarting from *The Critic*'s sarcasm, Frank Stone pronounced that the picture was one example of a 'perversion of talent' that was 'wasting the energies' of some promising men. 'Ignoring all that has made the art great in the works of the greatest masters, the school to which Mr Rossetti belongs would begin the work anew ... setting at nought all the advanced principles of light and shade, colour and composition,' he wrote. More particularly, *Ecce Ancilla* was weak, puerile, unintelligent, imitative. The Angel's head was insipid. There were 'fanciful scribblings on the frame, and other infantile absurdities'. Altogether it was a work 'thrust by the artist into the eye of the spectator more with the presumption of a teacher than the modesty of a hopeful and true aspiration after excellence'.[25]

This was partly true, but largely unfair. *Ecce Ancilla* is painted with hopeful and genuine aspiration. Writing to Scott, Gabriel joked off his hurt, saying his picture had been 'a great deal abused' and adding: 'the *Athenaeum*, which blarneyed me last year, is now dreadfully impertinent'.[26] He sent a (doubtless impertinent) protest to the editor, who declined to publish it.

The word got round. Although no monograms appeared on this year's pictures, when the Academy opened at the beginning of May, the 'mystic initials' were revealed in the press as those of the 'Prae-Raffaelite Brotherhood', a league of 'ingenious gentlemen who profess themselves practitioners of "Early Christian Art" ', according to the *Illustrated London News*, 'and who – setting aside the Mediaeval schools of Italy, the Raffaelles, the Guidos and Titians and all such small beer daubers – devote their energies to the reproduction of saints squeezed out perfectly flat'.

Other critics aimed chiefly at Millais's representation of the Sacred Family as working carpenters. Such 'pictorial blasphemy' made Stone 'recoil with loathing and disgust'. Great talent had been perverted to 'lamentable and revolting' eccentricity. He proceeded to give the lads a lesson in art history, denouncing 'the new school of English youths' as arrogant and insincere, seeking 'notoriety by means of mere conceit'. Abruptness, singularity, uncouthness, were 'the counters by which they play for fame'.[27] *The Times* echoed the attack. 'The attempt to associate the holy family with the meanest details of a carpenter's shop, with no conceivable omission of misery, of dirt, of even disease, all finished with the same loathsome minuteness, is disgusting,' its reviewer wrote; 'and with a surprising power of imitation, this picture serves to show how far mere imitation may fall short, by dryness and conceit, of all dignity and truth.'

'Such a collection of splay feet, puffed joints and misshapen limbs was assuredly never before made within so small a compass,' mocked the mighty *Blackwood's Magazine* at the beginning of July. Lower down the intellectual scale, Dickens's popular *Household Words* declared the painting mean, odious, revolting and repulsive.

'Millais's picture has been the signal for a perfect crusade against the PRB,' reported William in the Journal. So far, so good, in some ways: abuse is not necessarily damaging. 'Indeed, the PRB has unquestionably been one of the topics of the season,' he added with tacit satisfaction. Such was the publicity that the Queen asked for Millais's picture to 'be brought to her from the walls of the RA' which she could not visit on account of her recent confinement. God grant it had no ill effects, joked the artist.

To the art establishment, the boys of the Brotherhood were getting too big for their boots – or rather they claimed a bigger size than their experience warranted. It was largely a generational affair. Stephens responded with a counter-attack on contemporary landscape painting, like murky Old Masters with dismal trees and lead-coloured streams. 'Yes! there are Giants on the earth in these days; but it is their great bulk, and the nearness of our view, which prevents us from perceiving their grandeur,' he declared, with a parable about the true poetry of modern life, in which a young gentleman courteously escorted a dirty beggarwoman through city traffic. Such was worth a thousand unnatural landscapes.

This appeared in the fourth issue of *The Germ*, which bloomed one last time in May. 'We are to meet to overhaul the accounts on Thursday even[ing] next at 7 o'clock,' wrote George Tupper to Stephens, warning that the business should not degenerate into its familiar 'poetic-spouting-railing-trolloping-mystifying-smoke-scandal'. The final reckoning came on 17 May with a bill for over £30 on the first two issues.[28] With little regret, the magazine succumbed to its doom.

When the dancing master decamped, owing rent himself, Gabriel had to accomplish another swift flit. 'Mithered even to madness' he found a room at 74 Newman Street. Hunt had a new studio at the other end of town, on the river. At Whitsuntide Collinson – whose picture went unnoticed in the reviews – resigned from the Brotherhood, more in sorrow than in anger. Having rejoined the Catholic church, he was uneasy about the quasi-religious name and the formal association. 'It was for me to have judged beforehand whether I could conscientiously, as a Catholic, assist in spreading the artistic opinions of those who are not,' he explained. In addition, he was dismayed to be associated with pictures which helped dishonour 'God's holy saints' by making their sanctity a cause for ridicule. 'PS Please do not attempt to change my mind.'[29]

At this stage, relations remained friendly. But shortly afterwards, the engagement between James and Christina was brought to an end, causing a formal breach. Whether, in his religious fervour, Collinson decided to forgo marriage (as his sonnet about 'forsaking all other' suggests) or whether Christina was persuaded to release him is not now possible to say. The Rossetti family closed ranks. Fifty years later, when Christina's biography was being written, only Holman Hunt and one or two others remembered it. The break effectively ended Gabriel's friendship with James, however, and the influence of Catholic imagery on his art.

A new friend was William Allingham, a young poet living in his native Donegal where he was employed as a customs official. 'An odd, out-of-the-way little town, ours, on the extreme western verge of Europe,' he wrote. A literary lionizer, he corresponded with celebrities, including Leigh Hunt, and visited London each summer to see exhibitions, plays, people. Patmore had sent him *The Germ*. 'I remember very distinctly every breathing of the verses which were in the first number,' he wrote later. 'Real love of nature, and delicate truth of touch; with the quaint guild-mark, so to speak, of the PRB.'[30]

On his 1850 visit, he met the PRBs in person. 'London, Friday, July 19 – with Woolner, two Rossettis and Buchanan Reid in an omnibus to Chelsea, to Holman Hunt's lodging, large first floor room looking on river, near the old church,' his diary recorded, adding Deverell's name to the list; 'much talk on pictures, etc; we have coffee and fruit; some lie on the floor smoking.' The conversation veered wildly from topic to topic, and continued late. Their host had to be up early. 'As it was now late, and his guests showed no wish to depart, Hunt lay down on three chairs for a nap; but they only made merry of his drowsiness, proposed to sit on him, etc., and so the time lounged on till dawn was broad upon the river and its trailing barges, and D. G. Rossetti (usual captain on such occasions, and notorious night-bird) uprooted himself at last from some cushion or easy-chair, and all departed, after three o'clock, save myself, to whom Hunt had kindly offered a spare bed.'[31]

They talked poetry too, for Allingham had a slim volume ready for the press, with a title-page design which required engraving. Enlisting Walter's aid, Gabriel assisted and when Allingham returned to Ireland let him take the precious Blake manuscript on loan. Soon afterwards, William reviewed their new friend's slim volume.

Another new acquaintance was James Hannay, a Scottish-born naval officer turned writer, whom William described as kingpin of a rival bohemian set. Having next to no money, 'the PRBs were all high-thinking young men, and marked by habits generally abstemious', he explained. 'The Hannay set were equally impecunious but not equally abstemious', spending money in a devil-may-care manner. Hannay himself, who this autumn published a novel based on his naval experiences (which included a court martial for inciting riot) was a fellow 'of inexhaustible spirits', and never-ending anecdote, according to Hunt. Drink and literature were his two passions, and after a day's scribbling in the British Museum, he would muster as many friends as he could, to cruise public bars, make speeches at debating clubs, sally drunkenly into the pit of Drury Lane, and pelt the audience with oranges before being removed by the police, or order a special train to take him to Dover. All with such brio that his companions always bailed him out of trouble.[32]

Gabriel, who never took alcohol, liked Hannay for living so dangerously. Once, both penniless, they found sixpence in the street. Rossetti proposed a cheap meal. Hannay stared: it must buy them a drink. But Gabriel held out for food, and prevailed. They talked, with Hunt, about an illustrated edition of Poe, Rossetti also suggesting *Faust*, *Hamlet*, and the *Vita Nuova*. His translation was now 'in a state of terrific readiness'.

Both Millais's *Christ in the Carpenter's Shop* and Hunt's *Converted British Family* found buyers only with difficulty. No one even inquired after *Ecce Ancilla*, which returned unsold when the season closed. It is often said that its reception made Rossetti vow never to exhibit again, but there is no immediate evidence of this. Publicly identified as an up-and-coming artist – the first stage to fame – Rossetti had reason to feel pleased. 'We are most of us beginning again to work at our painting in the purpose of astounding Europe next year,' he had told Scott in May.[33] However, each of the leading PRBs now turned to more romantic subjects. Religious pictures did not hang well in drawing rooms, the Anglican church seldom sought graven images, while wealthy Catholics tended to favour artists of their own faith, or Old Master copies.

Millais spent the summer painting woodland, with fellow artist Charles Collins, who required an ornamental lily pool. Claiming that as true Londoners they were homesick for smoke, square vegetation, dead leaves and iron railings, Johnny joked about their aims. 'I cannot help feeling we have been asses to have followed the principle of nature,' he told Holman; 'it is so disgustingly laborious and unremunerative ...'[34]

Hunt meanwhile took lodgings with Stephens at Sevenoaks in Kent, for a forest background. Rossetti returned to *Kate the Queen*. 'I am now beginning a large picture containing about thirty figures, and concerning the love of a page for a queen, as treated of in one of Browning's songs – a subject which I have pitched upon principally for its saleableness,' he informed his aunt. 'I find unluckily that the class of pictures which has my natural preference is not for the market.' But his scale was ambitiously over-large, and the subject was soon put aside in favour of Beatrice and Benedick from *Much Ado*, which he would start painting 'in a very few days'. Then this too was superseded, by 'the most wonderful subject in the world', which he would paint 'immediately': a diptych of Dante's meetings with Beatrice on Earth and in Heaven. The latter required a landscape background with trees, and so on 23 October he left London to join Hunt and Stephens. 'My canvas is a whopper again, more than 7 ft long. Ai! Ai!,' he told Tupper.[35]

Within a day he was painting al fresco in Knole Park. It poured with rain. Would his mother send a spare pair of trousers, galoshes, and a rug? Further into the woodland, Holman was painting a vivid autumnal setting for his scene from *Two Gentlemen*. 'Hunt gets on swimmingly – yesterday indeed a full inch above the ankles,' Gabriel joked; he himself had rigged up an umbrella, somehow secured to his button hole.

In his memoirs Hunt recalled Rossetti's struggles with wind and rain, claiming that he stomped off in despair, leaving canvas, easel, stool and paintbox. But soon the weather improved, with sunlight beaming on the scattered red leaves and dappled deer. Then for three weeks 'Gabriel was ever a good-humoured and pleasant companion.' Summoned to visit, Woolner reported that he 'gets up at 7 o'clock, is painting his background [and] translates canzoni at a great rate of evenings'. Millais thought his new subject sounded wonderful. Next year, they would all easily 'spiffligate the sloshers'.[36]

When on 13 November Rossetti went back to London, he had a frieze of woodland at the top of his canvas, a quantity of new translations, and one or two original pieces, including a mock medieval ballad called *Dennis Shand*, aptly about the love of a page for a queen, and apparently inspired by the ancient mansion of Knole. There was a sonnet to autumn, and a lyric on a stand of firs, whose saplings were plumy cockades in a giant's cap. He returned to *Ecce Ancilla*, repainting the Angel's 'insipid' head and adding a left hand. He started a new design – 'Music, with dance of children' – from a line in *Richard III*.

Patmore had shown his *Vita Nuova* translation to Tennyson. Cockney rhymes were again disparaged, but otherwise Patmore was most encouraging, saying there would be no doubt of finding a publisher. 'I calculate on the triumph of being the first man in England who was ever beforehand with the Germans in translating any important work,' Rossetti boasted to Millais, only half ironic.[37]

Back in London, Hannay talked of going to India, Hunt of Jerusalem. Woolner wanted to sculpt figures representing the defeat of despotic power by moral strength. A slight acquaintance named Charles Cayley, former pupil of Professor Rossetti, had produced a translation of Dante's *Inferno*. Other events of the season included Eastlake's election as President of the Royal Academy, the Prince Consort's ambitious plans for next year's Great Exhibition, Wordsworth's posthumous *Prelude*, a new edition of poems by Elizabeth Barrett Browning and *Death's Jest Book* by Thomas Beddoes, with grotesque invocations to toads, snakes, crocodiles.

The second PRB anniversary was approaching. From Oxford Millais proposed Charley Collins for membership. Son of artist William Collins, Charley was brother to Wilkie, the writer, and a devout Anglo-Catholic. Well known to the Rossettis, he shyly admired Maria. But Woolner opposed his election, and in any case Deverell was also a candidate for the vacant place. Like Gabriel, Walter was busy on too many subjects, and sick with some urinary trouble, which occasioned indelicate jokes. He was also without studio space. Some rooms in Red Lion Square, Holborn, owned by William North's father, were affordable if shared, though Mr North added prissy conditions about keeping models 'under gentlemanly restraint' lest artists 'sacrifice the dignity of art to the baseness of passion'.[38] Gabriel and Walter took the rooms.

Though themselves virginal, the PRB understood the allusion to models. After inspecting Red Lion Square, Gabriel had run into Millais, Hunt and Collins, 'parading' up and down the Tottenham Court Road in search of pretty girls who would not shout for the police if accosted, the problem being that such young women would be prostitutes, looking for customers. Artists, moreover, were subject to special temptation; even now the widowed Madox Brown was living at 17 Newman Street with a young model named Emma Hill, who had just given birth to their daughter.

Missing only Millais, the Brotherhood met on 9 December. The year-end anniversary followed at Stephens's house. 'If the rest do not come we can wail together for the departed glory,' wrote Gabriel. 'Happy New Year to you! and PRB to Deverell, I suppose,' Tupper told Fred on 2 January 1851. But in fact the decision was postponed, no doubt because no one wanted to choose between Deverell and Collins. Hunt planned to devise election rules. '[W]hatever system is followed now will be looked upon as a precedent,' he told Stephens. 'Tomorrow I will call on Gabriel and Johnny, to make sure of having a full meeting ... Vivat PRB!'[39]

Eventually, on 9 February a full gathering of the Brothers agreed in principle that new members be elected by ballot. But no vote was taken. Instead they agreed to celebrate Shakespeare's birthday, and 'that anyone contemplating a public course of action affecting the Brotherhood shall mention the matter first to his colleagues'.

If the PRB was losing momentum, however, Gabriel Rossetti seemed to have lost direction. He now had several good designs, two of which were half-begun on canvas. He had new studio space. The exhibitions opened in March, but like his namesake in the *Vita Nuova*, he was 'like unto him who doubteth which path to take, and wishing to go, goeth not . . .' This year he would have nothing to present to the public, or to the reviewers.

CHAPTER FIVE

Run to Me, Delia

Gabriel Rossetti appeared to exist on virtually nothing, and credit. His material needs were few, since he bought no clothes, borrowing William's best garments when necessary, and ate often at home, or from street stalls. When rent or bills for painting materials fell overdue, he postponed payment. But now he was in financial difficulties. On the strength of a promised commission from the Marquess of Northampton, he had refused a further loan from good aunt Charlotte, and declined to send *Ecce Ancilla* to the provincial autumn art shows – a common practice that was 'a very bad thing for any artist' in his view, as it advertised to all that the picture had not sold. But when Northampton's interest evaporated, he was severely embarrassed.

Cut down, large canvases could be used for more saleable works. He began a third oil, a 'small genre cabinet picture'. Then, as Hunt recalled, he was obliged to abandon easel painting, although 'by the sacrificing generosity of relatives his urgent needs were supplied enough for him still to work at designs and little watercolour compositions'. According to his own testimony, however, Gabriel determined to be no further drag on his parents, by giving up painting altogether in favour of 'odd jobs' that would pay ready money. One was drawing on the wood for an illustrated edition of Longfellow, which was to be shared with Hunt, but came to nothing.[1] Through Hannay, Gabriel then did a little translation work on Mallet du Pan's memoirs of the French revolution. He was the more despondent for seeing Millais's new works: *Mariana in the Moated Grange* and the beautiful *Return of the Dove to the Ark*. Especially fine was a design for *The Deluge*, showing a feasting family unaware of the rising waters.

William remembered this as an especially difficult time. At the end of 1850, the family moved to a smaller house in Arlington Street just south of Camden Town, where, with Christina to assist, Frances Rossetti taught young pupils. 'There was our father incapacitated; our mother and Christina fagging over an unremunerative attempt at a day-school; Maria giving lessons in Italian etc., at two or three houses; myself with a small salary,' wrote William, whose earnings were the mainstay of the household.'

Brown wondered if the brothers had quarrelled. No, said Deverell, only he supposed William avoided calling 'oftener than he could help, because he was ordered peremptorily to hand over all the cash he had about him'. But how did Gabriel manage? Brown was intrigued. 'You know he lives in Red Lion Square along with Deverell, and purports to keep himself,' he wrote. In fact, Gabriel borrowed from his mother, and accepted a cheque from aunt Charlotte. 'I need not say of what incalculable value to me, at this juncture, will be the means of dispensing with further delay in my picture,' he told her gruffly. On 15 April he opened an account with Robersons, the premier artists' suppliers, with an order for pigments and a canvas.[2]

And yet no progress was made. 'Rossetti has just thrown up a *third* picture,' reported Brown in dismay; 'he has made some designs which are perfectly divine . . . finer than anything I have seen, but paint he *will not*. He is too idle.' On 21 March William told Allingham tersely that Gabriel 'will not exhibit' in the approaching exhibitions. Reviewing Deverell's *Hamlet* at the National Institution in April, William also noted a 'certain brooding insolence' in the Prince's aspect, an oblique comment on his brother, who was probably the model, and whose mood this spring echoed Hamlet's.[3]

Instead of painting, Gabriel mixed with Hannay's Grub Street crowd, who were planning a magazine. He went to the Eclectic Society where Hannay was a regular debater. With Millais and Hunt he attended a public demonstration of hypnosis, one of the sensations of the year. The other, which all sophisticated Londoners affected to disdain, was the forthcoming exhibition in Hyde Park, dubbed 'the large Glasshouse'. 'I expect all respectable families will leave London after the first month of the Exhibition, it will be so crowded with the lowest rabble of all the countries of Europe,' wrote Millais. As his brother's substitute on the *Spectator*, Gabriel reviewed the concurrent international art exhibition at Lichfield House with customary hauteur. 'The great mass of these pictures is such as we shall not attempt to criticise,' he began, 'belonging as they do to that class where examination and silence are the sum of criticism.' Those worthy of notice included Bonheur's *Charcoal Burners* in the Auvergne, 'the best work in the place . . . quite of the first class'. Gérôme's *Troubadour* was poetical and dainty, while *Boccaccio reading to the Queen of Naples* by Baron Wappers, under whom Brown had studied, was 'good enough' in execution but commonplace in conception. Delaroche's *Cromwell* was admirable in every respect except that of the Protector's face, to which Rossetti felt sure 'our great historian' Carlyle would object.[4] (Carlyle, sitting to Woolner, had recently remarked approvingly on the 'sense and sincerity' of the PRB's aspiration to paint from nature rather than ideal forms.)

British artists were poorly represented; taking a side-swipe at Stone, Gabriel complained that 'by young and unknown English artists, there seems to be scarcely anything'. In other words, the PRB and their associates had not been invited to exhibit.

By this date, the Red Lion Square rooms had been given up. Neither Gabriel nor Deverell could pay another quarter's rent. As Emma and her baby were now living in a cottage in Clapham, Rossetti moved his belongings to Brown's place in Newman Street – where six months earlier he had sat for the figure of Chaucer, perched on the scaffold tower sketching while Brown painted on, late into the night. Taken there by Alex Munro in order to meet Rossetti, painter Arthur Hughes recalled it as a vast and tenebrous studio, built out into the yard.

Brown, Hunt, Millais and Collins had their works accepted at the RA. It looked as if the attack would be as violent as last year. At the preview, William watched critics guffaw ostentatiously in front of PRB pictures, though he also noted that Millais's *Mariana* was 'a great favourite with the women'. On 7 May, *The Times* led the assault in familiar terms, castigating the 'offensive and absurd productions' of those who combined puerility in art with 'uppishness and self-sufficiency' and calling on the RA not to tolerate any more 'offensive jests' by those 'who style themselves PRB'. With similar sneers, the *Athenaeum* greeted Millais's 'old perversity' and Hunt's 'rearguard move'.[5]

But the tide was turning. Brown heard that Academicians Mulready, Maclise and Dyce, as well as the veteran John Linnell, had praised the PRB works, and then that Ruskin had written to *The Times* in their defence. 'This is the very thing we want,' commented William, when Hunt brought the news to Hannay's. At dawn, Hunt proposed a row up to Richmond. It was a fine Sunday morning. 'The lovely spring variations of green in trees and grass were specially delightful,' he recalled. So too were the bottles of champagne and claret they collected at his studio, in order to celebrate the change in critical fortune.

Though young, Ruskin was author of *Modern Painters* (1843 and 1846) and the newly-issued *Stones of Venice* (1851) and thanks to his prosperous father's wine business was a wealthy patron as well as an influential writer. Confidently, he asserted that other critics were wrong about the PRB: there had been nothing in art so earnest or so complete as their pictures since the days of Albrecht Dürer.

Throughout his life, everyone remarked on Rossetti's lack of envy towards his friends' successes. Keenly competitive, he nevertheless genuinely promoted others' interests and rejoiced on their behalf, seeing this as a spur to ambition, not to spite. But he was doubly disappointed to have no picture in the current exhibitions when it emerged that Ruskin was to follow his letter to *The Times* with a pamphlet on 'Pre-Raphaelitism'. 'It will no doubt be of much service to us,' he told Scott; though he feared he would not be individually mentioned, since it was doubtful that Ruskin had seen either of his exhibited works. William suggested he review the pamphlet. Better if William did it, came the reply; then he could mention Gabriel's name ('though of course not obtrusively') and dwell particularly on the fact that his religious subjects had been entirely original in conception.

Through a mutual acquaintance, he had finally been introduced to Browning – on a rare visit to Britain – who though short had a 'most stunning head' and well recalled the letter about *Pauline*. Otherwise London was empty. Hunt and Millais were in Surrey with Charley Collins, already working for the 1852 season. Hunt, whose *Two Gentlemen of Verona* received a prize at the Liverpool Academy exhibition and sold to a Belfast businessman, had two new subjects: a rustic courtship scene with moral symbolism and a moonlit picture of Christ outside a door, lantern in hand, to be called *The Light of the World*. Millais, whose *Mariana* went to a dealer, was painting a river-bank background for Ophelia. Cheerful and sun-tanned, they joked about the pretty girls in country lanes, and teased Collins for his religious self-denial in refusing blackberry pie. They expected a visit from Rossetti, but he did not show, so on visiting London the following weekend the three made straight for Newman Street, where they found Gabriel in very low spirits, as was not now unusual. Their genial, expansive PR Brother could so easily turn glum, disconsolate, unrousable. Millais, seeing him after another gap, described him as 'just the same', lounging with his legs flung up on the furniture, humming moodily. Another time, Stephens reported him in accustomed aspect, crumpled in an armchair 'scowling like a brigand'.[6]

He had been feeling unwell, 'exceedingly disordered and uncomfortable', he told William. Compounded of seediness and self-doubt, the condition was recurrent, aggravated by the stinking air of London's streets and sewers in summer. So when he heard that their new patron Thomas Combe of Oxford University Press had offered to pay for Hunt and Millais to travel and paint in Palestine, he responded with almost hysterical distress. 'Dear Holman ... Why did you not mention this when I saw you on Sunday?' he demanded. 'I hope to God – and I use the words most solemnly, as concerning one of the dearest hopes I have – that you are not going to start before the next exhibition, in order that I may at least have a chance, by the sale of the picture I shall then have ready, of accompanying you on your journey ...' Otherwise 'it would seem as if the fellowship between us were taken from me, and my life rejected'.[7]

These were 'the most serious words I ever wrote in my life', he added. On second thoughts: 'PS. You had better burn this letter, for I find it reads childishly.' On third thoughts, however, he was in earnest. 'Give my love to Millais.'

William and Woolner hooted at the idea of Gabriel going to Palestine; as atheists, they saw no point in authentic biblical landscapes. In truth, Gabriel could never have really relished such an expedition, and his appeal to Holman is thus eloquent of the fellowship he felt towards his Brothers in art, at a time when he was falling behind.

'I am not doing anything and probably shall cut Art as it is too much trouble,' he had told Walter defiantly. A literary friend of his father's commended the *Vita Nuova* translation to publisher John Murray, which briefly revived his spirits, but the silence which followed shows that this too proved a *non avenue*. For all his talent, Gabriel Rossetti sometimes seemed ill-fated.

Brown, too, was subject to moodiness and these months in the old studio behind Newman Street are one key to their lifelong friendship. Working on a picture of Jesus washing the Disciples' feet, Brown was struggling financially, and heading for a period in which he described himself as having been 'intensely miserable very hard up & a little mad'. Rossetti was perhaps not the best companion – he kept Brown up late talking, sometimes painted all night 'making the whole place miserable and filthy, translating sonnets at breakfast working very hard and doing nothing'. But he understood.

'All pictures that's painted with sense or with thought / Are painted by madmen, as sure as a groat,' Blake had scribbled in his notebook. With their depressive anxieties, Brown and Rossetti were both 'a little mad' at this time.

Sleeping in the studio three nights a week, Brown spent the others with Emma and their daughter Cathy, now a year old. He planned a picture of a young woman proudly presenting a new-born child to its father, to pose for which Emma came to Newman Street. Fond of her as he was, she was a complication Brown could have done without; as well as the cost, there was his elder daughter Lucy, now nine, to consider. Nor was he the only one of Gabriel's friends whose sexual desires had led to difficulties, for Hannay was also involved with a woman who had just borne him a child. 'Don't think me blind to the proper view of the matter,' Hannay protested to Allingham, saying he was truly remorseful for his 'absurd conduct' and fully aware of the temporal – i.e. financial – and spiritual consequences.[8]

Miss Lock had been paid off, and he was already courting a more respectable young lady, perhaps to guard against further 'absurdities'.

Gabriel approached such topics obliquely, working on his closet scene of dancing children to produce a watercolour with a sinister atmosphere of decadence and lust entitled 'To caper nimbly in a lady's chamber to the lascivious pleasing of a lute', from a line in *Richard III*, and planning a new subject, from the poems of Tibullus, which was both saleable and likely to secure a good place at the RA, he told his ever-inquiring aunt. In fact, it was an erotic scene, only slightly elevated by its classical source.

Perhaps one of the literary fellows introduced him to the lines in Book I, where Tibullus, absent on a military campaign, urges his mistress Delia to remain chaste, awaiting his return and then greet him eagerly, running with bare feet and long, loose hair. The scene is laid in one of the bedchambers adjoining the atrium of Delia's house, Rossetti explained later:

> She is seated on her couch, which she has vowed to Diana during her lover's absence ... At present she is resting languidly from her spinning, with the spindle still in one hand, while with the other she draws a lock of hair listlessly between her lips. The lamp is lit at the close of one of her long days of waiting and she is listening, before she lies down to sleep, to the chaunt of an old woman, who plays on two harps at the same time, as is sometimes seen in Roman art. Tibullus has just arrived, and is stepping eagerly but cautiously over the black boy who sleeps on the doorway as a guard. He has been shown in by a dark girl who holds him back as he enters, that he may gaze at Delia for a moment before she perceives his presence. A metal mirror reflects the light of the lamp opposite and on each side of the doorway are painted figures of Love and Night.

In an enclosed chamber, as music plays, a pair of lovers are coming together, drawn by mutual desire. As Tibullus approaches, Delia's eyes are closed with veiled longing and passive receptivity.

Rossetti ordered a canvas, and hired a lay-figure, on which to arrange the costumes. The first model for Delia was Emma, sitting awkwardly on a dining chair, hair neatly braided, on one of the evenings she came to Newman Street. The other drawings are of Elizabeth Siddall, sitting professionally with her hair undone, wearing a loose shift, eyes closed and a strand of hair suggestively between her lips.

Miss Siddall lived in Southwark, where her family had an ironmongery business. Like her sisters, she worked in dressmaking and millinery, but had artistic aspirations. Somehow, she became acquainted with Deverell's family and early in 1850 sat to him for Viola in *Twelfth Night*, wearing a tunic over Elizabethan-style hose. Soon she was one of Hunt's British Family succouring a Druid, and thence his Sylvia, holding a difficult kneeling pose.

The fellows teased each other about supposed attachments. Hearing that a country girl was sitting to Hunt for his shepherdess, they went hammering on the studio door, pretending to be her sweetheart. Hunt himself had initiated a practical joke the year before, when Lizzie Siddall was sitting for Sylvia, by getting Stephens to persuade Jack Tupper that she was Hunt's wife. An 'impromptu farce' according to Hunt, this was a 'disgraceful hoax' according to Gabriel, who insisted they apologise to Tupper. With mock regret, Hunt protested that Tupper would never have suspected him of 'passing off in such a character any but a modest-agreeable girl as Miss Siddal you see is, and not a common model'.[9] Indeed not, for she took an intelligent interest in art and had aspirations of her own. It was suspected she had fallen for Deverell, like many young women, but he had family as well as health troubles and was not seen much around the studios now.

Brown had first succumbed to Emma's charms when alone in the studio. On the days when Brown was in south London, Lizzie was unchaperoned at Newman Street, willing to let down her hair, take off her shoes and put on costumes. She was modest and respectable, yet independent.

As Dante had written of Beatrice: 'I felt a spirit of love begin to stir / within my heart, long time unfelt till then.' Gabriel was twenty-three, with no 'juvenile amours, liaisons or flirtations' behind him. Having never previously been smitten, he joked to Hunt around this time that like Dante Alighieri he was 'of little knowledge in such matters'. Later he would tell Brown that when he first saw Lizzie 'he felt his destiny was defined' and there are other references to a sense of predestination, of this being the beloved marked out for him, even partnered with him in a previous existence. 'I have been here before', he wrote in 1854:

> You have been mine before –
> How long ago I may not know:
> But just when at that swallow's soar
> Your neck turned so,
>   Some veil did fall – I knew it all of yore.

They may well have first met when Miss Siddall was sitting to Walter in the days of *The Germ*. Gabriel's over-reaction to Hunt's practical joke suggests susceptibility, as does an obscure poem enclosed in the same letter, about mistaking a face in a crowded reflection for one's own. 'Can you explain?' he asked abruptly. Printing the verses thirty years later, William paraphrased simply: 'A man is in love with a woman, without declaring himself and without her appreciating the fact.'[10] But only now did the attraction become imperative.

Emotionally, he was ready to fall in love, like Millais, Hunt, Hannay and the rest of the fellows, not with an ideal beloved but with a real girl who would make his heart beat so hard that, like the outlawed revolutionary in *A Last Confession*, he thought she would hear it. 'Suddenly her face is there', he would write in *Love's Nocturn*:

> Part the boughs and look beneath –
> Lilies share
> Secret waters there, and breathe.

Brown, seeing the drawings of Delia, may have guessed. Millais, perhaps seeing them too, asked Miss Siddall to pose for his *Ophelia*. The river background being complete, he was ready to add the figure.

In February 1852, in the Gower Street back room, she first lay with her head back and mouth slightly open – Ophelia died singing – to be delicately drawn in pencil. Then she put on a heavy, antique brocade dress and climbed into a tin bath-tub filled with water to simulate a river. Millais painted with deep concentration, intent on a perfect rendering before model and dress had to move. Candles warming the bath went out. Lizzie grew numb, until she could not move, so that she might have died of hypothermia, a virtual drowning to mimic Ophelia's. Her father was angry, threatening to sue. Something made it a story to be suppressed and recalled, after Millais's death, only by Arthur Hughes.

By common consent, *Ophelia* was a marvel, 'of the noblest order of perfection ... the idealism of loveliness' as William told Scott.[11] Only Gabriel dissented, perversely preferring Millais's other picture, which suggests jealous feelings.

Lizzie had copper-coloured hair and such translucent skin that when she looked down demurely, as Victorian girls were taught to do, her eyes seemed almost visible through the lids. She was tall and slim in an age that praised the petite: Allingham recalled her 'long thin limbs'. Her mouth was imperfect, the lower lip tucked under the upper, 'as if it strove to kiss itself' in Rossetti's more partial words. She spoke hesitantly, but laughed aloud, with a sideways sense of humour. Sometimes, she looked as frail and beautiful as Ophelia; at others, merely pinched and plain. Nor was red hair admired, being thought unlucky, even accursed. No one liked to mention freckles, which were considered blemishes. Amongst themselves, the fellows called her 'Miss Sid' or even 'the Sid' in jokey adaptation of the way beauties and courtesans were identified elsewhere in Europe. She called herself Lizzie. At twenty-two, she was just a year younger than Gabriel.

Soon enough, they were on first-name terms – an immediate sign of intimacy. In retrospect, William claimed they were engaged 'very probably before or not long after the close of 1851'. But as the imprecision indicates, there was no such formal or informal agreement, public or private. For good reason: it was a promise of marriage. As well as breaking hearts, men who broke an engagement could be sued for compensation. Gabriel was ready neither to marry nor to enter a sexual liaison. Hannay's bastard child and Brown's domestic situation were warning enough. In his present circumstances romance was out of the question. Moreover, even if no common model, Lizzie was not an eligible bride. Her family lacked class, culture, wealth. Even without snobbery, the Rossettis would not approve.

Dante's beloved Beatrice is forever out of reach. Tibullus stops on the threshold, so he may gaze at Delia unseen. Gabriel did not declare his feelings, either to Lizzie herself, or to his friends. While she was yet a model, he could, as Christina later put it, 'feed upon her face' as long as he wished. He could turn her head, reposition her arm, ask her to lean back in abandon: all the intimacy of love, without its reciprocity. For both, perhaps, the intense excitement of knowing but not saying.

When two years later Millais found himself comparably if far more complicatedly in love, he produced no paintings for the next exhibition season. Emotional perturbation is one reason why Gabriel Rossetti again had nothing to show in 1852.

Ruskin proved an invaluable ally to the PRB this year. 'Our position is greatly altered,' wrote William. 'We have emerged from reckless abuse to a position of general and high recognition.' Millais's works were triumphant, Hunt's well received. Even Brown, seized with last-minute determination, completed *Christ with the Disciples* and sent it with the *Pretty Baa-Lambs* to the Academy. Only Gabriel was unrepresented. Christina, staying in the country, voiced family concern: 'I think he ought to work now, and shine superior at the next Exhibition, with his P. R. Brothers. There will always be time for recreation,' she wrote primly, hoping also that the next year 'will show us his time has not been wasted'.[12]

He was homeless again, for Brown's tenancy at Newman Street ended in May. But his melancholy had passed and, thanks to new friends, he was about to begin a time he described as 'one of the jolliest of my life'.

Halfway up the slopes of Highgate's West Hill stood a pretty house called the Hermitage, with a Gothick garden cottage known as the Nest, in use as a studio. Hither, soon after Easter, Rossetti moved his traps yet again, at the invitation of Edward Bateman, a designer who had worked with Owen Jones on the Great Exhibition and was known among the Brethren as the Illuminator from his fondness for initials and borders. Bateman was engaged to Anna Howitt, a fellow artist currently studying in Bavaria, whose parents were the authors William and Mary Howitt. Gabriel knew them slightly. A veteran radical, William Howitt had kept the light burning in various periodicals. His *People's Journal* had incidentally printed the Holst engraving of a student dicing with Satan that had graced Gabriel's wall in 1847, while in March 1850 his *Standard of Freedom* had favourably mentioned *The Germ*.

Set back from the road behind elm trees, the Hermitage had a long sloping garden. The Nest had two rooms, the upper reached by an outside staircase, under a roof of thatch and rampant, picturesque ivy. With a 'gimcrack attempt at rusticity', stained glass and grotto work decorated the interior, together with country furniture and old china, making 'a most unique, quaint and pleasant abode, fit home for a painter' in Mary Howitt's words, though Rossetti himself described the accomodation as that of a 'savage bivouac'. For the few weeks of their cohabitation, he and Bateman seem to have done little serious work, though Bateman had a number of commissions, and Gabriel purchased more colours and brushes. On fine days they could walk over the Heath, skirting Lord Mansfield's park at Kenwood, and call on Brown, who had taken a painting room in Hampstead High Street. Indeed, looking from his back window, Brown could see the white spire of the new church just below the Hermitage.

Instead of oil painting, Rossetti completed *To Caper Nimbly*, and worked on more careful, inventive, expressive compositions in pencil and watercolour, sketches towards full-scale pictures depicting intense, arrested moments. At his best, everyone agreed, he was insurpassable in this field, his designs full of freshness and feeling. New ideas included Giotto painting Dante's portrait, Dante in exile, the medieval sorcerer Michael Scott, 'Yesterday's Rose' from a verse drama by Henry Taylor. One of the first, done at Highgate and given to Bateman, was a fine study of Mary being comforted by other women as her Son is condemned to death. Next came a very small, very intense scene of Beatrice refusing to greet Dante as she descends stairs at a wedding feast, one of several incidents in the *Vita Nuova* that dramatise the emotions of unacknowledged love.[13] The scene depicted is taut with tension, and Miss Siddall models for Beatrice. There could hardly be a clearer pictorial expression of Dante Rossetti's feelings, for those with eyes to see.

One evening at the Nest, Gabriel had a visit from William Bell Scott, on his annual trip from Newcastle for the London exhibitions. In the cool of the evening, climbing the wooden stair, he found himself in the romantic dusk 'face to face with Rossetti and a lady whom I did not recognise and could scarcely see. He did not introduce her; she rose to go. I made a little bow, which she did not acknowledge; and she left.'[14] This was Miss Siddall. 'Why he did not introduce me I cannot say.'

On occasion, Lizzie could be a hired model, of no account socially. But the contrast between the tacit declaration in the drawing and the silence in front of Scott is eloquent.

Bateman was preparing to leave for Australia where, according to the press, any healthy young fellow had a good chance of making his fortune in the goldfields. Scott's train from Newcastle had been filled with working men bound for the emigrant ships. Australia was a challenge, an opportunity and an adventure. William Howitt and his sons left in June. With Bateman, whose cousin was Governor of gold-rich Victoria, went Bernhard Smith, and Woolner, who had recently failed to win an important commission. On 15 July Hunt and the Rossetti brothers saw them off from London docks, on the three-month voyage, all 'plentifully stocked with corduroys, sou'westers, jerseys, fire-arms and belts full of little bags to hold the expected nuggets'.

Though the Brotherhood had ceased to meet regularly, Gabriel missed Woolner keenly. When instalments of his 'sea-log' reached England, its 'Woolnerian idiosyncrasies' set him roaring with delight. He thought of the travellers often, trying to imagine the 'extraordinary conditions' they were experiencing. Australia was indeed another world, wrote Tommy, inhabited by men who all carried firearms and looked like 'red French Republicans, much of that loose air and swagger'. En route to the goldfield, the overnight camps had a wild aspect, with fires blazing, meat frying, oxen being unyoked, whips snapping, dogs barking, guns banging away in all directions, shooting birds for the pot. Soon, they were hard at work, like navvies. 'Digging for gold is not play. My hand trembles so much I can scarcely write,' he reported after the first day. A man in the encampment was murdered. One of their own group drowned in a creek . . . He wished his friends at home would write.[15]

One evening that winter, walking home by Primrose Hill, Gabriel extemporised a sonnet recalling the annual PRB reunions:

> Woolner, tonight it snows for the first time.
> Our feet knew well the path, where in this snow
> Mine leave one track . . .
> Can the year change, and I not think of thee
> With whom so many changes of the year
> So many years were watched . . . –

But when he finally wrote, on New Year's Day, he had 'nothing to say except to hover round the old desperate desultory story' of his own failures. Compared to these, Woolner's adventures were heroic. None the less, his letters were long and cordial, revealing his strong urge to keep contact with the absent PR Brother, whom he sometimes called 'Tommaso' in Italian style, or more facetiously 'Woolnerius'. He drew verbal and visual sketches of those left in London: William dozing uncomfortably in an armchair, Hunt looking 'like a fellow who would have a try at anything, even to making the sun stand still', Brown painting in Hampstead. A week later, on Gabriel's initiative, they gathered again and agreed to meet in spirit, on 12 April, at either ends of the earth, for 'some act of communication'. In London and Melbourne each group would produce sketches ('mutual portraits preferable') or verses, for immediate dispatch, in token of abiding comradeship.

The promised portraits were duly done: Millais by Hunt, Stephens by Millais, Rossetti and Hunt by each other. 'I could not and need not say all that we conjectured about you,' wrote Gabriel; 'dear Tommaso, write as soon as you can and tell me all news, over which I wonder and puzzle.'

Gabriel's affection for his friends was golden, like the glittering nuggets the prospectors failed to find. 'We were just eight months too late,' Woolner explained. 'The numbers had multiplied vastly, the richest places were exhausted.' Rossetti was awed, nevertheless, by the dangers encountered and survived, by manliness tried and proved. If Woolner missed making his fortune, he told Scott, he had gained strength and self-confidence. Physically timid himself, Rossetti responded vicariously to the travellers' courage and initiation into hardships that literally separated men from boys, women, poets.

At the diggings Woolner had hardened more than his muscles. When he finally returned to Britain eighteen months later, much had changed. Always forthright, he had grown brasher, more determined, less idealistic. As he had not come back 'like a conquering hero, loaded with honours and with chariots of riches', he had to take up where he had left off, with some bitterness of spirit. The friendships resumed, but the intimacy of brotherhood had passed. The snow-covered path he and Rossetti had once shared now parted.

Ten years on, hearing that Tommy spoke disparagingly of him, Gabriel severed all contact. When, twenty years further, the topic arose of a funeral memorial to his brother, William remarked that the most appropriate artist would be the now-famous portrait sculptor Thomas Woolner, RA, 'were it not for the fatal objection that Gabriel of late years hated him'. One grief, one joy, one love, one hatred: Rossetti's relationships were never likely to be lukewarm. 'He always was most generous in his admiration,' recalled Hughes; 'but anything he did not like he hated as heartily.'[16]

When Bateman left for Australia, Mary Howitt and her daughters moved into the Hermitage and Rossetti lost his lodging. At home, his mother's little school failed to flourish – it was a common lament that there were more gentlewomen wishing to teach than pupils to pay – while his father was ever weaker, mentally and physically. Political hopes having collapsed, to family dismay Gabriele was now beset by and involved with anti-Papist groups seeking the conversion of Catholic Italy to the Protestant faith. To this end, he was composing a collection of hymns entitled *Arpa Evangelica*, encouraged by a nephew on his mother's side, Teodorico Pietrocola, who had arrived in Britain with unrealistic hopes of assistance from his uncle *il professore*. First falling in with Plymouth Brethren and then with others of a more evangelical persuasion, in due course Teodorico was ordained, and ministered to a Protestant congregation in Florence.

For the younger Rossettis, a new group of friends centred on the Orme family, living just north of Regent's Park. Mrs Orme, sister to Mrs Patmore, was a good-looking, well-endowed woman with a special fondness for young writers and artists; Gabriel compared her to the glamorous actress Isabella Glyn, whom he and William held in extravagant admiration. He gave his portrait of Woolner to Mrs Orme, and sent Woolner a sketch of her daughter Rosalind, one of a number of portrait drawings completed this autumn, which included his mother, aunt Eliza, Scott and Brown.

He was always welcome at the Hermitage, too, for though as a former Quaker she was rather critical of young Mr Rossetti's casual manner, as editor of Christmas annuals Mary Howitt was a literary talent-spotter, who had admired the poems in *The Germ* and encouraged his literary ambitions. One achievement this season was the publication of his poem *Vingt-et-un* in the *Athenaeum*. Hunt later told a story of Rossetti unexpectedly sharing a cab with the editor of a leading periodical and though the details are confused, this may have been a lucky encounter; newly titled *The Card-dealer*, the poem appeared on 23 October, with a note explaining the Holst picture that inspired it. In place of name, the signature was 'HHH', because someone – probably Mrs Howitt – said his style was very hard.

Thus prompted, Rossetti returned to poetry, versifying the medieval *Staff and Scrip* in ballad form, and drafting *Sister Helen*, a macabre companion piece for two voices derived from old tales of mystery and magic, in which a betrayed woman kills her faithless lover by melting his waxen effigy. The Howitts, who collected ghost stories and folklore, seized on it for publication.

Encouraged by her brothers, Christina had enrolled in drawing classes. Shortly after his eviction from the Hermitage, Gabriel asked her to send specimens of her handiwork while on holiday. But, he continued teasingly, 'You must take care not to rival the Sid, but keep within respectful limits. Since you went away, I have had sent me, among my things from Highgate, a lock of hair shorn from the beloved hair of that dear, and radiant as the tresses of Aurora, a sight of which may perhaps dazzle you on your return. That love has lately made herself a grey dress, also a black silk one, the first bringing out her characteristics as a "meek unconscious dove", while the second enhances her qualifications as a "rara avis in terris" by rendering her "nigro simillima cygno".[17]

Thus with Latin quotations and ironical hyperbole he alerted the family to the strength of his attachment. The Rossettis were satirical when it came to sentiment, finding much amusement in James Hannay's description of his new fiancée as 'the sugar-plum of the universe', though charmed by the young woman in person. By writing of Miss Siddall in equally extravagant manner, Gabriel deflected deeper inquiry. He did not invite Lizzie to meet his parents, nor did he visit her family.

Millais and Hunt returned from their summer painting season in Kent and Sussex, canvases ready for completion. For Rossetti the question of a studio was urgent, for more than one reason. So in Highgate and Hornsey, 'as well as at Hampstead, Islington, Highbury, Holloway and Muswell Hill', he searched diligently, before changing tack, to 'forage for cribs' in Southwark, and eventually finding an apartment just north of Blackfriars Bridge. The search ended, William wrote on 15 November, in rooms on the second floor of Chatham Place, virtually over the Fleet Ditch's confluence with the Thames. This was convenient for William's new office in Somerset House, along the Strand, for in theory it was the brothers' joint residence, William being thereby persuaded to pay what he considered the high rent of £60 a year, inclusive of attendance. There were two rooms, one for a studio, with a small bedroom and a balcony where Gabriel optimistically proposed to paint *al fresco*.

The block gave an excellent view of the annual Lord Mayor's Procession; in subsequent years, family and friends were often invited. More importantly, it was relatively close to Miss Siddall's home in the Old Kent Road. One of Gabriel's first acts on moving in was to invite her for an evening, tête-à-tête. Since she was coming, he informed William, he did not 'of course wish for anyone else' to call.

It was a bustling, noisy location. Buses and carts crossed the bridge constantly to Bankside, Bermondsey, Elephant and Castle. Cattle and sheep were driven north to the Smithfield slaughterhouses. Hard by were Ludgate Circus, Fleet Street, St Bride's and St Paul's, its sonorous chime marking the hours. Downriver, beyond London Bridge by the Tower lay the Pool of London, busiest of all harbours, and the ever-growing complex of docks: East India, West India, Canada, Canary. Upstream, steamers plied between the City, Westminster and Chelsea, while barges ferried coal, timber, bricks, sand and virtually every other commodity under the sun to wharves and warehouses. When the tide ebbed, as Arthur Munby observed one winter afternoon, mudlarks scavenged for coals among dead cats and broken crockery. Give or take a few years, it was the London of *Our Mutual*

Friend, with its smoky, smelly fogs, gas-lamps illuminating pools in the murk. One of Rossetti's first acts was to get the Chatham Place gas fittings fixed.[18]

Above all, it was a great place to invite the fellows. 'You cannot imagine what delightful rooms these are for a party,' Gabriel told Woolner, 'regularly built out into the river and with windows on all sides.' He borrowed a bed off Brown, begged the family's best mirrors as essential studio equipment and graciously accepted a lamp from aunt Margaret; it would bring her to mind 'not only when I look at the lamp, but when the lamp enables me to look at anything else', he wrote. Having somehow managed to pay £5 towards his Roberson's account in August, he now ordered a mahogany rack easel costing 50 shillings, together with a supply of fine drawing paper and crayons.

The first social event at Blackfriars was on 2 December. Hunt, Millais, Deverell, Collins, Stephens and Tom Seddon came. Brown defaulted, being now at some distance, either at Hampstead or at Hendon, where Emma and the baby were now lodging. A second party, on 30 December, was recorded in the diary of George Boyce, aspiring landscapist, who had bought the *To Caper Nimbly* watercolour and was curious to see the rooms. Fred Stephens, Alex Munro, Arthur Hughes, John Clayton, Henry Wells and Tom's brother John Seddon were there. But there were no works on view – 'which is his way' commented Boyce, half admiring, half doubtful. Instead, Rossetti showed his collection of Gavarni prints, some highly poetical illustrations by the Hon. Mrs Boyle, and the impressive face of Dante's death-mask.

Boyce found the atmosphere most beguiling. The view of lights from bridge and wharves reflected in the river was as picturesque as the conversation over roast chestnuts, coffee and hot spirits was delightful, thanks to the 'happy and gentlemanly freedom of the company'. In an all-male gathering, there was no false politeness, but no coarseness either; all spoke freely, warmly, cleanly. This was Gabriel at his happiest, at last able to repay hospitality and shine in his own crib. He himself did not smoke or drink; as Brown remarked later, 'tobacco, tea, coffee, stimulants' were all distasteful to him – indeed there was something provoking about the way, after hours of conviviality, Rossetti would end the evening by pouring himself a tumbler of cold water.[19]

New Year's Eve was spent *en famille* at Arlington Street, together with Hunt and Stephens. After the visitors left, Gabriel wrote to Woolner while William snoozed in his chair. This should have been the fourth PRB anniversary. Perhaps it was, after a fashion, but the circle was widening. On Twelfth Night he played host again. 'To Rossetti's, Blackfriars Bridge,' recorded Boyce. 'Met there W. Holman Hunt, J. E. Millais, J. P. Seddon,

Clayton, Munro, Stephens, Blanchard, C. Lucy, a Scotchman and a foreigner.' Seddon was an architect, Clayton a stained-glass artist, Blanchard a journalist. The Scot was possibly David Masson, scholar and secretary of the Friends of Italy. The foreigner was almost certainly cousin Teodorico. Holman Hunt spoke of leaving soon to paint in Syria. Millais had been 'taken up' by Ruskin and was currently painting Mrs Ruskin's head into his new picture, a dramatic scene set in the Jacobite era.

Primed with this year's success, Millais, Hunt and Brown had all applied for election to the RA, confident that, in Millais's earlier words, they would now 'spiffligate the sloshers'. But the latter had prevailed, electing Frederick Goodall instead. Fools were thus rampant, wrote William. Worse, added Hunt: any institution that elected artists like Stone, Scroggins and Snooks stood as an obstacle to all progress. Hunt called a meeting to discuss an independent PRB exhibition, including Brown, who was virtually a Brother and doubly needed in Woolner's absence. Gabriel excused himself. 'What between remissnesses and disappointments in my painting, it has come to that pass with me, that until I have done something decisive and got again into the field, I should feel like a pretender at any meeting connected with the artistic interests of the brotherhood,' he wrote. Of course, this was in confidence; he hoped in due course to achieve something.[20]

In fact, he had had some minor success. As well as Boyce, Henry Wells and John Seddon had bought watercolour sketches: *Beatrice denying her Salutation* and *The Youth of Dante*, showing Giotto painting the poet, with Guido Cavalcanti looking on. Encouraged, Rossetti sent the drawings to a show at the Old Water-colour Society over Christmas,[21] where they attracted a good deal of praise. 'I am now working with a vague reference to the Exhibition of this year, but on that vexatious subject shall defer speaking,' he told Woolner in the new year, having learnt not to brag of things as yet unachieved.

William summarised the fortunes of the Brotherhood for the last time in January 1853, explaining that 'though Preraphaelism and Brotherhood are as real as ever, and purpose to continue so, the P.R.B is not and cannot be, so much a matter of social intercourse as it used to be.' But this hardly mattered, since their critics were well-nigh routed. Even Gabriel seemed to be getting on at last.

CHAPTER SIX

Art, Friendship and Love

If the Brotherhood had served its chief purpose, it was not yet redundant, for it was thanks to the PRB that Rossetti made his next significant sale, to Francis MacCracken, the Belfast businessman who had bought Hunt's *Two Gentlemen of Verona*. Influenced by Ruskin's commendation, MacCracken was taken with the notion of owning other Pre-Raphaelite works. It did not at first look hopeful, for he liked neither watercolours nor Italian subjects, but would prefer a small oil, ideally from scripture, Shakespeare, or national history. Negotiating on Gabriel's behalf, Brown thereupon suggested *Ecce Ancilla*, tactfully retitled *The Annunciation* to suit Protestant sympathies. When Hunt also commended the picture MacCracken succumbed, 'unable to resist the temptation of possessing a work so highly lauded by two brother artists', but still nervous: the dimensions suggested an ill-proportioned, altogether singular work. 'I expect to be somewhat *horrified* at first sight, but I hope ultimately to be able to face and appreciate the beauty of his work,' he wrote bravely at the end of January, when the canvas was ready for shipment.[1]

Albeit an idiosyncratic buyer, MacCracken was representative of a new breed, as aristocratic patronage declined. 'The noble and wealthy ... believing that their possessions were threatened by a popular revolution which was to sink the rights of station and property in a general deluge of republican equality, had little time to attend to the remoter importance of the progress of national Art,' wrote Wilkie Collins, whose own father had suffered.[2] Into their shoes stepped the newly-rich in manufacturing and commerce – banking, textiles, shipping. Motivated partly by patriotism and partly by fear of being sold fake Old Masters, such purchasers favoured contemporary British art, also wishing to distinguish their taste from the patrician 'country house' style. Hence the great increase in sentimental and genre pieces, together with literary and moral pictures. Enterprises like the Art Union aimed to foster this change, promoting the purchase of work by living artists.

As a chance acquaintance noted in 1859, Rossetti did not think that 'the transference of the patronage of the Arts from the nobility to the mercantile and manufacturing men was an injury to the Arts'. Indeed, he declared it to be a benefit 'that the collections were disinterestedly made, etc etc.' and roundly challenged the supremacy of most 'Old Masters', declaring that, with the exception of a few men of genius, nothing had been done since Michelangelo worthy of the name of art. His interlocutor on this occasion, who had an old-fashioned collection that included a Reynolds, was then subjected to a characteristically imperious judgement. 'I can't think how a man like you can give a large sum of money for such rubbish as that!'[3]

Properly grateful to Hunt and Brown for their exertions on his behalf, he welcomed MacCracken in similar spirit. 'You have heard, I believe, that I have got rid of my white picture to an Irish maniac,' he told Woolner.[4] Refusing to let Ruskin inspect it before purchase, he none the less touched up the work, put a 'gilt saucer' behind the Angel's head in token of a halo and took off the 'Popish' inscription. And then he set about persuading MacCracken to buy from Deverell.

Some while later, in a sonnet based on Tennyson's *Kraken*, Rossetti parodied the patron as a ravenous figure, 'fattening on ill-got pictures' by the PRB. In William's words, this was pure fun, with no resemblance to the facts: as Gabriel well knew, MacCracken's patronage was the mainstay of 'his most struggling years' as an artist. At the same time, he shared the view expressed by Blake in a satirical squib he had transcribed from the notebook, which inquired of Wisdom:

> What's the first part of painting?' She said 'Patronage'.
> 'And what is the second to please and engage?'
> She frowned like a fury and said 'Patronage'.
> 'And what is the third?' She put off old age
> And smiled like a Syren, and said 'Patronage'.

As if condescending to grant favours, Rossetti often behaved arrogantly towards purchasers, but in this case there was some basis for mockery. With wildly scrawled and heavily underscored letters, MacCracken had the hallmarks of the crazy collector, causing Rossetti to dub him M'Crack-ed'un. He bought pictures without seeing them, with money he could not spare (Hunt had only just received the final instalment on *Two Gentlemen*), sometimes offering other works as part payment. At this point, however, the sale of what Gabriel had taken to calling his 'blessed white eyesore' was a confidence-restoring action, and the £50 purchase price was most welcome.

'*Victoria!*' he wrote to Deverell when MacCracken expressed interest in the unsold picture of Hamlet. 'Come round here tomorrow evening,' and a few fellows would join them in concocting a potent spell, like the witches in *Macbeth*, to secure the sale. Approaching his twenty-fifth birthday, the future looked brighter than for some time. As he told Woolner, 'there is a prospect of my getting on all right if I can make myself work.'[5] He would publish the *Vita Nuova* with etchings, and offer a new version of *Dante drawing an Angel* to the Irish Kraken.

He told Woolner he had deliberately introduced Beatrice into his drawing of Dante sitting to Giotto, so as to bring 'all the influences of Dante's youth – Art, Friendship and Love' into the same image. In his own life, a comparable conjunction now prevailed. The sale revived his artistic ambition. The departure of Woolner and Bateman highlighted the importance of friends. The budding romance with Lizzie fulfilled the trinity. Though Stephens, writing in April, detected signs of 'the old moodiness' in Gabriel, all other evidence indicates a return of the vigour, buoyancy and élan recalled by William at this period, when Gabriel was 'well alive to the main chance and by no means behindhand in contributing his quota to the cause of high spirits'.

'I have not seen you in an age. Can you not come down – to give you a long date – on Saturday evening?' Gabriel wrote to Brown on 1 March. Inspired by Woolner's departure, Brown was painting a picture of young emigrants, using himself and Emma as models. In preparation for marriage, Emma was attending a ladies' academy and on 5 April, the wedding took place at St Dunstan-in-the-West, close to Chatham Place. With Tom Seddon, Rossetti was a witness and possibly lent his apartment for the purpose, for when replying on 9 April to Emma's first formal invitation, he acknowledged receipt of the key. To avoid drawing attention to the discrepancy with Cathy's birth, the marriage was not announced.

Holman was a steamer-ride away up the river. 'From my lodgings in Prospect Place we sometimes were tempted by the brilliancy of the moon . . . to give up thought of bed and roam about during the night,' he recalled nostalgically, half a century gone. Once, following a 'glorious thunderstorm' he and Gabriel walked all the way to the ruined Elizabethan palace at Eltham, arriving at daybreak. Another time they rowed upstream towards Hampton Court, 'feeling with our fingers the black slimy piles of the timber bridges', gliding past dim lawns and dark willows. When Hunt rested on the oars, they felt themselves floating in blackness; then, 'on the swelling tide far behind the darkness we could discern white presences, neither boat nor sail, stemming forward abreast of us' – ghostly shapes finally revealed as swans, paddling silently ahead of the skiff. As it grew light, the tide turned, taking them back to Chelsea.[6] Here Hunt worked through the night whenever there was a moon, to get the right effects for *The Light of the World*.

Not far away, in Cheyne Row, lived Thomas Carlyle; Hunt recalled how Hannay would slip out during an evening at the studio to pay silent respects before the lighted window where his hero was presumed to be working. In the street the sage was seen walking slowly, immersed in thought. Once, he invited himself to Prospect Place, to see Hunt's pictures. To hear him talk was like listening to a page from his books, for he admitted no dialogue, no discussion, assuming all wanted merely to listen. As he spoke, Mrs Carlyle nodded vigorously to endorse the profound wisdom of her husband's every observation.

Carlyle's books, *The French Revolution*, *Past and Present* and *Heroes and Hero-Worship*, shaped much of the Victorian intellectual atmosphere, with its concern over the contemporary 'condition of England'. Full of wealth, of every sort of product, of supply for human want of every kind, 'yet England is dying of inanition!' he declared, attacking Mammonism, Idleness, Ignorance, Greed, the Corn Laws. In polemical style, he contrasted present conditions with those in the year 1200, arguing for a modern doctrine of fulfilling industry: 'Blessed is he who has found his work.' Currently, Gabriel was reading Carlyle's translation of Goethe's *Wilhelm Meister*. The hero's self-cultivation was amusing and amazing, he reported to Scott. 'On one page he is in despair about some girl he has been the death of; in the next you are delighted with his enlarged views of Hamlet. Nothing, plainly, is so fatal to the duty of self-culture as self-sacrifice.' The Romantic view did not chime with the religious. He found humbug too in St Augustine's *Confessions*, and in *The Life Drama* by Alexander Smith, a new Spasmodic poet whom he jealously described to Allingham as 'some Glasgow nobody of about twenty-three or twenty-four, with a bad squint'. Though often acute, his judgements were frequently waspish. The book of the season was Harriet Beecher Stowe's *Uncle Tom's Cabin*, which Gabriel irreverently dismissed as interminable. He made comic sketches and began a parody of a minstrel song:

> Dere was an old nigger and him name was Uncle Tom
> And him tale was rather slow;
> Me try to read de whole but me only read some
> Because me find it no go ...

'My brother had no very settled ideas about negroes, their rights and wrongs: he knew, and was much tickled by, Carlyle's "Occasional Discourse on the Nigger Question", published in 1849,' noted William, apropos but ambiguously, knowing that the *Discourse* is a fiercely racist diatribe, hardly as satirical as its extravagant tone would suggest.[7]

Mrs Stowe visited the Howitts, who were active Abolitionists. At this date a vigorous walker, Rossetti often took the road up to the Hermitage, where the Nest was now Miss Howitt's studio. 'You can scarcely imagine how elegant and habitable this room has been made,' he told Woolner, before leaving off the letter in favour of a walk in the fields with Anna Mary and her young sister. Another day, Anna took Mr Rossetti and Miss Siddall to visit cousins in Essex, with a drive and picnic in Epping Forest. The girls remembered Lizzie as very quiet, and Gabriel 'in rattling good spirits' standing up in the carriage with an Italian gesture of approval at every passing scene of beauty. Adducing popular physiognomy, Anna's cousin later remarked on the double aspect of his face – the 'intellectual and even spiritual' brow contrasting with the sensuous lips and 'heavy' Italian jaw. His eyes, she recalled, glowed with a lazy lustre.[8]

Miss Howitt was planning to paint a scene from Dante. The first serious female artist Rossetti got to know, she too had trained at Sass's before going to study under Wilhelm von Kaulbach in Bavaria and was full of artistic fervour and idealism. Gabriel made a quick sketch, showing Anna Mary as a slight, nervous young woman with bright eyes, leaning forward, hands a-flutter. But she was talented and sincere. In a story soon to appear in the *Magazine of Art*, she conjured up the possibility of a Sisterhood in Art to emulate the PRB. Gabriel promised he would get William to review her book, *An Art Student in Munich* and introduce her to Christina.

But his parents and sister were moving to Somerset. Frances Rossetti had taken a sudden decision, prompted by the promise of better teaching prospects at Frome, the closest town to aunt Charlotte at Longleat. Professor Rossetti's health and temper were deteriorating. Medical opinion was agreed on the curative effects of fresh air. Unwillingly, Christina accompanied them to the country, to assist with the day-school, but Maria stayed in London to housekeep for William. Before they left, Gabriel made a careful pencil portrait of his father peering short-sightedly at a page of notes, faithfully rendering the old man's look and habit as if aware he had not long to live.

He himself was full of projects, according to William. Plans for 'severe study', for visiting Florence, for a private exhibition at Colnaghi's. He now declared that exhibiting in public galleries was altogether a mistake, to which he would not again succumb. This was Gabriel all over, heroically cutting off his nose. Nevertheless, William observed, 'his future now seems in his own hands, if only he will use it'. Happily, not only had MacCracken liked the 'old white picture' (which Rossetti would one day claim as the ancestor of all the white pictures that multiplied in Whistler's wake) but so had the influential Liverpool collector John Miller. Moreover, Ruskin had commended the two Dante scenes shown at the Old Water-Colour Society, and thus fortified MacCracken offered a commission, for £150. Gabriel was so pleased that he resorted to ironic jocularity. Even if Ruskin were half-ignorant, like most critics, everything he said was valuable. 'O Woolner! – if one could only find the supreme Carlylian Ignoramus – him who knows positively the least about Art of any living creature – and get him to write a pamphlet about one – what a fortune one might make.'[9]

Presumably on the grounds that MacCracken might like a companion picture to *The Annunciation*, he ordered a new canvas and began a scene showing Mary in the house of St John. But in the event MacCracken could not actually afford £150. For Deverell's *Hamlet* he offered paintings by David Roberts and J. R. Herbert instead of money, which was amusing but not of immediate use, while his first payment for the 'white picture' came as a negotiable bill cashed only at a discount. Rossetti therefore sent a list of watercolour subjects, to which MacCracken replied in (allowing for pardonable exaggeration) 'a state of wild excitement', with directions to travel to Belfast at once. He would take the new version of *Dante drawing an Angel on the First Anniversary of Beatrice's Death*, for a more modest but highly acceptable 35 guineas. Begun in early summer, it was 'nearly done' at the end of September, but still lingered at the end of the year.

Though small, the picture is most impressive. Kneeling at a deep window alcove, absorbed in painting a tiny angelic head, Dante turns to see three visitors who have been watching him for some while. 'Perceiving whom, I arose for salutation, and said: "Another was with me",' he says in the *Vita Nuova*. Within, the light is subdued, playing softly on the figures. Beyond is bright sunlight, light blue through the window and intensely green through the door; Rossetti was starting to use a signature emerald, buffed in like all his pigments with hardly any water. Three small jars on the window-sill filled with red, blue and yellow paint set a pure, intense colour key. The figures wear richly-coloured garments, and their hands are linked in a linear rhythm that reaches through to Dante, roused by a touch on the shoulder.

'The excellency of every art is its intensity, capable of making all disagreeables evaporate,' Keats had written. Rossetti had the originality of genius, in conceiving his subjects. 'I do not wrap myself up in my imaginings,' he once protested; 'it is they that envelop me from the outer world, whether I will or no.' But he had the capacity to be so enveloped. As Hunt recalled, he also had 'the genius for taking pains'. Far from being lazy, as he feared, he was 'untiring in his application and in his wrestling with the difficulties of a design' until all the aesthetic elements of a composition were in harmony. How often, he once remarked at Prospect Place, the very feature for which a design was first undertaken had ultimately to be erased, for the sake of the whole. In commercial terms, this was a disadvantage; but as he told his mother, he could never get over the 'weakness of making a thing as good as I can manage'. *Dante drawing an Angel* was thus 'absurdly under value' in his own estimation. Placed in a 'spiffy jammy nobby stunning splendacious frame', it was finally released nearly a year after commencement.[10]

In his developing aesthetic, colour was the essential feature of painting, 'quite indispensable to the highest art'. No picture ever belonged to the highest order without fine colour, he told MacCracken; and some, like Titian's, were raised to a higher class by virtue of their colour. The only exception was Hogarth. Other artists – Wilkie and Delaroche, for example – were so poor in colour one might as well see their work in monochrome reproduction. In sum, 'Colour is the physiognomy of a picture; and like the shape of the human forehead, it cannot be perfectly beautiful, without proving goodness and greatness. Other qualities are its life exercised, but this is the body of its life, by which we know and love it at first.'[11]

The most beautiful colour combination, he said a few months later when Boyce handed him an opal, was green, blue and carmine, all inclining to purplish; but overall the tone should incline to yellow. With characteristic vehemence, he added that Giotto, Dürer and Hogarth were the three great names in art. What matter if this did not make complete sense?

By early summer Blackfriars lost some of its charm as Thames and Fleet Ditch began to smell. There was a cholera scare, with the first outbreak across the river in Southwark. Gabriel suffered a bad attack of boils, and another of thrush. The pills he took – perhaps a purgative – caused inconvenient side-effects, so the family doctor prescribed new medicine, and no doubt also change of air. 'I wish to get into the country immediately,' Gabriel told his mother, 'to go somewhere and walk a good deal.'

He ought to have gone to Frome, but what he ought to do was just what he could not do, partly because of the unspoken reproaches he unjustly attributed to his family. 'Read my letter again and you will see that I never said that you thought it a bore to write to me; but that my letters are so barren that *they* might well prove a bore to you to read,' remonstrated Frances Rossetti mildly.[12] But the mistake was Freudian: Gabriel did find it a bore to write, and worse to visit. Instead, he yielded to an earlier promise and went north with Scott to Newcastle, borrowing a carpet-bag and twelve pounds from trusty aunt Charlotte. It was a mistake. Newcastle was as grimy and morbidic as London. As Mrs Scott remained in London, he was spared her chatter; but there was an energetic dog, whom he detested.

The previous year, he had hoped to visit the Lake District. Now, he and Scott took the train to Carlisle, to see the ancient village of Wetheral with monastic cells carved in the sandstone rock. They stopped at Hexham, a sleepy, pleasantly quaint town. 'We sat and looked at the market place from the deep window of an inn some centuries old, and talked of friends for one pleasant hour, while sun and air seemed whispering together, and the "hovering pigeons" touched the street,' he recalled.[13] Though he claimed to have abandoned poetry, the cool, dark interior of Hexham's abbey church prompted a pair of sonnets for his sisters comparing the quietness within – and by extension the lives of women – with the heat and noise of the outside, public, male world:

> . . . on the carven church door this hot noon
> Lays all its heavy sunshine here without:
> But having entered in, we shall find there
> Silence, and sudden dimness, and deep prayer,
> And faces of carved angels all about.

As Scott sketched the ancient market-place, Gabriel was tempted to stay, send for his canvas and begin his next picture forthwith. Instead, the mood and their ultimate destination inspired a dreamy little drawing of a medieval woman in yellow holding a lute, and a colour sketch of two red-clad lovers on battlements, made in response to the sandstone city, where 'the sun shines red on Carlisle wall'. As ever, his impulse was to resist the modern world in favour of Keatsian fancies.

Gruff, misanthropic and extremely prickly, Scott felt artistically neglected. He was married (unwisely, as he saw it) to a voluble, unintellectual woman who provided no true companionship. An avowed free-thinker, he was liked only by those who admired bluntness, for he had few skills of flattery and looked scowlingly; travelling in Italy, country-women claimed he had 'the evil eye'. Alone with Gabriel for the first time, he felt the full fascination of Rossetti's irresistible if narcissistic personality. Though William called this imperious, in fact Gabriel had no need to command. When his sympathies were engaged, his good humour was reward enough. Teasingly, he dubbed his companion 'Scotus', to rhyme with Pictor Ignotus, the attribution on pictures where the painter's name is unknown.

'We had much talk of poetry, in the first place, and of friends in the second,' recalled Scott, who also wrote. They shared thoughts on the vexed question of 'self-culture' and the nature of Romantic ambition. 'Ought we to long for more than we possess, to seek for Babel's heights, or Jacob's stair, For lotus food, elixir happiness, or aught that may not flower in mortal air?' asked Scott rhetorically. 'Are they not all within us, towering there?' To such philosophical effusions, Gabriel preferred Scott's 'medieval' poems like *Saint Margaret* or *Woodstock Maze*. Best of all was *Rosabell*, the pathetic narrative of a street-girl whom Scott had befriended years before in his native Edinburgh. Indeed, it was so good it immediately felt his revising hand. 'Scott and I have looked through his poems together and have made some very advantageous amendments between us,' Gabriel reported regally. As a result, the poor girl's real name was deemed too fancy, and Rosabell Bonnally became *Mary Anne*.[14]

Once roused, Gabriel's energy doubled. The poem should include the encounter between Rosabell and her village swain on the city streets, he said. Scott demurred. Well then, said Rossetti, he would paint it, full of sentiment and pathos. Better still, he would illustrate the slim volume Scott must surely publish, showing the wretched woman recalling her innocent past:

> Come all ye pretty maidens
> And dance along with this . . .
> She heard them as they sang, she stood
> As she were dead while still they sang . . .

He sketched a group of girls dancing in the street, observed by a shawled figure, as a large rat scuttles into a sewer. The urban scene: prostitution and pestilence; cholera and corruption. He took the design away, but no etching was made and Scott's book a year later had only its author's illustrations.

Around 8 July Gabriel escaped 'beastly Newcastle', travelling by rail to Coventry, and thence on foot to Warwick's magnificent castle and Kenilworth, made famous by Walter Scott. 'I walked through some part of Warwickshire for a week or so, having great glory,' he told Woolner.[15] Climbing a hill towards dusk, he saw the setting sun transfigured into 'a fiery bush with coruscating hair' and loitered in the twilight composing a sonnet, as gold and silver faded from the sky. His penchant for night walks proved useful training, and as he tramped he made verses:

> Weary already, weary miles tonight
> I walked for bed; and so, to get some ease,
> I dogged the flying moon with similes.
> And like a wisp she doubled on my sight
> In ponds; and caught in tree-tops like a kite . . .

From the hedgerow, he picked a spray of honeysuckle, struggling with brambles to gain a single stem. A little further, it grew in profusion, with perfect blooms. 'So from my hand that first I threw,' he rhymed. 'Yet plucked not any more of them.' Somewhere below the actual words, the lines are charged with sexual feeling.

His destination was Stratford-on-Avon, then at the start of its tourist career. He stayed at the Red Horse Inn, from where he wrote to Scott, reinstalled at Hexham's White Horse. He went twice to Shakespeare's birthplace, and twice walked out to Charlecote, undeterred by heavy floods. The chapel and ancient graveyard at Alveston were islanded, under heavy clouds, he noted; it would have made a most solemn picture. But he was no landscapist and the only drawing he made was of a nursemaid wheeling a baby, sent to aunt Charlotte. 'Would it not make a capital picture of the domestic class to represent a half-dozen of girls racing the babies entrusted to their care – babies bewildered, out of breath, upset, sprawling at bottom of barrow, etc. etc.?'

This brief and solitary pilgrimage, so uncharacteristic of Rossetti's torpid physical self in later years, remained with him as a golden memory, and some kind of indefinite landmark in his life. Perhaps it just cleared the cobwebs and oscitation. But it was also a gesture of belief, not so much in rural England as in the past. As his friends observed, he half-pretended to live in the Middle Ages. The modern world was not 'poetic'; technological 'progress' held no attraction; he was assertively anti-modern. Affecting to turn the clock back before the eleven-day adjustment, he claimed his birthday fell on 'Old May Day', and wilfully ignored the emerging information on earth's antiquity, so ably synthesised by Charles Lyell's son in *Principles of Geology*, enlarged and revised in 1853. Both Scott and Hunt recalled how 'DGR' had 'no idea of the changed position of the historical forms or cosmogony of religion by geological and other discoveries'. He was not even convinced the earth moved round the sun, declaring that our senses did not tell us so, at any rate, so what did it matter? 'He then remembered Galileo ... "It might matter in a scientific way, oh yes!" ' but applauded Keats's 'magnificent' toast: 'Confusion to the memory of Newton!' and the reply, when Wordsworth asked why: 'Because he destroyed the poetry of the rainbow by reducing it to a prism.'[16]

Such Romantic archaicism, which included a feeling for superstition perhaps unconsciously absorbed from his father, was part self-conscious eccentricity, part homage to the lost sense of the numinous. As Max Müller would write in his celebrated 1856 essay on comparative mythology, 'if we could but believe again that there was in the sun a being like our own, that in the dawn there was a soul open to human sympathy ...'.[17] But it came also from Rossetti's interior world, first peopled by Ivanhoe and Rowena and then by Dante and Beatrice, and forever set in an imaginary past that had almost the immediacy of reality, as his rapt immersion in the tale of Chiaro or scenes from the *Vita Nuova* indicates. All through his life, he was fascinated by Poe's image of meeting one's self, as if existing in two time-spheres simultaneously.

Beyond this, resistance to science was a way of handling the very collapse of religious belief caused by modern knowledge. For, like many of his generation, he found himself marooned by the Victorian ebb of faith.

'You are doing Gabriel Rossetti an injustice in concluding that he advocated Christianity merely for argument's sake,' Millais told Allingham at the end of 1852, from which it may be assumed that in this period Rossetti's views were comparable to those of his Brethren. Millais and Hunt, who both sincerely endorsed the teachings of Jesus. 'It is an undeniable fact that the greatest good is to be seen in those that are the staunchest believers,' continued Millais. 'There is nothing in the New Testament desired of us but what must be apparently right to any educated person, and therefore why not follow it? even though you should not believe . . .'[18]

Morality was one thing, but faith another. What could one believe? Rossetti had included some meditations on this in *The Burden of Nineveh*, his poem inspired by the great Assyrian winged bull in the British Museum. What beliefs had been held when this creature was originally worshipped? Archaeology made the history of religions a matter of debate. Would Christianity be replaced in its turn? The conjunction was apt, for to his generation Nineveh was the city unto which Jonah declined to preach, as commanded by the Lord, before changing his mind inside the whale, whereupon he spoke so forcefully that the people abjured evil. According to the clergy, present-day London was equally wicked, heathen, unrepentant, doomed. Including all these allusions, Rossetti closed his poem by wondering if one day the massive sculpture would be re-excavated, leading unborn generations to believe that Britain worshipped at the shrine of the Bull, not the Cross. Whatever his doubts, he still thought and felt in scriptural terms, but at the same time the concept of empires passing away over millennia – Egypt, Assyria, Greece, Rome – suggested the possibility of an end to the Christian era. So much for religious certainty.

Later, Scott would assert that DGR was 'an old pagan' and in 1865 Rossetti himself wrote to James Smetham: 'I had better tell you frankly at once that I have no such faith as you have.' But, he went on, this was not from any lack of will to believe: he was by no means a 'confident denier', still less an 'apostle of opposition'. Finding doctrinal debate both painful and pointless, he refused further discussion. 'I abstain from it altogether,' he told Smetham firmly. 'This is all I feel able to say on the matter.' But he never declared himself an atheist, and indeed objected to such imputation. 'I once saw him very indignant on hearing that he had been accused of irreligion, or rather of not being a Christian,' recalled a later friend. 'He asked with great earnestness "Do not my works testify to my Christianity?" ' And he remonstrated when Swinburne proposed to publish some blasphemous verses, saying that while free from all dogmatic belief, he sincerely felt that Christ's supremely noble character was precluded from base uses.[19]

'That my brother was a strict doctrinal Christian is not a fact,' confirmed William; 'but he had an earnest reverence for a Christian ideal and a delight in Christian legend and symbol.' It was, however, just such distinctions that exercised the Victorian mind: could one be a Christian without accepting doctrine or attending church? Neither Maria nor Christina thought so, fearing their brothers would be among the damned.

Rossetti was not a theologian or a scientist. He would have preferred to live in an age of faith, where he might dissent subversively without threatening the superstructure. Instead, with a heart committed to the days of faith, he lived in an age when all belief was crumbling. Incapable of shoring up its pillars, he was left among the ruins, and part of his response was to ignore the modern world.

From Shakespeare's county he headed back to London. Despite his declaration, he had new exhibition pictures in mind, including that discussed with Scott, of a fallen woman recognised by her former sweetheart, which he offered to MacCracken.

Not many fellows were in town. He spent a day visiting Brown, now at Hendon, but then fell back into a listless Gothic humour. 'One feels again within the accursed circle,' he wrote to Scott, warming to his allusions; 'the skulls and bones rattle, the goblins keep mumbling, and the owls beat their obscene wings round the casting of those bullets, among which is the Devil's Seventh, though it should be hidden till the last. Meanwhile to step out of the ring is death and damnation.' Oh, he observed ironically, this metaphor was so fine 'something might be done with it – in charcoal . . .'[20] In such moods Rossetti was natural heir to Coleridge and de Quincey.

He had been away a month. Having not paid the rent before leaving, he had sent an urgent message to William from Newcastle. 'I want to tell you that Lizzy is painting at Blackfriars while I am away,' he wrote. 'Do not therefore encourage anyone to go near the place. I have told her to keep the doors locked, and she will probably sleep there sometimes.'[21] From Stratford, Scott received a caricature of a landlord rampant, with a tiny self-portrait thumbing his nose. But the anxiety was real, for Lizzie's presence at Chatham Place was unofficial, like her presence in Gabriel's life.

Drawings show that, as well as for *Beatrice denying her Salutation*, during 1852 she sat, or rather knelt, for two or three figures playing musical instruments and for studies towards a never-completed picture of St Elizabeth of Hungary. Hers is also recognisable as the figure of the female visitor in *Dante drawing an Angel*. But by the autumn of this year, she had stopped sitting to other artists, for when Charley Collins wrote to ask, she responded 'in the most freezing manner' that she now had 'other occupation'.[22] The inference is that Gabriel claimed his beloved exclusively. Early in 1853, he drafted a characteristically convoluted sonnet, which seems to describe the first acknowledgement of mutual feeling. 'As two, whose love, first foolish, widening scope, Knows suddenly, to music high and soft, The Holy of holies,' this begins, 'are now amazed with shame, nor dare to cope With the whole truth aloud, lest heaven should ope...' But, almost as if he were keeping a secret, there are few references to Lizzie in his correspondence at this date. As William noted, to those less intimate than himself and the Browns, his brother 'wrapped himself in impenetrable silence' regarding Lizzie.[23]

When she was expected at Blackfriars, no one else was welcome, and the impropriety of such intimacy was camouflaged by the 'other occupation' to which Lizzie referred, which must be her own endeavours at drawing under Gabriel's tuition, begun at the Nest. Later, she told friends in Sheffield that Walter Deverell had first formed 'a strong attachment' to her and that only after his death had she sought instruction from Rossetti. But this was either outright or wishful invention, perhaps to occlude her time as a model. It is more likely that, with artistic leanings of her own, Lizzie formed a 'strong attachment' to studio life that included other hopes, for all the artists she sat to were single and in her eyes very eligible, while Hunt's 'practical joke' on Tupper shows she was not unimaginable as a wife. As yet, however, any such possibility was disguised – to the outside world – by her informal position as Rossetti's 'pupil'.

The transition is visible in his drawings. Gradually, Lizzie appeared less as a model, holding poses or in costume, and more as herself, resting, reading, standing at the easel. And so by the summer of 1853, the relationship was such that she was installed at Chatham Place in Gabriel's absence, with his pigments and brushes, engaged on the beginner's task of a self-portrait. 'Lizzie has made a perfect wonder of her portrait,' he told Brown in August. 'I think we shall send it to the Winter Exhibition.' She was also beginning a picture for next year's RA (no less) from *The Lady of Shalott*.[24] In September he drew her at work, in a teasing sketch showing her with a drawing board propped against the back of a chair, leaning earnestly towards the facing chair on which he sits, hands in pockets, posing stiffly in a reversal of roles.

Her *Lady of Shalott* drawing is carefully inscribed 'E.E.Siddal Dec 15 / 53'. The slightly refined spelling of her name, always used by Rossetti, perhaps came from an initial mistake; neatly it signifies her transformation from milliner-model to pupil-artist. Her oval self-portrait is a small but striking work, from which she looks out with a lack of expression that comes from the steady gaze into a mirror but also seems to endorse William's description of her manner as that of one saying 'my mind and my feelings are my own, and no outsider is expected to pry into them.'[25] What with her reserve and Gabriel's caution, it is hard to judge when mutual declarations were made. 'Was that the landmark?' Rossetti inquired in a poem some months later, pondering 'the stations of his course' in life, which he had expected to rise before him, like shrines or citadels. No, he had missed the turning and must go back, seeking the spring where he had paused to drink. How could one tell what decisions would prove significant?

Lizzie told Gabriel how, in the crowded Siddall home above the ironmongery shop in the Old Kent Road, where knives and scissors were made and repaired, she had nowhere but an unheated bedroom in which to draw, shared with sisters Clara and Lydia. She told him how she had discovered Tennyson on a newspaper used to wrap groceries, and how as a toddler she had been helped across the street by a neighbour later hanged for a notorious murder. Gabriel enjoyed such tales, which shocked the prim and proper. Mixed with nervous, genteel shyness, Lizzie also had a sharp wit and a gift for comic observation; her mocking Cockney humour could always lighten his spirits. He saw her as a Cinderella, blessed with beauty and talent but doomed to a drab life, and surely to Lizzie, as to many others, Gabriel was a Prince, who could transform her life. To some extent she played on his sympathy. When he felt 'sick and queer' in London after his holiday, he learnt that she too had been ill, with no chance of benefiting from country air, and was roused to pity and self-reproach, in a pattern that would come to shape their lives. 'How truly she may say "No man cared for my soul",' he told Allingham a year later. 'I do not mean to make myself an exception, for how long I have known her and not thought of this till so late – perhaps too late.'[26] The implication of this oddly tortuous wording is that at some stage Lizzie lamented that no one cared whether she were ill or unhappy, nor whether she might nourish herself on art and literature, and so she might sink back into sickness, poverty and despair – even into soul-destroying immorality. Of course, her position was not as grave as that of Hannay's unfortunate Georgina Lock, or Scott's Rosabell Bonally, but evidently she needed protection, if not rescue. In this context, Rossetti's idea of painting the encounter between a 'lost soul' and her former sweetheart has a distinct poignancy.

Strangely enough, two of his PR Brothers were concurrently engaged on rescue missions of their own. Early in the year, Hunt had been seized with the idea of a worldly counterpart to *The Light of the World*, on moral awakening. 'As he that taketh away a garment in cold weather, so is he that singeth songs to a heavy heart' was the biblical text selected for the contemporary depiction of a fallen woman. Installed in a luxurious apartment as the paramour of a young swell, she is shocked into repentant recollection of lost innocence by means of the popular song 'Oft in the stilly night'.

It was a topical issue, for sexual licence was widely deplored. Just as widely, all censure was customarily visited upon the woman, according to the accepted double standard. 'The sin wandereth against me in the Infinite,' wrote Hannay, but in the immediate he was unpunished. 'I think with you that it *is* an artificial lie that a woman should so suffer and lose all, while he who led her to do so encounters no share of evil from his acts,' wrote Edward Lear to Hunt this autumn,[27] warning also that the subject might be misconstrued, since artists already had a reputation for licentiousness. But when Hunt secured a patron, he postponed his planned trip to Palestine in company with Tom Seddon, and set to work; by mid-October the elaborate background, painted from an authentic *maison de convenance*, was ready for the figures.

For that of the woman, Hunt employed a local girl named Annie Miller, daughter of an old soldier. Uneducated and unkempt, shy but bright, her good looks placed her in the very position of those tempted to a life of luxury as the fancy woman of some young gent. Unlike Miss Siddal, she was not from a respectable home and therefore proportionally more 'at risk'. When the sittings were over, Hunt found Annie lodgings, and arranged for Fred Stephens to take charge of funds to cover the cost of her self-improvement while he was travelling in the East. She could earn extra by sitting to selected artists (including Millais, Rossetti, Boyce and Michael Halliday) but she must be a 'good girl'. On his return, he would look for results. It was a quixotic enterprise, only partly disclosed. If he had eventual marriage in mind, he kept his own counsel, but the fellows knew of Annie's existence, as they knew of Hunt's success in selling both his pictures. Indeed, Gabriel reported to Woolner, Holman had become such a swell that his new works were 'celebrated already before the town has even seen them'. Hunt planned that both *The Light of the World* and *The Awakening Conscience* should appear unannounced at the Academy, after his departure.

To mark his going in January 1854, Gabriel gave him a photo of *The Girlhood*, which had been painted in their shared studio, inscribed with lines of enduring friendship. Millais ordered a signet ring with entwined initials for Holman to wear in memory of the PRB. 'What a leave-taking it was with him in my heart when the train started!' Hunt recalled. 'Did other men have such a sacred friendship as that we had formed?'[28]

But since his own return to London in November, poor Millais was in a wretched state, hardly able to work, with a momentous secret he could not disclose. In June he and his brother had gone with Mr and Mrs Ruskin to Perthshire, where he was due to paint the background for a portrait of his patron, standing by a rushing stream. It was an enjoyable, open-air time, marred only by midges and Ruskin's manifest dislike of his wife. The Millais brothers were at first embarrassed and then indignant. In their eyes, Effie was charming, cultivated, thoughtful and energetic. With playful but sincere courtesy they called her the Countess. She responded to their sympathy, and Millais's heart went out to her. At some stage, he learnt that her marriage was unconsummated as well as unhappy. They went on to Edinburgh, where Ruskin was to lecture. Then they returned to London, where Millais was due to complete the portrait of a patron who had now become hateful. There was no solution to Effie's plight, for divorce would ruin her reputation – and Johnny's too, if implicated.

Rossetti's rescue mission was less dramatic. 'Lizzy sits by me at work on her design, which is now coming really admirable,' he told Brown early in the New Year, shortly before Hunt's departure. Yet some decisions had been taken, if not announced. None of the three women – Lizzie, Annie, Effie – could go back to where they had been.

Gaetano Polidori died in December 1853, following a stroke. 'He was upwards of ninety years of age, but retained his mental faculties perfect, and even his bodily ones, to an extraordinary degree,' Gabriel told Scott, describing the real affection he felt for his grandfather. 'Our family may wait long now for so stout a branch.'[29] He was among those attending the deathbed: with his father incapacitated in the country and his uncles Henry and Philip variously unfit for the role, he was next in line as senior male and 'head of the family'.

Polidori's death set in train the others' return from Frome. 'You are right in supposing that I have missed them greatly,' Gabriel told Woolner. Lately he had received a visitor from Italy, calling on the only Rossetti in the London directory in search of the Professor, to whom he brought compliments from Vasto. Diligently Gabriel dipped into his father's *Arpa Evangelica* and wrote as filially as he knew how: 'How much I owe you, and how much pain I have given you, dearest father, in this and everything! Needless to ask your loving heart to forgive me; but I must always beg you to believe the deep and true affection with which I sign myself your loving son Dante Gabriel Rossetti.'[30]

The family was due back by March quarter-day. Then suddenly, his father suffered a paralytic seizure. Gabriel, William and Maria hastened to Frome, fearing the worst. Papa rallied, however. Unlike poor Deverell, who was now critically ill with kidney failure. Gabriel saw Walter for the last time a week before his death, and joined Brown, Stephens and Munro at the cemetery on 7 February. 'His was the happiest face when our circle sat together, and it is the first gone that may not return,' he wrote sorrowfully to Woolner, recalling their once-shared youthful hopes. 'None of us had known him so long or perhaps so intimately as I had.' It was the first real loss of his life. 'I have none left whom I love better,' he told Walter's sister, truthfully; 'and I doubt whether any who loves me so well.'[31] Both Deverell's parents being dead, his siblings were grateful for support. Gabriel joined with Millais and others to assist them financially, through sales and subscriptions; at Rossetti's request John Miller in Liverpool gave £50 for Walter's picture *As You Like It*.

'Poor dear Deverell in the dark earth, so blind, so dumb and so deaf,' wrote Hunt in macabre mode, sitting in his Cairo hotel before a dark, deserted square, and conjuring up the contrast with London, where Gabriel and William would be dining at a gas-lit chop-house in Fleet Street, amid horse-buses and hansom cabs. Was Millais nearby at Mike Halliday's studio in Adelphi? Brown was certainly with Emma and little Kate.[32] It was five years since the founding of the Brotherhood. With Woolner and Hunt absent, Deverell's death diminished the circle even further. In November, Millais had been duly elected an Associate of the RA, the first step towards full membership. 'So now the whole Round Table is dissolved,' wrote Gabriel to Christina, quoting Tennyson. In response, she memorialised the once-great PRB, erasing Collinson from the fraternity but including a jibe at her brother's failure to exhibit:

> The P.R.B. is in its decadence:
> For Woolner in Australia cooks his chops;
> And Hunt is yearning for the land of Cheops;
> D. G. Rossetti shuns the vulgar optic . . .
> And he at last, the champion, great Millais
> Attaining Academic opulence
> Winds up his signature with A.R.A.:
> So rivers merge in the perpetual sea . . .

Almost as a replacement, Millais proposed a new sketching club, on the lines of the old Cyclographic. Launched on 24 February 1854, its eighteen projected members included the remaining PRBs, together with Brown, Scott, Hughes, Munro, Collins, and older artists like John Leech, Richard Doyle and Mark Antony. Two women were proposed, Louisa, Lady Waterford, and the Hon. Mrs Boyle, who signed herself 'E.V.B', though in the event their places were taken by Anna Howitt and Barbara Smith.

William, as ever, was to be secretary. 'Might it not be made a first-rate thing?' Gabriel asked, urging Scott to join.[33]

But though William drew up rules and Millais provided a handsome portfolio, the Folio Club was slow to get under way – partly because Millais was so upset and miserable, desperately in love with Effie yet unable to confide in friends. He had nothing to send to the RA and could think only of going abroad. After much distress he had concluded that Ruskin was 'certainly mad or has a slate loose'; no sane man could so lack human affection. 'Do you think I can get off finishing his portrait without doing harm to The Countess?' he asked her mother. 'I would rather do anything than that his name should be dragged before the public,' wrote Effie in her turn, afraid of gossip; 'his character stands so deservedly high as the founder of a new school and in a great position in this country it would be a lasting sorrow to have that reputation tarnished in the slightest degree.'[34] As it happened, Ruskin was currently preparing for publication his Edinburgh lectures on the PRB, with all cordial references to his 'friend Mr Millais'. It was a tense psychological moment. On 7 March, having explained her marital status to Lady Eastlake, Effie prepared to sue publicly for an annulment. It was like a melodrama, commented Millais; or more truly a tragic farce.

CHAPTER SEVEN

Many Capital Plans

The texture of Gabriel's life was growing more complex, strands crossing and recrossing, literally and emotionally. From Chatham Place, deep in London at its most Dickensian, amid streets, alleys, inns, chop-houses, workshops, apartment blocks and stableyards housing a multitude of unknown and incurious individuals, an unmarried man could come and go without explanation. Observed only by landlady and crossing sweeper, his destinations remained unnamed, his business unrevealed. He could move across the city calling at whatever addresses he pleased without leaving a connecting trace among the atomised population. Urban life created compartmentalisation, like drawers that open only singly. In London, in the mid-nineteenth century, this experience became habitual and natural. Even well-known men could often circulate freely between appointments and entertainments, assignations and aleatory wanderings, donning a separate self for each journey. This suited Rossetti, who never liked to be where people could easily find him – especially if they were tradesmen with overdue accounts. Gabriel had better uses for his shillings and sovereigns, or 'tin' in current parlance.

With typical generosity, in the spring of 1854 he offered studio space to Arthur Hughes, and posed for the figure of Orlando; maybe it was then that Hughes heard the story of Ophelia's bath-tub. Lizzie was making a watercolour of *We Are Seven*. Though there was still no formal engagement, their romance was flowering and within a restricted circle Lizzie was acknowledged as his sweetheart as well as pupil. Among a few close friends she was 'dear Guggum', a pet name which has never adequately been explained but is eloquent of intimacy. 'Dear Lizzy's a Guggum,' Gabriel wrote in doggerel verses. 'What a Guggum is Lizzy!' Shortened to 'Gug' and also to 'G', it appears to have been used reciprocally, as in the babytalk of fond lovers, as if together Lizzie and Gabriel were 'the Guggums'. 'If you are in London any day, do look in at Chatham Place and see dear G's drawings – the one from Wordsworth is very advanced,' Gabriel told

Brown, after visiting the Photographic Society exhibition ('whither I had promised to take my pupil on this the last evening').[1]

Through Anna Howitt (whose picture of Margaret from *Faust*, his own old subject, was much better than Gabriel expected) they had a new acquaintance. Gabriel teased Christina, as yet languishing at Frome: 'Ah! if you were only like Miss Barbara Smith, blessed with large rations of tin, fat, enthusiasm, and golden hair, who thinks nothing of climbing up a mountain in breeches, or wading through a stream in none, in the sacred name of pigment,' he wrote. 'Last night she invited us all to lunch with her on Sunday; and perhaps I shall go, as she is quite a *jolly fellow*.'[2]

Aspiring *amateur*, Barbara Leigh Smith was also a social reformer of independent means and views – and the first truly liberated young woman Rossetti had met, whose wealthy father with a country seat in Sussex and a town house in Blandford Square had advanced views on female education. With Anna Mary and their friend Bessie, she had spent the previous summer in Wales, writing and painting together like any group of young men. Indeed, it was Barbara who, visiting Anna Mary in Munich, had proposed an Art Sisterhood to provide female artists with mutual support. Rossetti was impressed. Had he been more venal, he might have been seriously attracted by Miss Smith's plentiful rations of tin as well as her enthusiasm for art. It is, however, hard to envisage him making a marriage partnership with such a very strong-minded figure. Pale, demure, delicate, poor, Lizzie was quite different. The Howitts thought she was terminally ill.

Rossetti's attitudes towards women were relatively emancipated. His mother, aunts and sisters all worked for wages, without loss of gentility, and though he assumed masculine privilege, he was far from regarding women as essentially weak and subservient. He respected the ambition of artists like Anna Howitt and Joanna Boyce, George's sister, and was rather stimulated by Barbara's unconventionality. When invited to a soirée in Blandford Square, he responded by inviting her to call and see his works – a favour not promiscuously bestowed.

Through Barbara and Annie, he also met Bessie Rayner Parkes, aspiring poet who had been an early reader of *The Germ*, as well as critic Marian Evans, soon to become novelist George Eliot, and the American actress Charlotte Cushman. Among this feminist circle he was evidently perceived as an egalitarian young fellow. As a result, joked his friends, were not Miss Parkes and Miss Smith in danger of falling in love with him? Maybe. 'Dante Rossetti is my favourite of these young men,' Barbara told Bessie. 'I like the poetic narrow-minded thorough-artist Italian nature.'[3]

Gabriel was not unaware of his appeal. At the Belle Sauvage inn on Ludgate Hill, where he dined regularly with Allingham, who had quit his

Customs post for literary journalism in London, they vied for the waitress's favours. In any such contest, Rossetti was an easy, almost unconscious winner, probably unaware of the young woman's partiality until Allingham remarked on it. Thereafter, to tease his friend, he played back to her flirtations as she advertised the daily menu.

On 24 March, his outstanding Roberson's bill for £12 2s 9d was paid, which suggests he had received another loan from his aunt – or perhaps a share of his grandfather's legacy, for the payment coincided with his parents' return to London. They took up residence at no. 45 Upper Albany Street, east of Regent's Park. Aunts Margaret and Eliza lodged nearby, looking after uncle Philip. Soon afterwards, Gabriel invited Christina to Chatham Place to meet Miss Siddal. He also borrowed Christina's poetic notebooks to show Allingham, talking of sending them to a publisher, with Lizzie to illustrate. This came to nothing, but it did prompt Christina to forward a small selection of her own to *Blackwood's* in August. He also introduced his sister to the Howitts, and on at least one evening Lizzie, Gabriel, Christina and Allingham bussed and walked together up to the Hermitage and back. Christina was shy and over-formal; her friendship with Lizzie did not flourish. But she observed, in verses which seem to describe her brother's sweetheart:

> Not fair as men would reckon fair,
>   Nor noble as they count the line;
> Only as graceful as a bough
>   And tendrils of the vine ...
>
> And downcast were her dovelike eyes,
>   And downcast was her tender cheek,
> Her pulses fluttered like a dove
>   To hear him speak.

In his letters, Gabriel often sketched a dove in place of Lizzie's name.

Not 'noble as they count the line'. Miss Siddal's social status was still questionable. 'Now my dear I have got a strong interest in a young girl formerly model to Millais and Dante Rossetti, now Rossetti's love and pupil,' wrote Barbara to Bessie. 'She is a genius and will, if she lives, be a great artist. Alas! her life has been hard and full of trials, her home unhappy and her whole fate hard. Dante Rossetti has been an honourable friend to her and I do not doubt if circumstances were favourable would marry her. She is of course under a ban having been a model (tho' only to 2 PRBs) ergo do not mention it to anyone.' And, added Miss Smith, 'although she is not a lady her mind is poetic', which was all Mr Rossetti cared about.[4]

Insisting that Lizzie was sicker than she seemed, the Howitts arranged a consultation with the Swedenborgian Garth Wilkinson, who alarmingly diagnosed curvature of the spine. Dear Guggum was often unwell, Gabriel conceded in April, but hard at at work on a most poetical design. Together they invited the Browns to Blackfriars, but it was a long way, and Emma was newly pregnant.

Dante drawing an Angel was dispatched to MacCracken, going without the artist's permission first to Ruskin, which proved a lucky error. Early in April Millais finished Ruskin's portrait; one day, he called at Boyce's studio and after he left, Rossetti arrived, with two of his own designs. He and George talked about art and maybe wondered why Johnny was so much less enthusiastic about Ruskin than a year ago. Then two days later the great critic wrote, praising *Dante drawing an Angel* as a 'thoroughly glorious work' and 'the most perfect piece of Italy' he had ever seen. Ruskin had sent 'an incredible letter', Gabriel crowed to Brown, 'remaining mine respectfully (!!) and wanting to call'.[5]

Such patronage would be invaluable. Gabriel hurried back to Boyce, to work further on the drawings. A week later, Ruskin brought his father, who held the purse-strings; he pronounced *Beatrice denying her Salutation* to be 'celestial', but did not approve the lascivious subject of *To Caper Nimbly*.

Coincidentally, Rossetti was in touch with another patron, William Marshall MP, a 'millionaire' from Leeds, who had a select collection of old and new works in his Eaton Square house. He purchased the oil sketch of *Kate the Queen*, and in due course would take other works. But he may have insisted on confidentiality, for instead of crowing, Rossetti barely mentioned him in correspondence. Meanwhile, Allingham had a commission to edit an anthology of the old ballads he and Rossetti liked so much, with a cash advance towards woodblock illustrations. Borrowing thirty shillings of this, Gabriel took Lizzie to Hastings. With help from Bessie and Barbara, she was installed in lodgings, in a room large enough for 'eating and drawing and sleeping'. Then Gabriel returned to London, where his father was steadily sinking and the Ruskins' tragic farce was nearing its critical act.

On 24 April he lunched with Ruskin at Denmark Hill (but seemingly not with Effie), taking Allingham's *Day and Night Songs* and speaking of Miss Siddal, his pupil, whose works were of untutored genius. In return, Ruskin offered Rossetti his collected works and commissioned a watercolour similar to that of *Beatrice denying her Salutation*. Gabriel asked 15 guineas, a low price, perhaps a sprat to catch a mackerel. Jubilant, he hurried off, to Allingham's lodgings, Albany Street and the Hermitage in turn.

The following day, Effie Ruskin left the marital home to travel north with her parents, returning her wedding ring, house keys and account books. A day later, Professor Rossetti died, 'after much lingering delay', with all the family at his bedside. 'He had not, I think, felt much pain,' Gabriel told Allingham; 'but it has been a wearisome, protracted state of dull suffering, from which we cannot but feel in some sort happy at seeing him released.'[6] Watching his mother kiss her husband's closed eyes before the coffin was sealed, he wondered despite himself what the kisses had been like during his parents' courtship – suddenly, perhaps for the first time, seeing their lives in a longer perspective than his own.

He barely mourned: to most intents and purposes his father had died several months, if not years, before. The Rossettis were not unfeeling, but nor did they display emotion for the sake of show. Frances was dignified, and decided. She refused a public, patriotic wake by the Italian community in favour of private burial in Highgate Cemetery, quietly ordered all remaining copies of *Amor Platonica* to be destroyed, and looked about for a new occupation, perhaps more from habit than necessity. With her modest inheritance, William's increased salary and Maria's earnings, the reduced household was comfortable enough.

From Hastings, Bessie and Barbara sent urgent missives saying Lizzie must go into the Sussex Infirmary, though Lizzie insisted she was no worse. On the day of his father's funeral, Gabriel heard from Ruskin again, opaquely mentioning matters of which he had perhaps already heard or certainly soon would hear. Was this some grievous family misfortune? Gabriel asked Allingham, ignorant of Effie's flight and clearly fearing the Ruskin wine business was close to collapse. As soon as the funeral was over, he left for Hastings. 'I have been staying at the Inn here, but move today to Mrs Elphick's, 5 High Street, where Guggum is, and where my lodging will cost 8s,' he wrote home on 7 May. Everyone was most attentive and 'no-one thinks it at all odd my going into the Gug's room to sit there; and Barbara Smith said to the landlady how unadvisable it would be for her to sit with me in a room without fire.' If any impropriety was suspected, *honi soit*. The weather blessed them: the sunlit sea was smooth as enamel, with a cool breeze. Gabriel was writing at the unaccustomed hour of eight, having risen at dawn. 'Yesterday I saw the sun rise !!! over the sea – the most wonderful of earthly sights.'[7]

He used notepaper with a thin black border, reserving the deep edge for those outside the family to whom it would be indispensable. But he was quite unable to suppress his good spirits. His motive is easy to discern, as he turned from death and mourning towards light, life, love, released at last from the pall long cast over the family. He ought not to have raced off to the coast before his father was cold in his coffin, but this was precisely what he must do, as if escaping from the underworld.

'Together they form the most touching group I ever saw in my life,' noted Bessie. 'He is a slim Italian; English born and bred, but a son of Italy on both sides of the house – short, dark hair, lighter eyes, a little moustache and a beard; very gentlemanly, even tender in manner; with a sweet mellow voice.' Lizzie beside him was the tallest, slenderest creature, dressed in a lilac-coloured costume, 'with masses of red auburn hair looped up in a wild picturesque fashion . . .'[8]

Gabriel gave Bessie a copy of Christina's *Verses*, with a tactful account of Lizzie's health. 'Indeed, if anything she seems to me a little better,' he wrote. 'I have known her for several years and always in a state hardly less variable than now; and I can understand that those who have not had so long a knowledge of her, would naturally be more liable to sudden alarm on her account than I am.' But was Lizzie sickly at this date? She was slim, and very pale-skinned, and could look listless. At Chatham Place in the autumn, Brown noted her 'looking thinner and more deathlike and more beautiful and more ragged than ever'.[9] Despite all the diagnoses, however, there was no organic disease, and it may be that the appearance of illness added protective camouflage to an intimate holiday.

In the upstairs front room in Hastings High Street, Gabriel drew several finely detailed and expressive pencil studies of his 'dear dove': Lizzie reading, standing by the window, reclining in a chair. She wears a soft woollen dress with full, unhooped skirt and loose-fitting bodice with pleats falling from shoulder to waist and wide sleeves over deep cuffs – all the detail attesting to close, unhurried transcription. 'Wonderful and lovely', said Brown, 'each one stamped with immortality.' Rossetti's draughtsmanship was not flawless, but in these studies he excelled himself; together they seem to recreate a moment 'out of time' for two lovers in unwonted closeness, unfamiliar surroundings and perfect equipoise.

Often they were more energetic, rambling on the cliffs, walking on the beach, writing their names in the sand and on the rocks. Along the cliffs towards Fairlight was a resting-place romantically named Lovers' Seat. A similar spot forms the backdrop to one of Lizzie's drawings, of lovers listening to music. On East Hill they met a 'dark gipsy-looking girl' of about twelve, minding a younger sister, who later came to sit for Lizzie. One day they went to see Barbara and Anna Mary at Scalands, the Leigh Smith house near Robertsbridge, where Lizzie became the model, her hair decked with wild irises for the others to draw. She and Gabriel walked in the Scalands woods, in the late springtime, as in a dream-world. With soft, erotic imagery, his ode *Love's Nocturn*, begun this year, evokes the atmosphere of love almost too delicate to define. Only the last but one of twenty-two stanzas seems a direct expression of the impulse now shaping his life:

> Yet from old time, life, not death,
>   Master, in thy rule is rife:
> Lo! through thee, with mingling breath,
>   Adam woke beside his wife.
> O Love, bring me so, for strife,
>   Force and faith,
> Bring me so not death but life!

As conceived, the ode was in the voice 'of a man not yet in love who dreams vaguely of a woman who he thinks must exist for him'. But as Rossetti later realised, this was cloudily expressed; the poem should really invoke 'the love of a known woman'. He was twenty-six this month, and his father's death impelled him for the first time to imagine waking like Adam, beside a wife. They had a joint project, too, for Lizzie was also designing for the ballad illustrations. Having brought the woodblocks to Hastings, as earnest of intent, he had done little himself. 'I have been disgracefully idle,' he told Allingham. He assured his mother, however, that he was giving thought to the design of a paternal tombstone, as promised.

As Millais foresaw, his name was publicly linked to the Ruskin affair. Sending Rossetti a message from art dealer Gambart, he received in reply inquiries about the Folio Club and the scandal – for as Millais had been so intimate with Ruskin, he was surely privy to the truth. 'My dear Gabriel, I am obliged to leave here on Tuesday, so that I cannot see you just now,' he replied evasively. He was going to Scotland, to Derbyshire and then to visit Tennyson; would Gabriel join in illustrating the Laureate's poems? The poet seemed inclined to favour the Pre-Raphaelites, if the publisher agreed. As to the Folio, many apologies: he had been too plagued with callers and desperate to get away. He wished he, Gabriel and Hunt could go off and paint together, as of old. In the meantime, would Gabriel do him a watercolour he would be proud to hang? He would write again about 'the R. business'.[10]

He did not need to; the rumours were soon confirmed. When news of Effie's appeal on grounds of non-consummation became public, both Munro and Calder Campbell sent full details, which Rossetti relayed to Brown. 'Mrs R. will get a divorce it seems – her husband is – or *is not* – I know not,' he wrote fumblingly before hitting a better manner of expression. 'It seems Mrs R's seven years of marriage have been passed like Rachel's seven marriageable years – in hope . . . he seems to take it very cool, as he wrote to me during the row with a great deal about Art etc.'[11] All the same, it was difficult to reply. Thankfully, Ruskin had left for Switzerland, so there was no hurry in respect of his commission. From

Belfast MacCracken promised £50 for his watercolour in place of the agreed 35 guineas.

Hastings was stunning, but somnolent. 'I want to know something of all things. How do people talk of Hunt's picture?' he asked William. 'How is Collins hung? And is there anything worth description in the RA?' His colour box needed replenishment. Lizzie was a sweet companion, but the atmosphere of idleness proved enervating. 'I lie often on the cliffs, which are lazy themselves, not athletic as at Dover, not gaunt as at North Shields,' he told Brown. 'Sometimes through the summer mists the sea and sky are one; and, if you half shut your eyes, as of course you do, there is no swearing to the distant sail as boat or bird, while just under one's feet the near boats stand together immoveable, as if their shadows clogged them and they would not come in after all, but loved to see the land. So one may lie and symbolize till one goes to sleep, and that be a symbol too perhaps.'[12]

Of oblivion, perhaps. He had been in dreamland long enough; it was time to return to the world. Besides, he was out of tin, obliged to ask William to pawn his gold pin – possibly inherited from father or grandfather – to pay for the lodgings. A week later he tore himself away.

'In the summer of 1854 I had rooms in quiet shady little Queen Square, Bloomsbury,' Allingham recalled; 'and there one afternoon appeared, as it often did, the welcome face of Gabriel Rossetti. "Would I come out with him?" "With the greatest pleasure, if he could wait a little while." He took a book and sat silent. A quarter of an hour later (it was a scribbling book of mine that was in his hands) he had made a pen and ink drawing in it opposite to a translation of a poem of Heine's, twelve lines long, which he had never seen before.'[13]

The drawing, of King, Queen and Page, is inscribed '9 June 54'. It was medieval in theme, quaint in style, like one of the Border ballads for the projected anthology.

This year *Sister Helen*, Rossetti's 'ghastly ballad' of betrayal and revenge, appeared in the *Düsseldorf Artists' Album*, guest-edited by Mary Howitt. Allingham, Christina and Bessie Parkes were also represented. His own poem centres on an act of witchcraft as the story unfolds obliquely, in folkloric fashion, through a dialogue between Helen and her young brother, while she destroys the waxen image of her false lover. Each stanza has a repeated, slightly varied burden, which would become a favoured device, and the narrative left some things unexplained, which in Rossetti's view was one of the main attractions of traditional ballads. At Hastings, Lizzie sketched 'a splendid design' for the poem, depicting the climactic moment when the wax melts, the betrayer dies, and Helen is damned.

The ultimate sources for *Sister Helen* lie in Walter Scott's *Letters on Demonology and Witchcraft*, and Thomas Keightley's *Fairy Mythology*, a compendium of European folklore and long-time favourite with the Rossetti family. In Devon, Frances's cousin had written up a collection of such tales garnered by her antiquarian husband, some published this year in *A Peep at the Pixies*. From the west coast of Ireland Allingham had a stock of similar stories. Like ballads, tales of supernatural sorcery were to Rossetti quaint survivals of older time, well-nigh obliterated by the modern world of scientific progress. Akin to picturesque ruins and old furniture, their antiquity was value in itself. In addition, they spoke of prerational beliefs in strange and inexplicable events – beliefs that were fast vanishing yet never quite vanquished. Orthodox and rational minds were dismissive or hostile towards the supernatural, as encouraging superstition at best and at worst belief in the occult, thereby overtly challenging both reason and revealed religion. Yet mid-Victorian literature, art and drama was filled with such material, from the tales collected by the Grimms to those minted by Hans Andersen, from Maclise's *Undine*, purchased by the Queen for Albert's birthday, to Noel Paton's *Fairy Raid*, Francis Danby's *Oberon and Titania*, Dicky Doyle's sprites or Richard Dadd's fantasias. The stage saw *The Tempest* and *A Midsummer Night's Dream* rendered operatic by Halévy and Weber, as well as ballets like *La Sylphide* and *Ondine*, not to mention spectacular pantomimes. All deployed technical wizardry to create magical effects. Such fantasies seemed to dramatise the amazing, incredible inventions now bodying forth such as that which enabled the electric telegraph to 'put a girdle round about the earth' in forty minutes.

There is no evidence that Rossetti believed in fairies in the same way as Yeats, for example. On ghosts, he inclined to suspend disbelief, and once startled Scott by alluding, with apparent conviction, to the folk belief that the spirits of the dead migrated into the bodies of birds. As for sorcery, he reserved judgement, but used the theme over and again in poetry and painting. Among his favourite subjects was Michael Scott, a legendary wizard from the Scottish Borders who also makes a brief appearance in Dante's *Inferno* (thus uniting two of Gabriel's literary passions). First sketched in 1853, the subject haunted Rossetti's imagination and years later he drafted an account of Michael Scott's powers exercised on a maiden. 'He says how she loved him but would not sin', this begins; 'how hearing in her sleep his appeal from the shore she almost yielded, and the embodied image of her longing came rushing out to him; but how in the last instant she turned back for refuge to Christ, and her soul was wrung from her by the struggle of her heart. "And as I speak," he says, "the fiend who whispers this concerning her says also in my ear how surely I am lost." '[14]

Both Sister Helen and Michael Scott are doomed by the Faustian strength of their own desires, vengeance and lust. In time to come, Rossetti himself would literally hear demonic whispers in his ear, audible manifestations of inner impulses. And his antiquarian absorption in supernatural tales was also founded on their dramatisation of acute states of mind, like 'embodied images' of longing, fear and hatred. Especially when illicit or transgressive, intense emotion went beyond normal, rational representation. Moreover, by virtually ignoring 'Gradgrindian' knowledge through his schooldays, Rossetti kept in touch with the childhood faculty for mingling real and fictional, factual and fearful. In poetry and painting both, Gabriel transported himself to such a realm, where images are in many respects pictorial and poetic embodiments of inner visions.

Finding freelance journalism too arduous and uncertain, Allingham was going back to Ireland and his old post. Before he left, Rossetti made a cover design for his new book, to be called *Day and Night Songs*, showing noontide and evening, framed by a blue-and-green border of ivy leaves, and promised at least one wood-engraving for the volume, alongside Millais and Hughes. Such collaboration pleased him, like the exchange of sonnets in thirteenth-century Florence. 'How many capital plans we have!' he wrote when Allingham proposed a joint volume of poems and pictures, by himself and the former PRBs.

Which poem should he illustrate? 'Nothing so much spoils a good book as an attempt to embody its ideas, only going half way,' he told Allingham, before settling on *The Maids of Elfen-Mere*. Was this not founded on some Northern legend? he added; he seemed to have read it somewhere.[15] Indeed, it came from a tale in *Rhine Legends* (1839) about a pastor's son visited every night by three fairy damsels, singing and spinning. The maidens always depart before midnight, until the young man alters the clock to make them stay. Then they return no more, and on the surface of the mere that is their home three red stains appear.

In August, Rossetti sketched an *Elfen-Mere* design, showing the youth sitting on the floor clasping his knees and looking down; above him the three maidens are illuminated by moonlight. It was reminiscent of an earlier sketch showing the Fates holding scissors and similar in atmosphere and proportion to Lizzie's *Sister Helen*. A month or so later, *Elfen-Mere* was drawn on the wood, the composition altered so that the man turns his back to the spectator, his profile lit by a low light that also falls on the maidens' long white shifts and seems unearthly. The room-space is narrow and enclosed, and through three high window-openings are glimpsed rooftops, a church clock showing the hands at ten to twelve, and three dark shapes on moonlit water.

But to his dismay Rossetti misunderstood the nature of drawing on the wood. 'I have committed a stupid mistake in not drawing the actions reversed, so that, when printed, the figures will be left-handed,' he told Allingham on 15 October. Redrawing on a new block, however, he forgot

the clock-face, which when printed shows the time at ten past one –
admittedly on such a small scale that the mistake is hardly legible.

Dalziel Brothers, whose professional wood-engravers cut the block, later
complained that the drawing was not just in ink but also in 'wash, pencil
and coloured chalk', quite unsuitable for clean cutting. But in view of
Rossetti's technical description and the opinion of John Clayton, who
thought the design eminently adaptable to engraving, this seems mistaken,
perhaps defensively in view of the artist's eldritch shrieks when proofs came
to hand. 'That woodblock!' he wrote to Allingham in dismay. 'Dalziel has
made such an incredible mull of it in the cutting that it cannot possibly
appear.' The faces of the open-mouthed maidens resembled goldfish and the
treatment was both hard and flabby. It would have to go.[16]

Allingham demurred, insisting it was fine. Reluctantly Rossetti agreed to
printing, but tore the print from his own copy. Ironically, however, it was
his *Maids of Elfen-Mere* which made the little book famous, and was
recognised as a new departure in illustration. With their long tresses
cascading over their shoulders, and their lips apart, the maids 'appear
absorbed in a trance that is distinctly sensual', writes a recent critic,[17]
arguing that *Elfen-Mere* embodies the tension of unrealised desire, and the
conviction that any move towards consummation is fatal – as in the poem.
Sexual initiation means death for both sexes.

'It is a great secret in art never to hurry – don't you think so? Gabriel
does,' wrote Allingham to Hughes[18] when the book missed its Christmas
deadline. Though he was not the only defaulter, this approach was
characteristic. It is also defensible, for if, when complete, works of art look
as though they have sprung fully formed, in practice time, thought and
revision are usually required. Especially if, as often happened in his case, the
result was not all he had hoped for.

'I have got out my work this morning, but it looks so hopelessly beastly,
and I feel so hopelessly beastly, that I must try to revive myself before
beginning, by some exercise that goes quicker than the Fine Arts,' he told
Allingham in the summer. Not much interested in painting, Allingham had
suggested Rossetti publish a volume of verse. But all his best poems were
still 'in an aboriginal state', Gabriel replied; although some were 'very long
beginnings', none was finished.[19] Here was one newly minted, however. It
began with a contrived conceit of two men who love the same woman
changing from enemies to melancholy friends after her death, as a metaphor
for 'separate hopes' contending within a single soul, who end the poem as
tired travellers 'through high streets and at many dusty inns'. The lines were
cloudy, said Allingham, and they remain so despite later revision. But in
due course the sonnet was titled *Lost on Both Sides*, and it is likely that the

separate hopes are those of poetry and painting, ancient competitors within Rossetti. In despondent moods both seemed equally vain and dusty.

Interrupted when drawing an angel in memory of Beatrice, Dante Alighieri wrote a sonnet. Michelangelo composed poems as well as frescoes and sculptures. When dissatisfied with painting, Rossetti was always tempted to turn to verse, though this only aggravated the problem. 'I believe my poetry and painting prevented each other from doing much good for a long while,' he explained; 'and now I think I could do better in either, but can't write, for then I sha'n't paint.'

Nevertheless, a few weeks later he wrote a 'modern-antique' ballad called *Stratton Water*. Partly inspired by the flooded fields in Warwickshire a year before and partly by the ballads he and Lizzie were supposed to be illustrating, this is a piece of Scots pastiche (for which he admitted lifting 'an unimportant phrase here and there' from old texts). Like *Sister Helen* and the old *Bride-chamber Talk*, it is yet another tale of sexual betrayal and blighted love:

> 'They told me you were dead, Janet, –
>   How could I guess the lie?'
> 'They told me you were false, Lord Sands, –
>   What could I do but die?'
>   . . .
> 'O it's one half-hour to reach the kirk
>   And one for the marriage-rite;
> And kirk and castle and castle-lands
>   Shall be our babe's to-night.'

Allingham sent copious comments on the 'abruptnesses, improbabilities, prosaicisms, coarsenesses and others *esses* and *isms*' of the verse.[20] Gabriel promised to take the points into account, if ever he revised it. And so the poem was laid aside imperfect, like the rest.

His next sonnet, sent to Allingham and Hunt six months later, was subsequently given the apt title *A Dark Day*, evocative of the gloomy moods to which he was prone. Did they presage new doles, he wondered, or merely arouse old memories, like those of unanswered prayers? Perhaps time would soothe all prickly griefs, like the thistledown country girls were said to gather in order to make a soft marriage-bed. As in *Lost on Both Sides*, the imagery is both attractive and yet laboured.

Some writers, as they work through from concept to realisation, find a poem takes on its own momentum, in unpredicted ways, often emerging quite other than expected, almost as a self-created work of art. This had happened with *Hand and Soul*. Rossetti's verses, by contrast, frequently limped after rather than led their ideas, struggling for adequate imagery. When a poem began buzzing in his brain, he told Jack Tupper, he was struck by his 'utter inadequacy to the job of writing it down'.[21] Visually, the process seems to have been easier, but to some degree similar, for somewhere beyond his reach lay the perfect rendering, which might one day be achieved. Until then, both poems and pictures remained long or short beginnings.

So dissatisfaction compounded the restless alternation between verbal and visual art, and the curiously energetic irresolution of these years. The biographer is struck by the tortuous similes Rossetti deployed in verse and prose attempts to analyse himself. 'A man of many journeys must needs find his path crossed here and there by some old hobby each time grown seedier and sleepier,' he told Allingham a little later, in relation to past projects; 'and sometimes he may say: "Now will I saddle thee, for where our pastures lay, there they lie"; and no doubt so they do; but even one's hobby is not so soft to ride as to lay one's head on; and so they two snooze together. If either is ever woke up, it may be the hobby, which somebody saddles awry to fetch the sexton, to risk a cheap bell or so for him who is still asleep, and have him enough remembered to be forgotten . . .' Then he checked himself. 'This fine writing, you'll say, is wronging you of news.' Half a year later, he realised with some surprise that he had effectively 'given up poetry as a pursuit of my own'.[22] A dozen other projects had intervened, and he was indeed 'a man of many journeys'.

John Ruskin, who now seemed set to make Rossetti's fortune, was more interested in art than literature. To Hastings, Barbara Smith had brought the published version of his Edinburgh lectures on Pre-Raphaelite principles, delivered before the author had seen any of Gabriel's works. 'Pre-Raphaelitism has but one principle, that of absolute, uncompromising truth in all that it does, obtained by working everything, down to the most minute detail, from nature and from nature only,' it asserted confidently. Then, bearing evident signs of revision, a qualifying footnote added that where imagination was necessarily trusted to – as in depictions of past or imaginary scenes – truth to nature was achieved 'by always endeavouring to conceive a fact as it really was likely to have happened, rather than as it most prettily *might* have happened'. And finally, the text mentioned Rossetti by name, as one of the 'various members of the school' worthy to rank beside Millais, each possessing as much 'exhaustless invention' as 'the greatest men of old times'.[23]

Invention meant originality, the distinguishing faculty necessary to great art. Lesser artists aimed for a high degree of imitation, but 'the man whose mind a thousand living imaginations haunt, every hour' was apt to aspire higher. Rossetti certainly aspired thus: ideas thronged his brain, waiting only on realisation.

In May, Millais had urged him not to let anything interfere with his determination to paint something really large and fit for exhibition. The proposed subject, destined for MacCracken, was the encounter between a fallen woman and her former sweetheart – first mentioned to Deverell twelve months before, and then to Scott – which was to be 'a great modern work' combining social concern with a treatment both truthful and poetic.

If not large in size, *Found* was certainly so in conception. The scene is a city street at dawn, with the gas-lamps still lit. 'A drover has left his cart standing in the middle of the road ... and has run a little way after a girl who ... recognising him, has sunk under her shame upon her knees', against a churchyard wall, while he seizes her hands 'half in bewilderment and half guarding her from doing herself a hurt'. In the cart is a calf on its way to market, a symbolic correlative of the woman, as commodities 'bought and sold' in urban society. Maria Rossetti found an apt quotation, from Jeremiah: 'I remember Thee, the kindness of thy youth, the love of thine espousals.'[24]

Once designed, *Found* required models and a location. The background came first. In the autumn of 1853 Rossetti had contemplated going to Frome, telling his mother he would need a brick wall and a white heifer tied to a cart. But as was his habit, he let the season pass, and by June 1854 when he met MacCracken for the first time, the commission looked less and less secure. The Belfast manufacturer was in London to sell his other pictures – by Hunt, Millais, Brown, Goodall and the rest. 'He squeezed my arm with some pathos on communicating his purpose, and added that he should part with neither of mine,' Gabriel told Allingham with a frisson of relief. Sales like this made artists understandably nervous, as they watched the prices of their works plummet. 'I like MacCrac pretty well enough,' he continued, with half-ironic arrogance. 'I told him I had nothing whatever to show him, and that his picture was not yet begun, which placed us at once on a perfect understanding. He seems hard up.'[25] Nevertheless, MacCracken did not cancel the commission.

But now there was a further problem: Hunt's *Awakening Conscience* – a modern subject showing a fallen woman suddenly remorseful for lost innocence.

Painted in the last months of 1853, the picture remained unseen until its appearance at the Academy in May 1854, where it was one of the most talked-of exhibits despite or perhaps because of being so 'strong-minded' – the current term for socially controversial topics concerning gender relations. Ruskin sang its praises in *The Times*. 'The poor girl has been sitting singing with her seducer; some chance words of the song "Oft in the stilly night" have struck upon the numbed places of her heart; she has started up in agony,' he wrote. To many, the subject would appear coarse, or commonplace. But the brilliantly rendered details were based on true principles of the pathetic. Each 'becomes tragical, if rightly read', he continued. 'That furniture so carefully painted ... that terrible lustre ... those embossed books, vain and useless ... the torn and dying bird upon the floor; the gilded tapestry ... the picture above the fireplace, with its single dropping figure – the woman taken in adultery; nay, the very hem of the poor girl's dress ... has a story in it, if we think how soon its pure whiteness may be soiled with dust and rain, the outcast feet failing in the street ...'[26]

On seeing *The Awakening Conscience* in early June, Rossetti must have immediately understood the implications for his own picture. After this, *Found* would seem like a sequel, an imitation. Of course he was pleased for Hunt, but dismayed. Was he always to be outstripped by his PR Brothers? Besides, it was his idea first.

'I know that, so far from being envious of them, you are thoroughly happy in their success: but yet ... you have a kind of gnawing pain at not standing side by side with them,' replied Ruskin from Geneva. 'You feel as if it were not worth while now to bring out your modern subjects, as Hunt has done his first.' But, he went on, like a kindly tutor to a disappointed student:

> I firmly believe that, to whomsoever it may belong in priority of time, it belongs to all three of you rightly in right of possession. I think that you, Hunt and Millais, would, every one of you, have made the discovery, without assistance or suggestion from the other. One might make it quicker or slower than another, and I suppose that, actually, you were the first who did it. But it would have been impossible for men of such eyes and hearts as Millais and Hunt to walk the streets of London, or have watched the things that pass each day, and not discover also what there was in them to be shown and painted.[27]

It was an accurate observation. Though exhibiting nothing this year, Millais had produced designs on comparable themes: *Retribution*, in which a man is confronted by a pleading wife and infants as he pays court to another woman; *Virtue and Vice*, showing a poor seamstress tempted to a life of shame; and *The Race Meeting*, based on an incident witnessed by the artist at Ascot, 'a woman crying bitterly, evidently the paramour of the man lolling back in the carriage flushed with drink', his losses so great he can no longer afford to keep her.[28] Moreover, other artists were tackling such controversial themes.

The current Folio theme was 'Desolation'. When the portfolio reached Rossetti in August, Millais's design was of the Romans leaving Britain. But *The Castaway* by Anna Howitt showed a poor flower-girl, with a motto from Job: 'he cast me into the mire ...' This was 'rather a strong-minded subject ... symbolical of something improper', Gabriel reported to Allingham. 'Of course Miss Howitt is quite right in painting it if she chooses,' he added. 'I daresay it will be a good picture.'[29] But suddenly, everyone was doing fallen women.

So he hesitated to place his study for *Found* in the Folio, thinking rather to choose Hamlet's rejection of Ophelia ('deeply symbolic and far sighted, of course'). Then anxiety surfaced in a sudden outburst on rivalry and plagiarism. Expressed as a satirical drama, this opens with Mike Halliday alone in his Adelphi studio, writing to Millais. 'I've just got the Folio back at last from that lazy wretch Rossetti. In spite of your prophecy he really *has* put in a design,' he says, proceeding to describe *Found*. Scene Two takes place at the Collins' home in Regent's Park, where John Everett Millais, Esq., ARA, PRB, etc., is visiting. How odd, he remarks, that design of Gabriel's – the very same subject as his own. 'Did I show you my sketch for it? O didn't I?' Enter Stephens and the dialogue continues:

> *Steph*. Ah, have you seen Gabriel's design in the Folio? Stunning!
> *Mil*. No, but Halliday told me. We were talking about that. Ah! it was you, Stephens, that I showed that design of mine to?
> *Steph*. Which? That in the Folio? Yes! Stunning!
> *Mil*. No – one I did some time ago like Gabriel's, about a woman and market-gardener, finding her in the street.
> *Steph*. O, no. O. Let's see though ...
> *Hal*. Are you going to paint that design of yours, then?
> *Mil*. Yes, I've got the canvas. My brother couldn't come tonight because he was drawing the perspective for me.
> *Hal*. It'll be a bore for Rossetti.
> *Steph*. Ah! sorry for old Gabriel.
> *Mil*. Lord bless you, he'd never have painted it you know. You know him. Is he coming here tonight, Collins? Ah! he always keeps out of my way ... (*to Steph*.) O my dear fellow, you'll see when I paint this picture, it'll come the loveliest thing your ever saw in your life. I know of a brick wall to paint in it that's perfectly heavenly ...

In the final scene, set in 1855, a critic completes his review of the RA exhibition by comparing the impact of Hunt's *Awakening Conscience* to ... Mr Millais's *Found*. Both have 'the merit of perfect originality'; no other painters could conceive such powerful subjects. 'What say you to my dramatic powers?' Gabriel asked Allingham, wrapping up this *jeu d'esprit*. 'Not to speak of historical truth, prophetic verve, etc?'[30] And envy, we may add, with even a hint of paranoia.

As it happened, Millais's response to *The Awakening Conscience* was a blind beggar girl – a modern-life picture on vagrancy, an equally urgent social concern. And when, towards the end of the year he set to work on an urban scene, he chose the heroic subject of a London firefighter rescuing children from a blazing building. But the fear was telling. Millais, with immense technique and dispatch, had less inventiveness. Rossetti, blessed with ideas, intellect, sensibility, still took no place on the exhibition walls. Brown, writing a few weeks later, noted how Gabriel's bitter moods came on, occluding his geniality. 'After he has talked as much as his strength will bear, he becomes spiteful and crusty, denying everything,' he wrote; 'and when chaffed he at length grows bitterly sarcastic in his way, but never quite unpleasant nor ever unbearable.'[31] Of all his friends, Brown best understood the dissatisfaction that fuelled such spleen.

This helps to explain why he persisted with *Found*, when MacCracken was hard up and Ruskin, who discouragingly declared it a most 'painful' subject which might prove '*dreadfully* difficult' to paint, said he would prefer a watercolour of the Holy Family celebrating Passover. Gabriel had perforce to apply yet again to his aunt. 'I am afraid you will guess, before reading this letter, what it is likely to relate to,' he began, pre-emptively. 'I am in a very great difficulty for money . . .' In short, could she lend £25, or possibly £30?[32]

Good aunt Charlotte duly obliged. Gabriel paid his rent arrears and spent a few days with Hannay, visiting the abbey church at St Albans and prospecting for an eligible location, with wall and calf. But when he appeared at Brown's, one hot September day, he sought costumes for the Holy Family, instead of setting to work on 'the picture for which he has been commissioned by MacCrack since 12 months'. Then there was more procrastination, spent partly in discovering *Wuthering Heights* – 'the first novel I've read for an age, and the best (as regards power and sound style) for two ages, except *Sidonia*', he wrote. It was set in Hell '– only it seems places and people have English names there'. When asked about his work in early October, however, though 'as usual diffuse and inconsequent' in reply, he did inquire if Brown could find a willing farmer, with a white calf. 'Would he but study the *golden one* a little more,' commented Brown. 'Poor Gabriello.'[33]

In the end he found a wall first, staying with his father's friend Thomas Keightley in Chiswick and painting 'within earshot almost of Hogarth's grave – a good omen for one's modern picture!' Another favourable sign came from a passer-by, who said the wall reminded him of a picture in

Danzig, by two brothers whose name he forgot. Could this be Van Eyck? Rossetti asked, only to find afterwards that there was indeed such an altarpiece.[34]

The 'hateful mechanical brick-painting' took about a fortnight, interrupted by Woolner's return home and by a few days' illness, when Gabriel retreated to his mother's care. Cholera was growing epidemic and bodies left the Middlesex Hospital in vanloads. War was under way against Russia, in the Crimea. Reports of dreadful suffering reached London, and Eliza Polidori volunteered to join the nursing team.

'How very busy and bothered I have been,' Gabriel told Allingham in November, from Finchley, where the Browns were now living and where Mr Johnson of Manor Farm had an eligible white calf. As Ruskin predicted, painting was dreadfully difficult. 'He paints it in all like Albert Dürer hair by hair and seems incapable of any breadth,' noted Brown. 'From want of habit I see nature bothers him – but it is sweetly drawn and felt.' As at Sevenoaks the weather turned wet, and then cold. Secured in a net for five or six hours daily, the calf kicked and struggled continuously. Indeed, Gabriel joked, its experience of art seemed so miserable that it looked as if it were attempting suicide by strangling itself with the rope. At weekends he went into London to see Lizzie, again working on her own at Blackfriars. She drew herself and Gabriel as lovers listening to musical maidens and made a careful ink illustration to Browning's *Pippa Passes*, whose theme and dispositions echo those of *Found*. Then she again attempted oils, before changing to watercolour, for scenes from Wordsworth and Keats.

Again Gabriel ran out of funds. 'Please don't forget – but I know you won't,' he asked the ever-faithful, ever-reluctant William; '– as soon and as much as you can manage like a brick. I have an awful lot of claimants' – including the housekeeper who serviced the apartments at Chatham Place – 'not to speak of utterly unavoidable expenses here.'[35]

After five weeks Brown ran out of patience, for Rossetti proved an annoying expense in himself, borrowing his host's breeches and overcoat and consuming quantities of turpentine. The house was small, Emma heavily pregnant, the servant-girl untrained. Brown's elder daughter Lucy was due home for Christmas. The grocer's bill was unpaid, the silver spoons broken or melted, the carpet full of holes, Brown's dress suit destined for the pawnshop. In early December they came close to a quarrel after Gabriel teased four-year-old Cathy by threatening to put her in the fire. 'That ass of a child,' he began, as her fond parents entered the room. 'I don't choose you to call my child an ass,' retorted Brown. 'If you can't stay here without calling her names you had better go.'

Another night Rossetti kept Brown up until 5 a.m. talking about suicide, probably in response to news of William North's death. On 17 December, when Emma was within a week or two of her confinement and Gabriel, sleeping on the parlour floor, never rose until eleven, Brown said he must at least go home every night by bus. That would be far too expensive, objected Gabriel. He could walk, then, replied Brown. Unthinkable, said Gabriel. ('He thinks nothing of putting *us* to trouble and expence,' noted Brown.)

And so, eventually, he left, promising to return; could Brown collect the easel from Farmer Johnson? He neither returned, nor continued. In due course the picture came back to the studio and lay there unfinished.

Conceptually, *Found* is an important Victorian painting, filled with social and moral motifs for the viewer to read like poetic metaphors. The man's white smock contrasts with the girl's dark mantle. The edge of the wall forms a barrier between them, and she crouches beneath a graveyard while his head is silhouetted against the dawn sky. A discarded rose lies by a drain. Two birds gather straw from the cart, watched by a cat. The calf, 'trammelled in the net and helpless', is being carried to its death. The bridge alludes to Thomas Hood's poem on a drowned prostitute, and to Martha in *Great Expectations*, who likens herself to the river, flowing from the innocent countryside through the dismal and defiled city.[36]

Much has been written on the Fallen Woman theme, which sometimes seems to feature as the dominant trope of the Victorian age. For young men around town, it was a personal as well as social issue – perhaps because sexual laxity was both widespread and morally anathemised. Since, as Edward Lear observed, it was held that no woman could ever recover from a fall from virtue, yet no such punishment was visited on their partners, men were urged not to be the agent of another's perdition, but instead save her from the fate worse than death. This year, after their holiday in Hastings, Rossetti wrote about Lizzie in terms of deliverance. The subject was her health, but a moral metaphor is entwined in the words. How painful to think, he told Allingham, that perhaps her soul was 'never to bloom, nor her bright hair to fade, but after hardly escaping from degradation and corruption, all she might have been must sink out again unprofitably in that dark house where she was born'.

But what degradation had Miss Siddal escaped from? Her father's business in the Old Kent Road was an ironmonger's, not a brothel. Or had Lizzie represented herself as in need of moral protection as well as artistic instruction? Rossetti seemed to cast himself as rescuer. Yet he had just taken his pupil – or was it his paramour? – to the seaside, staying in the same lodgings. Often, she was in the studio, unchaperoned. All might be quite proper – as subsequent events suggest – but many would simply assume he was her seducer. At the very least, they were sailing close to the moral wind.

Found remained an important picture to him, its Blakean rather than sentimental pathos offering a powerful and lasting testimony to his artistic aims. As late as 1879, it was the one painting he still wished to finish for exhibition, to demonstrate that he was able to paint 'what is real and human'. But in the New Year of 1855, when the figures should have been painted, he felt perhaps too awkward to ask Lizzie to pose for the fallen woman, and too poor to pay a professional model. Moreover, its sale looked unlikely, for he now knew that MacCracken 'either is or professes to be too nearly ruined now to buy more pictures'.[37] And so, despite his 'many capital plans', once again Mr D. G. Rossetti would have no major work for this year's exhibitions.

It has often been asserted, without evidence, that Gabriel and Lizzie were sexually intimate during the years of their 'engagement', or conversely, that Lizzie refused all physical relations until a wedding ring was on her finger. Neither seems to have been the case, and, as later events suggest, it was probably Gabriel who held out against sex – unlikely though this seems in one so accustomed to indulge every impulse – for fear of being trapped into marriage. Had Lizzie fallen pregnant, he could hardly have abandoned her, and he was certainly not ready to be a worthy husband and father. So like many Victorian couples, they suffered the frustrations of a long engagement. At first, this was no problem, but inevitably, troubles would develop.

CHAPTER EIGHT

Ruskin and Browning

Returning from the Continent in autumn 1854 as a bachelor once more, Ruskin also had many plans. 'I am rolling projects over and over in my head: I want to give lectures to about 200 at once in turn of the sign painters and shop decorators – and writing masters and upholsterers – and masons – and brickmakers and glassblowers, and pottery people – and young artists – and young men in general and schoolmasters – and young ladies in general and schoolmistresses,' he told Lady Trevelyan. 'And I mean to lend out Liber Studiorum and Albert Dürers to everybody who wants them ... and to have a room where anybody can go in all day and always see *nothing* in it but what is *good*: and I want to have a black hole, where they shall see nothing but what is *bad*, filled with Claudes and Sir Charles Barry's architecture ... and I want to have a little Academy of my own in all the manufacturing towns – and to get young artists – pre-Raphaelite always, to help me ...'[1] In practice, this meant teaching art at the newly-launched Working Men's College, a philanthropic adult education endeavour founded by the Christian Socialist F. D. Maurice.

The first students had enrolled. The third-floor room in Red Lion Square was packed with stools and easels. Twice a week Ruskin made the men draw: a plaster ball, a leather ball, the cast of a leaf. Then twigs, feathers, stones, purple fluorspar in a tumbler of water, lichen and fungi from Surrey woods, stuffed birds with brilliant plumage, an illuminated missal. He brought all his treasures, and talked 'discursively and radiantly' on art, poetry, nature. The aim was not mere technical proficiency, but that all might be encouraged 'to note and observe, to perceive and not merely to see, the wonder and beauty of this mysterious universe'.[2]

'He is most enthusiastic about it and has so infected me that I think of offering an evening weekly for the same purpose,' Rossetti told Allingham. Ruskin dispelled his doubts about formal teaching, saying the students needed only to be guided 'in the simplest possible way', and on 22 January Gabriel took his first class – 'for the figure, quite a separate thing from Ruskin's who teaches foliage'. He started by setting the students – 'mostly real workingmen – carpenters etc – to draw directly from nature, one serving as model to the rest'. No plaster casts or drawing manuals: 'the British mind is brought to bear on the British *mug* at once, with results that would astonish you,' he told Hunt proudly. Almost all the students were more able than he had expected, and everything was very informal. 'I draw there myself and find that by far the most valuable part of my teaching, not only to me, but to them,' he added.[3]

'The masses of shade are the drawing,' he would say to those who wanted to rely on line. The first fact to notice was the shade on one side of the nose, then that on cheek and chin. Once, when a student drew the return of an eyelid, he protested. 'Get rid of that academic fribble! draw only what you see.'

There were three short terms a year, and classes ran from 8 until 10 p.m. Very soon, he began using colours. Two of the first students described how the class watched intently, as he threw his pencil with apparent recklessness about the paper, to produce a design that combined outline and shading. Then he filled a brush with violet carmine or a mixture of cobalt and vermilion and, having worked it on the margin until it was virtually dry, painted over the rough design to produce a rugged modelling, looking like an aquatint. Also with virtually dry colour, he next worked in chrome yellow, cobalt blue, red lead – loose yet vivid and luminous. Finally he would work over all with a wetter, more flowing brush, blending and softening the forms until the glowing effect was complete.

One evening, Thomas Sulman recalled, Mr Rossetti blocked in on scrap paper the design of the lovers on Carlisle Wall, sketching the motif in ink and then adding colour, predominantly reds. For flesh tones he used vermilion, emerald green and a little purple carmine. The students stared, as the work acquired a strange iridescence, which steadily deepened into the desired harmony. Afterwards they were sure he must add some glaze, too, even though Rossetti denied this.[4]

One week, Ruskin brought in a hamper of dead game birds – pheasant, duck, partridge, pigeon – to show how wings should be drawn if, despite his protestations, angels were to be thus depicted. He challenged the other teachers, Rossetti and Lowes Dickinson, to paint a bird each. Gabriel got the duck and after tying it to a drawing-board began sketching in his customary neutral tones. The next week he worked over this in bright chrome. The students wondered, seeing no yellow in the bird. Before it could be completed, however, the carcass was thrown out by the college housekeeper 'for sanitary reasons'.

J. P. Emslie remembered how Rossetti was eager for men to graduate from Ruskin's class to his own. ' "Mr Ruskin'll spoil their eye for colour if he keeps 'em so long at that pencil and sepia drawing," he would say, while

Ruskin in turn would observe that "Mr Rossetti is such a colourist that he wishes everybody to be the same, and would have people practise colour before they understand light-and-shade." ' But the arguments were genial, and Emslie recalled Ruskin also remarking how Rossetti lacked the professional jealousy that made most art teachers withhold some part of their knowledge. By contrast, he shared everything.

The class noted his own battered paintbox. Were Robersons or Windsor & Newton the best colourmen? asked one student rather ostentatiously. 'Ah, I don't know,' said Gabriel. 'I generally use the halfpenny colours from the oil shop myself.' This may not have been quite true – he shopped at Robersons unless his account was too long unpaid – but it certainly spelt out a helpful message to impecunious men. Moreover, his easy manner worked its usual magic. To George Campfield, he was a cheerful, 'laughing gentleman', more like a friend than an instructor. Emslie witnessed his 'magnetic influence' again and again among fellow students. He could inspire and thrill us, recalled Sulman, till they were happy to render him the smallest service. Unlike Ruskin, however, Rossetti 'did not want our worship'; though a natural leader, Gabriel did not seek disciples.

His evident enjoyment of the Working Men's College is underlined by the fact that, as Ruskin noted, unlike other artists he was happy to teach without payment. He kept up his regular evening there well into 1857, when the College moved to Great Ormond Street, and returned in 1861, in the interim recruiting Madox Brown as substitute. He encouraged Munro and Woolner to teach modelling, and for a while sat at least nominally on the College Council, along with Maurice, Thomas Hughes, Llewellyn Davies, F. J. Furnivall, J. M. Ludlow and Vernon Lushington. While he became friendly with several of these worthies, however, he was far from sharing the earnest philosophy of the College and resolute in his refusal to engage in its political programme. He never preached 'Mauriceism' – generally understood as the establishment of Christ's kingdom on earth. Art was his only religion. Indeed, his letters, which show that he read the daily and weekly press and kept up with cultural matters, contain virtually no references to public events after the death of Wellington. The Crimean War, the crisis in India, changes of government, all go unmentioned. And if a stranger to snobbery, with a natural egalitarianism stretching from marchionesses to models, he had no particular sympathy towards working men as such, joking cruelly about the smelliness of the lower orders. He found a certain breed of self-improving autodidact consummately boring; and bores he could not abide. Nevertheless he continued his class at the Working Men's College longer than many other activities in a demonstration of practical politics that was as personal as it was determinedly apolitical.

A cynic might suggest that his commitment to the Working Men's College in 1855 was calculated to appeal to Ruskin, the new patron. But any initial ulteriority was soon superseded by genuine feeling. As soon became clear, friendship with Ruskin was the key feature of this year.

Ruskin at this date was thirty-six, of medium height and exceeding thinness. 'I have sometimes laid a light grasp on his coat-sleeve and there seemed to be next to nothing inside it,' William remembered.[5] He had thick fair hair, eyebrows and side-whiskers, striking blue eyes and a keen, confident expression, with a genial smile despite a mouth badly scarred in a childhood accident. Temperamentally, he was rather solitary, despite a wide acquaintance. To many, his boyish dependence on elderly parents was surprising: though heir to considerable wealth, he had to ask his father for the money for each purchase, and Gabriel was astonished to find that in his son's absence Mr Ruskin senior opened all his letters. The relationship might be admirably filial, but to his male contemporaries, to whom independence was the marker of masculinity, it verged on the unmanly. And everyone knew of his *mariage blanc*.

As critic, Ruskin was developing the ideas contained in *The Stones of Venice*, which interpreted the political decline of the Venetian Republic through its fifteenth-century architectural transition from medieval to neo-classical – and saw in this a paradigm for the present British nation-state. The first thing to be done, he asserted, was to cast out all aspects of Greek, Roman and Renaissance form and reintroduce Gothic modes, so that 'the London of the nineteenth century may yet become as Venice without her despotism, and as Florence without her dispeace'.[6]

Rossetti was already a romantic medievalist. Building on Pugin, Ruskin's writings provided a theoretical basis for his preferences, praising those very qualities for which Gothic art was generally damned as quaint, primitive, confused. The inner spirit of Gothic, Ruskin proclaimed, was based on Savageness – primitive but vital imperfection, as opposed to lifeless perfection – Changefulness or variety, Love of nature, Obstinacy or forceful tension, Generosity or delight in ornamentation, and above all Imagination – delight in the grotesque and comic as well as the noble and ideal.

This section of *The Stones of Venice*, 'On the Nature of Gothic', was issued as a pamphlet for the College students. Inspiringly, its rhetoric soared like vaulting roofs from the springing of an arch, enlivened with exuberantly carved clauses. Gothic was not only the best, but the only rational style. 'It can shrink into a turret, expand into a hall, coil into a staircase, or spring into a spire, with undegraded grace and unexhausted energy; and whenever it finds occasion for change in its form or purpose, it submits to it without the slightest sense of loss either to its unity or majesty,' Ruskin proclaimed; '– subtle and flexible like a fiery serpent, but ever attentive to the voice of the charmer.'

Surprisingly, for all his love of old things, Rossetti took little interest in building styles. 'In Sculpture he only cares for picturesque and grotesque qualities,' noted Allingham, 'and of Architecture as such takes, I think, no notice at all.'[7] But in other matters, he and Ruskin shared the same pleasures: the prints of Dürer and Burgkmair, the naive, brilliantly-coloured art of illuminated manuscripts, the work of Giotto, Fra Angelico, Benozzo Gozzoli. Currently, Ruskin was a moving figure in the Arundel Club's scheme to copy and illustrate surviving fresco cycles, in Padua, Pisa and Florence. In turn, Rossetti impressed on Ruskin his own passions for Dante and other early writers. At the start of 1855, he raised the idea of issuing his translations through Ruskin's publisher, who might be persuaded to 'shell out something for them in a lump'. As ever, a cash advance would be a stimulus to completion. The projected title was 'Italian Lyrical Poetry of the First Epoch from Ciullo d'Alcamo to Dante Alighieri (1197–1300) translated in the original metres, including Dante's *Vita Nuova* or autobiography of his youth'.[8]

Above all, they shared the impulse to recreate the medieval habit of seeing and showing the symbolic within figurative representation. Rossetti welcomed a promoter and friend who understood what his 'quaint' endeavours were about, Ruskin in turn welcomed Rossetti's freedom from conventional ideas of picture-making. He gave Gabriel a list of preferred subjects, but warned that his father's strict business habits would not allow him to make payment in advance.

In February, Rossetti heard that MacCracken had to sell all his paintings. Though he affected nonchalance, calling MacCracken a fool, it made Ruskin's patronage all the more valuable, especially since there were many purchasers who, like MacCrac, sought guidance from the great critic. But he also had another plan, to which end, early in March, he showed Lizzie's drawings to Ruskin, with a careful, pathetic account of her history. Her father was a watchmaker, he said, and though not unkind her family was opposed to art, to which she was devoted; moreover, doctors said her health might fail at any time.

Philanthropically, to assist Miss Siddal, Ruskin offered to buy the drawings. What would be the right figure? Twenty-five pounds? suggested Rossetti, hoping this was neither too high nor too low. Thirty? replied Ruskin, and the deal was struck. It was a good year's wages to one in Lizzie's position. Gabriel was jubilant.

On 11 April they were invited to tea with the Ruskins. The house was large, with a lodge and coachhouse; a footman answered the door. There was a room full of Turners. But the tradesman's daughter was graciously welcomed. 'All were most delighted with Guggum,' Gabriel told Brown triumphantly. 'John Ruskin said she was a noble glorious creature, and his father said that by her look and manner she might have been born a countess.'⁹ Showing concern for Lizzie's health, Mrs Ruskin made her a gift of powdered ivory, to be made into a restorative jelly.

It was in the nature of an inspection, but the plan succeeded; the next day Ruskin came to Blackfriars with a generous proposal – either to buy everything Lizzie produced, or to give her £150 a year in exchange for whatever work she was able to produce. 'I think myself the second plan the best, considering that there may be goodish intervals when she cannot work and might run short of money,' wrote Gabriel, persuasively. Preferring independence, Lizzie was not so sure. But Gabriel insisted. 'She will be sternly coerced if necessary,' he told Brown. 'Meanwhile I love him and her and everybody and feel happier than I have felt for a long while.' Could Emma and Brown take tea on Saturday at Albany Street, where Lizzie was at last to be introduced? And would Brown go with her to Robersons, since he dared not show his own face there. 'D.G.R in glee' was Brown's terse comment.¹⁰

Thus Saturday 14 April saw what Brown called 'Miss S's first intervue' with Gabriel's mother. Lizzie was ladylike, but the Rossetti women did not warm to her, nor she to them. There was no mention of any engagement.

Ruskin wrote prettily to free Miss Siddal from any sense of obligation. He urged her to go to the country or to the Mediterranean, for her health. When she still demurred, he wrote again. Was she too proud to take money for which he had no use? Did she think he was helping her only for Rossetti's sake? Not at all, but only as he would try to save a beautiful tree, or a decaying Gothic cathedral. Thus, if she would consider herself a bit of wood or Gothic for a few months, he would be obliged. Duly coerced, Lizzie accepted the allowance.

At the same time, Ruskin asked Rossetti if he had 'any plans or wishes respecting Miss S' – marriage for example? – which income would facilitate. Rossetti's reply has not survived, but was evidently a dignified refusal. He would not wish to be Ruskin's pensioner.

Why does he not marry her? Brown wondered, on hearing the good news. But Lizzie could only receive an allowance if single. Conventional wisdom held that it was a woman's duty to obey her husband, a man's to support his wife; in Ruskin's own words, no woman should do more, no man should do less. If married, Rossetti could not permit his wife to accept another man's money. Meanwhile he too had an arrangement – Ruskin's offer to purchase whatever he produced, up to a certain value. Works commissioned included Rachel and Leah from the *Purgatorio*, and the Holy Family *Preparing for the Passover*, one of the projected scenes from the Life of the Virgin. 'Amongst all the painters I know, you on the whole have the greatest genius and you appear to me also to be – as far as I can make out – a very good sort of person,' Ruskin wrote. 'I see that you are unhappy, and that you can't bring out your genius as you should. It seems to me then the proper and *necessary* thing, if I can, to make you more happy, and that I should be more really useful in enabling you to paint properly and keep your room in order than in any other way.'[11]

He liked helping people, as a duty imposed on wealth, but insisted this was not philanthropy. 'I really do *covet* your drawings as much as I covet Turner's; only it is useless self-indulgence to buy Turner's, and useful self-indulgence to buy yours.' However, he added, he would not buy those which were 'more than nine times rubbed entirely out'. Some of those at Chatham Place were now very well worked.

Ruskin's motives were mixed. Rossetti must not imagine that this, or his involvement in the Working Men's College, was done in any way to regain his reputation. He would never fawn for public favour. But somewhere along the line, he admitted, he had lost or misplaced his affections; it was now his misfortune to have 'no friendships and no loves'. He hoped Rossetti would be a friend. And for some months the friendship flourished, on a frank, masculine basis. 'Mr Ruskin took keen delight in Rossetti's paintings and designs,' wrote William later. 'He praised freely and abused heartily, both him and them.'[12] Taken and given good-humouredly, the abuse sometimes nettled. Someone at the College asked if Mr Rossetti were industrious. Yes, Ruskin replied, if you call beginning work at nine in the evening and working till daybreak industrious. But what business was this of his? Moreover, Ruskin was given to asking 'troublesomeish favours'. Once, he summoned Gabriel urgently to determine the exact pigments used by Turner. Next, having invited Charles Kingsley, author of *The Water-Babies* and *Alton Locke*, he demanded that Rossetti send the preparatory study for *Found*. 'Please don't be ridiculous and say you've nothing fit to be seen,' he wrote.

Gabriel's reciprocal requests often met with refusal. Could Ruskin get Charles Wells's *Joseph* republished? No. 'Dear Rossetti, I think you are mistaken respecting that play', came the reply. Would Ruskin support the verse translation of Dante by Charles Cayley, former student of Professor Rossetti? By no means; '[n]o poem *can* be translated in rhyme.' Moreover, Gabriel's taste was 'as yet unformed in verse'.

At least they agreed over the RA, where Millais's *Rescue* was outshone by a picture of Cimabue carrying his work in a procession, 'by a new man, living abroad, named Leighton', as Rossetti informed Allingham, – a huge thing which the Queen has bought and which everyone talks of'. In Ruskin's view this compared with the best work of the Venetians. The main feature was 'nobly principal' while the figures of the master Cimabue and the boy Giotto 'attract full regard by distinction of form and face'.

Dante was also depicted. By rights, this was Rossetti's subject, for which he had shown a sketch in the 1852 winter exhibition in hope of a commission. Yet he could allege no plagiarism, because Leighton lived and worked abroad. And though at first he resisted, soon he came round to Ruskin's view of the painting. '[O]n looking more at it I think there is a great richness of arrangement,' he told Allingham, echoing also Ruskin's comparison with Paul Veronese and eventually concurring that at twenty-five Mr Leighton had the potential for greatness.[13] It was a sobering thought for Gabriel was writing on the eve of his own twenty-seventh birthday.

At MacCracken's sale, however, his *Annunciation* had fetched 76 guineas, while *Dante drawing an Angel* went for 50 guineas – to Mr and Mrs Combe of Oxford. And Ruskin's wider influence was bearing fruit. Miss Heaton, from Leeds, commissioned two scenes from Dante, for 20 guineas each. And Lady Waterford, whose talent he already respected, requested lessons. Flattered but unable to contemplate a marchioness in his chaotic studio, Gabriel declined.

Anna Howitt ran into Mr Rossetti and Miss Siddal at the Academy. She thought Lizzie looked marvellously well. But Ruskin insisted Lizzie be examined by Dr Acland in Oxford. 'Pray accept her and my thanks', wrote Gabriel to Acland. It was a useful contact, and when they went to Oxford he also met Benjamin Woodward, architect of the new museum there, who had truly Gothic ideas, and planned to commission carvings and frescoes.

Encouragingly, Dr Acland said that Lizzie's lungs were apparently sound, and diagnosed the main cause of her illness as 'mental power long pent up and lately overtaxed'. This accorded with current notions that female ailments were a direct result of serious study, a powerful argument in the debate over girls' education. It should be recorded that Rossetti did not agree with such arguments, but he could not challenge medical opinion. Prescribing extreme care, Acland advised Lizzie to go south for the winter, and abstain from all work. It is possible that he heeded Ruskin's opinion that young Mr Rossetti would work more assiduously if apart.

Ruskin himself was away from London, wrestling with the latest volume of *Modern Painters*. He resisted Gabriel's requests for cash advances; a drawing had only to be delivered and it would be bought. Where was the *Passover* picture? In his view, Gabriel was Grief, growling with discontent, and Ruskin was Patience on the monument, waiting for watercolours. Meanwhile, he bought the small golden *Lute Player*, wherewith to recompense Acland.[14]

The same month, Millais married Effie, at her home in Perthshire. The news was not secret but perhaps the least said the better, William told Allingham. This appeared to be the unconscious wish of one newspaper, which printed the announcement in the Deaths column. Soon, Millais wrote that he was blissfully happy, and planned to settle in Scotland for a year or so. No doubt Rossetti was relieved, for his new intimacy threatened the older friendship. It was hardly possible to be in close contact with both Effie's husbands.

Soon Ruskin's patronage impinged also on Gabriel's friendship with Brown. This summer there were several sociable gatherings at Chatham Place, where on one occasion guests sat on the balcony eating strawberries and ice, and on another, Scott, Hannay, Hughes, Munro and Martineau were joined by Brown, who stayed the night, finally getting to sleep at five. The next day, when Ruskin called unannounced, Brown was casually smoking a pipe, still in shirtsleeves. Immaculate in morning coat and clean stock, Ruskin talked 'divers nonsense about art, hurriedly in shrill tones' (privately, Brown made many jokes about his 'stonelessness') and then asked abruptly why Brown had chosen such an ugly subject for his last landscape. 'Because it lay out of a back window,' growled Brown, doubly dumbfounded because Gabriel had said that Ruskin liked the work. They all knew that if Ruskin were to praise it in print, Brown's prices would rise, and this year Brown was very much in debt. Henceforth, the antipathy remained fixed. In notes to Brown, Gabriel took to calling Ruskin the Great Prohibited, or GP, or 'the Initials', and offered sophistical consolation. 'Rossetti says Ruskin is a sneak and loves him, Rossetti, because he is one too ... but hates Woolner because he is manly and strait forward, and me too because I am ditto,' wrote Brown. 'He adored Millais because Millais was the prince of sneaks but Millais was too much so for he sneaked away his wife and so he is obliged to hate him for too much of his favourite quality.'[15]

The weather was very warm. From Oxford Lizzie went to Clevedon on the Somerset coast. When Gabriel joined her they visited the grave of *In Memoriam*'s Arthur Hallam, bringing home yellow flags, to plant in pots at Blackfriars. Then they went to stay with the Browns, where there was more dissension, owing to Gabriel's imperious conduct and his claims that Emma 'incited' Lizzie against him. A month later there was another characteristic event when he summoned the Browns to join him and Lizzie at Drury Lane. But '[w]hen we got there he had forgotten that after a certain hour we could not get in, so Emma & I paid 5/- & he & Guggum went home', Brown recorded. With baby Oliver, the Browns slept over at Chatham Place, amidst all manner of discomfort, compounded in the morning with another call by Ruskin. This time the Browns stayed out of sight. To cap everything, 'Gabriel being scant of tin we had to pay for all we had'.[16]

Rossetti could be a trying friend. And a difficult lover. His abuse of Emma for inciting Lizzie against him is the first recorded hint of trouble with his 'dear dove'. Given his reckless, feckless behaviour, it is hardly surprising if she was sometimes as annoyed as Brown. But perhaps there was more; for surely it was time to talk of marriage. It was a year since they had stayed together at Hastings and doubtless her family wondered when the wedding might be. Instead, it was arranged she should go south for the winter with a cousin of Mrs Rossetti's, travelling to Paris en route for Nice and possibly Italy. To assure the Siddalls that all was proper, Gabriel went to Guggum's 'native crib' in Kent Place for the first time, finding the house more comfortable than he had been led to believe. Having already spent most of her current allowance, he had to borrow yet more from Brown.

Robert and Elizabeth Browning, on a short visit to Britain, invited Mr Rossetti to dine. He took the opportunity to ask if he might bring William, writing persuasively that his brother had long looked forward to meeting them 'and would feel as much pleasure as I do in it, which I assure you is saying not a little'. They were not disappointed. Browning was a 'most glorious fellow', reported William; 'kind, vivid, witty, interested in everything worth being interested in and knowing something about everything worth knowing.' He and Gabriel got on famously, especially when Browning quoted from memory a couplet from *The Blessed Damozel* – written, as the author said, when his hosts had been his favourite poets.[17]

Mrs Browning was 'the very embodiment of fragile sensitiveness' to William and 'delightfully unliterary' to Gabriel, although her otherwise sensible conversation included the claim that she 'adored' Correggio. Both husband and wife were slight in stature. 'How large a part of the real world, I wonder, are those two small people?' mused Gabriel later; 'taking meanwhile so little room in a railway carriage, and hardly needing a double bed at the inn.' He asked if he might paint both poets, for next year's Academy. They agreed, though in the event Mrs Browning deferred her proposed sitting and Rossetti made only a watercolour portrait of Robert. At the studio, Browning was eager to see Gabriel's other works, including the oil sketch for *Kate the Queen*, and Lizzie's drawing of *Pippa Passes*. Gabriel carried his elation to the Working Men's College, late one evening. What was Robert Browning like as a poet? asked the students. 'Like? why, in his lyrics he's like Shelley, in his dramas like Shakespeare!' replied Rossetti.[18]

A second evening he and William were fellow guests with Tennyson – a privilege accorded to few – who graced the company with a reading of the newly-published *Maud*. Gabriel made a surreptitious sketch as the Laureate read, book in one hand, ankle in the other:

> I hate the dreadful hollow behind the little wood,
> Its lips in the field above are dabbled with a blood-red heath,
> The red-ribb'd ledges drip with a silent horror of blood,
> And Echo there, whatever is ask'd her, answers 'Death.'

The poet's voice was sonorously emotional, delivering the fiery passages with vehemence and weeping at moments of pathos.

'Truly a night of the gods,' wrote William later, for Browning followed on, with a spirited rendering of *Fra Lippo Lippi*, perhaps chosen in honour of the young PRBs, spiritual heirs to the Florentine painter. It was from *Men and Women*, his forthcoming collection of dramatic monologues that teased out the contradictory impulses of the contemporary condition: ambition, idealism, desire, shame, irreverence, belief. *One Word More*, another new piece, dedicated to 'E.B.B', demonstrated how in tune both poets were with Gabriel's own interests. What would one not give for Raphael lost sonnets or Dante's drawing of an angel? (which, whispered Browning to his wife, 'you and I would rather see – would we not? than read a fresh Inferno'). And a dense but profound evocation of the creative impulse linked it to love:

> no artist lives and loves, that longs not
> Once, and only once, and for One only,
> (Ah! the prize!) to find his love a language
> Fit and fair and simple and sufficient –
> Using nature that's an art to others,
> Not, this one time, art that's turned his nature.
> Ay, of all the artists living, loving,
> None but would forego his proper dowry, –
> Does he paint? he fain would write a poem, –
> Does he write? he fain would paint a picture,
> Put to proof art alien to the artist's,
> Once, and only once, and for One only,
> So to be the man and leave the artist,
> Gain the man's joy, miss the artist's sorrow.

There were not many people with whom Gabriel felt such affinity. Browning's poetry was his 'elixir of life'. By comparison Tennyson was a self-pitying sentimentalist, however fine his verse. He groaned over *Maud*'s reviews, repeating the same stories, all 'to the intense wonder of Browning, who as you know treats reviewers the way they deserve'. After a vivid verbal sketch of Tennyson's complaints against 'the literary cabals under which he is destined to sink one day', Gabriel described for Allingham how as he walked home with the Laureate they passed the Holborn Casino, a popular night-spot. ' "What's that place?" asks A. T. and on my telling him – "Ah!" he says, "I'd rather like to go there, but la!" (a minute afterwards) "there'd be some newspaper man, and he'd know me." ' [19] It was an object lesson in the delusions of fame.

The Brownings left for Paris on 18 October. Ruskin asked Rossetti to 'take a run into Wales' and make a colour sketch of rocks in a mountain stream, with rowan trees all scarlet in the autumn. 'If you are later than Wednesday, you will be too late; but if you can go on Wednesday, let me know by return.' He would send the money. Gabriel protested. He couldn't sit out in the open, painting from nature. Oh no, replied Ruskin – just look, make notes, 'work at home in the inn and *walk* among the hills.' Gabriel preferred Paris. He could take Lizzie the next instalment of her allowance. 'You are a *very* odd creature,' Ruskin replied. 'I said I would find funds for you to go into Wales to draw something I wanted. I never said I would pay for you to go to Paris, to disturb yourself and other people, and I won't.' Positively, Rossetti must not go until he had finished the drawings he and Miss Heaton had commissioned.

Naturally, Gabriel went, getting the money by producing, in less than a week, a Blakean picture showing the illicit lovers Paolo and Francesca from the *Inferno*. He travelled with Alex Munro, in order to catch the final days of the Exposition Universelle, France's answer to the 1851 Exhibition. Over five thousand British pictures were on show, including Millais's *Ophelia* and *Order of Release*, Hunt's *Light of the World*, Brown's *Chaucer at the Court of Edward III*. Sculptures included Munro's *Paolo and Francesca*, to which Gabriel's latest work paid homage. National pride was more or less upheld. 'Our show at the Exposition ... does us credit I think on the whole,' he told Miss Heaton, mentioning Millais, Hunt, C. R. Leslie, William Henry Hunt and J. F. Lewis. The big names among the French were still Ingres and Delacroix, the latter among 'the mighty ones of the earth', filling the central hall with 'religion, history, poetry, romance, drama, legend, still-life, wild sports, national manners and public events of the day'. Indeed, William noted, Gabriel seemed to have looked at little else. The German Ludwig Knaus caught his attention as a genre painter 'somewhere between Hogarth and Wilkie'; for the rest, nothing. [20]

The judgements suggest that Gabriel shared his brother's view of Courbet, exhibiting in a gallery close to the Palais des Beaux-Arts, as a 'jolly, careless, pipe-smoking French painter' of enormous vigour but no vision, and coarse technique, as of a scrubbing-brush. 'He sees as far into a mill-stone as another man – and no further; and is honest enough to paint, with a rough and ready freedom, exactly what he sees,' wrote William in his notice of the Exposition. 'But it never seems to occur to him that real sincerity in art must be exercised first of all in the invention of the subject; that his function is to translate the sentiment of things as well as to exhibit their conformation; or that love and reverence, far from the "hail-fellow-well-met" spirit, is the true artist's relation to Nature. The vitality of the English Praeraphaelites consists in their having remembered these fundamental truths ...'[21]

This was the first opportunity for the French to see Pre-Raphaelite work. Delacroix remarked on the originality of observation and feeling in *The Order of Release* and on the minute realism of Hunt's sheep in *Our English Coasts*. Critics however focused on the 'eccentricity' beyond originality of both artists, finding the display aggressively national. 'Their subjects are entirely English, their characters are all English ... it is all local and peculiar to the insular soil and genius of Great Britain,' wrote Ernest Chesneau. The precision both impressed and offended. 'Have you seen the English artist's hay?' visitors were quoted as asking, apropos of *The Return of the Dove*. 'Mr Millais cannot make up his mind to sacrifice a single detail, be it ever so devoid of interest.'[22]

'We enjoyed Paris immensely, in different ways of course,' Munro told Scott. 'Rossetti was every day with his sweetheart, of whom he is more foolishly fond than I ever saw lover. Great affection is ever so to the mere looker-on, I suppose.'[23] Gabriel was hardly so demonstrative in London; evidently he enjoyed showing Lizzie the sights, and perhaps she needed reassurance before their impending separation. He only half succeeded in introducing her to the Brownings, for Elizabeth was not strong enough to receive calls, but one day Gabriel invited Robert to call. And after seeing Lizzie and Mrs Kincaid off to Nice, Rossetti lingered in Paris, delighting in Browning's company and knowledge of European art. Together they toured the museums, and talked. Both were dismayed at the obtuse reviews of *Men and Women*, which critics found obscure, riddling, 'unpoetic'.

These two friendships, with Ruskin and Browning, provided valuable intellectual stimulation. In addition, the latter strengthened Rossetti's determination to stick to his individual vision rather than seek popularity, while the former's good-humoured 'abuse' sharpened his defiant singularity. Back in London by 24 November, he was generally pleased. *Found* remained untouched, alas, but not through sloth, for he had done 'more during the past year than for a long while previously'. The sum total was half a dozen finished watercolours and a replica of *Beatrice denying her Salutation*; the little portrait of Browning and one in sepia of uncle Henry;

and two detailed designs for future paintings. He had secured patronage for Lizzie, and regular earnings for himself. It was not bad for a season's work.

Intended for Miss Heaton, Ruskin took for himself the replica *Beatrice denying her Salutation*. Other works included *Matilda gathering flowers* and *Rachel and Leah*, both from Dante, and a couple in medieval dress who may be Hamlet and Ophelia. There followed the *Paolo and Francesca*, which as Ruskin recognised had an unfortunate bearing on his own marital history that would prevent his showing it to anyone, and a second equally tactless scene, of Lancelot and Guinevere embracing over Arthur's Tomb. Rossetti must have known both subjects were unsuitable, or perhaps chose them unconsciously, as an act of independence: Ruskin's patronage made him both grateful and resentful, for though stimulating, the relationship was not truly harmonious.

Rossetti followed his own direction, working intensively but slowly. Ruskin favoured observation, and a light, swift brush. 'If you make a careless couple of sketches with bright and full colour in them, you are sure to do what will please me,' he wrote. 'I tell you the plain truth – and I always said the same to Turner – "If you will do me a drawing in three days I will be obliged to you; but if you take three months to it, you may put it behind the fire when it is done." ' Well-meant, the advice was ill-judged. When Rossetti worked quickly, the results could be poor. The vexed, never-finished *Passover* was a case in point. Three times the head of Christ was scratched out and repainted, then it was cut out, patched and yet again redrawn. A *Nativity*, 'done in a week, price fifteen guineas', was also ill-received. A human arm was not as the Academicians drew it, but nor was it as Rossetti showed, wrote Ruskin sternly. 'Flesh is not buff colour – as Mr Herbert draws it – but neither is it pea-green, as you draw it.' The angels' noses were wrong, the Virgin's blue dress was ridiculously bright in full shadow, and (of the kneeling shepherd) one thing Ruskin especially disliked was the sight of 'dirty old men with the soles of their feet turned up'. Though the rest was lovely, the figures in *Rachel and Leah* were like dolls, sitting 'stiffly, in a Pre-Raphaelite way', while the replica *Beatrice denying her Salutation* was seriously flawed in execution; one of the heads was like a skull.[24]

Worst of all was *Arthur's Tomb*. Though Ruskin paid 20 guineas, he claimed he was going to make Rossetti do it again, 'without mistakes'. Browning liked it, however, which suggests he understood better what Rossetti was about in these watercolours of 1855. The figures are out of scale and squashed into a low horizontal space, echoing the shape of the tomb in a frankly medieval manner: the inspiration surely comes from the Gothic carvings, illuminated missals and early German woodcuts Ruskin was currently studying, praising, lending. With this encouragement, Rossetti was entering deeply into the medieval spirit, as he perceived it.

Reciprocally, and thanks in part to Rossetti's assistance, Ruskin was developing his ideas 'on many things' for *Modern Painters III*, published early in 1856.[25] One was to demote the 'false idealism' of the High Renaissance in favour of expressive 'grotesque idealism', through which the most important truths had been conveyed in all ages. 'No element of imagination has a wider range, a more magnificent use, or so colossal a grasp of sacred truth,' he wrote, adding that 'so far from the pursuit of the false ideal having in any wise exhausted the realms of fantastic imagination, those realms have hardly yet been entered, and that a universe of noble dream-land lies before us, yet to be conquered ...' It would be 'an infinite good to mankind' for this to be accepted, for through such expression 'an enormous mass of intellectual power is turned to everlasting use, which, in this present century of ours, evaporates in street gibing or vain revelling; all the good wit and satire expiring in daily talk (like foam on wine) which in the thirteenth and fourteenth centuries had a permitted and useful expression in the arts of sculpture and illumination.' Citing Dürer's *Knight and Death* and Blake's *Job* as powerful examples, he argued further that it was 'not only permissible, but even desirable, that the art by which the grotesque is expressed should be more or less imperfect ...' Indeed, 'no great man ever stops working till he has reached his point of failure: that is to say, his mind is always far in advance of his powers of execution ...'

Ironically, the imperfect watercolours he received from Rossetti were too grotesque, too primitive. Later, Ruskin shuddered at the extreme medievalism his praise of Gothic had stimulated, since what he really hoped for were pictures with sensitive drawing, elevated themes and fine colour that would justify his promotion of Pre-Raphaelitism as a 'new and noble school'. Nor did he mean to be a major purchaser, his patronage being aimed largely at extending influence with the public; when he asked for green to be taken out of the flesh tones of the *Nativity*, for example, it was to show an archdeacon with whom he wished to have 'some practical talk over religious art for the multitude'; for in his crusade against the age, Ruskin saw Rossetti as his standard-bearer, not as its *raison d'être*.

The mutual influence, however, also produced some signal successes. Close study of medieval illumination and contemporary texts such as the description of a meadow at the start of the *Purgatorio* led towards detailed observations in *Modern Painters III*. 'With the usual medieval accuracy,' Ruskin explained, Dante gives the precise colours in terms of paint: 'Gold and fine silver, and cochineal, and white lead, and Indian wood, serene and lucid, and fresh emerald, just broken ...' Clearly, the 'emerald' here meant the emerald green of the illuminators – 'the colours of the variegation are defined and illustrated by the reference to actual pigments' – while because the other colours were so bright, the ground was sober; 'and presently two angels enter, who are dressed in green drapery, paler than the grass, like newly-budding leaves.'

Shortly after this passage appeared, Rossetti began a new watercolour, for Miss Heaton, showing *Dante's Dream at the Time of the Death of Beatrice*. His long-favoured subject from the *Vita Nuova*, it showed the poet's vision of Beatrice on her bier: 'These idle fantasies then carried me to see my lady dead / and when I entered / With a white veil her friends were covering her / And in her mild look was a quietness / which seemed as if it said I have found peace.' In what Rossetti later called 'a chamber of dreams', clear green tones bind the composition together. Like angels, Beatrice's attendants are dressed in robes of emerald, setting off Dante in black, Love in red and Beatrice in white. To either side are stairways, one upward, one downward opening into daylight.

For the attendants, Rossetti employed a dark-haired model named Miss Lazenby, known to Stephens, and Annie Miller, Hunt's protégée, whom he had first drawn in the spring of 1854, soon after Holman's departure, and who had blossomed into a personable young lady. In Lizzie's absence, he asked if Margaret Hannay might pose for Beatrice. She came with her husband to Chatham Place. 'I am delighted to know that Gabriel is becoming more and more recognized,' wrote Hannay, 'and will be as prosperous as he is gifted and good, which is all his friends need hope for him.'[26]

'You insinuate a sarcasm against Gabriel's indolence,' wrote William to Scott a few weeks later. 'It is undeserved. For the past two years Gabriel had been working with exemplary perseverance, and Ruskin must possess nearly a score of his works by now.' Yet there was still no big piece. Early in 1856, Christina sent a story to the American *Crayon* magazine to which William, Fred Stephens and Anna Howitt also contributed. Loosely, *The Lost Titian* seemed to compare the great Venetian and two fictional companions to the three leaders of the PRB, in a glittering tale of worldly success and jealous envy. More particularly, the character of Giannuccione was lightly disguised as one 'who had promised everything and fufilled nothing'. His first picture was greeted with rapture, threatening to eclipse the others; 'but, when, year after year, his works appeared still lazily imperfect, though always all but perfect, Venice subsided into apathetic silence'. Millais's reputation progressed annually; where was DGR's masterpiece and the acclaim that had seemed his due?

Especially on dim winter days, when fog muffled all river traffic except the sound of barges grinding against the wall beneath his window, Rossetti's moodiness returned. 'Today here is neither a bright day nor a dark day, but a white smutty day – piebald,' he told Allingham; '– wherein, accordingly, life seems neither worth keeping nor getting rid of'.[27] He missed Lizzie. As daylight waned, the colours on the easel altered. Humming tunelessly, he 'daubed' till dusk and sat awhile over the fire before dashing out to eat at a chop-house. Then he would walk or, if anyone called, stay up late talking, as though reluctant to sleep. In Valentine verses which seem never to have been sent, he sketched a sorrowful self-portrait:

> Yesterday was St Valentine.
> Thought you at all, dear dove divine,
> Upon the beard in sorry trim
> And rueful countenance of him
> That Orson who's your Valentine?
>
> He daubed, you know, as usual.
> The stick would slip, the brush would fall:
> Yet daubed he till the lamplighter
> Set those two seedy flames astir;
> But growled all day at slow St Paul.
>
> The bore was heard ere noon; the dun
> Was at the door by half past one:
> At least, 'tis thought so, but the clock –
> No Lizzy there to help its stroke –
> Struck work before the day begun.
>
> . . .
>
> Come back, dear Liz, and, looking wise,
> In that arm-chair which suits your size,
> Through some fresh drawing scrape a hole.
> Your Valentine and Orson's soul
> Is sad for those two friendly eyes.

Coming home one evening after a late, aimless walk, the more despondent because he had accomplished nothing all day, he picked up a book of botanical woodcuts. It opened at a picture of the woodspurge, a plant he had never knowingly seen. He sat abstractedly. Then, annoyed at having 'wasted' a day, he drafted a poem. 'The wind flapped loose, the wind was still . . .' He imagined, or remembered resting by the roadside, maybe in Warwickshire, listening to time pass and staring at 'some ten weeds' between his knees:

Among those few, out of the sun
The woodspurge flowered, three cups in one.

From perfect grief there need not be
Wisdom or even memory:
One thing then learnt remains to me, –
The woodspurge has a cup of three.

Gerard's *Herball*, which is listed among Rossetti's books, warns graphically against the blistering properties of spurges, concluding with an 'old worne proverb' of the quaint kind he liked: 'Dear is the honie that is lickt out of thornes.' It was an apt theme for his day, and for his art. But the little poem seems to have been inspired not by Gerard, but by Ruskin, responding to a number of the idiosyncratic observations in *Modern Painters III*. Thus, on the question of Finish: 'If you will lie down on your breast on the next bank you come to, you will see, in the cluster of leaves and grass close to your face ... a mystery of soft shadow in the depths of the grass, with indefinite forms of leaves, which you cannot trace nor count, within it, and out of that, the nearer leaves coming in every subtle gradation of tender light and flickering form, quite beyond all delicacy of pencilling to follow.' And then, on the Pathetic Fallacy, the true poet – and painter – was 'the man who perceives rightly in spite of his feelings, and to whom the primrose is for ever nothing else than itself – a little flower apprehended in the very plain and leafy fact of it, whatever and how many so ever the associations and passions may be that crowd around it.'

'The primrose is for ever nothing else than itself.' 'One thing then learnt remains to me – The woodspurge has a cup of three.' Art, as Rossetti would observe some while later, 'must be its own comforter, or else comfortless'.[28]

He was halfway through *Modern Painters III*, Gabriel told Browning in January. In many places it was glorious – especially the attack on Raphael's 'False Ideal'. He half planned to join Lizzie, passing through Paris again. 'Somehow tonight everything on my table seems oily and unsavoury,' he lamented, amid a mess of painting equipment. In the words of *Fra Lippo Lippi*, he wished they were 'hip to haunch' together.[29]

To please Ruskin, who owned a number of illuminated manuscripts, he designed a new watercolour showing a medieval monk at work on a missal. Indirectly it drew also on Browning's poem, for had not Lippi begun his career in the Carmelite order? In *Men and Women*, Rossetti's other favourites were *Bishop Blougram's Apology*, *Karshish*, *How it strikes a Contemporary*, *Cleon* and especially '*Childe Roland*', which spoke eloquently of the artist's dreams and frustrations:

> Thus, I had so long suffered in this quest
> Heard failure prophesied so oft, been writ
>   So many times among 'The Band' – to it
> The knights who to the Dark Tower's search addressed
> Their steps – that just to fail as they, seemed best ...

His own new picture contained a dark tower. A knight and lady are praying together before he rides out to single combat with a black-armoured warrior by a black tower, as in medieval romance. It brought together the key themes of olden time, he told Brown: Religion, Art, Chivalry, Love. At last, Brown noted, Gabriel had found his sphere, 'as a lyrical painter and poet, and certainly a glorious one'.[30] They dined together on lobster.

Single combat with a black knight was the subject of a poem called *Winter Weather*, in a new magazine sent to Ruskin:

> Black grew his tower
> As we rode down lower
>   Black from the barren hill;
> And our horses strode
> Up the winding road
>   To the gateway dim and still ...

Devoted to art, literature and high-minded social criticism, the *Oxford and Cambridge Magazine* was produced by some young University men. It contained a tribute to Rossetti's *Maids of Elfen-Mere*, which, according to the anonymous contributor, was 'the most beautiful drawing for an illustration I have ever seen,' such as only a great artist could conceive. Why is the author of *The Blessed Damozel* and the story of Chiaro so seldom on the lips of men? if only we could hear him oftener, live in the light of his power a little longer ...'

This was just about the most gratifying thing that had ever happened, Rossetti told Allingham.

CHAPTER NINE

Morris and Burne-Jones

The author of the gratifying remarks was a young man named Edward Jones. 'I had no dream of ever knowing Rossetti, but I wanted to look at him,' he recalled later. Learning that his hero taught at the Working Men's College, he travelled from Oxford in January 1856 to attend an open meeting. Tea was provided at long tables, college-fashion. The visitor spoke to his neighbours, F. J. Furnivall and Vernon Lushington, and confessed his purpose. Rossetti was unlikely to appear, they said, having little taste for meetings. 'So I waited a good hour or more, listening to speeches about the progress of the College, and Maurice, who was president, spoke of Macaulay's new volume, just out,' recalled Ned; 'and then Lushington whispered to me that Rossetti had come in, so I saw him for the first time . . .'[1]

A night or two later Jones was introduced, at Lushington's chambers. Someone speaking disrespectfully of *Men and Women* was at once 'rent in pieces' by Rossetti. Later, Lushington asked laughingly if he would have all men be painters? Indeed yes, came the commanding reply – the only valuable occupation. The shy visitor admired his hero even more.

Invited next day to Blackfriars, he found Rossetti working on *Fra Pace*, the monk illuminating. They talked of the magazine and the author of *Winter Weather*, Jones's close friend William Morris, who was about to sign articles with Gothic Revival architect G. E. Street in Oxford. It took Gabriel back: the young men shared the same idealism as the PRB, whose own magazine was confessedly their inspiration. They were, he wrote 'the nicest young fellows – in *Dreamland*', since their miraculous magazine seemed to hail from such a place; it might easily be bound in the same volume as *The Germ*. Indeed, its founders described themselves as 'banded together in an exclusive Brotherhood of seven', as if in conscious emulation.[2] Generously he showed his drawings to Jones, an aspiring artist who had never been in a studio. 'They tossed about everywhere in the room; the floor at one end was covered with them, and his books . . . No one seemed to be in attendance on him. I stayed long and watched him at work, not knowing till many a day afterwards that this was a thing he greatly hated,' he recalled.

Expected daily, Holman Hunt returned at the end of January, 'looking older and altered, with a leonine beard', according to Christina. 'He came like a thunderclap on one of our family parties, luckily in time for chestnuts, cake, and a social glass of grog.' One day he called when Jones and Morris were at Chatham Place. '[S]uch a grand-looking fellow,' wrote Jones to his father; 'oh, such a man. And Rossetti sat by him and played with his golden beard passing his paint-brush through the hair of it.'³

Hunt had been away two years and like Woolner was altered in more than appearance by travel and privations. He recounted his painting exploits in the desert around the Dead Sea, gun propped against the easel. His English nationalism was more pronounced, his ambition tougher, while at the same time more singular. When Rossetti and Brown saw his pictures, they were impressed, if surprised, especially by *The Scapegoat*, into which Hunt seemed to have poured much personal intensity. It must be seen to be believed, wrote Brown, and only then 'can it be understood how by the might of genius out of an old goat and some saline incrustations can be made one of the most tragic and impressive works in the annals of art.' A grand thing, 'but not for the public', was Gabriel's verdict.⁴

Sharing with Halliday and Martineau, Hunt took rooms in Pimlico, a steamer-ride from Blackfriars. He proposed a group show, a *salon des indépendants*. Brown was interested, Rossetti was not, advising Hunt to send his pictures to the RA. When Hunt saw Gabriel's new things at Ruskin's on 21 February, he was full of reciprocal admiration, but perhaps understood the diffidence: all were small, intensely-worked watercolours, not exhibition pieces as currently understood. He appeared to have given up oil painting.

But the old association was not yet extinguished, for the three leading PRBs were now linked through their contributions to the illustrated edition of Tennyson's poems. Having extended the invitation via Millais, publisher Edward Moxon had finally found Rossetti at home a year past, explaining that as well the three leading PRBs, the illustrators engaged included older artists – Maclise, Mulready, Clarkson Stanfield, J. C. Horsley. Gabriel was contemptuous. 'The right names would have been Millais, Hunt, Madox Brown, Hughes, a certain lady and myself. NO OTHERS,' he told Allingham. And fresh from his struggles with *Elfen-Mere*, he had firm views on illustration, preferring non-narrative texts 'where one can allegorise on one's own hook on the subject of the poem, without killing, for oneself and everyone, a distinct idea of the poet's'. Seeing Hunt's name pencilled beside *The Lady of Shalott*, his own favourite, he had written to ask if they could both tackle it, in different episodes,⁵ and lobbied to have Lizzie included in the project, urging her merits on the Tennysons, via Woolner, who replied encouragingly but over-optimistically that the Laureate's wife was sympathetic. Over the months, Lizzie nevertheless worked hard at several designs, while Gabriel postponed his, the deadline being comfortably distant.

In March 1856, to illustrate a lecture on Dante, Ruskin lent *Paolo and Francesca* to a literary soirée at the London Institution, together with *Rachel and Leah*, now Miss Heaton's property. But he declined to purchase *Fra Pace*. 'Very ingenious and wonderful, but not my sort of drawing,' he wrote. If Gabriel wished to please him, he added, he would keep his room in order and go to bed at night.[6] Needing the tin, Rossetti set to work on *Dante's Dream on the Death of Beatrice*, asking Annie Miller to model for one of the attendant women. Could Miss Heaton kindly send £20 on account? It had five figures and 'a good deal of accessory matter'. And please would Boyce trace a picture of a windmill, for him to copy into the distant landscape view, and send it *forthwith*?

William was now engaged to Henrietta Rintoul, daughter of the *Spectator*'s editor. Gabriel's silence on the subject suggests he was not impressed by his prospective sister-in-law, while Lizzie and Henrietta were not introduced, as might have been expected. But William was increasingly developing a separate life, centred on art criticism and literary journalism. He no longer pretended to share the Chatham Place tenancy, leaving Gabriel to find the rent, and weeks might pass between his visits. He did not always know what Gabriel was up to, nor see his pictures in progress.

Gabriel was an affectionate brother, son and nephew, but family matters were not his priority, and their individual affairs seldom interested him deeply. He took Maria to meet the Ruskins, however – when, as it turned out, Ruskin was so attentive that Maria promptly lost her heart. Gabriel knew that after two attempts to place her poems, Christina had given up trying for publication, though she was still writing. When he was at home – and the family always gathered for Christmas – he heard her latest pieces; one of his favourites was a fantastical poem about 'the prudent crocodile' who, having devoured his kin, wept appropriately false tears; and he had forwarded to Holman her quaint request for a live specimen from the banks of the Nile. But he had never bothered to hand on the volume that Bessie Parkes gave him for Christina in Hastings, which she only collected when visiting Chatham Place. In the autumn of 1855 she took a short post as governess with a family in Lancashire, but her brothers were so uninterested in her affairs that, editing her letters years later, William had no recollection of her having left London.

Gabriel was invited to Albany Street whenever aunt Charlotte or uncle Henry were visiting. Always courteous towards Charlotte, he more or less ignored his uncle, whom he regarded as a nervous old fogey. Henry

Polydore's wife had recently left him, taking their young daughter, the Rossettis' only cousin, and this year they learnt she was planning to try her luck in America. Henry wrote in some distress, asking William to help regain cousin Henrietta. As a government servant William had a more convincing status in such matters, but significantly Gabriel was not even asked.

Though Gabriel might have written more frequently – his mother and aunts kept all his letters – messages were constantly passing between Chatham Place and Albany Street. 'Ask William if he'll come too. I have only had one shirt and one wearable collar this week,' he wrote to his mother on one occasion; evidently his laundry and mending were still sent home. At Chatham Place, housekeeper Mrs Birrell supplied cans of hot water, and cleaning services on request but, judging by Ruskin's response, neither the chaotic studio nor the rest of the apartment received much attention. Adding to the general clutter were quaint old curiosity-shop items, potential studio props.

'Come back, dear Liz,' he had written for Valentine's Day, knowing she would probably stay in Nice until May. Four days later, however, having invited the Madox Browns, with Lucy and Cathy, to join William and himself to see Kean play Henry VIII, he rushed off at the last minute to see his new 'discovery' at another theatre. Tall and shapely, with pale gold hair and refined, ethereal features, Miss Herbert was an actress of stunning appearance but limited talent, according to Ellen Terry. 'Did you ever see her? O my eye!' Gabriel wrote to Scott later. 'She has the most varied and highest expression I ever saw in a woman's face, besides abundant beauty, golden hair, etc.'[7]

Such extravagant admiration does not denote infidelity, but when Lizzie returned after seven months away, things had subtly changed. Was Gabriel irrationally annoyed at her long absence, or had it simply opened a gap between them? Superficially, all seemed well. Taking lodgings in fashionable Marylebone, Lizzie played hostess, inviting Allingham to dine one evening, before the theatre. A week or so later, the Browns too went to supper, admiring a splendid Indian evening cloak Gabriel had bought for Lizzie to show off at the Princess Theatre, where Kean's *Winter's Tale*, with eight-year-old Ellen Terry in her first professional role, was the hit of the season.

It was a marrying summer. Millais was holding forth on conjugal joys, and Charley Collins and Arthur Hughes were also new husbands. Writing to Hunt a few months earlier, Brown had warned that he would return to 'a maelstrom of matrimony'. There was a rumour about, added Stephens, that both the Rossettis were to marry – 'D. G. to a young lady, an artist. You will guess who.' Brown, however, was more knowledgeable, telling Hunt that Gabriel 'still prudently holds aloof from any measure of the kind likely to break in upon his artistic and poetic reveries'. Now, on Lizzie's return, Brown's comment was brief: 'they had better marry.'[8] When, if not now? This month Rossetti was twenty-eight. He had several wealthy patrons, dealers were starting to make approaches and he was full of ideas, for new 'modern subjects' and others on chivalric themes. And in addition he had his first, important, public commission.

In south Wales the ancient cathedral church of Llandaff was being rebuilt to serve industrial Cardiff. Architect J. P. Seddon, Tom's brother, persuaded the diocese to commission an altarpiece. Would Rossetti be interested? His two exhibited works had been on sacred themes. On 4 March Tom Seddon brought Henry Bruce, Member of Parliament and treasurer of the fund-raising committee, for a preliminary talk.

Bruce liked the 'earnest and serious style' of Rossetti's work. He asked for a list of three or four subjects and their prices. Talking to Tom, Gabriel had suggested a modest fee of £100, it being 'an opportunity of displaying his talent in a higher sphere than usually fell to an artist's lot'. Despite Llandaff's lack of funds, Bruce felt that £200 was more appropriate. 'I think you should be fairly paid,' he said; 'therefore do not stint yourself.'[9]

True fresco being impractical in Britain, it was agreed that oil on canvas was the best medium. 'You know that the reason oil pictures on walls turn dark is that the plaster has to be saturated with boiled oil, and that most painters use so much varnish and vehicle,' Tom told his brother, who evidently favoured tempera. 'Rossetti uses none . . . and if you want a proof of how colours stand, if paint clean and clear, look at Van Eyck's pictures and the old paintings on panels.'

The obvious models were the great Flemish altarpieces. That by Memling in the St John Hospital in Bruges had the Adoration flanked by Nativity and Presentation, its theme the triple worship of Christ by Virgin, Gentiles and Jews. Rossetti's first idea was thus for a triptych of the Nativity between King David and St Paul, psalmist and preacher, symbolic of the three cathedral functions of veneration, song and sermon. He went to talk to Ruskin, who promised a good sum for the subscription fund, and then wrote to Llandaff, asking £200 for the centrepiece, or £400 for all three pictures. 'I suppose this settles the business as impracticable,' he told Brown, half expecting to lose the commission. However, a week later the restoration committee cordially welcomed the proposal, subject to approval by Bishop and Dean, saying every effort would be made to raise the money.

It was 'a big thing, which I shall go into with a howl of delight after all my small work', Rossetti told Allingham. Currently, Hunt was busy with a comparable canvas showing Christ disputing with the rabbis in the vanished Temple of Jerusalem. Just about the greatest thing he had done, in Gabriel's view, this was over eleven feet wide, with a dozen figures. Suddenly it seemed as if the serious public art which the PRB had dreamed of was coming into being. Although the new Oxford Museum had funds only for sculpture (Rossetti helped secure commissions for Woolner, Munro and Tupper), a decorated church was being talked of, while its architect Benjamin Woodward, in discussion with a Manchester cotton magnate about a large philanthropic scheme, had further plans to cover a chapel with paintings 'from top to bottom and end to end'. Rossetti had visions of vast fresco cycles like those by Giotto and Gozzoli, full-scale copies of which were currently on display at the Crystal Palace. Benozzo Gozzoli was a god, he told Allingham.[10]

Amending the original design (which Llandaff thought somewhat 'popish') Rossetti completed a watercolour study within a week, adapting the Nativity done for Ruskin into a central Adoration (aptly for the cathedral, which was scheduled to reopen for divine service in twelve months' time) while the side panels now held images of David in youth and age. The aim was a 'condensed symbol' rather than a literal reading of scripture, as the artist explained:

> This triple picture shows Christ sprung from high and low, as united in the person of David who was both Shepherd and King, and worshipped by high and low (by King and Shepherd) at His birth.
>
> An angel has just entered the stable where Christ is newly born, and leads by the hand a king and a shepherd, who bow themselves before the manger on which the Virgin Mother kneels, holding the infant Saviour. The Shepherd kisses the hand, and the King the foot, of Christ, to denote the superiority of lowliness to greatness in His sight; while the one lays a crook, the other a crown, at His feet . . . Other angels look in through the openings round the stable, or play on musical instruments in the loft above.
>
> The two side-figures represent David, one as Shepherd, the other as King. In the first he is a youth, and advances fearlessly but cautiously, sling in hand, to take aim at Goliath, while the Israelite troops watch the issue of the combat from behind an entrenchment. In the second he is a man of mature years, still armed from battle, and composing on his harp a psalm in thanksgiving for victory.

The whole was called *The Seed of David*, following the Gospel tradition of Jesus's descent from the stem of Jesse. A very striking and original treatment, G. E. Street told the Ecclesiological Society.[11]

One wonders if any contribution came from Maria, for ingenious typological correspondences of this kind were popular in her High Church circles. The image of David may have come from Gozzoli's Pisan fresco, while the central idea was surely influenced by Ruskin's recent commendation of Titian's *Adoration* in the Scuola San Rocco in Venice. Thematically, however, Rossetti's imagery rather responds to Henry Bruce's Liberal commitment to social reform through education, religion and culture in his native South Wales, where industrialisation had resulted in conditions of grim squalor, poverty and ignorance. According to his biographer, 'sound judgement and impartial insight into social and economic questions made Bruce through his life a wise friend and counsellor of the working classes [who] did much to increase the activity and usefulness of the Church [and] seized every opportunity of educating the people about him to a sense of their position and their needs'.[12] He was also renowned for plain speaking. Perhaps he stressed the danger of class alienation in Cardiff and the Valleys. Certainly he was aware that Methodism was more popular than the established Church; Llandaff's rehabilitation was not merely an architectural project.

'Who shall ascend into the hill of the Lord: or who shall rise up in his holy place?' asks David's Psalm 24 in the Anglican liturgy. 'Even he that hath clean hands and a pure heart: and that hath not lifted up his mind unto vanity, nor sworn to deceive his neighbour ...' Traditionally, shepherds and kings are kept separate in Christian art. Bringing them together, with asserted equality, was a radical, Victorian notion, challenging orthodox iconography. Moreover, the contemporary moral message that in Christ the mighty shall be humbled and the lowly elevated is tacitly reinforced by Rossetti's flanking figures. David Pastor is a slim, unconfident youth, without wealth or power, clad only in his courage. David Rex sits in rich clothing on a peacock throne, but holds his harp in penitent mood. 'Blessed is he that considereth the poor and needy: the Lord shall deliver him in time of trouble ...'

At the same time, many of the altarpiece motifs are wholly canonical, such as the King kissing the Christ Child's foot – also seen, as it happened, in the *Adoration* by Paolo Veronese, recently acquired by London's National Gallery – or the golden-winged angels hovering in the roof of the stable, which pay homage to *cinquecentists* like Tintoretto, whom Ruskin so much admired. *The Seed of David* was thus both innovative and traditional, a tribute to Rossetti's powers of invention.[13]

Though it would be two years before Rossetti started painting in earnest, and six more before it was finished, the design was approved, and the artist newly confident. 1856 seemed to be going well.

Early in April, Millais came back to London, bringing his new pictures for the summer exhibition. He abused everyone – Holman for wasting his time in Palestine, Gabriel for getting an immense reputation *having done nothing to deserve it*, and Brown for refusing to send to the RA; how could anyone object to the Academy now Pre-Raphaelite work was so well received there? In response Rossetti scouted *Peace Concluded*, the most topical of Millais's works. Depicting a Crimean officer back in the bosom of his family in anticipation of victory celebrations on 29 May, it was a stupid affair to suit the day, he commented, 'but very big and earning him £900! without the copyright, for which he expects £1000 more'. However he admired *Autumn Leaves* and *The Blind Girl*, describing the first as a fine piece of poetic colour and elegiac feeling, as in Titian or Giorgione, the second as a moralised landscape in full PRB manner – 'most touching and perfect'.[14]

Millais was excitable, holding forth on the 'disgustingness of stale virginities' in relation to his fellow artists. Passionately indignant on the subject of Effie's sufferings, he told Brown among other things that Ruskin claimed she had been unfaithful, when the medical examination had 'perfectly substantiated the fact of her purity'. The indiscreet loquacity convinced Brown that Millais was telling the truth, but did not lower the barrier between Millais and Rossetti. First Johnny complained that for three years past Gabriel had shown him no new work. Then he said the real obstacle was Gabriel's silence regarding Effie, and his praise of Ruskin. But at Brown's urging he went to Chatham Place, where he was enchanted by the now-finished *Dante's Dream*, the projected altarpiece, and two new beginnings showing Mary Nazarene and Mary Magdalene in companion watercolours. Brown had 'never witnessed a mortal more delighted than he was with these admirable drawings. He kept returning to one after the other and bursting into such raptures as only Millais can.'[15] Afterwards, Gabriel promised Brown he would call when Millais returned to town with Effie. But there is no record of his doing so, and the old friendship was not sustained.

Holman needed to sell his big picture before he could take Millais's advice and marry. Though privately hoping to make her his wife, he had as yet made Annie no promises. Gabriel seems to have made plenty to Lizzie, at least in private. But there were arguments. When she and Emma decided to go to Ramsgate for the Whitsun weekend, Rossetti came hot foot to the Browns' new house in Kentish Town to stop them, in a very ill temper. Then, a month later, it emerged that he had been seeing Annie Miller.

Indeed, Hunt claimed, Gabriel, William and George Boyce had all been flirting with Annie. Lizzie complained to Emma of Gabriel's 'absurd' behaviour, while Hunt poured out his distress to Brown – all about Annie's love for him and his liking for her and how while he was away Gabriel had encouraged her to sit to other artists (a charge hard to substantiate and perhaps invented by Annie to excuse her own conduct). Recently she had been taken to 'all sorts of places of amusement' including Cremorne pleasure gardens, where she danced with Boyce, and on the river by William, apparently as forgetful of Henrietta as Gabriel was of Lizzie. Poor Hunt was in a fever about it all, and Gabriel seemed 'mad past care', commented Brown wonderingly.[16] Doubtless Annie was enchanted.

Rossetti's motives are obscure. Maybe he meant merely to jolt Hunt into taking note of Annie's needs. Looking 'siren-like', she was leaving Hunt's studio when Brown and Tom Seddon arrived for dinner on 28 July. A week later Gabriel restored good relations all round by forswearing further flirtation, so the whole business may have been merely a summer caprice. More probably, it was a signal to Lizzie that he would do as he wished, not as he ought; no man was more accustomed to please himself, said William, over and again. But it also marked Gabriel's first real quarrel with Hunt.

His world was still predominantly masculine, and as his PRB friendships faded he took possession of a new circle. Early this summer, Edward Jones moved to London. Lodging in Sloane Street, he worked on a drawing called *The Waxen Image* inspired by *Sister Helen*, and came often to Chatham Place, where Gabriel rechristened him Ned. One afternoon, he found Rossetti surrounded by piles of muddy books, thrown out of the window to make space. It being low tide they landed in the deep slime of the foreshore, and all day muddy scavengers trailed up the stairs in expectation of reward. In grumpy mood, Gabriel cursed books, and told Ned 'that no painter should have any, and that the only use for a book for a painter was to steady his easel upon if the floor was uneven, and to build up constructions for models to stand on or lean upon – and he urged me to get rid of books out of my life ...'[17]

Another day when Ned arrived, the studio floor was covered with discarded garments – coats, waistcoats, dress trousers – as Gabriel bargained with a pawnbroker. Three sovereigns were then presented to a destitute dramatist, whom Ned remembered haunting the hallway for many months in hope of further hand-outs. Rossetti's generosity to beggars was legendary. Walking with him past Charing Cross some years later, Luke Ionides watched him speak to a homeless and hungry woman in a doorway, and then empty all his coins into her hand, urging her to spend them on pleasures, not necessities.

He introduced young Ned to London's attractions. 'This play is a curse,' he would say in mid-performance, leaving abruptly for the Judge and Jury, a drinking den with topical satires. Ned preferred the theatre, but Rossetti said it was seeing life. Teasingly, one night he paid a whore to follow Ned home. 'I saw him talking to her as I looked back, and then she came after me and I couldn't get rid of her . . . it was no use, she wouldn't go, and there we marched arm-in-arm down Regent Street,' Ned recalled, remembering his terror. Perhaps for safety's sake, after a month in London (and exactly on the anniversary of Beatrice's death, in homage to a day held sacred by Gabriel) Ned engaged himself to marry Georgiana, fifteen-year-old daughter of a Methodist minister. Taken for an awestruck visit to 'the shrine of Rossetti at Blackfriars', Georgie noted only that Gabriel carried on painting and had olive skin. When in August her even younger sister was introduced, for a birthday treat, Gabriel gave her a copy of Hunt's etching from *The Germ*, inscribed to Louisa Macdonald with 'affectionate regards' for her eleventh birthday. 'We shall see the greatest man in Europe,' Ned said, taking a college friend to Chatham Place.[18]

To begin with, Ned simply watched while Rossetti painted. Then, one early day, holding out palette and brushes, Gabriel told him to make a head study of the boy model who was present. Dismayed, Ned rose to the challenge, and was afterwards grateful for the heart-warming confidence. 'As I walked with him in the streets I wondered what the crowd were so busy about that it could not stop to look at him,' he wrote later.[19] For his part, Gabriel recognised a kindred spirit, with intense ambition and comparable poetic visions of painting by the light that never was on land or sea. Like Chiaro, both drew images of their own souls, disguised as 'daubs' to the profane. 'He taught me to have no fear or shame of my own ideas,' Ned explained, 'to design perpetually, to seek no popularity, to be altogether myself.' In after-years, whenever he began a new canvas, he asked himself if Gabriel would have liked it.

Ruskin warned Rossetti that Ned would be his rival. Gabriel replied that he knew it. 'I could have sunk on the carpet for shame,' Ned recalled, '– so I wrote to Morris at Oxford and said he must come to be a painter too, for it was such a wonderful world, and only revealed to painters – and always Gabriel was saying, "If any man has any poetry in him he should paint it, for it has all been said and written, and they have hardly begun to paint it. Every man who has that gift should paint." That's how we began!' Thus Morris also felt the glow of Gabriel's personality, being half-persuaded he too could be an artist. '[N]ow as he is a very great man, and speaks with authority and not as the scribes, I *must* try,' he wrote in July. 'I don't hope much, I must say, yet will try my best – he gave me practical advice on the subject . . .'[20]

In this golden year when Ned vowed it never rained but was 'blue summer from Christmas to Christmas', Rossetti took to spending his Sundays at Sloane Street, when Morris came to London and read aloud while Ned drew. Their passion was for Malory, which kindled Rossetti's own. There were but 'two books in the world: the *Morte d'Arthur* and the

Bible', he declared. Malory indeed became an alternative gospel, with its beguiling, picaresque mix of battle, brotherhood, sorcery and sexual romance. The Knights of the Round Table, Lancelot of the Lake, Tristram and Isoud, the search for the Holy Grail, Arthur in Avalon. Like Childe Roland, in an unpromising world, they too were setting off on a comparable quest. Once, Christina had likened the PRB to the Round Table. Now, Gabriel became the most valiant knight in a new fraternity.

Morris was short and square, with an abrupt, emphatic manner and a mop of dark curly hair, on account of which he was called 'Topsy'. Ned by contrast was pale and willowy, in appearance a gentle dreamer, inwardly iron and granite. According to Rossetti, his new friends were 'both stunners as artists and bricks as coves'. Ned's designs were 'marvels of finish and imaginative detail, unequalled by anything unless perhaps Albert Dürer's finest works', he wrote; while Morris was 'one of the finest little fellows alive – with a touch of the incoherent, but a real man'. Though as yet unpractised in art, he had written 'some really wonderful poetry'.[21]

Indeed, Morris's rough-hewn yet romantic poems and stories in the *Oxford and Cambridge Magazine* were such as to challenge Rossetti in the literary field. His tales were of the olden days. 'I dreamed once, that four men sat by the winter fire talking and telling tales, in a house that the wind howled round', began *A Dream*, in March. 'Long ago there was a land, never mind where or when, a fair country and good to live in', opened *Gertha's Lovers*, in July. Like Rossetti's own earliest efforts, the poems were more chivalric; *Winter Weather* was followed by *Riding Together*:

> Up the sweep of the bridge we dash'd together,
> It rock'd to the crash of the meeting spears,
> Down rain'd the buds of the dear spring weather,
> The elm-tree flowers fell like tears.

'Morris's facility for poeticizing puts one in a rage,' Rossetti told Allingham in December. 'He has been writing at all for little more than a year, I believe, and has already poetry enough for a big book.' Stimulated, he retrieved *The Burden of Nineveh* from his own mass of manuscripts, for publication in the magazine. A reprint of *The Blessed Damozel* followed, and then *The Staff and Scrip*, which grew quite Morrissian:

> His sword was broken in his hand
> Where he had kiss'd the blade.
> 'O soft steel that could not withstand!
> O my hard heart unstay'd,
> That pray'd and pray'd!'

From New York, editor W. J. Stillman requested permission to reprint all three poems in *The Crayon*, and thus, between January and March 1857, D. G. Rossetti made his first appearance in the United States. Commending the poems' power of expression, depth of feeling and force of imagination, a note explained that the author was 'one of the leaders of the Pre-Raphaelite school in painting'.[22]

Morris had a private fortune from his late father's mining investments. In summer 1856, he bought Hughes's *April Love* from the Academy and Brown's *Hayfield* on Rossetti's recommendation. 'You know he is a millionaire and buys pictures,' Gabriel wrote with pardonable exaggeration. Just as those with talent should be painters so those with wealth should be patrons, as a matter of natural duty. Accordingly, when Ruskin declined, Morris bought *Fra Pace* and also *The Chapel before the Lists*, with the black tower. So Rossetti had a new patron, who was also a disciple.

He had other commissions, too. William Marshall agreed to buy *Mary Nazarene*. In early May the exhibitions brought Ellen Heaton, a good-hearted if gushing creature who prized her acquaintance with Ruskin and Browning. Seeking a less melancholy subject to complement *The death of Beatrice*, she agreed to commission the old design of *Mary in the House of St John*, which was well begun by the time she left town. Most importantly, another Leeds patron called Thomas E. Plint, a young art-loving stock-broker who this year began buying enthusiastically from the Pre-Raphaelite circle, commissioned a large work in oil. Not precisely identified, this was probably a version of 'Mary Magdalene leaving the House of Feasting', for which an advance of 100 guineas was agreed. 'Gabriel goes on swim-mingly,' Woolner told Allingham in September; '– just received a commission for a £400 picture, besides no end of applications for his watercolours.'[23]

Another new acquaintance was Charles Eliot Norton of Massachusetts, currently on an extended European tour, who was introduced by Ruskin and the Brownings. Founded on shared interests, friendship flourished, for Norton had passions for the *Vita Nuova* and Italian liberation. Although a Boston Brahmin, he expressed himself with Rossettian vigour. 'Milan and Venice are hemmed round by Austrian bayonets and Florence is discon-tented under the stupid despotism of an insane bigot,' he wrote, while 'Rome stagnates under the superstitious priests and Naples under the brutality of a Bourbon. I think I could roast a Franciscan with pleasure and it would need only a tolerable opportunity to make me stab a Cardinal in the dark.' Norton was very influential and particularly nice, Gabriel told Brown; 'you will like him much.'[24]

Gabriel urged Mr Plint and Miss Heaton to buy from Brown, and badgered his newspaper contacts for a favourable notice in the *Daily News* when one of Brown's pictures won a prize at the Liverpool Academy. 'Really Gabriello seems bent on making my fortune at one blow,' commented Brown. 'Never did fellow, I think, so bestir himself for a rival before, it is very good and very great to act so.'

Yet sometimes, even often, Brown saw an obverse, ill-tempered side. 'I could narrate a hundred instances of his most disinterested and noble minded conduct towards his art rivals which places him far above Hunt or Millais for greatness of soul,' he noted this spring, 'and yet he will on the most trivial occasion hate and backbite anyone who gives him offence ...' He had unequalled sympathy with other artists, agreed Burne-Jones, and boundless generosity towards those he liked; but also 'an immense power of humour and sarcasm', and a distinctly cruel streak. Like his namesake Dante Alighieri, 'who loved well because he hated', Rossetti's scorn was unrestrained. Those who offended him got short shrift. 'I hate Inchbold,' he wrote baldly, of a fellow artist. And what horrors Mike Halliday's pictures were! 'So dogmatic and so irritable when opposed', remarked Millais long afterwards, Rossetti was impossible as a boon companion.[25]

Sometimes, Gabriel pondered on his moodiness. In the summer, he was apt to ascribe it to the usual seediness brought on by city heat and smells. Invited to join William on vacation, however, he was too busy to get away. A few months later, Elizabeth Barrett Browning's verse novel *Aurora Leigh*, on the personal and professional travails of a woman artist, made him feel imperfect, worldly, knowledgeable in all the wrong ways. Everyone knew St Francis did not espouse Poverty in fashionable St James's, he told Allingham, while for himself, 'if a blind man were to enter the room this evening and talk to me for some hour, I should, with the best intentions, be in danger of twigging his blindness before the right moment came, if such there were, for the chord in the orchestra and the proper theatrical start'.[26] Something was at war within his soul.

Typically, Rossetti's impulsive, wayward behaviour simply took no account of others. A week after the *Daily News* puff, he arrived at the Browns' house, suffering from 'blue devils' and insisting that Brown therefore accompany him to an old house out in Essex once occupied by Guy Fawkes, which he had a fancy to visit. He was quite undeterred by the fact that Brown had a severe cold and Emma was already in labour. Born thirty-six hours later, the baby was named Arthur Gabriel; Rossetti and Lizzie were asked to be godparents.

Rossetti wrote good letters. Whether brief notes or lengthier, information- and opinion-packed epistles, they are lively and distinctive, in his unmistakable voice. Brown kept every one, as did the Rossetti family, Allingham and Boyce. But no letters to Lizzie survive, either because she lost or destroyed them, or because she kept them and he burnt them after her death. As a result, we have few immediate records of their relationship to add to what can be inferred from other sources. So we cannot know what exactly prompted Rossetti's sudden announcement to Brown in the autumn of 1856 that 'he intended to get married at once to Guggum & then off to Algeria!!!' Well might Brown exclaim, though whether marriage or Algeria were the greater surprise is hard to tell. Winter was approaching, and Barbara Smith was bound there with her sister and Bessie, who would have been pleasanter company than poor Mrs Kincaid. To Lizzie, Gabriel said they would marry when Plint's advance arrived. But the moment passed, for as she bitterly told the Browns later, 'lo! the money being paid, Gabriel brought it and told her all he was going to pay with it and do with it, but never a word more about marriage.'[27] Upset and enraged, she took herself off to Bath. Gabriel told people she had no fancy for Algeria, on account of the earthquakes, but perhaps she feared another long banishment.

Whenever Lizzie grew angry he was contrite, as if afraid she would leave him. Yet much of his behaviour was hurtful and heedless, as if he wished to be free. No one truly understood him, but this year Christina was sufficiently puzzled to weave something of her brother's conduct into a dramatic monologue on conflicting desires in a man's heart, with 'I wish we once were wedded – then I must be true' as its opening line. Gabriel doubtless did not himself know why he behaved so badly. 'As soon as a thing is imposed on me as an obligation, my aptitude for doing it is gone,' he admitted ruefully around this time; 'what I *ought* to do is just what I *can't* do.'[28]

He had in truth no time for a wedding or holiday, being busy on the now overdue Tennyson illustrations for Moxon. Deadlines were as bad as duties. 'I cannot endure his pestering,' he told William at midsummer, refusing to see the publisher. But thus prompted, he turned his mind from large triptych to tiny wood-engravings three inches square. His subjects comprised St Cecilia and King Arthur with the Weeping Queens (both for *The Palace of Art*) and a scene apiece for *Sir Galahad, Mariana in the South* and *The Lady of Shalott*. It is likely that Moxon hoped to publish for Christmas, the customary season for illustrated books.[29]

As with Llandaff, there were obvious sources of inspiration, the more so because wood-engraving occupied a special position in the world of Victorian illustration, often in contention with steel engraving, etching and even newer forms of reproduction. Among the immediate stylistic sources were modern German engravings by artists such as Alfred Rethel and

Ludwig Richter. 'Death, standing there, with his head thrown on one side, has two bones in his hands, which he uses as fiddle and fiddle-bow, playing so wonderfully that as you look at the drawing you almost seem to hear the wild terrible skirling of some mad reel,' wrote Morris this year in a vivid description of Rethel's image of cholera's first appearance at a masked ball.[30] But it was earlier exemplars to which Rossetti mainly looked, in accord with long-standing admiration. In Paris with Hunt in 1849 he had bought 'three stunning etchings' after Dürer, and in 1853 talked of going to Nüremberg with Scott, to see the master's house. Into *Dante drawing an Angel* he copied background details of a water urn, towel and brush from Dürer's *Birth of the Virgin*, and in *Fra Pace* paid direct homage to Dürer's *St Jerome*, complete with a domestic cat in place of Jerome's lion. He also knew, and later owned, copies of Burgkmair's woodcuts for *Der Weisskünig*, and an early sixteenth-century *Ship of Fools*.

It was a shared passion, for Ruskin was buying and lending Dürers on a prodigal scale – *St Jerome*, *St Eustace*, the *Melancholia*, *Knight, Death and the Devil*, the *Apocalypse*, *The Cannon*, *The Flight into Egypt*. 'To all enquiries how to proceed I generally make but one answer – buy an Albert Dürer – and copy it till you can't look at anything else,' he wrote. Morris and Jones pinned up woodcuts alongside brass-rubbings, and while Ned said his intricate ink drawings were designed to 'make people say that Albert Dürer has come back again',[31] Morris took up wood-engraving, hanging his tools in a looped strap as depicted by the master himself.

Rossetti's designs were ready by the end of October. He then spent the best part of a fortnight at Brown's studio, drawing them in reverse on the boxwood blocks. The process was necessarily slow, even for those with less fidgety habits; typically blocks were redrawn several times until judged satisfactory. At this stage, the block might be photographed, before going to be cut. Proofs came back, for the artist to correct by refining lines, altering tones, clarifying outlines. More cutting and further proofs followed. 'I cannot produce them quickly even if supposing I gave all my time to them,' wrote Millais on one occasion.[32]

As has often been remarked, the PRB illustrations for Moxon are quite distinct from those by the other artists, and share certain stylistic affinities, although Millais's work is noticeably suaver than the others'. Both Hunt's design for *Oriana*, which recalls Rossetti's *Arthur's Tomb*, and his *Lady of Shalott*, with dark swirling hair, bent neck and elongated figure (which seems curiously to foreshadow Rossetti's later images of Jane Morris) were masterpieces, according to Gabriel. The Gothic feasters in Millais's *Day Dream* seem echoed by his own weeping queens, while the Prince gazing at the spellbound lovers compares both with Lancelot looking on the Lady of

Shalott and the near-embrace of Angel and Saint in *St Cecilia*. These correspondences are coincidental, however, for Millais was working in Scotland and neither saw nor shared images with his fellow illustrators.

Ned recalled that when the block for *St Cecilia* arrived, Rossetti declared it one-sixteenth of an inch too short. Did that matter? they asked. 'Good God! What do you mean by that?' he yelled in reply; 'I could get a whole city in there!' Which is roughly what he did, taking one of Lizzie's ideas, moving her scene out on to ramparts and adding a wide perspective of soldiers firing a cannon, furled warships in the harbour, a turreted town, a military catapult in the castle yard, a dove, a sundial and a mail-clad guard with halberd munching an apple, oblivious to the dying saint and her heavenly companion. Confused? Intricate? Wholly original? 'Jolly quaint but very lovely', was Brown's judgement.[33] Plint liked it so much he asked for a watercolour version.

Like Blake, Rossetti was now out on his own as regards invention. In conventional terms, the drawing was eccentric and flawed – in anatomy, perspective, fall of light, framing. Without benefit of foreground, the spectator is thrust abruptly into the image, like the reader into one of Morris's poems. The figures are awkwardly contorted, expressionistically archaic in posture like those in historiated capitals. With stylised handling of spatial recession, all the Moxon scenes challenge received notions of illustration. 'Rossetti seems to revel in [the] wildest extravagances,' protested one baffled reviewer when the book appeared.[34] But they stay in the mind. As with *Elfen-Mere*, his Tennyson designs were strikingly original, reworking the medium of Dürer and Burgkmair in a manner appropriate to the poems' own archaism. (Appropriately, for a projected edition of Longfellow, he also drew a block showing Dürer in his studio.)

Mariana in the South appears to have been finished first. In the background, Gabriel again inserted the urn and towel from Dürer's *Birth of the Virgin*. For *King Arthur*, he persuaded Arthur Hughes to don a massive medieval helmet – 'upon the pretext of introducing it in a picture, but really in the hope of seriously damaging my brain', joked Hughes. It was finished around the end of November, and after being photographed on the block three drawings were dispatched, *St Cecilia* and *King Arthur* going to Dalziels, despite their alleged mangling of *Elfen-Mere*. By 8 December, Rossetti had second proofs of *Arthur*. 'But these engravers! What ministers of wrath!' he wrote Allingham with exaggerated indignation. 'Your drawing comes to them, like Agag, delicately, and is hewn in pieces before the Lord Harry.' One block – probably *St Cecilia* – came back ruined. 'O woodman, spare that block!' he apostrophised, parodying a famous verse of the day; 'O gash not anyhow; / It took ten days by clock, / I'd fain protect it now.'[35]

His preferred engraver was the veteran W. J. Linton, whose work he had admired for over a decade.

Comparison of the photographed blocks with the printed illustrations shows indeed how the complex drawings were coarsened during cutting; in the words of one commentator, 'how much subtlety and nervous force in the artist's line, how much of its freshness and spontaneity was lost in the mechanical line of the engraver'. Accustomed to reproducing the more sinuous line, regular shading and vignette framing of conventional illustration, engravers had problems with the new pictorial style. But it is also true that Rossetti made substantive alterations at proof stage, for Dalziels to implement. The crowns of Arthur's queens were altered, making each unique. Cecilia's organ acquired accessories and decoration, the guard a visor to his helmet, the saint a girdle to her gown and the angel a differently draped sleeve. Most strikingly, the angel, whose features are clearly visible in the drawing, has moved from gazing at Cecilia to kissing her forehead, in a close, ambiguous gesture.

However, Hunt and Millais had similar experiences; their proofs too are covered with corrections. 'Cut a slight touch beneath the iris which is too straight. Cut away something of the two harsh lines against the eye . . . Cut away entirely in the forehead,' wrote Millais. Moreover, mailed from Perth on 16 and 26 December, his *Cleopatra* and *Day Dream* show that Rossetti's four blocks were not the last completed. If indeed Moxon hoped for Christmas publication, his aim was thwarted by more than one illustrator.[36] When he died not long after publication, cruel jokes circulated to the effect that Rossetti's procrastination had killed him. This was not even figuratively true, although one element at least was accurate, for Gabriel was a difficult and demanding artist.

In December he followed Lizzie to Bath, reporting that rain made it a mud-bath. But after an absence, he and Liz always enjoyed each other's company; more than anything, she could make him laugh with what William called her light, chaffy, ironic conversation. Gabriel renewed his avowals of affection, persuading her he at least was not seeking release. Together, they worked on a watercolour to her design of the Holy Grail, showing Galahad with two angels in a flooded chapel. Inscribed with both names, this 'duet' delighted Ruskin, to whom it was presented.

He was reading *Aurora Leigh* – 'an astounding piece of work, surely,' he told Allingham. 'O the wonder of it! – and O the bore of writing about it.'[37] Astonishing to relate, Mrs Browning had taken up spiritualism – communication with the dead. Politely appalled, Gabriel had joined her husband one evening in laying rationalist siege to the whole notion. He had seen them frequently this autumn, observing how Browning collected stories in conversation like a portraitist sketching faces.

He still kept his life in separate compartments. Lizzie had not been introduced to his new friends, which suggests she was seldom at Chatham Place, where Morris and Jones were so frequently to be seen. They were now occupying the rooms Gabriel and Deverell had once shared in Red Lion Square, where he found a poignant reminder – 'an address written by us on the wall of a bedroom'. For the large, empty first-floor studio, Morris had designed some 'intensely medieval' furniture – 'tables and chairs like incubi and succubi', in Gabriel's words – including a circular table, a squat round chair and two immensely heavy high-backed thrones, 'fit for Barbarossa'. Immediately, Gabriel and Morris began painting 'figures and inscriptions in gules and vert and azure' on the chairbacks, taking subjects from Morris's poems.[38]

Next came a great settle, with three high cupboards above, which was delivered when they were out. 'When we came in, all the passages and the staircase were choked with vast blocks of timber and there was a scene. I think the measurements had perhaps been given a little wrongly,' recalled Burne-Jones; 'but set up it was finally, and our studio was one-third less in size. Rossetti came. This was always a terrifying moment to the last. He laughed, but approved.' He also elected to cover the settle with pictures. On four diapered panels, he painted four medieval ladies, representing the seasons. Further inspired, he worked at a sequence of watercolours showing knights and ladies, as from Malory, Froissart, *Lancelot du Lac*, the *Roman de la Rose*. Morris bought them; unlike Ruskin, he did not criticise the technique but entered fully into the spirit and wrote a 'stunning poem' for *The Blue Closet*.

In this picture, four women in medieval dress play and sing to curious musical instruments. 'The sharp accents of the scarlet and green seem to go with the sound of the bell,' wrote Stephens later; 'the softer crimson, purple and white accord with the throbbing notes of the lute and clavichord, while the dulcet, flute-like voices of the girls appear to agree with those azure tiles on the wall and floor.' Morris gave them names and a shadowy narrative:

> Alice the Queen and Louise the Queen,
> Two damozels wearing purple and green
> Four lone ladies dwelling here
> From day to day and year to year . . .

Alice and Louise were the names of Georgiana Macdonald's sisters, but the fantasy was set in that realm of romance where the spirit was both escapist and playful. As a friend later ventriloquised over Rossetti's depiction of the vanquished beast in *The Wedding of St George*: ' "Do you believe in St

George and the Dragon? If you do, I don't. But do you think we mean
nothing, the man in gold and I? Either way I pity you, my friend." '[39]

Calling frequently at 17 Red Lion Square, Rossetti was as happy as he
had ever been with the PRB. The frank admiration of the younger men gave
him a new pleasure, helping to drive away the demons. Together, they
created a glowing if disorderly space, wonderingly recalled by Georgie's
young brother Fred. The studio was 'generally in a state of noble
confusion,' he wrote; '– massive furniture of Morris's design, old pieces of
metal-work, easels, canvases mounted on wooden frames, armour, lay-
figures, pieces of tapestry and drapery, half-finished pictures, sketchbooks,
bits of Flemish or Italian earthenware, with here and there a hat, or coat, or
pair of boots. Near the fire-place was something like a clearing – an open
space, as it were, in the forest or jungle – with a table and chairs for joyous
meals, and for genial converse when work was done.'[40]

The maid of the house, employed to cook, clean, mend and run errands
for the residents, was Mrs Mary Nicholson, known always as 'Red Lion
Mary'. A woman of great character and shrewd good humour, she had
some literary tastes and was much taken with the young artists. When they
said she was too short to model, she offered to stand on a stool; but they
were polite: she was in fact too plain. 'She liked Gabriel and me, and cheated
for us always,' recalled Ned, adding that Morris got the worst bed and the
coldest water. Unfailingly, Rossetti's natural manner made him a favourite.

The end of the year was saddened by news of Tom Seddon's death in
Cairo. Meanwhile, having persuaded J. F. Lewis to support the candidacy,
Ruskin had decided that Rossetti must join the Old Water-colour Society.
'Consider what good you may effect by the influence of your work,' he
wrote. 'So pray do this. Write to Lewis instantly, saying you accept.' To the
Society's winter exhibition he would lend his *Beatrice*, Combe his *Dante*,
Morris his *Blue Closet*; 'and there we are, all right'.[41]

'I don't know what to do,' Gabriel told Allingham. Membership would
undoubtedly help sell his work, but might kill his name as an oil painter, for
like portraiture, watercolour was a second-rank genre. He had higher
ambitions and did not apply.

Though still lacking facility of handling, his command of form and colour
was growing into assurance. Of the qualities that make an exceptional artist,
Rossetti had that profound originality which is not factitious or opportun-
istic, coupled with absorption in his own ideas and a certain fearlessness.
Sensitive to criticism, he was not thereby made timid. 'He taught me to have
no fear or shame of my own ideas,' Ned repeated; 'and this not in any
words I can remember, but in the tenor of his conversation always and in
the spirit of everything he said.' And, added Ned: 'Everything was ready for
the making of a glorious creature – the perfect hunger for romance that was

spread abroad in the world at the time when he came into it, the mingling of blood in him, his own admiration and discrimination for all that was splendid, his surroundings and the things he was brought up among; the people of all sorts of cultivation that he must have known from his earliest days – never was anyone so started, so ready for a great career.'[42]

Throughout his life, Rossetti was repeatedly drawn to join and form homosocial groups which in both emotional and artistic terms evidently answered a deep need not for disciples but companionship. By their nature, such groups were temporary – each member having an individual route to pursue – and indeed Gabriel would not have liked it otherwise, since his desire for association was matched by an equal impulse for singularity; what others did was always what he could not emulate. As always, internal pressures conflicted.

CHAPTER TEN

An Old Song Ended

When Lizzie returned from Bath she took lodgings in Hampstead, not far across the fields from the Browns in Kentish Town. The next crisis came at the end of February.

Brown had revived the old idea of an artist 'college', with separate apartments and studios but shared common room and dining hall. Hearing that Lizzie had not been consulted, he called one evening, finding her mother and Gabriel with her at Eland House, to outline the idea. He explained that he and Hunt intended to initiate the plan, as two married couples, followed by Ned and Topsy. When he left, a great row erupted. The details are unclear, but it seems Lizzie was angered on many fronts: at not being consulted, at Gabriel's silence regarding the vexed issue of marriage, and at the thought of living in close proximity to Hunt and Annie.

'My dear Brown,' wrote Gabriel the next morning, 'when you first spoke on Tuesday evening of two married couples as beginning the scheme, I thought you meant Lizzy and me for the second; and, on finding you did not, I refrained from saying anything, simply because Lizzy has sometimes lately shown so much displeasure on my mentioning our engagement (which I have hoped was attributable to illness) that I could not tell how far her mother was aware of it, or how Lizzy would take my mentioning it before her . . .' Surely Brown should have spoken to him first? especially as he had 'expressly said' he and Lizzie would be married by the time the plan came about.

'She now says that she understood only a range of studios, and would strongly object to living where Hunt was, of which objection of hers I had no idea to any such extent,' he added. 'I have myself wished to keep him and her apart hitherto, as I do not think he has acted lately as a friend towards me in her regard, but that feeling would have left me once we were married. However, my wishes as to this scheme would entirely depend on hers, supposing that it would really affect her happiness; in which case I should cease to care for it or think of it. As it is, she seemed last night quite embittered and estranged from me on this account, whether for the moment or permanently I cannot yet tell, and it has made me most unhappy ever since, more so than anything else could make me.'[1]

Though Brown immediately accepted this explanation, it was almost certainly partial. Plainly, Gabriel had not told Lizzie they would be among the early occupants of the proposed 'college'. If she were bitter when he spoke of their 'engagement', this was probably because it was never mentioned in front of her mother. Hunt's offence towards Gabriel in her regard can only be guessed at: had Holman alerted Lizzie to last year's flirtation with Annie? In any event, the whole letter reeks of sophistry. If Rossetti were as desperately unhappy when they quarrelled as he claimed, the remedy lay in his hands.

After two days' cajoling, things were smoothed over once more. Gabriel warned Brown to keep out of the affair. 'This will be the best way of avoiding further difficulty. Will you tell Emma this in case you showed her my letter.' If Lizzie broached the subject, however, would Brown persuade her that Gabriel was not to blame. 'I cannot trouble her about it or feel any anger at her, only constant pain at her sufferings,' he wrote. 'Kind and patient she has been with me many and many times, more than I have deserved; and I trust this trouble is over. It is but too natural that her mind should be anxious and disturbed . . . PS. Will you burn my former letter, or at any rate not leave it about.'[2]

Once again, he claimed to be ready to marry, settling the matter the next evening with Brown and a few days later borrowing ten pounds for the marriage licence. But then he 'somehow' spent it all, on other things. 'Of course I am very glad to lend it him but he has quite lost her affection through his extraordinary proceedings,' wrote Brown, exasperated, noting also that between them Gabriel and Miss Sid owed him forty-two pounds.[3]

Meanwhile, Lizzie refused to see Gabriel. When the Browns walked over to Hampstead, she roundly abused him. Brown then collected Gabriel from Blackfriars while Emma went to let Lizzie know they were coming. 'But on getting there she would not see him nor me,' recorded Brown in his diary. 'At length I was admitted but could obtain no favourable speech from her and so Gabriel and I came away again leaving Emma. Gabriel in a sad state.'

But not too upset to go to his Thursday class at the Working Men's College and attend a meeting at which Maurice spouted and Ruskin jawed. The next morning, a note came saying Lizzie would now see him. He and Brown set off for Kentish Town, Gabriel wishing to take every hansom they saw. Then he and Emma went over to Hampstead, Brown joining them for supper – after which there was an 'unrepeatable scene' of recrimination.[4]

No wonder Brown was baffled. 'He does not know his own mind for one day,' he wrote. However, Gabriel was winning, for as Brown noted

Lizzie seemed to be relenting. In this respect, her angry despair is the clearest evidence against sexual intimacy, since this would have enabled her to shame him into matrimony. Surprising though it seems, in his twenties Rossetti resisted passionate urges, or sublimated them in Dantesque and Malorian fantasies. Like many of his generation, he half-believed that carnal desire was the fount of all sin, debasing man's higher nature.

By mid-April normal relations had been restored. At Easter, Gabriel was invited to the reconsecration of Llandaff Cathedral, followed by lunch at Bishop Ollivant's and a visit to Henry Bruce's home near Aberdare. Although he quite forgot this was the weekend of baby Arthur's baptism (where he was to be godfather) as usual he presumed on Brown's forgiveness. 'Will you tell Dear Guggum if you see her, that my first journey on Monday, after reaching town, will be to Hampstead, if I am able to get there before the Working Men's College hour,' he added; 'if not, on Tuesday day time I trust.'5

As in life so in art: the simultaneous attraction to and repulsion from marriage was played out in his work this spring. As well as the chivalric watercolours for Morris, he was at work on a *St Catherine* in oils for Ruskin, which is a picture not of the saint herself but of a costumed model, with martyr's wheel and palm, posing for a medieval-ish artist at his easel. Behind, a boy munches on a sandwich while holding up her velvet gown, and studio assistants work on a study of St Sebastian. Though sumptuously coloured, the picture's harsh lines and rough paint make it hard to like, while the composition seems deliberately, even aggressively, unappealing. This is partly due to its hasty qualities: with more work, the forms might have been pulled into harmony. But Rossetti's artistic hallmark of the intense, magnetic gaze or embrace between figures is missing. The painter looks at his canvas while the model gazes at nothing. Although facing each other locked into a small picture space, they occupy separate fields, divided by the long vertical line of the easel, and both are ignored by the background figures. Since the St Catherine model is drawn from Lizzie and Rossetti was of course a painter, the formal division here could easily figure as a visual metaphor for that between themselves. The analogy should not be taken further, but with hindsight one might suggest that Lizzie was being broken on the wheel of Gabriel's indecision.

In *The Wedding of St George*, the marriage theme is explicit. The couple are in a close embrace, while the dragon lies dead. Two angels ring the wedding bell, the white marriage bed is ready. Still in armour, St George is seated, holding his helmet to which Princess Sabra ties a tress of hair which she is in the act of cutting – indistinctly but surely symbolic of the conjugal act to follow. Her coronet forms a circlet of desire directly above the couple and George's great sword is in its black scabbard. On the walls hang

Dürer's accessory details, an almost cabbalistic signature forming vertical, triangular and circular strokes.

'One of the grandest things, like a dim golden dream,' wrote James Smetham on seeing the picture. All green, red and gold, with 'a sense of secret enclosure in "palace chambers far apart"; but quaint chambers in quaint palaces where angels creep in through sliding panel doors, and stand behind rows of flowers . . .'[6] The mood however is indecipherable rather than joyous, and between the couple and the bed stands a low wall covered with roses and a high diagonal bar, visually blocking access to the chamber beyond.

A similar stroke is visible in *The Tune of Seven Towers*, in which a pair of medieval lovers sit gazing inwardly, not at each other. Originally a square composition containing two figures in great oak chairs like those at Red Lion Square, this acquired extra space on either side, for a sorrowful attendant and a maid laying orange blossom on a marriage-bed. Again, both central theme and accessories offer a wedding image. Then, diagonally across the whole picture comes a long lance, as if cancelling the scene. The woman is playing music but the mood is of melancholy, not harmony. The man looks especially unhappy.

Finally, from this period, is a scene of Hamlet and Ophelia, showing the moment when their betrothal is cancelled. She redelivers his gifts of remembrance, while, as Norton wrote, 'he strips the leaves from a rose tree as he breaks her heart'.[7]

Produced at the time when Rossetti was under most pressure to fully commit himself, these works appear to express acute ambivalence, both desiring and resisting. His conduct was the same. No wonder Lizzie was enraged and despairing. For, as she probably understood well, he who is not wholeheartedly in favour of marriage is in fact against it.

Aesthetically, these works are among the most acclaimed in his whole career, for their formal qualities of colour and line as well as emotional power. Refusing narrative and easy sentiment, tones and forms build up abstract patterns that intersect with figurative images. Singled out by Roger Fry, champion of Post-Impressionism, they gestured towards the path British art so sadly failed to take. Small in scale, their intensity draws the viewer into their visual field, as into an enchanted world.

Morris wrote an aptly melancholy poem to *The Tune of Seven Towers*, but Ruskin was not pleased with *St Catherine*. 'I was put out to-day, as you must have seen, for I can't hide it when I am vexed,' he wrote. 'I don't at all like my picture now.' Catherine's cheek was a quarter of a yard too thin and the whole figure 'quite stiff and stupid'. If anyone else would buy the picture, Rossetti should let them have it, and do something more pleasing.

Or could he let Ruskin have the watercolour of Mary Magdalene just completed for Mr Marshall, which he much preferred?

Sulkily, Rossetti offered to repay the advance payment in cash. 'I don't want the money a bit,' countered Ruskin, in similar vein. 'You are a conceited monkey, thinking your pictures right when I tell you positively they are wrong. What do *you* know about the matter, I should like to know? You'll find out in six months what an absurdity that "St Catherine" is.'[8]

The debt stood over and the picture sold instead to Liverpool collector John Miller, whom Rossetti had met in January. Priced at 50 guineas for Ruskin, when Miller sold it at Christie's a year later, it went to Gambart for 45 guineas despite its supposed flaws.

This year, thanks to Brown, the idea of an independent Pre-Raphaelite exhibition finally got off the ground, in hired rooms at Russell Place, Fitzroy Square. Brown showed twelve works. Hunt, whose big *Saviour in the Temple* was regularly delayed by immediate needs, showed three small pictures and photos of his Tennyson designs. Millais, who sent as usual to the RA, contributed two small pictures and two portraits – a generous gesture of fellowship for one who had no need of mutual support. Lizzie, whose exhibition debut this was, sent three watercolours, two ink drawings and her self-portrait. Other exhibitors included Boyce, Collins, Hughes, Inchbold, Halliday, Martineau, Scott, Windus, Lowes Dickinson, the late Tom Seddon, and a new acquaintance, John Brett.[9]

Rossetti borrowed back *Dante's Dream* from Ellen Heaton, *Dante drawing an Angel* from the Combes, *Hesterna Rosa* from Fred Stephens, *Mary Nazarene* and *Mary Magdalene* from Marshall and *The Blue Closet* from Morris. He hung his Llandaff colour sketch, and the photographed Tennyson blocks. Moxon's edition was just published.

It was a reasonable showing and critics were curious, for in seven years Rossetti had, as Millais noted, gained an immense reputation with little to be seen for it. Formally untitled, the show was taken as 'a PreRaphaelite Exhibition, perhaps the germ of more important self-assertions and reprisals' according to the *Athenaeum*, as if expecting further warfare in the battle of the styles, and an overt attack on the Academy. Millais was called 'chief of the sect'; Hunt the apostle of the order; and Rossetti 'the original founder of the three-lettered race, who is generally spoken of by them in a low voice, and is supposed from the fertility of his allegorical sketches to be capable of doing anything, though he does not and will not exhibit in public.'

To the *Saturday Review*, the 'somewhat numerous contributions of

DGR, *Self-Portrait*, 1847

ABOVE DGR, *Frances Rossetti*, 1854
RIGHT DGR, *Gabriele Rossetti*, 1853

ABOVE DGR, *William Michael Rossetti*, 1853
RIGHT DGR, *Christina Rossetti*, 1866

ABOVE DGR, *Ford Madox Brown*, 1852

CENTRE William Holman Hunt, *Dante Gabriel Rossetti*, 1853

BELOW William Holman Hunt, *John Everett Millais*, 1853

ABOVE John Everett Millais, *William Holman Hunt*, 1853

BELOW William Allingham in the 1850s

LEFT DGR, *Retro me Sathana!* 1848

ABOVE DGR, *Dante drawing an angel on the anniversary of Beatrice's death,* 1849. Dante has the features of John Everett Millais, to whom the drawing was given.

FACING PAGE DGR, *Ecce Ancilla Domini!* 1850

DGR, '*Down behind the hidden village*': sketch of a gathering at James Hannay's lodging, contained in a letter to Walter Deverell, August 1851. Of the identifiable figures, Holman Hunt reclines on the left, DGR stands in front of the mirror, Hannay is seated extreme right. The central figure is the American writer Buchanan Read, reciting his own work, from which the quotation is drawn.

DGR, *Sitting to Elizabeth Siddal*, 1853

DGR, *The Maids of Elfen-Mere*,
woodcut from William Allingham's *The
Music Master*, 1855

DGR, *Elizabeth Siddal*,
1854, drawn at Hastings

Detail from J. R. Spencer Stanhope, *Thoughts of the Past*, 1858, showing view of river from Blackfriars.

DGR, study for *Found*, 1853

DGR, sketch for *Bocca Baciata*, in letter to George Boyce, 1859

DGR, *Fanny Cornforth with George Boyce at the easel*, 1858. Drawing made by Rossetti in Boyce's studio off the Strand. The portrait on the wall is that of actress Ruth Herbert, who also sat for Rossetti at this time.

TOP LEFT DGR, *Robert Browning*, 1855

ABOVE James McNeill Whistler, 1860s

LEFT Edward Burne-Jones and William Morris, 1874

BELOW LEFT Algernon Charles Swinburne

BELOW John Ruskin, 1863

Mr Gabriel Rossetti unquestionably constituted the main interest', since 'strange to say' his name had become known through work seen only by friends, or friends of friends. It revealed profundity of thought, tender feeling, ascetic severity, grave rapture, stern and deep pathos, with a use of colour that was simultaneously natural and symbolic. A truly poetic art, unlike any other. The *Athenaeum* agreed, with qualifications. 'His designs in this exhibition are mystic ones, full of thought and imagination,' it wrote, but they were also dangerously slight.[10] Sketches in watercolour, as opposed to full-size oils, were day-dreams compared to reality.

To some, however, day-dreams were more appealing than reality. One new recruit to the cause was sixteen-year-old Simeon Solomon, a student at the RA Schools whose imagination and draughtsmanship were already attracting attention. Within a few months, Solomon would produce a distinctly *Germ*-like drawing of Chiaro dell'Erma and the vision of his soul, and be numbered among Rossetti's disciples.[11]

Ruskin left the Russell Place exhibition abruptly on seeing a portrait of his ex-wife, and in his critical survey of the RA show, he launched a fierce attack on Millais's latest works. 'As it is possible to stoop to victory, it is also possible to climb to defeat,' he wrote; 'and I see with consternation that it was not the Parnassian rock which Mr Millais was ascending, but the Tarpeian.' The change, from the years of "Ophelia" and "Mariana", to 1857 'is not merely Fall – it is Catastrophe; not merely a loss of power, but a reversal of principle: his excellence has been effaced, "as a man wipeth a dish – wiping it and turning it upside down".'[12] Although Millais remained popular and successful, the tide of critical esteem was ebbing. And while Hunt enjoyed serious attention, to his chagrin this year when he applied for election to the RA, he received just one vote. In this context Rossetti had every reason to be pleased with his own position, even if so far his was largely *un succès d'estime*.

Charles Norton, briefly back in London, reviewed the Russell Place show, bought Lizzie's *Clerk Saunders* and commissioned from Gabriel a portrait of Ruskin and a watercolour of the artist's choice. (Later, at Harvard, students complained he let them study nothing but Pre-Raphaelitism – giving them the same knowledge of art as a caterpillar had of geography.) Currently involved in launching the *Atlantic Monthly*, he requested poetic contributions. Rossetti sent a poem – probably *Love's Nocturn* – but with other manuscripts this went astray in transit and was never used.[13]

His fame was spreading. Earlier this year a Newcastle industrialist known to Scott had inquired if he might purchase something (caustically, William remarked that he might have a long wait). Gabriel's Moxon illustrations were talked about ('Tennyson loathes mine,' he informed Hunt, though the following year the poet and his wife told William they liked *King Arthur* as well as any other in the volume.) Linton had an exciting proposal for an illustrated edition of both Brownings, while Gabriel thought of pictures for a reprint of Charles Wells's *Stories after Nature*. Nothing came of either proposal, but there was no shortage of things to do.

Morris was in Oxford painting *Tristram and Iseult*. (Someone with Rossetti's sense of humour gave it the mocking title 'Sudden Indisposition of Sir Tristram in the Garden of King Mark's Palace, recognisable as Collywobbles by the pile of gooseberry skins beside him, remains of unripe gooseberries devoured by him while waiting for Yseult.') Despite other commitments and lack of time, Gabriel decided on a holiday. 'Shouldn't I like to come to Oxford – and ain't I seedy!' he wrote. Then, suddenly, Ned reported, Gabriel and Topsy were 'full of a scheme' to which all else gave precedence.' As well as the museum, Woodward had designed a debating hall for the students' Union Society; the large bays above the gallery were 'hungry to be filled with pictures – Gabriel equally hungry to fill them, and the pictures were to be from the Morte d'Arthur, so willed our master.'[14]

The university was on vacation. All London responsibilities were postponed. 'What do you think I and two friends of mine are doing here? Painting pictures nine feet high with life-size figures, on the walls of the Union Society's new room,' Rossetti wrote early in August to Barbara Smith, who in Algeria had met a French doctor and was now Madame Bodichon. 'The work goes very fast and is the finest fun possible.'[15]

There were ten panels. Other artists were being recruited, to do a wall each. They were not paid – this was their gift to the seat of learning – but the Union Society authorised funds for materials, lodging and travel, together with refreshing supplies of soda water. A man was employed to mix colours and sweep up. Hunt dared not leave his work, and Brown was in worse straits, desperately short of money and grieving for baby Arthur who had suddenly sickened and died. But Ned and Morris were followed by Arthur Hughes and new acquaintances Spencer Stanhope, J. Hungerford Pollen and young Valentine Prinsep, besides Alex Munro, to carve the tympanum Rossetti had designed for a doorway.

Val was the son of Thoby and Sara Prinsep, to whose home, Little Holland House in west London, Gabriel had taken Ned barely a month before, to meet their resident genius, G. F. Watts, with whom nineteen-year-old Val studied. A decade earlier, Rossetti had noted Watts's designs for the Palace of Westminster. Next to himself, Watts was now the most visionary painter in London, full of high idealism and poetic feeling; indeed, recently Ruskin had identified Rossetti and Watts as founders of the 'new and noble school' he hoped for in British art. Currently Watts was painting a large fresco for Lincoln's Inn, on the theme of Justice. Rossetti was impressed, and eager to emulate such a prestigious project.

Arriving at Oxford, Val went to the High Street lodgings as directed, to find the assembled company, Rossetti wearing his familiar plum-coloured frock-coat with its deep pockets for books of verse. Dinner over, Gabriel, humming in his usual manner, curled up on the sofa. ' "Top," he said, "read us one of your grinds." "No, Gabriel," answered Morris, "you have heard them all." "Never mind," said Rossetti, "here's Prinsep who has never heard them, and besides, they are devilish good." ' Forty years later the scene was still vivid in Val's mind: Rossetti with his large dark eyes fixed on Morris, Morris reading at the table, fidgeting with his watch-chain, Ned scratching at a pen-and-ink drawing while the words rolled:

> Gold on her head and gold on her feet,
> And gold where the hems of her kirtle meet,
> And a golden girdle round my sweet;
> *Ah, qu'elle est belle La Marguerite.*

With Rossetti's encouragement, Morris sent four of his 'grinds' to the publisher Alexander Macmillan, to see on what terms the verses could be published.[16]

They had a wonderful summer. Among his boyish companions, Gabriel felt rejuvenated. Ned told Georgie that at eight each morning he and Topsy were roused by Rossetti and Pollen, shouting out insults and pulling off the blankets. In the Union, sometimes Pollen feared for his wits amid the constant rattle of banter and startling opinions, though at other times he and Rossetti painted on quietly together, by gaslight.[17] Once, the others were startled by a bellowing from below when Morris got his head locked inside the helmet he had ordered from a local blacksmith together with a chainmail surcoat. Another time, Rossetti teasingly sent Morris out to ask an innkeeper's daughter to sit, laughing when he was rebuffed. In the evenings, they joked, played cards, read poetry, arm-wrestled, and tried to evade invitations from Dr Acland, who was kind but *boring*, and for whom one had to dress. Once, when yet another invitation arrived, Gabriel swept Ned into a cab. They caught the London train and returned in the morning. 'We were back in Oxford by nine and at work again – and it was all his idea,' said Ned; 'and I thought – this man could lead armies and destroy empires if he liked; how good it is to be with him.'

'It is really very jolly work in itself, but really one is mad to do such things,' Gabriel told Brown. As the weeks passed, visitors came and went. Charley Faulkner and Crom Price, student friends of Ned and Topsy, were followed by Edwin Hatch, Birkbeck Hill and Algernon Swinburne, an odd, carrot-haired boy of wild poetic enthusiasms, son of a baronet. 'We have unearthed a new poet who is charming,' Rossetti wrote to Morris, briefly in Manchester for this year's celebrated Art Treasures exhibition.[18]

Out in the real world, Britain was learning, week by appalling week, of the terrible carnage exacted by the insurrection of sepoy troops in India. British officers, their wives, children and servants were besieged, captured, killed. In Oxford the fun continued. 'Rossetti was the planet around whom we revolved,' wrote Val; 'we copied his very way of speaking. All beautiful women were "stunners" with us. Wombats were the most delightful of God's creatures. Medievalism was our *beau idéal* and we sank our individuality in the strong personality of our adored Gabriel.' Term started, but the painters showed no disposition to depart. 'I wonder what other set of artists would work so hard for nothing, except fair fame and love of art,' wrote Hill to a friend. 'Munro tells me that if Rossetti had given all the time to small pictures that he has to his large one here, he would have made a thousand guineas.'[19]

For all the high spirits, the scheme had serious intent, catastrophically undermined by haste and insouciance. They knew full well that mural painting requires a smooth, dry, carefully-prepared surface, yet the Union walls consisted of raw, whitewashed bricks and mortar, rough-ridged, damp and insecure. 'But we began with enthusiasm, and repented, if we repented, afterwards,' wrote Ned. 'At any rate we had no misgivings, and when Gabriel willed a thing it had to be done.'

A second problem was that each bay was pierced by two windows, around which the composition had to be drawn. Tripartite schemes naturally suggested themselves. Spencer Stanhope, for example, chose Sir Gawain meeting three ladies at the fountain, placing Gawain to the right, one lady in the centre and two to the left. In a strong, well-articulated image despite his youth, Val Prinsep positioned Sir Pelleas between Ettarde and Nimue, while Morris depicted Sir Palomides watching Tristram and Iseult.

Rossetti chose scenes from the Holy Grail, making notes of five possible subjects from Malory. The first showed Lancelot failing on the threshold. 'He has fallen asleep before the shrine full of angels, and between him and it, rises in his dream the image of Guenevere, cause of all. She stands gazing at him with her arms extended in the branches of an apple tree.' He started a companion poem called *God's Graal*. 'Lancelot lay before the shrine ... There was set Christ's very sign / the bread unknown and the unknown wine / that the soul's life for a livelihood / craves ...' Who else in the world could have designed that image, embodying Lancelot's passion in the figure of the Queen in the Tree of Temptation, with Eve's apple in her hand? asked Ned wonderingly, years later.[20] A second image would show the

Grail attained by the spotless Galahad together with Sir Bors and Sir Percival.

Today, the murals are decayed almost beyond assessment, but nevertheless show Rossetti's confident transition to the large scale and his successful handling of a high, awkwardly-shaped area. In the first, the tripartite space is filled by the Grail Angel on the left and Guenevere in the centre, directing the viewer towards Lancelot asleep on the right, the whole held together by the Queen's outstretched arms. The second composition, never executed, was to deploy a line of figures, as the three knights approach the Grail, with a reinforcing frieze of angels. In their horizontal dispositions both designs are comparable to *Dante's Dream* and *Dante drawing an Angel*, conceived on a far more intimate scale. That both large and small succeed suggests that Rossetti was not mistaken in his ambitions.

The moral message of his subjects also contributes to their underlying seriousness of purpose. Not merely a quaint text, the *Morte d'Arthur* was an appropriate source for a mural scheme in more than one respect. For, thanks largely to the Queen and Consort, English chivalry had become the secular equivalent of scripture, reinvented for the Victorian age. In church, school, armed forces and fiction, medieval knighthood was regularly invoked as the Englishman's ideal, featuring in visual depictions of the nation just as the Augustan age invoked the imagery of classical Rome. Almost the first major works of art Gabriel had seen were the Palace of Westminster designs – Maclise's *The Spirit of Chivalry* and Dyce's 'Order of the Garter'. The latter was to show the Companions of the Round Table as personifications of certain moral qualities and choose for representation 'such adventures of Arthur and his knights as best exemplified the ... qualities which make up the ancient idea of chivalric greatness'.[21] Still in progress, Dyce's seven frescoes therefore celebrated courage, mercy, hospitality, generosity, religion, courtesy and fidelity. Currently, Tennyson was also adding morality to romance in the *Idylls of the King*, endorsing the masculine ideal through the Arthurian myth:

> To ride abroad redressing human wrongs,
> To speak no slander, no, nor listen to it,
> To honour his own word as if his God's,
> To lead sweet lives in purest chastity.
>
> . . .
>
> Not only to keep down the base in man
> But teach high thought, and amiable words,
> And courtliness, and the desire of fame
> And love of truth, and all that makes a man ...

Swinburne satirically called Tennyson's epic the Morte d'Albert, but what more appropriate subject for the young knights of Oxford, going out into the world as defenders of Queen and country, leaders of men and seekers after honour? The Oxford University Union was indeed a junior version of Parliament, where future ministers debated the affairs of the nation. Such historical, heroical parallels were much in fashion.

The young painters were more drawn to the Romance aspects. Ned liked the tales of enchantment – Merlin, Nimue, Morgan le Fay. Morris liked those of tragic, unrequited love. Gabriel was divided between the two heroes Lancelot and Galahad. In Malory they all liked the passion and toughness, for the most part free of moralism. Yet their images, and Rossetti's in particular, none the less endorse Victorian pieties. Lancelot fails to reach the Grail owing to his sinful love for Guenevere. Galahad is granted the vision by virtue of his purity. The Victorian hero is chaste and courageous, honourable and valiant.

Like the devil, however, Lancelot has all the best exploits. The third Malorian scene Rossetti chose was that of Lancelot surprised in the Queen's chamber by a posse of knights intent on killing him for treachery to his liege lord. 'Alas,' says Guenevere as they hammer on the door, 'now we are mischieved both.' Rossetti drew this scene in meticulous pen and ink. Morris put it into verse, as the unfaithful Queen challenges her accusers in *The Defence of Guenevere*. This summer, Flaubert's *Madame Bovary*, with its scandalous tale of an adulterous wife, was prosecuted for obscenity in France. In Britain, with the rest of the nation, the painters followed the sensational trial of young Madeline Smith, charged with poisoning her lover when a more prosperous marriage beckoned. Her beauty, according to Gabriel and his companions, was enough to save Madeline from the gallows. 'Oh, you wouldn't hang a stunner!' they chorused as Hill ventured a more conventional verdict.[22]

As the vacation came to a close, they moved to new lodgings in George Street. Crom Price's diary records that on 17 October Coventry Patmore came to see the murals, and the next day Rossetti was drawing the tall muscular Val as St George, squashed awkwardly into a medieval basket-chair, for a watercolour thirteen inches square. From the monumental to the miniature again.

Two or three weeks earlier, Gabriel had found the model whose dark colouring is given to Princess Sabra. Towards the end of the vacation, the Drury Lane theatre company presented a season of popular plays for the people of Oxford. One evening Gabriel and Ned were in the audience, when Rossetti's roving eye caught a tall girl sitting with her sister in the little gallery. He spoke, asking if she would come and sit. Not knowing what he meant, she agreed, but did not appear. Then Ned met her in the street, and went to speak to her mother. And thus Jane Burden was 'discovered' by the Pre-Raphaelites. Gabriel took her looks for the Princess, and drew her as Guenevere, head back, hands clasped at the throat. This was a departure, for the summer's talk had all been of stunners with golden hair like Madeline Smith. Val Prinsep was frankly surprised.

Seventeen years old, Jane lived in an alley off Holywell, opposite the Music Room. Her father worked in a nearby livery stable. She was poor, uneducated, speaking with a local burr, related to farmworkers on both sides of the family. Perhaps as a gift, or in payment, Rossetti drew her portrait as a pensive young woman, with neatly pinned hair, and inscribed it with her initials and age: 'J.B. AETAT XVII'. At the foot, he signed his own name: 'DGR Oxoniae primo delt. Oct 1857'. She didn't know Latin, but Oxford was full of such gnomic inscriptions. Later, he would design a bracelet which records their first meeting.[23]

And so Rossetti lingered on, unwilling to return to the work awaiting him in London. Hunt, Woolner and Madox Brown arrived, to see the murals, followed by Ruskin. Then without warning Gabriel was gone to join Lizzie in Derbyshire.[24] His walls at the Union – and Jane Burden – would have to wait until the next long vacation.

Lizzie had been staying in Sheffield, where her father came from. She attended his old chapel and took advantage of facilities at the local art school; joining their excursion to the Art Treasures exhibition in Manchester, she impressed the Sheffield contingent with her intimate knowledge of the Pre-Raphaelite circle, of which they had barely heard. Then she moved to Matlock, a small spa in the Peak District. When she wrote saying she was ill again, Gabriel hastened to her side.

They boarded at Lime Tree View, managed by Mr Cartledge high above the town at Matlock Bank. North-west ran picturesque Darley Dale, towards Bakewell and the great park of Chatsworth House, where the Duke of Devonshire had a magnificent collection of Old Masters and French furniture. Rossetti preferred Haddon Hall, whose flagged courtyard and medieval hall more nearly matched his conception of olden times. He seems to have relished the remoteness. For a week or so even the family were left ignorant of his address, until Ned forwarded Frances Rossetti's worries. There was not the least necessity for anxiety, Gabriel replied, without mentioning Lizzie, adding that he was in 'an interesting and beautiful part of the country'. The next day he sent his brother a familiar request for 'the loan of as many pounds as you can manage'. Repairs were in hand at Chatham Place, perhaps temporarily remitting the rent, yet board, lodging and laundry at Lime Tree View cost around half a guinea per person per week, not to speak of outings by rail and pony carriage. Did he perhaps Leeds, to offer Mr Plint his latest drawings. We know that Plint paid 80 guineas for *St George* and *Hamlet and Ophelia*.[25] A month later, Rossetti was able to repay Brown only three pounds of all he owed; creditors were pressing him on all sides.

He stayed in the North over Christmas, but early in the New Year returned briefly to London, where one evening there was a reunion at Red Lion Square. 'Come to-night and see the chair – there's a dear old fellow – such a chair!!!!' Ned urged Brown invitingly, promising 'victuals and squalor' and 'a stunner or two' making melody. 'Gabriel and Top hook it to-morrow, so do come …'[26] According to Georgie, the 'chair!!!!' had a cupboard above like those in his watercolour *Tune of Seven Towers*, in which Gabriel whimsically suggested owls might be kept. Perhaps inspired by Georgie's singing from *Échos du Temps Passé*, his next picture, *The Christmas Carol*, shows a fair-haired stunner fingering a portable clavichord. As she plays a seasonal tune, two more medieval women comb her improbably long hair. Her gown is red, theirs Gabriel's favourite green, the wall behind a deep blue. When he saw this image, Swinburne began a poem for it, echoing medieval carols:

> They held the gold combs out from her
>   A span's length off her head;
> She sang this song of God's mother
>   And of her bearing-bed.
>   Mary most full of grace,
>   Bring us to thy son's face.

'Greensleeves is my heart of gold' ran another olden song, traditionally attributed to Henry VIII. Gabriel began another chivalric watercolour, showing a Lizzie-like woman tying her green sleeves to a knight's helm. Then came *Before the Battle* in which 'a castleful of ladies' embroider banners that are fastened to knights' lances by the châtelaine, a tall, red-gowned figure. Below and behind, other women spin, card and weave, as in medieval depictions of textile arts. Long masculine lances and banners crowd the sides; the knights are riding out to war. Later, Rossetti excused *Before the Battle* as 'ultra-medieval'. But for the moment, he explained, these 'Froissartian themes are quite a passion of mine'.[27]

The image could well be inspired by Haddon Hall and visions of armoured horsemen clattering over the paved yard. Lizzie's companion drawing of a lady helping a knight fix a pennon to his lance has the landscape background of moorland that certainly suggests Derbyshire. In Ned Jones's *Knight's Farewell* similar figures are ignored by a young squire, absorbed in the pages of *Roman du Quête du San Grail*.

Gabriel's protégés were spreading their wings. Through his recommendation Ned had been commissioned to design stained glass for Powells of Whitefriars. One window showed Christ carrying the lost sheep, which nibbles the leaves round his hat. 'A lovely idea, is it not?' Rossetti wrote persuasively.[28] Plint had agreed to extend patronage to both Ned and Topsy, while the latter had found a publisher for his Froissartian volume, *The Defence of Guenevere and Other Poems*. At New Year Gabriel learnt that Morris remained at Oxford, painting Jane Burden as Iseult. Soon, he would propose marriage. A long-standing oral tradition claims that Rossetti encouraged this match, 'to keep Jane within the circle'. But the chivalrous marriage surprised many. A wealthy man like Morris had his pick of brides; why then choose a stableman's daughter? 'The idea of his marrying her is insane. To kiss her feet is the utmost men should dream of doing,' commented Swinburne ambiguously on 17 February,[29] quoting Morris's own words for *la belle Marguerite*. Externally, Morris was unromantic – he would be such a bear with women, thought Mary Nicholson, housekeeper at Red Lion Square. Inside, he was all knight errant, born out of his due time. 'If I were rich I would kiss her feet, I would kiss the place where the gold hems meet.'

Rossetti drew a caricature of Topsy, short and stout, presenting a ring to Janey, tall and slender. It was the first of many such humorous scrawls, all edged. Warm as their fellowship was, something in Morris grated on Rossetti, 'who would have expired if he mightn't tease and be a little cruel', in Ned's view.[30]

Later, as Gabriel figured it, they were knights and squires, Jane a peasant girl who proved a queen. 'The young King of a country is hunting on a day with a young Knight when, feeling thirsty, he stops at a Forester's cottage, and the Forester's daughter brings him a cup of water to drink,' he wrote. 'Both of them are equally enamoured at once of her unequalled beauty. The King, however, has been affianced from boyhood to a princess worthy of all love, and whom he has always believed that he loved until undeceived by his new absorbing passion.' Pleading his own cause, the Knight goes again to the cottage, to learn that the girl has fallen in love with the King, not knowing his rank. 'Ultimately the King goes to the girl and pleads his friend's cause ...' Thus ran the fiction. In fact, Rossetti did not need to plead Morris's cause. Even if Jane had fixed her thoughts on king Gabriel – not the first to fall under his spell – she was far too poor to refuse any suitor. All else is hindsight.

When he returned to Matlock and Lizzie at the end of January 1858, Rossetti took the translations he had so long talked of publishing. Together with the *Vita Nuova*, the poems now numbered some hundreds. Editing and polishing appear to have been his chief tasks into early spring, for though he took his colour-box and brushes, there was no studio at Lime Tree View. Maybe he was spurred by Morris's characteristic energy, for Gabriel did not like to be outdone. Through February and March he worked intensively on the final copy for what was now called *Early Italian Poets from Ciullo d'Alcamo to Dante Alighieri*, selecting, rejecting, wrestling with obscure readings and disputed attributions.

His aim was 'a full and truthful view of early Italian poetry' for English-speaking readers to complement their emerging acquaintance with early Italian painting. 'To compensate for much that is incomplete and inexperienced, these poems possess, in their degree, beauties of a kind which can never again exist in art; and offer, besides, a treasure of grace and variety in the formation of their metres,' he explained in his preface. Moreover 'the life-blood of rhymed translation is this – that a good poem shall not be turned into a bad one.' Literality was not the same as fidelity. And yet a good poem should not be turned into a better, for 'the task of the translator (and with all humility be it spoken) is one of some self-denial':

> Often would he avail himself of any special grace of his own idiom and epoch, if only his will belonged to him; often would some cadence serve him but for his author's structure – some structure but for his author's cadence; often the beautiful turn of a stanza must be weakened to adopt some rhyme which will tally, and he sees the poet revelling in abundance of language where himself is scantily supplied. Now he would slight the matter for the music, and now the music for the matter; but no, he must deal to each alike. Sometimes, too, a flaw in the work galls him, and he would fain remove it, doing for the poet that which his age denied him; but no, – it is not in the bond. His path is like that of Aladdin through the enchanted vaults: many are the precious fruits and flowers which he must pass by unheeded in search of the lamp alone; happy if at last, when brought to light, it does not prove that his old lamp has been exchanged for a new one – glittering indeed to the eye, but scarcely of the same virtue nor with the same genius at its summons.

At times a coherent text seemed impossible. He toiled on, however, and in May asked Patmore for the address of a printer who would set the work in type, so it could be read by others. 'I have had to find out all that is to be found for myself in the course of a good many years,' he told Norton; 'and I really feel it to be worth doing, as they are an immense accession.'[31] In fact, as later scholars have shown, his preference for fidelity rather than literality led him in many cases to transfigure his originals, producing a new creation in place of a translation, while a good deal of the contemporary scholarship on which he relied has been shown to be erroneous. Nevertheless the achievement was significant, introducing readers to the otherwise inaccessible charms of the *dolce stil nuovo*, and setting in motion a number of literary ripples.

But as these Matlock weeks stretched into months, the real business was the ending of his engagement. Though Lizzie's image was in both his latest watercolours, Gabriel at last faced the fact that his love for her was over.

For nearly two years since her return from Nice, he had repeatedly denied this even while his behaviour proved it, unable to make the break which would leave her in an unenviable position, as a sickly woman of twenty-nine with no fortune. But if he could not in honour abandon her, nor could he honestly marry without love. 'A little while a little love May yet be ours who have not said The word it makes our eyes afraid To know that each is thinking of,' he wrote in verses of farewell, marking love's passing in cadences borrowed from an Italian *canzonetta*:

> So it is, my dear.
> All such things touch secret strings
> For heavy hearts to hear.
> So it is, my dear.
>
> Very like indeed:
> Sea and sky, afar, on high,
> Sand and strewn seaweed, –
> Very like indeed.
>
> But the sea stands spread
> As one wall with the flat skies,
> Where the lean black craft like flies
> Seem well-nigh stagnated,
> Soon to drop off dead.
>
> Seemed it so to us
> When I was thine and thou wast mine,
> And all these things were thus,
> But all our world in us?
>
> Could we be so now?
> Not if all beneath heaven's pall
> Lay dead but I and thou,
> Could we be so now!

These images came from the days at Hastings, where they had carved their initials on the rocks, in token of love everlasting.

'I did love you once,' says Hamlet to Ophelia in the scene Gabriel had chosen to depict ten months before. 'Indeed, my lord, you made me believe so,' she answers. 'You should not have believed me,' he counters cruelly. 'I loved you not.' In *An Old Song Ended*, Gabriel completed the verses of Ophelia's madness. Lizzie was angrier, if her lines express her own feelings:

> Turn thou away thy false dark eyes
> Nor gaze upon my face;
> Great love I bore thee: now great hate
> Sits firmly in its place.

'And what's the thing beneath the skies we two would most forget?' he asked in *A New Year's Burden*. 'The love once ours, but ours long hours ago' came the melancholy answer.

This is a period of Gabriel's life about which we know very little. Later, he would describe his time at Matlock as a 'solitary stay in the country of some length', as if Lizzie had not been there. Yet on another occasion he wrote that 'both Lizzie and I lodged at Matlock Bank, for nearly a year'. Whatever hard decisions were being faced, or deferred, he was not happy. 'Your "Shady Hill" is a tempting address, where one would wish to be,' he wrote to Norton in Massachusetts. 'It reminds one somehow of the *Pilgrim's Progress* where the pleasant names of Heavenly places really make you feel as if you could get there if the journey could be made in that very way – the pitfalls plain to the eye and all the wicked people with wicked names. I find no shady hill or vale, though, in these places or pursuits which I have to do with. It all seems glare and change, and nothing well done . . .'[32]

'If you don't know at twenty, you never will know', ran his father's Italian proverb. 'If you don't do at thirty, you never will do.' Leaving Lizzie at Lime Tree View, Gabriel went back to London for the RA and his birthday on 12 May, full of renewed resolution. 'I am 30 this year, and want to try if I am ever to begin anything,' he told Scotus.

He took his translations to printers in Tooks Court. Munro told Allingham that Gabriel's 'Book of Translations' was 'veritably being printed by Whittingham', and selected proofs were sent to Norton, Swinburne, Patmore and Ruskin, while William was entrusted with the *Vita Nuova*. The translations from Cavalcanti went to Macmillan, in hope of publication. 'Before showing it to anyone else I should like to know whether you would be willing to undertake it and on what terms,' he wrote, adding that the whole contents would fill 400 pages. Encouragingly, cautious Macmillan suggested two volumes, with preface and notes, and a preliminary opinion from experts in the field, so in due course the texts went also to Aurelio Saffi, professor of Italian at Oxford, and the French scholar de Circourt, with whom Elizabeth Gaskell acted as intermediary. Meanwhile, Rossetti inquired if Macmillan would bear the whole expense of production and in addition pay him 100 guineas? 'I need hardly say that the book has cost me more time and trouble than several hundred would repay were it painting instead of poetry.'[33]

Ready cash was a pressing requirement. For nearly a year he had effectively idled, at Oxford and Matlock Bank. Already in debt to Plint and Llandaff, he could not proceed with their commissions without selling other pieces. Ruskin had promised £70 for his second Arthurian scene at the Union during the coming vacation, but as the first was still unfinished, this would hardly serve. When the writer Robert Brough wanted an illustration for his latest poem, Rossetti forwarded the text to Hughes, saying he was 'mad with half done (and even some half paid for) work'. But he had prospective buyers in Charles Norton, in Ruskin's friend Lady Trevelyan, and in James Leathart, the Newcastle industrialist known to Scott. *A Christmas Carol* was accordingly earmarked for Leathart, and *Before the Battle* offered to Norton. 'I hope that in colour it is one of the best things I have done,' Gabriel wrote, peremptorily frank. 'Meanwhile, (to be thoroughly impudent, all things considered) may I beg your answer at once … and (worst of all, to be thoroughly sordid) may I beg without mincing, that you will consider this drawing or another as ready to be delivered at once on your decision, and that you will let me have with your answer to this letter, by return of post if possible, the amount of the commission (50 guineas if I am not mistaken) for, to tell you the truth, my Oxford labours of love have resulted in leaving me a little aground.'[34]

The triple parentheses in an already long sentence betray his doubts, though there is no sign that Norton regretted his purchase. Contemplating the productions of Rossetti and his 'clique' this year, Ruskin however began to repent of his promotion of Gothic, feeling personally responsible, as he told Watts, for 'a good deal of this fatal medievalism' with its 'stiffness and quaintness and intensity as opposed to classical grace and tranquillity'. In this, Gabriel was not the worst offender. 'Your people all live on love, and crimson and gold,' Ruskin told Morris in response to *The Defence of Guenevere*. 'Do you suppose that in the middle ages there were no heads fit for using as well as hearts, or that people couldn't think inside of helmets?' He was sufficiently vexed to accuse Morris of leading Rossetti astray: all the excitement about colour and hair, 'blood and murder and bones and pokes with lances' was 'inconsistent with good painter's work and proper business generally'.[35]

The letter came from the Continent where, this summer, Ruskin experienced the deconversion or disillusion with religious belief that would lead him from art towards social reform. But in any case this year's exhibitions demonstrated what an eccentric path the Red Lion Square artists were following with their Froissartian themes. At the RA the lead picture was Frith's panoramic *Derby Day*, a social microcosm of the nation. In works combining exquisite natural detail with social compassion, two other canvases featured present-day paupers breaking stones by the roadside. John Brett's *Stonebreaker* was a parish boy in full sunlight, while Henry Wallis's was an old man, dying at dusk where he sat, which attracted much praise.

Beside these modern subjects treated with gravity and skill, dragons, medieval knights and stiff-necked ladies – however rich in crimson and gold – appeared decorative and irrelevant. It was time to leave the dreams of twenty for the deeds of thirty. Rossetti turned to his oil commissions, Plint's *Magdalene* and the Llandaff altarpiece. 'I feel quite emancipated in getting to work of so large a size,' he told aunt Charlotte, promising to show her 'something considerable' when she next came to town. His choice of words was perhaps unconsciously revealing, for he was also 'emancipated' from an engagement that now seemed mistaken. The old song was ended: it was time for new tunes, new women, new experiences. *Qui a trenta non fa, mai non farà*. And he has been chaste too long.

CHAPTER ELEVEN

Placatâ Venere

'If you don't do at thirty . . .' Boldly, he asked Ruth Herbert for a sitting. 'I am in the stunning position this morning of expecting the actual visit, at ½ past 11, of a model whom I have been longing to paint for years,' Gabriel bragged to Scott at the end of May. Such luck, so I must finish and get my things in order.' Miss Herbert – 'rightly Mrs Crabbe, though she doesn't live with her husband', as Boyce carefully noted – was appearing at the Olympic Theatre in comedies and burlesques, applauded for refinement of demeanour combined with the risqué nature of her parts, including travesti roles. 'Ah! if I were Millais, I would paint her in my next picture in her pure white silk dress, if I were Munro I would carve a lovely medallion from her profile,' gushed the *Illustrated Times*.[1]

Being women who displayed their bodies in public, actresses occupied an anomalous social position, as this month's hottest gossip underlined. Now at the zenith of his fame, Charles Dickens had left his wife, infatuated with nineteen-year-old Nelly Ternan, who played at the Haymarket and Lyceum. Miss Herbert's private life was also scandalous: separated from her stockbroker husband, she and her son were set up by a wealthy admirer near Eaton Square, while various other gentlemen vied for her favours; within months she would be pregnant by John Rochfort, ex-army officer and amateur artist.

Rossetti wanted to to use her for sacred figures: Mary Magdalene and the Llandaff Virgin. Ruskin approved. 'I want you to get her beautiful face into your picture as soon as possible,' he wrote, regarding the altarpiece. In exchange for sittings, Rossetti offered a portrait, and a large head in watercolour was under way by mid-June. A dozen more studies are known, among them one with a large pointing finger and the word 'stunner'. 'Once we were shown a small watercolour made by Gabriel of her, radiant in golden hair,' recalled Georgie; '– just the head and throat on an emerald-green background – and deeply did we feel the tribute rendered to her beauty when we read the names which he had written around the four sides of the little picture: "BEATRICE HELEN GUENEVERE HERBERT".'[2]

This was a face. 'If one could have that little head of hers Painted upon a background of pure gold', began one of Browning's poems that Gabriel read to Boyce in May. Such flattery was evidently pleasing to Miss Herbert, who enjoyed studio life and frank artists' admiration. Some sittings apparently took place at her residence, where Rossetti was struck by her way of feeding a pet bullfinch with seed placed on her tongue, rosily peeping from between her lips. A careful drawing and a sonnet record the intimacy of the scene, as she turned to her visitor, blushing prettily.

'I never saw such men,' recalled Miss Herbert years later, of Rossetti, Watts and their circle; 'it was being in a new world to be with them. I sat to them and was there with them, and they were different to everyone else I ever saw. And I was a holy thing to them – I was a holy thing . . .'[3] Theatre audiences were apt to behave lewdly.

For her benefit performance on 12 July, Rossetti drummed up support. 'Do you not know some lovers of golden hair and the springs of Preraphaelitism who would like to assist?' he asked Sir John Simon. 'She is a brave girl fighting against injustice in & out of the theatre, and greatly needs help, and deserves the best she can get . . . At any rate it is my duty to try and enlist you, after her great kindness in sitting to me.' Inscribed 'for the Benefit of Miss Herbert' is a sketch of the actress facing a grotesque gentleman in tails – perhaps a fellow performer – and three admirers in the stalls, who include an unmistakable William Morris. 'Now do go and get every one to go,' Rossetti urged journalist Bob Brough.[4]

When she praised his drawing of 'a loving couple on a sea beach on a windy day', he produced a sweet, lively watercolour copy in which the breeze almost lifts the crinolined woman off her button-booted feet, as her escort draws her profile in the sand with his cane. Based on a drawing of himself and Lizzie, who had walked together on the beaches of Hastings and Clevedon, this reworking, in which Lizzie's features are replaced by those of a mimsy blonde, marked a silent closure to their long engagement, over which the waters now washed. It is called *Writing in the Sand*. Symbolically, Hamlet was parting with the tokens of his love for Ophelia.

Briefly, Gabriel returned to Lizzie in Matlock, where he sorted another batch of translations for Macmillan. He left again shortly before her twenty-ninth birthday on 25 July, going to Oxford, as if to restart work at the Union. Instead, he drew a large and careful half-length ink portrait of Jane Burden. Although Jane later confirmed that before her marriage Gabriel never 'made love' to her in conversation, it was none the less a provocative act, for Morris was in France with Philip Webb, planning his new marital home. On his return, Topsy was noticeably moody and less convivial, as if unconsciously apprehensive.[5]

In London the summer heat grew intense and the 'river stink' unbearable.

Ned being taken off to Kensington by Val's mother, Gabriel moved himself into Red Lion Square, sharing for a few weeks with Crom Price. Still seriously intent on returning to work and mindful of the Trevelyans' outstanding commission, he sent a message via Arthur Hughes, offering *Mary in the House of St John* after the Crucifixion. Pauline Trevelyan replied positively. An early admirer of the PRB, she and her Casaubon-like husband were old friends of Ruskin and for their country house in Northumberland had commissioned work from several artists, including Scott, Hughes and Munro. In the *House of St John*, as Rossetti explained, the Virgin is 'standing in the embrasure of a deep window, at the coming on of twilight, and rising from her work to trim the lamp, suspended in the centre of the cross-frame of the window', so as to form a visual echo of the Holy Cross.[6] Laying aside the gospel he is writing, St John kindles tinder to provide a flame, symbolic of the Resurrection, as in the accompanying text: 'a little while and ye shall not see me, and again a little while and ye shall see me.'

The result was 'a beautiful solemn purple drawing', with what Simeon Solomon described as a forceful impression of intense repose after strife. The figures are finely grouped, their heads and hands within a circle edged by the high-arched window, balanced by diagonal lines of tension. Though cloaked and hooded, the Virgin clearly has Ruth Herbert's delicate profile. Behind her, the window gives on to a dusky view of Jerusalem.

Seeing the work in progress, Lady Trevelyan echoed Ruskin in finding it grand and deep, and thankfully not in the eccentric manner of the medieval watercolours ('very chivalrous and fine once in a way,' she told Scott, 'but not what one wants to see him spending years of his life upon'). Though Sir Walter had reservations regarding 'Pre-Raphaelite extravagance', they agreed to pay the asking price of 100 guineas,[7] and also that a replica be made for Miss Heaton, to whom the subject had been originally promised. She, presumably, could wait.

Rossetti's new sense of purpose was underlined in September by his sending works to the Liverpool Academy, the premier provincial exhibition, where so many new patrons were to be found. Ellen Heaton lent *Dante's Dream* and Plint *The Wedding of St George*, to hang alongside the *Christmas Carol*, priced at 80 guineas. (Leathart, just married, had declined the purchase.) It did not sell, but the venture marks a new departure.

At Chatham Place, Spencer Stanhope now occupied the apartment immediately below. With studies and an elaborate ink design, Rossetti worked on Plint's *Mary Magdalene*. 'The scene represents two houses opposite each other, one of which is that of Simon the Pharisee, where Christ and Simon, with other guests, are seated at table,' he explained later. 'In the opposite house a great banquet is held, and feasters are trooping to it dressed in cloth of gold and crowned in flowers. The musicians play at the door, and each couple kiss as they enter.' Suddenly stricken, Mary Magdalene turns away, tearing the roses from her hair, as her paramour tries to stop her. Boyce described it as Mary Magdalene jeered at by a lot of gay women – the current term for harlots – as she crosses to the house of Jesus, 'who is looking earnestly and absorbingly at her'. A beggar girl sits on the step, eating broken meats. 'A fawn crops the vine below Christ's window, and some fowls gather to share the beggar girl's dinner, giving a kind of equivalent to His words: "Yet the dogs under the table eat of the children's crumbs." '8

The elaboration of this image was typical of Rossetti's methods of work, as he grew increasingly absorbed. Compositionally, it is indebted to Dürer's 'Christ before the People' from the *Grand Passion*. Thematically, the scriptural subject is also linked to Hunt's *Awakening Conscience*, and thence to other images of contemporary social concern. To church-going Victorians, Mary Magdalene was the type of the repentant sinner, a notorious loose woman whom Christ forgave, saying, 'Her sins, which are many, are forgiven: for she loveth much.' Like the *House of St John*, it was a deeply serious work. The Magdalene has Ruth Herbert's features, Christ those of Burne-Jones. The Magdalene's figure was drawn from 'a strapping Scandinavian', a woman of the streets who humourously referred to Ned as 'Herr Jesus'.

Simultaneously, work was under way on the Llandaff triptych. Although John Seddon politely reminded Rossetti that the contract was for the centrepiece first, the side panels only when funds permitted, and though Frances Rossetti supplied a mother and baby, painting proceeded not on the *Adoration* but on *David Rex*, whose head was drawn from Morris. Gabriel hoped to exhibit it at the Hogarth Club in January. While he had been in Matlock, previous ideas for an independent salon had metamorphosed into an association. 'Some half dozen of our friends, with myself, are contemplating the formation of a club, chiefly artistic, with a non-artistic minority, for the purpose of social intercourse,' William informed Scott. At the club, members' works would be hung, for exhibition to fellow members, friends and patrons. 'We propose to limit the number of members to about 50; the names of 43 have definitely been proposed.'9 Guests could come by invitation only.

The name of Hogarth paid tribute to a famous British painter who, unlike Reynolds, was not identified with the RA, for the club was aimed chiefly at non-Academicians. To many, it appeared a Pre-Raphaelite enterprise, like the Russell Place show. At the inaugural meeting on 10 April, Brown, Jones, William Rossetti, and Spencer Stanhope formed the managing committee, with Fred Stephens as Honorary Secretary. Others present included Woolner, Boyce, Wallis, Hughes, Morris, and

W. S. Burton, with a similar muster on 4 May in Red Lion Square. Gabriel joined when he returned to town later the same month.

Though select, membership was relatively wide. Several Liverpool painters joined, grateful for the advantage of exhibition space in central London. Architects G. E. Street and G. F. Bodley were members, alongside Martineau, Prinsep, Jack Tupper, Inchbold, Pollen and Fred Leighton. 'Non-artistic' and honorary members included Ruskin, John Miller, Henry Bruce, Thomas Plint, Major Gillum (a friend of Browning), the Marquess of Lothian, Swinburne, Richard Monckton Milnes and author George Meredith (whose wife had recently run off with Henry Wallis, which suggests some curious encounters or evasions at Hogarth viewings). No women were proposed or invited. They would have benefited artistically from a congenial exhibition and meeting place, but their presence would have precluded the easygoing clubland atmosphere, where fellows could congregate after work, without ceremony. In addition, there were monthly meetings, weekly soirées and open days when female guests might be brought.

The first Hogarth exhibition, at 178 Piccadilly, was scheduled for the end of the year. Rossetti sent *Mary in the House of St John*, the old *To Caper Nimbly* refashioned as a Borgia subject, and a watercolour *Annunciation* from 1855, showing Mary washing clothes in a stream, which belonged to Boyce. Seeing this last picture, Plint spoke admiringly, in characteristic Yorkshire brogue stumblingly rendered by Prinsep, who was also present. ' "Nobbut Mr Rossetti, that's a fine scene," he said. "But couldn't you put a soonset floosh over the whole thing?" ' Gabriel responded with histrionic indignation, saying that with such views, Mr Plint should never be allowed to purchase anything. To Val's surprise, Plint was 'contrite and apologetic and in no way offended'.[10] Such was Gabriel's style, imperious and disarming.

'News, what news can I give you?' wrote Hughes to Allingham in December. 'Rossetti of course first, he's doing an immense *tryptych* (is that spelt right?) for Llandaff Cathedral – just beginning – it's awfully jolly – and also a big "Jesus & Mary Magdalene" – also awfully jolly; has actually tidied up his room and hung his drawings on the wall, which seems almost too good a joke, but truth is sometimes as strange as fiction, and so it *is*.'[11]

'If you don't do at thirty, you never will do.' We do not know where Lizzie was now living.

One day a few weeks later, Rossetti was about to set off for the Zoo, to draw the fawn who features in *Mary Magdalene*, when a visitor called, asking if he might see the William Blake notebook. The caller's identity is unknown, but he was a corn chandler by trade and his diary account of the meeting and consequent conversations in cabs in pursuit of the manuscript offers a vivid snapshot of Rossetti at thirty as he appeared to a stranger. Still slight in build, with now-receding hair, his eyes retained their dark circles and changeable moods. On this day, he proved generous, impulsive, opinionated. Pleased to meet a fellow enthusiast, he spoke of Blake as 'a man of genius – great, but there was no doubt he was wild or mad in certain respects'. The notebook was with his brother, he added, offering to take the visitor to Albany Street to collect it. In the cab, however, he countermanded the direction, saying the book was probably at Somerset House. 'Driver made some blunder in driving to the wrong doors, which caused Rossetti to expostulate, called the said driver stupid etc.'[12]

When it turned out that William had lent the notebook to a friend, the cab proceeded towards Regent's Park. En route, the corn chandler remarked on the decline of Art – the standard post-Raphael view that had prevailed in Gabriel's student days – regretting the transfer of patronage from the nobility to the manufacturing class. No, this was no injury but benefit to art, returned Rossetti; modern collections were more disinterestedly made. Nor were the arts in decline: had Blake had the opportunities for study now available, he would have been a far better painter. His companion demurred: Blake had all the Old Masters as instructors, just as if he lived today. Of course, Rossetti rejoined, he did not mean that the present age had the genius of the past, nor its powers of execution, but 'it possessed a far better knowledge of the principles of painting ... that with the exception of a few men of genius, since before Michelangelo nothing had been done worthy of the name of art – the principles were thoroughly wrong.'

Wrong? queried the corn chandler; surely all artists had the same nature to refer to? Michelangelo studied from the Greeks, replied Rossetti. And where did the Greeks get their knowledge of form? Oh, there was no trace of their paintings, only statuary, 'in short what I mean is there is more common sense in Arts in the present day'. They arrived at their destination, and if the recorded conversation is not entirely lucid it gives a flavour of Gabriel's style and views. Driving back to Red Lion Square, his companion got out at the British Museum. Altogether, he noted, Mr Rossetti's ready manner and remarks savoured more of the Corn Exchange than the studio.

Open, direct, down to earth: this was one side of Gabriel Rossetti. If his friends sometimes saw moodiness, he could equally be bluff and hearty. It was ten years since the boyish dreams of the PRB and Chiaro dell'Erma. If his soul remained Romantic, his outward manner had a distinct touch of the downright Englishman. When in 1859 a great Militia Movement was raised in response to fears of French aggression, he therefore volunteered to serve alongside Morris, Hunt, Millais, Leighton and Woolner, all of whom donned grey-and-silver uniforms and took part in military drills. 'DGR and Ned Jones have entered the Rifle Corps. Isn't that a lark?' Swinburne told Scott.[13] In the event, Gabriel's enthusiasm waned even more rapidly than the threat of an invasion, but his participation confirms that aspect of his character that endorsed conventional, masculine, patriotic pursuits.

Yet he was now thirty and to all intents a virgin. His latest religious images confirmed his reputation as a painter of sacred subjects. Personally, he was no coenobite with an ascetic horror of the world, but nor was he a libertine. As a young man, he had avoided irregular relationships like that of James Hannay. Sexual desire had not been sufficient to draw him into marriage, alongside Millais, Hughes and others of his generation. Whatever his natural urges, he was able to withstand temptation, rather than accept either self-disgust or marital responsibilities for the sake of sexual experience.

It has been so common to paint Rossetti as a lusty philanderer, living and sleeping with Lizzie in bohemian squalor, seducing Annie Miller in order to annoy Holman Hunt, and generally bedding all available models, that his celibacy requires more explanation. Yet he was not unique, for others in his circle, like William, Hunt, Allingham and Stephens, also remained chaste through their twenties, under the combined influence of morality and prudence.

Celibacy and matrimony were not the only alternatives; the artists were familiar with the recognised mode for irregular liaisons. William Frith kept a secret family round the corner from his legitimate one, while Augustus Egg had a mistress who was not introduced to friends even after they married. Closer to the PRB were the Collins brothers – Charley who in 1856 was involved in 'a disreputable kind of secret connection', and Wilkie who the same year set up with the young widow who inspired his *Woman in White*. Rossetti did not condemn, but refrained from following their lead, even though – despite her much-vaunted respectability – Lizzie was of the class that such 'kept women' came from. Her unconventional conduct – unchaperoned modelling, sharing lodgings and so on – suggests she was not afraid of sexual indiscretion; indeed, the freedom of her behaviour may indicate willingness in this regard, which was a traditional means of hastening a wedding. Her sister Lydia, for example, was four months pregnant when she married in 1860.

Gabriel thus seems to have been sexually cautious, despite the many moments in London, Paris and Derbyshire when it must have looked as if he and Lizzie were enjoying what the age termed 'conjugal relations'. Nor is there evidence of more casual liaisons, with servant girls or street walkers. Millais, who was himself a creature of impulse, conjectured that the reason Hunt was 'able to be so long virtuous' was that before doing anything 'he always held a sort of little council with himself,' to debate the matter. This was not Rossetti's habit, yet Val Prinsep, who this year accompanied him to dubious places like the Coal Hole and Cave of Harmony, knew him to be essentially chaste, if also unshockable. Despite limited experience, Georgie Macdonald was also confident that Gabriel, Topsy and her own Ned were 'as good as they were gifted', and unlike the usual run of men. 'The mystery which shrouds men and women from each other in youth was sacred to each of them,' she wrote.[14]

As a child of his time, and more particularly of a high-minded mother, Rossetti held an idealised view of love and a distaste for lust as a matter of masculine appetite. When his poems were attacked for sensuality, he protested vehemently that *au contraire* 'all the passionate and just delights of the body are declared ... to be as naught if not ennobled by the concurrence of the soul at all times'.[15] Sex without love was insupportable. At the same time, however, even sex with love was unmentionable in polite society and, especially, in mixed company. In art and literature, couples might embrace only. Within marriage, the considerate husband refrained from penetrative sex as often as possible. It was therefore difficult to bring romantic and physical desire together. The gap between body and soul was barely bridgeable.

But as Rossetti returned to London, having ended the engagement that kept sex on hold for so long, and turned from medieval fantasies to rejoin the world of men, he was aroused as he had been in Paris a decade before. Not exactly overnight, but very markedly, puritanism was on retreat in a city that now seemed dedicated to pleasure, hedonism, sexual freedom. Acquaintance with Ruth Herbert, a woman who was neither virginal nor vulgar but well aware of her own attractions, made him conscious that physical desire need not be idealised or sordid, but merely mutual.

'As when desire, long darkling, dawns,' he would write in a sonnet called *Bridal Birth*:

> Even so my Lady stood at gaze and smiled
> When her soul knew at length the Love it nurs'd.
> Born with her life, creature of poignant thirst
>   And exquisite hunger, at her heart Love lay
>   Quickening in darkness, till a voice that day
> Cried on him, and the bonds of birth were burst ...

'Bridal' was a way of saying 'sexual'. In the sestet, Love is full-grown 'and his warm hands our couch prepare ...'

Times were changing. Young men and women – servants, shop assistants, clerks, gents and 'swells' – were ignoring the moral prescriptions of their elders. They had money to spend and London's West End to entertain them – theatres, supper rooms, drinking and dancing venues: the Holborn casino, the Alhambra in Leicester Square, the Argyll Rooms in Windmill Street. In summer there were 'night gardens' like Cremorne, with music, dancing, casual encounters, fireworks, Christy minstrels, circus acts. There were the first music-halls, whose sudden rise and immense popularity was due, in Arthur Munby's opinion, to the free-and-easy atmosphere combined with a certain pretence of refinement. 'The amusements are agreeably varied,' he wrote; 'your real taste is gratified by nigger songs and acrobats; and beween whiles "operatic selections" put you for the time on a level with your betters and please your vanity. Besides, you are not compelled to sit silent and cramped as at a theatre or a concert: you drink and smoke pipes alongside your woman or wife, and chat and "chaff" to your heart's content.'[16] And all for sixpence a seat.

For fellows with the means to a tail-coat, the gentleman's garb, there were smoking rooms and 'cigar divans' where newspapers might be read and a discreet visit paid 'upstairs'. In theatres and streets, in the Strand, Haymarket and Regent Street, well-dressed gay women sought a 'friend' for the evening with whom to drink and dance as well as retire.

Rossetti began to explore, often taking young Val with him. 'There was seldom a day in which I did not see Rossetti,' wrote Prinsep of this period. 'We often dined together at the Old Cock or at Dick's or at John of Groat's in Rupert Street.'[17] Or they went to an eating-house behind the Alhambra before going on to one of the 'many now happily obsolete exhibitions' known as *poses plastiques* in Leicester Square, where they sat in the so-called green room with the girls in figure-revealing flesh-coloured tops and tights, sipping negus supplied by Rossetti ostensibly in exchange for a pose, though no Degas-like drawings have survived. Or they went to the Piccadilly Saloon, which opened at 2 a.m. and 'where ladies and gentlemen wildly and, I regret to say, generally tipsily, danced to the music of an old piano and a fiddle'. Every so often the alarm was raised, a man rushed in, waving a dirty napkin, the piano was shut up, the fiddle stowed away, and when the police inspector appeared the ladies and gentlemen were quietly conversing together.

Despite this, Val insisted, DGR was not 'fast' or dissolute. 'All three of these friends were the chastest of men,' he wrote. On his rare visits to such places, Ned fell asleep, while Morris showed no desire to 'see life' in this manner. Chaste as may be, however, Gabriel exhibited a perverse desire to see everything. A decade before, with Hannay and Charley Ware, he had dipped his toes into London's shadows. Now he was for full immersion.

With his 'healthy English education', Val was a boyishly energetic sportsman who took lessons from champion boxers. One evening they went to a benefit bout in the Rotunda Theatre across the river in Blackfriars Road. As a precaution, they left their watches and money behind, but as toffs were ushered to ringside seats. 'It was a wonderful sight to see Rossetti sitting among a lot of sporting "bungs",' recalled Val. 'He watched the sparring with his melancholy Italian eyes, humming to himself as was his habit', while each pair fought three rounds. One of the boxers was black. When he retired to his corner, 'he threw himself back on the chair and, while he was being fanned, turned up his eyes in quiet enjoyment of the cooling breeze. Suddenly I heard Rossetti's voice echoing through the house. "Look. What a lark! Uncle Tom aspiring to Heaven!" The whole house rose with cheers . . .'

One evening in the autumn of 1858, in the Strand or the Royal Surrey pleasure gardens, Gabriel spoke to a prostitute who was cracking nuts and flicked the shells in his direction. She had fine features, a wealth of corn-coloured hair and winningly bold manners. A veritable stunner, she was at once invited back to the studio, to pose, as she recalled, for the fallen woman in 'his calf picture'. And thence into his bed.

'As when the last of the paid joys of love Has come and gone,' Rossetti wrote in a graphic description of sexual intercourse:

> and with one laugh of satiate bliss
> The wearied man one minute rests above
> The wearied woman, no more urged to move
> In those long throes of longing, till they glide
> Now lightlier clasped, each to the other's side,
> In joys past acting, not past dreaming of . . .

Startlingly, the coital image was then used as a metaphor for the French army's self-interested liberation of northern Italy, but the displacement is transparent, and the sonnet goes on to allude to the 'bought body' of a 'loveless whore'. As Swinburne later confirmed, the 'fornicative' lines were written simply through DGR's wish to do into verse 'the animal sensation' of copulation, the political metaphor being 'an afterthought'. This thus records his first, overwhelming, sexual experience. The manuscript is dated 1859, and the whore in question had lodgings in Soho. She called herself Fanny Cornforth.[18] The calf picture was the unfinished *Found*, whose subject would bring him back to mainstream themes of social concern. Suddenly, her presence was everywhere in his art.

Venal, vulgar, prettily pouting, Fanny was fun. On 15 December, returning to town, Boyce called at Chatham Place to see Gabriel's new works. 'We went off at dusk and dined at the Cock, and afterwards adjourned to 24 Dean St, Soho, to see "Fanny",' he recorded in his diary. 'Interesting face and jolly hair and engaging disposition.' The next day he saw her again, sitting to Stanhope, who was copying Rossetti in depicting a fallen woman 'in two phases of her life'. Afterwards Fanny 'went up to Rossetti' and Boyce followed.

Boyce's quotation marks indicate that 'Fanny' was an assumed name, recently adopted; later she called it her 'art name'. She was really Sarah Cox, and on the Census return gave her place of birth as Steyning, near Arundel in Sussex, where, it has been said, her father was a blacksmith, though this is doubtful. She was twenty-four.

A month later Boyce ran into Fanny in the Argyll Rooms and took her to dinner. 'She was in considerable trepidation lest Rossetti should come in – and lo! he did so.' By now, the two men were in mock rivalry for her favours. In February they helped her furnish a new home near Waterloo station, a move which suggests that Fanny left Soho lodgings shared with other street girls for a place of her own; like Ruth Herbert's grander abode, this was partly paid for by her 'admirers', of whom Rossetti must have been the principal.

As so often under pressure of strong emotion, he composed a sonnet, entitled *Placatâ Venere*, which means 'Venus appeased', or 'lust satisfied'.

> So their lips drew asunder with fierce smart:
>> And as the last slow sudden drops are shed
>> From sparkling eaves when all the storm has fled,
> So singly flagged the pulses of each heart.
> Then their close bosoms sundered at one start,
>> As when a flower bursts open on its bed
>> From the knit stem; yet still their mouths, burnt red,
> Chirped at each other where they lay apart.

The lovers drift into post-coital sleep, dreaming of waters, woods and streams. The imagery was startlingly vivid. This was not a poem to be printed. William admired it, only thinking mouths chirping was 'a shade too graphic'.[19]

Thenceforth Fanny was in and out of the studios, at Chatham Place and elsewhere. On 2 March, she was in Prinsep's painting room hard by Lincoln's Inn, where Rossetti made two quick sketches. Another time she was at Boyce's in Buckingham Street, where Rossetti drew her leaning with arms clasped round Boyce's neck as he sat at his easel, in an eloquent image of easy informality. On 24 March the two men escorted her to the Zoo, and on 2 April they took tea at her lodgings. Greedily, Rossetti drew and painted her – as Princess Parisadé from the *Arabian Nights* for Ruskin, as a blue-gowned serving-woman in *The Bower Garden* for Plint, and as one of Beatrice's attendants, on the doors of the great Red Lion Square settle, now destined for the Morrises' new home in Kent.[20] Their marriage took place quietly in Oxford in April and though it has sometimes been alleged that Rossetti avoided the occasion, the truth is that neither Morris's family nor his London friends were present. After a honeymoon tour of Belgium the new couple rented rooms not far from Red Lion Square. On the settle doors, Beatrice was given Jane's features, but it is unlikely that she was introduced to Fanny.

Unmentionable though it was, prostitution was everywhere discussed. The 'great social evil' of the time was said to be undermining the fabric of society, destroying the family, polluting the streets. Streetwalkers should be cleared from the West End. Refuges offered rescue and rehabilitation. The churches were especially active in reclamation; at this very season, Gabriel's own sister Christina became a voluntary worker at the St Mary Magdalene Penitentiary for Fallen Women in Highgate. Future Prime Minister William Gladstone walked out late in the evenings, to persuade prostitutes to abandon their vicious ways. Men of the world demurred. This spring, shortly after inviting Rossetti to breakfast with some literary coves, the shy young lawyer Arthur Munby, who taught Latin at the Working Men's College, recorded a long conversation on the topical subject of 'repressing street vice'. He himself spoke in favour of 'the unmolested streetwalker, provided she be sober, well-dressed and not too importunate', while his friend John Ormsby observed that the so-called clearance of the Haymarket had simply moved women into a large and flourishing underworld of 'secret dens and night haunts' all over the West End.[21]

Rossetti was relaxed about his relationship with Fanny, feeling no need to keep her hidden from his male friends. He teased and bantered with her for, though her speech was 'common' and her grammar faulty, she was not dull; indeed, she was uninhibited in a frank, amusing manner. Puncturing pomposity, she made him laugh, keeping his bearish moods at bay. She loved food and flattery and could always be cajoled by a small gift. Above all he was grateful for her generous, undemanding sexuality, which measured affection in terms of treats and aspired only to the security of being set up by a nice gentleman. It may also have pleased his quirky sense of humour to have a 'mistress' who was a demonstrable whore. For her part, it may be inferred that Fanny lost her heart: whatever her previous history, she had never known anyone like 'Mr Rizetty'.

The moral complications sent him back to *Jenny*, drafted ten years before when the theme had been theoretical, a boastful boy's gesture towards worldliness. Now the fictional figure had become a real woman.

The poem's development was considerable, as it grew to nearly 400 lines. Still in the form of a dramatic monologue by the man on whose knee the eponymous woman has laid her sleepy head, it became a meditation on sexual sin and blame. The central images of the fallen woman as trampled blossom, carnal experience as a book to be read, lust as a toad within a stone, were retained, some passages repeated verbatim. But now was introduced the 'framework of incident' whereby a studious man, seeking relaxation, has sought entertainment in London's night-life and ended up in Jenny's room. As she dozes – grateful, as he supposes, that this client is neither drunk nor violent – he silently soliloquises on her physical attractions, mental degradation and the larger issues: society's scorn, the culpability of men, the whole urban traffic in women, the shame and the blame. Introduced too is the narrator's virtuous yet lively cousin Nell. Two sister vessels – two women – 'so pure – so fall'n!' – an unspeakable conjunction.

And yet why so scorned, so outcast, so damned? 'How atone, Great God, for this which man has done?' Thus discussed, Jenny becomes a cipher for a social problem, a semiotic sign of male 'lust, past, present and to come', a riddle from which the poet/narrator shrinks. So dawn breaks in Jenny's room where the lamp has burned all night. On this occasion, the bed is unused, though the narrator pays anyway. Slipping cushions under her head and scattering coins in her golden hair, he quietly leaves, acknowledging the complexity of sexual desire and commerce, from the carriage-borne courtesans in Hyde Park to the heights of classical culture, where sculpted images of Venus excite the appetite:

> Aye, or let offerings nicely plac'd
> But hide Priapus to the waist,
> And whoso looks on him shall see
> An eligible deity.

For a poetic instant, the coins in Jenny's hair turn her into Danae's equal, and their sound is ironically a pledge of affection:

> Jenny, my love rang true! for still
> Love at first sight is vague, until
> That tinkling makes him audible.

> And I must mock you to the last,
> Ashamed of my own shame – aghast
> Because some thoughts not born amiss
> Rose at a poor fair face like this?
> Well, of such thoughts so much I know:
> In my life, as in hers, they show,
> By a far gleam which I may near,

A dark path I can strive to clear.

Only one kiss. Good-bye, my dear.

Gabriel was well pleased with his poem – 'which I reckon the most serious thing I have written'.[22] Obliquely, it was a meditation on the hedonistic life he and others were currently leading. With its mixture of colloquial language, social comment, philosophical inquiry, sensuous imagery and modern sensibility, it addressed current issues in an innovative manner. Neither salacious nor censorious, it delved into the Browningesque ambiguity of the subject, brought its characters vividly to life, and reached a contemporary conclusion – the difficulty of clearing a path amid such complexities.

He wanted to send it, with other pieces, to the new *Cornhill Magazine* that Thackeray was editing for Ruskin's publisher. Once, Ruskin had believed that like art, poetry should eschew sordid subjects and aim at 'the suggestion, by the imagination, of noble grounds for the noble emotions'. However, since the overturning of his religious faith by Veronese's *Queen of Sheba*, he was now apt to assert that morality and art did not mix. 'To be a first-rate painter *you mustn't* be pious; but rather a little wicked, and entirely a man of the world,' he told Norton.[23] If he said the same to Rossetti, small wonder he was offered this newly-wrought poem, to forward to Thackeray.

'I have read *Jenny*,' Ruskin replied, eventually. But he could not commend it. The narrator was 'anomalous', he wrote; 'he reasons and feels entirely like a just and wise man, yet is occasionally drunk and brutal – no affection for the girl shows itself – his throwing the money into her hair is disorderly, altogether disorderly. The right feeling is unnatural in him and does not therefore truly touch us. I don't mean that an entirely right-minded person never keeps a mistress – but if he does, he either loves her, or not loving her would blame himself – no less than for her – in such a moralizing fit.'[24]

Furthermore, the versification was faulty and unmelodious. 'Fail' did not rhyme with 'Belle' nor 'Jenny' with 'guinea', he added pompously. 'You can write perfect verses if you choose and should never write imperfect ones.'

In literary matters, Ruskin's conversion to worldliness was limited, like his tastes; he admired Longfellow, and in *Modern Painters IV* had poured scorn on most modern efforts, saying it was far better to study poems of the past than to encumber the world with new, inevitably poorer ones. But he also misconceived *Jenny*'s purpose, which was not to create narrative or character, but to explore and contest the puritan/Puseyite equation of sexual desire with sin and damnation, the traditional conflict between body and soul, the tension between sexual love and lust. The very Victorian fear of man's 'higher nature' being degraded by 'animal instincts'. The problem of reconciling romantic love with conjugal congress. For an artist, the virtual impossibility of depicting such matters except in the most false, veiled manner. Or, clandestinely, in the explicitly pornographic print or sketch. No man about town was ignorant of indecent French photographs, ostensibly produced to assist artists. Only lately, Ruskin had helped the National Gallery burn a great quantity of 'grossly obscene drawings' by Turner, which perhaps tempered his enthusiasm for worldly wickedness.

'Say, is it day, is it dusk in thy bower, / Thou whom I long for, who longest for me?' opened Rossetti's next poem, a lightly disguised ode to sexual arousal, with swinging rhythms and rising pulses:

> What were my prize, could I enter thy bower,
>   This day, to-morrow, at eve or at morn?
> Large lovely arms and a neck like a tower,
>   Bosom then heaving that now lies forlorn.
> Kindled with love-breath, (the sun's kiss is colder!)
>   Thy sweetness all near me, so distant to-day;
> My hand round thy neck and thy hand on my shoulder
>   My mouth to thy mouth as the world melts away.

'Bower' was commonly used to signify 'bed' and hence consummation. Erotically transposed, verbs and adjectives carry the sense. And yet the poem holds back from the bower, deterred by 'waters engulfing or fires that devour'. Sex equals drowning or burning, corruption, pestilence, hell:

> Nay, but in day-dreams, for terror, for pity,
>   The trees wave their heads with an omen to tell;
> Nay, but in night-dreams throughout the dark city,
>   The hours, clashed together, lose count in the bell.

In the end, *The Song of the Bower* is a poem of severance, repudiation, sexual refusal. The speaker does not enter the woman, while yet yearning to do so.

Arthur Munby, whose secret life was with a strapping housemaid, fetishised strong arms scrubbing doorsteps and pans. In time, Rossetti's pictorial art hymned 'large lovely arms', naked, elongated necks, full-lipped mouths and willowy fingers, agents of sexual pleasure in themselves but also figures for less mentionable organs. And in pictures and poems he idolised loose rippling hair. Elizabeth Gaskell, in London with her daughters in June 1859 for an intensive social round, renewed her acquaintance. 'I think we got to know Rossetti pretty well,' she told Norton. 'I went three times to his studio, and met him at two evening parties – where I had a good deal of talk with him, always excepting the times when ladies with beautiful hair came in when he was like the cat turned into a lady who jumped out of bed and ran after a mouse. It did not signify what we were talking about or how agreeable I was; if a particular kind of reddish brown, crepe wavy hair came in, he was away in a moment, struggling for an introduction to the owner of said head of hair. He is not as mad as a March hair, but hair-mad.'[25]

Ruskin had identified the same passion in Morris's poems, writing 'what a blessed book it is for hair-deifiers!' Presumably as well as any other man he understood the code by which women's hair signified sexuality. Normally, hair was covered or neatly braided and pinned. Only in the bedroom was it loose and long, and visible together with the body hair never otherwise depicted. Culturally, too, hair was symbolic of vanity and wantonness: unbraided hair signalled sexual abandon, looseness of morals as well as locks. One of the stories of Gabriel's meeting with Fanny tells how he purposely dislodged her hair, so that it fell to her shoulders in a provocatively intimate gesture.

His next move was to paint Fanny as a Renaissance courtesan in a style indebted to Titian, taking as his text a quotation from bawdy Boccaccio, cited by Shelley as words that might cure a male prude: 'The mouth that has been kissed loses not its freshness; still it renews itself as doth the moon'. *Bocca baciata*, the mouth kissed by many men, is an apt figure for a whore. As if to underline the connection, one manuscript of *The Song of the Bower* is given 'Bocca Baciata' as its title.

In her full youthful beauty, Fanny was a fine subject. Even tight-laced William, who in later life disliked her, scrupulously insisted on her loveliness, sweet features and wealth of harvest-coloured hair. Boyce agreed to buy the picture for £40, a price suggesting that Rossetti did not regard it as saleable to the usual patrons. A pencil study of Fanny dated 23 July marks the date of the agreement.[26]

She herself was not the sole stimulus. At this year's Royal Academy, much attention was paid to a sequence of pictures by Leighton showing a Roman beauty with glossy dark hair, turning her head to engage the spectator. Identified only as La Nana, her 'backward yet proud look' was worthy of Lucretia Borgia, wrote Stephens in the *Athenaeum*. The same show also held Watts's dreamy half-length portrait *Isabella*, hailed by *The Times* as a 'masterpiece of the tenderer harmonies of blonde colouring', where nature was idealised without sacrifice of truth, and a perfect likeness was 'accompanied by something which we never saw in the face till the painter revealed its presence'.[27] In their different ways, both were an implicit challenge to all who aimed to blend beauty and feeling with a masterly touch.

During August and September, while most of the artists were out of town, Rossetti applied himself to *Bocca Baciata*, putting more work into it than he at first intended partly because his current unfamiliarity with oils led him to abandon the first version, painted with too much copal. But when Boyce returned to London in October the picture was ready for collection. It had a distinctly Venetian aspect, the figure shown half-length surrounded by flowers. 'Them be'inds merrygoes, as the fair original might say, in her striking rendering of the word marygolds,' he explained, mimicking Fanny's accent.[28] Ambiguously, in the language of flowers marigolds were held to signify grief and tears.

Rossetti had begun collecting fine fabrics, fringed and embroidered Indian, Chinese and Italian silks, velvets, damasks, satins. In *Bocca Baciata* the figure wears a late-sixteenth-century costume, the bodice unbuttoned. Her abundant hair is loosely fastened, with an ornament and a white rose, in a manner that would become a hallmark. She rests her delicately-gloved hands on a parapet, and beside them is Eve's apple, the ancient symbol of carnal temptation. It is only a small work, suitable for a gentleman's private room.

Creating this image excited him, partly because of its sexual element and partly because it was a new departure. Though Ruth Herbert came again to sit, *Mary Magdalene* was laid aside, apparently because Plint was now in financial difficulties and hesitating over the large commission. In compensation, James Leathart, who had finally purchased the *Christmas Carol* and ordered a watercolour of *Sir Galahad* based on the Tennyson block, was persuaded to take *Found*, for 350 guineas. Persuasion was needed: the subject was indelicate. 'The sainted Leathart seems to project giving me a larger commission, but after all funks the calf picture for the usual reason,' Gabriel reported to Scott on 1 November. Shortly after, however, the commission was in the bag. Fanny's head, mantle and gown were laid on the canvas. Though she told Boyce that Gabriel habitually sat up 'in a large chair o'nights', reading Balzac, it was a busy season.

Then Annie Miller reappeared, upset and anxious. Hunt had finally relinquished all ideas of marriage, and withdrawn her allowance. She wanted to model, 'determined on sitting again in preference to doing anything else'. Gallantly, Boyce employed her. 'Rossetti came in and made a pencil study of her. She looked more beautiful than ever,' he noted.[29] A competition for her sittings followed, in which Gabriel was the natural winner: more than once in the New Year, Boyce found that his arrangements with Annie had been usurped. 'Dear Boyce, Blow *you*, Annie is coming to *me* tomorrow. I'm sure you won't mind, like a good chap', began one typical message. 'Will you write to her again for another day. She would hardly consent to ill-using you in this style, but I bored her till she did.' Once, when Annie was sitting to Boyce, Rossetti dropped by towards dusk, to collect her for the evening. So Fanny was not Rossetti's only companion this winter.

New acquaintances included solicitor J. Anderson Rose; surgeon John Marshall, a good friend of Brown; painters James Smetham, Henry Holiday and Frederick Sandys; and literary lawyer John Skelton, who came regularly to London from Scotland and habitually called in the late afternoon, for a city walk and supper. Then, if they did not go to a play, they would knock up E.S. Dallas of *The Times*, for a game of whist. 'Rossetti liked a rubber,' Skelton recalled, 'though he was a poor player and rather addicted to abstruse speculations on the reasons which had induced him to play the wrong card . . .'[30]

From Oxford, the Union Society requested completion of the Arthurian cycle, but though the London artists expressed willingness, no action was taken, and in the end the Society employed another man to fill the remaining spaces with his own designs. 'I have not seen them, but I hear they are wonderful exceedingly,' wrote Rossetti, evidently thankful. In the studio, work proceeded on the Llandaff triptych. One naked infant model for the Saviour was 'squalling awfully' when Boyce called on 20 February. To the 1860 Hogarth exhibition, in new premises off Pall Mall, Rossetti sent three works, including the double panel of *Beatrice's Salutation* on the cupboard doors of the settle, still awaiting reassembly. Here, Beatrice's second attendant was drawn from Red Lion Mary, who had lamented that she was too plain and dumpy to be used as a model. Dear Mary, Gabriel is said to have said; she *shall* be in a picture. And so she was, 'much idealised and glorified, but decidedly Mary'. According to James Smetham, the Salutation in Paradise was glorious: 'The background is a rich rose hedge, with birds of paradise pecking roses . . . and singing birds singing lustily. There is a floor of tall buttercups, hyacinths and lilies . . .' on which Dante and Beatrice 'walk in knowledge, love and beauty evermore'.[31]

The second work at the Hogarth exhibition was a second Lucrezia. Having 'more than once' been asked if Boyce's little *Borgia* shown last year were for sale, Rossetti produced a sequel, showing Lucrezia washing her hands after poisoning her husband. In company with Ned and young Swinburne, who had been expelled from Oxford, he shared a fascination with evil, powerful women – witches and murderous queens, guilty of egregious crimes in which eroticism and cruelty met. Ned was painting Sidonia van Bork, anti-heroine of a cult classic by Meinhold for which Gabriel had a 'positive passion' in his early twenties, while Swinburne called Lucrezia his 'blessedest pet' and the Borgias his 'holy family'. Part-inspired by the portrait of Isabella d'Este at Hampton Court, with its elaborately-patterned costume, enclosed space and figures glimpsed in a room beyond, Gabriel's *Lucrezia* was an apt reversion to the 'medieval' mode, so Dürer's water cistern and brush made another appearance.

His main work at the Hogarth, however, was *Bocca Baciata*. 'A most beautiful head, a marigold background, so awfully lovely,' reported Hughes to Allingham, adding that Boyce 'will I expect kiss the dear thing's lips away before you come over to see it ...' According to Swinburne, who should have known, it was 'more stunning than can be decently expressed'. Because so many were loud in praise, Hunt was cautious. 'I shall be curious to hear your opinion,' he wrote to Thomas Combe. 'Most people admire it very much and speak to me of it as a triumph of our school. I have strong prejudices and may be influenced by them ...' In his view, if remarkably well-painted, the piece was virtually pornographic – 'still more remarkable for gross sensuality of a revolting kind', like an erotic print. Openly, it endorsed the principle of sensuous gratification – 'the animal passions as the aim of art'. Hunt would sooner give up art than paint thus.[32] It may be that knowledge of the model's relation to the artist coloured this reaction, though others' responses show that the image was generally seen as sensual and provocative, making explicit the new mood of sexual freedom.

In technical terms, the picture had taught Rossetti lessons in the difficult art of flesh-painting. Trying to avoid what he knew to be a 'besetting sin ... that of stippling on the flesh', he had worked rapidly, against his normal practice. As he told Ned, he still believed that pictures were 'all the better the longer they are in hand' but sometimes too many pains interfered with the true business of painting. 'I am sure that among the many botherations of a picture where design, drawing, expression, and colour have to be thought of all at once (and this, perhaps, in the focus of the four winds out of doors, or at any rate among somnolent models, ticklish draperies, and toppling lay figures) one can never do justice even to what faculty of mere painting may be in one,' he told Scott. 'Even among the old good painters, their portraits and simpler pictures are almost always their masterpieces for colour and execution, and I fancy if one kept this in view one must have a better chance of learning to paint at last.'[33]

The 1860 Hogarth Club exhibition thus marked a decisive moment in Rossetti's style and reputation. Simpler forms, broader treatment. Warm glowing colour. Less niggling and less narrative. 'Abandoning a style he had exhausted, he began a series of mature, expansive, coloristic works,' writes a recent commentator. Hunt had been in travail six years over *The Finding of the Saviour*, at last on public view. Once, Rossetti would have marvelled. Now he was so out of sympathy that he called it a 'sawdust picture' and a 'wooden puppet-show'. Following Ruskin, he preferred 'Veronese's flesh, blood and slight stupidity'; or even Millais, if Veronese were not to be had. It was half self-justification for altering direction. It certainly marked a parting of the ways. Gabriel had 'now completely changed his philosophy . . . leaving Stoicism for Epicureanism', wrote Hunt with barely concealed disdain. 'He executed heads of women of voluptuous nature with such richness of ornamental trapping and decoration that they were a surprise, coming from the hand which had hitherto indulged itself in austerities.'[34] *Bocca Baciata* was the first in the sequence of female images freighted with symbolic meaning that would in due course be described as 'Rossettian'.

In truth it was art that was changing, shifting with society towards visual pleasure, opulence, consumption, display for display's sake, almost in mimicry of the move from early Florentine piety to Venetian magnificence, as moral messages gave way to aesthetic beauties. As well as *Isabella*, Watts, whose avowed master was Titian, had produced a 'Venetian' portrait of Lady Somers, all crimson and purple. Leighton's beautiful Roman was entitled *La Pavonia*, in allusion to her peacock feather, emblem of luxury. So while *Bocca Baciata* may be 'a landmark in the emerging Aestheticism of the post-Pre-Raphaelite era', it was one among several signposts.

In retrospect, 1859 was a significant year in other respects also, of which the most conspicuous was the publication of Darwin's *Origin of Species*, with its newly-formulated ideas about natural evolution. Almost overnight, this contributed decisively to the erosion of faith: within a few years the whole edifice of Western faith would crumble. With hindsight, the religious nature of Rossetti's recent output appears almost anomalous. In addition, Darwinian theories of natural adaptation necessary for success and dominance legitimated the struggle for supremacy in many fields. Hitherto condemned, 'the survival of the fittest' justified ambitious and selfish individualism. By analogy, innovation in all fields was regarded as advantageous, and in due course the history of art was written as a progressive sequence by which stronger, more original artists supplanted the weaker or obsolete. Keeping ahead of the field became a key aim.

Rossetti did not instantly change course, continuing with chivalric and sacred themes for some time. But whatever his own preferences had been, the art market was changing. By contrast, fancy heads and Venetian half-figures grew ever more popular and saleable, thanks to economic prosperity and epicurean philosophies. This was only part of the picture, of course: art dealer Ernest Gambart gave 5,000 guineas for Hunt's *Saviour*, confident of profit from engraved reproductions. But among private patrons, moral and scriptural subjects were going out of fashion.

Rossetti needed to earn a living, so it was partly fortuitous that his personal discovery of sexual pleasure coincided with his first voluptuous picture. Both, however, were in the nature of signposts although, as yet, the destination was unclear. '[S]uch a small lamp illumes, on this highway, So dimly so few steps in front of my feet', ran the penultimate lines of *The Song of the Bower*. *Jenny*'s conclusion, too, points to an as yet obscure goal. 'In my life, as in hers, they show, By a far gleam which I may near, A dark path I can strive to clear.'

The return to verse made Gabriel think once more of publishing his poems alongside his translations. He copied them out, old and new, into a notebook, for Ruskin and Allingham to appraise. But the one redirection no one expected him to take, in the spring of 1860, was that of marriage.

CHAPTER TWELVE

Marriage

'Lizzy and I are going to be married at last, in as few days as possible,' Gabriel wrote to his mother on Friday 13 April, from Hastings. 'Like all the important things I ever meant to do – to fulfil duty or secure happiness – this one has been deferred almost beyond possibility. I have hardly deserved that Lizzy should still consent to it, but she has done so, and I trust I may still have time to prove my thankfulness to her.'

'We were a little taken by surprise', William told Scott frankly. The circumstances appeared as unpropitious as the date of the announcement. Lizzie was in a 'constantly failing' state of health, vomiting and seemingly 'ready to die daily and more than once a day'.¹ She was too weak to travel, and though by 17 April Gabriel had the special licence, to avoid waiting for banns, even a marriage ceremony seemed beyond achievement.

He was conscience-smitten. If he were to lose her now, if she were to die before the wedding, he told William, 'I should have so much to grieve for, and what is worse, so much to reproach myself with, that I do not know how it might end for me.' Thankfully he was in funds, for he could not paint and nurse Lizzie at the same time. Emma Brown offered to come, but Lizzie wanted only Gabriel.

But if this was one of the 'important things' he had always meant to do, was it to fulfil duty or secure happiness? With their history, Lizzie had hardly expected that he should still consent; as far as we can tell, they had not been in touch for twenty months. It seems that, as on earlier occasions, she sent a message saying she was very sick. Or that she appealed through Ruskin, wishing to see Gabriel one last time. When he found her so weak she might die any moment, what could he honourably do but promise marriage, 'in as few days as possible'? Then, if she died, he would have less to reproach himself with. We know nothing of the details, but it is possible that her condition appeared a direct result of their separation.

It is possible, too, that a certain degree of self-disgust attended Rossetti's London lifestyle. As well as Fanny, he was mixing with an increasingly amoral crowd of artists and writers, who openly mocked religion, virtue, honour. Men could be redeemed by matrimony which, as the Prayer-book said, was a remedy against sin and certainly better than debauchery. Millais and Hughes were fathers and householders. Younger men like Morris and Jones were already or soon to be husbands; it was reported that Munro was about to follow suit. Even William's staid courtship of Henrietta appeared closer to its conclusion following her father's death.

A month passed. Preparations were in train for a great muster of all Volunteer Regiments in Hyde Park. The Academy opened, with Millais's *Black Brunswicker* and *At the Piano* by a new man named James Whistler. By Lizzie's bed, Gabriel took up his old, unfinished poem *Bride-chamber Talk* (now retitled *The Bride's Chamber*), extending the dialogue between the two sisters – now named Amelotte and Aloyse – so as to defer the fateful wedding still further, and vividly evoke the oppressive, ominous atmosphere. 'Each breath was time that went away, / Each pause a minute of the day.' Everyday noises sound as at a distance, and the long-drawn-out tale echoes the suspended time where another bride-to-be drifted in and out of uneasy sleep. The poem's plot is that of sexual guilt – Aloyse has secretly borne a child and by a twist of fate must marry her now-hated seducer – but the theme is the inescapable past. Aloyse shudders, enfolding her old self within a changed heart.[2] In the silent sick-room at 12 East Parade, in daily, hourly anxiety, Gabriel dramatised an emotional correlative, in a story whose ending could not yet be written.

He hoped for a wedding on 12 May, his thirty-first birthday, but it was 23 May when he and Lizzie emerged from St Clement's Church as Mr and Mrs D. G. Rossetti. A local couple acted as witnesses; no friends were present.

Though she was still weak, they were going at once to France, to meet up with Ned and Georgie Jones, for a joint honeymoon. At Boulogne, the Maenzas were welcoming, as always, and naturally excited over Garibaldi's advances in Italy, reminding Gabriel of his ancestry. He composed a notice for William to insert in *The Times*, announcing the marriage between 'Dante Gabriel, eldest son of the late Gabriel Rossetti, of Vasto degli Abruzzi, Kingdom of Naples, and Elizabeth Eleanor, daughter of the late Charles Siddal, of Sheffield'. Was that correct? 'If the governor's birthplace is wrong at all, please alter,' he added.[3]

During the months of their estrangement, Lizzie's father had died, leaving the cutlery business to be run by his widow and elder son James, who appears to have been ineffectual. The younger son, Harry – said to be Lizzie's favourite brother – had learning difficulties, and both men ended their days on welfare. Lizzie herself seemed damaged: already, or very soon, she was dependent on laudanum, tincture of opium, to raise her spirits, calm her nerves, help her sleep. She retained a quirky sense of humour, however, and her aspirations in art.

They played with the idea of renting an ancient château near Boulogne, with a wonderful old garden. 'One might paint some very paying backgrounds for small pictures, and it is lovely beyond description,' Gabriel wrote. In Paris they stayed at the Hôtel Meurice before moving to cheaper lodgings in the rue de Rivoli. Due on 11 June, the newly-married Joneses did not appear, Ned having succumbed to fever immediately after the ceremony. As Lizzie was not fit for sightseeing, they spent much time reading, laughing together over Pepys's *Diary* and Boswell's *Johnson*, acquired two dogs (one called Punch in tribute to a passage from Pepys) and joked over literal translations on menu cards – turnback steak with tumbled potatoes, quail at the ashes. Gabriel got to the galleries and the Louvre, where he pronounced Veronese's *Marriage at Cana* 'the greatest picture in the world beyond a doubt'.

He had no paints, but could hardly be idle and while in Paris produced two detailed ink drawings, sketchbook size. Illustrating Boswell, one depicted the anecdote about Johnson's flirtatious evening with two young women, professedly Methodists. Decidedly reminiscent of the popular image of Uncle Toby and the Widow, this Hogarthian subject suggests that Rossetti was looking to extend his range. The other subject, however, sustains his mystical Romanticism. Entitled *How They Met Themselves*, it shows a pair of lovers in a wood at twilight meeting their doubles. The woman falls fainting, her face deathly pale with horror, while her companion supports her with one arm and tries to draw his sword against the encounter; 'in another moment, the lovers will be alone again, shuddering with fear at the occult significance of this strange and unnatural meeting', wrote a later critic in exposition of Rossetti's intention. 'It is not ghost-seeing: they are not confronted with apparitions but with realities like themselves . . .'[4] An ominous subject for a honeymoon, since in Northern mythology the *doppelgänger* motif presages death, but also an exorcism: less than a month before, Lizzie had literally faced death. Using the nursery term for ghosts, spirits, supernatural beings, Gabriel called it a 'bogie drawing', and added the dates of their meeting and marriage: 1851–1860.

It was nearly a decade since they had first met. Marriage, which he had so often evaded, brought him face to face with the past; how uncannily time had shaken everything, while appearances remained. The image in *How They Met Themselves* corresponds to the repeated motif in *The Bride's Chamber* of hearing one's own voice, seeing one's own face, embracing a changed heart. Rossetti acknowledged the link, later explaining that his design was suggested by a passage in the poem. Unable to find this, William surmised a stanza had been omitted, but the theme of recurrence was pervasive, and scarcely needed an exact parallel.

Despite the dates, the drawing was not a love-token. On returning to London, Gabriel sold it to Boyce, and later made two watercolour versions, one sold in 1861 and the other in 1864. It was amongst his most intense poetic designs, a true feat of imaginative realisation, the doubled meaning both literal and figurative.

Lizzie meanwhile made her own drawing for *The Bride's Chamber*, called *The Woeful Victory*, where a medieval lady like Aloyse watches as her true love is slain by her hated rival, whom she must now marry. Lizzie liked tragic romance almost as much as Pepysian comedy.

On the way home, they read the news of Bob Brough's death. He left a wife and two young children. Having spent all their funds in Paris, they drove straight to a pawnbroker, to raise a loan on Lizzie's jewellery, and then to Mrs Brough's lodgings. After that, wrote Hughes, who had the story from Munro, they went home 'with entirely empty pockets; but, I expect, two very full hearts'.[5] Like his other acts of charity, such generosity was long remembered by Rossetti's circle.

'Have you heard yet that I'm married?' he asked Allingham, 'one of the few valued friends' he and Lizzie had in common. Very soon, they were installed at 'a very nice little lodging' in Spring Cottage, Hampstead, close to Keats's house, and starting to socialise. 'Dear Brown,' he wrote on 15 July, 'Lizzie and I propose to meet Georgie and Ned at 2 p.m. tomorrow at the Zool. Gardens – place of meeting The Wombat's Lair. Can you and Emma and Lucy come too and dine after?'[6]

'I wish I could recall more details of that day,' wrote Georgie; '– of the wombat's reception of us, and of the other beasts we visited – but can remember only a passing call on the owls, between one of whom and Gabriel there was a feud. The moment their eyes met they seemed to rush at each other, Gabriel rattling his stick between the cage bars furiously and the owl almost barking with rage.' She recalled, however, that Lizzie was tall and slender, dressed in graceful and simple style, with neat jacket over hooped crinoline. They all went back to the rooms at Hampstead. 'I see her in the little upstairs bedroom with its lattice window, to which she carried me when we arrived, and the mass of her beautiful deep-red hair as she took off her bonnet: she wore her hair very loosely fastened up, so that it fell in soft heavy wings.'[7]

In the weeks that followed there were more such meetings between the young couples. One day they went to Hampton Court, and lost themselves in the maze. Another time, at Spring Cottage, Gabriel made a candlelight portrait of Georgie, later one of Emma also. Lizzie and Georgie talked of illustrating a book of traditional tales together, for Georgie practised wood-engraving. She recalled how, on evenings at Blackfriars, the men retired to the studio, as was customary, and how Lizzie seemed restless until Gabriel returned, when all nervousness vanished as he settled beside her on the sofa, the image of conjugal harmony.[8] Despite long avoidance, he embraced the married state happily, proving an uxorious husband, who tenderly protected Lizzie against illness and anxiety. Naturally, romance had faded, transmuted into domestic affection. But the image so often painted of Gabriel as an unkind, unfaithful spouse, is not supported by evidence; whatever else he may be blamed for, when married he was loyal and loving. For one accustomed only to pleasing himself, this was some change.

Early in August, 'Mr and Mrs Gabriel', as they would now be known in their social circle, were invited to Albany Street for the evening, to meet family and friends. Ned and Georgie and Mrs Bell Scott were there, Morris and Janey looked in on their way to catch a train. With the Rossetti sisters and aunts, and probably William and Henrietta, it was a party of about twelve. Little Mrs Jones played the piano and sang 'Greensleeves', reported Letitia Scott, but after all Lizzie did not appear, on this first visit to her in-laws. She was of course ill: an explanation if not an excuse. Gabriel sent for the family doctor. Within a month they would know that Lizzie was pregnant, and in need of additional care.

While Gabriel was away, or out, the Bishop of Llandaff called to see the altarpiece, on behalf of the Dean and Chapter. 'Oh lor,' replied the maidservant at Chatham Place, 'Mr Rossetti is married and does not paint now.' But of course he did, and by 23 July Seddon was able to reassure Bruce that he was at work again, 'after his matrimonial escapade'.[9] Boyce saw him on 30 July, painting from an Italian model, who may have been Gaetano Meo, a favourite with many of the set (and who was later quoted as saying that in Paris painters treated models as fellow workers, while English artists treated them as dirt – all except Rossetti and Burne-Jones, who treated models as human beings[10]). He now gave the Virgin dark colouring, making her more like a Jewish woman, in emulation of the historical authenticity in Hunt's *Saviour*, and using Jane as the model. Ruskin was horrified: the Madonna had 'black hair in ringlets like a George II wig' and a mulatto complexion, he told Norton: '*nigra sum*, not that he meant that, but he took a fancy to the face.'[11] Western Europe still imposed its canons of beauty on art, but Rossetti did not change his figure, though in due course he covered the ringlets with a snood.

For a few days, Lizzie went to Chatham Place to sit for a 'fancy head' called *The Queen of Hearts*, a deliberately naive study in pinks and reds with the flat quality of a playing card. Against a decorative diaper of hearts and crosses, the bare-shouldered beloved wore loops of coral. A week later, she went to Brighton with her sister Lydia, for sea air. Feeling well enough to go out in a pleasure boat, she sent a cheerful letter asking for her paintbox. 'My dear Gug, I am most sorry to have worried you about coming back when you have so many things to upset you,' she wrote. 'I seem to have gained flesh within the last ten days and seem also much better in some respects, though I am in constant pain and cannot sleep at nights for fear of another illness like the last. But do not feel anxious about it as I would not fail to let you know in time . . .'[12] They were looking for a new home, so far without success.

Fanny, meanwhile, who had taken to her bed on hearing of Rossetti's marriage, married a new or former boyfriend named Timothy Hughes, a Liverpool-born mechanic working for a Lambeth engineering firm. But in any case Rossetti no longer visited the old haunts. 'I literally see no one except Madox Brown,' he told Allingham; 'and even he is gone now to join Morris . . . and with them is married Jones painting the inner walls of the house that Top built.'[13] Designed to Morris's specifications, Red House was at Upton, near Bexleyheath, amid Kentish orchards, and was to be decorated throughout; Ned's subjects were from the Trojan Wars. Thinking of the Oxford Union, Rossetti imagined tall, grotesque figures in red vermilion, that would alarm the neighbours. Pregnant with her first child, Jane was mistress of the house and Morris in his element as a genial host. Still mostly in their twenties, the guests – Ned, Algernon, Charley Faulkner and others of the Oxford set – played boisterous games, hide-and-seek in the dark, throwing apples up and down the stairs.

After *The Queen of Hearts*, Rossetti started another head in the style of *Bocca Baciata*, with honeysuckles instead of marigolds. To tempt Gambart, he borrowed back 'poor old fat Fanny's head' from Boyce; but annoyingly the dealer would give only £50 for the honeysuckle head, saying he would pay more for *Bocca*, 'which everyone prefers – so I had better not have borrowed it'. Earlier, Gabriel had accepted a commission from Browning's friend Major Gillum, who had paid in advance for a *Hamlet* like Plint's and a Dante subject. As the first delivery date approached, Gabriel had done neither. Could he substitute a new drawing for the *Hamlet* and defer the Dante?[14] He needed to buy more time, in order to do something for poor, uncomplaining Plint.

The proffered new design was a surprising classical subject. 'The incident is just before Hector's last battle,' Rossetti told Gillum. Rending her garments because he will not heed her words, Cassandra warns him against the Greeks. Hector shouts orders to his men, while Helen arms Paris in leisurely fashion, Andromache stands with Astyanax; Priam and Hecuba listen in dismay. The ramparts are lined with catapult engines. One could never predict what Rossetti was going to do next. A heroic scene, for the kind of large-scale composition the French favoured, was almost the last subject expected from one absorbed in quaint, mystical medievalisms. In fact, the inspiration must have come from the current mural-painting plans at Red House, which were to accompany Morris's next book of verse, derived as much from Caxton and Chaucer as from the classics and entitled 'Scenes from the Fall of Troy'. Morris's projected subjects begin with these very same incidents.

When a challenge was offered, Rossetti's visual imagination was often driven to work out a treatment. The image composed, urgency vanished, and painting was postponed – as with the *Adoration* and the troublesome *Found*, both of which ought to have taken precedence over *Cassandra*. Happily, however, Gillum accepted *Cassandra*, which liquidated one debt.

Returning from his summer travels, Ruskin observed the courtesies to call on the newly-married couple, pleased with Lizzie's 'queenly' welcome and reinstatement as muse. It was very pretty to see how much better Rossetti drew his wife than any other model, he told Norton. 'When he was merely in love with her he used to exaggerate all the faults of her face and think them beauties, but now that he's married he just draws her rightly and so much more tenderly than other women that all his harshness and eccentricity vanish whenever she sits.'[15] Other acquaintances followed, including Anna Mary Howitt and her husband (since 1859) Alaric Watts. Henry Wells brought his wife Joanna, sister to George Boyce and an artist of greater talent than either husband or brother. Lizzie remarked on the Wellses' professional as well as marital partnership, later suggesting that Joanna was the 'head of the firm' in this respect. Perhaps to help Lizzie maintain her own ambitions, Gabriel hoped to foster this friendship. 'I am sure you would all like each other,' he told Joanna at the end of the year.[16]

On his return to London, George Boyce had also called at Chatham Place. He bought *How They Met Themselves* and *Dr Johnson at the Mitre*, framed, for £30, together with a new watercolour derived from Rossetti's old unfinished story of 'a woman dying while her lover is painting her portrait'. Executed with such dispatch that it was 'rough and incomplete in finish', but 'fine and touching in design and beautiful in colour',[17] this was entitled *Bonifazio's Mistress*, from a reputed incident in the life of the Renaissance painter. This distanced it, a little, from present reality, though it is a fit companion for *How They Met*. Like an amulet to externalise fear or avert fate, it shows the dying woman held so closely that she cannot fall.

Lizzie in fact was a good deal better, once the early weeks of pregnancy were over. Failing to secure a large old house at Hampstead, they resolved to take the adjacent apartment at Chatham Place, and open a door between, to get 'space enough on one floor' for both home and studio. Indeed,

Gabriel informed Norton, 'there is something so delightfully quaint and characteristic about our quarters here' that they were not inclined to move again.[18] It was familiar, and well serviced by housekeeper Mrs Birrell; Lizzie did not desire an 'establishment' of her own, with servants to supervise. By mid-November they were in residence, although the apartment was still rather spartan. Gabriel was 'happy and proud' to hang her watercolours in their gold frames round the so-called drawing room. They issued invitations for a small party. Coming in from Kent, the Morrises were to stay the night; Jane's baby was due in January. But the rooms were still in disorder; could his own family defer their visit? Oh, never mind; all were most welcome 'to tea and higgledy piggledy' after all.

There was evidently some friction, for Gabriel withheld from Lizzie an invitation from his mother that appears to have contained a rebuke – had Frances's daughter-in-law still failed to pay her respects in person? 'Nothing pains me more than the idea of our being in any way divided – which would indeed be a bad return for all I owe to my dear good Mother,' he wrote.[19] Clearly, his wife and his family did not get on. Lizzie hid behind invalidism and what William called her 'chaffiness' – a manner of turning all conversation with light, ironic humour that might mask mockery – while she no doubt found her sisters-in-law too pious and William too ponderous. This autumn, his engagement to Henrietta Rintoul was cancelled when, at last free from filial duties, she requested a celibate marriage; he thought this 'unreasonable' and was perhaps somewhat sour in consequence.

There was a moderate amount of socialising. Georgie recalled a large theatre party to see Boucicault's smash-hit, *The Colleen Bawn*, with its spectacular effects. They filled a row and the boy selling programmes was superstitiously afraid of the two redheads, Lizzie and Algernon. In December Lizzie went to Red House, where she added her contribution to the decoration. Gabriel joined her, to paint the remaining panel on the great settle, now re-erected in the drawing room. It was a time of much teasing, as well as creativity. Philip Webb, Morris's architect and friend from the days with Street, had designed tables, candlesticks and glassware to go with the house, and Janey – within three weeks of her confinement – was stitching large stylised daisies on dark blue serge hangings. In the first-floor drawing-room Morris painted a 'false tapestry' with little scrolls set among leafage, 'in which he meant next day to write his motto IF I CAN', as Ned recalled. 'But when he came down in the morning, all the labels were filled with AS I CAN'T and that pleasantry was of Gabriel's devising – and there was a scene – and it might have puzzled the discriminator of words to say which of these two was most eloquent in violent English.' Morris's rages were legendary, but Gabriel provoked them, much as he did the owl. He delighted in the fact that a nearby settlement was known as Hog's Hole. Seriously though, Red House was 'a real wonder of the age', 'more a poem than a house ... but an admirable place to live in too'.[20]

He began a long-remembered series of limericks, designed to offend:

> There was a poor devil named Topsy
> Who feared he was suffering from dropsy.
> He shook like a jelly, but the doctors cried 'Belly!'
> Then sad, but relieved, was poor Topsy.

'Oh, the joy of those Saturdays to Mondays!' recalled one visitor; 'the getting out at Abbey Wood station and smelling the sweet air, and then the scrambling, swinging drive of three miles or so to the house; and the beautiful roomy place where we seemed to be coming home.' The local gentry gossiped about the heathen neighbours who held parties on Sunday instead of going to church.[21] And Morris had a fine cellar.

Like Rossetti, Georgie was an abstainer, but the only eligible rhyme suggested otherwise:

> There was a young person named Georgie
> Whose life was one profligate orgy;
> So the water and brandy were always kept handy
> To efface the effect of each orgy.

His own name was even harder, but ingenuity prevailed:

> There was a poor bloke named Rossetti
> As a painter with many kicks met he;
> With more as a man, but he frequently ran
> And that saved the hide of Rossetti.

Gabriel's comments on others were vivid, Georgie recalled, and 'no faint portrait' of the speaker himself. One day he graded his friends according to the degrees of artistic vanity, placing himself, Swinburne and Ned in the first class, since none had any false modesty. When Ned, who often despaired of his work, queried his high position, Gabriel replied, 'Oh, Ned thinks even *his* pictures aren't good enough for him to have painted.' Another time he joked paradoxically that Ned was lazy because, having sat down to work, he did not easily rise again. Both men were perfectionists, with platonic hopes. 'I want a perfect thing and can't forgive imperfection at all, and my faults and sins, which are many, scream at me, and drown the praise,' Ned said later. 'Can't help it, made like that.'[22] Often, Rossetti was called lazy. But more often than not, when he sat down to work, it was hours before he got up again, unforgiving of imperfection. Morris, by contrast, worked intently but then abruptly moved to a new challenge, never regretful, never returning. With him, Gabriel's relationship was subtly competitive. 'They never throve together, those two, after the first year or two,' wrote Ned later. 'But in justice it was G[abriel's] fault, who loved to be unfair ...'

From the adornment of Red House grew the idea of a business. 'We are organising a company for the production of furniture and decoration of all kinds, for the sale of which we are going to open an actual shop!' Rossetti announced to Allingham in January 1861. 'The men concerned are Madox Brown, Jones, Topsy, Webb, P. P. Marshall, Faulkner and myself.'[23] Not intending to rival established firms like Crace's, they nevertheless aimed 'to give real good taste at the price as far as possible of ordinary furniture', and expected to start around May or June.

In fact, the firm began trading on 11 April, the seven equal partners each owning a nominal £20 share, with a capital loan of £100 from Morris's mother. Much of the work, if orders were secured, was to be subcontracted, but cramped premises were lesed in familiar Red Lion Square, providing just enough room for an office, showroom and workshop, with a kiln in the basement for firing glass and tiles. They circulated a prospectus to likely clients.

Morris, who claimed the initiative as his own – something he had 'long meant to do when I could get men of reputation to join me' – became manager, with mathematician Charley Faulkner in charge of the accounts. Peter Paul Marshall, surveyor as well as artist and son-in-law of the Liverpool patron John Miller, seems to have been recruited by Brown, though there is no record why the company was registered formally as Morris, Marshall, Faulkner & Co. Perhaps the other partners feared that a 'trade name' would affect their status as artists. Years later, Gabriel would jeer at Morris the shopkeeper, of petit-bourgeois renown. At the beginning, however, he was surely delighted when William Burges wrote in the press that the firm of Marshall, Morris and Co. [sic] was 'an association of architects and painters, who have set up a shop in Red Lion Square, in the same manner as the Italian painters, such as Giotto, did in the Middle Ages'.[24]

Partly to occupy his evenings, he had returned to his poems. The red-edged notebook bound in rough calf into which they were copied had returned from Ruskin only in September; with the unfinished *Bride's Chamber* added it was sent to Allingham. 'When I think how old most of these things are, it seems like a sort of mania to keep thinking of them still,' wrote Gabriel; 'but I suppose one's leaning still to them depends mainly on their having no trade associations and being a sort of thing of one's own.' In other words, pure art, unmixed with market values. Disingenuously, he claimed not to be planning to publish but merely wanting, 'even if they lie at rest, to make them as good as I can'.[25]

Allingham's comments arrived ten days before the manuscript, which caused alarm, these being the only copies. From Rossetti's reply the projected contents can be reconstructed. There was variety, romance, depth, music and feeling, with original subjects and innovative treatment. In one form or another he had some twenty-five pieces, including *The Blessed Damozel*, *My Sister's Sleep*, *Ave*, *The Card-dealer*, the ode to Wellington, *Autumn Song*, *Dante at Verona*, *A Last Confession*, *The Burden of Nineveh*, *Pax Vobis*, *Dennis Shand*, *The Staff and Scrip*, *Sister Helen*, *The Church Porches*, *Love's Nocturn*, *Stratton Water*, *The Woodspurge*, *Even So*, *A New Year's Burden*, *The Song of the Bower* and *Jenny*, plus more than a dozen sonnets, several written to pictures, and some rather juvenile items, including *The Portrait*, and a curious Wesleyan hymn. On the whole he agreed with Allingham it would be best to omit those deemed precious, pious or plainly unpoetic. *The Bride's Chamber*, however, was needed to make the book 'look as portly as may be from such a middle-aged novice'. He planned to get the poems set in type and publish at the same time as his translations. Enclosing some notes from Professor Saffi, he asked William to check the *Vita Nuova* for howlers.[26]

A first collection at the age of thirty-three, from one whose fugitive early pieces had brought a certain *réclame*? He was certainly hoping to publish.

To Whitley Stokes in February, he appeared 'fat and flourishing', with both literary and pictorial projects in hand.[27] As always, he was spurred by rivalry, for little Swinburne had completed two whole poetic dramas, dedicated to DGR, which were now being printed; so might disciples overtake their mentors. Gabriel described Algernon as 'Topsaic, with a decided dash of Death's Jest Book' (the macabre work by Thomas Beddoes), for Swinburne had Jacobean tastes for excess. As well as raving about Lucretia Borgia (Alboni was currently singing the role to great acclaim), at one gathering at Blackfriars he startled fellow guests by praising the Marquis de Sade's *Justine*, which he had not read. For the planned frontispiece to *Early Italian Poets*, he posed embracing an unnamed young model – 'I need not say in the most fervent and abandoned style ... When the book comes out I shall have no refuge but the grave.'[28]

With publication in mind, Gabriel began to cultivate links with the literary magazines, which were multiplying. Millais's friend John Leech was art editor on *Once a Week*, which published more poetry than most.

Thackeray's *Cornhill* was prestigious, but hard to penetrate, and recently Ruskin's idiosyncratic essays on political economy had been unceremoniously stopped as too 'socialistic' (but then, in Gabriel's view, who could read anything about such bosh?)[29] Publisher Macmillan had lately launched his own monthly, edited by David Masson, an old acquaintance of the Rossettis, and every Thursday evening held 'open house' at the magazine's office in Henrietta Street. Gabriel knew many of the regulars, including Whitley Stokes, Arthur Munby, and a new fellow named Alexander Gilchrist, biographer and reviewer on *The Critic*, who was preparing a book on Blake.

He did not intend to offer his own poems to such periodicals, but rather to prepare the ground for reviews. And then, early in 1861, he heard Christina's new pieces for the first time. She was still working with fallen women and while he did not challenge either sister's devotionalism, it formed a gulf, especially given the general retreat of faith. Poetry was another matter, however. Particularly a remarkable piece about 'two Girls and the Goblins':

> Morning and evening
> Maids heard the goblins cry:
> 'Come buy our orchard fruits,
> Come buy, come buy:
> Apples and quinces,
> Lemons and oranges,
> Plump unpecked cherries,
> Melons and raspberries,
> Bloom-down-cheeked peaches,
> Swart-headed mulberries,
> Wild free-born cranberries,
> Crab-apples, dewberries,
> Pine-apples, blackberries,
> Apricots, strawberries ...'

Like a primitive painting or woodcut, it tumbled straight in, creating its own vivid world. Yet it also moved subtly between registers, for those with ears to interpret. Most excitingly, it conveyed a daring, pulse-racing almost sensual sense of physical pleasure, in short, irregularly rhyming lines:

> She cried, 'Laura', up the garden,
> 'Did you miss me?
> Come and kiss me.
> Never mind my bruises,

Hug me, kiss me, suck my juices
Squeezed from goblin fruits for you,
Goblin pulp and goblin dew.
Eat me, drink me, love me;
Laura, make much of me;
For your sake I have braved the glen
And had to do with goblin merchant men.'

Persuading Christina to lend her notebooks, Gabriel asked Ruskin to commend the poems to the *Cornhill*. But again Ruskin proved useless. The verses were 'so full of quaintnesses and offences' that no publisher would take them. Homer, Virgil, Spenser, Milton, Keats – all wrote in regular verse; poets must obey the forms.

'Most senseless,' replied Gabriel, forwarding the note with disgust and refusing to give up. He wanted to try the goblins on Mrs Gaskell, who also wrote for the *Cornhill*. Suddenly, half his energies were diverted into getting Christina into print.

'Really, they must come out somehow.'[30] In fact, she had already acted, sending half a dozen short pieces to Masson. All at once, in the first week of February, Gabriel found that her 'lively little Song of the Tomb'– the sombre *Up-hill* – was in *Macmillan's*. At the Thursday gathering, the publisher read it aloud, with great satisfaction and applause. What else had she written? he asked.

'I told him of the poem Ruskin has, and he would like to see it if it does not go into the *Cornhill*,' Gabriel reported. 'He would also specially like to see *Folio Q*; can you get it or make another copy? or have you got anything else available? He asked whether you had much ready in MS, and I told him there was a good deal of poetry.' Rushing ahead, he told Christina to copy everything out and let him make a selection. 'I believe they would have a chance with Macmillan, or might with others, if they existed in a proper form.'[31] The only problem might be the devotional pieces; could these perhaps be placed in a separate section?

Christina had destroyed *Folio Q*, being told that the much-admired mystery tale unwittingly contained a dangerous moral message. But two weeks later, she sent copies of the poems. That Sunday, Stokes and Munby called, taking Gabriel out to dine and returning for tea, when he read her verses with some of his own. The verdict was highly favourable and he was even more convinced that Christina's could find a publisher, and a public.[32] So she duly sent her notebooks to Macmillan, who was especially taken with the one about the two girls. Gabriel offered a woodcut illustration and deftly renamed it *Goblin Market*. He foresaw a pretty little book, just right for Christmas sales.

Though sometimes driven to distraction by Gabriel's textual suggestions, Christina found them helpful, for he had a sure sense of looseness and redundancy. Her aim, she once told an inquirer, was conciseness; but Maria complained of obscurity, and so she had to steer towards clarity while not becoming banal. Like herself, Gabriel preferred vivid intensity, compression, things that didn't quite make sense. As a poet, he knew she was more natural and 'spontaneous' than himself, recognising the way her pieces seemed to spring to existence on their own, while his own verse was intensively even laboriously, worked. Though some have accused him of meddling, all the evidence suggests that at this stage in her career he was warmly and sincerely supportive.

Lizzie's pregnancy continued well. A maternity nurse was engaged, to care for mother and baby for the month after the birth. Then, in mid-April, the child stopped moving in the womb. Gabriel called the regular doctor and a specialist obstetrician; neither ventured a diagnosis, and Lizzie remained hopeful. 'So we can but wait, and trust for a happy termination,' wrote her husband. But on 2 May their baby daughter was born dead, at full term. She had died two or three weeks earlier.

In Gabriel's letters, to his mother, the Browns, Gilchrist, Allingham, all his concern was for Lizzie.[33] There were many accidents in childbirth, and too many maternal deaths; received wisdom held it was better to lose a baby than its mother. So he sent the news briefly, to his kind friends at Little Holland House, including Sara Prinsep's sister. 'My dear Mrs Dalrymple,' he wrote. 'My dear wife has just given birth to a still-born child. However, she herself is so far the most important, and seems as yet to have got through so much better than we ventured to hope, that I can feel nothing but thankfulness. God send she may continue to do well!'

But Georgie knew that the loss was 'not a light thing to Gabriel', and that the dead child continued to live in his heart.

The final version of *The Bride's Chamber* contains a birth that does not result in a baby – when Aloyse's child is taken away to hide her shame:

> I woke at midnight, cold and dazed;
>   Because I found myself
> Seated upright. with bosom bare,
> Upon my bed, combing my hair,
> Ready to go, I knew not where.
>
> It dawned light day – the last of those
>   Long months of longing days.
> That noon, the change was wrought on me

> In somewise – nought to hear or see –
> Only a trance and agony . . .

The black day was of his dead daughter's birth, marked *dies atra* in Rossetti's calendar; eight years later, this was written beside the sonnet *Death-in-Love*, whose imagery is of stillbirth. Here, 'birth's dark portal' groans, and all is new. Immediately, in words that personify the child's death but also suggest a midwife, a veiled woman plucks a feather from Love's wing, and holds it 'to lips that stirred it not', saying ' "Behold, there is no breath: I and this Love are one, and I am Death." '

The even more explicit *Stillborn Love* followed, with an hour 'which might have been yet might not be' and a sestet that metaphorically conjures the reunion of parents and baby:

> Lo! how the little outcast hour has turned
> And leaped to them and in their faces yearned: –
> 'I am your child: O parents, ye have come!'

Rossetti never ceased to mourn the death of his 'outcast' daughter. When a few weeks later Lizzie spoke of giving 'a certain small wardrobe' of unworn baby-clothes to Georgie, Gabriel pleaded with Georgie not to take them. 'Please,' he wrote. 'It looks such a bad omen for us – would you mind?'[34] Another child would surely follow.

But Lizzie never really recovered. When Ned and Georgie called, they found her rocking an empty cradle, hushing them. She took refuge in larger doses of laudanum. Gabriel was grateful to nurse Wheeler, to Emma Brown, and to Swinburne, who sometimes came to keep Lizzie company. He hoped to take her to the Academy, to see Hughes's *Home from Work*, Leighton's *Lieder ohne Wörter*, Watts's fine portraits, and perhaps especially Joanna Wells's *Peep-Bo!* Art was the only thing Lizzie seriously cared for, he would write later. But it is doubtful if she got to the exhibition, and within a few weeks Joanna Wells died, following the birth of her own third child. Lizzie went to stay with the Browns, then left without warning. 'Her departure must have surprised you as her return did me,' Gabriel told Brown.[35] To the Browns' daughters, she seemed to sit motionless by the fireplace, staring into space.

But though painting was necessarily interrupted, the translations were nearly all in print, filling five hundred small pages. Half a dozen copies were bound up, 'to use in getting a publisher'. Others went to William, Allingham, Ruskin, Scott, Munro and George Meredith, a new acquaintance who was impressed by the 'exquisite' quality of the work; Rossetti would 'rank as poet as well as artist from the hour of publication', he wrote.[36]

Gilchrist, to whom Gabriel lent the precious Blake notebook and recommended Georgie as a sensitive copyist of illustrations, advised on negotiations with Macmillan. Rossetti wanted an advance, and payment of the already incurred printer's bill. How much was that? asked Mac. 'Stiffish', was the answer – and Gabriel began to consider other publishers – Chapman & Hall, or Smith & Elder. Eventually Smith & Elder, Ruskin's publishers, offered to pay for printing but no advance; moreover, if he wanted a frontispiece he would have to pay for it himself. On 18 June Rossetti accepted, realising these would be the best terms available.[37] He thanked Macmillan courteously, implying that he had a received a better offer. In fact Ruskin had been influential, advancing £100 to cover the typesetting costs. Publication was set for the autumn.

As regards painting, he had plans for the next Hogarth show at the end of the year; viz: one good-size modern subject in oils, four heads or half figures in oil and two or three watercolours. The first was *Found*, for which he requested a further £50 on account, after seeing Leathart in London, though it proved an inopportune moment. The smaller oils included *Regina Cordium*, the honeysuckle head and another called *Fair Rosamund* after the medieval legend of Henry II's mistress, hidden in a bower. Of the watercolours, two were coloured versions of *Dr Johnson*, for the faithful Plint, and of *How They Met*, sold to lawyer J. A. Rose. Early in July he sold something – perhaps *Regina Cordium*, perhaps to Gambart, for around a hundred guineas. 'Of course it was a pity to let the picture go so much below its value, but it was unavoidable at the moment,' he told Lizzie, convalescing at Red House.[38] There were a lot of outstanding bills. He re-opened his account at Roberson's.

With a final push the Llandaff *Adoration* would soon be completed; the cathedral was due to reopen in September. Morris, Marshall, Faulkner & Co. had a major commission for church windows, of which Rossetti was delegated to design a *Sermon on the Mount*. (He drew Lizzie and Fanny for the Virgin and the Magdalene, Morris and Swinburne for St Peter and St John.) Professionally, things seemed well in hand. And as if to mark his steadiness, Gabriel resumed his class at the Working Men's College, where he had last taught in 1857.

Then on 11 July Plint died. Rossetti was grieved and then appalled when it was revealed that owing to his insolvency, Plint's executors were obliged to realise all assets, including the several hundred pounds advanced against pictures, already spent. Brown and Jones were in a similar plight. It was the worst moment for such a fix. The unfortunate thing, he confessed to William, was that 'owing chiefly to Plint's habit of pressing money on one for work in progress (of which I naturally availed myself, being always hard up) I am in debt to the estate for three pictures, to the amount of

680 guineas.' It was a huge sum, which he could never repay. To increase his dismay, acting for the Plint estate Gambart wanted to see the pictures and chose to disbelieve that Gabriel was out of town when he called. 'I never show work of importance in progress, and the principal picture I have in hand for Mr Plint's trustees is not nearly finished,' replied Rossetti pompously, knowing that the *Mary Magdalene* was barely begun, but adding a conciliatory promise.[39] Gambart's response was plain: if neither pictures nor money were forthcoming, the Plint heirs would sue.

Gabriel had visions of gaol. The altarpiece was due and Leathart had just made another payment towards *Found*. 'I am really just as anxious to do justice to the relatives of so excellent a man as Plint,' he insisted, refusing to deal through Gambart and instead writing directly to the trustees, to propose the delivery of works to the same value, by next April. 'They seem to think this feasible . . . but are going to refer the proposal to Gambart, so I do not know what it may come to.'[40] Asked to mediate, Ruskin (who did not know what debt was) took a light-hearted view. 'I hope somebody *will* soon throw you into prison,' he joked. 'We will have the cell made nice, airy, cheery and tidy, and you'll get on with your work gloriously.'[41]

Gambart was no villain and in other circumstances Gabriel would have gleefully collaborated on extracting high prices from patrons. At the same time, like many artists he resented both the dealer's profit and the use of art as commercial speculation. Rossetti calls him 'Gamble-art', noted Scott this summer. Next to a great love he needed a great hatred, observed Burne-Jones; a new limerick was swiftly devised, and in his design for *The Sermon on the Mount* Rossetti gave Gambart's features to Iscariot, inscribing his halo 'Judas Damnatus'.[42]

Another acquaintance also deemed a scoundrel was J. Farrell Hogg, a gentleman fraudster who had numbered Gabriel among his victims. A dramatic but shadowy figure in Pre-Raphaelite annals, whose extant letters suggest an unstable, combative personality, Hogg posed as an army officer and claimed to work for *Once a Week*, but was in reality 'an incorrigible swindler' against whom over a hundred complaints were lodged. Then, one Thursday in February, Munby recorded, the conversation at Macmillan's was interrupted when 'Dante Rossetti came in, hot from the capture of Farrell Hogg'.[43] Few more details are known, but the captive was released on bail. Then six months later Burges arrived at Chatham Place before Gabriel and Lizzie had breakfasted, saying Hogg was again in custody. At Michaelmas, he was sentenced to six years.

By this date, the *Adoration* was nearly finished. Working literally day and night, Rossetti delivered it with *David Rex* to Seddon's office in Whitehall on 12 September. Probably at John Miller's request, he agreed that the watercolour study, framed like a triptych, be shown at the Liverpool exhibition. Part personal publicity, this was also advertising for the Firm, who as well as ecclesiastical glass were offering painted panels, woodwork, church ceilings.

On his own behalf, he accepted a portrait commission from Mr J. Aldam Heaton, a textile manufacturer who had called earlier in the year, RA catalogue in hand, wishing to make Mr Rossetti's acquaintance. The portrait was to be of his wife, as 'Queen of Hearts', for 50 guineas. Hitherto Gabriel had not felt the need to cultivate a portrait clientele, so this marked a new step, in a recognised professional direction. It was a test of skill, too, both in catching a likeness and creating a work of art, as he noted in observing Watts's work in this year's Academy. With so much else on his plate, the timing was inconvenient, but outweighed by the potential rewards. Impressed, Scott observed approvingly that 'he ought to work at ten hundred horse power rather than get into debt – them's my sentiments'.[44]

Marriage made for responsibility; for once, Rossetti acted in businesslike manner, arriving at Woodbank, the Heatons' home near Bingley in Yorkshire, before the month was out. Mrs Heaton invited Lizzie too, but her uncertain condition ruled this out; instead, she went again to Red House, which cannot have been altogether easy for her, since little Jenny Morris was eight months old, and Jane pregnant again. Finished on 4 November, the portrait – less of a likeness than a reworking of the original *Regina Cordium*, presumably as the Heatons requested – was accompanied by sketches of their daughters, Winifred and Monica, aged nine and four. 'It's not a bit like, but beastly,' he scrawled on the former. 'I only send it supposing you wouldn't wish it to go in the fire, but if you do, put it there. Some day I'll do you a better, says your DGR'.[45]

Mindful of the 'shop' he also proposed a window design, showing Mrs Heaton as 'The Lady of Woodbank', holding a model of the house as in images of medieval patrons and donors, with a swan at her feet and meadows behind. This would be one of Morris, Marshall, Faulkner & Co.'s earliest productions: slightly modified in design, it was completed early in 1862.

Commissions of this kind, like portraiture, were the bread-and-butter of Victorian art: lesser genres, but indispensable to earning a living and a reputation. Somewhat lionised by local society, Rossetti was an amiable house-guest, despite his detestation of full-dress dinners. Back in London, his preferences returned – as for example when he invited 'a few blokes and coves – not to say worse' – Brown, William, Prinsep, Meredith, Rose, Gilchrist and Fred Sandys, to 'oysters and obloquy' at Chatham Place – 'and of course the seediest of clothes'. Another night he and Ned went to Gilchrist's in Chelsea, where Swinburne was 'even more meteoric' with alcohol than usual. Rossetti was a very jolly fellow, wrote William

Hardman, introduced by Meredith. 'I am going on Friday again, to a social reunion of artists and literary men.'[46] But such events did not mask the very real change: observers – and no doubt his family – would have noted with approval that DGR was at last settling down. In two short years he had moved from being a man who haunted London's night-life and consorted with women of the streets, to an attentive husband, business partner and portrait painter. Emotionally, too, he had grown up, through the ordeals of Lizzie's illness and the loss of their child. The transformation was great.

CHAPTER THIRTEEN

Loss

'It was DGR's idea; he saw money in it,' claimed Burne-Jones of Morris, Marshall, Faulkner & Co. But the Firm was not Rossetti's idea, nor did he expect it to make much money, although he clearly joined enthusiastically in the discussions that led to its launch, as well as in the activities that preceded it, such as the decorated furniture at Red Lion Square. Moreover, although Red House is commonly cited as the inspiration for the company, both Rossetti and Burne-Jones were also furnishing their homes in similar manner. At Chatham Place, the fireplace was newly surrounded by 'real old blue glazed Dutch tiles' to match the traditional willow pattern chinaware, and 'Japanese fans' made from peacock feathers were hung on the walls. Soon after the first Christmas at Red House, Gabriel designed for his own appartment a wallpaper of quite startling originality, with stylised trees reaching from dado to frieze. 'The stems and fruit will be Venetian Red, the leaves black,' he wrote. Fruit and stars would be outlined in yellow and the design printed on 'common brown packing-paper and on blue grocer's paper, to try which is best'. The whole effect 'will be rather sombre, but I think rich also. When we get the paper up we shall have the doors and wainscoting painted summer-house green.'[1]

Like many projects, this remained in the platonic realm; at least, no visitor records such a paper actually being printed or hung. But the plan surely contributed to the Firm's decision to produce wallpapers. Initially, it was proposed to print at Red Lion Square, using zinc plates, but eventually the work was subcontracted. Two of Morris's early papers – 'Trellis', designed in November 1862, and that known both as 'Fruit' and 'Pomegranate' – seem to have a vestigial link with the Chatham Place fruit trees.[2]

With regard to furniture, Rossetti had painted the two massive chairbacks for Morris, in addition to *Beatrice and Dante* on the settle doors and the quartet of panels showing the Seasons. Among his first designs for MMF & Co. was a painted panel *Annunciation* for a new church by G. F. Bodley, and more might have followed had orders been placed. In stained glass, which brought in the bulk of the Firm's early commissions, he had been approached by James Powell & Co. as early as 1857 as a potential designer. All these beginnings derived ultimately from architects like Woodward, Bodley and Street, who believed in a 'medieval' integration of fine and applied arts, but in essence the Firm was more like a modern design partnership. All the items – glass, furniture, wallpaper, tiles, etc. – were actually made and decorated by hired workers.

On Morris's death, nearly fifteen years after his own, Rossetti was quoted as having said that the founding of the Firm had been proposed 'as a joke more than anything else ... in fact mere playing with business'[3] – a statement which has been taken to mean that he was a half-hearted partner, who jeered at the 'shop' and contributed little to its affairs. But the remark, actually made in 1873-4, was intended to contrast the certainly amateurish beginnings of MMF & Co. with the successful enterprise Morris had built a decade later. Moreover, by 1866 Rossetti had more or less dropped out of active participation, and from 1874, when Morris decided to restructure the business, he relinquished all connection. But in the very early years he was certainly active, both in design and what might now be called marketing, though he was not the most assiduous attender at the monthly partners' meetings (more like convivial gatherings at the Jolly Masons, according to Faulkner).

The prospectus advertising the enterprise has long been regarded as partly of his drafting, with its 'imperious' prose style and emphasis on artistic quality:

> Although no doubt particular instances of success may be cited, still it must be generally felt that attempts at this kind hitherto have been crude and fragmentary. Up to this time want of artistic supervision, which can alone bring about harmony between the various branches of a successful work, has been increased by the necessarily excessive outlay consequent on taking an individual artist from his pictorial labour. The Artists whose names appear above hope by association to do away with this difficulty. Having among their number men of varied qualifications, they will be able to undertake any species of decoration, mural or otherwise, from pictures, properly so called, down to the consideration of the smallest work susceptible of art beauty.[4]

Though not naturally a team player, Rossetti nevertheless contributed on the same basis as the other partners, it being recognised from an early date that commitment to a house style and joint contributions to any project made individual design credits neither necessary nor wise. One man might design a figure for a window, for example, another the borders, background and canopy; a third decide the leading and colouring and a fifth supervise the whole assembly – and these in addition to the glaziers and painters who actually worked on the glass itself. Rossetti never demurred at this arrangement, and showed far less concern for 'his' designs than one might expect, given his Romantic temperament and concern for adherence to his ideas in, say, wood-engraving. For clarity, his contributions in his four years of active participation are outlined in this chapter, so it should be remembered that designs proceeded in parallel with painting commissions. Each design was paid for, the partners having individual accounts with the Firm that also enabled them to purchase items for their own use.

By the end of 1861 the workforce totalled five men and boys, the latter usually coming from the Industrial Home in Euston Road patronised by Major Gillum. It can be inferred that Rossetti was also responsible for recruiting the Firm's longest-serving employee, George Campfield, still on the payroll in 1899, who was a former student at the Working Men's College and had previously asked Rossetti to find him work.[5] One has a sense that Gabriel enjoyed this facilitating role, as he clearly did when recommending the Firm to customers. Through contact with men like Ruskin and Seddon, he was well placed to do so.

'Stained glass was the most obvious starting-point for business growth,' write the Firm's historians, and it was here that Rossetti made his largest contribution, with thirty-six large or multiple-figure cartoons between 1861 and 1864. The first major commission was for Bodley's church at Selsley, for which he was allocated two windows. The *Sermon on the Mount* was apt for a three-light window near the pulpit, and his initial design, which remained with the Firm until 1933, has a scrawled note to Morris suggesting this was a first essay in the medium: 'Dear Top. If you have to reduce it do it in pencil and then I'll draw it again. It strikes me now it's done there's no space for lead lines is there? Don't spoil this one as I'll make some use of it, if you find it too big. I'm waiting for the reduction to do the others, as then I'll get them exact. Note signs that I've added a little bit at bottom to get Christ in.'[6] Because the angled shape of church windows makes them often awkward to fill, in this case the central Gothic hood surrounds a standing figure of Christ, with seated disciples grouped around; each has an inscribed halo, in the manner of Gozzoli's *Virgin and Child enthroned among Saints*, in the National Gallery. In the *Sermon's* smaller lights to left and right are members of the multitude – a mother and child, an elderly woman, a man on crutches. The design required a little simplification: the actual window lost the landscape sketched in behind the figures – a touch that belonged more properly to painting – but is otherwise strikingly successful.

A similar-sized single-light cartoon for the *Visitation* contains Mary and Elizabeth flanked by their husbands; Christ and the Baptist *in utero* are indicated by small roundels, following medieval precedent, in a rare and touching depiction of pregnancy. One of the first windows completed, it was probably this cartoon that William Rossetti saw at Red Lion Square on 7 September, when Gabriel told him that Morris had 'found the real way of painting glass, by putting colour on the back of it'.[7] This may have been a non-technical way of describing one of the processes; in fact MMF & Co. bought red, blue and plain glass from Powells, creating yellow and green by means of silver oxide, but like the painting of features and patterns this was not a new discovery.

In some ways these early designs were primitive – partly in homage to their medieval prototypes – yet at the same time the work was innovative, and also commercial. 'Our stained glass ... I will venture to say, may challenge any other firm to approach it,' Rossetti told Norton in the New Year, 'and must, I think, establish a reputation when seen.' Enclosing a prospectus, he continued: 'we mean to do wonders – indeed are already making *some* way, though cautiously, of course only venturing as far as commissions actually in hand permit of outlay. I wish you could see a painted cabinet, with the history of St George, and other furniture of great beauty which we have in hand. We have bespoke space at the great Exhibition, and hope to make the best show there that a short notice will permit of ... Morris, and Webb the architect, are our most active men of business as regards the actual conduct of the concern: the rest of us chiefly confine ourselves to contributing designs when called for, as of course the plan is to effect something worth doing by co-operation, but without the least interfering with the individual pursuits of those among us who are painters.'[8] And, he added, he was about to leave for a meeting of the partners that very evening.

Already he was at work on his next order, for St Martin's in Scarborough, where Brown's *Crucifixion* was to be flanked by seven panels showing a typological narrative. 'I'm doing The Parable of the Vineyard for the shop-glass,' he wrote on 1 December, asking to borrow a book that illustrated an archaic winepress. 'If you've anything else in the Vineyard line you might include it.' But here, though the designs are vigorous and varied, the windows themselves are not so successful, for the small square panels, additionally broken by leading, are crowded with narrative figures, causing illegibility.[9] Three were set on each side of the main image, and the seventh below, with its appropriate legend: 'And they cast the son out of the vineyard and slew him. When the lord therefore of this vineyard cometh what will he do unto those husbandmen?'

Not surprisingly, Gambart featured as one of the villains and was no doubt also consigned, in wish if not execution, among the souls of the damned in the *Last Judgement* sequence, which Gabriel designed in nine panels for the same church.

The *Vineyard* window was completed by May 1862, and exhibited at the International Exhibition, in the space taken by MMF & Co. in the 'Medieval Court'. Here the *Building News*, which like other papers was critical or amused by the Firm's products generally, expressed approval of the glass, with some cavils. '[T]he work is, however, so lovely, and approaches so nearly the gemlike character of the old glass, that we are glad to admire heartily instead of seeking out faults,' it wrote, while the *Practical Mechanic's Journal* described the *Vineyard* as 'for the most part slovenly and unintelligible' but added that 'the exhibitors are certainly capable of better things ... [and] we are glad to find out that there are men in the profession prepared at all hazards to carry out their theories of art, and fling the challenge in the face of popular taste and fashion'. It may have been due to this mixed reception that the *Last Judgement* was not put into production or installed at Scarborough.

Planned to excel the 1855 Exposition Universelle in Paris, itself mounted in response to the Great Exhibition of 1851, the 1862 International Exhibition was threatened by the sudden death of Prince Albert in December 1861, and by the effects of the Civil War in America, which preoccupied the United States and cut off cotton supplies to the Lancashire textile industry. Neither event was of immediate concern to the Exhibition's Medieval Court, to MMF & Co., or to Rossetti personally, except insofar as Albert's death placed the aristocracy in mourning, and hence made them less likely to redecorate their homes, while the Civil War kept potential clients and contacts such as Charles Norton from visiting Britain. It was therefore a relief when the exhibition went ahead as planned, albeit with muffled fanfares, offering an important showcase for the Firm's work. As well as glass and embroidered hangings, MMF & Co. exhibited half a dozen pieces of painted or lacquered furniture, including the St George cabinet designed by Webb and painted by Morris, the Backgammon Players cabinet painted by Burne-Jones and the English Life 1810–60 bookcase decorated by Brown. Rossetti's contribution was an 'Egyptian'-style sofa made of white and ebonised poles and rails, with cushions covered in red serge decorated with musical notation, which was received as strange but striking.[10] He also contributed to the decorated drawings cabinet celebrating King René of Anjou, commissioned by John Seddon. Of the four large and six small panels depicting the fine and applied arts, Rossetti's allocation was the large 'Music' and the small 'Gardening'.

Demonstrating the collective nature of the output, MMF & Co. designs were typically available for reuse and adaptation. 'Music' therefore reappeared in stained glass when artist Birket Foster commissioned a King René window sequence. A year or so later, Rossetti and Brown also sold oil versions of their subjects to a private patron as easel paintings; MMF & Co. evidently did not hold exclusive rights.

The Heatons' commission for the window at Woodbank was one of the Firm's first secular windows, and Rossetti was indirectly also responsible for MMF's first large-scale domestic commission, from Walter Dunlop, who lived near the Heatons and presumably saw their window as well as the *Vineyard* at the International Exhibition. For Dunlop's home, Harden Grange near Bradford, thirteen panels roughly two feet square showing the story of Tristram and Iseult were made and installed in 1862–3, employing the services of Arthur Hughes and Val Prinsep as well as Brown, Morris, Rossetti and Burne-Jones. Rossetti's subjects were 'How Sir Tristram fought with Sir Marhaus the King's son of Ireland for the tribute of Cornwall and how Sir Tristram wounded him sore, of which wound Sir Marhaus died' and 'Tristram and Iseult drinking the Love Potion'. The first of these, showing two armoured men in close combat, was a spirited and successful design, the second simpler and more static.

There followed a third Yorkshire commission, from Charles Hastings, who ordered a large number of window panels for his house near Keighley, recorded on 18 February 1863 in the first surviving MMF minute book. They included windows for the dining room showing scenes from English history (St George, Richard I and Henry V), and for the drawing room showing the lady of the house flanked by the seasons and the fine arts. The history of the windows is obscure, but as there is no further record of the two kings listed for the dining room, it seems likely that in the event Mr Hastings was persuaded to take a full six-light sequence depicting the Legend of St George, for which Rossetti made all the designs. The fee was £5 apiece, and the compositions are vigorous, visually dramatic and spatially compressed, as would fit the square upper lights in a bayed fenestration series.[11]

The local connection Rossetti had initiated for the Firm yielded yet more commissions, including a number of windows for the church that became Bradford Cathedral. The minute book records that on 1 April 1863 cartoons for single figures in the east window were allocated: Jacob, Mary Magdalene and Martha to Rossetti, the Virgin and David to Burne-Jones. On 15 April the four major prophets were shared out: Ezekiel and Daniel to Rossetti, Isaiah and Jeremiah to Morris. As was agreed practice, Rossetti and Burne-Jones were paid £3 per figure, Morris only £2.

When the Magdalene design was delivered, however, the Firm had a problem. Probably with tongue half in cheek, the minutes record on 22 April how it was agreed 'the managers write to Rossetti asking him to alter the costume of his Mary Magdalene for Bradford East [window] on account of its inappropriateness for its destination'. No designs survive, but the window suggests that the saint became more heavily draped. Martha is a working woman, with headscarf and sleeves rolled to the elbow.

Among the Patriarchs and Prophets, Rossetti's figures took their allotted place, easily but not strikingly distinctive in their handling, for variety within bounds was a feature of MMF's work, and the glass painters in Red Lion Square copied each design faithfully rather than attempting a homogeneous look. Jacob, unusually, is shown as a young man, with a wallet and bowl. Ezekiel is signalled by his flames.

Other ecclesiastical designs include The Sacrifice of Isaac and Joseph lifted from the Pit for Peterborough Cathedral, Christ in Glory for St Paul's, Manningham, St Jude for Southgate and a Crucifixion for Dedworth, near Windsor, that became one of the Firm's staples. Designs for Joshua (looking like a Crusader) and St Alban (in Saxon costume) exist, but are not thought to have been executed. Altogether, there are over thirty major designs, comprising some of the most effective figures and compositions to come from MMF in the early years. Hitherto largely known as a small-scale painter, filling densely patterned spaces with overworked detail, in his glass designs Rossetti showed a clear grasp of the necessary principles of simplicity and vigour, with flattened perspective and conventionalised settings.

His other contributions include one in the familiar Morris & Co. range of rush-seated chairs, with arms and a circular seat, always described as the 'Rossetti chair' in the Firm's catalogue, as well as some of the tiled calendar of Months installed at Queens' College, Cambridge. It is likely too that Rossetti was responsible for securing one of the Firm's ecclesiastical ceramic commissions, for the tiled reredos at Findon, Sussex, through his connection with the client, Lady Bath.

Above all, he was instrumental in 1866 in obtaining for MMF the commission to decorate public rooms in St James's Palace and the South Kensington Museum (now the V&A); and as Linda Parry observes, 'one can only marvel at his success in convincing a royal court not known for its love of avant-garde design and a museum that had only moved from temporary headquarters a few years before, that a new, inexperienced firm of decorators was capable of carrying out work of the quality and standard demanded.'[12] These took the Firm into the second phase of its life, although by the time both Palace and Museum were finished Rossetti had more or less ceased his active role as designer. If, in 1873, he looked back in some amazement at the Firm's success, there is every reason to suppose that he was proud of his part in it.

While Gabriel was with the Heatons in the autumn of 1861, Alexander

Macmillan wrote to say that he would like to publish Christina's poems – 'at least I would run the risk of a small edition, with the two designs which you so kindly offer'. If Rossetti would kindly call, they could go over the poems and make the final selection; the designs must of course feature *Goblin Market*, the title poem and chief attraction. Back in London, the two men met, and on 17 November Gabriel returned the manuscript, with a frontispiece design – for *A Birthday*. But the title-page would feature goblins, he assured the publisher; could he have two woodblocks by return of post? A fortnight later, the frontispiece had changed, and one of Rossetti's happiest designs, showing Laura clipping her golden curl for the goblins – rat-faced, cat-faced, weasel- and parrot-faced – was ready for the engraver, together with the title-page showing the sisters asleep in each other's arms.[13]

He promised more, but there was scarcely time, especially as he had elected to design the binding also, and decreed that the blocks be cut by the Firm where Charley Faulkner was a willing, if inexperienced, wood-engraver. 'Do not be at all fidgetted about it,' Gabriel told him on 9 December. 'It seems to me that with your steady eye and hand it cannot be too difficult.'[14] But unsurprisingly *Goblin Market and Other Poems* was not ready in time for Christmas and indeed Gabriel had other priorities, including his own translations.

A plump volume of 450 pages, price twelve shillings, *Early Italian Poets from Ciullo d'Alcamo to Dante Alighieri* was finally issued in December 1861 by Smith & Elder from the pages set in type by Whittinghams. It contained the biographical notes requested by Macmillan, and a short preface, acknowledging inter alia Rossetti's ancestral connections. Well might he feel divided from his youth in finally relinquishing the only contribution he expected to make 'to our English knowledge of old Italy'. It was fourteen years since he had begun the task, before the PRB had formed or *The Germ* sprouted. Now, those friends were dispersed. Then, his father was angry with his casual habits. Now, he was a married man with a sick wife. He was less whimsical, more down-to-earth. And he was learning to be satisfied with imperfection, for the sake of getting things done. One day, according to a brief postscript, he hoped to research the libraries of Europe and continue his work. But he was not by nature a scholar and he was better pleased to put the work to bed rather than keep it longer at his side like a fretful child. Ironically, Italy's exiles were now free to return: thanks to Garibaldi and Mazzini, a new political order prevailed, and the occupying armies were departing.

Why, you wretch, wrote Professor Rossetti's old friend Thomas Keightley on receiving his copy. Throughout the *Vita Nuova*, Gabriel had treated Beatrice as a real woman, in defiance of everything his father had written! Well, he had published neither to praise nor bury Papa's work, though perhaps some element of redress crept in; the poetry of Dante's period was worth resurrecting, even if its chief commentator had been led astray by conspiracy theories.

As no one was willing to pay, the illustrated title-page had been dropped, probably to the benefit of the book as a serious work. Gabriel feared that a rival *Vita Nuova*, costing only 7s 6d, would divert buyers; and so perhaps it proved, for sales were slow. Otherwise the work was received well, with respectful commendation. Not only had the translator caught the spirit of Dante with a remarkable fidelity but he had discovered a whole circle of poets unknown even to students of Italian literature, infusing all with a dignity borrowed from their great compatriot, wrote the *Spectator*, so 'the base coin is fused and recast, to be used with the old stamp, but with a nobler metal . . .' *Fraser's* review filled a dozen pages, while the *Athenaeum* requested more scholarship, but concluded 'with the kindest feeling towards the author, who has produced a handsome, an original and a very interesting volume, which will always give him an honourable position among the cultivators of Dante-lore'.[15]

But when these words appeared, Rossetti was in no position to appreciate them.

Through summer and autumn, Lizzie had remained fragile but not dangerously ill. While he was away, painting Mrs Heaton, she left Red House without warning, returning to Blackfriars. Urgently he asked his mother to take round some money; knowing that as well as behaving erratically she was consuming large quantities of laudanum, he did not like her to be alone. But, he noted, she was always plucky; he trusted she would pull through these troubles as in the past. Briefly, they considered an immediate remedy, asking if they might adopt Nell Farren, a red-haired girl who came sometimes to model and later became an actress. It is not known whose desperate notion this was, but in any case Nellie already had parents.

There are hints that, throughout their marriage, Lizzie was 'difficult' and demanding, insisting on Gabriel's presence and scaring him with the prospect of 'another illness like the last'. Invalids can often be tyrannical, and fellow guests at Red House sometimes observed how cowed Gabriel seemed when his wife spoke sharply. Friends and family 'knew who had been the real martyr of that foredoomed marriage', wrote Helen Rossetti Angeli eighty years later. Lizzie's recorded behaviour was assuredly disruptive, perhaps hysterical, and half-informed gossip as to her ill-tempered, jealous nature, suppressed during Gabriel's lifetime, resurfaced very quickly after his death.[16] But as the incident with the empty cradle indicates, she was almost certainly suffering from post-natal depression, in addition to the fluctuations in health and spirits caused by opiate addiction. Gabriel was clearly very worried.

Sometimes, she was able to sit. Shortly before Christmas he drew her head as that of Princess Sabra, embracing her gallant saviour in another version of *St George*, for Ellen Heaton, whom he had also seen in Yorkshire. He drew Lizzie seated, too, for a figure of Beatrice entranced. Later, her abstracted state made him envision her again as Ophelia, led away from King and Queen in her first madness. 'Can you say to me some word I shall say to him?' he had made her ask in his *Old Song Ended*. 'Say I'm looking in his eyes / Though my eyes are dim.'

Swinburne was a welcome visitor, for she needed company. 'I used to come and read to her sometimes,' he wrote, recalling especially her delight in the competition for a legacy in Fletcher's *Spanish Curate*. Her pleasure was quick and keen and intelligent, with no wish to bowdlerise the bawdy Elizabethan dialogue. A new edition of Child's *English and Scottish Ballads* – a favourite with both – was out, and Algernon collaborated with Gabriel on a pastiche of 'The Laird o' Waristoun', perhaps also to entertain.[17] They went to the theatre, and out to dine, which was easier than eating at home, and Lizzie was not too sick to be never left alone. After dinner, Gabriel could go out, to meetings of the Firm, to his Monday class of working men, now in Great Ormond Street, to Macmillan's Thursdays in Covent Garden. Tragically, his new friend Alex Gilchrist had died suddenly, after catching scarlet fever from his children. Gabriel promised to assist his widow in completing the *Life of Blake*. Meanwhile, the endpapers of *Early Italian Poets* advertised the imminent appearance of 'Dante at Verona and Other Poems' by D. G. Rossetti.

It was a Monday when he and Lizzie went to meet Swinburne at the Sablonnière restaurant in Leicester Square. In the cab, Lizzie seemed sleepy, and he wanted to turn back, but she insisted. During supper her mood alternated between flightiness and drowsiness, as it often did, and when they got home around eight she seemed agitated. But this too was usual, and both Mrs Birrell and her niece were downstairs. Before nine, as she was getting ready for bed, he went out again, to the College. He stayed on talking, to make up for lateness, or else went somewhere else, for he got back to Blackfriars only at 11.30. He took off his boots so as not to disturb her. The empty laudanum bottle beside her, Lizzie was asleep, snoring unnaturally, unconscious.

He sent at once for the doctor hard by in Bridge Street, who had attended her confinement. Unable to rouse her, Dr Hutchinson prepared his stomach pump, to flush out the narcotic. Gabriel summoned other doctors, sent a messenger to the Siddall home in Southwark, and when her sister Clara arrived set off himself for Kentish Town, to fetch Brown. Perhaps by now he anticipated the worst. Not long after their return, Lizzie died, at 7.20 in the morning of Tuesday 11 February.

'I can scarcely believe the words as I write them,' Georgie told her sister, 'but yesterday I saw her dead. I went down directly I heard it and saw her poor body laid in the very bed where I have seen her lie and laugh in the midst of illness.'[18] Unable to face visitors, Gabriel did not appear.

She had taken a massive overdose. 'The poor thing had been in the habit of taking laudanum for 2 or 3 years past in considerable doses, and on Monday she must have taken more than her system could bear,' William told Fred Stephens. Whether by accident or design cannot be determined. 'My impression was that she did not do it to injure herself but to quiet her nerves,' Gabriel told the coroner when asked about her habit. 'She could not have lived without laudanum.' She was not especially depressed, had just ordered a new mantle, and had talked of going out of town in a day or two. Emphatically, she had not spoken of wishing to die.

The coroner's routine questions, to the widower and witnesses, including Swinburne and Mrs Birrell, were designed firstly to exclude suspicion of foul play and then to judge if death were accidental or self-inflicted. Compassion for the family urged the former if at all possible; suicide carried a stigma. A compassionate verdict was returned.

But Gabriel had not told the inquest, nor anyone but Brown, about the note. Later, some said it lay on the table, others that it was pinned to Lizzie's nightdress. According to Lucy Brown's daughter, it asked Gabriel to 'take care' of Lizzie's simple-minded youngest brother. It was not mentioned because, if she left a note, she must have intended to die. Given her post-partum history, this is wholly plausible; indeed, in trying to make sure she was not on her own, Gabriel had surely feared such an outcome.

'His most intimate friends know well that she intentionally poisoned herself,' wrote a young woman in 1882, who almost certainly had not heard directly from an intimate friend; so the secret was not closely kept.[19] Out of deference to both families, however, the 'accidental overdose' was maintained as the official cause of death.

As was customary the coffin lay open for friends to pay their respects. Poetically, William saw her exactly as Dante described the dead Beatrice, looking so very quiet and humble 'that she appeared to say, I am at peace'.

It was twenty months since Dante Gabriel had seen his Beatrice nearly die daily at Hastings. At first in shock, on the second or third day he was suddenly seized with the notion that she was not dead after all, but still in a laudanum-induced trance. He summoned Brown's friend, the surgeon John Marshall, who related how Rossetti cried, 'Oh Lizzie, Lizzie, come back to me!', standing by the coffin.

On the day of the funeral, the apartment at Chatham Place was full of people. Shortly before the coffin was closed, going alone into the room, Gabriel placed in it Lizzie's Bible and his own calf-bound manuscript book, as a last offering. 'I have often been writing at these poems when Lizzie was ill and suffering, and I might have been attending to her, and now they shall go,' he told Brown. Brown remonstrated, and asked William to intervene. But William was uncharacteristically moved. The feeling did Gabriel honour, he replied, and he should act as he felt.

It was a grand, unreasonable gesture. The publication of the poems was already announced. What did their sacrifice signify? It was hardly true that they had taken priority over her sickness, or made him neglectful. Nor had they been written to her or for her; they were not love poems. Yet some atonement was clearly due. If only he had done more. 'If I were to lose her now, I do not know what effect it might have on my mind,' he had written from Hastings. 'I should have so much to grieve for and (what is worse) so much to reproach myself with, that I do not know how it might end for me.'

He had been under great stress. First, Lizzie's near-fatal illness. Then the death of their child. The great debt to Plint. And this loss, so often feared and yet sudden. How would it end, indeed? What had he now to live for? Some time in the following weeks he wrote out an old lament in Poe's most lugubrious manner:

> Never happy any more!
> Aye, from the saying o'er and o'er,
> It says but what is said before,
> And heart and life are just as sore.
> The wet leaves blow aslant the floor
> In the rain through the open door.
>   No, no, no more . . .
>
> Never happy any more!
> Put out the light, shut the door,
> Sweep the wet leaves from the floor
> Even thus God's hand has swept her floor . . .

No. He erased God and wrote in Fate. But the tone was all wrong, such as a boy reading Keats might write.[20]

'Beatrice is gone up into high Heaven, / The kingdom where the angels are at peace; / And lives with them; and to her friends is dead,' his namesake had written in the *Vita Nuova*. Perhaps Rossetti simply had no heart to go ahead. Effectively, Lizzie's death silenced his poetic voice.

Before he even knew Lizzie, he had fantasised about yearning for a beloved damozel in heaven. Where was she now? Vain indeed to conjecture about reunion, since science had undermined so much once held infallible.

He laid poetry aside, inhumed with the notebook. But years later he said farewell, in *First Love Remembered*:

> Peace in her chamber, wheresoe'er
> It be, a holy place:
> The thought still brings my soul such grace
> As morning meadows wear.
>
> Whether it be small and light,
> A maid's who dreams alone,
> As from her orchard-gate the moon
> Its ceiling showed at night:
>
> Or whether, in a shadow dense
> As nuptial hymns invoke,
> Innocent maidenhood awoke
> To married innocence:
>
> There still the thanks unheard await
> The unconscious gift bequeathed:
> For there my soul this hour has breathed
> An air inviolate.

Maudlin, maybe, but heartfelt; as William noted, the sentiment did him honour. Later in the year, when asked to contribute to a fund-raising anthology, he sent *Sudden Light*, from the time he had first taken Lizzie to Hastings.

She was buried in the family plot at Highgate, above the father-in-law she had never met, thus joining in death a family she had hardly embraced in life. Later, they said Gabriel was haunted. More probably, Lizzie's death reawoke other sorrows. He had not properly mourned his father, who had died just as his love for Lizzie blossomed. There were other regrets, faults and derelictions too late to amend. In language lurid with self-accusation, the sonnet later published as *Lost Days* bore the burden of regret for all he had meant and failed to do:

> The lost days of my life until to-day,
> What were they, could I see them on the street
> Lie as they fell? Would they be ears of wheat
> Sown once for food but trodden into clay?
> Or golden coins squandered and still to pay?
> Or drops of blood dabbling the guilty feet?
> Or such spilt water as in dreams must cheat
> The undying throats of Hell, athirst alway?

> I do not see them here; but after death
> God knows I know the faces I shall see,
> Each one a murdered self, with low last breath.
> 'I am thyself, – what hast thou done to me?'
> 'And I – and I – thyself', (lo! each one saith,)
> 'And thou thyself to all eternity!'

Lost, fell, lie, squandered, trodden, spilt. Guilty, undying, athirst, murdered. To all eternity. The poem, Rossetti said twenty years later, might be a favourite 'if I did not remember in what but too opportune juncture it was wrung out of me'.[21]

It had been a year of untimely deaths: a widowing cloud had taken Mrs Browning, Plint, Joanna Wells, Alex Gilchrist, the Prince Consort. Rossetti had to leave Blackfriars. At once. He could think only of living with his family and painting at Brown's; beyond that he had no plans. Others cleared the rooms and the studio. Lizzie's clothes went to her sisters, her songbird to Albany Street, her half-painted Gothic jewel box to Janey Morris, as a memento.

CHAPTER FOURTEEN

Tudor House

'I already begin to find the inactive moments the most unbearable,' Rossetti told Mrs Gilchrist on 2 March. 'Of my dear wife I do not dare speak now, nor to attempt any vain conjecture whether it may ever be possible for me, or I be found worthy, to meet her again ...' He was saddened, shocked, thrown off-balance. But he did not fall into the suspended animation that commonly attends bereavement. 'Some writers have supposed that Rossetti was constantly mournful and dejected after his wife's death ... but the fact was not so ... and I shall not pretend that it was,' wrote scrupulous William.[1] Gabriel buried grief, like belief, as painful and unproductive. Nothing could reverse Lizzie's death, and the rest of his life lay before him.

Others felt relief for him, no longer tied to an invalid. 'Thank God!' said someone, overheard by young Lucy Brown.

As if intended as a sign, the old house that the PRB had once thought of renting was again available. 'You must know Cheyne Walk in Chelsea and may perhaps be aware that it is a place which Gabriel and indeed Prae-raffaelism generally – has always had a special itch for,' William told Scott. 'One house in particular, Tudor House, the remains of a mansion built by Queen Catherine Parr, has always allured him.' The price was £225 for the lease, from Michaelmas, plus £100 a year to the landowner, Earl Cadogan. It would be a sin to let it slip, said Gabriel.[2] On 24 March he entered into negotiations through Anderson Rose.

Chelsea was too far 'out of town' for casual callers, but quiet and historic, with the Royal Hospital and Physic Garden close by. He envisaged a reunited family centred on himself – as the womenfolk thought right and proper, in almost Italian manner – with mother and sisters to look after household affairs. None of the four siblings was now attached, and he had no thoughts of remarriage. The dreadful event 'must cast a gloom over all the future for me', he wrote in response to Linton's condolences.

Work was a welcome refuge: he was now 'thankful for obligations ... which were a source of anxiety before'. He still had many debts to meet. At the sale of Plint's pictures on 7 March, his honeysuckle head, entitled *Burd*

Alane, fetched £68 5s, while the drawing of *Dr Johnson at the Mitre* made an even more respectable £75, suggesting that his stock as an artist was secure.[3] In deference to his widowhood, *Regina Cordium*, imaging Lizzie, was withdrawn from the sale.

For a few weeks he walked daily to Kentish Town to paint at Brown's, producing a wistful little oil head taken from the housemaid, in *Regina Cordium* mode, and another called *Monna Rosa*. Probably at the request of Noel Paton, he sent two similar works to the Royal Scottish Academy in Edinburgh. Then he took a temporary studio in Newman Street, the artists' old stamping ground, but it didn't suit, so in April he transferred the lease to Swinburne and rehoused himself at 59 Lincoln's Inn Fields, until Cheyne Walk should be vacant. The apartment had large and lofty rooms, which he filled with antique furniture. Here he worked on *After the Ninth Hour (At the Foot of the Cross)* and *Bethlehem Gate (The Flight into Egypt)* for Ellen Heaton, and a watercolour of Tennyson's *Mariana*, with old William Marshall in mind. Rose, who was a collector as well as a solicitor, inquired about a replica of *Paolo and Francesca*. They were all old subjects, good to be getting on with. Munby, inviting Rossetti to Sunday breakfast in June on the occasion of Whitley Stokes's departure for India, thought him 'recovered, outwardly at least, from the loss of his wife'.[4]

He was much in male company, for custom decreed that the recently widowed were not invited to evening parties. With such companions, he did not appear to mope, but in slightly world-weary manner reverted to the hedonism that preceded his marriage. On Easter Monday, for example, he went with William and Boyce to Greenwich, to see Thornhill's Painted Hall in the Naval Hospital and watch the London populace at play in the Park. One game was kiss-in-the-ring, where young men and women took turns to chase each other, exchanging favours for kisses. 'Gabriel catching sight of a girl with a paintable face, made up to her and got her address,' noted Boyce.[5] A few weeks later he spied another lass at the International Exhibition, with the same result.

At the Exhibition, Morris, Marshall, Faulkner & Co. had their place in the Mediaeval Court. Rossetti's *Vineyard* panels were on view, with his Egyptian sofa and the great King René cabinet. Among the pictures were Hunt's *Light of the World*, Brown's *Last of England*, Millais's *Vale of Rest*, Leighton's *Cimabue Madonna*, Constable's *Haywain*. His own discovery was the work of Belgian artist Henri Leys, painter of medieval scenes and sites.

William, advising a change of scene, proposed a trip to Italy, with himself and Scott and perhaps Christina. For the first time in their lives, the political situation made it possible for the Rossettis to visit their ancestral land. But Gabriel was too apathetic to be eager and in the event William and Scott went alone. Showing more independence than had been foreseen, Mrs Rossetti and her daughters declined to move to Chelsea, not wishing to be so far from the aunts, their church, Maria's pupils or Christina's penitentiary. Gabriel then asked Boyce to share the house with himself, William and Algernon. 'You and I are among the most lastingly get-on-ables,' he wrote persuasively, but in vain; instead Boyce took over the Chatham Place apartment. In his place, George Meredith, currently living in Surrey, accepted the invitation to use Tudor House as a pied-à-terre. 'I am to have a bedroom there, for my once-a-week visits,' he wrote. It was a 'strange, quaint, grand old place, with an immense garden, magnificent panelled staircases and rooms – a palace ... We shall have nice evenings there.'[6]

Rossetti, dear fellow, was better, but still somewhat shaken. 'Mention it not – he buried his MSS poems in his wife's coffin, it is whispered.'

In the 'penny box' outside Quaritch's bookshop, Gabriel had discovered a quaint little production, Edward Fitzgerald's free translation of *The Rubáiyát of Omar Khayyám*. Swinburne took it on a visit to Meredith, where, sitting in the sun, waiting in vain for DGR to arrive, they read alternate stanzas. In the evening, applying Omar's rhyme scheme to the Tannhäuser theme, Swinburne began *Laus Veneris*:

> Asleep or waking is it? for her neck
> Kissed over close, wears yet a purple speck
>   Wherein the pained blood falters and goes out;
> Soft, and stung softly – fairer for a fleck.
>   . . .
> Night falls like fire; the heavy lights run low,
> And as they drop, my blood and body so
>   Shake as the flame shakes ...

At Swinburne's Newman Street housewarming on 11 July, Gabriel, Boyce, Munro, Rose, Ormsby, Meredith and Fred Sandys heard their host recite his pulsating, anaphoric verses. Rossetti thought Swinburne 'certainly destined to be one of the two or three leaders who are to succeed Tennyson and Browning'. And at last Algernon had procured de Sade's *Justine*; one morning in August he and Gabriel shrieked together over its grotesque obscenities. 'I thought I must have died or split open or choked with laughing,' Swinburne told Milnes.[7]

Rossetti moved into Tudor House on 22 October, Swinburne and William coming two days later. Aunt Charlotte, in Sussex with Lady Bath, was asked to find a suitable couple to house-keep. More furniture came from an antique dealer, together with bedsteads from home, one being that in which Gabriel himself had been born. 'I have reclaimed my studio from the general wilderness and got to work,' he told Brown on 2 November.[8] The nine months' limbo was over.

The first time Boyce called at Cheyne Walk, he found Fanny there. The second time, he found her and Gabriel 'at home'. The kindest explanation is mutual comfort amid the passive depression that often attends bereavement: what did anything now matter?

A studio assistant presented himself in the shape of Walter Knewstub, who came via the Working Men's College and RA Schools and at the end of the year paid a premium to become 'something between pupil and assistant'. His first tasks were to plug draughty windows and doors, and to find a model for *David Pastor*, the outstanding wing for Llandaff. Meanwhile Rossetti was working on a *Joan of Arc*, for J. A. Rose. His model was Agnes Manetti, who may or may not have been one of the paintable young women approached in public places.

His next commission was a portrait in oils for the Leatharts, who like the rest of the world had come to London in the summer for the International Exhibition. Inviting Rossetti to dinner, they offered to buy both *Mariana* and the replica *Paolo and Francesca*, and requested a portrait of Mrs Leathart, for a fee of 80 guineas. Nothing seems to have been said about *Found*, which had not been touched.

James Leathart was a metallurgist and self-made man, director and partner in a Newcastle leadworks, husband of a much younger wife, and father of the first of fourteen children. Over time he amassed a sizeable contemporary collection, mainly from the Pre-Raphaelite circle, and it has been argued that art gave him, like other industrialists, access to aesthetic experiences denied to business life, demonstrating entry into the cultured classes. After several postponements, Rossetti arrived on Tyneside in early December, staying with the Scotts and going daily to the Leatharts outside Gateshead. Though remaining on formal terms in correspondence, he liked Leathart well enough and found Maria Leathart a pleasant, obliging sitter as well as 'a very pretty little lady' and a great lover of pictures. He ordered Edward Lear's *Book of Nonsense* for her daughter. The small half-length proved more troublesome than expected, however; failing at first attempt, he began again, using a different pose. After four weeks, including Christmas, he could struggle no longer and returned to London, bringing Mrs Leathart's dress to continue work from. 'I will not pretend to say that I think it perfect,' he wrote with unaccustomed candour when dispatching the finished picture.[9] The problem was 'lack of animation', giving Mrs Leathart a rather wooden look despite her informal pose; but overall Leathart was satisfied. One day, Rossetti would make female portraiture a speciality, though not in oils; as yet his technical command was wanting.

Creatively, he was still marking time. But he was anything but idle, for this autumn and winter his evenings and all other 'inactive moments' were devoted to a therapeutic labour of love almost equal to that of his Dante translations, which similarly took him back to the ardours of youth. The task was the biography of William Blake, left unfinished on Alex Gilchrist's death, and now being completed by his widow.

Gilchrist had moved from law into literature; husband of Anne and father of four, he lived near Carlyle in Chelsea. Marking him as 'a man to seek out' on reading his life of William Etty, Gabriel had met Alex in 1860, responding with warm mutual sympathy and active assistance with his new project. It was no doubt Rossetti who arranged for Gilchrist to see the Blake collection owned by the grain merchant who had called at Chatham Place, and certainly he who asked Woolner for details of a conversation with a woman who had met Blake when young. 'As I remember it,' replied Woolner, 'he looked at her very kindly for a long while without speaking, and then stroking her head and long ringlets said "May God make this world to you, my child, as beautiful as it has been to me." She thought it strange, for he was old and shabby, but in after-years she understood well enough what he meant.'[10]

By spring 1861 Gilchrist was one of the fellows Rossetti most looked forward to seeing at Macmillan's Thursday evenings. That summer they co-operated on obituary notices of Benjamin Woodward and Joanna Wells, and in his capacity as art reviewer on *The Critic* Gilchrist briefly mentioned *The Seed of David* when it was exhibited in Liverpool. As the *Life of Blake* proceeded, he borrowed the precious notebook and consulted over the selections of poetry and prose to be included in the volume, for most of Blake's writings were currently unobtainable. From a second manuscript, Rossetti copied out *Auguries of Innocence*:

> To see a World in a Grain of Sand
> And a Heaven in a Wild Flower,
> Hold Infinity in the palm of your hand
> And Eternity in an hour.
>
> A Robin Red breast in a cage
> Puts all heaven in a Rage.

Hard to imagine a time when this was not known to the world.

Of the others, he advised Alex to include *The Smile*, *The Golden Net*, *The Land of Dreams* and *The Crystal Cabinet* but judged *Mary* 'too vague and queer' and *William Bond* too incoherent, while *Long John Brown and Little Mary Bell* was simply too obscene. 'Merciful Powers! if indeed

Macmillan had a branch house in Holywell St!! or our editor's name were Swinburne!' he wrote.[11]

By November 1861 he had read the first chapters in proof 'with much pleasure and corresponding impatience' and when he heard that Gilchrist had caught scarlet fever from his children, he was quick to offer his and William's services in any matter that required immediate attention. Then on 3 December came the terrible news that Gilchrist was dead. 'I truly valued and loved your husband,' Rossetti told his widow, 'more than I think I had ever felt towards anyone on the same length of acquaintance or, I should say, friendship, for such I believe it was on both sides.'[12] He offered an obituary memoir to preface the so-nearly-completed biography.

With Lizzie's death a few weeks later, mutual sympathy strengthened, and when in due course Anne Gilchrist, who had removed with her family to Shottermill in the Surrey hills, started on the task, Rossetti promised a conclusion as well as a memoir, and editorial advice throughout. It was a welcome occupation, though it proved more difficult than he foresaw, given the fragmentary and scattered nature of Blake's works, and the complexity of his chosen symbolism. The trickiest parts were the sections dealing with the Prophetic Books, which as yet lacked all scholarly apparatus and easily appeared nonsensical. He offered notes on the illustrations for *Job* and *Jerusalem*, to complement Gilchrist's explication; meanwhile *The Gates of Paradise* needed repunctuating. Distractingly he had also to cope with Swinburne's fervour to rearrange, augment, indeed entirely redraft Gilchrist's analysis of *The Marriage of Heaven and Hell* and *The Book of Thel*. And what about *The Book of Los* and *Urizen*?[13]

By the autumn he was beginning to repent of his promises, for he had many other commitments. Should he choose between the memoir and Job? Mrs Gilchrist preferred Job. 'Gabriel took it up with a will in my presence the other evening,' reported William on 8 December, 'making all needful notes and leaving little or nothing to be done except throwing them into shape for reading, which he *intended* to accomplish before starting for Newcastle.'[14] Five days later it was in the mail, while William compiled a checklist of the pictorial works.

The task was challenging but worthwhile. Blake featured nowhere in current histories of art and literature. No edition of his poems existed, apart from an unillustrated, freely reordered version of *Songs of Innocence and Experience*. The engraved and coloured works had never been catalogued. His life was seen as spent in obscurity and isolation, the urban equivalent of an Ettrick shepherd who never found fame, living his last years in two bare rooms in Fountain Court, with his devoted wife Catherine. His writings were glossological extrapolations of Ossian, Swedenborg, the Book of Revelation and Joanna Southcott, his pictorial works those of a gifted lunatic, with no wider value. He was known, too, as one who conversed with saints and angels, literally. Leigh Hunt told the story of how, walking down Cheapside, Blake doffed his hat and bowed to an unseen pedestrian. 'Oh! that was the Apostle Paul.' Reading Edward Young's *Night Thoughts*, Blake echoed the question aloud: 'Who can paint an angel?' 'Michelangelo could', replied a voice. 'And how do *you* know?' asked Blake. 'I sat to him: I am the archangel Gabriel,' came the answer, amid a shining vision.

Gilchrist disputed this presentation, aiming in his biography to show that Blake was 'the most spiritual of artists, a mystic poet and painter' whose life and work were alike 'new, romantic, pious ... animated by the same unbroken simplicity, the same high unity of sentiment'. Combating Blake's exclusion from cultural history, he devoted a chapter to 'the vexed question of Blake's madness', arguing that the notorious visions were products of imagination, not insanity. Declaring that he 'would infinitely rather be mad with William Blake than sane with nine-tenths of the world', he placed Blake among the visionaries of all ages 'whose exceptional powers had been accepted as a matter of course in gifted men and turned to serious account': saints, seers, spiritual leaders.

Rossetti was impressed, if not wholly convinced. He feared Blake's verbal and visual eccentricities must appear the product of a cracked mind. In respect of the proposed selections of poetry, he took licence to amend and delete lines, 'the better to make its merits tell', extending this dubious editorial principle even to published works like the *Poetical Sketches* of 1783, where 'frequent imperfections' in prosody led him to correct the metre, claiming to do this 'without once in the slightest degree affecting the originality of the text.' (Ten years later, in response to criticism, he conceded that he would not do this again.) *Songs of Innocence and of Experience* nearly fared worse, for here he wanted to omit 'inferior' pieces such as the chimney-sweep in *Experience* – the 'little black thing among the snow / Crying 'weep! 'weep! in notes of woe!' – on the grounds that it was 'tinged merely with the commonplaces of social discontent'. In the end, however, he printed both books entire, and even added to *Songs of Experience* an extra 'Cradle Song' found in the notebook, unilaterally deciding that it was meant to complement the first. 'Here, then, is the whole,' he wrote; 'and assuredly its beauties, surpassing in degree and perhaps unparalleled in kind, not only greatly outweigh its defects, but are also clearly separable from them.'

The unpublished writings were more genuinely problematic, for here texts were corrupt or confused, and Mrs Gilchrist was unsure which of her husband's choices to follow. Yes, Rossetti replied, to *The Ghost of Abel*; and one or two extracts from the *French Revolution*. And yes to the 'woman taken in adultery' from the *Everlasting Gospel*; it was 'one of the finest things Blake ever wrote' and had nothing to shock readers except the opening (where Mary Magdalene is discovered in 'an adulterous bed'). But why was the text different from his own? And where was *My Spectre*? The *Mental Traveller*, on the other hand, was 'a hopeless riddle' and should be dropped.

Anne Gilchrist was educated and broad-minded; later, William would find her an enthusiastic supporter of Walt Whitman. But she lacked Rossettian confidence, and eventually handed over full control regarding the Selections, which soon included facsimiles of *Job*, *Thel* and the *Songs*, as well as William's comprehensive catalogue. Packets sped back and forth between London and Shottermill, holding clean and corrected proofs. Soon, Macmillan objected to the length. Rossetti was angered. How could Mac allow various busy people to waste their valuable time? 'It would be an infinite pity that the *Life of Blake*, coming at last, should not include a properly and competently edited collection of his writings,' he wrote. The solution was to expand the work into two volumes, which naturally allowed for even more Selections. Thus printed for the first time in Volume 2 were twenty-seven new poems, including *Auguries of Innocence*, together with fragments culled from manuscript sources, demonstrating Blake's range of lyric, satire, prophecy and aphorism. In this way many of his most reboant lines entered the language. They included: 'Sooner murder an infant in its cradle than nurse unacted desires;' and

> Does the Eagle know what is in the pit?
>> Or wilt thou go ask the Mole?
> Can Wisdom be put in a silver rod
>> Or Love in a golden bowl?

*

> I give you the end of a golden string
>> Only wind it into a ball
> It will lead you in at heaven's gate
>> Built in Jerusalem wall.

Rossetti proposed epigraphs, checked title-pages, supervised illustrations. By the end of May 1863, virtually all was complete. 'The book will, I verily believe, among all of us, have been done as much justice as was possible,' he assured Anne Gilchrist, 'and will still bring out your husband's full intentions regarding it.'

So it proved, for Gilchrist's *Life* was a landmark biography, and can be credited with starting the process that brought Blake into the canons of English literature and art, and spawned a scholarly industry. 'See how well

the Blake is being reviewed. There will be a good many important notices,'
wrote Macmillan on publication. 'As nobody knew about Blake, and the
book had its way to fight, this is not bad. It goes on selling too.'[15] Rossetti's
part in this achievement was significant, and his meddling with the texts
may be forgiven, if not excused.

What of his own relation to its subject? Like his Italian translations,
Blake was a discovery he had made for himself, when 'as a lad' he had found
the jumbled notebook lines which spoke so vividly to the painters of the
PRB. 'Imagination is my world this world of Dross is beneath my notice
and beneath the notice of the Public,' wrote Blake, grandiloquently. 'I
demand therefore of the Amateurs of art the encouragement which is my
due if they refuse theirs is the loss not mine and theirs is the Contempt of
Posterity . . .'[16] So Rossetti was proud to introduce the Selections as a feast
'spread first of all for those who can know at a glance that it is theirs . . .
who can meet their host's eye with sympathy and recognition, even when
he offers them new, strange fruits grown for himself in far-off gardens
where he has dwelt alone, or pours for them the wines he has learnt to love,
in lands where they never travelled.'

He revelled in Blake's unpredictable imagination, his conjunction of
quotidian and ecstatic, his fierce irony and sudden humours. The Rossetti
who startled strangers with rhetorical quotations or declared that the sun
went round the earth felt a natural affinity to the author of *The Proverbs of
Hell*. The Illustrated Books, with their mysterious half-printed, half-painted
technique were truly miraculous in concept, line and colour. 'No littleness
here because the scale of work is a small one,' he wrote. No finer example of
poetic effect in art could be found than in *The Song of Los*, 'where a youth
and maiden, lightly embraced, are racing along a saddened low-lit hill,
against an open sky of blazing and changing wonder.'

Above all, Rossetti's account of Blake enables us to understand more of
his own aesthetic, as it had developed in the 1850s, through the use of
glowing colour and symbolic imagery. Blake's colour was an integral aspect
of the more fantastic images, he wrote, embodying conceptions that no
other artist had dreamed of. Indeed, Blake achieved depictions of the most
abstract truths of natural science by legitimate pictorial means, so that for
instance 'we are somehow shown, in figurative yet not wholly unreal shapes
and hues, the mingling of organic substances, the gradual development and
perpetual transmission of life'. Some 'old skeleton folded together in the
dark bowels of the earth or rock, discoloured with metallic stain' was
juxtaposed with 'some symbolic human birth of crowned flowers at dawn,
amid rosy light and the joyful opening of all things'. Such true mysticism
should be cherished: only linger over the *Midsummer Night's Dream* plates,
and gain back things once known, 'too delicate for memory or for years

since forgotten: the momentary sense of spring in winter sunshine, the long sunsets long ago, and falling fires on many distant hills . . .'

He was not uncritical, smiling for example at 'the intensity of comic decorum' in Blake's engraving of *The Horse* as, 'absolutely snuffling with propriety', the animal came face to face with a young lady. Often, the writings were too repetitive to be worth much; others were incoherent or bewildering. He preferred the successes, particularly the short poems and the watercolour designs. Colour and metre were 'the true patents of nobility in painting and poetry, taking precedence of all intellectual claims', he wrote; 'and it is by virtue of these, first of all, that Blake holds in both arts a rank which cannot be taken from him.' And though he transcribed from the famous notebook several of Blake's jibes against Rubens, Reynolds *et hoc genus omne*, he also registered his own maturer assessment. For all the mockery of great names, he wrote, 'I have my strong suspicions that the same amount of disparagement of them uttered *to* instead of *by* our good Blake would have elicited on his part a somewhat different estimate. These phials of his wrath have no poison, but merely some laughing gas in them . . .'

In his concluding chapter, Rossetti added to his assessment of Blake's influence other neglected geniuses: Fuseli, Holst, David Scott and Charles Wells. Beyond their common marginalisation and his admiration, the relevance to Blake is slight, though not invisible. More interestingly, they form a lineage to which Rossetti might belong. Reading the *Life of Blake*, one is struck by correspondences with his own life. Both had dual beginnings in poetry and painting, early interests in Gothic art, Dürer and the Italian Primitives. Both had fits of nervous perturbation and verbal pugnacity, despite a generally benign demeanour; both were seized with irrational hatreds and found it easier to forgive enemies than friends. Both could be irreverent and pious, serious and whimsical, earthy and idealistic. Both could be high-handed with patrons. Rossetti did not see visions, but within a few years of working on Blake he was hearing voices. Both artists spent some years in rustic seclusion which included an aggressive, unsettling altercation. Towards the end both lived in some obscurity, shunning the public, with a small group of devoted supporters.

Both also displayed a peculiar independence of mind, with idiosyncratic creative imaginations that seemed to have wills of their own. 'I shut myself in with my soul / And the shapes come eddying forth', was a fragment from Rossetti's own notebook. Where others, rationally, demurred, he gloried in Blake's paradoxical assertions. 'If the fool would persist in his folly he would become wise'. As artist, Blake was a supreme, if unwitting, example of Romantic individualism, true to his inner nature, unable to bend himself to the age. In a letter of 1799 he outlined a position which *ceteris paribus* had been Rossetti's. 'I find more and more that my Style of Designing is a Species by itself, and in this which I send you have been compelled by my Genius or Angel to follow where he led,' he wrote to a patron; 'if I were to act otherwise it would not fulfil the purpose for which alone I live.'

Oddly comparable to the Prophetic Books were Professor Rossetti's obsessive, mystical, unread and unreadable commentaries on Dante. Gabriel had discovered Blake's notebook when his father's fortunes were at their nadir, and in some ways his youthful response to Blake seems both a displacement and the adoption of an alternative or artistic father-figure – the mentor he had not found among his teachers – whose poems and pictures showed it was possible to create both, and reach distant shores.

Years later, when Mrs Gilchrist revised her husband's book, Rossetti looked again at Blake, and composed a sonnet celebrating one who, intent on the 'unfettered irreversible goal', was content with wifely loyalty and a bare cupboard filled with 'the cloud / Of his soul writ and limned'. But the phrases are half-hackneyed; and one senses that his fascination with the subject was exhausted by the intensive immersion of 1863. For Blake's failure in his lifetime was a warning of the poverty and ridicule visited on those who obeyed only inner dictates. Incoherence, narrowed vision and bare cupboards were the result. Gilchrist might have preferred to be mad with mystical Blake than sane with mundane mankind, but Rossetti was altogether more worldly. He wanted to paint the shapes of his soul, and also to prosper.

At Cheyne Walk, Tudor House was set back from the Thames but faced 'all the boating bustle and longshore litter' of moorings, slipways, jetties and sheds. There was no embankment wall and sometimes equinoctial tides flooded the cellars. Impressive gate piers and railings proclaimed the house's antiquity, as did the flagged forecourt and Queen Anne doorcase. Inside opened a hallway of noble proportions, with doors to parlours and a double staircase, together with a passage leading to the large rear room designated as studio, with a tall window and a flight of iron steps to the garden. Outside was a lime tree avenue, an ancient mulberry (reputedly Elizabethan) and over an acre of grass.

Upstairs the grand seven-bay drawing room stretched across the front of the house, giving a fine view of the river and Surrey side, with summer shade from old trees in the Walk. Behind, a room overlooking the garden served as breakfast room, and next to it Rossetti's own dark bedroom, hung with curtains and eventually containing a great black chimneypiece with shelves and ledges reaching to the ceiling. A guest room lay off the half-landing, and on the top floor 'hardly less than a dozen' other rooms, some very commodious. Below stairs was a spacious sequence of kitchens, pantries and servants' quarters, with 'an oddly complicated range of vaults' in front, which had perhaps once led through to the river-bank.

One of the ground-floor parlours became the dining room, the other Swinburne's study. For his weekly visit, Meredith had the use of two rooms, while William slept over on Mondays, Wednesdays and Fridays, in his own room. Knewstub had both a bedroom and a painting room, though was naturally much in the main studio. The first requirement was domestic staff – a woman to cook, a man to carry coal, black boots and run errands. 'The third couple I got by advertisement, and are just going to rid me of themselves after driving me half crazy with their stupidity,' Gabriel told Mrs Gilchrist in May, hoping she could help. 'Our household consists of four men, two of whom only, myself and Mr Swinburne, are at all constantly inmates . . . I have hitherto been giving 15s a week with board to each couple.'

Mrs Gilchrist obliged with a cook and housemaid, and in due course a man named Pope was also employed. For a while the joint household functioned amicably, no doubt because there were few occasions when all four male inmates were simultaneously present. Both Swinburne and Meredith were in residence on 13 March 1863, however, when Boyce called to collect his *Borgia* drawing, and on 30 April when he dined there with Leathart and others, in the 'most exquisitely fitted' drawing room. Soon after this, however, Meredith departed, more or less officially. Reminded of the quarter-day in June, he acknowledged his recent absence from the house, promising his rent money on Monday. But this was probably his last contribution.

There was a quarrel. It was rumoured that, when put out at night, Meredith's boots were exchanged; that once when he called Rossetti a fool, he had a cup of milk flung in his face; that when he saw the enormous breakfast Rossetti ate, it raised his gorge. 'At any rate, it was agreed that, whatever happened, he was disgusted and walked out of the house, never to return.'[17]

Meredith, who had just published his controversial *Modern Love* sequence, detailing marital disintegration, was energetic, hale and hearty. In later life, he claimed to have liked Rossetti greatly. 'His talk was always full of interest and rare knowledge,' he said; 'and he himself, his pictures and his house, had I think an immense influence for good on us all, and on English life and work.' However, Rossetti had strong prejudices, strongly expressed, often without foundation. And his breakfasts were indeed unspeakable: 'eleven a.m. Plates of small-shop ham, thick cut, grisly with brine: four smashed eggs on it . . .'

Heated discussions over meals between three opinionated men naturally led to friction. Swinburne is said to have thrown a poached egg at Meredith for disparaging his hero Victor Hugo. Nor was Meredith self-effacing; Whistler told the tale of how, 'witty as well as brilliant', the novelist jested about Rossetti's pictures in the presence of several patrons. Playful, no doubt, but overstepping a limit. 'The evening ended less pleasantly than it began.' Perhaps this was the quarrel. There was no absolute breach – early in 1864 Meredith brought his son to sit to Rossetti – but their personalities were incompatible. Rossetti was 'rich, refined, royal-robed', in Meredith's ironic epithets, in contrast to his 'wild, bluff, coarse self'. Then there was Swinburne, both rich and wild, royal and coarse, but particularly wild. Small of stature, he had a large head topped with a ginger bush. Unable to keep still, he fidgeted continually and gabbled incessantly. The young American observer Henry Adams called him a tropical bird, 'high-crested, long-beaked, quick moving, with rapid utterance and screams of humour'. When sober, his manners were impeccably patrician, but all too often he was drunk; once, Gabriel was woken by a tremendous knocking at three in the morning to find Algernon on the doorstep, held up by a peeler and attended by a posse of street urchins. 'Screaming and splashing about', he was manœuvred into bed. Other tales have him chasing Simeon Solomon round the house naked, and sliding down the banisters. 'It is an emancipated ménage,' Scott informed Pauline Trevelyan.[18]

Meredith doubted whether Swinburne would do anything except make a great noise. He was just a child, said J. H. Pollen. A very very *spoilt* child, responded Mrs Pollen. His conversation was lurid. Meeting Fred Sandys in Newcastle, Rossetti told him that Algernon was 'madder than ever'; at all times, in all companies, his conversation invariably turned to 'the relations – not exactly of the sexes – but of each sex with itself'. Some while later, after witnessing a characteristic tirade of blasphemy and indecency, Arthur Munby pondered the contradictions, reluctantly concluding that Swinburne was 'so far from all sobriety and restraint, from all ordinary moral sanctions and beliefs, and yet so full of genius, of noble enthusiasm for freedom and beauty and so genuine and kindly in his way ...'[19]

Rossetti's surprising tolerance is illustrated by one tangled incident sometimes known as 'the imbroglio', when, it appears, Holman Hunt was told that Rossetti boasted of 'procuring abortions,' and sought to alert Brown of this dangerous gossip. Assuming it came from Swinburne, Brown told Burne-Jones, who informed Rossetti, who then gently remonstrated with Swinburne, who agitatedly denied being the source. Inferring that Algernon had been too drunk to remember, Rossetti dropped the subject, only to find Swinburne insistent on confronting his slanderers. No, no, Hunt told Brown, the story came 'from other sources'. But, replied Brown, suddenly himself cast as rumour-monger, 'I should never have whispered a syllable of it had I dreamed there was any doubt about it having been Swinburne who said it at Monckton Milnes' . . .' The truth can probably not be known – but the whole sorry affair shows that everyone thought Swinburne capable of such calumnies, and that Rossetti was relatively unperturbed, telling Brown it would be useless to try to correct or counteract the 'foolish scandal and tattle.'[20] It seems likely however that the affair contributed to his growing prejudice against Hunt.

'This house goes on getting more settled and I more restless, he told Allingham in August. 'I see hardly anyone. Swinburne is away. Meredith has evaporated for good, and my brother is seldom here. There is only one more to unite with me in good wishes to you.'[21] This was of course Fanny – perhaps an additional reason for Meredith's evaporation.

Loving Gabriel, Fanny had been devastated by his marriage. On the rebound, she herself had married soon after. But Mr Hughes did not suit, or was insufficiently indulgent, and it takes little imagination to see Fanny offering herself as a model again, to Boyce, or Burges, or other of the artistic gentlemen. And now at Cheyne Walk there were no obstacles but decency. However unfounded the belief may be, Rossetti had only himself to blame for the assumption that he had not kept his marriage vows, for it was shocking that within months of his wife's death his mistress was installed in his house. 'Fanny says she would like to know what I am saying to you as I am writing such a lot, so I had better leave off before I am scratched about the nose and eyes,' he wrote to Red Lion Mary early in 1863.[22] The allusion to jealousy is eloquent; and as he was writing about curtains and bell-pulls that needed cleaning and mending, it is clear that Fanny's role in Cheyne Walk was not that of housekeeper, despite the euphemistic bestowal of this title in after-years. What the servants thought, expecting a household of four single men, can only be guessed. When necessary, she could be invisible; Tudor House was large enough. But as Allingham recorded the following summer, she was definitely an inmate, present when he arrived to breakfast at eight thirty. Afterwards, Fanny went to inspect the hens, which appeared to be her special care; then all lounged in the garden, joined by Swinburne and Whistler. The day before, when Allingham arrived Rossetti was painting from another model and Fanny appeared only after dinner, when the conversation turned to Scott, who following an illness had become quite bald. ' "O my, Mr Scott is changed!" exclaimed Fanny. "He aint got a hye-brow or a hye-lash – not a 'air on his 'head!" ' Rossetti laughed immoderately at this, Allingham recorded, 'so that poor Fanny, good-humoured as she is, pouted at last – "Well, I know I don't say it right." '[23]

Rossetti drew her again and again, standing, seated, sewing, eating grapes, reclining on a couch, hair loose and outspread. Changing her hair colour, Swinburne cast her as Faustina, alluring and amoral empress:

> Lean back and get some minutes' peace;
>   Let your head lean
> Back to the shoulder with its fleece
>   Of locks, Faustine.
>
> . . .
>
> You could do all things but be good
>   Or chaste of mien;
> And that you would not if you could
>   We know, Faustine . . .

Of course Fanny Hughes was neither Faustine, nor Bocca Baciata, nor Lucrezia Borgia. Not even poor Jenny, who sold herself for a guinea. She was a fair-featured, frankly amorous young woman, with some misplaced pride but no false shame. If Rossetti laughed at her dropped h's and Dickensian pretensions, in this period he became genuinely fond of Fanny, not least because she made him laugh. He never seems to have felt that in doing so he was betraying Lizzie's memory. Fanny and her kind belonged to another world.

There have long been apocryphal tales that Rossetti had at least one illegitimate child, who survived to produce descendants. So apocryphal are these tales however that they have not made it into print, nor is it easy to determine when the notion first circulated. This is surprising, since Rossetti's life and loves have always been subject to notorious assertion, and writers who say Lizzie was his live-in mistress, or committed suicide because he went to see Fanny, would hardly have balked at a bastard child, especially if descendants exist. Yet if there was such a birth, it seems unlikely that Rossetti knew, for he always mourned his childlessness and would surely not have left offspring unprovided for. Famous figures often provoke such claims, of course, and one wonders, perhaps, if Fanny had a child, before or after her marriage to Timothy Hughes, that gave rise to such fancies. On the other hand, Rossetti supported Fanny until his death, and nowhere in his correspondence is there any hint of an unacknowledged infant. At present, the notion remains an insoluble mystery. That it is believed at all, however, testifies to the nature of Rossetti's posthumous reputation. Here was a man with many secrets to be disinterred.

Close by, first in a small cottage and then along in Lindsey Row, Whistler was living with Joanna Hiffernan, *la belle Irlandaise*. A companion or rival to Fanny, with next to no education but vivid intelligence and charm, Jo was red-haired and white-skinned in the Celtic manner. Whistler painted her dressed in white, with loose dishevelled hair and a drooping posy, which appeared emblematic of lost virginity.

Whistler was a new figure on the London art scene. James, Jimmy, or Jemmy, he was a raconteur, a *blagueur*, a dandy, who affected idleness but worked extremely hard at both painting and etching. Five years younger than Rossetti and American by nationality, he was the son of a military railroad engineer and had spent his childhood in Russia and Britain before becoming a West Point cadet – like Poe before him. He then worked as a government surveyor, until at twenty-one he arrived in Paris to study art, meeting George du Maurier, Edward Poynter and others from Britain, including Leighton, Thomas Armstrong and Alecco Ionides, as well as Frenchmen Henri Fantin-Latour, Alphonse Legros, Carolus Duran, Henry Oulevey and Ernest Delannoy. He worked at copies in the Louvre, made etchings of the students' *vie de bohème* and drew from the model under Courbet. Arriving in London in 1859, he lived first with his married sister and then in a squalid Newman Street studio, which in summer 1860 was made over to du Maurier. 'Jemmy has left me his bed, his sister's sheets and towels, 2 chairs a table and lots of wonderful etchings to adorn the walls,' du Maurier told his mother, 'besides the use of a dress coat and waistcoat quite new (when he doesn't want it himself).'[24]

Whistler was witty, entertaining, intolerant, gloriously arrogant, an individualist of the first rank. Rather remarkably, his path had not directly crossed Rossetti's hitherto. For a year or two, indeed, Swinburne had been itching to introduce them, eventually succeeding in the August after Lizzie's death, to his great satisfaction, saying he had always known Whistler would be exactly the man Gabriel would like. Well, Rossetti replied, he could not say that was precisely the fact, though he was certainly glad to know him. The distinction was nice, for Whistler, who notoriously cultivated the gentle art of making enemies, was not the sort of person whom one liked. His conceit was extreme and his political views could be hard to stomach, among the generally Liberal-minded artistic circle. The American Civil War was in progress and Whistler provocatively defended slavery. Invited to dinner, Gabriel appealed to a friend for support. 'Don't leave me at the mercy of the Confederacy,' he wrote. (Later, in a doubtful compliment, Jimmy would describe Rossetti as 'the only white man in all that crew'.)[25]

But he was undeniably amusing, and moreover a most original and serious painter, whose work challenged the prevailing mode rather as the PRB had done a decade earlier, with an unusual technique, taking infinite pains to achieve an impressionistic effect. 'It was interesting to watch him at work,' recalled Luke Ionides. 'He would compose his colour on the palette, and put on some touch; then he would stand off, and recompose his colour. It was almost like working in mosaic, and yet when it was finished it bore no trace of the way the effect was obtained . . .'[26] In summer 1862 his *White Girl* caused a small stir, on being exhibited independently after rejection at the RA. Like *Bocca Baciata*, it was suggestive but ambiguous, and both are now seen as seminal works in the emergence of Aestheticism.

Whistler greatly admired *Bocca Baciata*, urging that it be exhibited in Paris, and after they became near neighbours in Chelsea, Rossetti got to know him well, frequently strolling along to Whistler's in the evening, or sending an invitation to dine. In January 1863, he ordered a set of Whistler's etchings and admired Jo's painting on pebbles. In May, when William and Boyce called at Lindsey Row, they found Whistler and Jo at home, joined afterwards by Gabriel and Fanny.

When Whistler's mother came to Britain, Jo had to leave Lindsey Row for lodgings. As du Maurier recorded, Jemmy's brother-in-law then turned moralist, refusing to let his wife visit a house formerly polluted by Jo's presence. Similarly, Fanny was banished whenever a 'respectable' woman came to Tudor House. Among men, her presence was acceptable, but their wives or sisters would be insulted; for like Jenny she was indeed a fallen rose 'shut in a book / In which pure women may not look . . .'

In June of the first summer at Tudor House, the camera of William Downey recorded Ruskin's visit to Cheyne Walk at the same time as Bell Scott. Taking a chair into the garden, the photographer invited Ruskin to sit, as doyen of the group. 'Sit in the presence of Rossetti? Never!' replied Ruskin. So the men stand as an awkward trio, Scott like a comic policeman, bowler hat firmly over his bald pate, Ruskin and Rossetti with arms firmly linked. Afterwards, Ruskin made a strange boast of the pose, saying that Rossetti leaning on his arm was 'a truth-telling position'; although of course, he added, Rossetti's 'power and genius' hardly required his aid.[27]

The same afternoon, Fanny recalled, Ruskin and Scott carried a cheval glass into the garden, placed it among the bushes and helped Rossetti pose her against it, with a mirrored reflection for the photographer to catch. It was a favourite motif: in the autumn, when Whistler was working on his second picture of Jo, also standing before a mirror, Gabriel painted Fanny braiding her hair before a glass, in a similar white shift, with notes of blue and red. He gave this a title, or pretext, from his own translation of Fazio degli Uberti's ode to his mistress:

> I look at the crisp golden-threaded hair
> Whereof, to thrall my heart, Love twists a net;

...

> I would give anything that I possess,
> Only to hear her mouth say frankly, 'Yes.'

Swinburne's lines for Whistler's *Little White Girl* might have been written for either picture, either woman:

> She knows not where.
> Art thou my ghost, my sister
>   White sister there,
> Am I thy ghost, who knows?
> My hand, a fallen rose,
>   Lies snow white on white snows ...

Fazio's Mistress is a key work in the aesthetic transformation of Rossetti's art, whose component parts bring together his multiple preoccupations. Even more than *Bocca Baciata*, it is 'Venetian' in inspiration, manifestly in homage to Titian's image of Laura de Dinati in the Louvre. But its title alludes to the earlier world of Florence, with Uberti's poem to Angiola of Verona, with her white neck, shoulders, bosom. Above all, however, despite its historicising elements, the work is modern: merely the faithful likeness of a woman drying her hair, as Gabriel told Fanny later.

He told Miss Heaton the picture was 'chiefly a piece of colour ... showing a lady plaiting her golden hair'.[28] But this was no lady; and there could be no clearer proof of Fanny's presence in Tudor House than this and other images of her *toilette*. These are pictures from intimacy, not modelling, and they are among some of the best Rossetti painted.

At another photo-session, he got the photographer to take a group picture of the Cheyne Walk housemates, also in the garden. Fanny leans back, in her finest, widest crinoline, nervelessly holding a rose. Gabriel and William stand on either side, like supporters, while Swinburne is dwarfed on a low chair. With its literal eye, photography can kill illusion. Algernon is a clown, William a bald curate with nervous clasped hands. Gabriel looks like a seedy conjuror, who has organised a curious display.

By the end of the summer, Rossetti was feeling as well as looking seedy. When William 'dropped in with a request that I would accompany him to Belgium for a week', he agreed to a seven-day tour, during which William kept his customary prose diary. A chief object was the international art exhibition in Brussels, where he hoped to see more work by Henri Leys, who sadly did not exhibit. At the Belgian National Gallery, however, there was 'a very sufficient quantity of things to look at': seven or eight hundred paintings of the Old Master genre. Much Rubens (now no longer reviled) including a fine portrait of a noblewoman, a small 'martyrdom of many ladies' which sounds of interest to Swinburne, two fine Veroneses, an admirable Rembrandt, three rooms of old Flemish works, a good triptych by van Orley, a notable series by Philippe de Champaign, and the head of 'a beautiful young man, with peculiar and delightful costumes', ascribed to Giorgione, of which Gabriel made a quick note.[29]

The Jardin de Zoologie offered equal attractions: elephant, bison, lion, camel and a brown bear who obeyed commands, besides a large lake for wildfowl.

In Antwerp there were also pictures and animals – more Rubens, a Titian of Alexander VI, and in a notable private collection a delightful Pieter de Hooch and a nude *Prometheus* attributed to Velázquez, with beautiful brown-and-grey flesh tones. William was convinced, Gabriel more doubtful. A so-called Raphael *Virgin* convinced neither. Leys's projected frescoes in the City Hall were not yet started, while other works by him were packed up ready for removal. Again, the Zoo was splendid, with as many animals as in London, and a wonderful series of coloured parrots and macaws. There were two lion cubs, a young elephant, a blue-faced baboon, a rhinoceros and many antelope. The brothers dined on oysters at the restaurant Bertrand – 'a very good house, the reverse of cheap', noted William, who kept accounts.

They also raided 'old and out-of-the-way' shops for antique brass pots, gilt brooches, a large jar with blue birds, a Dutch Bible with old prints, a bed valance. Ghent in turn yielded an earthenware pot and two brass sconces. In Bruges the Hôtel du Commerce boasted a carved staircase with balusters in the shape of swans swallowing bulrushes. Unable to buy these, Gabriel took a sketch. Here they saw again the Memling altarpiece whose astounding finish and ecstatic poetry had overwhelmed Gabriel in 1849, the Van Eyck *Virgin and Child with SS Donatian and George*, and Memling's famous *châsse* – which seemed to have been repainted since last viewed. In between the Hospital and the Academy they bought two peacock fans and then, laden with purchases, headed for home. Waiting three hours in Lille they saw half an opera, and reached Calais by midnight. The next day a smooth sea brought them over the Channel in less than two hours, to Gabriel's great relief, for he was always a poor sailor.

The pots, sconces, fans and fabrics were for Tudor House, which was rapidly filling. Dining there this year, Munby so marvelled at the drawing room 'hung with curtains of old Indian chintz from end to end, and quaintly furnished with Japanese cabinets and Italian and Dutch pictures' that he could not stop walking up and down, absorbing 'the aroma of its manifold romance'. Tea was served in antique china, 'upon a carven table' by the light of massive Elizabethan candlesticks. On his next visit, a fire blazed in the antique grate, and all round pictures, ebony cabinets and silver-gilt dishes and flagons gleamed strangely against the dark wainscot panelling. Altogether an impressive scene, worthy of DGR's genius.

Modern pieces made by the Firm mingled with old. In July 1863 Rossetti reported the arrival of a sideboard of his own design, 'which licks all creation'. Swinburne added other items: a lacquer screen, painted mirrors, pictures on alabaster. 'When I return to Chelsea I shall enrich the house with various glories of Chinese origin,' he told William in October.[30] But the main passion was for porcelain. From the willow pattern ware he and Lizzie had used at Chatham Place, Gabriel graduated to antique blue-and-white Nankin china: platters, bowls, squat ginger jars, tall lidded pots nicknamed Lang Elizas, cups, teapots, slim-necked flasks. 'My Pots now baffle description altogether,' he crowed hyperbolically to Brown the following spring, 'COME AND SEE THEM.'[31]

One spur was competitive rivalry with Whistler, the subject of countless anecdotes. Many recalled how each tried to outwit the other in picking up choicest pieces from curiosity shops as well as the Oriental warehouse in Regent Street where Lazenby Liberty worked before opening his own aesthetic emporium, and the store in Sloane Street owned by Murray Marks, who soon became a main supplier. Whistler also bought in Amsterdam and Paris, and when Rossetti visited one famous Parisian boutique in autumn 1864 he was told by the proprietress, 'with a great deal of laughing', of Whistler's consternation at his impressive collection.

At Cheyne Walk, Gabriel began to entertain, occasionally in some style. On 30 April, when the four original housemates were in residence and Leathart was the principal guest, Boyce, Ned, Rose, John Marshall and painter George Chapman were also invited.[32] On 12 May, his thirty-fifth birthday, the diners were Swinburne, Munby and G. E. Street. On 16 July Monckton Milnes and Alphonse Legros joined Whistler, Boyce, Swinburne and William. Legros entertained the company with extracts from French comedy and opera, while Swinburne spouted French verse of his own devising. Another regular visitor was James Smetham, a sincere, religious and wholly unsuccessful painter, whom Rossetti had first met through the Working Men's College.

'Rossetti had a soft, southern, Italian voice, which was most persuasive when he advocated living among beautiful things of one's own choice,' wrote Luke Ionides, whom Whistler introduced. 'His own house was full of them: some copies of Italian chairs, some very fine old blue-and-white china, some good Chinese red lacquer, and several pictures.' Once, Luke was at a dinner-party in Tudor House when a fortuitous silence fell and a fellow diner – identified only as a well-known artist with a high-pitched voice – was heard saying, 'I had rather any day meet a lioness bereft of her whelps than a woman who has lost her virtue.' Then the soft voice of Rossetti answered, 'Nonsense, man, nonsense! I've met many and all very nice indeed.'[33]

There was no lioness or cubs at Cheyne Walk, but in the years from 1863 the garden housed a veritable menagerie of animals, purchased in the same spirit as the antique furniture. 'Being fond of "beasts" and having a large garden, with plenty of space for accommodating them either in the open or in corners partitioned off, he freely indulged his taste,' William wrote later, opening a list.[34] The Pomeranian puppy named Punch, a grand Irish deerhound named Wolf, a barn-owl named Jessie, another owl named Bobby ... rabbits, dormice, hedgehogs, two successive wombats, a Canadian marmot or woodchuck, an ordinary marmot, armadilloes, kangaroos, a deer, a white mouse with her brood, a racoon, squirrels, a mole, peacocks, wood-owls, Virginian owls, Chinese horned owls, a jackdaw, laughing jackasses, ungulated grass parakeets, a talking grey parrot, a raven, chameleons, green lizards and Japanese salamanders ...

'Persons who are familiar with the management of pets will easily believe that several of these animals came to a bad end,' he went on. 'Punch the puppy would get lost; one or other bird would get drowned; the dormice would fight and kill one another, or would eat up their own tails and gradually perish; Wolf the deerhound could get no adequate exercise and was given away; the parakeets were neglected at some time when Rossetti was absent from home, and on his return they were found dead. Other animals, from their burrowing or reclusive habits, disappeared. An armadillo was not to be found, and the tale went – I believe it to be not far from true – that ... he turned up under the hearthstone of a neighbour's kitchen, to the serious dismay of the cook ...'

Owing to neighbours' complaints, the Cadogan estate added a new clause to ground leases, forbidding householders to keep peacocks.

There was also a zebu or Indian bull, the size of a small pony, seen by Gabriel and William at Cremorne pleasure gardens and purchased for £20. On arrival, the beast tore through the house, pulling on its rope, before being tethered to a tree in the garden. When Gabriel went out to inspect, it charged angrily, causing him to dodge behind a bush like a terrified toreador. Eventually he escaped up the iron steps into the studio, leaving the zebu snorting and straining and looking likely to uproot its tree. It was resold at once.

Whistler told this tale, as well as one respecting a wombat, brought to table with the brandy and cigars when Swinburne read from *Leaves of Grass*. But Whistler conflated events, for the wombat came later, as a much-prized addition to the private zoo. Joking that it might be trained to wash the windows, Gabriel talked of buying an elephant, and almost acquired a lioness after all. 'Gabriel is thinking about buying a lion – really and truly having found one, a bargain, at a menagerie in Ratcliffe Highway,' Burne-Jones told Allingham in 1865. 'He has also bought some more blue pots, though he said he wouldn't . . .'

Small wonder that both ménage and menagerie at Cheyne Walk passed into legend.

CHAPTER FIFTEEN

Pot-Boilers and Paris

Such frivolities were accompanied and funded by developments in Rossetti's professional practice, which had begun on marriage and were now extended. Previously, he had painted for himself, following an individual vision and selling to a restricted circle of discerning friends and patrons. Henceforth, as befitted an artist in his mid-thirties who had always meant to be successful, he looked more to the market. An accompanying symbol of this established status came in the letterhead Rossetti now designed for his professional stationery, incorporating his father's family motto 'frangas non flectas' (break not bend). A pair of linked roundels contain his monogram, D and G encircling a sturdy R, and a stylised, leafy tree.

'Gabriel is at present in great force and plenty of commissions, so he is serene in this respect,' reported Scott in July 1863. A year later Rossetti confirmed this, telling his aunt he was 'getting quantities of commissions now, and never was so nearly prosperous before'.[1] If he kept an account book with titles, dates and payments, it has not survived; to see what 'quantities of commissions' meant in practice, a list of works produced, sold and contracted for during the mid-1860s has to be reconstructed, from which it can be seen that he was indeed very busy, particularly with small 'fancy heads', or ideal portraits in the *Bocca Baciata* mode. 'He has made several beautiful studies from divers women,' noted Boyce in March 1863, and as the genre required a regular supply of models, Rossetti began to build up a stable of attractive young women with paintable faces, like those accosted at Greenwich and South Kensington. Among those so 'discovered' were Agnes Manetti, Ellen Smith, Marie Ford and Ada Vernon.

Generally speaking, prices were determined by size, medium and complexity of subject, oils being more expensive than watercolours and pictures with figure groups fetching more than single figures or heads. Over the months in question, Rossetti's prices rose noticeably, and with them his reputation. Nationally, it was a period of continuing economic expansion and confidence, when art-buying increased, though from time to time a downturn in manufacturing or finance caused retrenchment. Major buyers included textile magnates, shipowners, brewers, bankers and the like.

During 1862, the oils *Girl at a Lattice* and *Monna Rosa* were followed by the watercolour *Paolo and Francesca* replica, sold to Leathart for over 100 guineas; *Bethlehem Gate* for Ellen Heaton; and *The Heart of the Night*, offered in turn to William Marshall and James Leathart for around 50 guineas and eventually sold to George Rae, a Merseyside banker. In September *After the Ninth Hour, Monna Rosa* and *The Farmer's Daughter* were sent to the Liverpool Autumn Exhibition, raising Rossetti's profile in this most prosperous region.

After Mrs Leathart's portrait in 1863 came five oil heads: *Belcolore, Joan of Arc, Helen of Troy, My Lady Greensleeves,* and *La Castagnetta*, together with a duplicate *Helen* and the watercolours *Lady in Yellow* and *Sweet Tooth*. As the fanciful and often confusing titles indicate, all were 'ideal portraiture' in a genre which had a mixed pedigree. Stretching back to images of Renaissance courtesans, it included the 'keepsake' or 'book of beauty' mode as well as works like Holst's *Ginevra*, and fluctuated in critical esteem. Currently it was a popular product in the artistic repertoire. The Prince of Wales owned Leighton's *Bianca*, a study of innocence and beauty in whites and pink, and this year the same artist made a splash at the Academy with his *Odalisque* – the depiction of a gorgeous woman, in William Rossetti's words, in which 'golden hair close gathered in the white headdress . . . the bosom half revealed . . . the ornamental scarf and peacock fan . . . roses, gilded domes, pink and blue sky and turquoise and chocolate butterflies' all went to create a stunning image.[2]

It was time to capitalise on Gambart's liking for *Bocca Baciata* and reach new clients. Despite his earlier misgivings, in relation to the Plint estate Rossetti had found the dealer a businesslike fellow. He was pleased when Gambart approved Mrs Leathart's portrait and impressed when he resold a replica *Lucrezia Borgia* for 100 guineas, having paid 50. Later in the year Gambart appears to have also taken *Fazio's Mistress, The Gate of Memory* and a *St George and the Dragon* worked up from the stained-glass design. As well as ideal heads, he could find buyers for small figure groups and crayon studies. All in all, Gabriel reported, the dealer 'understands pictures to some extent and their marketable qualities perfectly' and was therefore well able to judge whether something would sell, even without a 'name' to back it.[3]

With Knewstub to assist, Rossetti's rate of production rose rapidly, especially as many works were replicas and copies in other media from earlier designs. This was standard practice in the Victorian art world, where coloured reproduction was not otherwise possible, Old Master copies were a recognised genre and a painter's reputation was often based on his most sought-after works. While some patrons wished to possess a unique piece, others were content with duplicates, if done by the artist himself. In the tradition of the Renaissance workshop, studio assistants usually began replicas, leaving key areas and final touches for the artist to complete, and though subsequently such works were devalued in market terms, there was usually nothing false or inferior about them. Starting with the *Lucrezia*, Knewstub progressed to other works, among them watercolour versions of *Dante and Beatrice in Eden*, *La Belle Dame sans Merci* and *How They Met Themselves*.

Naturally, original commissions were also welcome. As the 1863 exhibition season opened, Miss Heaton called, asking if Mr Rossetti were able to produce a posthumous portrait of his wife. No, he replied, perhaps reluctant to return to those many poignant drawings. Instead, he proposed 'a Dantesque subject I have long meant to do', showing Beatrice seated with scenes from the *Vita Nuova* in the background 'in the manner of old Italian painters'. Would she like this, 'about the same size as the Joan of Arc?' The head, from Marie Ford, was already laid in.[4]

A second request came via Alex Munro from Lady Ashburton – old friend of Pauline Trevelyan – for 'some Dante subjects' in watercolour. In response, Rossetti proposed a replica of the *Salutation on Earth and in Heaven* from the Red House settle – 'about the same size again'. The two scenes would be framed together, 'with the symbolic figure of Love, as I before designed it, painted on the gilded upright dividing the two pictures'. So again the settle doors were detached and came to Cheyne Walk. By October the copy was ready for delivery. Simultaneously, Rossetti sold the original panels to Gambart, for 200 guineas (as they actually belonged to Morris, payment probably went to the Firm). Gambart sold the work on, for 350 guineas, and in due course it was bought by the painter Frederick Burton, and then by Leathart.[5]

When, in October, the photographer Rev. C. L. Dodgson asked the Rossettis to sit to him as artistic celebrities, Gabriel persuaded him in return to take some photographs of his drawings, and a portrait of the model Helene Beyer. These were to show prospective clients, and no doubt were seen in December by George Rae, calling to discuss a commission. With some persuasion, Rae agreed to take the picture originally conceived as Beatrice seated but subsequently redesigned as the Queen of Sheba or Solomon's Bride, already offered to Ellen Heaton. In compensation, and to fulfil Miss Heaton's wish for a portrait of Lizzie, Rossetti proposed a new Beatrice, based on 'a life-size head of my wife in oil begun many years ago'. With the aid of earlier studies, he now thought he could succeed posthumously. At the same time he borrowed back Miss Heaton's watercolour *Dante's Dream*, to make a copy from which he might one day paint a large oil. Then Mr Clabburn, a friend of Sandys from Norwich, commissioned a small *Mary Magdalene*, paying partly with the peacock and hen. Gorgeous beyond expression, replied the grateful artist.[6]

Despite telling Munro he intended to give up watercolour, this medium remained Rossetti's staple. By the end of 1863, he was discussing with Gambart a two-year contract to supply pictures on a fortnightly basis, for 40 guineas apiece. In January 1864, *Monna Pomona*, drawn from Ada Vernon, was sold to Constantine Ionides and the similar *Brimfull* went to John Mitchell of Bradford. Saying his business was with 'men of name', and warning that Rossetti's distinctive style was being deployed by others, the dealer urged him to join the Old Water-Colour Society in order to become better known. But again Gabriel resisted, unwilling to 'become ticketed as a watercolour painter wholly or even chiefly', and saying he intended to mount a solo show of all his pictures 'for exhibition by themselves some day'.[7] So, by March the contract was still unsigned. 'I want your advice in the matter,' Rossetti told Brown. Gambart's success suggested better terms should be negotiated, and accordingly he now felt that 50 guineas should be the price. Gambart replied in 'a rather injured and very long letter', but agreed.

Further subjects were adapted or recycled, including a watercolour *Wedding of St George*, from the stained-glass design, which went appositely to Emily Epps (a family friend) as a wedding gift from her husband. *St George and the Dragon*, which Gambart had failed to sell on behalf of the Plint estate, was now bought by Henry Tebbs, husband of Emily Seddon.[8] *Drawing the Lot*, from the same sequence, was laid aside apparently on Gambart's advice that such 'painful' subjects were unpopular. Other works in 1864 included *Roman de la Rose*, based on the *Early Italian Poets* design, a new version of *The First Madness of Ophelia*, an original design called *Morning Music*, and a small watercolour of the 'Gardening' panel on the Seddon cabinet, retitled *Spring*.

The more works Gambart sold, of course, the greater grew Gabriel's expectations. 'I should not usually be offering you a smaller drawing at all,' he wrote in respect of the tiny *Spring*; 'but am needing a sum of 150 guineas just now, and could easily obtain more than this for the two larger drawings alone by sending them to a private purchaser, but this would cause delay . . .'

In May, production was briefly interrupted when he caught mumps, but he was soon back at work, completing *David Pastor*, the remaining Llandaff wing. Most significantly, he also negotiated three major new commissions, all for Yorkshire businessmen. The first was with Walter Dunlop of Bingley, who had ordered the *Tristram* window sequence from MMF & Co. and was now persuaded to commission *The Ship of Love*, a large oil showing Dante and Cavalcanti with their ladies, for the fine price of 2,000 guineas.[9] The second client was Dunlop's business colleague John Heugh, who bought two unidentified watercolours, and agreed to commission two larger works – one a sacred subject (probably a version of the Mary Magdalene begun for Plint), the other showing Aspasia teaching Socrates to dance. The third was John Mitchell, who commissioned a female nude in oils.

Smaller commissions this season included a portait in oils of handsome Mrs Heimann; two watercolours for Ellen Heaton: *Sir Galahad, Sir Perceval and Sir Bors*, originally designed for the Oxford Union, and a replica of *Joan of Arc*; and an oil copy of *Music* from the King René cabinet, commissioned by J. H. Trist, a Brighton wine-merchant, for 80 guineas. Started by Knewstub, this was completed at the end of August. 'I finished Trist's pot-boiler today, and lo, the pot shall boil for a season,' Gabriel reported to Brown, hoping that Trist would not 'cackle like twigs on a campfire' when he saw it. 'I have been at work on it exactly eight days, so it pays better than most, though cheap.' In fact Trist was pleased, and paid promptly. Further sales on this scale included three variations on the popular motif of the woman at her *toilette*, all of which seem to have sold to Northern patrons via Gambart. The dramatic *Fight over a Woman* was however rejected by Gambart as a subject 'likely to prove unpopular'.[10]

'Rossetti is making an incredible lot of money and number of small works,' Scott reported to the Trevelyans, adding that this had recently resulted in the purchase of 130 further pieces of blue china, at the cost of £50. So, although obliged to admit to George Rae that he had made no progress whatever on Solomon's Bride, it was with some pride that Gabriel himself told aunt Charlotte he hoped 'henceforward to do almost exclusively large works in oil', having sufficiently established himself so as to give up 'small things and water-colours I never should have done at all, except for the long continuance of necessity for "pot-boilers".'[11]

In fact, the small works and high rate of production were partly to fill the inactive hours with occupation rather than grief, partly in order to provide cash-flow while working on larger pictures, and partly because all this while he was also liquidating his £700 debt to the Plint estate, which he had promised to repay in cash or kind. Although at the end of 1863 he complained of a 'cheeky' inquiry from the Trustees, surviving records of his account with Rose show regular payments at roughly half-year intervals thereafter, totalling £580 by the end of 1866.[12] Even allowing for interest, together with the pictures already delivered, it looks as if the outstanding amount was repaid in full by this date. It was an impressive feat.

Another debt was to Major Gillum, for money advanced on undelivered works. Early in 1864 Rossetti wrote proposing pictures or a refund 'at dates fixed by agreement during the same time that I am paying off the Plint debt'. Gillum and his wife then called, saying they preferred pictures, and were willing to wait. No further works were delivered, however, and the matter must have been otherwise settled. In view of Rossetti's sense of gentlemanly honour – whatever his high-handed tone towards patrons – it is probable that this debt was also repaid in full, possibly in the shape of items from the Firm. Or it may have been allowed to lapse by the generous Gillum, whose affection for DGR was undimmed; in 1882 he purchased several works from the artist's sale.[13]

A third outstanding matter was finally concluded when *David Pastor* was delivered to Llandaff. Payment – the last £100 – was received in October, when Rossetti went to Wales to see the whole altarpiece in position and touch up the previous panels. The pale stonework of the reredos did not show the triptych to advantage, but his suggestion that the surround be painted black was hardly feasible.

Thus, though Rossetti is often accused – and accused himself – of laziness and procrastination, in a period of thirty months during 1862–4 he produced and sold nearly forty small-to-medium-sized works, including eleven in oil. Estimating unknown prices conservatively, and including both advance payments and those for older works, his earnings can be assessed as around £3,000. Spread over three years, and deducting the debts to Plint and others, this is not an astronomical sum, but it was healthy and well in excess of his needs. For comparison, the more flamboyant Whistler is thought to have earned around £300 a year in this period, while in June 1864 Leighton's conspicuous success at the RA, *Dante at Verona* (a Rossettian subject, surely?) which secured his election to the Academy, was sold by Gambart for 1,000 guineas, of which presumably at least half went to the artist. Furthermore, during this period Rossetti was also producing designs for the Firm, and working on Gilchrist's *Life of Blake*. Like his neighbour in Lindsey Row, a certain nonchalance concealed assiduous industry.

His prices had increased, from 30 to 100 guineas per watercolour, from around 50 to 80 for a small oil, and to anything over 200 guineas for a medium to large work. This, as he readily acknowledged, was the result of the new-style marketing. In November 1864 he outlined the position to James Smetham, who for personal reasons was never able to function commercially. 'As to the dealers, I never went near them myself, but at last one or two have come to me, and one – Gambart – seems disposed to take anything of a small kind I will let him have and has thus benefited me immensely, having doubled my prices in the market in a very short time,' he explained, 'so that I now get for small works I suppose as high a price (considering the time they take me and the steadiness with which I can dispose of them) as anyone. I have also got a ready market for larger things at proportionate prices from private persons, but the dealers are not so fond of these as small ones. I mention all this to show I consider it the best thing possible for an artist to get into the dealing world, and indeed not to believe anything of a decisive kind can be done without it ...'[14]

Reading the market, Gambart also encouraged the production of unframed drawings, which were 'all the rage' at the end of 1864. 'The great thing with dealers just now is to get men of name to make moderate-sized water-colours for mounting,' Gabriel added. 'Of these they make portfolios – one of each man – and sell the collection together to cotton spinners and the like. It is far more profitable to them, and to artists too, than anything else can be.'

Moreover, unlike other dealers, Gambart paid on receipt rather than on resale. This year, for example, he entered a contract with the Belgian artist Laurens Alma-Tadema, for the supply of twenty-four paintings, to be delivered regularly, on a rising scale of prices that averaged £80. 'He is, as far as I have found him, a straightforward man and an immediate paymaster,' Gabriel confirmed.

Gambart also sold discreetly, preferring that clients and customers should not compare notes. He showed discreetly too, so works did not languish publicly unwanted in his saleroom. Moreover he did not demand an exclusive contract, but allowed Rossetti to sell directly if desired. All created a degree of opacity useful to both artist and dealer if not to historians, since without full records it is impossible to tell which works passed through his hands, or ascertain exact prices.

Once, Gambart had been a vampire and a demon; now he was honest Ernest, the artists' benefactor. But if he was not Mephistopheles, nevertheless the deal he brokered cost something. In steering artists towards more saleable subjects, he encouraged Rossetti to produce ideal portraits in an essentially formulaic manner – the innumerable 'visions of carnal loveliness with floral accessories' – and thereby become known as a painter of 'beauties'. Later, when people complained that all the faces in his pictures looked alike, William protested that insofar as the works were similar the reason lay in the taste of the buyers. This was indeed true: customers liked decorative images of young women with beguiling titles, and the assurance that they were drawn 'from nature'. Artistically, the genre would once have been scorned by the PRB as 'sloshy', however, while a sizeable proportion of the public saw such works as sensuous, pandering to increasingly vulgar tastes as the easygoing decade advanced. But steadily, by this means, Gabriel established the distinctive female image, freighted with symbolic meaning and enigmatic emotion, that is now known as 'Rossettian'.

From his own disparaging references to 'pot-boilers', some commentators have contended that in the later part of his career, Rossetti 'consciously sacrificed his artistic integrity for pragmatic ends'.[15] The implication is that he was now selling his soul rather than painting it. But the matter is complex. Some of the works of this period are undoubtedly inferior and formulaic; but many are triumphs of mood and colour. Moreover, despite his success with Dantesque and chivalric watercolours, his ambition had never been to create small visions only, in the style, say, of Samuel Palmer or James Smetham. Like Blake, his imagination soared; in many cases the jewelled drawings were meant as colour sketches for bigger pictures. Their replicas and reworkings were a means of buying time for the creation of larger, more elevated subjects, filled with poetic feeling. So too the fancy heads that followed *Bocca Baciata* fall into the strategic category, as attractive pictures to attract patrons, or at worst produce ready money. For while Rossetti had always disdained vulgarity and mere commercialism, he also had a horror of failure and penury, fearing the fate of Haydon, and that of his own father. Millais too is often damned for painting pretty pictures, sentimental scenes, bread-and-butter portraits whose main merit was saleability. But the alternative might have been not to paint at all: the art world was full of promising men who had given up in favour of a salaried position, or who struggled on precariously. At worst, an artist who could not sell starved in a garret with canvases stacked around, but this Van Goghian figure was not much admired in the Victorian era, where artistic success was measured by wealth, sustained output, eminent clients and magnificent houses. The position of unworldly genius was already occupied by G. F. Watts, secure in the Prinseps' patronage. Never unworldly, Rossetti did not intend his talents to be constrained by poverty or dependency.

At the same time, throwing himself into painting in these months after Lizzie's death, with intent to make money, may also have been a reaction to his loss. Wherefore high art, ambition, idealism? Vanity, vanity, all is vanity, saith the preacher . . . Ideal heads and watercolour replicas were mechanical, undemanding. Only as he came out of numbness, as it were, did his true creative energies return. Two years was the customary mourning period. And in this time, the art world had visibly altered. Moral and romantic subjects gave place to works of colour, form and visual beauty – an aesthetic hedonism to match the age. Rossetti had no wish to be isolated or left behind. Nevertheless, painting for the market posed real dangers to his creative imagination: it may well be that he needed a longer spoon.

Publicly, his status remained insecure. George du Maurier, meeting him at Simeon Solomon's studio in spring 1864, noted that he was now 'head of the Pre-Raphaelites, for Millais and Hunt have seceded; spoilt so to speak by their immense popularity', while as Rossetti never exhibited he was comparatively unknown; 'this strange contempt for fame is rather grand'.[16] A little while later, his name was conspicuously absent from a 'first class though not exhaustive list' of artists itemised by Francis Palgrave for the *Saturday Review.* Perhaps this was one reason why he now set about painting a most striking, uncharacteristic subject. Somewhat ironically, at precisely the time that his largest sacred work was completed for its cathedral, his first female nude was on the easel.

The patron John Mitchell was a Yorkshire import-export merchant of progressive Liberal views, typical of buyers from the ranks of 'cotton spinners and the like' whom Rossetti had commended to Smetham. Although 'the decentest of the lot' in Rossetti's view, he was 'looked down on as a cad rather', presumably owing to his unrefined tastes. (When urged to take a picture from Brown, Mitchell preferred an ancient pot-boiler known in the studios as 'doggie is jealous'.) This led him first to buy *Brimfull,* a 'keepsake' style watercolour in which a girl flirtatiously raises a glass to a man standing in the viewer's position. Acknowledging payment, Rossetti remarked coyly that he wished the image was 'really as handsome as the original who sat for her'. He had made 'many such studies of beautiful female heads', he added; priced at 10 to 25 guineas, in a portfolio these drawings would create a perfect ' "Book of Beauty" direct from nature'.[17]

'A Book of Beauty' was a compilation of prints from famous art works, each showing a celebrated woman from history or legend. But instead of portfolio drawings, Mitchell's commission was for a life-size Venus, naked amid flowers. Putting all else aside, Rossetti enthusiastically started work. Visiting Chelsea on 26 June, Allingham 'found DGR painting a very large young woman, almost a giantess, as "Venus Verticordia".' The title means 'turner of hearts' and according to William the model was 'a handsome and striking woman, not very much less than six feet high', who normally worked as a cook and whom Gabriel had approached in the street.[18] Her name is not known.

First, he drew a large red chalk study, not much smaller than the final canvas, showing the half-length figure behind a ledge in traditional Old Master manner. Her arm concealing one breast, she holds an arrow and an apple, Venus's attributes, and stands before an arbour of roses. Within the composition is also a sonnet, pinned as it were to the trellis, identifying the goddess of Love as a personification of the physical desire that arouses, enslaves and destroys men:

> She muses, with her eyes upon the track
> Of some dazed moth or honey-sucking bee;

Haply, 'He is not one of these,' saith she.
Alas, the apple for his lips – the dart
That follows in brief sweetness to his heart ...

Lately, Swinburne had written *Laus Veneris*, inspired by the Tannhäuser tale, and *St Dorothy*, in which Venus-worship features as a pagan ritual. Both were among the poems sent this year to Macmillan with Rossetti's endorsement. 'Don't swear more than you can help,' Gabriel warned in September when the inevitable rejection arrived.[19] The publisher's pudency was renowned; not surprisingly he funked all such lascivious themes.

Visually, Rossetti's Venus is a large, arresting, bare-breasted woman rather too close to the viewer for comfort. Though very little naked flesh is actually visible, she points the arrow plainly at her exposed nipple, making the provocative eroticism explicit. He was of course already halfway there, with half-length, close-up figures: *Bocca Baciata, Monna Pomona, Fazio's Mistress, Monna Rosa*, even *My Lady Greensleeves*, are but draped heralds of this Venus. Her verbal counterpart appears in *The Painter of Modern Life* by Charles Baudelaire (whom Swinburne had recently met) in a vivid evocation of the Parisian demi-mondaine. Against light either from hell or the aurora borealis, this begins – 'red, orange, sulphur yellow, pink (to express an idea of ecstasy amid frivolity) there arises a Protean image of wanton beauty. Now she is majestic, now playful ... now tiny and sparkling, now heavy and monumental ... She is a perfect image of the savagery that lurks in the midst of civilisation.'[20]

Despite his apparent indifference to fashion, Rossetti was responding to the mood. Both nudes and neo-classicism were making a comeback in art, though moral voices were still raised against public representations of nudity, held by many to be an especially French vice and perennially regrettable in the Great Masters. William Etty, the last pre-Victorian painter of naked women, was still a by-word for indecency in fine art. Edward Poynter's *Siren* of 1864 barely challenged prevailing views: though naked to the waist, the pose obscured both breasts. Somewhat surprisingly, however, Watts's *Study with Peacock Feathers*, which Rossetti may well have seen on the easel and was exhibited in 1865, frontally presents a Boucher-like figure leaning back with one arm invitingly raised.

If not on gallery walls, openly erotic images were of course available to men, 'under the counter' or in specialist print-shops in the shape of nude photographs, many marketed as 'artistic studies' like life drawings, to assist painters, others discreetly or fully pornographic.[21] In 1860 two hundred stereoscopic coloured prints by Auguste Belloc foreshadowing Courbet's *Origine du monde* were seized by the French police. In those of Louis-Camille d'Olivier, dating from the mid-1850s, some figures were placed before mirrors, the better to display their charms, not unlike the poses chosen by Rossetti and Whistler for Fanny and Jo.

The chief inspiration for *Venus Verticordia*, however, came from Titian's Venetian courtesans, whose thin shift has frequently slipped off the shoulder to reveal one breast – the effect Rossetti reproduced – and perhaps also the the nude versions of the *Mona Lisa* in circulation in the nineteenth century. Another antecedent was both more ancient and more local. In June 1863 two versions of Botticelli's *Venus Pudica* were sold at Christie's; in one the golden-haired goddess adopts the classic *pudica* pose, in the other she held a diaphanous drapery across the hips, which a recent owner had filled with an obscuring garland of roses. Both works were acquired by the Ashburtons, whose picture collection Rossetti much admired. At around this time, Rossetti purchased a profile portrait by Botticelli of Smeralda di Bandinelli, and was always loud in his praise of the artist. *Mona Lisa*'s 'equivocal smile' was, however, not to his taste at all; he preferred the peculiar 'fixedness of expression' that had first impressed him in Holst's *The Wish*.[22]

In the histories of art, the female nude is one of the classic categories, a challenge to every painter and sculptor, almost a rite of passage. When in 1865 Fred Stephens wrote of the *Verticordia* on Rossetti's behalf, he invoked the great exemplars. 'She is a Venus after Chaucer's heart, not the grave mother of the grand Greek school, still less a small meretrix like the Venus de' Medici or the pert women of the late Renaissance, but one of the true Renaissance, that glorious Indian summer when Art halted awhile before it fell completely.'[23] The ostentatious assertion illustrates the play Rossetti was making for a position among the masters of the female nude. In contrast with the glabrous, air-brushed nudes generally deemed admissible in contemporary art, the somewhat coarser painting of *Venus Verticordia* certainly posed a challenge.

By July, the picture was well advanced. In the foreground, the ledge was heaped, or replaced, with a bank of honeysuckle, rising so as to obscure everything below the breasts, yet simultaneously symbolising sexual desire through the flowers' curling petals, cream and deep red, with a directly erotic appeal. They were, however, troublesome to obtain. 'I got three different parcels of honeysuckles from three different friends in three different parts of England, none of which were any use,' Gabriel told his mother. 'Then I got some from a nursery at Waltham Cross which were not much use either, and lastly from the Crystal Palace. All with much delay and bother. But the picture gets on well now.'[24]

By 23 August, he was proposing a halo for Venus's head. 'I believe the Greeks used to do it,' he informed Brown. One senses Swinburne behind the sacrilege, although the golden nimbus over loose-flowing hair echoes the many depictions of Mary Magdalene in the Western tradition – the one figure in which artists could combine the sacred and the profane. 'I'm doing a Venus; which I mean to make a stunner,' Rossetti informed Macmillan in the autumn.[25]

As female nudes go, *Venus Verticordia* is neither remarkable as a nude nor as a triumph of art – one senses the same awkwardness with the naked form that Gabriel experienced when drawing at the Maddox Street life class. But its sensual impact is considerable, especially through the figure's bold demeanour, provocatively meeting the spectator's eye, and through the overheated tones: pink, tawny, orange, yellow, red.

Ruskin certainly perceived this. Denying that his taste had changed because he praised *Found* and hated the Venus, he explained further: 'I purposely used the word "wonderfully" painted about those flowers. They were wonderful to me, in their realism; awful I can use no other word – in their coarseness; showing enormous power; showing certain conditions of non-sentiment which underlie all you are doing – now – and which make your work, compared to what it used to be – what Fannie's face is to Lizzie's.'[26] The message was oblique but unmistakable. Rossetti had not 'used to be' a sensual painter. In this sense, *Venus Verticordia* was a clear statement.

Rae declined a smaller watercolour version, saying 'Ettyism' was not to his taste. Rossetti protested, denying the presence of any such quality[27] and Rae was persuaded. Or perhaps he parted with the required 100 guineas in the hope of seeing his *Beloved*, commissioned a year since and as yet untouched.

Flushed with success and anticipated riches, Rossetti began to behave like a successful artist. 'Could you tell me what the cost of building a thoroughly good but not showy studio in my garden ought to be, and most of all, how long it would take?' he asked Philip Webb on 1 July, apparently thinking of a Crystal Palace-type structure. 'Do you think one of any kind could be run up in a month or so? I have got some commissions for large works and cannot possibly paint them indoors.' The following month, however, caution prevailed, as Mitchell failed to remit money for the *Venus* and Heugh hesitated over the *Magdalene*. Euphoria was easily dissipated. 'As soon as I set about doing my best, I get bankrupt at once,' he wrote despondently to Brown. 'The only thing is to stick to the watercolours and earn whereby to live.'[28] Plans to visit Florence for authentic backgrounds to Dante's *Ship of Love* were quietly shelved. Instead, and after many postponements, he took Fanny to Paris.

'Paris is very much altered since I was last here,' he told his mother,[29] prosaically echoing Baudelaire's lament: '*Le vieux Paris n'est plus; la forme d'une ville change plus vite, hélas! Que le cœur d'un mortel.*' The *grands projets* of the Second Empire were in train, masterminded by Haussmann for Napoleon III. The city was being emptied of its poor as slum districts were cleared while grand boulevards, hotels, railway stations, town mansions, parks and gardens were built for the beau monde. Suburban communities were absorbed and workers sucked in from the provinces, doubling the population. Ambitious sewerage and water systems tackled the city's reputation as *Paris puant*, so that Louis Napoleon was praised for having found it stinking and left it sweet. Visitors flocked to sample the delights of shopping, dancing, cafés, theatre-going, horse-racing, and carriage rides. It was an era of conspicuous display, amid an atmosphere of high spending, high living and high prices. Fashionable society followed the Empress Eugénie, or the *demi-monde* of celebrated courtesans like La Paiva and la belle Otéro. Chez Nadar, the famous photographer's emporium, was a landmark of this new bourgeois metropolis of *luxe* and *richesse*, in a tall modern building of glass and red-painted ironwork at 35 rue des Capucines.

Not to be outclassed, Gabriel and Fanny stayed first at the Grand Hotel, *l'orgueil du Paris nouveau*, which occupied a full block on the same boulevard, close to the new Opéra. A huge establishment with 750 rooms and a circular *salle à dîner* with 300 covers, its reading room had newspapers from all countries and a 24-hour telegraph service. It was flanked by *magasins de luxe* – confectionery chez Boissier, millinery chez Laure, the latest gilt and velvet wall-coverings chez Maigret, sumptuous dolls and clockwork toys chez Giroux. Perhaps the style was too high. After a week or so they moved to a more modest hotel in the rue Lafitte, amidst art galleries and dealers.

Twenty-five years earlier Rossetti had been here with Hunt, students racing through the Louvre, haunting the print-shops and watching the cancan. Four and a half years before, he and Lizzie had been on honeymoon. This time – despite Fanny – he was on professional business, as an artist, perhaps to stay awhile, assess the market, seek out a new clientèle. He took enough work to last three months, and had half a plan to go on to Florence, for a view of Dante's Arno.

Whistler had long talked of contemporary French art and artists, and his regular moves with Jo between London and Paris signalled a new cosmopolitanism; in 1863 he took Swinburne to meet Baudelaire and visit Manet's studio. Settling in London later that year, Alphonse Legros had quickly become one of the Chelsea artists, warmly befriended by Rossetti, who displayed his works in his own studio, and arranged for Legros to copy Old Masters for Lady Ashburton.

In Paris in the late 1850s Whistler and Legros had been companions with Henri Fantin-Latour, as the Société des trois. After Delacroix's death in August 1863, Fantin conceived the idea of a Salon picture showing younger artists and writers paying tribute to the Master, in the 'new generation' spirit. The planned group included himself, Legros, Manet, Bracquemond, Baudelaire, Champfleury, Duranty and Whistler. Whistler suggested including Rossetti too, whom he said had a 'fine head' and a 'great talent'.[30] Gabriel agreed, in principle. On 3 February, Whistler told Fantin that they were coming, but a fortnight later Rossetti withdrew, pleading pressure of work. *Hommage à Delacroix* duly went to the Salon, where it caused a stir, and a month or so later Fantin came to London, where he sold six pictures and received two portrait commissions. He also met Gambart, who offered to buy the *Hommage*. In the London art world, 'connections are everything', he commented, evidently quoting his hosts; 'people must be made to buy, buying must be made fashionable'. There was, naturally, much talk of Paris, where a Delacroix memorial exhibition was being held at the Galerie Martinet.

So when Gabriel Rossetti arrived in Paris, Fantin took him in charge. 'I can't leave him to his own devices, his having so kindly received me in London,' he told Legros. 'We have been together to the Louvre, to the Luxembourg, chez Manet, chez Courbet (the studio as he isn't in town) and more than once to the Café de Bade, so he's seen all the fellows.'[31] Plying Fantin with questions, Rossetti wanted to meet everyone, hear about all the new work. Manet promised an introduction to Alfred Stevens, who wished to meet Rossetti and would show him Millet's work.

Fantin and Stevens had studios in the St Lazare *quartier*. Manet's was further west, in the newly developed area beyond the parc Monceau. While they looked at pictures, Fanny presumably stayed in the hotel. In the evenings, they visited the ritzy cafés clustered on the boulevard des Italiens – Tortoni, de Bade, La Maison Dorée, Café des Anglais – or sought further entertainment in the cabaret theatres, cafés-concerts and *cirque d'hiver*, where a few years since M. Léotard had introduced the flying trapeze. It was a brief taste of the life of the *artiste-flâneur*, as commended by Baudelaire. 'Baudelaire is away or I should have met him,' Gabriel reported to Swinburne, whose compliments he had promised to deliver. Months before, Swinburne had sent his review of *Fleurs du Mal* to the author, although unbeknownst to either, Baudelaire's thanks were languishing undelivered in Nadar's pocket.

'Fantin is anxious to see anything you may have written about his Delacroix picture. Is there anything, and where?' Gabriel asked William. It had been his own first task to see the *Hommage*, on which he complimented the artist warmly. Fantin was not deceived, however; why the devil should Rossetti, the Pre-Raphaelite, like such a picture?[32] And indeed, Gabriel's private opinion to William was that, despite a good deal of very able painting, the work overall was 'a great slovenly scrawl like the rest of this new French school – people painted with two eyes in one socket through merely being unable to efface the first, and what not.'

By the 'new French school' he meant the successors to Delacroix who followed Courbet in choosing contemporary subjects and a rough, realist style. It was their handling to which he objected: the lack of finish, the loose brushwork, the empty spaces, the lack of glazes to pull a composition together, and the general effect of a colour sketch. The pictures by Manet, the school's leading light, were the worst, he said, and those by Courbet, the founder, were not much better. But, he added, 'Don't tell Whistler what I say of Fantin's picture.' For face-to-face he was his charming self, *vraiment très aimable*, despite the lack of artistic rapport. 'We like hardly anything in common,' observed Fantin genially.[33]

Yet in many ways the two men were quite alike. At twenty-eight, Fantin was intensely serious about his vocation, haunted by fear of sloth and temptations that might keep him from the exalted heights to which he aspired. Like Rossetti, too, he was prone to moods, swinging between arrogance and despondency; later in life he became something of a recluse. Both also deplored politics; after an evening at Paul Meurice's salon spent discussing 'democracy', Fantin roundly declared that Art had nothing to do with such matters.[34] And although committed to painting 'from nature', both artists hated working out of doors, their pictures being strongly studio-bound. The works Fantin had taken to London included two large imaginative scenes, brightly coloured hymns to sensuous pleasure, full of light and movement, quite 'unreal' in conception. *Fantasy* (or *La Féerie*) was like something from the *Arabian Nights* and the *Venusberg* from *Tannhäuser* a *fête champêtre* with nymphs in a nebulous landscape. Bought by Alexander Ionides, the latter formed a link with Rossetti's own *Venus*, through Swinburne and Wagner, though Rossetti signally did not share Fantin's passion for music. Currently Fantin was preparing a successor to his Delacroix picture called *Hommage à la verité*, which was to allegorise the Higher Realism by showing a group of artists raising their glasses to the naked figure of Truth. Rossetti, who had an eye for the risible, may have foreseen the mockery that would greet this grandiose failure. Meanwhile, with Parisian condescension, Fantin smiled at his visitor's undeveloped taste in art. 'Gérôme, I fear, is almost the one he likes best,' he told Legros, adding that when at the Galerie Martinet someone had praised Delacroix and Whistler in the same breath, Rossetti's amazement knew no bounds.[35]

To friends at home, Gabriel offered a sweeping assessment of the contemporary scene. 'There is one man named Millet who can't sell his pictures except to someone who buys him up cheap and at whose house I saw a collection of them, really glorious things,' he told Swinburne. 'Really there seems to be no one else alive except Ingres who's nearly dead and Gérôme whom one can't stand for ever as he doesn't paint. Delacroix gains every time I see him. He is a real great man though often wonderfully shaky.' For the rest, 'the whole of French art at present is a beastly slop and really makes one sick' or 'simple putrescence and decomposition'.

In part, this was plain prejudice and English nationalism. Being abroad always roused the bulldog in Rossetti. Not long since, moreover, the painters of London had been drilling with the Artists' Rifles to protect Britain from French aggression. They were not likely to genuflect before Parisian painting; indeed, Rossetti told Rae, the current state of art in France was 'quite calculated to put English artists on their mettle to make a good run for the lead'.[36] It did not help that the French were largely uninterested in contemporary British art, and still identified Pre-Raphaelitism only with Millais and Hunt. But the shallow vulgarity of Rossetti's remarks betrays a more complex response, suggesting that he was unsettled by what Fantin's 'jeune école' was doing.

'We form a group and make a noise because there are lots of painters about and one is easily overlooked,' wrote Fantin to his main English patron, Edwin Edwards. 'We gain strength in numbers, and grow more adventurous.'[37] This, more or less, had been the PRB strategy, and there were many ways in which Courbet and his successors, working independently of the Academy, extending the range of art to encompass modern subjects and history painting imbued with a sense of past realities, committed to painting from actual rather than ideal forms, and arrogant of artistic individuality, shared similar goals to those of the Brotherhood. Indeed, to stress the affinity, William later quoted from Courbet's artistic manifesto of 1855 as epigraph to his book on the PRB: 'I wish simply to draw from the full knowledge of tradition the reasoned, independent expression of my own individuality.'[38]

They differed in their means, however, using a dark palette, free brushwork and rough finish, and in their respective valuation of form and feeling. As Fantin perceived when describing how well and sensitively Rossetti spoke about art, he nevertheless like most British artists valued 'sentiment' – subject and emotion – too much, and 'savoir' – skill with form and colour – too little. The new French painters resolutely refused to render modern-life scenes in a moralising manner. Their portraits contained no anecdote and no flattery. Though regarded as realists, they disdained photographic exactitude, believing in the primacy of nature and the authenticity of the artist's experience to provide convincing visual form. Smooth finish was deplored; according to Baudelaire, what was complete (*fait*) was not necessarily finished (*fini*) and something highly finished might not be complete at all.[39]

Rossetti knew some of this from Whistler and Swinburne, who were promoting the new French aesthetic in London. Visiting the studios and salons as well as the galleries, he perceived plainly how this was an avant-garde of new departures and new challenges. Finding himself so much more in tune with Delacroix than with Manet, his own preferences and aims suddenly seemed traditional rather than innovative. British artists had been overtaken, and his negative reaction was defensively competitive.

Hence his reaction to Courbet, whom *au fond* he admired and whom he later described as 'this really meritorious man'.[40] As it happened Courbet was out of Paris for most of 1864, but his *Demoiselles de Village* was on view chez Martinet, and his studio was opened on request. 'C[ourbet] was away but I saw various works of his – by far the best an early portrait of himself about 23 or 24 resting his head on his hand,' Gabriel reported to William. 'It is rather hard and colourless but has many of the fine qualities of a Leonardo.'[41] Recent landscapes and scenes of stag-hunting were not likely to interest him, nor the earthy anti-clerical satire *Return from the Conference*. A work like *Trellis*, combining a pretty girl with a cascade of flowers, was more to his taste, while the erotic appeal of the controversial *Demoiselles au bord de la Seine* – especially the demoiselle in her petticoats – had surely by some indirect means influenced his own *Bocca Baciata*, just as Courbet's *Venus and Psyche*, rejected by the Salon for indecency, must also have contributed, via Whistler, to the *Verticordia*.

More than these, however, Rossetti responded to the painter whose *Gleaners* had been reviled by French critics as 'scarecrows in rags', but who was now about to become celebrated. 'I have been especially delighted with the works of one Millet, whose name (Gallicè) is curiously identical with that of our best English painter,' he told George Rae, adding that he was sorry he could not bring samples home. 'He has warm admirers here, but almost entirely among artists.'[42]

This somewhat belated discovery underlines how, though Jean-François Millet had first shown at the Salon in 1840 and long been a leading figure in the realist school alongside Courbet, neither his name nor his works were yet widely known. He had, however, shown works in London in 1851 and 1856 (though as Rossetti remarked, never at Gambart's French Gallery) as well as at the 1855 Exposition. In 1863, three pictures, including *Le berger ramenant son troupeau* and *Une femme cardant de la laine*, were at the Belgian Academy, where no doubt Rossetti had noted him as an artist to seek out; indeed, this may have been one motive for visiting Paris. As Millet lived in Barbizon, special arrangements had to be made to see his works in the capital, where the now-famous *Angelus* would soon be on view. The canvases Rossetti saw are unrecorded, but one can readily understand why he responded to the gravity of Millet's forms and the purity of his feeling, as well as to his softer brushwork and subdued but glowing colour harmonies.

His abuse of French painting was therefore all directed at Manet, whom Fantin declared the key figure in Paris. As Manet did not have to sell his works, the studio in rue Guyot must have contained most of the major canvases to date: *Guitarrero, Mlle V en costume d'espada, Lola de Valence, The Street Singer, The Dead Toreador, Music in the Tuileries, Les anges au tombeau de Christ, Les Gitanes,* and possibly Jeanne Duval afloat in a vast expanse of white crinoline. Above all there were *Déjeuner sur l'herbe,* shown at the Salon des Refusés in 1863, and *Olympia,* awaiting exhibition. Seeing such works en masse probably added to the shock.

If Rossetti saw the series of *faux-naif* marine paintings inspired by the battle between American warships off Cherbourg, he would not have been impressed, although in another mood he might have noted the resemblance between Manet's black fishing-boats and his own poetic image of them like flies on a window-pane. From his recent struggles with roses and honeysuckle, he might also have acknowledged the sensuous strokes of Manet's *Paeony* series, then in progress, with their magniloquent blooms, apt symbol of the lush transience of Second Empire style, in perfect harmony with Manet's generous, heavy-laden brush.[43]

Also awaiting exhibition was a large religious image showing a deliberately unidealised Christ being mocked by men drawn from the lower ranks of contemporary soldiery. Did Rossetti recognise a renewed attempt to render a sacred subject with startling realism while simultaneously paying tribute to the Great Past? His own *Ecce Ancilla* and Millais's *Carpenter's Shop* of 1850 were unacknowledged forerunners in the genre. When shown, Manet's *Christ* provoked similar attacks, denounced for ignoring the principles of drawing, and for celebrating the most 'ignoble, low and horrible' specimens of humanity.

In theory, Rossetti was still interested in a major rendering of a modern religious subject. In practice, like Manet, he now abandoned the attempt.

Like Manet, too, he had recently attempted a nude. But *Venus Verticordia* could hardly be compared with *Déjeuner sur l'herbe* or *Olympia,* two provocative works that called into question the whole tradition of female nudes in classical landscapes or the boudoir, representing idealised figures of desire, by stripping away the High Art camouflage, much as Mrs Grundy might do at home. In *Déjeuner sur l'herbe,* according to one critic, a commonplace whore, stark naked, lounged brazenly on the grass with two students *en congé,* 'misbehaving to prove themselves men'. Audaciously, it brought homage to Raphael and Giorgione (the same *fête champêtre* to which Gabriel had addressed a sonnet in 1849) together with the new realist manner, reversing Academic practice to turn the ideal into the actual. In *Olympia*, an even more unmistakable whore lay on her day-bed. A shameless *Vénus de nos jours*, Victorine Meurent, whom everyone knew as Manet's model, was a modern, realistic nude that simultaneously invoked the Great Past and undermined all future excursions in the genre.

One of the works Rossetti had brought to Paris, and the only one he completed there, was the small crayon version of *Venus Verticordia*, which he had insisted to Rae had no touch of Ettyism about it. But why such a coyly erotic presentation, half masked by a classical title and waist-high floral display? Manet's approach was more honest – and, of course, innovative. It could hardly be more unsettling. Curiously enough, more-over, the two artists had produced remarkably similar images of their models: both Manet's 1862 portrait of Victorine wearing a white top and a blue ribbon in her hair and Rossetti's 1863 portrait of Fanny in white shift and blue ribbon plaiting her hair were similar in size and colour, with a restricted palette. Each model is set close to the picture plane against a dark ground, positioned to show a single golden ear-ring. More and more it begins to appear that Rossetti's foul-mouthed abuse of French slop arose from anxious rivalry. '*Hypocrite peintre*,' he might have said, paraphrasing Baudelaire, '– *mon semblable* – *mon frère*.'

Later, he called Manet a conceited ass – and indeed the Frenchman was a dandy and boulevardier, a conspicuous 'swell' in British terms, surrounded by a clique of admirers. Arrogant self-regard was bolstered by indepen-dence, for Edouard Manet did not need to paint pot-boilers, or please patrons, or fear falling prices. No wonder if Rossetti was envious. Face to face, each was courteously friendly. Preparing for the 1865 exhibition season, Manet spoke of sending to the RA. Rossetti insisted on acting as his agent, to ensure the works were delivered on time. So in due course Manet sent '*deux grands tableaux*' to Chelsea.[44] One contained a guitar, and was either the *Guitarrero* or *The Street Singer*; the other could have been *Lola de Valence*, or the large *Races at Longchamp*, which may have seemed appropriate for the horse-loving British. In the event, neither work was hung, though it appears the guitar picture was at least accepted. This was a hazard of the Academy, which regularly admitted more works than it had wall space for, but also indicates that Rossetti's exertions on Manet's behalf were hardly vigorous, since the whole point of his intervention was to ensure this sort of thing did not happen. None the less, his involvement in the matter throws an intriguing sidelight on his attitude to works which outwardly he had slammed as stink, slop and putrescence. Clearly, he recognised Manet as a member of the same artistic fraternity.

He could not, after all, settle to work in Paris. Within a month he was back in London (having lost some weight) and returned to the easel,

attired in his familiar long painting coat, to start work on a new picture of
Fanny, a study in blues. In many ways, nothing could be more different
than Manet's images of Victorine. But in *The Blue Bower* Fanny too has
tawny hair, a creamy complexion and steady gaze. Behind her head is a wall
of blue-and-white Chinese porcelain, draped with passion-flowers, and her
fingers strum fictively on a stringed instrument derived from a Japanese
koto probably purchased in Paris. Above all, the picture is an acknowledged
essay in form and colour, without subject or sentiment. 'There is nothing to
suggest subject, time, or place,' wrote Stephens, evidently quoting the
artist's own words. 'Where we thus leave off, the intellectual and purely
artistic splendour of the picture begins to develop itself ... The green and
chestnut-auburn, the pallid roses of the flesh, and the firmamental blue of
the background are as ineffable in variety of tint as in their delicious
harmony ...'[45]

'*Volupté, sois toujours ma reine! Prends le masque d'une sirène Faite de
chair et de velours.*' Baudelaire's jewels were pink and black, but his pagan
prayer found a response in the skin tones and soft fabrics of Rossetti's blue-
and-white bower.

CHAPTER SIXTEEN

The World Beyond

Among the outstanding commissions was *The Beloved*, for Mr Rae. Taking it up with renewed vigour, Rossetti now proposed to fill the background with a procession of girls in a challenging perspective, and to insert the figure of a black child in the foreground – a straight steal from *Olympia*, explained in painterly terms. 'I mean the colour of my picture to be like jewels,' he wrote, 'and the *jet* would be invaluable.'[1]

The Beloved was an ambitious but ambiguous piece, as its source suggests. While the sacred Song of Solomon is a religious allegory, it is also an erotic text. 'My beloved is mine and I am his: let him kiss me with the kisses of his mouth,' began the lines inscribed on the frame. The visualisation of a woman unveiling her charms was distinctly sexual, and though the attendants were perhaps designed to diminish the 'bridal' atmosphere, as in *Olympia* they rather heightened it. Nevertheless, in due course it became the star picture in the collection of a respectable banker, and its story illustrates both the complex elements of Rossetti's changing aesthetic at this moment in his career, and his relationship with loyal, sympathetic patrons.

Born in Aberdeen and widowed young, in the early 1860s George Rae had a new wife, a new home in Birkenhead and a substantial income. Introduced by John Miller, he had purchased the watercolour *Heart of the Night* and in summer 1863 brought Mrs Rae to Tudor House with a view to further acquisitions. Both were charmed by the artist and his works, but with Scottish caution Rae refused to pay more than 100 guineas for the little *Greensleeves* (it went instead to Gambart for the Plint estate) or 200 guineas for the two-panel replica *Salutation*, which was then bought by Lady Ashburton. When in December he invited himself again to Chelsea, evidently with serious intent, Rossetti suggested he first look at *Helen of Troy*, owned by another Liverpool businessman, no doubt in hope that he would order something similar.

Rae fancied a medieval-romantic figure subject, however; he especially admired Miss Heaton's *Dante's Dream*, exhibited at Liverpool in 1858. He also stipulated a price limit of 250 guineas. Together they looked at works in progress and at those projected: the oil of Solomon's Bride, with two attendants; a design for Tristram and Iseult drinking the love potion; and a scene from *Hamlet*. To add to the display, six of the chivalric watercolours belonging to Morris were also on offer, at 50 or 60 guineas apiece. To raise funds, Morris was selling his picture collection, and was about to accept Rae's offer for Hughes's *April Love*.

Rae agreed to an oil, and a week later Rossetti proffered either *The Beloved* (as 'The Bride' was now called) for 300 guineas, or *Tristram and Iseult* for 350 guineas. In response, Rae made some general remarks about high prices, which Rossetti countered by denying that his current rates were disproportionate, Rae being willing to pay up to 100 guineas for the little *Greensleeves*, and by citing his confrères in the PRB, whose works were about twice the price of his own.

The argument was evidently cogent; by mid-February Rae agreed to take *The Beloved* for £300, thus beating down the price by a mere £15. Rossetti promised to deliver by the end of the year – Rae saw the work as a Christmas gift for his wife – with payment in three equal instalments. He envisaged two sustained painting periods, separated by an interval for other work. Seeing Morris the same day, he ascertained that the watercolours were still for sale, writing at once to offer these, plus a small *Damsel of the Sanct Grael*, for a total of 250 guineas, with a token amount of £35 for retouching. 'No opportunity is ever likely to occur again of obtaining such drawings of mine at such a price, since they are all good specimens of my work,' he wrote. 'I could easily sell them all to Gambart at a higher rate, were they in mounts instead of being fixed on strainers and framed.'[2]

Rae closed with this bargain for what he called 'six and a half Rossettis', proposing like a wise trader to defer payment till the end of the year. The watercolours were duly dispatched on Easter Thursday. Sketching a diagram, Rossetti advised that all eight watercolours now owned by Rae hang close together, frames touching, to intensify the effect. 'In all modesty, I think I may congratulate you on the possession of these drawings,' he added when Julia Rae's approval was reported.

Owing to Mitchell's *Venus*, no more work was done on *The Beloved*, however. Instead, at the end of September, Rae was offered the watercolour *Venus*, for 100 guineas: '*N.B. very cheap.*' Doubtful, Rae asked if drapery could be introduced to veil the nudity (the picture was after all to hang in a drawing room). By no means, replied Rossetti; did Rae want the work or not? At the same time, he promised to work on *The Beloved*, so there would be 'no doubt of Mrs Rae's receiving her Xmas present' as planned.

Against all his banking instincts, Rae sent a whole fifty-pound note to Paris, instead of two halves, which would not be exchangeable there; in due course he received the watercolour which effectively formed Julia Rae's Christmas gift and also initiated the Aesthetic transformation of their collection. Six months later 'little Venus Verticordia' was 'our dear and charmingest of all'.

Conscious of contract law, Rossetti acknowledged that Rae could now refuse *The Beloved*, but none the less requested the next instalment of money, so he might start work again. If he could find a model, he was especially eager to paint in 'a little black girl carrying a cup before the bride'. Together with the additional figures behind, representing the biblical maidens that bear the Bride company, this gave fresh interest to the picture, he confessed ingenuously, as if otherwise the work bored him. Rae replied generously with a further £100 on account, requesting progress reports. 'We shall look with especial interest for the announcement that the black model has been discovered,' he wrote.

Such confidence from a patron was very gratifying. Shortly, the Raes were due to take a three-month voyage to Italy and Egypt. Telling them not to miss the works of Gozzoli, 'the greatest of all Tuscan painters', nor those of Carpaccio in Venice, Rossetti reported that he was about to begin painting the girl, from a mixed-race model known to Brown. On the Raes' return in March he announced that the picture was 'very forward', adding, 'I never did a better thing.' The four extra maidens were now in place, including one painted from a dark-skinned woman named Mrs Eaton, who was employed by several artists during the 1860s, while the girl had been replaced by a 'pure black' boy. The drawings of both children are exceptionally fine.

The boy was a slave child, travelling with his American master and spotted on the steps of a London hotel. Surprising as it may sound, he owes his presence in *The Beloved* not only to Manet's *Olympia* but also to current Abolitionist campaigning, which adds a now barely discernible political aspect to the picture. From 1861 to 1865, writes a recent commentator, Britain watched as America seemed to tear itself apart over black slavery. In response, 'English public men, politicians and writers of all qualities and degrees, gave an extensive airing to their views on the Negro.'[3] According to Henry Adams, many if not most Britons rushed to support the 'rebels' against the Union, while William Rossetti noted that his own countrymen were apt to declare their allegiance with the words 'I am a Northerner' or 'I am a Southerner'.[4] The subject also featured on the Academy walls, with Richard Ansdell's *Hunted Slaves* and Eyre Crowe's *Slave Market in Richmond, Virginia*. Among Gabriel's circle, Abolition claimed support from William, Christina, Brown and Burne-Jones, as well as Holman Hunt, Browning and the Lushingtons. On the other side stood

Carlyle and Ruskin, with Whistler in typically combative mood, having a brother serving as surgeon in the Confederate army.

Generally speaking, when they argued, Rossetti merely laughed, refusing to take sides. Not ordinarily sympathetic to the oppressed races of the world, and perhaps sharing Ruskin's view that the chief use of black boys was to be painted by Van Dyck and Veronese, his precise views on the Civil War, American slavery and racial difference are hard to discover, although it is also true that he who does not speak against slavery effectively supports it. In the early months of the war he wrote opaquely to Norton saying that it was surely 'painful to an American to see what is to be seen with you now', before adding that the subject was 'a matter so out of the current of my ideas that I am quite incompetent to speak of it'.[5] (An active Abolitionist, Norton perhaps wondered what expertise was required to condemn slavery.)

Subsequently, Rossetti was among those targeted as 'men of influence' by campaigner Moncure Conway, who came to Britain in 1863 to raise support for the Northern cause and met Gabriel the following year. In his memoirs Conway numbered both Rossettis in the anti-slavery camp, although it will be remembered that Whistler described Gabriel as 'the only white man' in the liberal London crowd, which does not suggest he was a conspicuous 'friend of the Negro'. It is, however, hard to imagine that he could introduce a black child into a painting, just at this moment, with no awareness of its political import. For the Abolitionist campaigns focused strongly on the cruel sale of slave children at around the same age as his model. When the young African-American came to Cheyne Walk to pose, he cried copiously. Rossetti remarked only that the tears made even darker streaks on his skin, but aunt Charlotte immediately wondered if the child were weeping for his 'mammy', having been forcibly separated from her.

Nor does it seem likely that George and Julia Rae would have welcomed a pure black child into their picture had they favoured the South. As the American war interrupted cotton supplies to the textile industry, and thus reduced the business profits of Liverpool, economic interest played across humanitarian sentiment, but much of Merseyside supported Abolition, and it may be inferred that Rae did so too, for at the time that he agreed to buy *The Beloved*, he also commissioned *The Coat of Many Colours* from Madox Brown, with its explicit allusion to a brother sold into slavery.

The issue is further nuanced because the American conflict coincided with the growth of an influential if specious discourse on 'race classification' in the Western world whereby racial difference was systematically promoted to justify European superiority, through a descending chain of proclaimed perfection that placed the European 'race' at the pinnacle and the African as lowest on the evolutionary scale. The inclusion of the finely-painted child, and indeed, the global play of racial references within *The Beloved* as a whole suggest a covert – even unconscious – reference to these socio-political theories, from a half-liberal artist who resolutely insisted he was merely concerned with the jewelled surface of his work. Each of the maidens has a darker skin than the fair Bride, so that the six figures together span the spectrum, while the green Japanese kimono and red Peruvian hair ornament gesture towards further ethnic groups. Given its contemporary context, the picture's ambiguities multiply.

Coming to London for the 1865 exhibitions, the Raes were privileged to see *The Beloved* in its forward state, and wrote metonymically of being introduced to the picture, as if to a human addition to their household, hoping she would arrive in time to astonish friends who were due to visit. Not yet satisfied, however, Rossetti prevaricated. He had also started on a new stunner, price 400 guineas. If Rae advanced 100 guineas on this, *The Beloved* would be ready all the sooner. Privately Rae perhaps groaned, but paid up. In the autumn, when he inquired again, Rossetti admitted that he was thoroughly depressed at his utter failure to keep his promise. However, he went on, in the next few days he would paint the flowers and foliage; after which remained only the finishing, which alas could not be hurried.

Perhaps to keep himself to the task, he invited Fred Stephens to see the canvas, together with *The Blue Bower* and *Venus Verticordia*, and thus there appeared in the *Athenaeum* for 21 October a long description of the work, hymning the Bride's beauty and brilliance of colour. 'Coming near, she draws from before her face, with a graceful action of both hands, the bridal veil of blue and white that was gathered about her head, so that the beautiful countenance is displayed in all its price of ivory-white', this declared; 'the lately-startled blush appears to spread from chin to brow; that brow is crowned by a geranium-coloured and golden aigrette on each temple, which spreads fan-like, and trembles as she moves ...'[6]

The 'harmony of colouring' was exquisite: the green silk gown lying 'in singular felicity' next to the golden-bronze hues of 'the little negro girl', whose black hair and tawny skin in turn formed an admirable foil to the fairness of the bride, with the four other maidens 'of diverse tints' completing the contrast. Moreover, *The Beloved* had a tender, delicate rendering of expression, with more beautiful drawing and modelling than was usual in English art. Its theme was the power of female beauty to arouse men, and altogether the work demonstrated the special powers of a remarkable artist.

This surely whetted the Raes' impatience, but Rossetti refused another visit in November, and still failed to finish by Christmas. In truth, though he altered the background figures' position he had set himself a real perspectival problem in depicting a procession head-on, which was never fully solved, and the work remains visually awkward. However, it was finally finished, framed and sent in February 1866. 'She is inexpressibly lovely, we *all* think, and the whole picture is a miracle of art, beauty and splendour,' wrote Rae warmly; his wife was transported, and both wished for art's sake 'that you might live and paint a thousand years'.

The picture was displayed on an easel – Mrs Rae was said to worship before it as at a shrine – and Rossetti was asked to add a rail to the frame, so that a curtain might conceal and reveal the glory. Moreover, although financially stretched, Rae was eager to buy further works.

The Raes must rank among the most perfect patrons Rossetti could have imagined. It has been customary to portray him as inconsiderate, unscrupulous and even something of a scoundrel for his treatment of clients, as he repeatedly demanded payment and postponed delivery, raising his prices and always claiming that works were vastly improved by delay. Manifestly, these customers did not complain, feeling indeed honoured to possess paintings of such beauty. 'I was one of the few who recognised his genius from the first,' Rae boasted later. 'I am proud to think that I am the possessor of probably the largest collection of his works.'[7]

Rossetti himself was so pleased with *The Beloved* that he arranged its brief display in London, both at Cheyne Walk and at the Arundel Club. Family, friends and fellow artists were invited; those who came included G. F. Watts and Arthur Hughes.[8] All must have wondered why Gabriel did not exhibit in the normal manner.

Roughly twice a year, Gabriel entertained all the family, usually around Christmas and then in the summer, to enjoy the garden. On one occasion in 1864, Christina and Henrietta Polydore joined the Heimanns and other old friends called Harrison, promising however not to insist on seeing the studio – no doubt owing to *Verticordia*. They noted the fruits of success – Gabriel was starting to put on weight.

From Paris, at the end of the year, he brought Christina a Japanese netsuke and a framed print showing a 'nest of crocodiles', in homage to her grotesque, fantastical vision of a cannibal beast. She was currently in Hastings, with her cousin and uncle Henry, close to where Gabriel and Lizzie had first lodged, and her winter's work included the preparation of a new volume of verse, to follow *Goblin Market*. Having a high estimate of her powers, Gabriel had reappointed himself literary adviser and agent, eager to see her reputation extended, and while vainly urging Mac to publish Swinburne, had also pushed his sister forward. At first, she resisted, having insufficient new material, but – perhaps while recovering from

mumps in spring 1864 – Gabriel looked through her notebooks again, and
made a fresh selection, noting 'queer rhymes', derivative phrases, repeti-
tions. 'On almost all points I succumb with serenity,' she replied,
responding poem by poem, and questioning only a few omissions. Would
he reverse his verdict on *Come and See* and *The Bourne*? 'Following your
advice, I have copied from Granpapa's vol. *Vanity of Vanities, Gone for
Ever* and the *Lady Isabella* sonnets,' she added. 'Don't you think this last
would do very well as sequence to the one called *A Portrait*? But please rearrange as seems well to you ...'⁹

Then she retracted, at risk of seeming 'a perfect weathercock'. Why rush
before the public with an immature volume? She would prefer to wait a few
months (or years if necessary) until there was 'a sufficiency of quality as
well as quantity'; was this not the best plan? she wrote. 'Not that the
brotherly trouble you have already taken need be lost, as your work will of
course avail when (and if) the day of publication comes.' But the pressure
was on: a 'new star' had risen in the ranks of poetesses. Jean Ingelow's
Poems, published by a rival house, went into edition after edition. *Goblin
Market* was being reprinted, but a new collection was very desirable. In her
way Christina was as competitive as her beloved brother.

> Too late for love, too late for joy
>   Too late, too late!
> You loitered in the road too long,
>   You trifled at the gate ...

Her new title poem, *The Fairy Prince who arrived too late*, was a
melancholy reversal of the Sleeping Beauty, in which the heroine does not
wake:

> The enchanted princess in her tower
>   Slept, died, behind the grate;
> Her heart was starving all this while:
>   You made it wait.

Gabriel suggested this be expanded, to include the prince's long journey,
beset by snares, diversions and obstacles, as well as the princess's long wait.
Deftly handled, it would augment Christina's reputation as a writer of
poetic fantasy to rival Keats.

The idea appealed, and some time during late summer or autumn
Christina set to work on what soon became known as *The Prince's Progress*,
partaking not only of Perrault but also of Bunyan, for this is also an
allegorical journey towards the Everlasting City. They discussed the

episodes that would tempt and delay the prince. Gabriel favoured his having to fight in the lists like a knight errant, but then agreed to a Faustian sojourn with an Alchemist falsely offering the elixir of eternal life. By the time Christina reached Hastings, only this section remained to be done. 'True, O Brother, my Alchemist still shivers in the blank of mere impossibility,' she wrote on 23 December, imitating the *Arabian Nights*; 'but I have so far overcome my feelings and disregarded my nerves as to unloose the Prince, so that wrapping paper may no longer bar his "progress".'

To assist, Gabriel sent a teasing caricature based on a *Times* review, which had remarked that 'Miss Rossetti can point to work which could not easily be mended'. Harking back to Christina's juvenile rages, this showed her in the parlour, dancing with anger and a hammer, smashing furniture, mirror, window-pane and ornaments, including a carved elephant who has lost half his trunk in the onslaught.[10]

At the end of January she delivered 'an Alchemist still reeking from the crucible', who fitted snugly into his niche. 'He's not precisely the Alchemist I prefigured,' she added; 'but thus he came and this he must stay: you know my system of work.' Gabriel still hankered after a jousting contest, however. 'How shall I express my sentiments about the terrible tournament?' Christina replied in exaggerated distress. 'Not a phrase to be relied on, not a correct knowledge of the subject, not the faintest impulse of inspiration incites me to the tilt: and looming before me in horrible bugbeardom stand 2 tournaments in Tennyson's *Idylls*.' But she agreed to delete the Prince's anachronistic pipe – 'immolated on the altar of sisterly deference'.

With characteristic warmth, and maybe a little chagrin in memory of his tardy goblins, Gabriel offered two illustrations for the new volume. He also speedily produced a redrawn title-page for *Goblin Market*'s second edition, which he asked Charley's sister Kate Faulkner to cut. 'She is a professional engraver,' he insisted to Macmillan, suggesting a fee of £2.[11] And then through the early months of 1865, drafts and comments passed back and forth between Chelsea and Hastings, as Christina wrote and revised, and Gabriel strove to ensure that the collection demonstrate the best powers she could command. He overestimated her capacity, she protested, joking that he would next request a classic poem in hendecasyllabics or quantitative hexameters. No, seriously, she questioned whether she possessed the poetic power with which he credited her: the 'latent epic' might emerge through his 'unflagging prodment', but he should please remember that the impossible seldom happened. The tone was humorous; in such matters they understood each other.

A fair amount of scholarly ink has been used in discussing Gabriel's 'influence' and 'interference' in Christina's writing. She herself later wrote that 'in poetics, my elder brother was my acute and most helpful critic', while also insisting that she read everything aloud to her mother and sister, whose responses were equally valued.[12] For most of her career, however, she worked independently of her brother – he indeed being otherwise occupied – and, if variations between her poems in manuscript and print are attributable to him, his advice was largely confined to deleting superfluous stanzas and supplying new titles; only occasionally did he suggest alterations to the verse. His most active involvement, however, was certainly during this period, in preparing 'vol. 2'; although, as only Christina's side of the correspondence survives, his interventions must be inferred from her responses.

From her available stock, he 'ousted' several poems he particularly disliked, such as a hectic group describing martyrdom and captivity, of which she was particularly fond. And he firmly vetoed a long dialogue poem exploring female discontent, apparently fearing lest she become a moralising, middle-brow poet with a social or 'woman question' agenda, in the mould of Bessie Parkes, Isa Craig, or Adelaide Procter. Originally entitled 'A Fight over the Body of Homer', the poem was overlong and had a complex, even contradictory argument. But, while it raises the questions, it articulates no feminist position and ends with a clear endorsement of submission to both gender and devotional humility, underlined by its eventual title, *The Lowest Room*, and its concluding message:

> Not to be first: how hard to learn
> That lifelong lesson of the past;
> Line graven on line and stroke on stroke;
> But, thank God, learned at last.

Gabriel continued to hate the poem, later taking his sister to task for its 'falsetto muscularity', and was dismayed when she published it a decade later. 'That vile trashy poem "The Lowest Room" I told her was only fit for one room, viz. the bog,' he wrote crudely; 'though I had made her leave it out of the *P's Progress* vol. . . . now the world will know that she can write a bad poem.'[13]

Naturally, he held out for high standards. But one suspects that his intemperate response arose from the poem's uncomfortable voicing of the restricted life choices open to women like his sisters, for by invoking Maria's juvenile enthusiasm for the Homeric heroes, the text replays her transition from ardent aspiration to self-imposed renunciation. As he grew older, Gabriel's views on gender equality became ever more conventional, but somewhere in his heart he was never reconciled to the suppression of his sister's strong intellect.

In respect of Christina's poems, he also had reservations about *Under the Rose*, a monologue in the mode of George Crabbe, on the subject of illegitimacy. Following his comments, she meekly returned the text, 'pruned and re-written to order', saying that if he still felt it was too coarse, it too would go. His objections centred on the subject, and the 'undesirability' of women writing on matters that they knew nothing about – those books into whose pages pure minds must not look. But, Christina protested, 'I yet incline to include within female range such an attempt as this. Moreover, the sketch gives only the girl's own deductions, feelings, semi-resolution ...' she wrote, 'and whilst it may truly be argued that unless white could be black and Heaven hell my experience (thank God) precludes me from hers, I yet don't see why "the Poet mind" should be less able to construct her from its own inner consciousness than a hundred other unknown quantities.'[14]

This seems unarguable; Gabriel had essayed similar dramatisations in *Jenny, Sister Helen, A Last Confession*. No one said certain subjects were off-limits for male poets, and it is hard not to feel that he was being prissy as well as obtuse. The newspapers and novels of the day were filled with stories of seduction and desertion, illegitimacy, infanticide, foundlings' discovery of their paternity, married men haunted by cast-off lovers, women pursued by their hidden past. These were the themes of drama and balladry too; several poems in Christina's first volume had dealt with the same topics; and in this respect *Under the Rose* was no different. Perhaps, however, its critique of male behaviour and the double sexual standard caused discomfort. 'But I could almost curse my father,' says the narrator:

> Why did he set a snare
> To catch at unaware
> My Mother's foolish youth;
> Load me with shame that's hers,
> And her with something worse,
> A lifelong lie for truth?

Following Christina's defence, Gabriel allowed the piece to remain. Soon, she grew impatient for the volume to be sent to Macmillan, whatever its flaws. He continued to tinker and tweak. She mimed a paroxysm of frustration. By 4 April, the manuscript was dispatched, Gabriel having offered to see the book through the press. He had already given the *Athenaeum* an advance notice: 'Miss Christina Rossetti will soon publish by Messrs. Macmillan, another volume of poems, of about the same bulk as that entitled "Goblin Market" ... Like the latter, the new book will be illustrated by two designs by Mr D. G. Rossetti. The proposed title is "The Prince's Progress and Other Poems".'[15]

This unauthorised pre-publicity, one may infer, was partly to prevent the volume being rejected by Macmillan, towards whom Gabriel adopted an imperious manner, quite unlike his sister's courtesy. 'I hear you have not adopted the colour I chose from a set of specimens sent, for the binding,' he wrote of the *Goblin Market* reprint; 'which is all right if it sells the book better. But I hope to find that there is a mistake in a report I hear that my design for the binding has been somehow clipped or altered. This should no more occur without my sanction than an alteration should be made in engraving my drawings.'[16]

This time, he was not behindhand with the illustrations, but when she saw the designs Christina was dismayed that he had failed to give the prince his 'curly black beard' or the princess her veil. And this caused delay, for Gabriel neither amended his designs nor drew them on the blocks. 'Your woodcuts are so essential to my contentment that I will wait a year for them if need is – though (in a whisper) six months would better please me,' she wrote, later jesting that her prince, 'having dawdled so long on his own account, cannot grumble at awaiting your pleasure'.[17] In the event the volume did not appear for a further twelvemonth.

> Too late, too late!
> You loitered on the road too long,
> You trifled at the gate ...

Despite his lack of a curly beard, Gabriel might perhaps have recognised his own portrait in that of the procrastinating prince, who dallies in 'his world-end palace ... taking his ease on cushion and mat', rather as he himself did, not far from the World's End west of Cheyne Walk, equally apt to be tempted by figurative alchemists and alluring women. For his family, and especially his younger sister, Gabriel had always been a prince. Now, she and Maria were more concerned with spiritual than earthly glory, fearful lest their golden brother fail to reach the Eternal City. He refused to talk about the salvation of his immortal soul, and his behaviour gave no sign of concern. His mother and sisters prayed for him.

Working on Christina's poems did not prompt him to return to his own, but he did look up and copy out the verses Lizzie had left – a handful of lyrics, ballads and fragments. Now, at the third anniversary of her death, he was ready for memorials. He bought and begged back her drawings, hung the framed watercolours and collected the studies and sketches in a portfolio, to be photographed. Several friends had requested mementoes, and a permanent record of her art was in order. 'Short, sad and strange her life; it must have seemed to her like a troubled dream,' wrote Allingham on receipt of his copy. 'She was sweet, gentle, and kindly, and sympathetic to art and poetry. As to art-power, it is not easy to make as much as a guess; and this portfolio hardly helps. But it is very interesting, at least to those who knew her.'[18]

'How full of beauty they are, but how painful: – how they bring poor Lizzie herself before one, with her voice, face and manner,' wrote Christina of the poems. But the idea of publishing them did not seem feasible. '[B]eautiful as they are they are almost too hopelessly sad for publication *en masse* ... talk of my bogieism, is it not by comparison jovial?'[19]

Gabriel's favourite was a 'sweet and pathetic' ballad imitation:

'And mother, dear, take a sapling twig
    And green grass newly mown
And lay them on my empty bed
    That my sorrow be not known.

'And mother, find three berries red
    And pluck them from the stalk
And burn them at the first cock-crow
    That my spirit may not walk.

'And mother, dear, break a willow wand
    And if the sap be even
Then save it for sweet Robert's sake
    And he'll know my soul's in heaven ...'

One assumes he did not polish the verses overmuch when copying them out; but he had hardly hesitated to smooth Blake's lines, nor to improve his sister's, and these have a very finished look. They were apt too, for Lizzie's spirit was walking, and Gabriel wanted to know her soul was in heaven. According to John Marshall, 'for two years he *saw* her ghost every night!' – a claim that led Marshall's melodramatic daughter to conclude that no doubt Mr Rossetti 'had a wretched life since his wife's death fr[om] poison she took herself!'[20]

Those who socialised with him in Paris or London would not have thought him wretched. On 10 February this year, Boyce dined with a large group of friends at the Arts Club, afterwards adjourning to his rooms at Chatham Place. 'The two Rossettis, Clayton, Wells, Walter Field,

F. Burton, Henry Wallis, Val Prinsep,' he recorded. 'The evening went off comfortably, though Mrs Birrell told me afterwards that on this very evening 3 years ago Mrs Gabriel Rossetti was taken so ill and died here.'[21] This must have been the first time her widower had been back to the apartment. He was out of mourning, and appeared fully restored. Maybe it was the deliberate exorcism of rooms he had thought never to revisit; ghosts did not walk among pipe smoke and art gossip.

But John Marshall was a reliable source, presumably repeating what he was told; it is fully possible that sleeping or half-waking, Rossetti was haunted by unquiet images of Lizzie.

Rational William thought so, feeling that she was very constantly present to his brother in these years. 'Poignant memories and painful associations were his portion; and he was prone to think some secret might yet be wrested from the grave,' he wrote,[22] in language betraying more than it says, for the patent meaning is that Gabriel half-believed in communication with the departed, like so many of his contemporaries. Spiritualism flourished, proffering literal messages from those who had 'gone before', rapped out from tables, or voiced by more or less convincing mediums.

Back in 1855, Gabriel had combined with Browning to attack spiritualism. But bereavement made for susceptibility. The first seance he is recorded as attending was staged in December 1864 by the Davenport Brothers, travelling illusionists who in this period 'electrified London with their performances', according to William, by communing with spirits while securely roped within a cabinet. Gabriel sent an account to Christina, from whose reply it may be inferred that he was inclined to credit a supernatural, or at least magic agency. 'To me the whole subject is awful and mysterious,' she wrote, expressing the bewildered hope that 'simple imposture' was the answer. It was, but the Davenports were not unmasked until 1868.

Browning's *Mr Sludge* (published this year) confessed to cheating – yet echoed Hamlet: There are more things in heaven and earth . . . By autumn 1865, the astonished Scott learnt that William now quite believed in the communications of spirits, thanks to home sessions at Tudor House. 'It seems Gabriel's wife is constantly appearing (that is, rapping out things) at the seances at Cheyne Walk – William affirms that the things communicated are such as only she could know.' Sceptical, Scott joined in, and found it 'simply childish'. He held fat Fanny responsible; and no doubt she knew more about Lizzie than William surmised.[23]

As geology and evolution undermined revealed religion, it became less and less possible to believe in 'heaven', or give rational assent to personal immortality, let alone communication from beyond the grave. Rossetti refused to discuss such matters, detesting all 'arid or disputatious' arguments, either from atheists or believers, so it is hard to establish what he thought. In his elegy for Algernon Stanhope in 1847, he had written in good faith of the child's soul being borne 'up through the sun to God', and in due course he appears to have inclined towards a Neoplatonic or Wordsworthian notion of the enduring soul, that brought dim memories from previous lives during its sojourn in the body. At this date, however, his ideas seem merely wishful. He dared not even surmise whether he and Lizzie would be one day reunited, he told Mrs Gilchrist. 'What can be done except to trust to what is surely at least a natural instinct in all,' he wrote, 'that such terrible partings from love and work must be, unless all things are a mere empty husk of nothing, a guide to belief in a new field of effort, and a second communion with those loved and lost?'[24] But in his heart he knew the prospect was vain; so much had changed, so quickly: in just over a decade, all the premises of faith had been washed away. As much as anything, this raised a barrier between himself and his sisters, fervent believers in life everlasting. However, he had never really disbelieved in ghosts; rather, as with all tales of supernatural, unexplained phenomena, he half-hoped they existed. And so, despite doubt, he was evidently willing to hear from Lizzie, even through the bogus means of a seance. When he asked, she replied that she was happy. At the end of the year, William participated again at the house of a family friend, where messages again came from Lizzie, though Gabriel was not present. If her spirit was not restless, many people evidently thought it might be. In time, Rossetti confessed himself haunted, telling Scott at the end of his life that for two whole years he saw Lizzie every night 'upon the bed as she died'.[25] Possibly a post-traumatic flashback, this vision had the reality of a hallucination.

It was now time for a memorial picture, drawn from the book he had made his personal text. In the *Vita Nuova*, Dante loses Beatrice without ever having gained her; and on the anniversary of her death is absorbed in drawing the image of an angel. Having told Ellen Heaton he could not paint Lizzie's portrait from memory, late in 1863 Rossetti had rediscovered a life-size oil sketch, intended as a prospective Beatrice. 'It is only laid in and the canvas is in a bad state, but it is possible I might be able to work it up successfully, either on this or another canvas, and should like to do so if possible,' he wrote. The picture was to represent Beatrice falling asleep by a sundial, whose shadow marks the hour of nine. 'You probably remember the singular way in which Dante dwells on the number nine in connection with Beatrice in the Vita Nuova. He meets her at nine years of age, she dies at nine o'clock on the 9th of June 1290.'[26]

In the end however Miss Heaton did not want the picture, and it was only in 1865 that the canvas was taken up again. Again, this seems part of the mourning process. In feeling and general iconography, the image accords with Victorian funerary practice. Its text, taken from Dante, quotes the opening verse of *Lamentations*: 'How doth the city sit solitary, that was so full of people! how is she become as a widow!' The picture's title, *Beata Beatrix* – Blessed Beatrice – brings together two signature themes – Dante's beloved and the lover yearning for the Damozel in heaven.

A new client, the Hon. William Cowper-Temple, became the patron; his wife was an old acquaintance of Ruskin's. As Commissioner of Works, Mr Cowper had employed MMF & Co. at St James's Palace and recently he had inherited the Hampshire estate of his natural father, Lord Palmerston. 'I have a picture in hand which though as yet in an early stage I should like to show you,' wrote Rossetti in July 1866, and the commission, for 300 guineas, was sealed by 3 August 1866, when he dined with the Cowpers. They were people of taste, he told his mother, 'and it is pleasanter sending a poetic work where it will be seen by cultivated folks than to a cotton-spinner or dealer'.[27]

'You will remember how much Dante dwells on the desolation of the city in connection with the incident of her death,' Rossetti explained to Mrs Cowper; 'and for this reason I have introduced it, as my background, and made the figure of Dante and love passing through the street and gazing ominously on one another, conscious of the event ... whilst the bird, a messenger of death, drops a poppy between the hands of Beatrice. She sees through her shut lids, is conscious of a new world, as expressed in the last words of the *Vita Nuova*, "*Quella beata Beatrice che gloriosamente mira nella fascia die colui qui est per omnia soecula benedictus.*" '[28] The dominant colours of purple and green are those of grief and hope, with strong red accents denoting love.

By the end of 1866, when it was admired by Ruskin, the picture was well under way, but painting proceeded slowly over the next few years. More than with any other work, completion was deferred for the sake of that unattainable perfection that attends important projects – and by the emotional content. A duplicate was begun in 1867, a finished chalk version was done for William Graham in 1869, but not until 1870 was Rossetti ready to relinquish his image of Lizzie as Beatrice. By this time, he had a well-developed notion of its subject, writing to Mrs Cowper-Temple to emphasise that it was a symbolic, not literal representation of Beatrice's death, showing her as a spirit 'suddenly rapt from Earth to Heaven'. Behind lies Florence, with Dante and the figure of Love, holding a flaming heart, separated for ever. This was Dante Gabriel's most explicit identification of his namesake's idealised love for Beatrice with his own for Lizzie.

Is she fair now as she lies?
   Once she was fair;
Meet queen for any kingly king,
   With gold-dust on her hair.
Now these are poppies in her locks,
   White poppies she must wear;
Must wear a veil to shroud her face . . .

Christina's words seemed obliquely, unintentionally, to refer to Gabriel's loss. Life was not art, but how else to register grief and change? After death 'God knows I know the faces I shall see,' he had written in *Lost Days*: 'Each one a murdered self, with low last breath. / "I am thyself, – what hast thou done to me?" ' Was he already beginning to hear voices? His ghosts were internal.

Materially, life in Chelsea in the mid-1860s was good, for a princely painter with a large house and no dependants. He was working hard – looking through his diary, he found only twelve days between June and October 1865 not spent at the easel – but the evenings were full.

After his large, late breakfast, he was in the studio till daylight faded. Then, the day's work over, he dined out, or at home with Fanny and a friend or two. 'Any day you can, look in and take pot-luck with me at half past 5,' ran a typical invitation to Rose. Always hospitable, yet disliking ceremony, his correspondence contains hundreds of such messages, many to the get-on-able Boyce, a frequent guest. For a time, Fred Sandys was a housemate, but the friend Gabriel most wished to lure towards Chelsea was of course Madox Brown, who since the end of 1864 had been living in a fine, large house in Fitzroy Square, but was repeatedly urged to move.

Fashionable London was moving westwards. Having been severely shaken by the sickness that killed their second child and nearly took Georgie too, Burne-Jones (as Ned now signed his name) was living in Kensington, while the Scotts were nearby, having left Newcastle. They brought with them Scott's new soul mate, Alice Boyd, who shared their London home over the winter and spent the summers in ancestral Ayrshire. Cheyne Walk was too far for unannounced calls; nevertheless, social traffic on the river-bank was brisk. If Ned cared to call tomorrow, Gabriel told Georgie at the end of January, he would find 'Topsy more or less rampant' – that is, upright. At a typical dinner-party at the Burne-Joneses' in March, his fellow guests were Morris, Legros, Edward Poynter and Rebecca Solomon.

He dined frequently at the Arts Club in Hanover Square and at the Arundel Club in the Strand, which partly took the place of the defunct

Hogarth, in promoting 'the association of gentlemen of literary, scientific and artistic pursuits and tastes'; its 1865 spring exhibition featured drawings of the finest stained glass in England. And to signal his general embourgeoisification, he joined the Garrick Club, where men (or rather gentlemen) of literary, artistic and theatrical tastes mingled. Millais, Woolner and Prinsep were already members.

In mid-March, Gabriel welcomed Georgie's sister Alice and her new husband John Kipling on a visit to the studio, and shortly afterwards hosted a dinner, transformed into an evening party as the numbers grew to encompass the Joneses, Morrises, Browns, Munros, Hugheses, and Warington Taylors as well as William, Webb, Scott, Legros, Stephens and Swinburne. 'Just fancy large panelled rooms, narrow tall windows with seats, a large garden at the back, at the front a paved court, with tall iron gates and lastly the Thames in a flood of moonlight,' wrote Georgie's third sister Agnes to her family at home. In fixing the date, Gabriel forgot it was Easter Week, so his mother, sister and aunts could not come, but the less religious had a very jolly evening.[29]

Still fairly convivial, meetings of the Firm were increasingly businesslike. Despite his rough-and-ready demeanour, Topsy proved an admirable director, in Gabriel's view, and had especial flair for translating designs into windows, wall-coverings and textiles. But the order book was expanding and Morris was overstretched. Himself too busy to contribute more designs, Rossetti approached Frederic Shields of Manchester, a new acquaintance known for his scriptural illustrations, as a potential designer of church glass and also supported the employment of Warington Taylor as a much-needed business manager, offering £25 from his own pocket towards the extra salary, to encourage the others.[30]

Within the Firm, relationships were, as they say, robust, along with language. Once, Gabriel remonstrated with Webb for being grossly abusive about a fellow artist – and then tempered his protest by assuring Webb that as the abuse was friendly it was entirely 'as it should be between members of a firm headed by Topsy and sentinelled by Taylor'. Morris in particular was renowned for his expletives.

The blue-and-white passion continued, giving rise to numerous stories. One evening, Gabriel dined with friends who served salmon in a noble dish, evidently a prized piece. When the cover was removed, recalled fellow guests, 'Rossetti started, leaned over to examine the dish, took it in both hands, turned it upside down to see the marks, and exclaimed "The very dish I was going to get tomorrow!" ' Elated with her triumph, the hostess at once forgave the fish unceremoniously tipped on to the tablecloth, and the episode passed into Pre-Raphaelite folklore.[31] He also introduced others bitten by the same mania, including Henry Huth and Henry Thompson, to amiable Murray Marks, the half-Dutch art and antique dealer, who knew how to obtain fine quality ware and became a valued if sometimes exploited friend. 'I do not think I was ever so impressed by anybody in my life,' wrote Marks. 'As I looked at him entranced, I thought of Shakespeare. He was the most amusing and at the same time the most intellectual man I ever met.' *Venus Verticordia* was on the easel, and Marks was overwhelmed. He began seeking other items of interest – old stamped leather, oriental furniture, brass bowls – and acted as credit agent by accepting Rossetti's bills. Gradually the services widened: did Marks know a good plumber? could he get a lamp fixed?[32]

At Cheyne Walk, Pope was dismissed. It was a pity, Rossetti told Rose, 'but he cheeked me one day and I had to give him warning'. Disrespect led to usurpation of authority, besides the more usual faults of drunkenness and petty theft. In a household as irregular as Tudor House, with no wife to take charge of cupboard keys or laundry lists, servants could easily live well at their employer's expense. Not to mention Gabriel's habit of stuffing shillings and sovereigns and even banknotes into a drawer, to be taken out when required. As yet he had no bank account, using Rose when necessary to cash and draw cheques. But after his dismissal Pope toured the local traders, telling of Mr Rossetti's careless ways. Annoyed by the sudden demands for payment, Rossetti then accused Pope of wasteful, maybe fraudulent, housekeeping and warned against his employment at the Arundel Club.[33] Loader, his replacement at Cheyne Walk, seems to have been more respectful, and lasted longer.

Fearful of a return 'to the primal elements of chaos', Gabriel persuaded Swinburne to look elsewhere for lodgings, but he was still a frequent visitor. This spring he issued *Atalanta in Calydon*, a virtuoso poem 'noticeably free' of sensuality, to his friends' relief, yet not timid. As Scott robustly told Lady Trevelyan, the 'paganism and licence' were quite right for the classical subject. But Swinburne meant to be more outrageous. A little while later, preparing his first lyric collection, he addressed numberless stanzas to Dolores, our Lady of Pain, a blasphemous Dame de Sept Dolours, dismissing the 'lilies and languors of virtue' for the foul 'raptures and roses of vice'. Even Ruskin was briefly impressed. 'I went to see Swinburne yesterday and heard some of the wickedest and splendidest verses ever written by a human creature,' he wrote on 8 December. 'I don't know what to do with him or for him – but he mustn't publish these things . . .'[34]

'Dolores' was said to be inspired by the actress Adah Mencken, for whom Algernon had conceived a wild passion, much to his friends' amusement. An adventurous, witty woman, Mencken was currently performing as Mazeppa, the hero of Byron's poem, strapped as if naked to a galloping horse. She held court in London, receiving her admiring 'slaves', and Ned made naughty caricatures of Ye Poet and ye Ancient Dame (Mencken was thirty). Rumour said that Rossetti and Fred Burton offered money if she could seduce Swinburne, who for all his sexual fantasies was celibate, if not chaste; later Algernon laid claim to 'a somewhat riotous concubinage', but the real scandal came when compromising photos of the pair began to circulate.

In this permissive decade, all was good for a satirical story, over the port and cigars. So too was Whistler's sudden departure for Valparaiso, to smuggle in naval mines for Chile's war against Spain, and the tale of the homeward voyage, when 'he got into a shindy with a swell Marquis-Nigger, whom he took exception to and whose head he punched, for which he was put under arrest'. When Whistler boasted of this racist assault, his dinner companions shifted uncomfortably, but only William remonstrated. As was his habit, Gabriel laughed at Jimmy's effrontery; and, as Whistler was badly in need of tin, he urged Rae to buy his *Lange Leizen of the Six Marks*.

In June 1865, when the Plint trustees sent another batch of pictures to auction, Rossetti's little oil *Greensleeves* held its price, in marked contrast to John Brett's celebrated view of Warwick Castle, which had cost Plint 400 guineas and fetched only £20. Both Gabriel and Gambart were quietly pleased; and Gabriel was pleased with Gambart for keeping up his values in the market. But why had Ruskin parted with some of his watercolours, he wanted to know? He would buy them back if Ruskin wished to sell.[35]

'What a goose you are to go about listening to people's gossip!' replied Ruskin, who was currently absorbed in mythology and mineralogy. He had not parted with anything. 'Am I so mean in money-matters that I should sell Lizzie? You ought to have painted her better, and known me better.' The works in question were on loan to a girls' school, because he was often there. He would give – not sell – them back 'any day that you're a good boy'; in the meantime, would Gabriel paint Dante's Boat for him instead of for money?

Wrong-footed, Rossetti took slight umbrage. He demanded to know when and where his works were lent. They should talk, but Ruskin's taste had evidently changed: clearly he no longer liked Rossetti's work. 'Do not think I am changed,' replied Ruskin; he liked the old watercolours as much as ever, but Rossetti's style had altered, like Millais's. 'The change in you may be right – or towards right – but it is in you – not in me.'

Politely, Rossetti demurred, prompting Ruskin to a fuller critique. Originally, he wrote, Rossetti had set out to paint with the precision of Van Eyck or Holbein; now he appeared to emulate the 'display' of Titian or Correggio. Worse, he was painting coarsely, daubing and smearing his colours, ignoring the accurate fall of light, bending the truth for the sake of effect. 'I cannot bear the pain of seeing you at work as you are working now,' he wrote. 'But come back to me when you have found out your mistake.'

The blend of frank affection with irritating condescension was hard to accept. Pressed again, Ruskin replied with his critique of *Venus Verticordia*, continuing bluntly, 'I tell you the people you associate with are ruining you.' He meant Whistler, Jo, Swinburne, Sandys. 'Come and see me now,' he concluded. 'I have said all I wish to say, and can be open.' Rossetti replied with equally barbed candour, observing that Ruskin's stature as 'a great man' gave him leave to lecture others. The sparring remained good-humoured, but social relations cooled. 'Rossetti and the rest I never see now,' Ruskin told Norton in August. 'They go their way and I go mine.'

Months later, Ruskin put out an olive branch, calling at Cheyne Walk on William's advice to admire *Beata Beatrix*. The visit was cordial, but ten years' friendship was effectively over. Henceforward Rossetti and Ruskin rather avoided than sought each other's company. Nevertheless, the exchange had influence: Gabriel put more care into his painting and, while keeping to the 'Venetian' mode, endowed his sensuous themes and forms with more seriousness, so that a soulful, 'Rossettian' face displaced the coquettish sweethearts.

A new and infinitely more obliging acquaintance claimed the place Ruskin left vacant. Charles Howell was certainly someone Brown should know, Rossetti wrote in May 1865, inviting both to dine with Marshall and the Millers. Now in his mid-twenties, Howell had first arrived in London from his native Portugal in 1857 and met the Rossettis through the swindler Hogg, whom he helped unmask. Implicated in the Orsini conspiracy to assassinate Louis Napoleon, he vanished for a while; and now reappeared, living with an aunt in Brixton and apparently on his wits, for there was no sign of an income. Yet he was engagingly generous and willing to do whatever was required – to secure Chinese pots, hold a pose, find a costume, negotiate a loan.

By June he was 'my dear Howell,' while Fanny's cockney rendition furnished Mr 'owell with an instant nickname. 'News is scarce here,' Rossetti wrote in midsummer. 'P.S. The Lumpses has been to Brighton and Shoreham, but "never seed no Owl." '[36] The Lumpses was Fanny, and the familiarity is eloquent; as Whistler said, Howell had a gift for immediate intimacy. Soon, he was swapping Sadean epistles with Swinburne. 'Write – and communicate to the ink une odeur mélangée de sang et de sperme,' he was adjured. Soon, Gabriel was commending Howell to all comers. Often as not Boyce found him dining at Tudor House – with the Whistler brothers and Legros, or with Gabriel and Fanny. He introduced his cousin Kate as his intended, and sometimes slept at Cheyne Walk. A peculiar charm always surrounded the Owl, as if favoured by fate; by the end of the year, he was Ruskin's secretary and assistant. A few months later, with hyperbolic sincerity Gabriel asserted that all friends voted Howell 'a treasure and a joy of our lives'.

CHAPTER SEVENTEEN

Prosperity

In early summer 1865, Rossetti secured a sitting from Janey Morris – perhaps proposed during the great evening party in April, for Gabriel had not been to Red House in over three years. 'A drawing of me of 1865 must be a very good one, all the best were of that date about,' she wrote later. She was the 'very Queen of Beauty', he told Rae, projecting a new picture, which was to have no subject but itself. Then, no doubt owing to the distance, he hit on the idea of a photographic session as well. 'My dear Janey,' he wrote on 5 July. 'The photographer is coming at 11 on Wednesday. So I'll expect you as early as you can manage. Love to all at the Hole.'[1]

He raised an awning in the garden, a spacious airy tent where visitors took tea. Being left largely to its own devices, the garden was already overgrown, as he preferred. A wilderness in most people's eyes, to Rossetti it was an Eden – the simile made even more apt by the menagerie, which would soon include the shrieking peacocks. Within the awning was a Japanese screen, a chair and a couch; here Janey stood, sat and lay in a score of carefully composed positions. The poses resemble Nadar's publicity shots of La Paiva and the young Sarah Bernhardt, where the sitters also possess features seen to advantage in profile and a mass of wavy dark hair. Bernhardt reproached Nadar with making her look '*laide et noire*' and the pictures of Janey have the same striking quality, quite unlike conventional depictions of simpering Victorian 'beauties'.[2] In repose, her face seemed pensive, perhaps with silent yearning, but the definition of dark eyes and brows, with strongly modelled mouth and chin, gave her image an arresting, ambivalent quality comparable to Swinburne's invocation of raven-haired Faustina.

However, Rossetti's vision of Jane as queen of beauty was laid aside for the present; striking as the photographs were, it was perhaps not easy to transfer the images to canvas without further study from life. In time, he would return to the subject.

After a bout of illness, Morris had decided he must live closer to the business. So Red House was up for sale after just five years' occupation, and by autumn 1865 both family and firm were relocated in Queen Square, a few blocks north of Red Lion Square. The following June Gabriel again asked Jane to sit, but the projected painting, now to be a portrait, was no closer to realisation and no drawings date from this period.

Meanwhile Gabriel continued to draw from other models, including Fanny, Ada Vernon, who lived in the King's Road, laundry-maid Ellen Smith and young women like Augusta Jones, Miss Burton and Miss Robertson, of whom virtually nothing is known. Emily Renshaw was spotted in the street by Rossetti and Knewstub; fancying her looks, they followed her home and asked permission to make portraits. Deeply suspicious, her father gave reluctant consent. Rossetti drew her head for the watercolour *Verticordia*, which is said to have upset Knewstub, who had swiftly fallen in love and objected to seeing Emily represented as a nude figure. 'The less said the better,' he wrote of this image in later life.[3]

Ellen Smith sat for *Washing Hands*, a curious anecdotal picture about the end of a love affair, in which 'the lady, I think, is the first to have the strength to act on such knowledge', Rossetti explained. 'It is all over, in my picture, and she is washing her hands of it.' This was for Mr Craven of Manchester, who already had *Hesterna Rosa* and a half-length *Aurora*, and whom Rossetti described as a grave and '(let us say in a whisper) rather stupid enthusiast' with a mystic reverence for the English watercolour school. While not rich, he was 'a very good paymaster and not a haggler at all', and therefore a thoroughly good fellow.[4]

Which was more than could be said for Messrs Dunlop and Heugh, from whom nothing had been heard for nearly twelve months. What was the reason for the silence? He wrote to both, and to his surprise Dunlop replied that such a long time had passed he had almost forgotten about *The Ship of Love*; he implied the transaction had lapsed. Sir, replied Rossetti, this was improbable; how could Dunlop 'forget' a commission for a picture costing 2,000 guineas? When Dunlop ignored further indignant letters, Rossetti drafted a reply to relieve his feelings in schoolboy fashion. Dunlop's face showed he was a weakling. His behaviour stank. 'Take care you do not come here again. I could probably enforce legally what you seek to avoid, but dirty conduct is like other slops and cannot be stirred with nasal impunity.'[5]

Heugh, who had commissioned two watercolours, replied with studied insolence. He was under no obligation to take works after so long a delay. On his high horse, Rossetti rejoined. 'When you commissioned these drawings, I naturally supposed you did so because you liked and wished to possess my work, in which case the delay of a year could not well alter such feeling,' he wrote. 'You could scarcely have supposed that all other work would be at once postponed to this for you; nor can you surely imagine that, should I now choose to relinquish these distinct commissions from a repugnance to working for a capricious and uncivil person, my work will therefore go a-begging ...' Disdainfully, he concluded that Heugh lacked taste, manners, and honesty.[6]

He was angry not merely on account of the lost income. A cancelled commission was a professional blow. Of course, it was his own fault, for he had delayed starting these pictures in order to work on Mitchell's *Venus*, Rae's *Beloved*, and *The Blue Bower*. Moreover, Leathart's *Found* was still untouched, and poor Maj. Gillum was still owed a *Hamlet*. Of course no artist would easily turn down a commission, but Rossetti was in danger of accepting far more orders than he could ever execute. But as if unable to stop himself, he began yet another head-and-hands, entitled *Bellebuona*, with an eye to a new client recently introduced by Mr Miller. Mr Leyland was director of a Liverpool shipping line – who with greater economic status at this date? Would he like this work, at 150 guineas? He did not, and in November it too went to Gambart. The title meant 'both fair and good', Gabriel explained, but the fanciful name was typical of those he was now bestowing on what were essentially variations on a single theme.[7] Later, he added a branch of ilex and renamed the picture *Il Ramoscello*.

With private patrons queuing up, he had no reason to fear loss of income or reputation. Lately, he had reaffirmed his decision not to exhibit, saying that while 'rather misplaced pride' in youth had led him to avoid the Academy, owing to its 'unfair' practices, he had long since learnt that the anxiety of deadlines was unsuited to his temperament. Increasingly, however, this attitude appeared cowardly, for public exhibition and the press criticism that went with it were in some sense a sign of artistic virility. To shun exhibition was either pretentious or timid; either way, not a manly course, for a confident artist had no fear of exposure. Almost in the same breath, Rossetti acknowledged that 'competition and due appreciation' were an artist's best privileges.[8] Moreover, the publicity raised one's profile.

This was the point when he turned to his old PR Brother on the *Athenaeum*. Hitherto, Gabriel had been content for William to keep up the friendship; now Fred Stephens was invited to Cheyne Walk and given privileged access to the works in progress, with useful items of information for the paper's 'Fine Art Gossip' column, such as the fact that Morris Marshall Faulkner & Co. had secured the prestigious commission to redecorate St James's Palace from the Commissioner of Public Works, together with an order for public drinking fountains. A week later, Stephens's long article on Gabriel's recent work appeared in the magazine.

'Mr Rossetti exhibits his pictures in his studio and on the walls of his employers – nowhere else,' this began combatively. Long columns of fulsome exposition followed, taken verbatim from the artist himself, stressing the sensuous and 'purely artistic' qualities of the works, without subject or story, and concluding that the pictures described showed Mr Rossetti 'in the rare character of an original designer of merit, who has made an unfrequented path of Art his own'.[9]

While not wholly satisfied – had the *Athenaeum*'s editor knifed Stephens's copy? he asked, objecting to the rather qualified conclusion – Gabriel was pleased, and offered to show Fred his next pictures. Flattered, Stephens followed up with briefer praise of *Bellebuona*, 'a study in ashy green and pearly hues of grey' showing a virginal girl of eighteen with a charmingly chaste expression, an implicit contrast to the sensuous *Bower* and *Venus* of the previous notice. In addition, Mr Rossetti was also working on a larger picture of Perseus and 'the nearly nude' Andromeda, reclining by the impluvium of their palace, with the Medusa's head reflected in the water.

He was not exactly working on this; rather fishing for a commission. The articles offered valuable advertisement. For those who knew Mr Rossetti either by his sacred works, *Ecce Ancilla* and *The Seed of David*, or his Dantesque and Arthurian themes at Russell Place in 1857, the change in both style and subjects signalled a distinct aesthetic departure, in line with the emergent classical revival seen most prominently in the works of Leighton and Albert Moore. Too long on the margins, Rossetti seemed now to be entering the mainstream, with a careful piece of publicity.

Pleasantly puffed up, he was then not displeased to hear it gossiped that Gambart had sold *The Blue Bower* to a Manchester businessman for 1,500 guineas! Such a phenomenal mark-up on the 200 guineas he had received would clearly raise his prices. Indeed, he boasted to uncle Henry, 'already I am getting commissions and effecting sales to greater advantage than hitherto, and such advantage cannot but continue on the increase for the present.' Moreover, it enabled him to crow to Dunlop over the cancelled *Ship of Love*. 'Had you not proved a recusant to your bargain,' he wrote, 'I should now have found myself very seriously a loser by fulfilling it.' And he promptly asked Gambart for 500 guineas for his next picture. But this was quite out of proportion to previous prices. And indeed when Gambart heard the enormous price – now 1,600 guineas – he was said to have obtained for *The Blue Bower*, he was distinctly displeased. Who started this mischievous and mendacious story? The rest of the tale being correct, the figure must have 'been guessed at in a remarkable way', he wrote crisply; perhaps Rossetti had supplied it himself? If so, they could not continue in business.[10]

Chastened, Rossetti defended himself, but promised to 'observe silence' in future. Mollified, Gambart, who had in fact sold *The Blue Bower* for

£500, continued as agent. Gabriel, in turn, admonished Howell 'not to tell a soul' about new transactions, his exaggeration having caused such trouble. Meanwhile, unwilling to forgo his raised hopes, he put a price of 550 guineas on a new life-size female figure he called *Palmifera*. It would really be his best yet, he asserted, painted from a 'glorious' new model. When Rae hesitated, he extended the offer to Leyland, the shipping magnate. When Leyland declined, he dropped the price to 400 guineas, and secured Rae after all.[11] It was to his advantage that patrons should compete for his works.

'Who *was* or is Palmifera?' Rae inquired. It meant 'palm-bearer', Rossetti replied, 'to mark the leading place which I intend her to have among my beauties.' With their trophy attitude to art, purchasers were tempted by new faces. In response, artists sought out attractive young women in rather the same way as film companies later created starlets. And thus came about the 'discovery' of Alexa Wilding, the glorious new model for *Palmifera*.

As Gabriel told the story, one evening on his way to the Arundel Club he followed a young woman in the crowd. After a distance she turned into a side street and he spoke, explaining that her face was of exactly the type required for his next picture. She agreed to a sitting, but at the appointed hour no one came. Perhaps he wrote, for in early April Miss Wilding replied with genteel formality from her home near St Paul's to say she had 'her Mamma's permission to sit for any picture' and would be available in three weeks' time.[12]

In the meantime, however, he had secured Janey's sitting and perhaps did not reply. A season passed and then, riding in a cab with Howell, Gabriel saw Miss Wilding again and jumped out in pursuit. This time she came. With no experience of the art world, 'to find that by simply sitting still in a comfortable room she could earn more money than a week's work at her ordinary occupation of dressmaking would bring, was a great surprise to her. With very little persuasion she gave up her situation and at a liberal arrangement sat to him entirely.'

For Rossetti, paying a retainer of a pound or two a week was an investment that would save having to pursue other stunners in the street.

As was soon apparent, although very good-natured, Alexa had no conversation and little curiosity about the world, being content to sit like a sphinx, as if day-dreaming. Some months later, Boyce ran into her in Cremorne Gardens, and on another occasion learnt that she now lived with an aunt, and that her father had been a piano-maker. In the studio, it emerged that she had ambitions to be an actress – which was perhaps why she changed her baptismal name of Alice into the more glamorous Alexa. While she showed no visible dramatic talent, in art her lack of animation was an asset, and through modelling she achieved sufficient distinction. Gabriel grew fond of her, but knew she was a ninny.

From her suggestively vacant features came yet another work, offered first to Mitchell and then to William Blackmore, who already possessed *Helen of Troy* and *Fazio's Mistress*. Representing 'a Venetian lady in a rich dress of white and gold . . . in short the Venetian ideal of female beauty', he explained, this was 'probably the most effective as a room decoration which I have ever painted'. He called it *Monna Vanna*, in oblique reference to the poetic mistress of Guido Cavalcanti, named Lady Giovanna. Again, a full play of allusions inspires the work, which is also purely Aesthetic and modern in its refusal of narrative. The figure's face recedes behind an opulently painted sleeve recalling Renaissance works, and a brown and golden feathered fan. Ropes of coral wind between her throat and fingers.

To the *Gazette des Beaux-Arts* early in 1866, Rossetti was the 'high priest' of Pre-Raphaelitism. But the French were out of date: as Gabriel told Brown in April, 'the epoch of preraphaelitism [sic] was a short one which is quite over yet and will never be renewed'. The new Aesthetic art was in creation, in the manner Whistler would succinctly describe. 'As music is the poetry of sound, so is painting the poetry of sight,' he wrote; 'and the subject matter has nothing to do with harmony of sound or colour.'[13] Art need have no subject but itself.

'Public success depends on the things that precede it. One of them is to live for years in an intense professional atmosphere, and I know of no instance of a successful painter with the public where this has not been done,' noted James Smetham in June 1864. For himself, 'studio life in its widest sense – haunting the clubs, sketching clubs, lecture rooms – the company of dealers and patrons' was 'utterly revolting and impossible'; yet necessary to 'that growing murmur of influence that is the preliminary of fame, secures votes and interest of the Academicians, and influential partisans – that which dictates the tone of reviews and critics – that which draws and rivets the attention of the buyer and excites the curiosity of the saleroom'.[14]

Did this advice come from Gabriel? 'I am told that you must join a club, "The Garrick", "The Arundel",' Smetham added later, '– that you must meet the Littérateurs at 2 a.m. (when you have been asleep 3 hours) and that you must cram them and tell them what to say or your picture won't be hung or won't be noticed if it is hung.' In such practices Rossetti was rapidly becoming an adept.

He had first met Smetham through Ruskin and the Working Men's Collage, when Smetham had perceived Rossetti as 'blunt, simple, hearty', albeit also 'impulsive and fiery and very clever'. A nervous artist, who worked on a tiny scale, producing visionary works that recall those of Blake and Palmer, Smetham was edgily gratified to be welcome at Tudor House. 'And do, please, let more distant forms be dropped on both sides, being, as we are, almost ten-year-old friends,' Rossetti warmly.[15]

'As I find everyone calling you Gabriel, I must take the liberty of falling into the same rut,' Smetham replied, adding frankly that the only two men 'concerned directly in Art' whom he had wished to know were 'Ruskin by his works, and D.G.R by his sum-total'. Ruskin was too well-off and too well-known to be bothered with bores, he knew, but Rossetti offered true sympathy. 'My dear Gabriel, if you have got any kick *in you*, pray kick out soon, and don't let us get into a mess. I am quite sure *you* are all right in respect to generosity and nobleness, but I'm not so sure that I am,' he wrote. 'Professionally I should be very glad of a niche in the charmed circle wherein you are fixed. For want of it – since 1855 – life has been a scramble instead of a joy.'[16]

As a devout and rigorous Methodist, Smetham foresaw friction between himself and the 'pagan' Chelsea circle, who not only ignored moral subjects in art, but often seemed without all perception of morality. But regularly, on Wednesdays, he travelled from his home in Stoke Newington to share in the wide-ranging talk. He was there four times in December, first with Stephens, Howell and Swinburne ('drunk'); next with Scott, Horace Scudder the American biographer, and Swinburne ('blasphemous'); then with Brown, William, Legros and Shields; and finally with Boyce, Burton, Burne-Jones, Hughes, Chapman and Rose, when the talk was of Topsy's poems.

Though impulsively generous, Gabriel was not usually sympathetic towards lame ducks. But something in Smetham touched him. He refused to let others mock, and unfeignedly, if unwisely, expressed interest in his friend's writings. Thus encouraged, Smetham proffered a selection of the devotional 'ventilators' in which he wrote out his circling thoughts. Gabriel had not anticipated religious debate; in courtesy to Smetham's evident sincerity, he explained his decision never to engage in such. He also offered frank advice. 'I am afraid you will think no better of me for pronouncing the commonplace verdict that what you lack is simply ambition,' he wrote, incidentally outlining his own view.[17] Ambition was not a fault, leading to the sin of envy, as Smetham seemed to fear, but the essential spur to achievement. Anger and self-hatred followed when one failed, or someone else did better; then analysis, self-interrogation and finally renewed determination. Success required singlemindedness.

Alas, Smetham proved beyond help, though for the rest of the decade he found the evening visits to Cheyne Walk a sort of lifeline, where he sat quietly amid the conversation, as if briefly liberated from the swirling perplexities in his mind. To meet Rossetti, Brown, Burne-Jones, 'appetising Boyce' and the rest was 'all charm and zest', he wrote later. 'None of these men can touch paper, pen, lead pencil, chalk or brush but something fresh, natural, powerful oozes out at their finger ends.'[18]

For his part, Rossetti sincerely admired Smetham's talent. When in 1869 his *Hymn of the Last Supper* was at the Academy, Gabriel wrote to enlist Stephens's sympathy. 'The lamplight in the picture and the balance of all its masses are singularly masterful and successful,' he explained, while the sacred sentiment and simplicity of feeling were reminiscent of the early Italians. 'If you could make it one of the things mentioned in your preliminary notice it would be of great service to Smetham, and I believe that you will agree that he deserves it.'[19] Then later, when Smetham was locked into catatonic psychosis, Rossetti took his tiny oils to Cheyne Walk and urged his own patrons to buy, if only out of charity for Smetham's intelligent, stoical wife on whom the full burden of family maintenance had fallen.

Spendthrift Frederick Sandys was the obverse of James Smetham. A year younger than Rossetti, he was born plain Fred Sands in Norwich (where he still had a home and a wife). They had first met in 1857, when Sandys published a graphic parody of Millais's *Sir Isumbras at the Ford*, showing a Pre-Raphaelite donkey with Ruskin's initials carrying the Brothers Millais, Hunt and Rossetti. He had exceptional talent, especially in draughtsman-ship, and virtually no scruples regarding money or morals; much of his life is still obscure, but during 1866 he lived more or less continuously at Tudor House. A large, heavy man with short yellowish hair parted in the middle, he affected a world-weary manner. Already his work had taken on a Rossettian cast, with Arthurian subjects like Vivien and Morgan le Fay, and female heads called *Cassandra* and *Helen*. Outdoing both Rossetti and Whistler, he had a model and mistress of gipsy origin, named Kiomi Gray; Boyce found them both at Cheyne Walk one evening, along with Gabriel and Fanny. Kiomi's unusual remarks passed into legend: later Gabriel recalled her assertion that 'a toad wasn't made for a side-pocket' and her calm explanation that she had stoned a raven to death, for amusement. He used her as model for one maiden in *The Beloved*, and seems to have found Fred a congenial companion, despite a formidable alcoholic intake. After dining with Sandys, Gabriel joked, everyone would see double.

He himself was not immune. After all his years of abstinence, he was now sampling wine and whisky. On Whit Monday 1866 Rossetti and Boyce took an excursion to Rye House in Hertfordshire, travelling by hansom cab and arriving around five in the afternoon. The fifteenth-century gatehouse, where in 1673 a plot against Charles II was hatched, formed the centrepiece of pleasure gardens on the model of Cremorne. But they had difficulty finding food, and 'Gabriel, somehow or other, perhaps by taking whisky etc., on an empty stomach, got rather drunk and quarrelsome and fell down in the dark passage leading to the dungeons and lost his overcoat.'[20] Boyce pulled him up before he was trampled underfoot, and 'after some fuss, the overcoat was regained, though torn'.

He dined regularly at tables where wine and spirits flowed. Howell ingratiatingly pressed crates of rare Madeira upon him. A typical all-male evening at Tudor House, with after-dinner whist, brag and copious alcohol, lasted till five in the morning.

Even in such company, Swinburne's excesses were now extreme, and starting to worry his friends. 'Gabriel and William Rossetti think he will not live long if he goes on as lately without stopping,' Scott told Pauline Trevelyan, who in turn warned Algernon. Everyone was talking about his drinking, his profanity, his sado-masochistic poems. What infamous wickedness, Swinburne replied, to invent or repeat such lies. Monckton Milnes's remonstrations were simply denied; what on earth had called down such an avalanche of unrequested advice? He scouted Rossetti's friendly words too, and was heard around town ranting against Gabriel 'in a very unhappy way', according to Scott. Then in March there was a messy episode at the Arts Club when, drunkenly unable to find his own hat, he tried all the others, stamping on them in turn. 'This is the first I have heard of the matter,' he protested when William warned of expulsion.[21] Inebriation brought insouciance, as Swinburne simply refused responsibility for what he could not recall.

But the 1860s were permissive, worldly years. Like religion, moral conduct was a private matter, more appropriate for womenfolk and children. Uprightness was unfashionable, even underbred. To philander, or cheat, or slander was a matter of manners only. Those who sinned egregiously were blackballed, but the latitude was wide. Against this background, affable and prosperous, Rossetti took his place as an established artist and man of the world, assuming appropriate responsibilities. One of the moving spirits behind a committee to raise a subscription for the elderly, poverty-stricken illustrator George Cruikshank, he privately also sent money to assist W. S. Burton, hung William Davies's landscapes in his own studio in the hope of making a sale, and did his best to promote Knewstub as well as Smetham. Rossetti's charities were not numerous, but in the right mood he was an easy touch, and towards impoverished fellow artists his sympathies were always warm. He even on occasion recommended one of Inchbold's pictures to a patron.

As a clubman, he met Millais from time to time, and also Woolner, Leighton, Dicky Doyle, Sir John Gilbert and others. He dined with Bryan Procter, and walked part of the way home with Tennyson. Early in 1866 he went to breakfast with Leighton, to preview the *Syracusan Procession* – a curious parallel to his own *Beloved* in theme – and immediately recipro- cated with a dinner invitation. It is probable that on these occasions Rossetti was urged to exhibit, for Leighton wished to promote an inclusive art scene. And it may well be that Rossetti passed this on to Stephens, who within weeks prefaced his notice of the RA summer show with regret for the absence of artists of such power as Rossetti, Madox Brown, Burne-Jones, implying that the Academy should make overtures. The RA should be representative and 'comprehensive of every shade of opinion – an equal field where all might be tested, to the advantage, doubtless, of these resolute absentees', he wrote.[22]

Looking back, Leighton described the 'strangely interesting' Rossetti as 'a considerable influence in the world's art' in the 1860s. Not returning the compliment, Rossetti dismissed Leighton's painting as having an impasto like scented soap and face-powder,[23] though this may belie envy and it is easily inferred that Leighton was one of those whose success spurred him to renewed ambition. Resisting attempts to set them against each other, Leighton persisted in his regard and when Rossetti's death fell during his time as President of the RA worked hard to mount a speedy retrospective for an artist never previously seen on the Academy walls.

Meanwhile Rossetti throve as never before. Despite his hatred of 'togs', his dress suit was more and more in use, for club dinners and evening parties, though he drew the line when bidden to wear historical costume to a great fancy dress ball at the Gambarts' on the eve of Derby Day 1866. As the date approached, the art world was abuzz with anticipation. W. P. Frith, whose *Derby Day* was the 'painting of honour' at the ball, planned to go as John Evelyn, complete with dangling sword and wife in period costume. At Gambart's house in St John's Wood, a parquet floor was laid in the picture gallery, and two marquees erected in the garden, with a special gas supply to give glittering illumination. Six days before the ball, a major finance company crashed, losing £19 million of its investors' funds, spreading panic and dismay. One of the victims was Holman Hunt, whose *Finding of the Saviour* was also due to hang at the great party. Then, the morning before, a gas explosion tore down the back of Gambart's house: bricks, pictures and statuary were hurled into the air and one of the servants died from her injuries. To the devout, it was a punishment for prodigality. 'Hope nothing of yours was blown up at Gambart's; did the Devil fetch away anything of Gabriel's?' Stephens asked Hunt with ill-placed jocularity.[24] But it does not seem that any work of Rossetti's was on display. Nor does any comment of his on the providential escape survive.

A month later came a bathetic sequel, at Madox Brown's home in Fitzroy Square. 'I was very sorry to bolt in that way from such a really jolly party,' Gabriel wrote. 'But, Brown, if you had known!' As a sketch vividly disclosed, in the middle of the evening his dress trousers and waistcoat had split down the back.[25] Clutching his tails lest every movement expose his disgrace, he had left without ceremony. Prosperity and indulgence spelt ever-increasing plumpness.

According to *Fraser's Magazine*, the literary *cause célèbre* of 1866 was Swinburne's *Poems and Ballads*, which he insisted on publishing against all advice. The critical storm broke in August, when the *Saturday Review* described the book's author as the libidinous laureate of a pack of satyrs, singing to the unnameable lusts of sated wantons. The *Athenaeum* claimed he was a poseur who promoted immorality for the sake of publicity, and implied effeminacy. The *Pall Mall Gazette* alleged he was 'maudlin drunk on lewd ideas'. The poems that gave most offence included those dramatising Sappho's love as overtly lesbian, the grotesque *Les Noyades*, and *Hermaphroditus*, inspired by a statue in the Louvre:

> Sex to sweet sex with lips and limbs is wed,
> Turning the fruitful feud of hers and his
> To the waste wedlock of a sterile kiss ...

In the clubs and at dinner tables where such things could be discussed, the book was denounced, usually unread, as a cesspit of depravity and perversion. Fearful of prosecution for obscenity, publisher J. B. Payne decided to withdraw the volume. Simultaneously furious and elated, Swinburne was in his element as a Sadean martyr to free speech. He made arrangements to reissue with Hotten, a disreputable publisher of semi-pornography.

Allegations flew. Scott thought the smoking-room gossip that Swinburne was 'unmanly' was physically true. Woolner denied having urged Payne to suppress the book. William began a public defence of the notorious volume. Gabriel devoted an afternoon in company with Sandys trying to persuade Swinburne to omit the more offensive pieces and keep clear of Hotten. This advice rejected, he attempted to distance himself from the debate, claiming he was too busy to meddle further in the matter, or act as 'reporter, apologist, or antagonist' for either side. Then Ned heard Tennyson say that the unpleasant element in Swinburne's verse was, in his view, due in part to the influence of Rossetti. (No doubt the other culprit was Milnes.) Ned relayed this to Gabriel, who at once composed a rebuttal. He was certainly not guilty of encouraging Swinburne's excesses, he told Tennyson. 'As no one delights more keenly in his genius than I do, I have also a right to say that no one has more strenuously combated its wayward exercise in certain instances,' he insisted, 'to the extent of having repeatedly begged him not to read me such portions of his writings when in MS.'[26] Indeed, he recalled saying so to Tennyson when coming away from the Procters', and was dismayed that less credence was given to his own words than others' unsupported allegations. 'I cannot now myself submit to misrepresentation in a quarter where I should much regret it,' he wrote, for Tennyson's opinions were influential.

With a hint of mockery, Gabriel began calling Algernon 'the Bard'. Now lodging in Marylebone, Swinburne was still often at Chelsea where all too frequently there were drunken incidents, when he became abusive and accident-prone. The amazing providence of topers, declared William after one such contretemps, when Swinburne reappeared a day later, nursing no bruises and airily dismissive of the row.

Gabriel talked of taking a holiday. A standing invitation came from Penkill Castle in Ayrshire, where Scott now spent his summers with Miss Boyd, its chatelaine. Allingham offered to find lodgings in Lymington, where he was now customs officer, but Rossetti's affection, once so lively, was fading into irritable familiarity. He dithered, and then in October went with Sandys to Winchelsea, one of the old Cinque Ports on the Channel coast, now a picturesque backwater. The half-ruined, ivy-clad church was as quiet as the quarter sessions, which they watched being opened by Mayor and aldermen with splendid robes and silver maces dating from Edward III's time. Solemnly, the Mayor informed the absent populace that there were no cases to hear. 'This may give you some idea of the pleasant doziness of the place, which is more to my taste I think than any other I know,' Gabriel told his mother. 'Everyone is eighty-two if he is not ninety-six.'[27]

One day they took a dogcart to Northiam, to see a medieval house – where Rossetti was amazed to find a Holbein painting in excellent condition, clearly a lost pendant to the well-known portrait of Sir Henry Guilford by the same artist.[28] Outside was an exceptional topiary garden. Topiary, in fact, filled the village, and Gabriel was particularly struck by a box tree grown in the shape of an armchair at the door of a cottage. Its owners were old and poor, so he paid a sovereign and the chair was dug up and dispatched to Chelsea, for Loader to plant. The village 'looked on with a rather evil eye', because the chair was a local celebrity and had been the old couple's proudest possession. Gabriel had a flicker of conscience: it was so beautiful and unique; he would send another sovereign when he got home. Perhaps he did. Perhaps not, for the transplanted chair soon died, inevitably.

By 23 October he was back in London, looking brisker and better for the break and talking of taking a house in the country – an old house – as a rural retreat. He had a barn owl in the studio, and a veritable aviary in the garden, with 'fierce foreign owls' and ravens as well as peacocks, pigeons and hens. Unannounced, Gabriel gave a cat to Christina, unable to keep it penned. The white mice escaped from their cage, and the hedgehogs that Kate Howell sent were loosed in the garden, proving troublesome indoors.

Kate had also furnished a supply of white roses, for the new picture that Mr Leyland had commissioned. An avowedly sensuous subject, it depicted Lilith, the first, apocryphal wife of Adam, by whom 'he begat nothing but devils' according to Jewish legend, but borrowed in this instance from Goethe's *Faust*, which Gabriel knew so well:

> Beware of her hair, for she excels
> All women in the magic of her locks
> And when she twines them round a young man's neck
> She will never set him free again.

Conceived as a counterpart to Rae's *Palmifera* (beauty of body and soul respectively), *Lady Lilith* was commissioned in April 1866, to be delivered in six months. The price of 450 guineas was paid in full at the end of July. Rossetti set to work over the summer, sending Loader to collect the roses. 'The picture represents a lady combing her hair' he told Leyland. 'Its colour is chiefly white and silver with a great mass of golden hair.' To Smetham he said simply 'my picture with the hair'. Fanny was the model.[29]

Lady Lilith is the most Swinburnian of all Rossetti's pictures, and at the same time one of the most unpleasant of all his carnal beauties, despite its iconic status in illustration and exhibition. The subject is a modern, self-absorbed Venus, contemplating her own features, representing malign but compelling femininity – the 'haughty luxuriousness of the beautiful modern witch's face, the tale of a cold soul amid all its charms . . .' as Fred Stephens later wrote. 'She has passion without love, and languor without satiety – energy without heart, and beauty without tenderness or sympathy for others – for her lovers least of all.' Rendered largely in whites, the colour range recalls that of *Ecce Ancilla*, but here the purity is that of the heartless Snow Queen, relieved by slashes of sexual red. Great display, as Allingham noted of Swinburne's *Poems and Ballads*, 'so elaborated, so violently emphatic, so really cold-blooded'.[30] Rossetti's *Lilith* invites a comparable judgement, with additional speculation that notwithstanding its presentation of 'beauty' the feeling that informs the image is deeply hostile to womanhood. Indeed, Rossetti later wrote that the sonnet written for the picture was based on belief in 'the perilous principle of the world being female from the first' – that is, that all sin and temptation were derived from woman, as in Judaeo-Christian tradition.[31]

Other works in hand were the Venetian lady with sumptuous sleeve and a new *Regina Cordium*, sold to Mr Trist for what seems a very reasonable £170 considering its size and elaboration: all the background space is filled with an espalier of cherry sprigs, on a golden ground. In addition, he had 'other small things in a forward state and still for sale', which included a loosely-painted *Fiammetta*, offered to Boyce for 80 guineas before going to Gambart. After all the alarms of 1866, he concluded that 'this panic year, strange to say, promises to be much my best as yet'.[32] With 'a goodish sum' in hand, he opened an account in December, with the Union Bank.

Rossetti's finances are difficult to disentangle. At this date he had for some time managed the equivalent of an overdraft by repeated bills of exchange, as well as habitually buying on long credit from Murray Marks and others. Altogether, however, he computed his income for 1866 as around £1,800 in payments and advances, which was somewhat less than the £2,050 he had earned in 1865, but his debts were lower now the Plint trustees were at last paid off. Aggregated income does not represent net figures, but a gross income of £1,800 was nevertheless extremely healthy, at a time when a typical manual wage was £50 a year, and £350 covered the necessities of a middle-class couple with one or two servants. It was substantially more than the £600 that Morris currently received from his inherited mining investments, albeit modest alongside Ruskin's reputed income of over £20,000 a year following the sale of his father's wine business.

From his earnings, Rossetti thus could afford £2 a week for Alexa, small payments to Lizzie's relatives and generosity towards friends. At the end of their Winchelsea excursion, Sandys calculated that he owed £60, which Rossetti ignored. It was an expensive holiday, if this was Sandys's half-share in the joint expenditure on rail fares, carriage hire, hotel rooms, etc.; more probably the debt included earlier subventions to the notoriously improvident Sandys.

On Christmas Day, Gabriel dined at Albany Street with the rest of the family, and on the last day of 1866 his mother and sisters were snowbound at Chelsea after a heavy fall. Years later, Christina recalled such gatherings warmly. 'Family or friendly parties used to assemble at Tudor House, there to meet with an unfailing affectionate welcome,' she wrote. When he chose, her brother 'became the sunshine of his circle, and he frequently chose to be so. His ready wit and fun amused us; his good-nature and kindness of heart endeared him to us.'[33] Friends endorsed this, Georgie Jones recalling Rossetti as 'a prince among men', who brought pleasure to every company.

Whistler was his only rival at 2 Lindsey Row, along the Chelsea riverside, where the blue-painted dining room was decorated with purple Japanese fans and the drawing room had pink and yellow walls, with white woodwork whose paint was still drying on the day of his first dinner-party. One Sunday a ship with spreading sails was painted in the hallway, to be joined in time by a golden dado sprinkled with pink and white petals. In the grey and black studio a tall screen was painted with bridge, church and a great gold moon.

Though for the most part Whistler's impact on Gabriel's art is barely visible – the iconic *Princesse du Pays de la Porcelaine* surely being influential – Rossetti admired the American artist's work as well as his aesthetic ideas. Whistler's Breton coast scene was unsurpassed in both truth to nature and pure colour, he told Leathart, urging him to buy. With Anderson Rose, Rossetti was made executor of Whistler's will, drawn up in Jo's favour ahead of Whistler's expedition to Valparaiso, during which Tudor House also provided secure lodging for several canvases. Temperamentally, one might not have expected a smooth friendship between two opinionated, egotistic artists with no dislike of making enemies, but somehow they seem to have been kindred spirits. When, early in 1867, Whistler struck Legros for calling him a liar, Rossetti was asked by others to mediate, writing to deplore such 'brutal' conduct. Whistler was not pleased: 'I wish it had never occurred to you to go to Rossetti and ask him to be judge or umpire,' he told Luke Ionides. But he wrote more in sorrow than anger to Rossetti, and was rewarded with firm, if wordy, affirmations of support. 'I should assuredly not have volunteered any written opinion on your affairs; and moreover am quite ready to admit that, in the absence of such supposed incentive, I might by doing so have justly been considered intrusive,' wrote Gabriel; 'I must also admit that the exact words you give – "Ce n'est pas vrai" – seem to me also to be inevitably the precursors of blows, and only to be spoken if at all by one prepared for them.'[34]

Shortly afterwards, when Whistler used his fists against a second victim, Rossetti again remonstrated. 'Even apart from my general feeling on such matters on which I have said enough already, I cannot but deplore that your indignation, though I believe it was just, has led you to do what must cause so much pain to others besides the offender,' he wrote. But six months later, when the Burlington Arts Club acceded to demands that Whistler's membership be withdrawn, both Gabriel and William resigned in support. Whistler thanked them both for 'the noble way you stood by me and did battle for me'. A distinct mutual regard is evident in the correspondence, with what one senses is some awe on Rossetti's part for Whistler's readiness to hit out so literally in defence of his 'honour'.

As 1867 opened, *Venus Verticordia* was not yet complete, *Palmifera* hardly begun, *Lilith* three months beyond the promised delivery date. In the interim Leyland was offered a new, smaller work, apparently conceived around this time with the seasonal title of *A Christmas Carol*. A fine picture of Ellen Smith playing a musical instrument, this was finished by mid-February. In the event, it appears that Leyland took instead another work drawn from Ellen, called *The Loving Cup*, which has the same bright clarity and precision.[35] With Trist's *Regina Cordium*, these works form a trio of attractive, winsome girls, less aloof than *Monna Vanna*, less self-absorbed than *Lilith*.

At the same time, for Frederick Craven, who clearly preferred incident to pure aesthetics, Rossetti resurrected his old subject of Delia and Tibullus, offered as a watercolour figure-subject, for around 300 guineas, with an advance of 100 guineas on commission. Rossetti redrew the sleeping Delia from Alexa, introduced an attendant slave curled up asleep, studied from an African boy found in a seamen's hostel in docklands, and to complete the domestic atmosphere added an anachronistic household cat. 'My dear W, have you any photos: of pussey cats asleep?' he wrote hastily, having parted with the Tudor House moggie.[36]

In March, a letter from Mitchell prompted the hurried return of *Venus* to the easel and the rather drastic decision to repaint the head. But then, rather unaccountably, Gabriel turned instead to a revised version of *Morning Music* from 1864, apparently done as a pot-boiler. It was bought – perhaps via Gambart – by 'the demon Dunlop', with whom Rossetti had forsworn all dealings. A fortnight after this, he was doing a duplicate *Paolo and Francesca*, probably also for Gambart. Seven days later, he had started *The Loving Cup* and another new subject (soon abandoned) showing Margaret finding the jewels in her chamber, from *Faust*. The next idea was a reversion to the Trojan scene of Cassandra warning Hector while Paris dallies with Helen. Instead he set to work on a portrait of Leyland's wife clipping roses from a bush growing in a large Chinese jar, which was begun in May and tackled with dispatch. 'I have now given the figure a flowing white and gold drapery, which I think comes remarkably well, and suits the head perfectly,' he wrote on 18 June. 'I think I cannot do better than call the picture again Monna Rosa and adopt a quotation from Poliziano which fits it perfectly . . .'[37] By 5 July, it was virtually finished.

An important new patron, Leyland's own story was a remarkable one. Born poor in Liverpool, he was he was the son of a convict transported to Australia. Dour in demeanour and ruthless in business, he was also an accomplished musician and linguist, and an art patron who constantly refined his collection of pictures, furniture and ceramics. Now aged thirty-five, he was about to become seriously rich as sole proprietor of a shipping line; Rossetti, Whistler and Burne-Jones would all be beneficiaries.

Knewstub had departed, intent on pursuing his career. Rossetti had done his best to assist, sending his pictures to the Arundel Club, introducing him to Gambart and Mrs Cowper, and commending Knewstub's talent for caricature to *Punch*. The parting was amicable, though when Knewstub asked if he might return to Cheyne Walk as a fellow painter rather than pupil-assistant, he was told that his rooms were now occupied by Sandys. His family however believed there was an estrangement, caused by Knewstub's 'desire to remove Emily Renshaw from the bohemian circle around Rossetti'. To do so, he married her before he could afford to, against the wishes of his parents, who promptly disinherited their son.[38] Rossetti is unlikely to have felt responsible, however, and was genuinely pleased when Knewstub's fortunes took a turn for the better around 1870.

But with all the commissions, he needed a new assistant. One candidate was a young man named Charles Murray, who had approached Rossetti in 1866. At this date barely seventeen years old, 'little Murray' was well below average height, working as 'the boy' in an engraving firm, with scant knowledge of painting. Rossetti suggested he might undertake a small task for Frederick Burton, but it was for Burne-Jones that Murray first worked, copying a picture of St Theophilus, and to whom he returned after failing with a replica *Beata Beatrix* early in 1867.[39]

In his place came Henry Treffry Dunn, an older and as yet utterly unsuccessful artist. Originally from Truro and now in his late twenties, he was easy-going, unambitious, theatre-loving. Somewhere or other he met the ubiquitous Howell, from whom it was a short step to Cheyne Walk. Preceded by some of his landscape sketches, Dunn presented himself to Rossetti in May 1867. Shown by the servant into the small parlour, he saw mirrors of all shapes, sizes and designs, a china cupboard full of Spode ware and a mantelshelf of black lacquer, its panels painted with golden birds, beasts, fruit and flowers. When Rossetti appeared, Dunn noted first the long loose jacket, with capacious pockets, and an old-fashioned fob watch on a gold chain. He was also struck by the warm, musical voice and informal, unassuming bonhomie. They proceeded to the studio, where half-finished works were on the easel.

Somewhat to Dunn's dismay, a watercolour replica was the first task on offer. 'I was in considerable doubt as to whether I could do it or not,' he recalled – watercolour being so much less amenable to scraping and repainting than oil. But he welcomed the opportunity, 'so arrangements were made there and then for me to come and make a beginning'.[40]

Finding Dunn a fellow admirer, Gabriel took down the precious Blake notebook and let his visitor leaf through the pages. The *Hypnerotomachia*

Poliphili followed. Then William arrived, glad to find the proposed assistant also a smoker. Howell appeared too, coming from Whistler's in search of a drawing with a gold background, which appears to have been one of the portraits of Ruth Herbert.

Dunn was then shown Rossetti's portfolio of studies, sketches and finished drawings, each accompanied by a lively flow of recollections and anecdotes, about Ruskin, Browning, Tennyson. Like others before him, he felt the effect of a certain glamour. Beyond that, he was struck by the total atmosphere of Tudor House, with its congeries of old furniture, china, metalware, antique fabrics. In the studio was a chest holding necklaces, brooches, featherwork, crystals and a wardrobe full of costumes and draperies. All were artists' props, for whatever took Gabriel's fancy he tended to buy against the day it might be painted. In time, the cellars were filled with unwanted and unused items, like the dusty junkshops whence they had come.

Dunn remarked particularly on the collection of musical instruments, all old and mostly stringed – mandolin, lutes, dulcimers, and a strange-shaped Japanese koto. 'Yet in all the after-years that I lived in the house I never heard a note of music. It had no home there,' he recalled, adding that Rossetti shared Dr Johnson's view that of all noises music was merely the most bearable.

Soon, Harry Dunn was invited to live at Tudor House, where he speedily established himself as household as well as studio assistant. If he was paid a salary, he left no details. As Burne-Jones had paid Murray 25s. a week, plus £60 for his first copy (which Rossetti considered a reasonable arrangement), it is likely that Dunn received a similar amount, perhaps with board and lodging in lieu of wages. With all the work in hand, it was useful that Dunn proved capable. 'The degree to which he has improved in copying my things is extraordinary, and I now perceive that he will prove most valuable to me,' Gabriel wrote in August.[41]

Dunn's first task was a watercolour *Beata Beatrix*, which does not at this date appear to have had a destination. No fewer than three replicas of *The Loving Cup* followed during 1867, together with two reduced versions of *Lady Lilith*, and before Mitchell's *Venus* was delivered the following year, a watercolour copy was sold elsewhere.

The slightly manic picture-making continued, with *The Rose*, a watercolour of a girl leaning from a window, *Joli Cœur*, a small oil of Ellen Smith coyly fingering a heart-shaped pendant; a watercolour of *Tristram and Iseult drinking the Love Potion* for T. H. McConnell, who now owned the *Vineyard* cartoons; and a careful chalk head called *Peace*. When *Tibullus and Delia* was delivered to Craven in July, a new work called *Rosa Triplex* was commissioned to hang with it.

The same month Rossetti was taken by Mike Halliday to Havering in Essex to meet an important new client, and came away with a commission from 'Mr Matthews the great brewer (who is Ind Coope & Co)' for the proposed picture of Perseus with Andromeda and the Gorgon's head. The price agreed was 1,500 guineas and Matthews came to Chelsea to approve the design. 'It is a very straightforward work, and will not involve delay or great labour; so this is a capital thing for me,' reported Rossetti to Brown. 'Now what I want is a studio.'[42] He meant a purpose-built space, with full north light, platform, storage racks, sinks and stoves, like those being created by all the best artists in Kensington and St John's Wood.

At last he felt able to cancel Leathart's commission for the untouched *Found*, and thus 'shake off the nightmare' hanging between them. Would Leathart accept his £250 refunded, with a small work worth £50 as interest? Leathart resisted. He would prefer the picture, completed without further delay. 'I am vain enough to believe you would be as glad to see the picture upon my walls as upon almost any other – at all events none would be prouder of it than I would,' he replied. But Rossetti could not oblige.[43] Nor was the promised 'little picture' ever delivered. They remained friends, but Leathart had no more works from Rossetti. To compensate, he bought the *Salutation* panels from Fred Burton, telling his wife that it was 'the very thing that we wanted to render our little collection unique as a gathering of some of the best works of a set of artists who have made so much noise and had so much influence upon English art during these last 15 or 20 years'.[44]

With a core of loyal patrons, many other eager customers, and a ready market for pot-boilers, Dante Gabriel Rossetti might well congratulate himself on his position in the contemporary art world as he entered his fortieth year. 'What you don't have at forty, you never will have', concluded his father's Italian proverb.

CHAPTER EIGHTEEN

La Pia

Spring 1867 saw the death of aunt Margaret Polidori, for long a shadowy though far from silent presence at Albany Street, owing to her involuntary hyena-like laughter. Summoned to her deathbed, Gabriel paid his last respects; it was close on thirteen years since the death of his father in the same house. Then, he had been young, disorganised but optimistic, still full of untried powers, in love with Lizzie. Now he was approaching middle age, sadder as well as richer and stouter, his whimsicality hardening into eccentricity even while worldliness tempered his idealism.

Teasingly, he had taken to addressing his mother as 'Good Antique – soon shortened to "Teak" – in playful honour of her venerable age; at sixty-eight, she was as old as the century. She now chose to move to the Bedford Estate in Bloomsbury, where no shops or public houses were permitted and the streets were sentinelled by gatekeepers, and from midsummer 1867 was rehoused at 56 Euston Square, with her daughters, sister Eliza and and son William, who typically spent two or three nights a week at Chelsea. Here, as Dunn recalled, he kept a jar of tobacco on the mantelpiece, to which all and sundry helped themselves.

Lizzie's watercolours hung round the dining room, and in the autumn of 1867 Gabriel distributed the folios of her photographed drawings and sketches to a few close friends, including Howell. The year before, chaffing Boyce over a misdirected letter, he had admitted that he often unthinkingly began letters as if from Blackfriars, and even gave the address to cab drivers. But early in 1867, he allowed Howell to sort all the miscellaneous correspondence brought from Chatham Place. Valuable autographs were kept; the rest burnt. Five years on from the tragedy of 1862, the past was being sealed.

To many, Mr Rossetti must have appeared a most eligible widower – in Victorian terms still young. Browning, in his fifties, was currently fending off the importunities of widowed Lady Ashburton. Holman Hunt, who at the end of 1865 had married Fanny Waugh, Woolner's sister-in-law, was now also widowed, with a young son to care for. Annie Miller, incidentally, had made an advantageous marriage to one Major Thomson, cousin to Lord

Ranelagh. 'I have met her husband, who seems a very good gentlemanly fellow,' Rossetti assured Stephens.[1] Domestically, Tudor House would benefit from a wife, to act as hostess and manage servants; indeed, Gabriel was currently talking to Dunn about a new method of housekeeping. But he gave no sign of seeking a new soul mate, and was verbally hostile to the whole idea. 'I loathe and despise family life!' he told Allingham, who yearned for the comforts of marriage. And when Howell's wedding to Kitty finally took place this year, Rossetti rather condoled than congratulated, and declined to attend, claiming to be such a 'bogey' that he would blight their happiness.[2]

With few exceptions, his social life in the clubs and studios remained largely masculine. He sought out pretty models, paid them liberally and flattered their vanities, but remained unsusceptible to more intimate charms. He tended to avoid evening parties where well-bred young women might be met, while Fanny's irregular presence at Cheyne Walk gave a clear signal that he was not available: any lady tempted to fall in love would soon be disabused by her male relatives, who knew the score.

One young lady however was at this date 'very graciously disposed towards him' and would have accepted had he proposed. She was Marie Spartali, a member of the wealthy and cultured Greek business community in London who, headed by the Ionides family, became conspicuous art patrons in this period, and good friends to many in the Pre-Raphaelite circle. Tom Armstrong recalled a garden party at the Ionides's house in summer 1863 when he, Rossetti, Whistler, Legros and du Maurier were first introduced to Miss Spartali and her sister Christine. 'We were all à genoux before them,' he wrote, 'and of course every one of us burned with a desire to paint them.'[3]

When Whistler secured Christine Spartali as his sitter for *La Princesse du Pays de la Porcelaine* Marie acted as chaperone, and the following year began taking lessons in art from Ford Madox Brown, in the studio at Fitzroy Square, alongside his children. In 1867 she made her exhibition debut at the Dudley Gallery. Tall and stately, with a grave, intelligent beauty, she too was sought after as a model. 'Of all the women who elicited Gabriel's admiration, Marie Spartali was probably the most gifted intellectually,' wrote William's daughter Helen; 'austere, virtuous and fearless, she was not lacking in caustic wit and a sharp tongue ... as decided in her outlook and sympathies as she was later in life.'[4]

At an early date, Rossetti became aware of Marie's reciprocal admiration, and her tacit hope of marriage – later confirmed by Marie's father. A few months later, he himself touched obliquely on the subject in a sonnet called *Love's Baubles*, in which the figure of Love is surrounded by ladies 'thronged in warm pursuit'.

Marie was in her early twenties, well-educated, well-connected, from a rich family, and above all sympathetic towards a life devoted to art. She loved poetry too, and for all her caustic opinions had a fully conventional view of womanly submission to masculine authority. She was liked and admired by most of Gabriel's friends. In many ways it would have been an excellent and advantageous match. Yet, if he was tempted, he showed no inclination to succumb, even while remaining eager to secure Marie's services as a model.

At the end of his life, Rossetti hinted that he had long been impotent. If so, this was probably as a result of the attack of mumps, whose complications, for about a quarter of adult male sufferers, include orchitis or hydrocele, involving the discomfort of swollen testicles. In about half such cases this is accompanied by partial testicular atrophy – though not usually by sterility. Rossetti is known to have suffered from a recurrent hydrocele in middle life, and so it is very possible he was, or believed himself to be, sexually impaired, though not necessarily lacking in desire. He had a passionate nature. His affections were warm and open, his emotions unrepressed. And he was painting, over and again, images of female beauty designed to delight and enrapture. *The Beloved* unveiled herself for her bridegroom. *Venus* held a dart to pierce the onlooker's heart. *The Loving Cup* was raised in a toast to dalliance, '*douce nuit et joyeux jour à cavalier de bel amour*'. *Lilith* twisted her tresses round a young man's heart, never to set him free.

At any given time, he talked of painting more elevated subjects, which the steady income from pot-boilers would have enabled him to pursue. Instead, he preferred to produce carnal 'beauties' one after another, in varied but essentially constant mode. Bust-length, half-length, three-quarters: sumptuously or simply attired young women, their hair outspread, their gowns open, their flowers at full bloom. Of course they were eminently saleable. But though formulaic, the works are invested with a good deal of their creator's own feeling. Chaste or seductive by turns, his female figures attest to some emotional need, some sublimation of unfulfilled longing, as if the artist were searching, through painted metaphor, for an ideal beloved, creating her images to assuage an inner need to, or for, love – a face to give visual shape to displaced desire.

'Have you seen, at heaven's mid-height / ... Venus leap forth burning white?' he wrote in a poem for Craven's *Aurora*. 'So my bright breast-jewel, so my bride, / One sweet night, when fear takes flight, / Shall leap against my side.'

It seemed almost a compulsion. No sooner was one such image half completed than another came crowding on to the easel. But when a real bride presented herself, it seems fear was not put to flight. And there was of course Fanny, of whom he was genuinely fond and whose familiar presence in Tudor House could not be reconciled with thoughts of marriage.

There were signs that not all was well beneath the successful surface. One symptom, or rather symbol, was the disastrous death-rate in the garden menagerie. 'The fate of our beasts at Chelsea has been a most calamitous one,' William noted in February 1867 when the small owl they named Jessie had her head bitten off by the raven. Then he listed the other casualties: two parakeets, a Jersey lizard, a dormouse, a tortoise, two robins, a salamander, a rabbit, two pigeons, etc. etc.[5]

Some died naturally, some were killed by mistrustful servants, some were attacked by other animals, some escaped and died of unknown causes. Loader's dog was killed by the deerhound. The young kangaroo was assumed to have murdered its mother. The armadilloes burrowed into the next-door garden where bait laced with prussic acid was laid for them. The bait disappeared, and so, it was hoped, had the armadilloes, recalled Dunn; but no – after three months they reappeared looking mangy and sick, having shed their scales. Eventually they were dispatched to the Zoological Gardens, where one hopes they were better treated.

Dunn also recalled a wire cage in which a packing case covered with a marble slab contained a raccoon. Rossetti removed the stone 'and then, to my astonishment, he put his hand in quickly, seized the "coon" by the scruff of its neck, hauled it out, and held it up, in a plunging, kicking, teeth-showing state for me to look at, remarking "Does it not look like a devil?" ' Subsequently it caused 'a world of trouble and annoyance' by recurrently escaping – raiding the neighbour's hen-roost, and finding its way into drawers and closets where it chewed manuscripts into shreds.

As Dunn observed, neither Rossetti brother had any particular affection for, or understanding of, their live Noah's Ark, whose inhabitants were valued for quaint or grotesque qualities, not as pets. The creatures were neglected and yet expected to perform on demand. Held responsible when they escaped, they were considered ungrateful when they died. It was all most surreal.

The management – or mismanagement – of household matters was equally chaotic. Unable to reconcile expenditure with tradesmen's bills, Rossetti was frequently brought down by what he regarded as inexplicable dereliction on the part of his servants. 'For the life of me I could not see why with his ample income there should not always be a good balance in his hands to meet every requirement,' recalled Dunn, adding that it did not require great acuity to see that, somewhere, 'there must be great waste and improvidence in the housekeeping'. He offered to check the domestic accounts, for which Loader was formally responsible. But this of course was an affront to Loader, the only person willing to make cages and catch animals when necessary. 'It has struck me that as I really do not wish to lose Loader but do wish to curtail expenses if possible, the best plan would be to give Loader so much a week for all provision expenses,' wrote Rossetti to Brown, seeking advice. 'The question is, what should the so much be? Do you think £5 a week ought to be sufficient, or at any rate £1 a day?'[6]

Later, Harry Dunn claimed to have halted 'the extravagance that was going on below stairs'. This may have been so, although Dunn also had his own reasons to exaggerate depredations 'downstairs', while Rossetti's unsystematic expenditure, on animals, bric-à-brac and china, was surely a contributory factor; an 1867 estimate of household expenses prepared by Warington Taylor, indexing the amounts due to butcher, baker, greengrocer and others, ended with a note: 'this does not include Wild Beasts.'[7] Other monies went on Fanny's maintenance, payments to Howell and loans to Sandys. As in the days of penury, so in those of wealth: Rossetti's attitude was notably casual, though Brown once observed he was fond of buying things simply because they were expensive.

On his visits to London, Allingham often preferred to sleep on the Burne-Joneses' sofa rather than amid the disorder of Tudor House. Overcoming his fastidiousness on one occasion this autumn, he endured a bibulous dinner with Gabriel, Fanny, Brown and Howell, the last telling outrageous tales and smutty stories. Later in the evening, when Dunn and Howell descended to the kitchen in search of supper, they found 'a mouse eating a haddock'.

'My old regard for D. G. R stirs within me, and would be as warm as ever *if he would let it*,' Allingham had earlier remarked, noting his friend's cantankerous irritability.[8] Increasingly, Gabriel's geniality was eclipsed by querulous moods, when nothing would please him.

At least part of this was due to general 'seediness' if not actual ill-health. Dunn was soon aware of his employer's nervous hypochondria, claiming that anxiety over trifling symptoms made Rossetti 'a veritable *malade imaginaire*'. One day, he was agitated and distressed by the unfounded conviction that he had cancer of the tongue; on another, he was sure he had a ruptured navel. Not all was imagined, however; the discomfort of the swollen hydrocele was very real, and no doubt responsible for his 'slopperty' way of walking, and habit of lounging full-length on a sofa, 'lolling about like a seal on a sandbank', according to Smetham.[9] Moreover, something less definable was now also troublesome. Perhaps it was attributable to growing corpulence: Gabriel consulted his medical adviser John Marshall, who advised a diet high in protein (including kidneys and oysters), vegetables, fruit and light wines and low on carbohydrates, eggs, coffee, chocolate, beer and spirits. It made little or no impact. By August

1867 he was suffering sufficiently to invite himself to stay with Allingham for health's sake. He arrived at Lymington wearing 'a ventilating hat, something like a policeman's helmet', and looking stouter than ever. He also complained of eye-trouble, and though he brought *Venus Verticordia*, hoping to find some roses, the painting-case remained unopened.

While Allingham was at work, he read *The Mill on the Floss*. Despite invitations, he refused to cross to the Isle of Wight, where the Spartalis as well as Tennyson had a home, and Mrs Prinsep's sister Julia Cameron wished to add D. G. Rossetti to her list of eminent photographic sitters. '[H]e entirely objects to be sea-sick, and doesn't want to see either Mrs Cameron or Tennyson,' noted Allingham. They took some walks, however, and amongst other excursions Rossetti went to see Leighton's church fresco in Lyndhurst. He enjoyed a dusty furniture shop, bargaining over an old mirror, and in a cottage garden found another box-tree chair; but this time the owner would not sell. For most of the visit, however, he seemed desultory and bored.

'Then a walk,' Allingham recorded. 'R. walks very characteristically, with a peculiar lounging gait, often trailing the point of his umbrella on the ground, but still obstinately pushing on and making way, he humming the while with closed teeth, in the intervals of talk, not a tune or anything like one but what sounds like a *sotto voce* note of defiance to the Universe. Then suddenly he will fling himself down somewhere and refuse to stir an inch further. His favourite attitude – on his back, one knee raised, arms behind head . . . He very seldom takes particular notice of anything as he goes, and cares nothing about natural history, or science in any form or degree. It is plain that the simple, the natural, the naive are merely insipid in his mouth; he must have strong savours, in art, in literature and in life. In poetry he desires spasmodic passion, and emphatic, partly archaic, diction. He cannot endure Wordsworth . . . Shakespeare, the old Ballads, Blake, Keats, Shelley, Browning, Mrs Browning, Tennyson, Poe, being first favourites, and now Swinburne. *Wuthering Heights* is a Koh-i-noor among novels, *Sidonia the Sorceress* "a stunner" . . .'[10]

In truth, Rossetti was far from well, confessing to eye-strain and 'confusion in the head'. A country retreat was advised, but as the symptoms seemed worryingly worse rather than better, with his eyes particularly sensitive to sunshine, he distrusted an open-air prescription. Back in London he arranged to see an oculist. But 'I mention this quite in confidence, as it would be injurious to me if it got about', he told Allingham. 'The only two to whom I have named it are Brown and Howell, and I do not mean to say more about it.'[11] Clients would not come to a purblind painter.

In retrospect, the 'confusion in the head' was more ominous. Immediately, however, insomnia was the greatest curse, upsetting all equilibrium. Something was seriously wrong.

Anxiety grew when a letter came from Mr Matthews the brewer, with second thoughts about Perseus and the Medusa. His initial misgivings were confirmed: the image of a severed head, however classical, was too gruesome for the drawing room. Would the artist suggest a different subject?

The commission was of importance, being a subject and a price that would raise a painter's profile. Rossetti replied in his most tactful tones, explaining that 'the head, treated as a pure ideal, presenting no likeness (as it will not) to the severed head of an actual person, being moreover so much in shadow (according to my arrangement) that no painful ghastliness of colour will be apparent, will not really possess when executed the least degree of that repugnant reality which might naturally suggest itself at first.' Indeed, he continued, perhaps with reference to dramatic works like Delaroche's *Execution of Lady Jane Grey*, or reports of Manet's latest offering, *The Execution of Emperor Maximilian*, 'the kind of French sensational horror which the realistic treatment of the severed head would cause is exactly the quality I should most desire to avoid'.[12] He sincerely hoped Mr Matthews would feel reassured. But no, Matthews could not take Medusa; would Mr Rossetti please propose a new subject?

Rossetti could not afford to forgo the commission, with its promise of 1,500 guineas. What about *Dante's Dream* instead; this was 'among the subjects' he most wished to accomplish in his lifetime. It contained five figures, so the price would have to be 2,000 guineas, but if acceptable, he would start work at once.

Like a simple businessman, however, Matthews wanted work of the same value. He would take *Dante's Dream* at 1,500 guineas, or smaller works up to the value of 1,200 guineas, which had been his original ceiling. Rossetti would not conceal his disappointment. He was sure they had agreed on 1,500 guineas, 'at Havering that evening' with Mike Halliday as witness. He would do the *Dante* on a reduced scale for this price, but Matthews must appreciate how much the artist lost thereby. The *Medusa* had been announced; any new purchaser would know it had been rejected elsewhere. He trusted Matthews would take this into account when pondering the new offer.

It was a long and conciliatory letter, but Matthews was annoyed. 'The tone of your correspondence is so unsatisfactory to me from the disposition which it shows to tie me down hand and foot for a certain outlay that it makes me half disposed to withdraw my commission entirely,' he replied crisply. 'I will not do this, but I am determined that I will in no way be fettered.' Surely Mr Rossetti had the courage to do his large-scale *Medusa* without a specific commission?

Dear Sir, responded Rossetti, 'Pray acquit me at once of all intention to "tie you down hand and foot" to any plans whatever.' He had too much pride to continue once mutual confidence was lost, therefore he must 'decline at once to paint you any picture at all'. When Matthews wrote again, he returned the letter unopened.

Matthews had in fact sent an apology. Halliday came to mediate. Placated, Rossetti replied that, after all, he would be happy to paint either of the pictures proposed. But mutual confidence was lost; no new commission was agreed.

In fact, Gabriel had already moved on to other ideas, and was now designing a picture of *La Pia*, for which Janey Morris had agreed to sit. By 23 January, he was at work on compositional studies and very soon was as enthusiastic about this subject as he had been about *Medusa*, wanting urgently not to be 'thinking of pot-boiling for the moment'.[13] Perhaps stung by Matthews's reference to courage, he thus projected a major painting without first securing a client.

The sorrowful Pia de' Tolomei from Siena, who is encountered in the fifth canto of *Purgatorio*, was imprisoned by her jealous husband in a castle in the Maremma, where she died of fever or, as some said, of poison. 'This in his inmost heart well knoweth he,' she tells Dante, 'With whose fair jewel I was ringed and wed.' The subject was not only Dantesque; a decade earlier, a play of the same title ran in London with Ristori in the main role, which may have influenced Rossetti's decision to pick a subject from the *Commedia* rather than his preferred *Vita Nuova*. Perhaps the sombre cast of Jane Morris's features in repose struck his fancy; or something in her current situation recalled that of La Pia. From the outset, subject and sitter were linked.

'My dear Janey, Next Wednesday was the day I hoped to see you,' he wrote on 6 March. The arrangement was for an extended sitting of four or five days, with the Morrises to stay at Cheyne Walk throughout. First he would draw her head, then paint directly on to canvas. 'I know exactly what I have to do as to the action of the figure, which, my dear Janey, is a very easy one, so you shall be punished as little as possible for your kindness.'[14]

Mother of Jenny aged seven and May aged six, Jane was now twenty-seven. Since her father's death in 1865, her sister Bessie had lived with the Morrises, now 'above the shop' at 26 Queen Square, not far from the Rossettis in Euston Square. Meanwhile, the Burne-Joneses had moved closer to Chelsea, taking a large old house named the Grange in North End

Road, Fulham. On 4 March, they hosted a great housewarming party, with all 'the circle'. Ned 'invited all the world and had azaleas and orange trees to decorate his studio,' Scott reported to Alice. 'Howell was major-domo and the supper was sumptuous. Everybody was there, that is everybody of the *true creed* ...' Shortly after the guests left, however, nemesis issued a warning against ostentation when the studio ceiling crashed to the floor. 'Had we all been there, the new school as Brown said, might have been extinguished,' continued Scott; 'he, Gabriel, Holman, Hunt, Morris, Swinburne, little Simeon, Jones and myself might have been squashed at one go.'[15] Not to mention wives, daughters and sisters, also present.

On Friday 13 March, Janey's sitting began. In the evening Morris arrived from work, and was joined by the Howells. On Tuesday, the Morrises were still in residence when Leyland brought a fellow businessman, partner of William Graham MP, to the studio. Leyland bought a *La Pia* study, the visitor agreed to a watercolour *Venus Verticordia*, and in conversation William discovered that Morris's political views were as democratic as Ned's and his own. By Thursday, *La Pia* was succesfully started on canvas, and the Morrises had departed. The following week, when Boyce came house-hunting in Cheyne Walk after a severe illness, he found Gabriel alone with Fanny, together with some beautiful drawings of Alexa and Janey. But Fanny's reign was ending. With teasing reference to her name and girth, Rossetti affectionately called her his Ele*Fant*. When not at Tudor House, she lived in her own residence in Royal Avenue, for which Gabriel paid.

On 1 April, Jane and Gabriel were fellow guests, along with Morris and William, at a seance held by the former Emily Seddon and her husband, lawyer H. V. Tebbs.[16] The medium was the celebrated Mrs Guppy who not long before had presided over a session attended by Holman Hunt, when in total darkness competent drawings of a crane, an angel and a griffin were produced 'by the spirits'. Later, Mrs Guppy would specialise in materialisations; on this occasion it seems to have been mainly rappings, perfumes and a mysterious light seen by Janey at least. In general, however, the atmosphere was one of muffled hilarity. A cynic might suggest that Topsy's scepticism scared off the spectral beings, for he certainly had no inclination to credulity. Janey inclined to suspend disbelief, for she had idiosyncratic notions that included the transmigration of souls, and was intrigued by omens and signs.

Around 12 April, Jane returned for a second sitting. The project was now well known among painters and patrons. 'Rossetti has the Morrises staying with him in order to paint Mrs M as La Pia from Dante's Purgatorio,' Brown told Rae. 'With Mrs Morris for model and Rossetti for the painter and such a subject, you can imagine some of the tragic, fearful beauty of the picture!'

Perhaps Morris sensed what was going on, for his teasing rivalry with Rossetti took on a sharper edge. He was reportedly enraged when, this month also, Gabriel acquired from Howell a pretty cabinet that he himself had coveted. It might not matter much, but male vanity was involved.

At some later date, Rossetti sketched into one of the miniature memorandum books that he always carried a design for what looks like a bracelet of linked rosettes. Beside this is pencilled 'Sept 57 ⊗ April 14 1868', as if for an inscription.[17]

What happened on 14 April? September 1857 was the month that Jane Burden met the jovial crew at Oxford, when she was with Bessie at the temporary theatre in Oriel Street and when she sat for the figure of Guenevere, her dark hair and strong features seeming apt for the Queen whose love for Lancelot undid the whole Round Table. Being young and poor, she was impressionable enough to find romance in common courtesies, and there seems little doubt that, like so many others, she fell for Mr Rossetti's charm before she learnt of his engagement. When his friend Mr Morris proposed a few weeks later she was in no position to refuse, despite being very little 'in love' with him.

Thereafter, though her feelings remain hidden, in all probability she retained a *tendresse* for Gabriel, who had praised the beauty of a scrawny girl with sallow skin and thick dark hair, and plucked her from obscurity. Since marriage, through the days at Red House, the founding of the Firm and the move to 26 Queen Square, she had grown into a quietly assured wife and mother who also played her part in the business, executing and supervising embroidery commissions. There were seasonal visits to her in-laws in Essex, and when she could Jane went to the theatre, concerts and opera, having a great liking for drama and music, which her husband did not share. Most at ease among friends, she was like them teasingly tolerant of Topsy's incongruous temperament, by turns generous, explosive, genial or gruff, and proud of his growing reputation as a poet. Quiet in company, she nevertheless had a marked taste for jokes, tall tales, ghost stories and extraordinary dreams, and a sensitive sympathy when required, succeeding socially as both hostess and guest, without any desire to shine. The close circle of friends long recalled the evenings at Queen Square, when the table was set for dinner, with blue china, old silver, green glass.

Meeting the Morrises in the late 1860s, Henry James saw Jane with a gaze already conditioned by art. Imagine a tall lean woman in a long dress of some purple stuff without hoops or stays, 'with a mass of crisped black hair heaped into great wavy projections on each side of her temples, a thin pale face, a pair of strange, sad, deep, dark, Swinburnian eyes, with great thick black oblique brows, joined in the middle and tucking themselves away under her hair, a mouth like Oriana in our illustrated Tennyson, a long neck without any collar and in lieu thereof some dozen strings of outlandish beads,' he wrote to his family in New England. 'It's hard to say whether she's a grand synthesis of all Pre-Raphaelite pictures ever made – or they a "keen analysis" of her – whether she's an original or a copy. In either case, she is a wonder.'[18]

Following the abandoned 'Scenes from the Fall of Troy', Morris had returned to writing, with an extensive project of verse tales that began with *The Life and Death of Jason*, published in January 1867. 'Rarely but in the ballad and romance periods has such poetry been written, so broad and sad and simple, so full of deep and direct fire, certain of its aim, without blemish, without fault,' wrote Swinburne in the *Fortnightly*; 'the verse for a little is as the garment of Medea steeped in strange moisture as of tears and liquid flame to be kindled by the sun.'[19] Sales were good, prompting the completion of the next volume, recasting legends from classical, romance and Northern sources. Parts I and II of *The Earthly Paradise* thus appeared in April 1868, the time of Jane's second sitting for *La Pia*. Gabriel had given up poetry, but perhaps felt a twinge of envy, and began to refer to Morris as 'the Bard and Petty Tradesman' in homage to his two professions. The latter, it seems, was less a jibe than a commercial description gleefully seized upon by members of the Firm, including Morris himself. Gabriel sent a caricature of Topsy in both roles to Jane, with suggestions for a third. 'As it is now the fashion for successful men in any walk of literature to start a newspaper at once,' he joked, 'will you endeavour to make the great original "seriously incline" thereto? Fancy the numbers of editorial chairs which would be smashed in the course of a week!'[20]

Over these years, as Gabriel was married and widowed, moved to Chelsea and tacitly set up with Fanny, his relationship with Jane had hardly developed; she was 'dear Janey', a member of the circle, 'Top's wife', a statuesque and graceful figure who did not gush or gossip (much) and was free of many irritating female affectations. Her looks were striking: he loved to draw her features, neck and long mobile fingers. There was ongoing talk that one day he would paint her properly. At one of the Browns' evening parties, Whistler noted Gabriel and Janey 'sitting side by side in state, being worshipped in an inner room'. In June 1863 she had spent a day being photographed, and two years later sat for a sequence of portrait drawings. In June 1866 Rossetti told Brown he was due to begin Jane's portrait 'on Saturday', but no picture followed.[21] Now at last, with *La Pia*, there was realisation.

For reasons that remain obscure, Janey had withdrawn emotionally from her husband. Surviving sources give the smallest of hints. 'If you want my company (usually considered of no use to anybody but the owner) please say so,' wrote Morris grumpily to a friend on 3 February.[22] Otherwise the trouble was well concealed. As Red Lion Mary had long ago observed, Morris had no talent to cajole or flatter where women were concerned; as a spouse he was often brusque and preoccupied with business affairs. Although Morris loved his wife dearly, and held to a romantic view of gender relations, Rossetti was prompted to cast Jane as La Pia, prisoner of a cruel husband. Writing of the picture a couple of weeks later, Swinburne described the figure 'looking forth from the ramparts of her lord's castle, over the fatal lands without':

> her pallid splendid face hangs a little forward, wan and white against the mass of dark deep hair; under her hands is a work of embroidery, hanging still on the unfinished frame; just touched by the weak weary hands, it trails forward across the lap of her pale green raiment . . . in her eyes is a strange look of sorrow and fatigue, without fear and without pain, as though she were even now looking beyond earth into the soft and sad air of purgatory: she presses the deadly marriage ring into the flesh of her finger, so deep that the soft skin is bloodless and blanched from the intense imprint of it.[23]

At some stage, Jane must have confided her discontent, and made it plain how much she liked Gabriel's company; maybe 14 April marked the day they acknowledged a mutual feeling. The sonnet *Broken Music* contains a vivid figure of a mother, hardly daring to believe she has heard her child's first words, who sits breathless, elated, but with averted gaze, in order to hear them again – a figure which must express Rossetti's sudden wonder.

Over the next few weeks, Jane's sittings at Tudor House became a regular habit. She was there on 20 April, when Boyce called, and when Emily Tebbs sent another séance invitation Gabriel replied that both he and Mrs Morris, 'who is again staying here', would gladly come, promising this time that their gravity would be worthy of the grave itself.

He sent Jane's daughters a pair of dormice, joking that if the girls 'loved them very much I daresay they will get much bigger and fatter and remind you of Papa and me'.[24] By early May, it was agreed that as well as *La Pia* he would paint a straight portrait, to hang in Queen Square. Jane was making a blue silk dress for the purpose, towards which Gabriel designed a simple panel embroidered in gold. She also stitched a cushion for La Pia's embroidery, hanging listlessly from a frame and emblematic of the figure's state.

At the end of May she presided over a large evening party, at which the usual circle was present, together with Kate Faulkner, Wilfred Heeley (an old friend from Oxford days) and the bookseller F. S. Ellis. Allingham proposed 'Earthly Paradise' as toast and theme, which Ned inscribed on the menu card; it appeared an apt description. There was a storm of talking until after midnight, when Gabriel and Allingham left. Call at Chelsea tomorrow and we'll go up to my mother's, said Gabriel warmly, no doubt also planning to drop in at Queen Square, with appropriate thanks for the evening.

They met again on 1 June, when Rossetti hosted a dinner for half a dozen men, including Boyce, Webb, Howell and Morris, with Jane as the only woman present. The large marquee was again set up in the garden, furnished with cushions and sofas. For the rest of the month, sittings were suspended, owing to more urgent commissions, but by now Jane was the model for several subjects besides *La Pia*. When William Graham expressed a wish for a Beatrice, he was offered another version of her image.

By 24 July, the 'blue silk dress' portrait was nearly finished. The Morrises went on holiday to Suffolk. Abruptly, Rossetti took up Leyland's invitation to visit Speke Hall, persuading Howell to go too. But he was hardly in a state to do so, for his eyes and head were suddenly much worse. Now there was a sort of mist over his vision, with swirling shapes when he closed his eyes. He felt he was going blind, or mad, or both.

Speke is a magnificent sixteenth-century mansion on the Mersey estuary east of Liverpool. Built round a courtyard, it has black-and-white gables with elaborate patterning, wide brick chimneys, low dark rooms with heavy wainscoting, a great hall with screens passage, a dry moat, a priest's hole. Decayed and neglected, it had been rescued and refurbished and was leased to Leyland, who added papers and fabrics from the Firm. It was just the sort of place Rossetti liked – 'a glorious old house, full of interest in every way'. But he was unsociable, morose, quite unable to shake off his fears. Leyland was concerned and Howell annoyed, complaining to William of Gabriel's 'total and absolute indifference to *everything*' during their stay.[25] In the few days they were away, he managed to miss Manet's unannounced flying visit to London, which was perhaps just as well.

Back in town Rossetti consulted an eminent oculist named Bader who told him there was no organic disease. 'He says the affection is cerebral, and he trusts to diminish it.' Eye-drops were prescribed, to Gabriel's alarm enlarging the pupils; but another consultation produced the same diagnosis: his sight was not threatened. The same opinion came from leading ophthalmologist Sir William Bowman. Next, Rossetti saw a physician named Gull, who arranged for the swollen hydrocele to be surgically lanced. 'This was done with every appearance of success and no pain worth speaking of,' the patient reported to William. Moreover, his head also felt immediately relieved, 'as if from the same cause'.[26] It seems remarkable that no medical man mentioned the most likely causes of his troubled vision – hypertension and diabetes, both of which had afflicted his father.

His nights remained terrible, with 'whirling, flickering and something like approaching apoplexy'. The Howells, now in Southwold with the Morrises, urged him to join them, but this was impracticable. Brown suggested Coblenz, for the sake of a famous oculist. Dr Gull, who thought the brain was affected through overwork, commended Harrogate. Gabriel asked if Allingham could join him – anywhere there were 'no impending female photographers or even poets laureate'.[27] Despite distress, his sense of humour did not desert him. And he managed a little work, mainly on drawings.

'Of course I know that he was madly in love, and can believe in anything in the way of hypochondria on that score,' William later wrote of this period, trying to distinguish his brother's real and imagined maladies.[28] There does not seem to have been much secrecy, although while Jane was in Suffolk, Gabriel sent letters clandestinely, via Howell, who liked intrigue. These can only have been love-letters, which Topsy must not see. Janey responded. It was excitingly, erotically dangerous. That it coincided with a crisis of vision might be Freudianly interpreted as signifying something Gabriel's conscious mind did not want to acknowledge. He was falling in love, beginning an affair, 'making love' to the wife of his close friend and business partner.

Why embark on such a romance? The repercussions were easy to predict and, although impulsive in many ways, Rossetti was seldom reckless.

Perhaps, when he sensed – or was told of – her unhappiness, he was dismayed, as the one who had brought her into 'the circle', and celebrated her beauty. Perhaps, to chide Morris, he would be her cavalier. Or maybe he did intend to 'steal' Jane from Topsy. Later, Ned said nothing pleased Gabriel more than to 'take his friend's mistress away from him . . . I'm quite sure there's not a woman in the whole world he couldn't have won for himself.'[29] Yet at the same time Rossetti had a strong sense of masculine honour, in which loyalty to friends ranked high. By any standard, adulterous treachery was the act of a blackguard, not at all in same league as rivalry over an antique cabinet or piece of prize china. If he broke up the Morrises' marriage, all friends and even some clients of the Firm would be obliged to take sides – against him. As he later learnt, in regard to Howell, some conduct was inexcusable.

There is no sign whatever that Rossetti wished or feared such an outcome. Indeed, he seems partly to have been playing a troubadour role, as a courtly lover worshipping an unattainable *donna Giovanna*. Later, he accused Jane of never quite taking his devotion seriously. One possibility is that he allowed himself to adore Jane romantically precisely because she was married, like Beatrice. A platonic love or *amitié amoureuse* served many purposes, especially for a man whose physical virility was impaired.

It is equally possible that the main impulse came from Jane, who loved being loved and certainly reciprocated. Had she not wished it, the romance could not have flourished. There are indeed hints that Rossetti struggled against Jane's allure. *The Orchard Pit*, schemed out for a prospective poem in 1869, is the tale of a man who despite his betrothed's restraining hands fights his way towards an enchantress whom he foreknows will cause his death, while in *The Doom of the Sirens*, conceived the same year as the plot for a Wagnerian drama like *Tannhäuser*, a Bride and a Siren fatally contend for possession of a Prince.

Inevitably, there was a crisis with Fanny who, Rossetti reported, had 'got into a rage somehow'. The reason is not hard to guess, and indeed Fanny herself remained predictably and permanently jealous of Jane.[30] Hitherto she had had the freedom of Tudor House, except when forewarned that 'ladies' were invited. Like Whistler's Jo, her 'official' lodgings were elsewhere, but she certainly regarded herself as *maîtresse en titre* at Cheyne Walk. Now Janey's visits were regular, Fanny's access was curtailed, to ensure the two women were never in the house together. Her anger was entirely comprehensible.

Returning from holiday, Jane came for a new sitting, to complete the portrait. Then, on 1 September, Rossetti set off with Dunn for a walking holiday in Warwickshire, revisiting Stratford, Warwick, Kenilworth. His previous tour, fourteen years before, had remained a golden memory. But this time it was miserable. The disturbance and weakness in his sight worsened, and no amount of fresh air over ten days helped him to sleep. Calling at Euston Square on his return, he played down his problems, saying his insomnia was slightly less, and only his eyes were really bad. But this was far from the truth. His next visit to his mother happened to coincide with a call from Woolner. William was worried, given the animosity now existing between the two erstwhile friends, but the encounter passed off amicably, and Woolner recommended a surgeon who had helped his own eye problems. From Ireland Fred Burton sent advice too, suggesting the ophthalmic nerve was affected by an overwrought nervous system; rest should be the cure.

Marshall prescribed a soporific, and it was around this time that Rossetti began to take whisky to help him sleep. Advised also to take exercise, he developed the habit of walking after dark, with vigour but little pleasure, through the streets or across Old Battersea Bridge. But the more he suffered from symptoms that medical opinion effectively dismissed, the more desperate he grew. How could nothing organic be wrong? Moreover, he now felt pain at the back of his head, which one specialist had stated would indeed indicate a physiological cause. At this rate, he would be blind by Christmas.

'*Chi a quarenta non ha, mai non avrà*': now he was forty, his father's aphorism held no reproach, for he had achieved fame and fortune, and felt no wish for a family. But the onslaught on his sight and mind were ominously reminiscent of Professor Rossetti's collapse in 1843, when insomnia and anxiety had preceded the catastrophic clouding of his sight, followed by a long, miserable decline.

At the start of the year, Gabriel had insured the Tudor House contents – pictures, furniture, china – for £3,000, and the works in his studio for £2,000. This proved foresightful – a month later a burglar was caught on the roof (stealing lead, as it emerged) – and indicative; for he did not want his assets undervalued. 'He talks of making a deed of gift of all his property to me; so that, whatever may befall himself, I may be empowered to do the best for all parties concerned,' William confided to his diary on 15 September.[31] Furthermore, Gabriel was 'strongly opposed' to a posthumous exhibition, 'on the ground that he has never done anything to satisfy his own standard'.

Such 'gloomy anticipations' were eloquent of the tenor of his thought. Writing to Browning in July, he had spoken of the 'sheer nausea' he felt on looking at his painting.

Dr Bowman called again on 22 September, repeating his optimistic diagnosis, prescribing rest and taking a watercolour *Bocca Baciata* for 150 guineas. The next day Gabriel left for Scotland, staying overnight in Leeds for the sake of a major loan exhibition. Among 'a good many things worth seeing', he listed Carpaccio's *Landing of Queen Cornaro in Cyprus* and some splendid heads by Titian, Bellini, Moroni and Velázquez. Best of all was the 'glorious glorious glorious' *Mystic Nativity* by Botticelli, which was probably the chief object of his visit, and subsequently entered the national collection.[32]

Penkill Castle, where he arrived on 25 September, just as Scott rather ungraciously planned to return to town, was an ancient peel tower in a secluded glen of the Ayrshire hills, in Burns country. The ancestral seat of the Boyd family, it was rebuilt from a ruin by Alice's brother Spencer, whom Rossetti had met in London. Sadly, Spencer had died, leaving Alice as chatelaine and somewhat upsetting the plan for Scott to spend his summers there, officially as Spencer's guest. Now, they merely ignored Mrs Grundy, finding that most visitors were neither deterred nor scandalised. For Miss Boyd, with whom Scott had first become acquainted in 1859, was now his permanent partner in all but name. Friends – including the morally-minded Rossetti women – accepted this unconventional arrangement, because so respectably condoned by Letitia Scott. Most of Scott's male friends greatly preferred Alice, a sensible, sympathetic and gracious woman, with a sincere feeling for art and a genuine, if hesitant talent. Independently wealthy, she was devoted to Scotus and a good friend to Letitia. In the winter, the threesome shared a London residence, becoming known in 'the circle' as the Sun, Moon and Star. Rossetti particularly liked Alice, and on this visit came to appreciate her qualities. For her part, Alice brought out the best in Gabriel, so that his letters to her are among the finest he wrote – genial, judicious, wide-ranging and informative.

Letitia Scott was sometimes at Penkill, but at this late stage in the season the only other guest was Alice's elderly aunt Miss Losh. 'This is a truly heavenly place, for beauty of scenery,' Rossetti reported to Howell, 'and all private. Such a glen of running stream and lovely woods and such nooks for loving in if there were only the material.'[33] There were corners asking to be painted, too, if he were better, while his hosts were both 'the dearest and best of friends'.

For the first time in many years, he actually rested, spending his days strolling in the grounds and glen beside the Penwhapple burn. In the evenings Alice read aloud, and they played whist. The weather was splendid and the company congenial – for Miss Losh, though his mother's age, was 'a nice, cheerful, intelligent old thing'.[34] For her part, Miss Losh took a fancy to Gabriel and, in response to his gloomy fears that he might never paint again, pressed loans upon him. She offered a thousand pounds; and with some embarrassment he accepted five hundred, knowing she was wealthy, unmarried, anxious to assist.

By early October he was sleeping better and his brain was calmer, though there was 'wavering and swimming' in everything he looked at, with marked distress in the right eye. But this same day he walked the five miles into Girvan with Scott and Alice to collect the post. On the beach, they rested on the spars of an old wreck, while Gabriel read aloud from Smetham's new volume of verse.

Thanks to the usual go-between, he continued to correspond with Janey. Occasional alarms arose over near-discovery, and as none of these secret missives survive both must have been sufficiently scared to make sure the letters were destroyed. The whole risky business led to flights of fancy, and elaborate circumlocutions. A year or so later, *The Love-letter* is a sonnet addressed to one such piece of correspondence:

> Warmed by her hand and shadowed by her hair
>   As close she leaned and poured her heart through thee . . .
>   . . .
> Sweet fluttering sheet, even of her breath aware, –
>   Oh let thy silent song disclose to me
>   That soul wherewith her lips and eyes agree
> Like married music in Love's answering air . . .

To Scott, however, he talked of suicide, if his sight should fail. Death, imaged in verse a few weeks later,[35] was a new companion:

> To-day, Death seems to me an infant child
>   Which her worn mother Life upon my knee
>   Has set to grow my friend and play with me;
> If haply so my heart might be beguil'd
> To find no terrors in a face so mild . . .

According to this figuration, Love, and Song, and Art were now all virtually extinguished. But neither humour nor malice were altogether eclipsed by such gloomy thoughts. He amused the company with exaggerated accounts of Topsy's uncouth behaviour – his legendary rages, his sartorial self-neglect, his swearing. When Brown reported Morris's views on the cause of Gabriel's malaise (overindulgence), Rossetti retorted with a squib set in the dining room at Queen Square satirising Topsy's own appetite:

Alarums, Excursions. Morris discovered ringing a bell with violence. Enter Brown.
B. How are you, Morris? Have you heard how Gabriel is?
M. (*dancing*) I wish to God Gabriel – no I mean the cook – was in Hell! Don't you, Janey dear? Damn blast etc etc. Oh ah! Don't you know? Gabriel's all right again. Damn blast etc etc – of course you'll stay to dinner old chap. I don't know though if we're to have any. Janey dear, it's all your fault . . .

Dinner arrives and Jane carves, only to have Morris wheedle the choicest cuts for himself. She complies. 'What were you saying, Mr Brown?' All conversation is lost in the sound of Morris's unmannerly eating: 'Oh ah! Gabri – obble obble – Gabri – uuch uuch – Gabri – obble obble obble obble . . .'[36]

Barely comic, the dialogue dramatises the tension now existing between the two men. Even if he did not know of the clandestine correspondence, at one level Morris no doubt did wish Gabriel in hell.

'I can't resist sending another enclosure, which you will manage I know if possible,' Rossetti wrote Howell on 22 October. 'You know what the service is to me and what my gratitude must be to you . . .'[37]

On 2 November he and Scott departed, leaving Alice and her aunt to close up Penkill for the winter. It was cold and wet. Waiting for the train, their flask of whisky and hard-boiled eggs were stolen. When they reached Carlisle, after midnight, Scott told Alice, 'we liquored up, you may be sure.' Back at Cheyne Walk, the habit continued, Gabriel liquoring up freely and regularly, sometimes with Brown and sometimes with Scott, who noted how Rossetti's low spirits were raised by whisky. The deterioration in his sight had halted. Now, he explained to William, he saw distant objects as if through a veil, 'like the curling of smoke or the effervescing of champagne', although the flashing lights behind his eyeballs were waning.[38]

He did not immediately call at Queen Square because, Scott told Alice, 'he understands they are watched'. So he had told Scott of his passion for the beautiful Mrs M, and Scott had told Alice, adding that in his opinion all disturbance of health and temper was due to 'an uncontrollable desire for possession' of Janey. Other people were also talking; Letitia Scott reported how Mrs Street, the wife of Morris's architectural mentor, had spoken plainly 'about Gabriel being so fond of Mrs Top'.[39]

They met only in others' company. 'I called on Topsy, who was howling and threatening to throw a new piano of his wife's out of the window,' Gabriel told Miss Losh, continuing the supposedly satiric vein of Penkill. A week later, he told Alice of an evening party at the Ionides' where Morris 'seemed depressed and complained of deafness, but on a large plug of string being taken out of his ear, he revived a good deal and even scratched himself in places apparently inaccessible. When I left, he was being prepared for departure, and Janey had nearly succeeded in fishing the paper-knife up from the base of his spine . . .'[40]

Was it necessary to paint Morris as a buffoon? On 25 November the Scotts hosted a dinner-party, inviting G. H. Lewes, William Burges, John Morley, editor of the *Fortnightly* and Mrs Lynn Linton, as well as the Morrises, Bessie and Gabriel. All began well: Gabriel was genial, Lewes an assured conversationalist, Morris in 'great spirits'. Having temporarily laid aside *The Earthly Paradise*, he was now translating Icelandic Sagas. But when the time came to go in to dinner and Scott was due to escort Jane, Gabriel first seized her arm and then hurriedly dropped it, 'Morris looking at him all the time'. At table Rossetti turned sideways towards her, when etiquette even among friends decreed that dinner guests talk equally and generally. Scott was sure the other women noticed.

'However, I have concluded that they (G & J) will not go further than they have gone,' he reported to Alice. 'She is certainly the most remarkable looking woman in the world, and *in expression* lovely. Of course, a woman, under such circumstances, before people, is a closed book, still I think she is cool.'[41]

Coolly, Jane proposed to resume her sittings. Early in December, she and her husband came again to Cheyne Walk for a few days. To do otherwise might confirm the gossip. As well as La Pia, she was now Pandora. Indeed, she was the model for everything in the studio, Scott told Leathart, citing 'ten life-size heads of Janey Morris either painted or drawn in chalk in progress, and nothing else visible, or likely to be, as far as one can see'.[42] Once Jane had left, Gabriel urged Howell not to let the drawings go to clients until they had all been photographed.

'Was I most born to paint your sovereign face, / Or most to sing, or most to love it, dear?' he would ask in a sonnet. In both media he flattered her grossly. 'Famous for her poet husband, outstandingly famous for her face, now may she be famous for this my picture', was inscribed in Latin on the portrait that was to hang in the marital home. 'Beauty like hers is genius,' started a sonnet, again invoking 'this sovereign face, whose love-spell breathes/Even from its shadowed contour on the wall.' And in due course he wrote The Portrait, which blended verbal and visual images:

> O Lord of all compassionate control,
>   O Love! let this my lady's picture glow
>   Under my hand to praise her name, and show
> Even of her inner self the perfect whole
>   . . .
> Lo! it is done. Above the long lithe throat
>   The mouth's mould testifies of voice and kiss,
>   The shadowed eyes remember and foresee.
> Her face is made her shrine. Let all men note
>   That in all years (O Love, thy gift is this!)
>   They that would look on her must come to me.

In the Vita Nuova, Dante's grieving heart had been reawakened after Beatrice's death, by 'a young and very beautiful lady' looking down from a window with a gaze full of pity. In response, he wrote a sonnet invoking the 'compassionate control' of the woman's eyes:

> And afterwards I said within my soul:
> 'Lo! with this lady dwells the counterpart
> Of the same Love who holds me weeping now.'

Swinburne was less sympathetic to romantic replacement. Six months later he wrote of the 'corroding effect of the poisonous solvent of love' on the later works of Andrea del Sarto, in which the 'inevitable and fatal figure' of Lucrezia del Fede recurs with little variation. According to this argument, which seems aimed in Rossetti's direction, '[n]othing now is left to him to live for but his faultless hand and her faultless face – still and full, suggestive of no change, in the steady deep-lidded eyes and heavy lovely lips', making Andrea's art like herself: 'rich, monotonous in beauty, calm, complete, without heart or spirit'.[43]

At Penkill, when Gabriel talked of suicide, Scott had suggested that should
he be unable to paint, he might return to his first love, poetry. Gloomily,
Gabriel had remained silent. But now, Scott observed in November, 'he is
really doing so.' He was of course 'poet as well as painter and was a poet
before he was a painter' and if his vision were permanently impaired, 'it
would be a great thing to get him to be the poet again'.[44]

Six years before, Rossetti had consigned his poetry to Lizzie's coffin.
Now he was versifying like a lovesick student. In December he wrote a
quartet of sonnets entitled *Willowwood*. Poetically, the sequence is oblique
and over-elaborate in its contrivance, but it speaks clearly of joyous, newly
achieved love. Despite the homophonic allusion to widowhood, when the
poetic figures are disentangled, their physical imagery is of love consummated in a long and slowly uncoupling kiss:

> I sat with Love upon a woodside well
>> Leaning across the water, I and he;
>> Nor ever did he speak nor looked at me,
> But touched his lute wherein was audible
> The certain secret thing he had to tell:
>> Only our mirrored eyes met silently
>> In the low wave; and that sound came to be
> The passionate voice I knew; and my tears fell.
> And at their fall, his eyes beneath grew hers;
> And with his foot and with his wing-feathers
>> He swept the spring that watered my heart's drouth.
> Then the dark ripples spread to waving hair,
> And as I stooped, her own lips rising there
>> Bubbled with brimming kisses at my mouth.

And now Love sang ...

> So sang he: and as meeting rose and rose
>> Together cling through the wind's wellaway
>> Nor change at once, yet near the end of day
> The leaves drop loosened where the heart-stain glows, –
> So when the song died did the kiss unclose;
>> And her face fell back drowned, and was as grey
>> As its grey eyes; and if it ever may
> Meet mine again I know not if Love knows.
> Only I know that I leaned low and drank
> A long draught from the water where she sank,
>> Her breath and all her tears and all her soul:

> And as I drank I know I felt Love's face
> Pressed on my neck with moan of pity and grace
> Till both our heads were in his aureole.

'For then at last we spoke,' he wrote later; and love 'then from the heart did rise'. *At Last* is also the title of another sonnet, registering the 'sacred sweetness' of love after the hard toll claimed by Fate. New light, new warmth, new bliss.

A year later, Rossetti asserted that the best of his poems came from the heart, under the impress of 'strong feeling'. He also said that the first twenty-six sonnets in *The House of Life* sequence 'treat of love'. Several of the most powerful and prominent of these treat fairly explicitly of physical love, not merely envisioned but achieved. And as these postdate his passion for Jane, it seems biographically legitimate to inquire how they relate to that relationship.

The sequence as published begins with *Bridal Birth* and *Love's Redemption* (both written by mid-1869) on love's awakening as an ecstatic, holy sacrament.[45] *Lovesight* (1869) invokes physical contact with lines redolent of intimacy: 'when in the dusk hours (we two alone) / Close-kissed and eloquent of still replies / Thy twilight-hidden glimmering visage lies / ... O love, my love!' The diction is deceptive, for the poet is in fact alone, with the glimmering image of the beloved, as in the studio at twilight, rather than close-kissing the lady herself. But the imagery is replete, as also in *The Kiss* (1869) where the poet refers to his own body and soul, saying the latter has worn 'wedding-raiment' as 'even now my lady's lips did play / With these my lips ... / I was a child beneath her touch – a man / When breast to breast we clung, even I and she ...' If fanciful, the diction is also literal – lips, touch, breast, breath, blood – and invokes the literal heat of mutual desire in a close embrace, like a kiss that precedes coition.

Nuptial Sleep is the most physical of the sonnets, describing sexual intercourse. Originally *Placatâ Venere*, it dates, as we have seen, from around 1859, but positioned in the midst of a new sequence it underlines the carnal nature of love here in *The House of Life*. The post-coital *Supreme Surrender* follows, in which 'Along the love-sown fallowfield of sleep / My lady lies apparent ... / and no man sees but I.' The sexual imagery is oblique but derived from the traditional symbolism of the female furrow ploughed by the male. The physical bliss of coition is the 'harvest' reaped from love's field, endorsed by the subsequent and remarkably direct images of 'the hand now warm around my neck' and 'across my breast the abandoned hair'; and finally that of two hearts lying next to each other.

Love's Lovers (1869) describes the lady's love as pure and unmixed. *Passion and Worship* (1869) brings physical love together with idealised adoration, as the personified emotions of the title are made to enter 'even where my lady and I lay all alone'. Physical passion claims precedence, but the lady says both are plighted to her equally. Traditionally and biblically, 'lay' is the term used for sexual congress.

In *A Day of Love* the poet and his beloved are together for a day. In *Love-Sweetness* he itemises her 'loosened hair' about his face, her 'sweet hands around his head,' her 'sweet glances' and 'her mouth's culled sweetness' which returned 'On cheeks and neck and eyelids, and so led / Back to her mouth . . .'. Sweeter than all these is the mutuality of love, 'the confident heart's still fervour'.

Somewhat further down the sequence is *Secret Parting* (1869) in which, when the lovers speak of Fate, the beloved falters. 'But soon, remembering her how brief the whole / Of joy . . . / Her set gaze gathered, thirstier than of late, / And as she kissed, her mouth became her soul.'

Especially at the start of *The House of Life*, passion is cast in an immediate tense: the poet's beloved is not a lost or *lointaine princesse* but a very present sexual partner. If this does not describe an actual experience in 1869, it would seem imaginatively to create one. There seems no doubt that the passion between Jane and Gabriel was very physically felt. It seems unlikely that it was translated into sexual action, however, for as well as the inhibiting effect of the hydrocele, the only possible location was the Tudor House studio, with its mess of oils and varnishes, easels and mirrors, cupboards and chairs, and the ever-present risk of being disturbed by Dunn, or a servant, or even a raccoon. It cannot be proved, but one might infer that the passion was all the more strongly felt for being denied direct physical expression.

It is in any case solecistic to infer that because Gabriel Rossetti wrote of physical passion at a time when he was in love with Jane Morris the poems describe their actual intimacy. As he himself remarked, 'to speak in the first person is often to speak most vividly'; but poetry is not autobiography. Swinburne's graphic contemporaneous invocations of desire reflect imagination, not experience. Moreover, Rossetti's professed theme, in poetry and painting at this date, was the union of body and soul, the indivisibility of desire and idealisation in true love between man and woman.

Yet undeniably, the return to verse, in the form of love sonnets, coincided with clandestine passion for Janey. And it is hard to read the poems without visualising an actual 'lady' who sleeps, sits, kisses, and is physically present. Elsewhere in his poetry, she is Lilith or Helen, Jenny or the unnamed Damozel – physically invoked but dramatically distanced from the poet. Here she has no such fictive persona. Of course, sonnets present particular problems of interpretation, deriving as they do from a verse form which laid claim to heartfelt emotion whilst being practised within a highly artificed sphere (as if those composing messages for Valentine cards should feel and speak *in propria persona*) yet by the nineteenth century was widely regarded as a vehicle for personal feeling, especially in light disguise, as in Elizabeth Barrett's celebrated *Sonnets from the Portuguese*. So if Gabriel was not writing of his love for Janey, one is hardly surprised that many interpret it thus. 'Of course, I know that he was madly in love,' commented William matter-of-factly.

CHAPTER NINETEEN

Life-in-Love

While Gabriel and Jane were conducting their half-acknowledged romance, Ned Jones had also fallen in love, with a flame-haired temptress, the stuff of legends. 'She was born at the foot of Olympus and looked and was primaeval ... and I was being turned into a hawthorn bush in the forest of Broceliande,' he wrote later, linking ancient and medieval mythology. In fact, she was Mary or Maria Zambaco, granddaughter of Constantine Ionides, with a fortune from her late father and a loving mother in Euphrosyne Cassavetti, sometimes called 'the Duchess'. As a girl, she was Marie Spartali's coeval and companion. According to the briefly smitten George du Maurier, at seventeen Mary was 'rude and unapproachable but of great talent and really wonderful beauty'. At eighteen she married Demetrius Zambaco, physician to the Greek community in Paris, where her son and daughter were born. But in 1866 she returned to her mother's house in Kensington, alone. To console her, the Duchess offered to pay for a picture and took her to meet Burne-Jones. Hers was 'a wonderful head', Ned wrote later, with a striking profile and large, melting eyes. Two things had power over Ned: beauty and misfortune, commented Georgie ambiguously; 'indeed, his impulse to comfort those in trouble was so strong that while the trouble lasted the sufferer took precedence over everyone else.'[1]

The pair planned to elope. 'I believed it to be all my future life,' Ned told Gabriel a few months later. Mary's face, Mary's head, Mary's hair, Mary's hands dominated his drawing, painting, feeling. She was the sorceress Circe, the nymph Phyllis, the enchantress Vivien, Beatrice, Venus. But Ned had not the courage to leave wife and children, nor to risk alienating his friends and patrons. 'It was a glorious head,' he wrote later, self-excusingly; 'only it didn't do in English suburban surroundings.' In his picture of Phyllis and Demophoön, the anchored nymph with Mary's unmistakable profile holds desperately to her fleeing lover.

In January 1869, on a supposedly final walk together from the Ionides' house in Holland Park to her own home near Little Venice, she attempted to jump from the bridge over the Regent's Canal. 'M. Z. provided herself with laudanum for two at least, and insisted on their winding up matters in Lord Holland's Lane,' reported Rossetti to Brown, who was in Manchester. 'Ned didn't see it, when she tried to drown herself in the water in front of Browning's house etc – bobbies collaring Ned who was rolling with her on the stones to prevent it, and God knows what else.'[2]

Shaken, Ned sought Morris's help, and agreed to go abroad quickly, so that Mary could not stage another ambush. This left 'the Greek damsel beating up the quarters of all his friends for him and howling like Cassandra', according to Gabriel. His informant was Janey, who confirmed that Ned was 'really bent' on breaking with Mary. And one incidental result of his precipitate flight was that, in Morris's absence, Jane could not come to Cheyne Walk. 'Janey has stopped her sittings by order during foreign service – just as I supposed,' Gabriel told Howell. In fact, Topsy and Ned got no further than Dover, where Ned fell ill, before creeping back to London, and, whatever his resolve, Ned was unable to stop seeing Mary altogether. Later in the year he was at work on 'the loveliest series of drawings he ever did' – delicate, flowing pencil studies of Mary's head and tumbling hair, like a beautiful Medusa. Tender and intimate, their affinity with Rossetti's images of Janey is evident. Unable to make love more openly, both men drew to express and record desire, as well as perpetuate portrait sittings *à deux*.

'How nice it would be if I could feel sure I had painted you once for all so as to let the world know what you were, but every new thing I do from you is a disappointment, and it is only at some odd moment when I cannot set about it that I see by a flash the way it ought to have been,' Gabriel would soon write to Jane, revealing more than artistic wishes.[3] If love could not be 'the way it ought to have been', portrait-drawing was a substitute.

Hoping their spouses' passions would pass, Georgie and Morris supported each other stoically, silently. A year before, they had watched another marriage crash from the tracks when Warington Taylor, the Firm's business manager, lost his wife Fanny to another man. Taking all the blame upon himself, he wanted Janey to visit Fanny, 'and tell her what she alone can tell her ... only a woman can speak to a woman', as he told Webb, ashamed to ask Morris's permission directly. Webb then asked Morris, who asked Jane, who agreed. It was a delicate matter, for Morris might have felt the irony of himself having a wife who loved another, but at the height of things everyone seems to have been involved, including Rossetti, who had stern words with Taylor. 'Gabriel has told me rightly what I was – he has hit me so hard,' Taylor reported to Webb. 'He never was so splendid, so noble, so grand, as on Friday when he told me what a scoundrel I was. And now after all this she takes me back again. She is more a goddess than ever . . .'[4]

'I am delighted to hear that you had a nice interview with Gabriel, he is – if he chooses – very straightforward and his intellect is very keen,' replied Webb, circumspectly; 'and I take it for granted you were sure of what he was saying at the time.' Not everyone saw Taylor as a scoundrel and Fanny as a goddess. In the event, she returned, though it is feared more for the sake of a legacy than for love, and the crisis was averted.

With such marital and extramarital passions raging around them, the relationship between Janey and Gabriel looks less dramatic. There were no scenes, no threats, no running away, no scandal. And perhaps because he was handling things differently, Rossetti showed scant sympathy towards Ned while the affair with Mary was critical. Nothing was said, but while praising his picture of Circe as 'the greatest work exhibited this year',[5] Gabriel composed a sonnet that interpreted Circe's power as that of animal passion, which made beasts of men.

For his part, Ned hated the way Gabriel now sneered at Morris. 'If you gird at Top I grow impatient and feel cross – if it's before strangers I feel explosive and miserable,' he wrote.[6] Nevertheless, he made caricatures of Morris, to amuse Mary, and drew a rotund Rossetti tiptoeing after tall thin Janey with armfuls of cushions, like a comic *cavaliere servente*.

The old friendships were beginning to fracture. Morris scowled and barked more than usually, often at the wrong targets. 'I am afraid I was crabby last night, but I didn't mean to be, so pray forgive me,' he wrote to Ned after one such incident; '– we seem to quarrel in speech now sometimes, and sometimes I think you find it hard to stand me, and no great wonder, for I am like a hedgehog with nastiness – but again forgive me for I can't on any terms do without you.'[7]

Had modern divorce laws prevailed, Jane could have paired up with Gabriel, Ned with Mary and Morris with Georgie, though not without all pain. Looking back in old age, they might have smiled at mid-life passions. Men in their thirties 'are more apt to desire what they have not than they that be younger or older', remarked Morris later, with the wisdom of sixty.

Rossetti acutely felt the consciousness of 'most good things' having passed, while others could never now come. 'For the last 2 years I have felt distinctly the clearing away of the chilling numbness that surrounds me in the utter want of you,' he told Jane early in 1870; 'but since then other obstacles have kept steadily on the increase, and it comes too late.'[8]

Through the agency of editor John Morley, his pathetic sonnet *A Superscription*, with its lament for what came too late, was published in the *Fortnightly Review*:

> Look in my face; my name is Might-have-been;
>   I am also called No-more, Too-late, Farewell . . .

So too was *Winged Hours*:

> Each hour until we meet is as a bird
>   That wings from far his gradual way along
>   The rustling covert of my soul, – his song
> Still loudlier trilled through leaves more deeply stirr'd:
> But at the hour of meeting, a clear word
>   Is every note he sings, in Love's own tongue;
>   Yet, Love, thou know'st the sweet strain suffers wrong,
> Through our contending kisses oft unheard.
>
> What of that hour at last, when for her sake
>   No wing may fly to me nor song may flow;
>   When, wandering round my life unleaved, I know
> The bloodied feathers scattered in the brake,
>   And think how she, far from me, with like eyes
>   Sees through the untuneful bough the wingless skies?

The startling image of love like a bird flying between the lovers until shot down suggests the fragility of a relationship that might at any moment be destroyed by anger, even violence, and 'come to a smash altogether', as Gabriel described Ned's tussle with Mary on the towpath. Written around the same time, it is possible that fear of a similar eruption, scattering bloody emotional fragments, informed the poem.

If the poetry was reborn from Rossetti's growing passion for Jane, its midwife may be identified as Morley, for it was only after dining with him on 18 November that Gabriel actually returned to verse. Ten days on, William noted in his diary that 'Gabriel, being still, from the state of his eyes, unable to resume painting, has been looking up his poems of old days, with some floating idea of offering some of them to the *Fortnightly Review*, and at any rate with a degree of zest which looks promising.'[9] Morley, it emerged, was looking to make 'poems of some substantial length' a feature of his magazine; a little while later he asked Rossetti to approach Browning, who had just brought out *The Ring and the Book*.

At first Gabriel merely looked out his old manuscripts. But early in December, when Janey came again to sit, inspiring *The Portrait*, the promise of publication caused his literary spring to rise once more. On 18 December William recorded the completion of *Willowwood* – 'about the finest thing he has done. I see the poetic impulse is upon him again: he even says he ought never to have been a painter, but a poet instead.' The next day, while visiting the family, Gabriel wrote 'a sonnet upon Death'. It was the first of a pair called *Newborn Death*, sent to Allingham on 23 December for comments, as of old. Owing to the trouble with his eyes, he was looking up his 'ravelled rags of verse', Rossetti explained, 'and writing a few new ones, to make a little bunch in a coming number of the *Fortnightly* – not till March however, as they are full till then.'[10]

By the New Year, he had written *Winged Hours, Inclusiveness* and *Sleepless Dreams*, which invokes both the misery of insomnia and the glimmering pulse of new love, in 'night desirous as the nights of youth!' From the ravelled rags of earlier work, he selected five sonnets sounding a personal, elegiac note: *Broken Music* from 1852, *Known in Vain* from 1853, *The Landmark* and *Lost on Both Sides* from 1854, and *Lost Days* from 1862:

> I do not see them here; but after death
> God knows I know the faces I shall see,
> Each one a murdered self . . .

There followed *A Superscription*, on what might have been, and by 24 January a neat 'little bunch' of sixteen sonnets was ready for printing. To dignify the heterogeneity, they were given a collective title suggestive of Swinburnian magniloquence: 'Of Life, Love and Death: Sixteen Sonnets'. *Willowwood* stood first. 'Your sonnets charm me more and more,' wrote Morley on 20 February. Sandwiched among heavy articles on current affairs and current science (Huxley and Tyndall were *Fortnightly* contributors) they were published on 1 March. Apart from a few fugitive appearances in anthologies and the *Oxford and Cambridge Magazine*, this was the first public evidence since *The Germ* that Dante Gabriel Rossetti was an original poet as well as a painter.

Like Dante *nel mezzo del cammin di nostra vita*, he was at a crisis-point. 'With most good things gone and others that will never come now,' he wrote sorrowfully to Norton on his next birthday. A few months before, he had read Swinburne on a drawing by Leonardo, showing Youth and Age meeting; or, 'it may be, of a young man coming suddenly upon the ghostly figure of himself as he will one day be; the brilliant life in his face is struck into sudden pallor and silence, the clear eyes startled, the happy lips confused. A fair straight-featured face, with full curls fallen or blown against the eyelids; and confronting it a keen, wan, mournful mask of flesh . . .'[11]

Once, with Chiaro, Rossetti had seen painting as a means of self-expression. But over the years this had become a profession, shaped by market forces rather than inner needs. Even the pictures of Jane had their commercial aspect, inevitably. Poetry, by contrast, was pure, uncorrupted, straight from the soul. The Romantic movement, and more especially the writings of poets popular in his youth like Felicia Hemans and Letitia Landon, had made 'the affections' the proper province of poetry. Much as the young Rossettis had mocked such 'effusions', sentiments of loss, longing and love found expression most appropriately in verse. At Lizzie's death, a shutter had been closed on Gabriel's feelings, symbolised by the burial of his manuscript book. Now, he was under pressure of a love that could not be publicly avowed. Janey was like Dante's *donna della finestra*, the compassionate lady at the window, and the resumption of poetry therefore signalled the opening of the emotional shutter, the reawakening of his 'heart' and the need to speak.

Besides the idealised desire for love, the other great impulse of Rossetti's life was ambition – the desire to excel. Always, he had measured himself against other men and been spurred by their success. In the years since 1862, new poetic reputations had risen: this season, both Swinburne and Morris, the protégés whose advent a decade earlier had prompted him to prepare the volume that now lay in Lizzie's coffin, had new poems in the *Fortnightly*; even Scotus had recently published verse here, too. While at Penkill, Rossetti had seen an article by Smetham on Alex Smith and Sydney Dobell, recalling the enthusiasms of his youth for 'masterpieces of the condensed and hinted order so dear to imaginative minds', and had also read Smetham's own poems with mounting admiration. 'I certainly think you ought to do something with your literary powers which I think equivalent to those you possess in art,' he wrote, as if advising himself.[12]

And though love was dominant in his emotions, the sombre *A Superscription*, on things not done, was also about failure: 'Look in my face; my name is Might-have-been ...' Holding a seashell to his ears, a figure looks into a cloudy mirror, which shows only 'a shaken shadow intolerable, / Of ultimate things unuttered the frail screen.' It was followed by *Newborn Death*, predicting the end of Art and Song, and the involuted *Vase of Life*, originally titled 'Run and Won', where the speaker compares the slow pace of his own life to that of one who is by comparison a victorious athlete. This figure 'rich in faculty and bold in enterprise' is a man of genius, according to William. He turns life masterfully in his hands, filling it with the achievements of his career, so that finally the vessel will be like an heroic funeral urn. And William 'always suspected' that in writing this, Gabriel had in mind 'his own early colleague in the race of life and of art, the illustrious painter Sir John Millais'.[13]

Currently, Millais's reputation was enjoying a revival. It was no longer possible to regard him as having sold out to sentimental, meretricious success. A few months hence, William described his *Vanessa* at the RA as 'most splendid – perhaps his finest piece of work' and Gabriel was not far behind in commendation.[14]

But the sestet of 'Run and Won' was more ambiguous and obscure. Here the urn of life has been filled 'with wine for blood, / With blood for tears, with spice for burning vow, / with watered flowers for buried love most fit.' Whatever this means, the urn is not heroically valued: the unnamed man of genius is minded to 'cast it shattered to the flood' but instead keeps it whole, yet unfilled. Somewhat camouflaged, this is surely also Rossetti's account of himself as one who began 'alert for the great race' but had not filled his life with achievements. He would have shattered it, as he talked of suicide to Scott; but now his career 'stands empty till his ashes fall'. Writing to Smetham from Penkill, Rossetti had sadly remarked that if his condition continued, he would have to consider his painting 'at an end'. At the age of forty, he would be quitting 'the race of art', if not life.

Many things thus came together in the resumption of poetry at this critical point: the rebirth of love, acute intimations of mortality, unfulfilled ambition, the sense of failure.

With the *Fortnightly* pages, Gabriel sent his mother an extraordinary letter based on the extended conceit that the poems were sheeted ghosts rattling their bones in a pantomime dance. 'Dear Darling, I send you my sonnets, which are such a lively band of bogies that they may join with the skeletons of Christina's various closets, and entertain you by a ballet,' he wrote. 'Their shanks are rather ghastly, it is true, but they will keep their shrouds down tolerably close, and creak enough themselves to render a piano unnecessary. As their own vacated graves serve them to dance on, there is no danger of their disturbing the lodgers beneath; and, if any one overhead objects you may say that it amuses them perhaps and will be soon over, and that, as their hats were probably not buried with them, these will not be sent round at the close of the performance ...' In any case, he concluded, 'in the long run the cock crows, or the turnip-head falls off the broomstick, or the price of phosphorus becomes an obstacle, or the police turn up if necessary ...'[15]

Being haunted by such 'bogies' was aptly descriptive of unpublished poems exhumed from what now seemed a previous life, but even more so of those still buried. The imagery is so vivid as to shock, and makes one wonder why, given such a metaphorical cast of thought, Rossetti's images in verse are often so difficult to see with the mind's eye, and so awkwardly developed. For example, *The Morrow's Message*, written this year, also uses the bogey figure, in conversation with the poet:

'Thou Ghost,' I said, 'and is thy name To-day? –
     Yesterday's son, with such an abject brow! –
     And can To-morrow be more pale than thou?'
While yet I spoke, the silence answered: 'Yea,
Henceforth our issue is all grieved and grey,
     And each beforehand makes such poor avow
     As of old leaves beneath the budding bough
Or night-drift that the sundawn shreds away.'

Then cried I: 'Mother of many malisons,
     O Earth, receive me to thy dusty bed!'
     But therewithal the tremulous silence said:
'Lo! Love yet bids thy lady greet thee once –
Yea, twice, – whereby thy life is still the sun's,
     And thrice, – whereby the shadow of death is dead.'

The problem is not simply the poetic diction of brow and avow, night-drift
and malisons, whatever they may be; nor that of personification, which as
the 'bogie letter' shows, can be startlingly lively when well realised. The
pale and abject figure named To-day is presented through confusing
conventionalities, as old leaves beneath new buds, as a mist dispelled at
dawn, and above all as 'a tremulous silence' that speaks in nevertheless
ringing tones. Buried within his speech is the 'cock-crow' of the letter,
when ghosts traditionally disappear, but there is nothing so striking as the
turnip-head falling from the broomstick, or the police arriving to chase
away the importunate players. Love, who bids the lady greet the poet, is
virtually invisible, added to the cast-list only by great effort on the reader's
part. Despite the dialogue, the whole drama is heard through a curtain of
muffled words.

     Only months before, Rossetti had praised verse 'of the condensed and
hinted order so dear to imaginative minds', and his poetic aim was, as Keats
advised Shelley, 'to load every rift with ore'. On returning from an early
holiday this summer, William noted his brother's manner of composition,
which was perhaps sufficiently singular to warrant description: 'His
practice with poetry is first to write the thing in the rough, and then turn
over dictionaries of rhymes and synonyms so as to bring the poem into the
most perfect form.'[16] This suggests a method based on the translating
technique of *Early Italian Poets*. Gabriel's own account owed more to
picture-making. The highest form of finish in poetic execution, he said later,
came 'where the work has been all mentally "cartooned" as it were,
beforehand, by a process intensely conscious, but patient and silent – an
occult evolution of life'.[17] As in visual art, so in verse: an intense, almost

trance-like period of conception, succeeded by careful, apparently obsessional tinkering, during which the concept seldom underwent drastic
revision, but details were added, deleted, repositioned, and the text
'finished' with words whose sound and sense heightened the colours and
feeling of the whole. Hence came the 'tattooed' proofs, equivalent not to
pictorial sketches and studies but rather to the various stages of a painting
towards completion. And, as in painting, somewhere beyond the mind's
reach lay a perfect, platonic version of each poem.[18]

Ironically, the eye-trouble that had prompted the return to poetry was
somewhat abated, and Gabriel was back at the easel. 'You'll be glad to hear
I am now decidedly on the mend,' he told Alice. Although when
summoned to jury service at the Old Bailey he lost no time in procuring
affidavits and certificates to prove he was unfit to serve, his mood lightened,
and his social life resumed, with frequent if not nightly 'liquoring up'.
Within a few months, he was telling old Miss Losh how more 'than for
many seasons past', he had become 'quite a diner-out'. He went to evenings
at Simeon Solomon's, to yet another seance at the Tebbses', to a party with
eighty guests at the Procters'. He took Brown to visit Smetham in Stoke
Newington, and came close to honouring a performance of Christina's
poem *Songs in a Cornfield*, set as a cantata, with his 'very unusual presence
(at a concert!)'[19]

He saw Swinburne and Whistler, Burne-Jones and Leighton. He
arranged for his mother and Charlotte to visit Queen Square and order a
memorial window for aunt Margaret Polidori. He contributed to a
subscription for Inchbold and exerted himself on behalf of Alice Boyd,
whose picture was rejected by the RA. He saw the Nortons, and met Anne
Gilchrist again at Euston Square. From time to time, he saw Browning, and
also the former Barbara Leigh Smith, who for ten years now had been
married to Dr Eugène Bodichon, dividing her life between Algiers and
England. He drew Aglaia Coronio's daughter Calliope – 'the little gypsy'.
Partly thanks to his practice with Jane, he had evolved a suave style of
portrait drawing, in black or sanguine chalks, which greatly pleased and
flattered the sitters. He welcomed Rae to Cheyne Walk, and went to Little
Holland House, after 'an unconscionable while', to appease Mrs Prinsep by
dining in the garden, admiring Watts's works, and envying Val's studio. He
dined in company with Matthew Arnold at the home of Fanny le Quaire.
He had, he told his mother in the summer, 'an extraordinary number of
engagements' and dinner-parties, and though he added that this was 'in
hopes of shaking off ennui', fellow guests found him sociable and amusing.
He refused, however, to soften his hostility towards Hunt and Woolner,
whom he believed were badmouthing his work to Mr Craven, though
William demurred. Particular venom was reserved for Hunt's *Isabella*, a

morbid image of his late wife as Keats's heroine weeping over the basil pot, whom Gabriel described as looking like a charwoman. '[H]ow grimy and sweaty is the poor thing's face,' he wrote sneeringly, 'and how she must yearn for her beer.'[20] Maybe he was envious: it was said Gambart had paid £2,500 for *Isabella*, with plans also to publish an engraving.

On his own account, in late May Gabriel replied warmly to Leathart, who had heard from Rae that he was painting again. 'I had two finished pictures here when he last visited me; and one (which you know in a forward state, the "Lilith") has left me since,' he began; '– the other is a portrait of Mrs Morris, which I fear I must in common decency send to her and Morris, its owners, before the time you name; but it *may* still be with me. For the rest, I shall be most happy to see you and Mrs Leathart and can only hope there may be *something* for you to see.' However, the 'long spell of troublesome health' which had prevented him from working for some time, had also retarded the refund on the cancelled *Found*. 'To an artist, interruption of work is generally curtailment of means; but I hope the delay may not be very much longer.'[21] He had not yet visited the Academy exhibition, in its centenary year, but he had already seen many of the season's best products – including Watts's 'most noble' *Endymion*, which 'alone should have made the year worthy to commence a new century', and Burne-Jones's *Circe*, which must be 'the *greatest* work exhibited this year'. Of the rest, Scott's *Veil of the Temple* was admirably composed and full of elevated feeling, Hughes's latest work was charming, and at the RA Sandys had a fine portrait of an old lady and a most striking Medea.

William Graham, merchant trader and MP for Glasgow, agreed to commission *Dante's Dream* in oils for 1,500 guineas. Leyland agreed to take *La Pia*, and Rossetti even resurrected the old idea of visiting Italy, for the sake of authentic landscape. Confidence was further boosted by the gratifying responses to his sonnets from friends old and new. Browning, while gracefully refusing Morley's forwarded request for poems ('you know my old ways') was gracious if unspecific towards the *Fortnightly* sonnets. More warmly, he alluded to previous expressions of sympathy arising from their respective bereavements. 'As for all the "other precious, precious jewels" that you made me bright with in your letters,' he wrote. 'I can't speak of them now nor at any time – nor would you wish it.'[22]

Their terms of correspondence remained 'ever affectionately yours' and face to face with the author Rossetti admired *The Ring and the Book*. Privately, however, its 'prosaic reality' was not to his taste – more like Seven Dials gin than pure cognac, he told Allingham, adding: 'this *entre nous*'.[23] When they met at Euston Square, with Jean Ingelow and a few other guests, Browning talked of John Donne, whose intricate, abstract, morbid and vivid imagination surely fed into Rossetti's:

Who ever comes to shroud me, do not harm
Nor question much
That subtle wreath of hair, which crowns my arm;
The mystery, the sign you must not touch . . .

But Donne was quite out of fashion, and anyway Browning was praising his *Progress of the Soul*, a sequence of sonnets charting the satirical, heretical, pythagorean journey of the soul through the plant, fishy and animal worlds of transmigration. Coarse in imagery and sour in feeling, this was like a parable of evolution *avant la lettre*, and there were not many at Euston Square that evening who would have shared Browning's enthusiasm.

Some old friends departed this year: Robert Martineau, who died suddenly, and Mike Halliday. Millais reported that Alex Munro was also dying at Cannes. A new friend was John Nettleship, who had turned to art in his mid-thirties. His heroes being Blake and the PRB, he drew 'strange designs of God creating Evil' and had an especial gift for depicting animals. The combination of originality and unworldliness appealed; Rossetti invited friends to meet, advise and assist. William, who was deeply and keenly working on an edition and biography of his own hero Shelley, suggested illustrations to *Prometheus Unbound*; curiously enough, *The Progress of the Soul* would have afforded a good opportunity for Nettleship's talents. Later in the year, Rossetti asked Watts and Leighton to inquire why his application to the RA Schools had been ignored.

Warington Taylor warned against the imminent bankruptcy of the Firm, if the partners did not change their habits. 'My dear Gabriel, the members of the firm are ruining it – we cannot go on if they do not pay up their debts,' he began. 'The personal extravagance of the members used to be spasmodic, now it is confirmed and habitual . . . every member directly or indirectly eggs the others on to fresh extravagance. "I have got this, you must have one" "order it at once" that sort of thing.' Exiled from London by ill-health but still responsible for the accounts, he claimed the books were only balanced with extreme finesse and the whole enterprise might crash – especially as Howell had started taking goods on credit, for resale elsewhere. Unlike Burne-Jones and Morris, Rossetti's own finances were not entangled with those of the business, and he responded to Taylor's warnings with humour rather than alarm, sending a caricature of the 'Rupes Topseia' like its Tarpeian namesake in Rome, from which a corpulent Morris is being hurled. On the hill above, MMF & Co. is a crumbling building where the partners crouch behind a banner saying 'we are starving'

while the gaunt figure of Warington Taylor wails like Cassandra. Taylor
sent it on to Webb. 'But after looking at it you will still have to turn back to
the main question,' he wrote; 'we want vigorous stern action if the firm is to
be saved.'[24]

This year Charles Norton brought his young compatriot Henry James to
Cheyne Walk – 'the most delicious melancholy old house at Chelsea on the
river'. Prickly, patrician, ironic, 25-year-old James chose to be fascinated by
the antique in Europe. 'When I think what Englishmen ought to be, with
such homes and haunts!' he wrote to painter John LaFarge. 'Rossetti
however does not shame his advantages. Personally, he struck me as
unattractive, poor man. I suppose he was horribly bored!' But they spoke
of LaFarge's illustrations, which Rossetti admired, perceiving a transatlantic
disciple. And to please Norton, who had agreed to return Lizzie's *Clerk
Saunders* in exchange for a drawing, James was favoured with a sight of the
studio. The pictures, he reported, were 'all large, fanciful portraits of
women, of the type que vous savez, narrow, special, monotonous, but with
lots of beauty and power. His chief inspiration and constant model is Mrs
William Morris (wife of the poet) ... a woman of quite extraordinary
beauty of a certain sort – a face, in fact, quite made to his hand. He has
painted a dozen portraits of her – one in particular, in a blue gown, with her
hair down, pressing a lot of lilies against her breast – an almost great
work.'[25]

No such image of Jane clutching lilies is known, but otherwise James is
describing the oil portrait that hung at Queen Square, where she sits in
profile, hands clasped to the throat, with a vase of white roses before her.
The other pictures were Jane as La Pia, Jane as Mariana, Jane as Pandora,
Jane as Beatrice, together with a dozen large drawings in chalks and pencil.
Her image indeed filled the studio; not surprisingly, when Norton escorted
James to Queen Square, the young visitor wondered if Janey were the
original or a copy.

As it happened, she was prostrated on the sofa, suffering from toothache
and other ailments. After Ned's crisis over Mary, her sittings had resumed,
with the Morrises twice staying at Cheyne Walk in February and March.
But as Gabriel's afflictions abated, hers increased. In May, Scott found him
'down in the dumps ... lounging about the room shouldering everything
with his hands in his pockets because Janey was ill and unable to come'.
When she and Topsy came again to Cheyne Walk in June, Jane was too
weak to sit. Doctors recommended the Rhineland spa of Bad Ems. 'Imagine
my Husband at a fashionable German watering place!' she wrote to Susan
Norton[26] but gallantly Morris agreed to escort his suffering wife there for a
six-week stay.

Some time this summer Gabriel wrote *Secret Parting*:

Because our talk was of the cloud-control
   And moon-track of the journeying face of Fate,
   Her kisses faltered at their ivory gate
And her eyes dreamed against a distant goal:
But soon, remembering her how brief the whole
   Of joy, which its own hours annihilate,
   Her set gaze gathered, thirstier than of late,
And as she kissed, her mouth became her soul

Thence in what ways we wandered ...

'The lovers have met in secret and have parted in secret, with an incertain outlook as to their meeting anew,' explained William later.[27]

On 14 July Gabriel drew Jane reclining listlessly on the sofa, head on hand. Three days later the Morrises left for Germany, Bessie and Lucy Madox Brown going with them on the outward journey. At Ems, Jane took baths and drank glasses of spa water. Morris walked in the woods and worked on *The Earthly Paradise.* 'The accompanying cartoon will prepare you for the worst, whichever that may be, the seven tumblers or the seven volumes,' joked Gabriel, drawing *The M's at Ems,* where Jane submits to the medical regimen while Morris reads his latest epic.[28] Among their friends, Topsy's fluency was a byword. Georgie recalled pricking herself with pins to stay awake while listening to each new *Earthly Paradise* tale.

There was now no go-between. Writing for Morris to read if he wished, Gabriel's letters to 'Dear Good Janey' were openly affectionate. She in turn sent reports on her health. When the bulletins were bad, Gabriel worried. When they were good he rejoiced. He would bless the spa in his prayers, he wrote on 14 August: 'it seems quite a shame to call it Bad Ems on the envelope and I should write Good instead if I thought the postman had an intuitive soul ...'[29]

For the most part, Gabriel's correspondence was cheerful and chatty, with a full if not revealing account of events in London, including a call from Macmillan with the American publisher Ticknor Fields, and visits to the Ionides' where Ned was probably seeing Mary. 'I suppose Bessie and Lucy are enjoying themselves vastly. Love to them as well as to dear Top and to your dear self.' He wrote on Val's sketch of Marie Spartali, which took four hours; on the Van Eyck altarpiece at Ghent; on an accident to P. P. Marshall's finger; on Ned's latest picture, 'a most beautiful single female figure in profile' (la Zambaco); and of a dinner in the marquee at Cheyne Walk, at which Val took Howell's role as raconteur of tall stories, 'but did not add the final charm of saying they had all happened to himself'. In Jane's absence Marie Spartali was finally sitting to Rossetti, accompanied by an elderly chaperone whose conversation with the Cheyne Walk parrot amused both artist and sitter.

Occasionally, franker feeling strove for expression. 'All that concerns you is the all absorbing question with me, as dear Top will not mind my telling you at this anxious time,' he wrote on 30 July. 'The more he loves you, the more he knows you are too lovely and noble not to be loved: and, dear Janey, there are too few things that seem worth expressing as life goes on, for one friend to deny another the poor expression of what is most at his heart. But he is before me in granting this, and there is no need for me to say it. I can never tell you how much I am with you at all times. Absence from your sight is what I have long been used to; and no absence can ever make me so far from you again as your presence did for years. For this long inconceivable change, you know now what my thanks must be.'[30]

'Of course do not say a word of any kind in answer to this foolish part of my letter,' he added hastily. Had Jane responded in kind, she had been obliged to censure his love-talk. Their relationship depended on the gossamer fiction that mutual passion was not adulterous desire.

Earlier in the summer he had written a new ode, invoking love as a mystical lily blending the sensuous with the ideal:

> Between the hands, between the brows
>   Between the lips of Love-Lily,
> A spirit is born whose birth endows
>   My blood with fire to burn through me;
> Who breathes upon my gazing eyes,
>   Who laughs and murmurs in mine ear,
> At whose least touch my colour flies,
>   And whom my life grows faint to hear.
>
>   . . .
>
> Ah! let not hope be still distraught,
>   But find in her its gracious goal,
> Whose speech Truth knows not from her thought
>   Nor Love her body from her soul.

Meanwhile Morris, readily enduring the tedium of Ems if it would benefit poor Jane, worked at retelling the triangular love-story from the Laxdaela Saga as *The Lovers of Gudrun*. Tricked into marriage with her lover's best friend, Gudrun urges her husband to kill him, thereby leading to the deaths of both, in an inevitable tragedy. According to Morris's rubric, this was the story of 'how two friends loved a fair woman and how he who loved her best had her to wife, though she loved him little or not at all'.

Rossetti's words: 'the more he loves you, the more he knows you are too lovely and noble not to be loved' had an acute edge in their own triangle.

'The deeper I got into the old tale the more interested I found myself,' Morris told Norton, adding that when it was finished he felt emotionally drained.[31] It was the best and the most important thing he had written. Deeply wounded but knowing he could not compel Jane's affection, Morris drew strength from Nordic stoicism. Gudrun's words at the end of her life: 'I did the worst to him I loved the most' offered oblique solace.

Simultaneously, Gabriel's passion overflowed into projected paintings. As soon as Jane could resume sitting, he intended to paint her full-length as Pandora. 'I also want beyond everything to paint another portrait picture of you: a little more severe in arrangement than the first – as I am sure I can do something more worthy of you than I have yet managed,' he wrote in July. At the end of August, he had a new idea: 'I have been conceiving a great desire to paint you as Fortune and have the design clearly in my head,' he told her. It was in fact the old inspiration, from Holst's *Wish*: 'Fortune will be seated full-faced dealing cards on which will be visible the symbols of life, death, etc. Behind her will be her wheel . . .'[32]

By now, Rossetti was almost sure he wanted to publish and stake a claim to poetic recognition after all. Friends like John Skelton reminded the world that such had been promised as long ago as 1861. After seven years, *Early Italian Poets* had sold out, yielding a modest profit that repaid Ruskin for his subsidy. It was rumoured that *Tinsley's Magazine* was preparing articles on each of the Rossettis, to follow pieces on Morris and Swinburne. Henry Longfellow came to Cheyne Walk, convinced (and courteously not disabused) that Gabriel Rossetti was the painter and his brother the poet. Even worse, Matthew Arnold expressed admiration for W. B. Scott's literary powers.

Morris's new publisher, bookseller F. S. Ellis, had become a helpful friend, patron and occasional banker; he was ready and willing. Insisting he was preparing 'for private circulation' only, Gabriel went back to his manuscripts – the ballads, sonnets and songs from the 1840s and 50s. Some were already famous by repute, like *The Blessed Damozel*, *Sister Helen*, and the unpublished *Jenny*.

In the decade since his last publishing endeavour, poetic tastes had altered. Then, the 'Art-Catholic' mode of PRB days had given way to the medieval mood of the mid-1850s, which had now been succeeded by emergent Aestheticism and renewed Classicism. Brusque Browning and mellifluous Tennyson had been joined by sonorous Arnold and elliptical Meredith, as well as Morris and Swinburne and Christina Rossetti. All these influenced the style of Rossetti's resurgent poetic impulse. Walt Whitman did so negatively, for while Gabriel tried not to mock William's enthusiasm for the free-flowing radical sentiments of *Leaves of Grass*, henceforth he shunned formal innovation.

In youth he had been attracted to romantic, mysterious and sometimes macabre ballad themes, to Keatsian odes like *Love's Nocturn*, and to dramatic monologues like *A Last Confession* and *Jenny*. Now his style became compressed, ambiguously inwrought and verbally Mannerist. In part, this was a reversion, with echoes of both the Dantean aesthetic and Spasmodic opacity, to the 'condensed and hinted' mode that had pleased him in his student days.

As if inching towards publication without looking, in mid-July he told Jane he had given Ellis 'a number of scrappy poems and sonnets to print that I may keep them by me in an available form and perhaps be induced to do more'. By 4 August he had fifty available sonnets. He feared however he would never match Topsy, who was no doubt 'roaring and screaming through the Parnassian tunnels' at his usual speed.[33]

Working to get all he had ready before leaving for Penkill, he aimed to start with a 'reprint' section, 'viz: – the *Blessed Damozel*; *Nocturn*; the *Burden of Nineveh*; the *Card-Dealer*; the *Staff and Scrip*; *Ave*; *Sister Helen*; *Stratton Water*; *Dennis Shand*.' Most had been previously printed; all were revised, 'to great advantage'. The second part was to be new work subtitled 'Songs and Sonnets towards a work to be called *The House of Life*' (building on the *Fortnightly* sequence, this would contain fifty sonnets, including *Placatâ Venere*, and eleven songs, among them *The Song of the Bower*). Other sonnets, on pictures and the like, would follow, and finally *Hand and Soul*, which was 'much more of the nature of a poem than anything else'.

There remained the longer, unpublished poems from the past – *A Last Confession*, *Dante at Verona*, and *Jenny* – whose latest versions lay in Highgate Cemetery. He had 'very imperfect' manuscript copies of these, he told Jane on 30 August; 'but I cannot remember many important alterations which I had once made in other copies now lost; and this has deterred me as yet from tackling them.' Then he drafted an explanatory note, to inform prospective readers that most of the poems were written between 1847 and 1853. 'They are here printed if not without revision yet much in their original state,' this continued. 'They are some among a good many then written, the rest of which I cannot print having no complete copies. "Sonnets & Songs" consist chiefly of more recent work.'[34]

But the note was cancelled, for steps were in hand. Some nine months before, at the end of 1868, with customary willingness Howell had offered his services in retrieving the notebook bound in rough grey calf from

Lizzie's coffin. 'I will reflect further on the poem question and send you the letter if I come to that conclusion,' Rossetti replied, with thanks. Other avenues were explored. 'Did I, years ago, give you a MS. copy of a poem of mine called *Jenny*?' he asked Lushington, of the Working Men's College days. 'To some one I gave it, and have a faint notion it may have been you.'[35]

In mid-August, just before leaving for Scotland, he instructed Howell to proceed. 'I feel disposed, if practicable, by your friendly aid, to go in for the recovery of my poems if possible, as you proposed some time ago. Only I should have to beg *absolute* secrecy to *everyone*, as the matter ought really not to be talked about. If you think this feasible, will you let me know what letter from myself is necessary,' he wrote, adding: 'P.S. If I recover the book I will give you the swellest drawing conceivable.'[36]

He reached Penkill earlier than last year, in order to return home around the same time as Janey and because his symptoms were worsening again. It was as if in her absence his troubled sight, insomnia and obsessive thoughts returned. In this state he could not paint. Welcoming him as before, Alice and Scott were doubtless also relieved he had his proofs from the printing firm of Strangeways to correct. These, he told Miss Losh, he was 'tattooing in the usual agonized state which such things bring to me'.

There followed a detailed editorial exchange with William, who could be relied on for constructive criticism.[37] 'I have been reading your poems all the evening with intense pleasure: they are (as I know from of old) most splendid, and ought to be published without any more seriously motived delay,' he replied. Some, like *The Staff and Scrip*, 'to which my memory was entirely faithful but rather blurred, are even better than I would have affirmed'. His criticisms were minor: Egyptian civilisation antedated Nineveh, and Lemprière's classical dictionary said Venus was surnamed Verticordia because she turned women to chastity – 'just the contrary sort of Venus from the one you contemplate'. He disliked the 'ivory gate' in *Secret Parting*, thought 'Luna' too rococo in *Plighted Promise*, and pointed out that 'occult' was a loose rhyme for 'difficult'. He identified grammatical errors in some Italian verses and anachronisms in *Hand and Soul*; there being, for example, no record of twelfth-century artists painting from the living model.

Gabriel was inclined to ignore such quibbles. More problematic was the eclipse of revealed religion, which made much of his early work appear 'discouragingly angelic'. *Ave* was an example, though the vividness of the verse saved it from mere devotionalism. As a defence against scoffers, however, he proposed a footnote: 'This hymn was written as a prologue to a series of designs. Art still identifies herself with all faiths for her own purposes: and the emotional influence here employed demands above all an inner standing point.' Did William think that would help? William did, but Swinburne protested, seeing it as a sop to believers.

Then there was the issue of explicit carnality. Originally among the pieces sent to Strangeways, *After the French Liberation* was now omitted from the proofs. How about *Placatâ Venere*, the sonnet on sexual congress? It was one of the best, but William had best remove it if showing the proofs *en famille*.

By all means include *Placatâ Venere*, replied William, so long as only private circulation was involved. If published, it should be renamed: the title was even more indecorous than the verses. Gabriel suggested *Nuptial Sleep*, which would 'help it to stand fire'. But what of the last line, where the post-coital lovers 'chirp' at each other with their mouths: was this clear, or if clear was it pleasant? Would 'yawned' be better, or simply 'kissed', or perhaps 'moaned'? It was now that William confessed he had never liked 'chirp'; it was too expressive. Finally Gabriel hit on 'fawned' – which some would think even more vivid.

The poems were being thus selected and amended when Dunn forwarded the copy of *Tinsley's Magazine* with the article on Gabriel. It made for peculiar reading. 'After twenty years, one stranger has learnt that one exists,' Rossetti told Brown. None the less, the notice was welcome, although it raised a problem. In his new selection, Rossetti had excluded the 'fearfully pious and sentimental' *My Sister's Sleep* as 'that rather spoony affair'. But as *Tinsley's* reviewer praised it (in rather spoony terms) as a vivid deathbed scene of simple pathos, the piece would have to be reprinted or, having been thus noticed, it would be sure to get into print again, unaltered. Could William or Christina copy it from *The Germ* and send it to Penkill, for him to revise? Christina obliged, and Gabriel purged the poem of its most 'Catholic' elements; the moon, for instance, becoming a 'crystal cup' instead of an 'altar-cup'. *The Staff and Scrip* became less chivalric, more melancholy. *Nineveh*'s focus altered, from faith to art.

'Well, dear Janey, I am going out for my daily tramp now, and only wish you too were capable of such daily constitutionals,' he wrote on 30 July after a long revising session, bidding her also remember how much she was loved 'by Your affectionate D. Gabriel R.'[38]

In the steep-sided glen below Penkill castle, the Penwhapple burn curled and fell through rocky crevices. How good it would be to see Jane there, 'at ease and liberty' in fresh air and seclusion. The weather was too hot and the Scottish insects very troublesome – he noted how ant-stings soon faded but midge-bites grew worse – but in the glen he discovered a cool half-hidden cave overhanging the stream – 'the very place for Topsy to spin endless poetry in, and for you to sit in and listen to the curious urgent whisper of the stream . . .' As yet he himself had written little, but '[y]ou may be sure I shall send you anything worthy to be sent'.[39] In late-summer solitude, he imagined the sound of the stream, onomatopoeically rendered, as a sotto voce message:

> What thing unto mine ear
> Wouldst thou convey, – what secret thing,
> O wandering water ever whispering?
> Surely thy speech shall be of her.
> Thou water, O thou whispering wanderer,
> What message dost thou bring?

In *The Stream's Secret*, a long Tennysonian ode, the speaker, parted from his beloved, expresses his hopes and fears. He has his heart's desire but does not know if their love will be fulfilled. He refuses to contemplate giving her up: love cannot be controlled. She gave him permission to speak; their love is mutual but they are now apart. When will they meet? He imagines the joy of being together, in images of shelter, rest, fullness, birds singing after rain, silence, a close embrace. He will be enfolded by love physical and spiritual; they will become one: fulfilment is imaged as transcendent quietness after passion.

But will this come about? He recalls the past, wasted and cold, but hope fills the hours until they meet. He is growing old, so their happiness should come soon. But night is falling; death approaches. Therein, however, lies consolation, for in death they will be together, eternally embracing:

> Each on the other gazing shall but see
> A self that has no need to speak:
> All things unsought, yet nothing more to seek, –
> One love in unity.

A final thought: is she weeping too, with the same feelings?

Both *The Stream's Secret* and *Willowwood* find inspiration in the fluid, flickering, reflective, trembling qualities of water to express and explore love that is both mutual and unfulfilled, ecstatic and fearful, uncertain yet hopeful. Like the reflection in a pool, or the tumbling sight and sound of a stream, this love cannot be fixed, held, secured. Fulfilment can be imagined, but never achieved. Swinburne had written recently of great artists like Michelangelo: 'They have known the causes of things, and are not too happy . . . the sorrow and strangeness of things are not lessened because to one or two their secret springs have been laid bare and the curses of their tides made known; refluent evil and good, alternate grief and joy, life inextricable from death, change inevitable and insuperable fate ...'[40] He might have been speaking of the prevailing tenor of Rossetti's verse.

Scott and Alice, to whom some poems were read aloud, were occasionally asked for their views – and Alice gathered up many page proofs from Gabriel's room afterwards. But their guest's mental state was troubling. He was feverish, unrested, as if battling with inner agitation. The oddest thing was a remark to Scott, as they walked in the castle grounds where chaffinches are as common as sparrows. Chirping, one landed on his hand. It was Lizzie's spirit, he said quite seriously, with a message or warning. He did not tell Scott how by the toll-house on the road, he heard children scrambling for pennies from the gentlemen call out 'foul names' in his direction. But another day, when they drove with Alice to a picturesque ravine known as the Devil's Punchbowl, abruptly both his companions were seized with fear that Gabriel was about to leap, in a sudden Romantic embrace of Death. He thought so too, before the momentary seizure passed as he turned to clasp Scott's hand. Retreating from the edge, all three sat down, 'without a word but with faces too conscious of each other's thoughts'.[41]

Later, Scott wrote of Rossetti at Penkill unpacking 'the fearful skeletons in his closet', as the two men sat over their whisky, but specific confidences are not recorded. Discreetly, Scott suggested that 'disturbing causes' might be 'softened away by time' – perhaps meaning that desire would fade. As if in reply, in *The Stream's Secret*, Rossetti protested against the 'vain behest' that his 'burning heart should cease to seek', declaring: 'I will have none thereof.'

But he did not hurry back to welcome Jane home, now feeling that he would 'soon get into very regular habits of production' by remaining in Scotland. Already, he had four new sonnets on pictures of his own (including *Cassandra* and *Mary Magdalene*) and a curious ballad called *Troy Town*, based on a classical legend in Lemprière about how Helen of Troy, while Queen of Sparta, dedicated to Venus a cup moulded to the shape of her breast. Years before, Browning had told him the tale, as a subject for a poem. Then, he had wanted to paint it; now it flowered in verse.

Read to his hosts (Scotus thought it splendid), *Troy Town* seems to have inspired a similar piece on Lilith called *Eden Bower*, which gained fourteen of its fifty stanzas during Rossetti's stopover with Miss Losh on the homeward journey. Both pieces are rather bold and Swinburnian in their celebration of erotic, fateful, irresistible forces.

In the *Fortnightly*, Swinburne had described one of Michelangelo's designs – a woman's head 'fairer than heaven and more terrible than hell', with serpentine ornaments like scales and hair 'shaping itself into a snake's likeness as it unwinds, right against a living snake held to the breast and throat'. The image, he continued, depicts a mystic marriage 'between the maiden body and the scaly coils of the serpent, so closely do the snake and the queen of snakes caress and cling . . .'[42] Far more grotesque than his own visual rendering, Rossetti's lascivious Lilith is a near-relation to this Lamia:

> 'Fold me fast, O God-snake of Eden!
> (*Eden Bower's in flower.*)
> What more prize than love to impel thee?
> Grip and lip my limbs as I tell thee!'

Impelled by destructive energy, the poetic Lilith is demonic in her energy. Perhaps, as Fanny had been the model for the painted version, her sexual jealousy of Jane contributed to the vengeful hatred of Eve that drives *Eden Bower*.

Back in London on 20 September, after a month away, Gabriel found 'everything as it should be, and even better'. The servants had cleaned and redecorated the house and, joy of joys, a wombat had been added to the domestic zoo. 'He is a round furry ball with a head something between a bear and a guinea-pig, no legs, human feet with heels like anybody else and no tail. Of course I shall call him "Top",' he told Miss Losh. 'He follows one about everywhere and sidles up and down stairs along the wall with the greatest activity. He is but a babe as yet . . . I know you would pronounce him a perfect darling.'[43]

A day or so later, Ruskin called, wanting to interest Rossetti in schemes of social reform – a fellowship of those who would gift a tithe of their income to utopian projects. Nothing was less to Gabriel's taste. He read his new poems to the family, obtusely ignoring the fact that blasphemous sexual imagery would offend his sisters deeply. *Eden Bower* drove them from the room, he told Scott with amusement. *Troy Town* can hardly have been more acceptable. William, however, thought both poems 'very fine'. Gabriel confided that his ambition now lay in poetry, for in painting he would always be outclassed by Millais and Burne-Jones.[44]

The fact that Gabriel was writing poems unsuitable for female listeners illustrates the gender gulf of the time, which inevitably separated him from his sisters. As a subject of verse or conversation, sexual relations were 'off-limits' in mixed company. Among men, they were often of correspondingly vigorous interest, with 'free talk' a marker of masculine sociability. Rossetti seems seldom to have initiated such topics, but he was clearly tolerant and amused. When, this autumn, Byron's incestuous relationship was revealed (or at least hinted at) in the pages of *Macmillan's Magazine*, he wrote robustly to William, anxious on behalf of his own work on Shelley, that 'if Byron f——d his sister he f——d her [sic] and there an end – an absolute end in my opinion as far as the vital interest of his poetry goes, which is all we have to do with.'[45] Doubtless, this was all that concerned his own verse too.

While at Penkill, arrangements for recovering the notebook had hardly progressed. Howell, who generally thought everything feasible, delayed answering and then spoke of difficulties. Exhumation was strictly regulated, to prevent grave-robbing activities like those of Burke and Hare in the 1830s. Formal application must be made, to the Secretary of State, with the grave-owner's knowledge and consent.

Mrs Rossetti was the grave-owner, and Gabriel decidedly did not want to inform her of the plan. But, he suddenly realised, the new Home Secretary was his old friend Henry A. Bruce, treasurer of the Llandaff fund-raising committee and now a senior member of the Liberal government. (Meeting Rossetti a few months earlier, John Morley found him unaware that a general election was in progress.) On 3 September, Rossetti asked Howell to forward his personal letter of application. Bruce was in Perthshire, but on 13 September replied saying he would do his utmost to assist, the circumstances justifying departure from the 'strict rule'. On returning to London the next day, he formally lodged the application ('Rossetti, D. G., for leave to open his wife's grave in Highgate Cemy. to take out a M. S. poem') and on 16 September signed the licence ('for leave to exhume the body of the late wife of Mr D. G. Rossetti interred in a grave in the Highgate Cemetery for the purpose of obtaining a book placed in the coffin . . . by virtue of the power vested in me by the 25th sect. of the Acts 20 and 21 Vic., cap.81 . . .')[46] On 19 September, Rossetti left Penkill, to arrange the macabre business. Life was imitating the art of his youth; this was the stuff of Holst, Poe, Bürger's *Lenore*. With disturbed displacement, as he travelled south, Rossetti poured out his hectic, sexual verses on Helen's breasts and Lilith's serpentine coils.

'The grave is at Highgate Cemetery – the exact spot can be found at once by enquiry at the lodge,' he told Howell. Besides the manuscript book, Lizzie's Bible was with her. Yet still he hesitated, wondering fearfully what condition books and body would be in. Medical reassurances gave him courage and, once the formalities were complete, he furnished the letter of authority:

28 September 1869 / In accordance with the order granted by the Right Honourable Henry Austin Bruce, Her Majesty's Secretary for the Home Department, for the exhumation of the body of my late wife, Elizabeth Eleanor Rossetti, buried at Highgate Cemetery: I hereby authorize my friend, Charles

Augustus Howell, of Northend Grove, Northend, Fulham, to act in all matters as he may think fit, for the purpose of opening the coffin and taking charge of the MS volume deposited therein. / Dante Gabriel Rossetti / 16 Cheyne Walk, Chelsea.

Then the Cemetery raised an objection 'as to there possibly being papers the removal of which involved a fraud'. Popular novels were full of secret wills and documents buried in family vaults. A lawyer was required to witness the items taken from the tomb. Tebbs agreed to perform this service; in return Gabriel offered a portrait drawing of Emily, his 'even older friend'.[47]

Also present at the disinterment on 5 October was Dr Llewellyn Williams, engaged by Howell to disinfect the manuscript, lest any contagion be transmitted from the dead to the living. The men employed by the funeral company removed the grave slab. They dug down in the narrow space to Lizzie's coffin, identified by its brass name-plate (Gabriele Rossetti lay beneath). Howell reported that 'all in the coffin was found quite perfect'. This has been taken to mean that her flesh was uncorrupted (preserved by opium as if in formaldehyde) and her hair still red-gold. Maybe this was the case, though it is unlikely. More probably 'quite perfect' meant simply that the coffin and its contents were undisturbed. The book was removed. The lid, earth and stone were replaced. The workmen were tipped. One imagines a rather silent group leaving the cemetery.

The book, however, was not 'quite perfect'; Rossetti was warned that it was 'soaked through and through', and that some of the writing was obliterated. He would get it in a fortnight.

He told Janey, Scott and Dunn. Howell told Ned and Topsy. From Penkill, Scott told William, writing on 11 October the underlined words 'He has recovered the M.S. of his poems', before reopening the envelope to add a postscript: 'he may not have yet broken the subject to you. If so, I ought not to have done so . . .'[48]

Eight days after the 'ghastly business', Gabriel gave William a full account. The principal reason for secrecy, he explained, had been 'the impossibility of mentioning so painful a matter to our mother'; or having to invent a pretext to move Lizzie's place of burial. He could not have asked William to assist; indeed, only Howell could or would have done it. But 'no mistrust or unbrotherly feeling' had led him to keep silent. As well as those already informed, Brown, Swinburne and Watts were to be told, but it was 'very desirable' that the rest of the Rossetti family should remain ignorant. For the present, he would merely tell people that the rough drafts of lost poems had proved more usable than foreseen. Inevitably, however, 'the truth must ooze out in time'. 'I have begged Howell to hold his tongue for the future; but if he does not I cannot help it.'[49] It was not, after all, illicit or shameful, merely distasteful.

There was 'no reason at all why you should mention the matter to me beforehand', replied William; 'you and I know each other of old, and shall continue to do so till (or perhaps after) one of us is a bogey.' He warned however that Howell had 'a very blabbing tongue'. As to the deed: his frank opinion was that his brother had acted rightly both when consigning his manuscript to oblivion and when resurrecting it. 'Under the pressure of a great sorrow, you performed an act of self-sacrifice: it did you honour but it was clearly an act of supererogation. You have not retracted the self-sacrifice, for it has taken actual effect in your being bereaved of due poetic fame these $7\frac{1}{2}$ years past: but you now think – and I quite agree with you – that there is no reason why the self-sacrifice should have no term.'

Such jesuitical reasoning was not William's normal style. Doubtless he felt no desire to condemn, but inadvertently his words pointed up the purpose of the disinterment: a desire for poetic fame that must be called self-seeking. No sin in that, among men of the world. But implicitly, it broke faith with Lizzie, to whom poetic fame had been sacrificed in the funeral gesture. Had Gabriel not declared, as she lay in the open box, that he had often been working on the poems when he could have been tending her, and so 'they should go'?

Now they were back. Another fortnight passed before Swinburne was told. 'I hope you will think none the worse of my feeling for the memory of one for whom I know you had a true regard. The truth is, no one so much as herself would have approved of my doing this,' Gabriel wrote. 'Art was the only thing for which she felt very seriously. Had it been possible to her, I should have found the book on my pillow the night she was buried; and could she have opened the grave no other hand would have been needed.' This was true, and not equivocal, and rewarded by Swinburne's response. 'My dear Gabriel, I cannot tell you how rejoiced I am at the news,' he began. 'None could have given me a truer or deeper pleasure . . . I can say to you now what of course I could never hint before, how often my thoughts have run in the line of yours as to what her own hope and desire in the matter would have been, who loved art so nobly and well. Your expression of such a feeling touched a chord in mine which till now had been only of fruitless and desperate regret.' Like William, he then proceeded to justify Gabriel's action to him, rhapsodising on Art as 'the most precious and serious pleasure of life', of which humanity should never be deprived. To retrieve the poems was a matter of 'grave delight', and he was 'glad and grateful to you with all my heart for the resolution'.[50]

Yet in despite of the assertions, the disquieting nature of the event undermined their words. From Gabriel's initial image of the poems rattling their bones like 'pantomime ghosts', to his anticipation that the truth would ooze out as from the sodden manuscript; from William's vision of the Rossetti brothers as 'bogeys' and Swinburne's punning use of 'grave delight', to Gabriel's own macabre invocation of Lizzie's hand opening her own coffin to restore the book to his pillow – the exhumation had a haunting power. As Gabriel confessed in thanking Swinburne, he had undergone 'so much mental disturbance about this matter', with many 'conflicting states of mind'.

He had his first sight of the manuscript at Dr Williams's house. Still wet, it had a dreadful smell, from decay and disinfectants. Many leaves were stuck together. Some were legible. But *Jenny*, the poem he most wished to recover, had 'a great worm-hole right through every page of it', so that only the ends of the lines were intact. 'I do not think it would be any use giving it to an ordinary transcriber,' he told William, 'and propose to take the copying in hand myself, probably with Dunn's assistance for the easier parts. I do not know if you would have time or inclination to assist in so unpleasant a job. If so you could do some of the more difficult parts while I did others.' With help, 'the whole might be done in a day or two and the original burnt. The best would be to work all together here . . .'[51]

The book was duly delivered and the grisly task accomplished. Despite worm-holes, the 'missing' poems were transcribed: *Jenny, A Last Confession, Dante at Verona* and *The Bride's Chamber*. Gabriel was especially pleased to rediscover the 'passion and reality' of *A Last Confession*. 'It is the outcome of the Italian part of me, and I am glad it is not lost,' he told Algernon on 30 October, having already added 130 new lines. A fortnight later he dined at Brown's, with W. J. Stillman and Marie Spartali. 'The chief *raison d'être* of the gathering was for Gabriel to read some of his poems to Miss Spartali,' noted William, though Stillman, formerly of *The Crayon* and lately a journalist covering the Cretan insurrection, was equally interested in the evocation of nationalist fervour in *A Last Confession*.[52]

This piece was also a tribute to Lizzie, whose awakening love in the early 1850s had partly inspired the poem's heroine, with her quick yet lingering speech and big eyes that turned half dizzily 'beneath the passionate lids'. Indeed, all the 'old' poems brought Lizzie back to mind, if only because they belonged to Gabriel's youth. And her shade hovered over new ones too. 'The *Life-in-Love* refers to an actual love with a reminiscence of an earlier one,' he explained to Alice, stressing the universality of such experience, which Scott had suggested was too personal to have wide appeal. However common, the sonnet resounds with very particular reminiscences to those in a certain circle, as the poet's loneliness before the new love's advent is likened to a 'poor tress of hair' which is all that remains from the past:

Even so much life endures unknown, even where
'Mid change the changeless night environeth,
Lies all that golden hair undimmed in death.

'The vivid hair of the dead woman is a figure of the continuing presence of the dead among the living,' writes a recent critic,[53] as well, it would seem (syntactical ambiguities make *Life-in-Love* an especially opaque text), of the reviving power of the new love. By this means, the lost love informs the new, rather as, in the letter to Swinburne, Lizzie was envisaged returning the manuscript with her own hand.

The Love-Moon, the sonnet placed next in the sequence, traces a similar segue between old and new, answering a vocalised rebuke:

'When that dead face, bowered in the furthest years,
    Which once was all the life years held for thee,
    Can now scarce bid the tides of memory
Cast on thy soul a little spray of tears, –
How canst thou gaze into these eyes of hers
    Whom now thy heart delights in, and not see
    Within each orb Love's philtred euphrasy
Make them of buried troth remembrancers?'

'Nay, pitiful Love, nay, loving Pity! Well
    Thou knowest that in these twain I have confess'd
Two very voices of thy summoning bell.
    Nay, Master, shall not Death make manifest
In these the culminant changes which approve
The love-moon that must light my soul to Love?'

How should Rossetti be judged? There was no good reason why a poet, let alone an individual *in propria persona*, should not think back to a lost love while celebrating the new, and indeed feel again the same heart-delighting emotion. Especially if the 'buried troth' were that for a dead beloved, who could not return. In Victorian Britain the experience was familiar enough. True, the Romantic concept was that of the faithful lover in *The Blessed Damozel*, ever awaiting heavenly reunion. In Romance, however, no one aged or changed. In the actual world, even the tide of memory ebbed away, casting scarcely a 'spray of tears'.

With anguish, he had balanced conflicting views and while recognising that 'digging up one's wife' aroused revulsion had concluded there was no disrespect in retrieving his notebook. Moreover, the recovered poems do not betray Lizzie, either as texts or gestures, for they were not love poems. Rationally, therefore, one might agree with Gabriel's words when all was done that the exhumation was 'less dreadful than might have seemed possible'.[54] Emotionally, however, posterity has never forgiven him. His action has been registered and condemned by many who hardly know his name as poet or painter, and made into the defining moment of his story.

He set to work revising the poems, more or less assured that he could now fill a respectable volume with a variety of pieces. He wanted to leave a mark on the sand before the sea of oblivion washed over him.

CHAPTER TWENTY

Poems and Reviews

Rossetti has been described as a writer whose endless alterations to his poems in proof display 'a repetitive profusion that no printer or publisher would tolerate even from his best-selling author today'.[1] The usual implication is that he was neurotic, uncertain, self-important. But as we have seen, this refinement was an integral element in his method of composition. 'I can never see my own work clearly till in print,' he told Swinburne plainly.[2] The method had worked well, if expensively, with *Early Italian Poets*, and now, uncertain as to whether he could in fact produce an original volume of sufficient quality and quantity, he used it again. The early proof versions may therefore be regarded as successive typescript drafts, as the poems moved into final form.

'I have been working on what may be called the flea-bite principle,' he had told Janey on 30 August. Topsy would scorn this 'fidgetty fretting over old ground' but 'when one suffers from the vain longings of perfectibility' such 'repeated condensation and revision' was never-ending. As in painting, he was a poet who conceived an ideal beyond the limits of actual achievement. The 'vain longings' for perfection made him feel that no work ever hit the mark, nor even came near. With Samuel Beckett he might have said: 'Try. Fail. Try again. Fail better.' He worried his texts like his canvases, and as he had bullied his sister over *The Prince's Progress*, urging her to produce a new masterpiece, so he beat his own brains for the exact, evocative, exceptional phrases.

As they emerged, the revisions were sent to William and Swinburne for further comments. The process was lengthy, intense, the reverse of casual or slapdash. And costly: Rossetti paid for the composing, correcting and repagination, as well as for 'hiring' the type while it was set up at Strangeways and therefore unavailable for other jobs.

Rossetti was a good critic, not indulgent towards his own works: selection and revision were always necessary. But an additional reason lay in the fact that so many of the texts were at least a decade old. While in many respects his poetic tastes – for Dantescan sonnets and Scots balladry –

remained, other judgements had matured. Thus, to take a minor example that showed major revision, they discussed the old sonnet on Giorgione's *Venetian Pastoral* or *Concert Champêtre* in Paris.[3] Alternate lines here indicate the 1849 version, with the 1869 phrasing in italics:

Water, for anguish of the solstice – yea
     Water, for anguish of the solstice: – nay,
Over the vessel's mouth still widening
     But dip the vessel slowly, – nay, but lean
Listlessly dipt to let the water in
     And hark how at its verge the wave sighs in
With slow vague gurgle. Blue, and deep away
     Reluctant. Hush! Beyond all depth away
The heart lies silent at the brink of day.
     The heart lies silent at the brink of day:
Now the hand trails upon the viol-string
     Now the hand trails upon the viol-string
That sobs; and the brown faces cease to sing,
     That sobs, and the brown faces cease to sing,
Mournful with complete pleasure. Her eyes stray
     Sad with the whole of pleasure. Whither stray
In distance; through her lips the pipe doth creep
     Her eyes now, from whose mouth the slim pipes creep
And leaves them pouting; the green shadowed grass
     And leave it pouting, while the shadowed grass
Is cool against her naked flesh. Let be:
     Is cool against her naked side? Let be: –
Do not now speak unto her lest she weep –
     Say nothing now unto her lest she weep,
Nor name this ever. Be it as it was: –
     Nor name this ever. Be it as it was: –
Silence of heat, and solemn poetry.
     Life touching lips with Immortality.

The revised last line was very fine, remarked William; but he preferred the original. The new line bent too far towards the Ideal – 'which is not to me at all the effect of the picture, but only poetry by way of intensity, or one might say *saturation*'.

Gabriel was unmoved; the old line now seemed to him 'quite bad'. 'Solemn poetry' belonged 'to the class of phrases absolutely forbidden' in verse. 'It is intellectually incestuous – poetry seeking to beget its emotional offspring on its own identity,' he wrote. 'Whereas I see nothing too "ideal" in the present line. It gives only the momentary contact with the immortal which results from sensuous culmination and is always a half conscious element of it.'

The revision remained. But one may agree with William and feel, besides, that Life touching lips with Immortality is yet another rhetorically posturing image impossible to visualise. Overall, moreover, in gaining suavity the sonnet lost sharpness. However, both versions are Keatsian; the 1849 lines showing a mix of high-flown naivety and vigour (the unpoetical gurgle as water enters the narrow neck of the pitcher) while those of 1869 have a surer sense of pulsing movement towards the arrested climax.

Other revisions were decided improvements; the long, rather spoony *Portrait*, for instance, was condensed into 'a good short poem' that seems now to express a good deal of concentrated feeling for Lizzie. In the early weeks, when proofs consisted of some 200 pages, including *Hand and Soul*, William was chief assistant. After the buried poems' recovery and the removal of the prose tale, Swinburne took over as chief confidant and constructive critic. 'Do pitch into me when I need it,' Rossetti urged on one occasion; 'remember that my verses are not yet my remains . . .'[4]

Swinburne was currently living with his parents in the country, to dry out and complete his own next volume. He sent responses interleaved with what Gabriel called (with some degree of irony) 'delightful farragoes of blasphemy and indecency', including a sacrilegious hymn to the Virgin and the scatological *Bogshire Banner*, a parodic provincial newspaper. (If he did not share Algernon's taste for the excremental and flagellatory, Rossetti appears to have tolerated it.) But his poetic critiques were both warm and detailed; Rossetti was grateful and heartened. Among other things, Swinburne approved of the archaisms, such as *Jenny*'s 'purfled buds', which William had queried. 'I was going to remove it, but shall not if you like it,' replied Gabriel. So 'purfled' stayed – a perfectly good, if old-fashioned word. Going carefully through the text, however, Swinburne found fault with 'many a double-bedded morn'. Surely, this could 'only mean that there are two beds, implying separate sleepers; which is chaste but startling, as a suggestion', he wrote. 'Also it sounds to me to have just a shade or breath of coarseness – escaped so exquisitely elsewhere.'[5] He proposed 'double-pillowed' to give the idea of two heads waking together, with hints of a long succession of sleeping partners.

'Pillowed makes the couplet just right, and I shall certainly now use it,' replied Rossetti. But he rejected the suggestion that 'But yet the pity of it!' from *Othello* be added as epigraph, alongside Mistress Quickly's 'Never name her, child!' on the grounds that these two Shakespearean characters would sit ill together – 'and I want to put Mrs Q. instead of *Merry Wives* etc., to remind the virtuous reader strongly whose words they are that his own mind is echoing at the moment.'

Another debate centred on Helen's breasts in *Troy Town*. 'It's an absurd piece (I daresay) of hypercriticism,' responded Swinburne; 'but it does strike me that to call a woman's breasts "the sun and moon of the heart's desire" sounds as if there were a difference between them, much in favour of one. It's a burlesque notion, I know, but . . .' How about 'the glowing spheres'? asked Rossetti, acknowledging the point. Eventually, however, Swinburne raised his embargo, and the sun and moon remained. Should he add a note to explain the *Troy Town* legend, Gabriel then asked, to prepare the reader for 'so outlandish a notion' as a cup resembling a bosom? And was it possible that in *Eden Bower* the metre of the opening lines (a sort of anapaestic trimeter) might mislead the reader into stressing the second syllable of 'Lilith'? 'One line, please, by return,' he wrote when the next query arose; 'and pardon these babyish bulletins.'[6]

To elucidate the motive of *Sister Helen*, he toyed with Swinburne's favourite device of a cod quotation from Old French, which briefly appeared in the proofs before being finally ejected, and he held a last-minute consultation with Allingham over the name of Sister Helen's faithless lover Keith, which featured in another supernatural ballad by Sydney Dobell. Rossetti had a horror of seeming to imitate. 'Holm', 'Neill', 'Kerr', 'Weir', 'Hearne', 'Lyle' and 'Carr' were considered, before Keith was stuck back, in despair.

Two small pieces emerged from oblivion by another route: Burne-Jones recalled verbatim two translations that dated from around 1860, when Georgie and her sisters frequently sang from a collection of Old French songs.[7] But even while Rossetti prepared designs for the binding and endpapers, knowing that publication could not be delayed much beyond Easter or a whole season would be lost, he yet hankered to add an impressive piece from the platonic store. On a dismal Valentine's Day in foggy London, just before telling Ellis to announce that 'Poems by Dante Gabriel Rossetti' would 'appear shortly', he told Swinburne he had 'serious thoughts of going into retreat for a few weeks almost immediately . . . and trying if I can hammer anything out before the inevitable day of publication is at the door'.[8]

On 11 March he left London, returning after a long absence to Scalands, the Leigh Smith estate in Sussex, where Barbara had built herself a commodious cottage with a studio which was available to let each winter while she was in Algeria. This season it was taken by 'William's Yankee friend' Stillman, who had once helped to publish Gabriel's poems in *The Crayon* and was now courting Marie Spartali. He was, observed Gabriel, a congenial but 'entirely unobtrusive man, who will leave me quite to myself'.

The aim, during two or three weeks' solitude, was 'one more poem to beat the rest hollow.' Rossetti had various subjects in mind for his *capo lavoro*, some half-begun. There was *The Orchard-pit*, a spooky tale begun at Penkill and perhaps inspired by the abandoned churchyard at Old Dailly. Another idea was *The Doom of the Sirens*, in the form of a choral drama. Or *The Harrowing of Hell*, in which Adam and Eve, David and Bathsheba and other unlucky lovers (and perhaps by implication himself and Jane) were to be rescued from damnation through Christ's redemption. William doubted that this could be made convincing, and the projected piece died in utero.[9]

Instead, Gabriel turned back to his old theme, *God's Graal*, first projected in the Oxford days in emulation of Malory and medieval French romances. Now the same tale was the subject of Tennyson's latest poem, *The Holy Grail*. 'O thou the Laureate that wast once so good / Fallen in the practice of this cursed King, what shall be said to thee?' Rossetti wrote parodically. Once again Tennyson's characters were milk-and-water, so in reaction, he foresaw 'additonal zest' in completing his own poem which, he promised Swinburne, would underline 'the marked superiority of Guenevere over God'; that is, the loss of the Grail would be reckoned a small price relative to the love of Guenevere – and thus reverse Tennyson's mimsy moral. This scorn should however be read against his continuing high regard for the Laureate's overall achievement, for to Swinburne a month earlier Rossetti cited those living poets with whom he would be humbly proud to rank: 'the four I mean above all are Tennyson, Browning, yourself and Morris.'[10]

For his own *God's Graal*, he had looked up an old French version of *Lancelot du Lac* printed in 1533, with a vivid and intriguing account of the first kiss between knight and queen. 'Lancelot has been doing some wonderful deeds of arms as an unknown knight, and Guenevere calls him to her to ask him of his adventures,' he reported. 'Galahalt then steps forward, to persuade the Queen to kiss Lancelot. She makes difficulties, but eventually does so in a corner, as if taking counsel.' The ending was 'the funniest part ... which is, not that the Queen and Lancelot go to bed together, but that he and Galahalt do! What this may mean I do not pretend to fathom ...'

Like the proposed *Harrowing of Hell*, a new poem justifying Lancelot's love for Guenevere had evident personal resonance, in its theme of a noble, overmastering, tragic passion for a woman whose husband is the hero's companion at arms. In Oxford, and in the Firm, Topsy and Gabriel were members of the same Round Table, with primary fealty to each other. But at Scalands the Grail remained elusive. The medieval form of Rossetti's 1857 fragment proved too limiting, maybe too lightweight, for what he now wished to say; and 'time runs short'. Perhaps he was intimidated by Tennyson after all, or by reports of the 'splendid' Tristram and Iseult poem that Swinburne was reciting to everyone. Instead, he went back to *The Stream's Secret*, inspired by the glen at Penkill. By 15 March this had grown to a dozen manuscript pages, sufficient to fill an extra printer's gathering of sixteen sheets, and had developed into a long ode of hope and foreboding. It was like *Love's Nocturn*, he told Swinburne, but weightier and more passionate.[11]

The poem's uncertainty echoed the impasse of his relationship with Jane. Over the winter, their meetings had been infrequent and unsatisfactory. Moreover, his health had grown even shakier – literally so, for in November he reported constant tremor in his hands, which he took to be a disease of the nerves, portending paralysis. Marshall prescribed iron tonics. The eminent Sir William Jenner ordered a stricter regimen: no spirits, bed before midnight, leisured country life with no 'regular professional work' for six months. Warning against opiates, he prescribed another medicine for insomnia.

Christina too, had been ill, though she also managed a visit to Penkill and had two new books in preparation – a delightful collection of original nursery rhymes and a volume of short stories, headed by one that Gabriel accurately described as 'in the Miss Austen vein'. 'Of course I think your proper business is to write poetry,' he added with brotherly candour.[12]

For Gabriel, Jane suggested Italy, which he still spoke of visiting 'this year', and where the Nortons were staying. 'His health is bad and I fear will become worse unless he takes some precautions at once. I wish he would come out to Florence, I wish we could all come before you leave,' she told Susan Norton at Christmas. 'He is suffering from his eyes and intense nervousness and general weakness. His work does not go as rapidly as formerly . . .'[13]

When Jane came to sit, he could only handle chalks. In January, she had found him in a morose and sorry state, too depressed even to escort her home. 'The sight of you going down the dark steps to the cab all alone has plagued me ever since – you looked so lonely,' he wrote remorsefully the next day, angry with himself, when she was the one person he wished to see. Why, just when her presence softened the 'chilling numbness' of his life, had other obstacles steadily increased? It all came too late. It was twelve months since the prophetic *Superscription*: 'my name is Might-have-been; I am also called No-more, Too-late, Farewell.'

Four days later he wrote even more dismally, arranging to deliver the latest chalk drawing. 'Dear Janey, I expect this has come into my head because I feel so badly the want of speaking to you. No one else seems alive at all to me now, and places that are empty of you are empty of all life,' he lamented. 'But more than all that for me, dear Janey, is the fact that you exist, that I can yet look forward to seeing you and speaking to you again, and know for certain that at that moment I shall forget all my own troubles nor even be able to remember yours. You are the noblest and dearest thing that the world has had to show me; and if no lesser loss than the loss of you could have brought so much bitterness, I would still rather have had this to endure than have missed the fulness of wonder and worship which nothing else could have made known to me.'

Jane gently explained she could not always be with him. 'I really feel, seeing you so little, as if I must seem neglectful and careless of all you have to endure,' he replied. 'But I hope you believe that it is never absent from my thoughts for a moment and that I never cease to long to be near you and doing whatever might be to distract and amuse you. To be with you and wait on you and read to you is absolutely the only happiness I can find or conceive in this world, dearest Janey; and when this cannot be, I can hardly now exert myself to move hand or foot for anything. If I ever do wish still to do any work, it is that I may not sink into utter unworthiness of you and deserve nothing but your contempt.' He would come to Queen Square on Saturday, or failing that, on Monday.[14]

To his surprise, Jenner's medicine seemed to work; at least his nights were no worse. He also took daytime walks in Battersea Park, when the weather served, rather than only after dark, for with 'constant pains in the eyes and head' as well as tremor, he had not lifted a brush for months. 'I do not think you or any one understands the extent to which my eyesight now interferes with my work,' he told Brown. 'Every moment is an effort.'[15] Nevertheless, he was frequently alone in the studio into the early hours, long after Dunn and the servants were abed. One night, he heard a child whimpering beyond the door. It came closer, and retreated, up and down the passageway, with no sound of footsteps. When the noise ceased, he went to look, but there was nothing. It was almost certainly the raccoon, prowling the house at night in search of food. Dunn eventually found it nesting in the drawer of an old armoire. But when, months later, this explanation was offered, Gabriel refused it. No, the sound was that of a child, a ghostly child.

His stillborn daughter would have been nine this spring. The supernatural visitation took place around the anniversary of her mother's death. To Dante, nine was a mystical number.

In fact, the season was not all gloomy. The Scotts, with Alice their Star, had moved to a large house at the other end of Cheyne Walk, where regularly Rossetti dined and joined in a rubber of whist. Through Barbara

Bodichon he met George Eliot and G. H. Lewes, lunched with them at the Priory and welcomed them to Tudor House, showing his drawings for Pandora, Beatrice, Cassandra, Mary Magdalene. Then he sent photos, evidently hoping to secure a commission, for George Eliot, who was beginning *Middlemarch*, was especially interested in the Magdalene, with her own tentative theories 'about forms of eyebrow and their relation to passionate expression' that seemed to chime with his pictorial renderings. Otherwise, he did not much like the Leweses, probably sharing Henry James's view of 'this great horse-faced bluestocking' and certainly having always found Lewes 'a horrid fellow ... a monster of physical ugliness and mental showiness' from their first meeting 'in bohemian circles' in the early 1850s.[16] Admittedly, he had fond boyhood memories of Lewes's wife Agnes, whose father had been a good friend of Professor Rossetti, and who at the age of seventeen had induced a bashful ten-year-old Gabriel to dance with her.

Another task this spring was a portrait drawing of Mary Zambaco, commissioned by her mother. Gabriel did it mainly to please Ned, whose failure to make good his promises to Mary was replaced with a sentimental fantasy of thwarted romance. 'I was so glad to have such a portrait, and for you to know her a little better – if ever so little,' Ned wrote, apologising for his own silliness. 'I can't say how the least kindness from any of you to her goes to my heart ...' For his part, Gabriel came to sympathise a little more. 'I think I have made a good portrait of Mary Zambaco, and Ned is greatly delighted with it,' he told Jane. 'I like her very much and am sure her love is all in all to her. I never had an opportunity of understanding her before.' Altogether he made four fine chalk studies. 'And she is really extremely beautiful herself when one gets to study her face. I think she has got much more so within the last year with all her love and trouble.'[17]

Like other friends, Ned was worried by Gabriel's condition. 'Keep well and strong,' he concluded. 'I feel as if I depended on you so much.' In turn, however, Rossetti felt that mentally and physically he depended on Jane. And his decision to join Stillman in Sussex in March was prompted largely by the fact that two days earlier, Jane and her daughters had gone to Hastings to escape the late-winter fogs. One of Gabriel's first acts on reaching Sussex was to travel on to see her.

Surrounded by woodland, Barbara's cottage was simple but spacious. Stillman recalled Rossetti's characteristically imperious behaviour when they arrived, going through the rooms. 'I will take this,' he said of those that suited him; 'you may have that.'[18] The front door opened straight into the living room, with an open fireplace and walls lined with bookshelves. Above the fireplace was a poignant reminder of earlier days: three pencil sketches of Lizzie, wearing an awkward garland of irises. Drawn by Barbara and Anna Howitt, they recorded the date, 8 May 1854, when he and Lizzie had come to Scalands for the day, in the dawn of their romance.

Stillman, with his 'grave, dark face', proved a pleasantly taciturn companion on walks in the snowy lanes, or before the fire indoors. Surely his name derived from a hereditary trait, Rossetti told Barbara. As he knew, his widowed housemate too had troubles. After a chequered career, he was without employment; his wife had killed herself in Crete, leaving three children currently in the United States, one with a bone disease. To Marie Spartali, his support for Greek liberty was heroic, but her parents vehemently opposed this 'unfortunate attachment' (and indeed wrote to Rossetti, Brown and others, urging them to intervene). But if preoccupied, Stillman was resilient and reserved, a man's man in the circumstances. Gabriel likened him to Don Quixote and himself to Sancho Panza.[19] With permission, they sampled the extensive Bodichon cellar, more liberally than was intended. Stillman kept some notes, but four months later Rossetti could only make good his obligations to the various vintages by sending cases 'in three simplified classes of sherry, claret and champagne'.

'By the bye,' he wrote to Barbara soon after arriving, Stillman said there was 'a British beauty' to hand, a local gamekeeper's daughter. Could she be asked to pose? A sitting or two would produce drawings worth 50 guineas, plus a sketch for the girl in lieu of payment. 'But ought one to ask?'[20] Barbara evidently gave her blessing, for a head study of Sophie Burgess was duly completed.

'Once more the changed year's turning wheel returns ...' He started a sonnet, comparing the season to a crinolined young woman. 'And as a girl sails balanced in the wind, / And now before and now again behind / Stoops as it swoops, with cheek that laughs and burns – / So Spring comes merry towards me here ...' But it received 'no answering smile' from himself, whose wintry mood was as bleak as the weather.

He drew Stillman's portrait also, and envied him. Marie was 'a noble girl – in beauty, in sweetness, and in artistic gifts', he wrote; 'and the sky should seem very warm and calm above, and the road in front bright and clear, and all ill things left behind for ever, to him who starts anew on his life-journey, foot to foot and hand in hand with her.'[21] What might have been, had he been able to start his life anew with Janey ...

'Now you *will* swear,' he told Ellis on 18 March, proposing at this eleventh hour to change the order of his poems, that the book might begin with *The Blessed Damozel* instead of *Troy Town*. The advice came from 'a specially trustworthy source', who may have been Janey. How much would it cost to cancel and reprint the two sheets involved? He would pay. Publication was firmly scheduled for the end of April.

As his eyes and head continued to hurt, on 5 April he went to town to see a new ophthalmologist, Dr Critchett, who found signs of normal ageing only, and recommended rest. Professionally, Rossetti had been resting his eyes for nigh on eighteen months. He spent the rest of the day in London with Swinburne, listening to the 'glorious new poems' that would appear in *Songs before Sunrise*. One was called *Hertha*:

> I am that which began;
>   Out of me the years roll;
> Out of me God and man;
>   I am equal and whole:
> God changes, and man, and the form of them bodily;
>   I am the soul . . .
>
>   I the grain and the furrow,
>   The plough-cloven clod
> And the ploughshare drawn thorough,
>   The germ and the sod,
> The deed and the doer, the seed and the sower, the dust which is God.

For once, Algernon was not drinking. How good it would be to see him always sober! commented Gabriel.

The Morrises came to Scalands overnight, and it was agreed that Jane would return, to enjoy the spring air. She stayed at Fir Bank, another house on the estate, easily reached by paths and private roads, and presumably saw Gabriel on a daily basis for three intimate weeks, until he himself had to leave. Morris ungrudgingly came to escort her home, all travelling back to London together on 9 May.[22] Now, lady, husband and lover were as well-established as Guinevere, Arthur and Lancelot.

Whether it was her company or the spring, his pains ceased, and he began suddenly to feel quite improved. He was also sleeping better, thanks to a new soporific known to Stillman. Though not to be used for more than three consecutive nights and not always restorative, twenty grains of chloral hydrate dissolved in three ounces of water lifted the curse of insomnia and lightened his spirits.

He even began to respond to nature. 'I have been drawing regularly, though not many hours, for several days, and am beginning to feel more cheerful,' he told his mother on 18 April. 'The air is delicious – the weather very hot just now while the sun lasts, but exquisitely cool in the evenings.' He sent wild flowers wrapped in moss, adding: 'as to the primroses, the country is already smothered in them. The white violets came in a swarm, and are now almost gone. The blue ones are everywhere now, and the wood anemones, of which I send a few, are most delightful, as well as the wild daffodils. Lambs have tails and begin to prance a little . . .'[23]

Reluctant to leave Scalands, he looked for a substitute. 'The leisure and pleasure of work in the country is something new for me – no interruptions, no invitations, no anything which is the bane of studious enjoyment,' he wrote during Jane's stay at Fir Bank. 'I feel almost tempted to set up my tent in the country altogether.' Locally, there were several eligible houses, one a most jolly old place, but expensive at £130 a year, another 'a splendid old mansion' now a farmhouse. 'I am seriously thinking about it,' he told Brown. 'There are fine big rooms and windows and a good east light to paint in and the house is perfectly noble.'[24] He put down a deposit, planning to return in the summer, hoping Jane would join him.

The precious collection of Gabriel's letters that Janey carefully guarded in subsequent years now includes none from this period – nor any for the next five years. Were they too revealing to preserve? 'I have no intention of destroying any more,' she wrote towards the end of her life, when concerned with their safe-keeping.[25] Those lost would have been among the most passionate, but perhaps also the most poignant. One can only guess, but Jane does not at this date seem to have shared the conviction that all was 'too late' for their love to flower; instead she appears to have been contriving ways and means. As he wrote in an unpublished sonnet called *At Last*, it could be that Fate's hard toll was paid. 'Oh! as I kneel, enfold mine eyes even there / Within thy breast', he wrote. 'And let our past years and our future meet / In the warm darkness underneath thine hair ...'[26] Once more, the outlook was hopeful. And his *Poems* were about to be published.

But there were the reviews to come. Stillman rightly judged Rossetti both 'the most gifted of his generation' and the most self-absorbed. Yet if 'the centre of his own system', Rossetti was not deluded by conceit, having an accurate sense of his own merits and limitations. 'An artist often hates his own best work in the same way as an envious soul hates the great work of others: it is equally a perpetual reproach,' he once wrote in a notebook.[27] And if in some moods he was sanguine, even boastful, in others he was full of doubts and fears.

'I am anxious that some influential article or articles by the well-affected should appear at once when the book comes out, for certain good reasons,' he had written in February to his old friend Skelton in Edinburgh, who wrote for *Fraser's*. A few key notices, appearing early, would prevent his book being ignored or panned in the prestigious papers. A year before, Skelton had lamented the 'lost' volume once promised to the world; now he was happy to undertake a review.[28] So too was J. F. McLennan, an even older friend from the Hannay days. Even so long after Byron and Keats, the 'Scotch Reviewers' still held a powerful place in literary journalism.

Swinburne, of course, wanted to review *Poems* for the *Fortnightly*, where he had just published *Monna Lisa*. Morris had the same thought. 'Top wants to do a notice of my book,' Gabriel told William. Would the *Academy* be willing? What about the *British Quarterly*, too, where William himself sometimes wrote? 'Do you think Scotus could get the job?' By 22 March he knew also that Sidney Colvin was to review for the *Pall Mall Gazette*, and Joseph Knight for the *Globe*. Both were new friends, partly cultivated for the purpose.[29] Young Buxton Forman, author of the *Tinsley's* articles, was another likely name. With all these in the bag, the 'outside journals', where he had no useful contacts – the *Athenaeum*, *Spectator*, *Saturday Review* – would not matter so much.

To an extent, such manipulation was normal practice. Despite the cultural prestige of poetry, the sophisticated reading public was relatively small; one thousand or even five hundred copies of a new volume was reckoned a good sale, and much depended on reviews. 'Even being laughed at is better than being ignored,' Christina had told Macmillan on the eve of *Goblin Market*'s appearance.[30]

Gabriel did not expect his *Poems* to sell well, but he wanted a *succès d'estime*. And with Swinburne's experience over *Poems and Ballads* still reverberating, he had reason to fear that if not ignored he would be attacked. The dramatic monologue *Jenny* dealt with the unmentionable subject of prostitution. Sonnets like *The Kiss*, *Nuptial Sleep*, *Supreme Surrender*, were avowedly carnal, describing coital events seldom if ever heard in polite verse. So it was wise to worry about the reviews. But the anxiety ran deeper. As a lad, Gabriel had witnessed his father's excitable, histrionic reaction to reviews, and the way Professor Rossetti, after labouring over his texts for years, had been professionally destroyed by the critical response when his great theories about Dante and the Masonic tradition were dismissed and ridiculed. His son's sensitivity to reviews, of his painting as well as poetry, surely owed much to this frightening example.

To his father, critical hostility was evidence of a conspiracy. In the narrow circles of literary and artistic London, Gabriel knew also that personal partiality coloured much reviewing. Indeed, though he could be disinterested, his own intemperate responses to individuals and their works frequently sprang from animosity. And now, perhaps through something Fred Stephens said when Sir Charles Dilke became its proprietor in 1869, he believed the *Athenaeum* was ill-disposed towards him. If publication and favourable publicity in the first reviews were timed together, he told William at an early stage, 'Dilke might perhaps be bilked yet ...'[31]

Furthermore, a hostile Scotch reviewer was already stalking the Rossettis in the person of Robert Buchanan, for whom the normally mild (though not indifferent) William had already developed a 'peculiar abhorrence'.

Like many another man of parts carving out a career in literary London, Buchanan was a jobbing journalist and hopeful poet, who wrote and reviewed for the *Athenaeum, Morning Star, All the Year Round, Temple Bar* and *Fortnightly*. His slim volumes had lately met with considerable acclaim. He was on good terms with Lewes and Browning. And for several months now he, Swinburne and William had been sparring in the literary columns. According to Buchanan, the *fons et origo* of the quarrel was 'an insulting allusion' by Swinburne to the poems of Buchanan's boyhood friend David Gray, who had died in 1860, although a worse provocation was probably Swinburne's mockery of Buchanan's own verse as 'idyls of the gallows and the gutter' and 'songs of costermongers and their trulls'.[32] The dramatis personae of Buchanan's *London Poems* (1866) included Nell, whose man is hanged for murder, and Liz, a poor flower-girl dying in childbed.

Buchanan's revenge came in 1866, when he described the author of *Poems and Ballads* as 'quite the Absalom of modern bards – long-ringleted, flippant-lipped, down-cheeked, amorous-lidded ...' Swinburne's verse was 'deliberately and impertinently insincere', inspired by pornography, or by Petronius, he wrote in the *Athenaeum*. 'Here, in fact, we have Gito, seated in the tub of Diogenes, conscious of the filth and whining at the stars.' There followed an unsigned satirical squib in the *Spectator*, which amusingly mocked Algernon's excesses:

> Up jumped, with his neck stretching out like a gander,
>   Master Swinburne, and squealed, glaring out through his hair,
> 'All virtue is bosh! Hallelujah for Landor!
>   I disbelieve wholly in everything! There!'
>
> With language so awful he dared then to treat 'em,
>   Miss Ingelow fainted in Tennyson's arms;
> Poor Arnold rushed out, crying 'Saecl' inficetum!'
>   And great bards and small bards were full of alarms:
> Till Tennyson, flaming and red as a gipsy,
>   Struck his fist on the table and uttered a shout:
> 'To the door with the boy! Call a cab! he is tipsy!'
>   And they carried the naughty young gentleman out.

The usually well-mannered William, who had earlier rejoiced that Buchanan's 'Caledonian faeces' were not to 'bedaub the corpse of Keats' in a pocket edition, called this comic doggerel 'vomit', and opened his long defence of *Poems and Ballads* with a gratuitous attack on 'the poor and pretentious poetaster now causing storms in teapots' called Robert Buchanan. Then the sparring abated, until in January 1870 Buchanan sneered at William's book on Shelley, citing absence of new information, coarseness of style and substance, textual emendations and the inclusion of juvenilia.[33]

To Gabriel, this was a 'hideous and bestial attack', even from 'that foetid quarter of the editorial anus' called the *Athenaeum*. He feared he would fare likewise. Thereafter the schoolboy scatology continued, nourished by the *Bogshire Banner*, to which shady paper's editor he confirmed the reviewer's identity. Buchanan was almost certainly 'the special atom of the excremental whole [sic] from which the scent which took us both unawares emanated', he wrote; it was therefore crucial to fix reviews of *Poems* in order 'to catch the obscene organ of his speech at the very moment when it is hitched up for an utterance, and perhaps compel the brain of which it is also the seat, to reconsider its view'.[34] Furthermore, he offered new verses to an old rhyme:

> Who slunk by night to a flash ken,
> And bilked poor Molly Magdalen
> And got a fresh pox there and then?

For the reviled Buchanan was also a rival, whose *London Poems* contained modern monologues not unlike *Jenny*.

Gabriel hated to appear in any way a follower. Years before, he had disputed precedence with Holman Hunt over the Fallen Woman theme in art. Not long since he had remonstrated with Fred Sandys for taking themes for Helen of Troy, Mary Magdalene and Lucrezia Borgia from 'designs made long ago' by himself, claiming that artistically he would 'sustain great injury' by subjects being forestalled. (Sandys responded belligerently, sending £50 to repay Rossetti for their long-past excursion to Winchelsea and pompously 'resigning his friendship'.[35])

It is easy to dismiss such touchiness as artistic jealousy, but the issue was of significance, for originality of subject was the main card with which Victorian artists played for fame. Poaching was as much feared as deplored. And so, too, in poetry. Although *Jenny* had been written long before *London Poems*, it might well seem derivative. Lest he appear the imitator, Rossetti grew increasingly obsessed with organising his reviews in order to outflank Buchanan's 'spite'. He told Ellis that, with luck, the 'Arse-ineum' would be caught off-balance, his planned utterance 'a silent emanation [with] nothing but the smell to enjoy'.

As it happened, their supposed enemy had suffered a nervous collapse and retired to the west of Scotland; Buchanan was not currently reviewing for the *Athenaeum*. On 27 March Rossetti learnt that veteran critic Westland Marston had asked for the book, 'with friendly intentions'. The threat evaporated.

All this worrying went on while he was still hoping to compose a new masterpiece, introducing 'a few further fidgetty changes' to the final text, and worrying equally obsessionally over the printing and binding, having like Morris an artist's idea of the well-made book. From Sussex, he raged impotently at delays which meant that finished copies could not be ready in advance of publication on 23 April, so that paper-bound ones went to reviewers. Then came a vile blunder by the block-cutter, when the binding was cut too wide across the spine, necessitating an extra gathering of blank leaves. Moreover, the stamped O in 'POEMS' and 'ROSSETTI' was 'monstrously big', throwing all out of proportion. Too bad: 'the thing must be shovelled out somehow,' he told Ellis peevishly on 15 April; 'I confess to a passion for managing my own affairs, and thought I had done so in this case.'[36]

Entering into the Rossettian spirit, Joseph Knight was whipping up support among the editors. 'It is a pity to defer sending the books out. Easter is so good a time,' he told Ellis. 'When Parliament reassembles you will not get half the notices.' He himself promised to review *Poems* for the *Globe* and the *Graphic*, as well as the *Sunday Times*. 'Not easy to write three, is it?' he added laconically. To forestall others, he arranged to get the *Globe* notice into print a day or two before publication, as did Sidney Colvin in the *Pall Mall Gazette*. Skelton was on schedule for *Fraser's*. Swinburne sent his review to Morley on 15 April. Morris finished his shortly after a lonely Easter weekend in London. Brown thought it good, he told Jane, although a less guarded comment reveals his real distaste for the task. 'I have done my review, just this moment – ugh!' he wrote to Aglaia Coronio.[37]

There was certainly something rum in Morris reviewing a book by the man who was currently enjoying a country sojourn with his wife. But by the same token, the review helped curb gossip; and in any case Morris, being a successful poet in his own right, was eminently suited to review a new volume from the same 'school'. His exclamation of disgust is likely to reflect not only personal embarrassment but also a well-attested scorn of all critics. 'To think of a beggar making a living by selling his opinions about other people!' he once declared.[38] Unlike Rossetti, Morris set no store by reviews.

If rather hurriedly at the end, *Poems* by D. G. Rossetti was duly launched. On 25 April, he travelled up from Scalands to inscribe gift copies at Ellis's shop in Covent Garden, afterwards lunching with Morris. 'I have just parted from Gabriel (and oysters) at Rules,' Morris told Jane, adding that the book already boasted 250 advance orders. Jane undoubtedly knew this, for Gabriel returned to Scalands by the four o'clock train. He saw no one else, though it was the eve of his mother's seventieth birthday, and even forgot to inscribe this in her copy.

Only authors and their mothers read all reviews. Mrs Rossetti's cuttings file began to bulge. 20 April: *Globe*; 21 April: *Pall Mall Gazette*; 30 April: *Athenaeum*, *Fraser's Magazine* and *Fortnightly Review*; 1 May: *Sunday Times*; 9 May: *Telegraph*; 14 May: *Academy*, *Saturday Review*, *Graphic*; 26 May: *Standard*; 1 June: *New Monthly Magazine*; 11 June: *Spectator* . . .

The book had 'imagination, passion, vivid reality of nature . . . and special subtlety in seizing the half-glimpsed suggestions of thought and feeling', wrote Marston. The poet's genius delighted in tracking feelings to their furthest retreats, and in grasping their most delicate, evanescent traits. In the sonnets, 'it is true that owing to Mr Rossetti's fondness for seizing phases of emotion as airy and shifting as the tints of sunset, some of them may escape the mind of even the most poetical reader, unless he catches at once the writer's point of view and follows him with the intuition of sympathy rather than with the mere vision of intellect.' But this super-subtlety, recording 'life between the mysteries of Love and Death', produced a rare and noble result, imbued with beauty.[39]

The volume was 'lighted by the authentic fire of the imagination', and the poems 'are almost without exception products of the high poetic faculty in certain of its highest and most intense moods', pronounced Skelton. 'This cardinal fact being conceded, I am ready to own if required that – not free from quaintness, eccentricity, mysticism of a sort – it is a publication in certain aspects fitted to startle and perplex that British Philistine with whose features Mr Matthew Arnold has made us familiar.'[40] He quoted lengthily from *The Blessed Damozel*, *Ave*, *Sister Helen* and the less lubricious sonnets, before concluding that here was a gift of a very high order of vision, directness, simplicity, concentration and insight – 'none higher, none rarer'.

The subject of *Jenny* was 'difficult for a modern poet to deal with, but necessary for a man to think of', wrote Morris firmly; 'it is thought of here with the utmost depths of feeling, pity and insight.' Not confusing poet with author, he stressed the dramatic nature of all the pieces, and ended with a ringing endorsement that they were the 'most complete' lyrics of their time: 'no difficulty is avoided in them – no subject is treated vaguely, languidly, or heartlessly: as there is no commonplace or second-hand thought left in them to be atoned for by beauty of execution, so no thought is allowed to overshadow that beauty of art which compels a real poet to speak in verse and not in prose. Nor do I know what lyrics of any time are to be called *great* if we are to deny that title to these.'[41]

An acute ear might detect some discomfort in the repeated negatives here, as if the critic could not quite commend positive values; but elsewhere in his intelligent and judicious review Morris also wrote of 'realizing mysticism', intensity, concentration, patience, energy, beauty and magnificence. *The Stream's Secret* in particular had high musical qualities 'and a certain stateliness of movement about it which coming among its real and deep feeling makes it very telling and impressive'.

Morris's review was, like its author, 'direct and complete' and an honour and a profit to the book, Rossetti responded. Marston was 'very good and kindly', while Skelton was inane but well-meaning and obviously useful.[42]

In swooping periods over eighteen close pages in the *Fortnightly*, Swinburne was effusive, but also attentive and perspicacious. He devoted space to the poems' religious tenor, for example, as well as detailing the particular 'masculine tenderness' of *Jenny*. He gave a nuanced reading of the poet as painter, painter as poet, true to the distinctions of each art. With a more positive vocabulary than Morris he too praised majesty and melody, energy and emotion, strength and sweetness, affluence and simplicity, depth, light, harmony, the flesh-and-spirit union of manner and matter. And he concluded with a personal tribute to Rossetti's standing among the younger generation:

> Born a light-bearer and leader of men, he has always fulfilled his office with readiness and done his work with might. Help and strength and light and fresh life have long been gifts of his giving, and freely given as only great gifts can be. And now that at length we receive from hands yet young and strong this treasury of many years, the gathered flower of youth and ripe firstlings of manhood, a fruit of the topmost branch 'more golden than gold', all men may witness and assure themselves what manner of harvest the life of this man was to bear . . .[43]

This was 'too overpoweringly flattering', protested the light-bearer himself. But gratifying: Gabriel was buoyant once again. 'Dear old Darling of 70,' he wrote to his mother; '[y]ou will be glad to hear that the first edition is almost exhausted and that Ellis is going to press with the second thousand copies', together with a few special large-format copies. Moreover, the book had already earned £300 – 'which is not so bad for poetry, particularly if it goes on'. Altogether he was 'wonderfully better'.[44]

There was no glimpse of Buchanan. Even an underwhelming notice in the *Saturday Review*, attributed to Palgrave, was 'grudgingly civil' – stupid and incompetent, but not hurtful. Such notices indeed served only to underline the general acclaim.

It is as well that, though Rossetti sent Browning a copy of *Poems* and received thanks, he did not hear the elder poet's frank opinion. 'Yes – I have read Rossetti's poems – and poetical they are – *scented* with poetry, as it were like trifles of various sorts you take out of a cedar or sandal-wood box; you know I hate the effeminacy of his school – the men that dress up like women – that use obsolete forms, too, and archaic accentuations to seem soft – fancy a man calling it a li*lý* – li*liés* and so on,' he told a friend in June; 'Swinburne started this, with other like Belialisms – witness his harp-playér, etc. . . . then, how I hate "Love" as a lubberly naked young man putting his arms here and his wings there, about a pair of lovers – a fellow they would kick away, in the reality.'[45]

But for the while, all was strength and sweetness. Years later, the critic Walter Pater recalled how Rossetti's volume 'came at last to satisfy a long-standing curiosity' regarding their author, whose poems where spoken of but largely unseen, like his pictures. 'For those poems were the work of a painter,' he continued, 'understood to belong to, and to be indeed the great leader of, a new school then rising into note.'[46]

CHAPTER TWENTY-ONE

Painter and Poet

At a stroke, it seemed, D. G. Rossetti had transformed from painter into poet. As Scott observed, poetry had been his first link with Gabriel, and within weeks Rossetti echoed this, saying he 'ought never to have been a painter but a poet instead'. More truly, however, he had become a poet as well as a painter, and by the end of 1869 was already envisaging a dual career. 'When I publish poetry I may very possibly take a fancy to exhibit some pictures about the same time,' he told old Miss Losh.[1]

But in practice he had done no new painting for many months, and his creative impulses in visual art were in abeyance, perhaps terminally. He was obliged to refashion his professional identity. 'My own belief is that I am a poet primarily, and that it is my poetic tendencies that chiefly give value to my pictures,' he wrote on the eve of publication; 'only painting being – what poetry is not – a livelihood – I have put my poetry chiefly in that form.' At the same time, 'the bread-and-cheese question' had led to a good deal of his painting 'being pot-boiling and no more'. Whereas 'my verse, being unprofitable, has remained (as much as I have found time for) unprostituted'.[2]

'I have often said that to be an artist is just the same thing as to be a whore,' he remarked later. This rather startling view of his art – not vouchsafed to patrons – was surely an exaggeration, signifying only that an artist who wished to sell work had to please the purchasers. However, it helps illuminate his view of poetry as a medium for the deepest and most abstract ideas and feelings, expressed through language with its own aesthetic techniques of imagery, assonance, rhyme and metre. At the same time, from boyhood he had a dual verbal and visual imagination, which was rarely satisfied with one art form.

Roughly speaking, Rossetti's verse falls into three categories – narrative or lyric pieces of relatively simple (though sometimes elliptical) structure and language; discursive longer works on relatively public themes; and compressed, densely-wrought sonnets with abstract or ideal motifs that yield their meaning with difficulty. Similarly, in art, he ranged from small but not merely decorative works through ideal portraiture, allegorical figures and dramatic scenes. He was customarily identified as a 'poetic' painter, in the sense of choosing non-realistic subjects and a heightened style, but this did not mean his pictures were illustrations to poems; indeed Rossetti always insisted on an independent pictorial conception even where actual texts were cited, and by the same token, vehemently asserted that his poetry was not pictorial, but entirely free of 'the trick of what is called word-painting' in the sense of vivid verbal description of scenes, colours, chiaroscuro. In terms of their forms and concerns, the poems were poetic, the paintings pictorial. The poetry might be that of a painter and the pictures those of a poet, but the art forms were distinct. On this issue Swinburne relevantly invoked the lost sonnets of Raphael and the extant ones of Michelangelo to assert 'the double glory' of Rossetti's genius, which equally showed 'no confusion of claims, no invasion of rights'.[3]

However, when Rossetti spoke of putting his poetry chiefly in the form of painting, he meant that both strove to realise dramatised inner feeling. 'As with recreated forms in painting,' he wrote, 'so I should wish to deal in poetry chiefly with personified emotions; and in carrying out my scheme of the '*House of Life*' (if ever I do so) shall try to put in action a complete *dramatis personae* of the soul.'

By the soul, he appears to have meant what is now called the self – the modern, Western, post-Romantic reflexive sense of individual identity. By 'personified emotions' we may understand visual and verbal images expressing the experiences, thoughts and feelings of that self, so that these appear like interacting characters in the inner life-drama of the soul.

Between the printing of his first sonnets in the *Fortnightly*, subtitled 'Of Life, Love and Death', and the preparation of his 1870 volume, Rossetti conceived the notion of calling his new poems 'The House of Life'. To begin with, the architecture of this scheme was not fully in place, although one obvious inspiration was the *Vita Nuova*, which can be read as a sequence of *sonneti* and *canzone* interspersed with a prose explication, all together creating an emotional autobiography. Other models are to be found in the Songs and Sonnets of Petrarch, Spenser's *Amoretti*, the 154 Sonnets of Shakespeare, and the 44 *Sonnets from the Portuguese*. By the time of publication, Rossetti's sequence comprised 61 pieces, but was explicitly described as still in progress: according to the head-note, the 50 sonnets and 11 songs were 'towards a Work to be called "The House of Life" ' which would in due course be divided into sections. When later completed, the songs were in fact dropped, in favour of a simple sequence of 100 sonnets, (in evident homage to the lost 'century of sonnets' by Raphael, to which Browning's *One Word More* alluded). Rossetti's sequence was presented in two parts: 'Youth and Change' dealing almost exclusively with love, and 'Change and Fate', with more diverse themes.

The title, however, invokes another metaphor, not that of a drama with characters, but that of life as a house. Gabriel never gave any explanation for his choice of title, according to William who, knowing his brother was 'fond of anything related to astrology or horoscopy', glossed its meaning as equivalent to astrological notation, with the phases of Youth, Love and Change passing through 'the House of Life', as the sun (say) is said to be 'in the house of Leo'.[4] This is ingenious and plausible, though uncorroborated by the poems, which show no such schema. Alternative inspiration may have come from Donne, whose own title 'Songs and Sonets' was close to Rossetti's description of his sequence at this date, and who wrote thus in *The Canonization*:

> And if unfit for tombs and hearse
> Our legend be, it will be fit for verse;
>   And if no piece of chronicle we prove,
>   We'll build in sonnets pretty rooms;
>   As well a well-wrought urn become
> The greatest ashes, as half-acre tombs,
>   And by these hymns, all shall approve
>   Us canonized for love ...

In Rossetti's case, Life would thus be conceived as a house with many mansions, or a dwelling with different rooms, the varying moods and moments occupied by the soul. To build a poetic architecture on this structure was to make each poem a room, or local habitation, for a multiplicity of moving emotions; passing from one to another in the permutation of self into selves, according to chance and change. Doors are chosen, or closed. The soul experiences and expresses grief, joy, hope, despair, discretely but also within a unity that is the 'house' or individual consciousness.

Browning saw himself as a poetic dramatist, giving voices and histories to different characters, entering into worlds apparently very unlike his own. In *Pippa Passes* the heroine's journey offers a moving image of the city's inhabitants. *The Ring and the Book* tells one story from differing perspectives, as in a court of law. Like *Pippa*, Rossetti's narrative pieces *Jenny, Dante at Verona, A Last Confession,* even *Eden Bower,* are verbally recreated forms of characters in their author's imagination, whose world he enters. *The House of Life* is by contrast as it were a single story told from within, in multiple moods. Figuratively somewhat like the real Tudor House, the sequence resembles a mysterious residence through which the poet wanders, with rooms that open from each other and many mirrors giving the illusion of other spaces, similar but subtly altered, with unexplored cellars beneath and attics above. There is a lot of emotional furniture – memories, regrets, desires, hopes – and a great deal of self-scrutiny both in self-addressed words and in the reflecting glasses whose ancient silvering returns an often shadowy image.

One wonders if, at a subliminal level, sonnets like rooms were linked to pictures in rectangular frames, each a confined 'space' for verbal or visual articulation of an idea or feeling, each replete with symbol and ornament.

Though Rossetti would write that his *House of Life* was 'a whole poem' in which each item was 'one sonnet-stanza'[5] (the Italian *stanza*, meaning 'room', furnishing another source for the architectural figure), he also disclaimed any premeditated plan, preferring to build his poetic structure piecemeal. 'I hardly ever do produce a sonnet except on the basis of special momentary emotion,' he told Scott in 1871, acknowledging that each was prompted by a specific impulse or experience rather than written to a preconceived plan. Each, in the phrase later used to introduce the sequence, was 'a moment's monument'. Some emotion was dominant, and he wrote a sonnet regarding it, added William. 'When a good number had been written, they came to form, if considered collectively, a sort of record of his feelings and experiences, his reading of the problems of life – an inscribed tablet of his mind.'[6]

On this basis, the soul whose emotions are personified is a split, fragmented self, which dramatises other moods and feelings as other persons. 'Whence came his feet into my field, and why?' inquired *He and I*, added to *Poems* in proof stage. 'How is it that he sees it all so drear? / How do I see his seeing, and how hear / The name his bitter silence knows it by?' Once, the field had nourished his own soul. How should this other find it lifeless?

> He, or I?
> Lo! this new Self now wanders round my field,
>   With plaints for every flower, and for each tree
>   A moan, the sighing wind's auxiliary:
> And o'er sweet waters of my life, that yield
> Unto his lips no draught but tears unseal'd,
>   Even in my place he weeps. Even I, not he.

Eloquently, the sonnet entitled *Inclusiveness* was originally positioned to open *The House of Life*. Here the different moods are like a succession of 'changing guests' who eat at a common table, each life 'a soul's board set daily with new food', and shared experience like a house with different inmates:

> May not this ancient room thou sit'st in dwell
>   In separate living souls for joy or pain?
>   Nay, all its corners may be painted plain
> Where Heaven shows pictures of some life spent well;
>   And may be stamped, a memory all in vain
> Upon the sight of lidless eyes in Hell.

William, incidentally, noted that the title was misleading. 'The gist of the sonnet ... is that one same thing has different aspects and influences to different persons and according to different conditions,' he wrote.[7] It might be the modern condition, but all his life Gabriel had been subject to contradictory, alternating, capricious impulses that he struggled in vain to integrate. 'Lo! the soul's sphere of infinite images! / What sense shall count them?' he asked in *The Soul's Sphere*.

'These fragments have I shored against my ruin,' a later poet would memorably write. Much has been said of the post-Romantic disintegration of the self, the industrialised atomisation of man, the vain struggle for psychic cohesion.

Virtually all the love sonnets in *The House of Life* were inspired by Janey, since all except one postdated the emergence of Rossetti's passion for her. However, they cannot be read as emotional autobiography, or unmediated personal expression in the confessional mode. All are carefully artificed poems within a chosen verse structure whose content is traditionally elaborate, condensed and complex. Since his late teens Rossetti had known the formula, most strikingly deployed in the *dolce stil nuovo* by Dante, to blend the idealisation of Love with what is claimed to be direct experience. He also knew Shakespeare's notoriously compressed Sonnets, whose meanings still defy agreed interpretation, and in the years after 1870 he drafted several versions of a statement designed to prevent his own being read too personally. 'To the Reader of The House of Life,' begins one note. 'These poems are in no sense "occasional". The "life" <recorded> involved is neither *my* life nor *your* life, but life <representative> purely and simply as tripled with Love and Death.' Later, this evolved into a longer statement which declared, truly, that 'to speak in the first person is often to speak most vividly', and added that 'these emotional poems' dealt with 'life representative, as associated with love and death, with aspiration and foreboding, or with ideal art and beauty. Whether the recorded moment exist in the region of fact or thought is a question indifferent to the Muse, so long only as her touch can quicken it.'[8] Works of art are works of art.

DGR with his sister Christina, mother Frances and brother William Rossetti in the garden at 16 Cheyne Walk, September 1863, photographed by C. L. Dodgson (Lewis Carroll)

DGR with Algernon Charles Swinburne (left), Fanny Cornforth and William Rossetti, in the garden at 16 Cheyne Walk, 1863

DGR with William Bell Scott and John Ruskin, 1863, photographed by William Downey

DGR, *St George and the Dragon*, stained glass window design, 1861–2

DGR, *Golden head by golden head*, title page to Christina Rossetti's *Goblin Market*, 1862.

DGR, '*Miss Rossetti can point to work which could not easily be mended*': DGR's caricature of his sister Christina, 1866, quoting from a review of her poetry in *The Times*.

RIGHT DGR, study of unidentified African-American boy, 1865, for *The Beloved*. This boy was spotted at the door of a London hotel and employed to pose for the figure of a child holding a vase of roses in the finished picture now in the Tate Gallery.

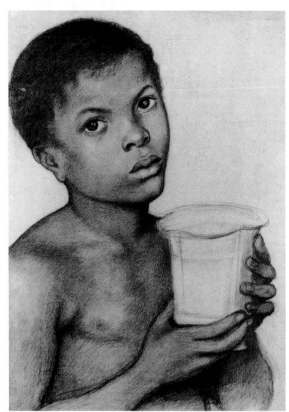

BELOW LEFT DGR, study for *Sweet Tooth*, 1863, drawn from Agnes Manetti, one of the models Rossetti employed during the 1860s.

BELOW RIGHT DGR, study of Kiomi Gray, 1865, for *The Beloved*. Kiomi Gray was a Romany woman who also modelled for A.F. Sandys.

Jane Morris, 1865, from a sequence of photographs taken at Cheyne Walk.

DGR, 1863, from a carte-de-visite photograph.

DGR,
Proserpine, 1874

DGR, *The M's at Ems*, 1869, caricature drawn when Jane and William Morris ('the M's') were at Bad Ems in the Rhineland.

Ford Madox Brown, *DGR as seen August 18, 1879*

DGR, *The Wombat's Death*, 1869, showing himself mourning for his pet wombat. The drawing is accompanied by verses reading: 'I never reared a young Wombat / To glad me with his pin-hole eye / But, when he most was sweet & fat / And tail-less, he was sure to die!'

Henry T. Dunn, *D. G. Rossetti and Theodore Watts in the Drawing-room at Cheyne Walk*, 1882, done partly from memory after DGR's death.

May Morris, *Kelmscott Manor*, 1877

RIGHT Frederic J. Shields, *DGR at the Easel*, 22 May 1880. DGR is shown painting *The Day-dream*

BELOW DGR, *Self-Portrait sketch*, late 1870s

ABOVE DGR's tombstone, designed by Ford Madox Brown, in the churchyard at Birchington-on-Sea, 1998

RIGHT DGR, *The Question*, 1875, study for a projected painting.

Thus in his poems as in his pictures, Rossetti aimed to draw from within a vivid expression of feeling that could be shared with the world. To bring 'various thought' within the 'rigid structural limits' of the sonnet form was 'an effort of precisely the kind which must ever be most tempting to the practised artist', he told John Heraud this year, speaking more for himself than in general. And he warned John Payne that the 'pouring forth of poetical material is the greatest danger for the affluent imagination', both concrete form and 'immense concentration' were required before the raw materials of verse were transformed into a poem.[9] The aim was not merely to express, but to blend thought and image in Coleridge's crucible, and with such alchemy to make something unique.

Heraud and Payne were among a number of younger writers who had sent their slim volumes to Mr D. G. Rossetti, hoping to flatter and be flattered. Though he was old enough to know better, Gabriel was flattered, and ready to condescend. 'I see you allow yourself the wide range of treatment which seems to me necessary if an unfettered scope of ideas is to be dealt with,' he wrote in July on receipt of Heraud's *In-Gathering*, before drawing attention to the solecism of starting a sonnet with a couplet. In November, when Payne sent *The Masque of Shadows*, humbly inscribed as 'a token (such as it is) of admiration of Mr Rossetti's genius', he was invited to dine and offered similar words of encouragement and warning. 'The Building of the Dream' was a romance full of 'imaginative picture work' but length and looseness were to be avoided, or 'the time is apt to come soon when the poet finds that he has written as much as anyone can ever read ...' Payne was gratified but not convinced, and continued to pour forth, preferring the exuberant Swinburnian model. With every volume Rossetti proffered the same advice and long after his death Payne responded in kind, asserting that Rossetti had talent but no genius. 'He laboured at his work. He would write a sonnet twelve times. There was no spontaneity in him.'[10]

A third newcomer was Arthur O'Shaughnessy, whose *The Epic of Women* contained verses of such uneven merit that some remained opaque after several readings. Was the oddly named *Bisclaveret* about sin? Rossetti asked, while praising the poem's terseness of language. It was in fact about a werewolf, replied the author. Of course, 'after your word of enlightenment, light it is', responded Rossetti; but surely the word should appear somewhere, to guide the reader? However, he continued graciously, 'obscurity is a little byword which we modern bards have a habit of passing round to each other as we used to do slips of paper in school-time. Each opus in turn gets caught as the holder of it by our Schoolmaster the British critic and duly rapped on the knuckles.' Yet critics were in reality 'poor trembling drudges' liable to be summarily dismissed like teachers later on in the term; poets did well to ignore their scolding.

Later, he would laugh when O'Shaughnessy, who verbally affected the wilder shores of Swinburnian transgression, married in conventional manner. It was comic to see 'so lawless a bard, who almost grudges sympathy to any views short of Baudelaire's, suddenly pairing off with the excellent, homely and not juvenile Miss M.', he wrote.[11] For the moment he greeted the young writer as further evidence that a 'contemporary English school of poetry' was coming into being, with a respect for style 'as a settled and technical quality – a gauge of craftsmanship without which admission to the guild cannot be granted'.

'New bards are rife,' he told Alice on 1 November, after dining at Fitzroy Square in the company of several, including Payne, O'Shaughnessy and Nolly Brown, who to his father's immense pride also displayed literary talent. He judged that their advent indicated 'a decided advance on the practice of the art *as* an art in our day – that is I mean they *contribute* to the result which I think is becoming apparent in poetic craftsmanship.'[12]

Yet another recruit was the son of Westland Marston, the veteran critic to whom he, Morris and Swinburne had reason to be grateful for critical recognition. Blinded in infancy, Philip Marston was now twenty. '[A] good deal of interest will no doubt be felt in him when he comes forward as a poet,' Rossetti wrote, urging Ellis to publish the boy's work. 'The book will no doubt be reviewed *everywhere* and much talked of.'[13]

'We modern bards'; 'the contemporary English school'; a new guild of poetic craftsmanship: evidently he sensed a new wave of supporters. Twenty years since, he had aspired to launch a brotherhood of poets as well as painters, using *The Germ* alongside the PRB. A decade later, Morris and Swinburne had adopted him as mentor. The high hopes of youth were much in mind as *Hand and Soul* was reprinted in the December *Fortnightly*, introducing a new generation to Chiaro dell' Erma who desired to draw (a pertinent pun) images from the depths of his heart and soul, and had a vision of a fair woman, clad in green and grey.

Not all the nascent poets were young, and another new acquaintance took Gabriel back to his days of youth. Now sixty-two, Thomas Gordon Hake was author of *Vates, or the Philosophy of Madness*, first published in 1840, which had seized Rossetti's adolescent soul. When Dr Hake reviewed *Poems*, friendship followed. It was very pleasing that his book should count among its reviewers a poet whose work had elicited his eager interest and curiosity in boyhood, wrote Gabriel. Could Hake come to dinner next Thursday?[14] Reared in an older school, Hake held to outdated formal correctness, and criticised metrical irregularities in *The Stream's Secret*. Rossetti begged to disagree, arguing that on the contrary, variety of modulation was 'absolutely a law in passionate lyrical poetry'. Then, volunteering to advise on Hake's own projected volume, he discovered the full depth of the gulf between them, for Hake's verse partook of the most contorted Della Cruscan qualities, harking back to the 1790s. In a 'choral work' called *Madeline*, the form was perfect throughout, but the subject as baffling as O'Shaughnessy's werewolf, with a succession of half-identified figures leading to an intricate tale of seduction and revenge. 'The mixture of real historical personages with events which in ordinary phraseology must be termed magical ones, and the strange and apparently arbitrary adoption of such an identity as Laura's where only a beneficent spirit of some sort was needed – nay the very name Laura which ... was undoubtedly borne by a human lady to whom Petrarch's homage has generally been imputed – seem to me to pile up difficulties unnecessarily,' Rossetti wrote, struggling with the story. Personally, however, Dr Hake (now retired from medicine) proved a cordial guest, with a wide range of interests.

Soon it became the habit for 'literary fellows' to read new verses to the assembled company at Tudor House, just as once Hunt, Deverell, Jack Tupper and members of 'the Hannay set' had brought their latest productions to the studio. In such company, Rossetti had a sympathetic sounding-board and stimulus for his own composition. With characteristic generosity, however, he urged the merits of all on editors as well as publishers, always willing to use his name helpfully, although sad to say his generosity was greater than his judgement; none of the new-fledged bards became swans. Briefly, he harboured visions of a mutually supportive group who would all publish with Ellis, alongside himself and Morris. Ellis declined to take Payne or Hake, but he did welcome Christina, whom in 1870 Gabriel persuaded to leave Macmillan. Still invalid, she saw *Commonplace*, her collection of short fiction, appear at the same time as her brother's *Poems*. Delighted with the success of *Poems*, Ellis urged Gabriel to prepare a second collection, and agreed to reissue *Early Italian Poets*.

Ellis had also agreed to publish Swinburne's new volume, *Songs before Sunrise*. Dedicated to Giuseppe Mazzini, Italian patriot and statesman, whose devoted disciple Swinburne had become in the intervals between periods of inebriation, the volume contained red republican hymns to political liberty in every country of Europe, with those featuring France the most intemperate. In private, Rossetti had happily bandied blasphemy with Algernon. Now he was dismayed to find that the proposed volume was to contain *Before a Crucifix*, on the deity worshipped by the downtrodden French peasantry, and a double sonnet on Napoleon III, ironically entitled *The Saviour of Society*. Hastily, he took steps to warn Ellis. 'The "Christ" anathematised in the *Crucifix* is the priests' corrupted and falsified God –

not the true one,' he explained. 'But still this might not appear clearly to everyone to whom the phraseology would give a shock.' The double sonnet was even worse, and might even be liable to prosecution. Alarmed, Ellis withdrew his offer to publish. Annoyed and agitated, Swinburne declared that he would go elsewhere, which threatened to break up the 'little group of authors' that Gabriel was fostering. He therefore undertook to persuade Algernon to omit these pieces from his collection; after all, he told Ellis, with a fine flash of bilingual punning, what else could be done when *Poeta nascitur non fit* for publication?'[15]

Arguing that Swinburne's genius deserved a wider circle of readers than could be won by verses designed to offend, Rossetti also disclosed the limits to his own tolerance. Though the *Saviour* sonnets were consummately written, their theme would bring down a storm of obloquy that no aesthetic criteria could defeat. Moreover, the supreme nobility of Christ's character ought to exempt it from being used in such a manner: here, even his own sensibilities were offended. He might no longer believe in revealed religion, but the teachings of childhood remained powerful: Christ's name was sacred. 'Do, do, my dear Swinburne, withdraw these Sonnets,' he pleaded, speaking frankly. 'This is my birthday, by the bye,' he added in a postscript: 'So make me the birthday gift I ask of you ...' It was an odd request, and Swinburne demurred. 'I cannot understand how anyone, friend or foe, can see anything in it but an indignant protest against the blasphemous misapplication to Bonaparte of the traditional titles of Christ,' he wrote later.[16] But whether in deference to Gabriel's birthday or his argument, he agreed to withdraw the sonnets.

In return, Rossetti took Swinburne briefly under his roof again. It was a mistake, as he might have known had he been present at the Arts Club on 2 May when Arthur Munby ran into Algernon. They spoke of Gabriel's *Poems*, Swinburne's review, Victor Hugo and Cardinal Newman. Then 'the wild poet got upon Christianity, and foamed and danced as his manner is'. When a clerical member came in, Munby succeeded in diverting Swinburne on to Shakespeare's Sonnets, which 'however led to worse talk; he expressed a horror of sodomy, yet *would* go on talking about it; and an actual admiration of Lesbianism ...' He was in fact heading for a crisis, which may have been the reason he was allowed to stay at Chelsea during June. 'Gabriel and Fanny have nursed me up again,' he reported with amnesiac insouciance to William. 'I am staying here in Cheyne Walk for a few days.' A day or so later, when he came in drunker than ever, Rossetti remonstrated sharply, vainly hoping he would sign the pledge. Swinburne then returned to his lodgings, where a week later windows were smashed in a violent attack of delirium tremens. Brown answered an urgent summons, a male nurse was engaged, and Admiral Swinburne once again came to collect his errant son.[17]

Poor dear little Swinburne, commented Gabriel; how would it all end? If it went on any longer, commented Scott, 'he had better die'. At Cheyne Walk the servants received orders to tell unexpected visitors that Mr Rossetti was 'not at home'. Woolner was a surprise casualty of the ruling, when he called to add his congratulations to those publicly heaped on *Poems*. But when in August Swinburne sent two new sonnets dedicated to the memory of Armand Barbès, a leader of the July Revolution, Gabriel and William judged them 'decidedly fine', always hoping that sobriety would restore the friend they knew. Gabriel even made a brief, oblique reference to the Franco-Prussian War, regretting that *Songs before Sunrise* was as yet unpublished, now that Louis Napoleon's nemesis had arrived.[18]

The war made Ellis delay the republication of *Early Italian Poets*. Meanwhile, Gabriel rested on the laurels of poetic fame, and returned to painting. To mark his new status, G. F. Watts asked him to sit for the portrait series of Eminent Men he was creating, to bestow on the nation. Well-lit, with his high-domed forehead rising above dark, pensive eyes, Rossetti's head is invested with a sculptural nobility and intellectual demeanour resembling Shakespeare's, while full lips beneath untrimmed whiskers betoken a sensuous spirit.[19] This, at any rate, was the common opinion: physiognomic theories and personal acquaintance both asserting the dual nature of DGR's character.

Confidence flowed back with the success of *Poems* and regained strength of sight. The *Times* review of the RA this year had hailed Burne-Jones as chief of the 'exclusive' school which Rossetti himself had always thought to lead. Illness and absence had thus nibbled at his reputation; now, he determined to achieve his long-projected *chef d'œuvre*, the large oil version of Beatrice lying dead, *Dante's Dream*. While poetry enhanced his fame, by the same token he needed to re-establish his position as a painter, lest he be said to practise both arts but master neither.

William Graham had commissioned the work a year since, for 1,500 guineas. Several other commissions were outstanding, including *Beata Beatrix* for the Cowpers, *Sibylla Palmifera* for Rae, *Pandora* for John Graham and two further works for William Graham, *Mariana* and *Found*. The last of these was being enlarged, and with assistance from Dunn and Murray work was under way on others, but *Dante's Dream* took precedence. Graham had repeatedly urged that Rossetti should complete and exhibit 'important' works, in order to influence the direction of art and make his name 'a household word amongst those who know true genius when they see it'.[20] Though now somewhat sceptical of 'genius', Gabriel's long-standing vision of his vocation had lately received indirect support from an Oxford scholar, writing on Leonardo in the *Fortnightly* in terms that echoed Rossetti's own view of art at its highest. Leonardo used sacred legends 'not for their own sake, or as mere objects for pictorial realisation, but as a symbolical language of fancies all his own', wrote thirty-year-old Walter Pater:

> Other artists have been as careless of present or future applause, in self-forgetfulness, or because they set moral or political ends above the ends of art; but in him this solitary culture of beauty seems to have hung upon a kind of self-love, and a carelessness in the work of art of all but art itself. Out of the secret places of a unique temperament he brought strange blossoms and fruits hitherto unknown; and for him the novel impression conveyed, the exquisite effect woven, counted as an end in itself – the perfect end ...

Big pictures were demonstrably ambitious. Leighton's *Syracusan Procession* was fourteen feet wide, Millais's *Jephtha* four feet by five, Hunt's *Isabella* six feet high. To date, the largest of Rossetti's finished works were only three feet square, and most contained but a single half-length figure. Graham stipulated that *Dante's Dream* be no more than six feet wide, to hang in his London house, but within this the figures could be virtually life-size. Rather than be simply scaled up from the watercolour, still jealously treasured by Ellen Heaton, the whole composition required reworking. Dunn was instructed to get the studies together. Several items from the common stock of medieval costumes kept by Morris were retrieved from Murray – a tunic and underkirtle for the women, 'an angel's long dress for Love' and a gown for Dante. Brown advised on the use of benzine in place of linseed oil, and on the proper proportions of the figures. 'My soul is vexed with the following point,' Rossetti explained. 'The women in my picture being 62 inches high, will it do for the man to be 65 inches, or should he be taller? I've got him traced on the canvas, and fancy he looks all right, but am rather nervous about begining to paint him.'[21]

He ordered new pigments, including the expensive ultramarine made from lapis lazuli. Alexa came to model for one attendant, Marie Spartali for the other. Dante's head was drawn from Stillman and Howell, and Beatrice from Janey, reclining with head thrown back against a pillow and hands clasped to the throat. While draperies were painted from studies, heads and hands were done 'from nature' – that is from the model – and Gabriel claimed to be able to paint a head in a single sitting, which William rather doubted. To either side of the bier, vistas of Florence are glimpsed, showing medieval roofs and towers. The Netherlandish windmill of the watercolour vanished, and Dunn was set to construct a wooden model to ensure the half-seen staircase was in correct perspective. In each opening, a red-winged bird flies free.

The most awkward part was the personified figure of Love, a quasi-medieval winged boy carrying Eros's quiver. Centrally placed, he leans low to kiss Beatrice's lips while holding Dante's hand, a linking gesture symbolic of the poet's love for the lady. Figuratively, in keeping with traditional iconography, this is coherent and taken from the lines Rossetti himself translated from the *Vita Nuova*:

> Then Love spoke thus: 'Now all shall be made clear:
> Come and behold our lady where she lies.'

Love's first incarnation was young Edward Hughes, nine-year-old nephew of Arthur, before his face was 'discarded as having too much of the Greek Adonis about it'. Then came sixteen-year-old Johnston Forbes Robertson, son of a dramatist known to Rossetti. There were three sittings, of ninety minutes each, Rossetti keeping his model entertained throughout with lively and interesting talk. Later, he recalled Rossetti's yellow ivory skin, deep-set smudged eyes and flatteringly adult conversation. 'At the first sitting I remember he said, "I am sorry, my dear Johnston, there is no beautiful creature for you to kiss." I can feel my blushes now.'[22]

Although time was inevitably spent dining out, receiving congratulations and sitting to Watts, for most of the summer Gabriel was in his own studio, 'fully occupied' with *Dante's Dream*. 'A big picture is glorious work, really rousing to every faculty one has or ever thought one might have, and I hope I am doing better in this than hitherto,' he told Fred Shields in mid-August. 'In another fortnight or so I shall have all the figures painted on the canvas and only the glazing of the draperies left to do.' He would leave the background till later, planning to spend a month or so out of London after completing the figures. Despite painting so consistently, he was feeling well. 'I feel no inconvenience with my eyes now, though working good hours and never missing a day.'[23] *Laus deo*, the affliction appeared to be over.

As painting progressed, sanguine plans were made for the future. After *Dante's Dream*, he would paint up both *Mary Magdalene* and *Cassandra*, compositions now nearly a decade old. He would do the Medusa picture too, and finish *Found* and *La Pia*. Further stimulus was provided when a review of *Poems* in the August issue of *Blackwood's* characterised the author as a poet 'who keeps his productions for some twenty years in the dark, before he condescends to unfold them to the common eye ...' and likewise 'a painter, so contemptuous of common public opinion that he refuses to exhibit his pictures'.[24] As regards poetry, the reviewer – veteran

Margaret Oliphant – was mistaken, for the poems had not been wilfully withheld. As regards painting, however, the point was valid, for Rossetti's well-known refusal to exhibit easily suggested egoistic pride. For too long, he had produced cabinet-style pictures for private consumption; now *Dante's Dream* made a more serious play for public recognition.

At over ten feet wide by seven feet high, the canvas was almost twice the size specified. It blocked up the whole studio, squeezing other pictures into dark holes and corners. He aimed to complete by the year's end. 'I haven't shown it as yet to anyone, thinking it best to keep it to myself till finished,' he told Aglaia Coronio on 7 October.[25]

Indeed, he was such a slave to the work that other matters hardly impinged, and he told Shields he had felt only transient distress – 'indeed I might almost say none at all' – when reading the *Blackwood's* review. France's declaration of war against Prussia in July and subsequent capitulation at Sedan were barely remarked, even though William and Swinburne were as fully *engagés* as it was possible for neutral Britons to be, hailing the downfall of Louis Napoleon, and many like Christina shared the national mood of 'horror at this horrible war', hoping that in victory the Prussians would be magnanimous and not subject Paris to military occupation.

Although in later weeks his sympathy was roused for the Communards and for Courbet in particular, Gabriel's only expressed concern in 1870 was the damage to the English art market caused by the flight of French artists seeking refuge as German armies advanced. The simultaneous influx of artists' models was a compensating benefit. British painters exchanged details. 'My dear Ned,' wrote Rossetti tersely. 'Another French model called on me yesterday ... Address: Mlle Léontine, chez Mme Galliant, 3 St George's St, Battersea Park.' A third, lodging in Soho, was taller, but did not look very promising. 'I haven't yet seen her stripped. Dunn found her.'[26]

When the farm near Scalands went unvisited all summer, Scott surmised that this was because Janey could not be persuaded to join Rossetti there, which may have been the case. But she came to Cheyne Walk to sit from 25 to 27 July, and again on 12 August, so it is more likely that Gabriel felt no need of a vacation. '[T]he luxury of working after so much enforced idleness has been so great to me that I know I shall not be able to leave off,' he told Barbara on 29 August. 'No doubt Scalands and the neighbourhood must have been looking most lovely all this time, while I have seen no daylight hardly except on the surface of my canvas.'[27] For once, this was a boast, not a complaint. Whatever he might say about pot-boiling, as Holman Hunt had noted long ago, his rapt attention to the process of painting when his faculties were fully engaged marks his seriousness as an

artist. He was suitably modest, telling Alice in November that he hoped
Dante's Dream was 'rather better' than his previous pictures. 'And that is
really all I do hope,' he added, 'for to suppose one is producing a
masterpiece as the next work following what so far one perceives to have
been otherwise, is a thing one does not do after 40.' Nevertheless, the
process was satisfying in itself: 'I cannot at all get rid of my absorbing
interest in what I do as mere occupation.'[28]

By the end of the year, progress on *Dante's Dream* made for an interval
that allowed *Beata Beatrix* to be finished and delivered to the Cowpers, at
long last. Writing to Miss Losh early in 1871, Rossetti gave a cheerful
account of his affairs. His disturbed vision had vanished. 'I have even
worked a good deal in the evenings since the short days set in,' he wrote.
'Accordingly, as you may suppose, I have got through a great deal of
painting, both in the finishing of work which had been hanging on hand
during my long seediness, and in progress with the large picture which is
now approaching completion.' After such long anxiety he could hardly
trust it, but now painting brought only pleasure. 'I shall certainly, either
this year or the next, take some steps to exhibit some of my things which I
think best worth showing.'[29]

He also told Shields – and no doubt others viva voce – that he hoped to
'get up a public show' next year, to include another large picture, hopefully
the *Magdalene*. 'The big *Dante* is nearing completion, but won't, I suppose,
be done quite so soon as I thought, as I knocked off lately to finish several
other things on hand.' These, which included the *Mariana* and a *Beatrice*
for William Graham, were now finished and he was busy on *Pandora*, for
Graham's uncle. This large and sombre image, which shows Janey holding
the casket from which the mischiefs of the world have escaped, was 'mighty
in its godlike terror' according to Swinburne.[30] Judging that all the new
works achieved 'great advance in colour and execution', Rossetti was
confident that *Dante's Dream* would be his best picture yet. 'Perfect it
won't be, but better it will be,' he wrote.[31]

As always, however, a sense of failure accompanied completion. As he
noted around this time, the true artist would always be the first to perceive
the defects in his own work. But the plans to exhibit prove how far the
painting did in fact approach his ambition to carry off a major project.
Dante's Dream also offered the fulfilment of Rossetti's.

Having taken less than a year, it was finished to all intents and purposes
by May 1871, lingering only for the highlights and glazes that drew the
whole together and had to dry thoroughly between applications. Brown
was the first to see it, early in June, when he apparently advised greater
colour contrasts. 'I am quite bent on making the picture thoroughly forcible
and well relieved as a primary necessity,' replied Rossetti, adding that the

background vistas were 'getting light again as I go on, and will be quite brilliant eventually'.[32] Next year, he would certainly exhibit it – maybe even at the RA.

Opinions differ on the merits of the picture, which owing to its size is seldom exhibited outside its permanent home in the Walker Art Gallery, Liverpool. The largest of Rossetti's paintings, *Dante's Dream* is in fact the least discussed today, when critical comment is usually confined to comparing its 'thoroughly confident Renaissance style' with the quaint medievalism of the watercolour version – often in the latter's favour.[33] The overblown manner is out of fashion – yet many comparable works, by Pre-Raphaelite, Olympian, Aesthetic and Symbolist artists have returned from oblivion to critical scrutiny. Neither the theatricality nor inherent improbability of the scene should be a bar to appraisal. *Dante's Dream* sits well alongside productions of the same era like Watts's *Paolo and Francesca* or William Blake Richmond's *Sleep and Death carrying the Body of Sarpedon*; and even against Burne-Jones's *Laus Veneris*, whose pose echoes that of Beatrice.

Like several works from his early period, the spatial handling is reminiscent of the flat, emboxed quality of the theatrical scenes he began with as a boy, their rectangular lines echoing those of the stage. The figures stand as in a frieze, Love and Beatrice thrust visually forward from the recessed bier by their red and white garments. Love may be awkwardly large, but his embrace is the symbolic focus of the scene; sympathetically read, his action echoes that in countless images of mourning over dead saints, which are identified as a compositional source, while the openings to the sky above and on either side of the central group recall the many Nativities of Western art. The atmosphere is sombre, not sensuous: Dante's gaze is answered by his beloved's closed, blank eyelids and the colour harmonies of the finely painted draperies glow soberly. Falling on Beatrice's face, white gown and cascading golden hair, a somewhat mysterious light-source illuminates also the attendant figures, as if from spotlights to either side.

However, though the picture is not a failure, it yet fails to enthrall. Beatrice looks uncomfortable, half-propped up on her deathbed, simul-taneously lifeless and swooning. Love, moreover, embodies the ado-lescent clumsiness of Browning's lubberly lad as he bends to kiss her, his right hand stretching back to grasp Dante's, his awkward left arm holding the arrow that points from Beatrice's heart to Dante's but seems likely to pierce everyone's flesh. His pink wings are half-tangled in the white veil that Beatrice's ladies are lowering on her bier, and above all, his corporeal presence imparts an unsettling suggestion of necrophilia.

None the less, the achievement was undeniable. This was what Rossetti had long aspired to paint: a large, original work, drawn from the *Vita Nuova* that he had made his own heritage. If more post- than pre-Raphael in style, it nevertheless expressed the reverence he felt for historic art and literature, in his heart and soul.

'In all that thou doest, work from thine own heart, simply,' he had made the golden-haired image of Chiaro's soul say in the recently republished *Hand and Soul*. 'Set thine hand and thy soul to serve man with God . . . take thine Art unto thee and paint me thus, as I am, to know me: weak as I am, and in the weeds of this time; only with eyes which seek out labour, and with a faith, not learned, yet jealous of prayer. Do this; so shall thy soul stand before thee always, and perplex thee no more.'

Faith had deserted Rossetti, and with lost health Art had seemed likely to follow. Now, with labour undertaken for love not lucre, his faith in painting was restored.

All in all, by the beginning of 1871, Rossetti's life had regained equilibrium. The physical pains and mental fears of 1868–9 were vanquished. His *Poems* were in their fifth edition. A new acquaintance named Franz Hueffer was arranging publication in Germany. The prestigious *Westminster Review* carried yet another commendatory article, by Sidney Colvin. Younger bards were clustering around, seeking leadership. *Beatrix*, *Palmifera* and *Mariana* were complete, as well as *Dante's Dream*. Masterpieces were perhaps not out of reach.

He felt renewed affection for the family, endeavouring to visit more often. 'I am afraid you must have been expecting me tonight,' he apologised on 24 January after failing to reach Euston Square; 'but believe, dearest Mother, that you are very often in my mind when I am away from you. I have been blessed with your love so long that I could imagine no good world, here or elsewhere, without it; and I blame myself a thousand times for the many days that pass without my seeing you.' The older he got, the more Gabriel appreciated his mother's silent, undeviating love for him. But even though he saw her briefly on 27 April – perhaps at the Scotts' – he again forgot it was her birthday. Frances Rossetti said nothing, and in the evening Gabriel wrote unhappily to apologise, remembering 'how this day once provided, for four children yet to be, the dearest and best of mothers'. He did not mean to be neglectful, concluding: 'With all truest love and every heartfelt wish for you today, my dearest Mother, I am your most affectionate Son, Gabriel.'[34]

With comparable affection, he endeavoured to assist his sisters' various projects. Recently, Maria, who continued to teach Italian (and around this date numbered Janey Morris among her pupils) as well as devote herself to church work, had addressed her intellectual gifts to an introductory guide to the *Divine Comedy*, entitled *The Shadow of Dante*. Willingly, Gabriel designed the binding and frontispiece for a book that complemented his own translation of the *Vita Nuova* and underlined the family identification with Dante, its members numbered among 'those that haunt / The vale of magical dark mysteries' frequented by their father.

He also attempted to promote Christina's literary career. *Sing-Song*, her nursery poems, were 'admirable things, alternating between the merest babyism and a sort of Blakish wisdom and tenderness,' he told Swinburne, exhibiting unexpected tenderness of his own. 'I believe no one could have written anything so absolutely right for babies but herself.' But in the event, the success of his own *Poems* only emphasised the failure of her stories in *Commonplace*, and Ellis was discouraged. Moreover, in pursuit of his plan for a cosy group centred on the publisher, Gabriel had asked Alice Boyd to do the illustrations for *Sing-Song*, which proved beyond her competence. Ellis then withdrew his offer, and though in the end the book appeared in 1871 as a joint venture by Christina's American publisher Roberts Bros and the London firm of Routledge, with drawings by Arthur Hughes engraved by Dalziels, one cannot but feel that Gabriel's interventions were less than helpful.

This summer, Stillman and Miss Spartali, newly married, left to visit America. The Whistler brothers were in London, dining at Cheyne Walk with the sculptor Edgar Boehm. A colourful compatriot of Stillman's named Joaquin Cincinnatus Miller, author of 'Kit Carson's Ride' and other *Songs of the Sierras*, proved an adventurous spirit, with tales to top Whistler's. News came of the Louvre being torched by 'revolutionists' in Paris, and funds were solicited for destitute artists and writers. Chariclea Ionides brought her niece to Tudor House, and then her fiancé Edward Dannreuther. Elizabeth Rovedino sent begging letters to the Rossettis, presuming on her father's old acquaintance; both Gabriel and William responded. From Italy cousin Teodorico sent news that the nation wished to honour *il professore* by removing his remains for reburial. Gabriel, on whose behalf the Highgate tomb had already been plundered, had no objection, but the women of the family reacted with pious horror. The Moxon publishing firm, for whom William was compiling a series of anthologies, collapsed suddenly. Whitley Stokes returned briefly from India, with a long beard. On 23 June the great Russian novelist Turgenev came to dine at Cheyne Walk, talking of Shakespeare, Byron and Lermontov. He was older than they expected, tall and handsome with a head of white hair, speaking good English and especially taken with the newest recruit to the menagerie, a Canadian marmot.

Gabriel went to South Kensington, where another International Exhibition was in train. *Notes and Queries* carried an odd correspondence about the meaning of his own little *Greensleeves*, which had surfaced at Agnew's. He promptly borrowed it back, 'gave it a good daubing all over' and returned it with a new title. Swinburne came to London to see the Comédie Française, and immediately fell into old habits, raving with delirium and swearing so noisily by Blake's Urizen that his fellow lodgers decamped in protest. Yet again his father was summoned.

Howell, who had been dismissed from Ruskin's service the previous autumn for unspecified offences (being a gentleman of the old school, Ruskin declined to elaborate) had now fallen out, terminally, with Ned. By this date, most were aware that Howell was a sharp operator, albeit a charming fellow, given to dubious, even duplicitous dealings and weaving a tissue of inventions as camouflage. If he said something had been lost at sea, almost certainly it was destroyed by fire, wrote Georgie Burne-Jones later. But now he had done something unforgivable, beyond looseness of tongue or fraudulence in money-matters. According to Whistler, Charles (who naturally knew a good deal about the Zambaco affair) had engineered a social encounter between Georgie and Mary, an insult to the former that broke all the rules of etiquette. Ned turned against his erstwhile friend with ferocity, to ensure Howell was frozen out of 'the circle'. Gabriel, like others, received a demand that Howell be cast off, as an act of friendship, leading to a frank 'face-to-face row' when Ned insisted.[35] Having himself no quarrel with Howell, Rossetti was disinclined; but Ned was so urgent that he felt obliged to acquiesce, by letting his intimacy with Howell lapse. Howell angrily demanded an interview, to denounce those who were libelling him all around town.

Christina was so sick she could not attend to her proofs. 'Would you believe that through all my illness I only saw Gabriel twice?' she told Kate Howell in July. 'You know his nocturnal habits are not adapted to a sickroom.'[36] He himself reported that his sister was a 'sad wreck', but quite unsubdued in spirit, which suggests the brave face she presented on his rare visits. She went to the seaside to convalesce, though her condition was by no means cured. Meanwhile, after a year's hard labour at the easel, Gabriel had a far more exciting summer in prospect.

During the painting of *Dante's Dream*, he and Janey had seen each other at regular though not frequent intervals, and had enjoyed at least one long weekend in July 1870, when three portrait drawings of her reclining on his sofa were drawn and dated. Two more were done on 12 August, and one on 29 November.[37] Early in 1871 she sat again, and Rossetti talked of issuing large photos of his 'life-studies of female heads' in chalks – a series of twelve for 12 guineas sounded a marketable idea. But not surprisingly this never happened: if at one level Rossetti wished to publicise both his art and his muse, at another he desired more fervently to keep both from the vulgar gaze.

Morris's last *Earthly Paradise* volume had appeared at Christmas – having sold a thousand copies before publication, to Gabriel's envy. By spring he was so immersed in the Sagas that he planned a two-month trip to Iceland, perhaps envisaging a seaside resort for 'the wife and kids' during his absence. But it seems Jane preferred a country retreat. It was over a year since the sojourn at Fir Bank; and now the plan – how arrived at, who knows? – was for a joint tenancy with Gabriel, in some secluded region. The summer stretched ahead.

Once the decision had been taken, Morris applied himself to house-hunting. In the Thames valley above Oxford, he located an available house of the 'out-of-the-world' kind that Gabriel had always sought but never expected to find in an agent's advertisement. It was 'a heaven on earth', Morris told Faulkner on 17 May: a stone-built Elizabethan manor, with 'such a garden! close down on the river, a boat house, and all things handy'.[38] Three days later, they all went to inspect it, travelling by train from Paddington to Faringdon and thence by hired carriage to the little village of Kelmscott. It must have been a curious visit, for two men and the woman they both loved. But the house was perfect, and the next day Gabriel told William he and Topsy planned to rent it on a yearly basis. There was some urgency, but when Topsy chose to act, he did so with dispatch. The lease was signed and before the end of June Morris escorted Jane and the girls there, engaged servants, ordered supplies, and arranged for local workmen to redecorate and furnish, with supplies from the Firm.

The shared tenancy cost £75 a year. For this, Morris acquired a summer residence for his family which he would visit at weekends, and where he could indulge his boyish delight in coarse fishing. For Rossetti, it was to be 'country-quarters', where he could work in the summer, leaving his traps over the winter. And both these objectives disguised the true aim, which was to enable Janey and Gabriel to live together, out of sight of prying gossip, for the warmest months of the year.

As if such house-sharing were nothing out of the ordinary, an air of studied casualness is evident in surviving references to the arrangement. It masked a new disposition, comparable to that of Scott and Alice at Penkill. 'Please, dear Janey, be well and happy,' Morris wrote in farewell. Six days later, Rossetti left London. In his absence, Philip Webb was to supervise alterations to the Tudor House studio – a project that provided further camouflage for the summer in 'love's bower'.

Kelmscott at midsummer was indeed a haven, as out of the world as might well be imagined, like something from a fairy-tale. The village was a collection of farms and cottages, seemingly untouched by modern life, and the Manor was almost outside the village, on the cart-track to the infant Thames. Surrounded by paddocks and water-meadows, it was enclosed in a walled garden. There was an adjacent yard, with a handsome dovecot and thatched barns where hay and haywains were stored. Indoors, it was a Sleeping Beauty house, with a screens passage, flagged floors, ancient wooden stairs and an upstairs room hung with old Flemish tapestries. Outside, in the kitchen courtyard, was a stone-roofed, three-seater privy.

Janey imagined the barns might move if you stroked them, like furry cats flexing their backs. Gabriel thought the manor 'purely Elizabethan', though Morris, who knew about these things, said it was 'much later'; building styles changed slowly in such a quiet neighbourhood. It had been inhabited only by the family that built it 'in old times', whose coat of arms was on the chimney-breasts, and altogether everything was so well-worn that little seemed to have changed since the sixteenth century. The riverside garden was perfect: without irony, Gabriel told Miss Losh it was 'simply an "earthly Paradise", appropriate you will say to our old friend Top.'[39]

The village was 'about the doziest clump of old grey beehives to look at you could find anywhere', and the solitude was 'almost absolute', Gabriel told Scott. Few of the hundred or so Kelmscott inhabitants were ever seen, especially if one kept to field-paths. There were beautiful walks for miles around, but little incentive to wander far. 'It's so flat that to see anything is not easy, and when you do see it, it isn't worth seeing,' he told Webb. But to Oxford-born Janey, the countryside was comfortingly familiar and 'home-like'. Her mother's family came from the next village, Alvescot.

She busied herself with home-making. The rooms were repainted and papered, fireplaces were removed and retiled with the Firm's products, new curtains and cushions hung and embroidered. 'The place looks now as if it had been in our use for years,' Gabriel wrote after four weeks' residence. They ordered tins of paint: grey, red, white and a 'good tint of green'.

He made his studio in the largest, airiest room in the Manor's north wing, where the ancient, faded tapestry – 'there since the house was built' – told the story of Samson. 'There is one very grisly subject, where his eyes are being gouged out, while a brass barber's basin lies at his feet containing his shorn locks, and Delilah looks over her shoulder at him while the Philistine leader counts out her wages to her,' he told Dr Hake, smiling at the baroque style.

They had brought quantities of books. Jane's daughters were devouring a Waverley novel daily, while their elders, who included the girls' governess, were 'doing' Shakespeare, reading scenes aloud, in the house and in the garden. 'Her babes are dear little things, and amuse themselves all day long,' Gabriel told Brown.[40] Holidays with children were a new and poignant experience. Young Jenny was now ten and May nine. 'I should have had a daughter just that age,' he remarked, with reawakened feeling for the child born dead in 1861 between the two living girls.

Though he intended to work on Graham's watercolour replica of *Beata Beatrix*, he at first did little painting, for once allowing himself true leisure and relaxation. As was his wont, he rose late and ate a large breakfast-cum-lunch in which eggs featured prominently. He and Jane consulted over decorating and furniture, sending to London for mirrors and tables. Then he read, or wrote, or simply listened to the activities of house, garden and farm. In the late afternoon he walked, usually with Janey, over the fields and along the river, down to Radcot Bridge and back, or upstream towards Buscot and Inglesham.

One day they discovered 'a funny little island midway in one walk, which can be reached by a crazy bridge'. Like the cave at Penkill, it served as a convenient spot for jotting down sonnets. In the small boathouse belonging to the Manor there was a punt, which also proved conducive to poetry. In it Gabriel composed a pastoral 'ballad or song or something' that tells a tale of innocence and betrayal, young lovers and an illegitimate child, drowned with its mother in the tangled weeds. Each pathetic action mirrors one of the river's moods:

> Between Holmscote and Hurstcote
>   A troth was given and riven,
> From heart's trust grew one life to two,
>   Two lost lives cry to Heaven;
> With banks spread calm to meet the sky,
>   With meadows newly mowed,
> The harvest-paths of glad July,
>   The sweet school-children's road.

If any troth was given this glad July, between Janey and Gabriel wandering on the river-bank, it did not result in a baby. Obliquely, perhaps, the verse reflected an imagined notion of what might have been.

Naturally they were circumspect. As well as the girls' governess, servants Allan and Emma McClounie from Cheyne Walk were in the house, to cook and clean, alongside two 'native retainers' and local workmen; and while Gabriel may not have seen them, a host of inquisitive villagers certainly watched the summer residents with interest. Years later, gossip alleged that at Kelmscott, Mrs Morris and Mr Rossetti 'used to lie in the rye furrows', but this diverting image must be fanciful, for at no time was their relationship openly sexual. Once in later years, when Georgie Burne-Jones, distressed by popular rumours that they had been lovers, asked a direct question, she received a direct denial from Jane. 'If you ever hear this discussed, I should like you to repeat what I have told you,' Georgie then instructed her own daughter.[41]

But sexual intimacy takes many forms, and there are numerous hints that the relationship between Jane and Gabriel, this season at Kelmscott, was not merely platonic but also physical – if perhaps not expressly copulative (to use one of Swinburne's terms). They took long walks together, and were alone in the evenings, once the children and servants were in bed. Every floorboard in the Manor creaked, but there was room for privacy, both indoors and out.

Jane heard twice from Topsy, enjoying the spare Icelandic landscape, rough living and egalitarian society. From what Gabriel called 'the unpronounceable capital' he wrote of the voyage, with porpoises and whales and 'great ice mountains with rivers of ice looking as if they were running into the sea', and four weeks later from Stykkisholm came a vigorous account of 'riding over the wilderness in the teeth of a tremendous storm of snow, rain and wind'. It was nothing like Kelmscott, he told his daughters, truly. 'I slept in the home-field of Njal's house, and Gunnar's, and at Herdholt: I have seen Bjarg, and Bathstead and the place where Bolli was killed, and am now half an hour's ride from Holyfell where Gudrun died.'[42] For his part, while not envying Top's adventures, Rossetti seems to have been impressed – not least because of an Icelandic newspaper that featured the arrival of 'Wm. Morris, Skald', which means 'poet'. He 'really ought to go by no other name for the future', Gabriel told Brown, with less jibing than heretofore.

At Kelmscott, when the weather grew hotter, he exchanged his waistcoat for a workman's loose shirt and painted at a leisurely pace. After completing Graham's *Beatrix*, he started a small oil of Jane holding willow branches before a Kelmscott scene: the winding river, with its punt peeping from the little boat-shed, and in the background the roofs of the Manor and the church bell-cote. To his mind, Kelmscott church, glimpsed through some wild apple trees, looked 'just as one fancies chapels in the *Morte d'Arthur*'. By analogy, the Manor was a kind of Joyous Gard, in what was either a wilderness or an Eden. In the *Water Willow* picture, the gables of the house rise above a curtain wall that makes it look like a moated grange.

The painting was made to fit an antique frame. Janey thought it was for her, but some years later it was sold with little hesitation when a patron offered a good price. 'I was mortally sorry to part with the Kelmscott picture,' Rossetti wrote frankly, 'but after one or two disappointments in business matters lately, felt that there was no alternative.'[43] Janey, it may be inferred, was even sorrier: when the little picture went to Murray for repair in the 1890s, a copy was made for her.

They took to walking at twilight, and Gabriel wrote of these walks, with 'hand that clings in hand', 'two souls softly spanned with one o'er-arching heaven', two passionate hearts and two bodies that 'lean unto / Each other's sweetness amorously . . .' Often, the garden close was sufficient, with its 'fat cut hedges' that seemed to 'purr and shimmer' in the sun,[44] and deep green grass where in the cool of the evening plump toads were observed, panting silently, with tender liquid eyes. After a while, time slowed down and their little world contracted. As long as the mail arrived regularly, it no longer mattered that tradespeople did not deliver, or that the carrier charged six shillings for each journey from Faringdon. The isolation and tranquillity were perfect.

'Your hands lie open in the long fresh grass', began the sonnet entitled *Silent Noon*:

> Your eyes smile peace. The pasture gleams and glooms
> 'Neath billowing skies that scatter and amass.
> All round our nest, far as the eye can pass,
>   Are golden kingcup-fields with silver edge
>   Where the cow-parsley skirts the hawthorn hedge.
> 'Tis visible silence, still as the hour-glass.

'Think through the silence how when we are old / We two will think upon this pace and days,' this continued. 'And clasp unto our hearts, when tempests lour / This close-companioned inarticulate hour.' As Pater had written: 'Art comes to you professing frankly to give nothing but the highest quality to your moments as they pass, and simply for the moment's sake.'[45]

Time stood still. Over the weeks, a whole sequence of sonnets appeared, eventually to be copied into a notebook and presented as a love-gift to Jane.[46] Feeling 'Elizabethan enough' to match the house, they read Plutarch as well as Shakespeare. When Browning's new book *Balaustion's Adventure* arrived, Gabriel entertained the household with a dramatic reading on the lawn, lasting ninety minutes. He amended the title to 'Exhaustion's Imposture', and told his mother that the text consisted largely of Euripides' *Alcestis*, 'interlarded with Browningian analysis' that bore no relation to things Greek.[47] Alcestis is the model wife who offers to die for her husband. Another classical analogy was unwittingly in Rossetti's mind when he referred to Morris's travels in Iceland as truly Odyssean. But if Jane were Penelope, Gabriel was her only suitor. Though it seems incredible, for two whole months no one else seems to have come to Kelmscott.

CHAPTER TWENTY-TWO

Catastrophe

Rossetti also drew the girls – large, careful portraits of each, in a manner to please the most doting Mamma. Jenny buried herself in books, he said, and was less observant. But May, easily his favourite, was 'quite a beauty', with 'a real turn for drawing when she gets a little less lazy'.[1] Perhaps Jenny observed more than he thought, half-resentful that Mr Rossetti was there when her father was not, or that he appropriated the Waverley novels which were her passion. May however enjoyed the long sittings in the studio, and posed well and patiently. 'When he was in a silent mood there was the tapestry to look at,' she recalled, 'and if he happened to place me opposite Samson having his eyes gouged out, or Samson pulling down the gates of the temple, I was absorbed indeed.'[2] Sometimes, Mr Rossetti would talk, flatteringly, as to an adult, really seeming to listen to her replies.

This summer he had intended to concentrate on poetry. A new collection was half-promised to Ellis for Christmas (an unauthorised announcement to this effect appeared in the *Athenaeum* on 12 August). Hence the long walks, composing lines in his head, as well as the 'funny little island' for sonneteering. But he was less productive than planned, not finding the Oxfordshire surroundings conducive to the completion of *The Orchard-pit*, first projected at Penkill. In one of his lengthy letters to Scott, four hundred miles away in Ayrshire, he lamented the failure. 'I wish I could get some serious verse-writing done here, but begin to see that I shall not,' he wrote on 25 August. 'In fact, I cannot carry it on with painting to do also, at any rate not unless I am quite alone.' Jane's company and some painting 'task-work' had intervened, keeping him away 'from the other Muse, who, I believe, after all is my true mistress . . .'[3]

In fact, besides the river-ballad, he had already produced a little song in Italian, several sonnets, six Shelleyan stanzas 'done from Nature', and an ode on the mystery of existence. The Shelleyan piece was *Sunset Wings*, inspired by the whirling flight of starlings at dusk, 'clamorous like mill-waters, at wild play':

> Save for the whirr within,
>   You could not tell the starlings from the leaves;
>   Then one great puff of wings, and the swarm heaves
>   Away with all its din.

Rossetti was never a Nature poet. The swooping flock and dying light serve
as figures for abstract concepts: 'ever-eddying' Hope, and Sorrow, in the
eventual darkness that covers all. The influence came from *Hertha*, whose
denial of theism nevertheless affirms belief in some Supreme Being 'as fast
as Swinburne tries to erase it'.[4] Cast in less prophetic diction, *The Cloud
Confines*, Rossetti's ode on the mystery of existence, dispatched to Scott on
9 August, was 'a poem not long but meant to deal with important matters'.
Its theme is the immortality of the soul, and the unknowable place of 'man'
in the cosmos:

> The day is dark and the night
>   To him that would search the heart;
>   No lips of cloud that will part
> Nor morning song in the light:
>   Only, gazing alone,
>   To him wild shadows are shown,
>   Deep under deep unknown,
> And height above unknown height.

No word comes from the dead to confirm 'whether at all they be'. The
pitiless nature of war and strife remains a mystery. Love proves fugitive.
What is life's purpose?

> Our past is clean forgot,
> Our present is and is not,
> Our future's a sealed seedplot,
> And what betwixt them are we?
>   Atoms that nought can sever
>   From one world-circling will –
>   To throb at its heart for ever,
>   Yet never to know it still.

Scott queried the final word. Rossetti protested, but revision crystallised his
drift:

> Oh, never from Thee to sever
>   Who wast and shalt be and art,

> To throb at Thy heart for ever
> Yet never to know Thy heart.

But did this invoke a personal God? 'I don't think it need do so,' he added hesitantly, as if unconvinced.[5] When Scott rejoined, he offered his current thinking on the vexed question of immortality, apparently derived from contemporary science, as expounded by Tyndall. 'Dearest Scotus, I cannot suppose that any particle of life is extinguished, though its permanent individuality may be more than questionable,' he wrote. 'Absorption is not annihilation; and it is even a real retributive future for the special atom of life to be really re-embodied (if so it were) which its own former ideality had helped to fashion for pain or pleasure. Such is the theory conjectured here.'

Of the physical properties of atoms and molecules, Rossetti's grasp was no doubt slight. But by this date he evidently held to a Neoplatonic view – perhaps also influenced by Jane's belief in reincarnation – of souls migrating through living beings, together with an intuitive apprehension of a world beyond that of the senses. However, he continued, it was probably better not to squeeze such ideas explicitly into verse, but purposely leave things vague. He tried other formulations, such as atoms throbbing at the heart of the Eternal Will, before finally deciding to reprise the first refrain:

> We who say as we go, –
> Strange to think by the way,
> Whatever there is to know,
> That we shall know one day.

It was not original, but a deliberate echo of Byron's famous lines in *Childe Harold's Pilgrimage* quoting Socrates: 'Well didst thou speak, Athena's wisest son! "All that we know is, nothing can be known." '

'Would God I knew there was a God to thank when thanks rise up in me!' Gabriel jotted down one day, deeply unwilling to accept the unbelief that was spreading through the age, with its implications of extinction. Janey meanwhile was reading Goethe's *Elective Affinities*. 'What? Is nothing real?' she protested to Webb. 'Must everything that is delightful change and leave nothing behind? I can't believe it . . .'[6]

'Let no priest tell you of any home / Unseen above the sky's blue dome,' Gabriel wrote in lines sent to Hake on 2 September:

> To have played in childhood by the sea,
> Or to have been young in Italy,
> Or anywhere in the sun or rain
> To have loved and been beloved again,
> Is nearer Heaven than he can come.

But timeless bliss was coming to an end. A week later Morris returned, with presents for Jane and the girls, a diminutive Icelandic pony, and many travellers' tales. He stayed only briefly, enjoyed a day's fishing on the river, prompting Gabriel to a comic caricature of Topsy as an Icelandic *skald*, in the Kelmscott punt.

To relieve his feelings, Gabriel plotted a new narrative poem, called *The Cup of Water*, whose folkloric nature harks back to the days of Red Lion Square.[7] A young king is hunting with a companion when, feeling thirsty, they take a drink of water from a forester's daughter, and both fall instantly in love with her unequalled beauty. The King, affianced to a princess, sacrifices the girl to his companion, who proceeds to propose. The girl, however, has fallen in love with the King, not knowing his rank. So the King goes to plead for his friend, explaining also his feelings. She then agrees to marry the knight, who is made an earl, on condition that each year the earl's wife will bring the King a cup of water, on the same spot and at the same date. Before the third anniversary, however, the wife dies in giving birth to a daughter. Sixteen years later, her daughter prepares to offer water to the King, in honour of the ancient pledge. But as he is about to take the cup he is aware of a second figure in her exact likeness but dressed in peasant's clothes, who steps forward as he leans from his horse, looks in his face with solemn words of love and welcome, and kisses him on the mouth. He falls forward on his horse's neck, and is lifted up dead.

But once plotted, the outline was laid aside. Instead, he grew deeply engrossed in a long poem about a magic crystal, which had been germinating in his mind like a picture and was now slowly 'floating paperwards'. Evidently conceived as a title-poem, it was to have 150 stanzas. 'The poem clawed hold of me and had to be done,' he told Scott. And though he claimed elsewhere that long poems were built slowly, 'like Solomon's temple, section by section, without the sound of a hammer', this one raced to completion like a Crystal Palace. By 23 September it was finished and named: '*Rose Mary* – 3 Parts, 160 stanzas'.[8]

A fanciful historical narrative, *Rose Mary* is reminiscent of Edgar Allan Poe, Coleridge and Scott. Gazing into a magic crystal, the eponymous heroine sees her husband-to-be safely evading an ambush. In fact, he is killed: the stone, obtained by her Crusader father at the cost of at least one immortal soul, reveals the truth only to maids. Rose Mary, who has anticipated her wedding, sees the vision contrariwise. Then, on Sir James's body, her mother finds a lock of hair and letter from one Jocelind, proving he also betrayed his beloved. Recovering from a deep swoon, Rose Mary smashes the crystal with a sword. As the spell breaks, she falls dead, and a voice welcomes her to heaven: through the stone's destruction, her immortal soul is saved from perdition.

Rossetti had first dreamed of this poem a long while since, perhaps even before *Sister Helen*, whose supernatural and incantatory elements *Rose Mary* shares. 'You may remember my using the name long ago for some rubbish destroyed,' he reminded William. Whatever that may have been, the inspiration went back to youthful reading of the *Arabian Nights*, where the first thing seen in a magic glass is a figure sweeping with a broom. 'This I have used,' he wrote.[9] Long ago, too, he had been fascinated by the tale of Michael Scott, a ballad magician who uses his powers for seduction. The key ingredient however came from a neighbour in Chelsea, who claimed to possess the 'original dreaming stone' of Dr John Dee, Elizabethan necromancer. Dunn recounted this story, telling how he went to see the stone, 'a small, unpretentious bit of crystal' with an awesome reputation. Gazing into its centre, he discerned nothing, but the owner 'had seen much and written much more from the pages of antiquated lore that it had unfolded to her – Hebrew, Sanscrit, and heaven only knows what else had been opened up to her enlightened vision.'[10]

The unnamed seer was doubtless Gabriel's 'old and sentimental friend', the former Anna Mary Howitt, now living with her husband at 19 Cheyne Walk and immersed in spiritualist pursuits. (Her family heard how through her agency Lizzie sent yet more messages for Gabriel.[11]) Rossetti was intrigued. The visionary stone was called the magic beryl, which both belongs to the gemstone family that yields the emerald, and is one of those listed in the Book of Revelation. Before Rossetti bestowed its name on Rose Mary's crystal ball, Dr Hake furnished some mineralogical details. 'I had no idea what the stone was really like,' confessed Rossetti, 'but perceived that for my purpose the elements must be somehow mystically condensed in it as a sort of mimic world.'[12]

The plot of his poem 'turned on the innocence required in the seer'. It was a story of his own devising, he explained, 'with, I hope, good emotions and surprises in it'. At first he aimed to interleave the stanzas with a burden, more elaborate than in *Sister Helen*, *Eden Bower*, or *Troy Town*, which would be 'distantly allusive to the story in a sort of gradually culminating way'. But as the poem grew longer, the burdens threatened to overtax the reader and were dropped in favour of a single, steadily intensifying narrative.

Even within its fantastical genre, the ballad is rather foolish. From the storyline Scott half-suspected as much. 'My poem, *The Beryl Stone*, has not a comic side, Scotus, or at least not an intentional one,' Gabriel replied reprovingly on 15 September; indeed, it was 'so consumedly tragic' that he had modified the intended course of the catastrophe to avoid 'unmanageable heaping up of the agony'. His own words should have sounded a warning, as well as William's observation that there seemed no reason why the shattering of the stone should also cause the death of the heroine. Instead, Rossetti was confident of success, saying only that 'being a sort of Scotch or Border story' with a supernatural theme, it ought to have been done at Penkill.

The burdens are pure Kelmscott, however. Alliterative and assonant, they dwell on its key attributes, the river and garden, water and murmuring sweetness:

> Water-willow and wellaway
> With a wind blown night and day.
>
> The willow's wan and the water white
> With a wind that blows day and night.
>
> . . .
>
> A honeycomb and a honeyflower
> And the bee shall have his hour.
>
> A honeyed heart for the honeycomb
> And the humming bee flies home.

He lingered a fortnight longer. 'Of course I'm leaving here just as I was getting into the poetic groove,' he wrote on 2 October, 'and I know were I to stay I should have a volume ready by the end of another three months. But it may not be.' The wheat fields were down to stubble, while autumn rains flooded the meadows. 'I went out in a boat on the fields I used to walk over,' he told friends[13] as he returned to the real world, where, he learned, the *Contemporary Review* had just published an unfriendly review.

Joaquin Miller recalled a dinner at Tudor House towards the end of his time in Britain. 'We dined so late we missed all relish for breakfast,' he noted, remembering also the flowing wine and odorous cigars. Stillman was there, with others, including a little man hidden among accumulated bottles, who may have been Swinburne, an admirer of Whitman, who must have been William, and perhaps also O'Shaughnessy.

Rossetti, 'the master', sat relatively quietly. 'I am an Italian who has never seen Italy,' he told his guests. 'Bella Italia!' Then the talk turned to poetry. Gnomically, Rossetti observed that 'silence was the noblest attribute in all things; that the greatest poets refused to write, and that all great artists in all lines were above the folly of expression.' Fellow diners chimed in. 'Unheard melodies are sweeter,' said one. 'Unwritten poems are divine,' said another.[14]

What is poetry? came the cry. Bending close, the master spoke. 'Poetry is soul set to music,' he said; none should be despised. 'All poetry is good. I never read a poem in my life that did not have some merit, and teach some sweet lesson.'

A poem should be a picture, proffered Miller. True, responded Rossetti; 'I also demand that it shall be lofty in sentiment and sublime in expression. The only rule I have for measuring the merits of a written poem is by the height of it. Why not be able to measure its altitude as you measure one of your sublime peaks in America?'

They spoke of Homer's *Odyssey*, and of the 'soft vowel sounds' in ancient Greek, rendered in English by alliteration and assonance. Then Rossetti returned to his theme. 'To me, every man or woman who loves the beautiful is a poet. The gift of expression is a separate affair altogether. I am certain that the greatest, the sweetest and the purest poets on earth are silent people – silent as the flowers. Pictures of the beautiful are as frequent to all really refined natures as are the flowers of the field. Yet only one in millions has the gift, desire and power of expression.' And he concluded:

'Oh, it is a beautiful, beautiful world! Only let us have capacity to see the beauty that is in it, and we will see nothing that is ugly at all – nothing that is evil at all.'

If Rossetti ever spoke thus preciously, it was not in his natural character. Plainly, however, he and his companions struck the American visitor as ineffably affected, spouting about the Pure and the Beautiful as the brandy passed from hand to hand. Indeed, one suspects barely disguised mockery.

Contradictorily, what struck the young Sidney Colvin, Fellow of Trinity College, Cambridge, now flexing his critical muscles in literary London, was Rossetti's 'round, John-Bullish, bluntly cordial manner of speech, with a preference for brief and bluff slang words and phrases'.[15] In retrospect, this seemed scarcely in keeping with the character of a man whose works proclaimed him 'the most quintessentially, romantically poetic of painters and writers'.

Deeply superstitious, Rossetti seldom tempted fate by presuming upon his powers. Despite all appearances to the contrary, he was more liable to self-deprecation than boasting. But the reception of *Poems*, now eighteen months past, had wrapped him in a coat of confidence. A new volume, whenever it appeared, would surely sell well. So at first, the hostile article in the *Contemporary* was a mere midge-bite.

Delighted with the rebuilt studio, he rejoiced to be 'now for the first time in possession of a splendid painting light'. All the family, including uncle Henry, came to a party on 23 October and saw both studio and the splendid *Dante's Dream*, in a fine carved frame. He was 'immediately' to start on other large projects.

He read his new poems 'to great and general applause' from Scott, Ned, and others, including his new friend Franz Hueffer, who was now living nearby and courting Cathy Brown. To Gabriel's delight, Maria was earning praise for her lucid exposition of Dante, while Christina's *Sing-Song* seemed also destined to do well. Dismayingly, however, Christina's illness had left her permanently disfigured, with browned skin and a goitrous, pop-eyed look, so she 'looked suddenly ten years older'.[16] Though illness afflicted all his female relatives this autumn, Christina was much the worst, suffering a serious relapse that led to fears for her life. Gabriel was sufficiently concerned to suggest she spend the winter at Kelmscott, optimistically claiming that though the Manor might be marooned by floods, the house itself was not damp. He was of course wrong, but Christina was anyway unable to move, being under the daily care of doctors.

Soon after his return to London, Janey came to stay overnight at Chelsea – to Scott's great surprise when invited by Morris to dine that same evening at Queen Square, together with Gabriel, who excused himself as 'already engaged'. 'Is this not too daring, and altogether inexplicable?' wrote Scott to Alice. Yet over the early months of 1872, Gabriel seems to have seen Jane only infrequently. On 6 January he sketched her on the sofa, and on 12 March he asked Howell to obtain tickets for the Queen's Theatre, where *Black-Eyed Susan* and *The Last Days of Pompeii* were playing. His request for the box to contain a comfortable armchair suggests this was for Jane. This was not wholly in the spirit of Ned's demand for total severance from Howell, but Gabriel had complied only with reluctance, and this spring both he and William supplied testimonials to assist Howell in a new art-dealing venture.[17]

Dante's Dream received further finishing touches. Come the spring it would certainly be exhibited 'in some way or other'. Indeed, he graciously floated the idea of sending it to the RA, if they would make the first move. To prompt an invitation, trusty Fred Stephens was therefore asked to publish an account (or should it be an advertisement?) of the picture in the *Athenaeum*. 'The picture is a serious effort – surpassing, in scale and care, any former one of mine – and professes to hold its own against any modern work whatever,' Rossetti wrote proudly, while more modestly informing Shields that he was 'far from blind' to its shortcomings, but none the less believed it was 'really much better' than anything he had done hitherto.[18]

Soon he was entertaining even grander notions, of election to the

Academy. He told William that if he were at any time invited to become an Academician, he would decline – because it would not suit him to take his turn supervising the students and yet he would not like to occupy the post 'without discharging its ordinary duties . . .'

It is hard to judge how realistic this notion was, or even whence it arose. He was in touch with Leighton, always anxious to enlist the ablest artists in the national academy, and occasionally with Millais, whom he later blamed – according to Whistler – for failing to nominate him when an opportunity arose.[19] All such discussions were of course conducted confidentially, often indirectly. It is possible that, had *Dante's Dream* gone to the 1872 Academy, Rossetti's name could have been proposed for election. As it was not shown, further speculation is idle – but the very possibility is an index of his rising aspirations – and maybe also a hint of mania.

As Graham foresaw, when delivered the picture was too large to hang anywhere but on the staircase, where it could not be seen. Rossetti took it back to Tudor House, promising a smaller version and other works in exchange. Meanwhile, his main work this winter was a pair of new pictures drawn chiefly from Alexa Wilding. 'New pictures for the future always, I say,' he told Leyland, having cancelled the commission for a replica *Palmifera*. 'I know I am out-growing my former self to some extent, as one should in ripening years, and had much better be doing new things only.'[20]

He discarded the medieval Michael Scott, persuading Leyland to commission the Dantescan *Ship of Love* instead. Before that however came a life-sized '*Lady with Violin*', offered to Leyland in January as 'chiefly a study of varied greens'. More precisely, it was an Aesthetic picture, a pictorial allegory of Art, showing a woman composing music Messiaen-like while listening to a songbird's notes. All art aspires to the condition of music, as Walter Pater would soon declare.

The image partly derived from an old Italian source – the symbolic *Iconologia* of Cesare Ripa, where Art is personified as a female figure with a flame rising from her brow. Green, the symbolic colour of hope, is Art's colour too, since Art conquers Time to keep all fresh. 'I mean to call the violin picture *Veronica Veronese*, which sounds like the name of a musical image,' Rossetti added, apparently attempting a harmonic verbal variation in sound while also producing a complex pun, for 'Veronica' means 'true image' as well as being the name of a common wild flower known as eyebright, while 'Veronese' refers to the painter whose opulent colour-sense is dominated by green and pale blue, lemon yellow and silvery white.

To the frame, he attached a textual fragment ascribed to a largely fictitious Renaissance source, which purports to inspire the image and does in fact describe how the lady Veronica, swiftly inscribing the notes on her page, pauses to listen further, searching for the supreme, still elusive, melody. '*C'était le mariage des voix de la nature et de l'âme – l'aube d'une création mystique*,'[21] he wrote, in a teasing, Swinburnian display of fake erudition. More seriously, text and picture combine to present a work allusive of all the arts: poetry, painting, music, song.

The depiction of the mystic dawn of artistic creation was completed in record time, being nearly ready for Leyland's splendid new London house by mid-March. The second major work was equally swift. Surely inspired by Kelmscott, *The Bower Meadow* utilised a very old canvas, showing a distant woodland background. Once intended for the meeting of Dante and Beatrice in Paradise, this had lain in his studio for twenty years, since his return from the sodden fortnight with Hunt at Sevenoaks. Now, it was painted with two women fingering antique instruments. At first, Love holding a songbird was placed between the musicians, but this motif was too close to that of the *Veronica*, and soon replaced by two women dancing, so that Music and Dance became the correlative of Art.

Both possess the qualities of time and movement denied to painting, which yet strives to convey these through graceful gesture and flowing drapery. Long ago, Rossetti had been enrapt by the dancing nymphs of Mantegna's *Parnassus* in the Louvre, in a sonnet later revised and republished. His *Bower Meadow* dancers echo Mantegna's, and also those of Botticelli's *Mystic Nativity* where angelic figures circle in the sky and embrace mortals on the ground. In the *The Bower Meadow*, a single, unexplained female figure dances solitary in the distance, mysteriously leading to the high wall of woodland beyond.

Although a musician, Leyland declined the picture. Completed by March, it was sold to dealers Pilgeram and Lefevre for 700 guineas, and thence, ironically, to 'the demon Dunlop', with whom Rossetti had refused to have further dealings, and who gave Pilgerams his watercolours of *Hamlet and Ophelia* and *Roman de la Rose* in part payment. Aldam Heaton thought he was a fool to do so, but *The Bower Meadow* is a fine, richly atmospheric work in subtle greens and pinks, imbued with aesthetic emotion.

There was no invitation from the RA to exhibit *Dante's Dream*, and as the exhibition season of 1872 approached, Rossetti made no alternative plans. In May came good news, however, when Gambart announced that he wished to publish a print, to be engraved by Auguste Blanchard, who had done Hunt's *Isabella* and *Finding of the Saviour*. In terms of 'name and fame', this was almost as good as star billing at the Academy; only a few months before, Rossetti had told Scott of his desire to reproduce his original compositions lithographically, so as to secure immortality. Thus, he wrote, 'one might really get one's brain into print before one died, like

Albert Dürer, and moreover be freed perhaps from slavery to "patrons" while one lived'.[22]

Gambart proposed to commission a replica of the work for 1,000 guineas, to include the copyright. It was a tempting offer, but Rossetti was reluctant to cede copyright, which could make the main picture harder to sell. Nothing was decided. There were new canvases on the easel and in his mind. 'Praised be the gods, I feel something like growing strength for work in me,' he had lately told Leyland; 'and if I can get some new things done now, they will be a precious deal better than any as yet, I know well.'[23]

All seemed set fair for his 'ripening years' as a leading poet and painter. In a few weeks he and Janey would return to Kelmscott. Yet all through the winter of 1871–2, the attack in the *Contemporary* had been eating into his equilibrium, to disastrous effect.

With hindsight, the obsession had been rising steadily, like the insistent waves of a flood tide that eventually liquefies a sandcastle. But right until the surging moment, it had seemed well within limits; Rossetti's rationality had been sapped imperceptibly. Now his mind was like a wind-lashed ocean, occasional lulls only masking the turbulence within.

'The Fleshly School of Poetry: Mr D. G. Rossetti' by Thomas Maitland that had greeted him on his return from Kelmscott was a vigorous piece of flyting, in a robust tradition of literary abuse. It hit shrewdly, wittily, and below the belt at the eroticism and artifice of *Poems*.

It began with an outline of the players on the stage of English poetry. If contemporary poets were characters in *Hamlet*, with the Laureate as Prince, then DGR was obviously Osric, flamboyant, fashionable, but of no serious account. The other members of the new, self-important 'fleshly school' were Mr Swinburne, who had already been arraigned for indecency, and Mr Morris: all dedicated to amorality, according to Maitland. 'The fleshly gentlemen have bound themselves by solemn league and covenant to extol fleshliness as the distinct and supreme end of poetic and pictorial art,' he explained; 'to aver that poetic expression is greater than poetic thought, and by inference that the body is greater than the soul, and sound superior to sense; and that the poet, properly to develop his poetic faculty, must be an intellectual hermaphrodite, to whom the very facts of day and night are lost in a whirl of aesthetic terminology.' Moreover, the poets in question had arranged 'to praise, extol and imitate each other' and thus fairly earned for themselves the title of the Mutual Admiration school . . .'[24]

Worse, they had encouraged a swarm of disciples who had caught the affectations of their elders as easily as the measles.

Homing in, the attack then reached its chief target: Mr Rossetti, 'known for many years as a painter of exceptional powers, who, for reasons best known to himself, has shrunk from publicly exhibiting his pictures'. Judging from the few photographs available, he appeared to conceive unpleasantly and draw badly. His verses showed 'the same combination of the simple and the grotesque, the same morbid deviation from healthy forms of life, the same sense of weary, wasting, yet exquisite sensuality'.

If Mr Swinburne's outrageousness was that of a naughty boy, the physicality of *Nuptial Sleep* was shameless. 'Here is a full-grown man, presumably intelligent and cultivated, putting on record for other full-grown men to read, the most secret mysteries of sexual connection, and that with so sickening a desire to reproduce the sensual mood, so careful a choice of epithet, that we merely shudder . . .' It was not poetic, nor manly, nor even human, to write on such topics; it was 'simply nasty' for a man who was 'too sensitive to exhibit his pictures, and so modest that it takes him years to make up his mind to publish his poems, [to] parade his private sensations before a coarse public, and [be] gratified by their applause.' Whether writing of the holy Damozel, or of the Virgin herself, or of Lilith, or of Helen, or of Dante, or of Jenny the streetwalker, Mr Rossetti was 'fleshly all over, from the roots of his hair to the tip of his toes'. Moreover, what astonishing women the fleshly poets encountered. 'Females who bite, scratch, scream, bubble, munch, sweat, writhe, twist, wriggle, foam and in a general way slaver over their lovers, must surely possess some extraordinary qualities to counteract their otherwise most offensive mode . . .'

Then there was the affected versification, accenting the last syllable in 'Love-Li*lee*' so as to produce a sort of cooing whistle, and rhyming 'dry and wet' with 'Haymar*ket*'. Poetry should be 'perfect human speech': such archaisms were 'the mere fiddlededeeing of empty heads and hollow hearts' as well as indicators of falser tricks and deeper affectations.

At first, Rossetti expressed only derision. He had feared such an attack in 1870 but now, after eighteen months of good reviews and healthy sales, it had little power to injure. 'Have you seen our contemptuous *Contemporary?*' he asked Ellis. 'What fools we must be! For it seems proved that we are greater fools than the writer, and even I can see what a fool he is. For once abuse comes in a form that even a bard can manage to grin at without grimacing.'[25] According to William, he even laughed at the parody of his burden in *Sister Helen*.

But who was the writer? Thomas Maitland was an unknown name in literary journalism. Ellis guessed at the old bogey, Robert Buchanan. 'Can you judge?' Gabriel asked William. The *Contemporary* was owned by Alexander Strahan, Buchanan's publisher. Did the Common Skunk and Scotch Fox share the same identity? 'If it be, I'll not deny myself the fun of a printed Letter to the Skunk.'

If contemptuous, however, he was also distinctly nettled. On 19 October, he burst in on the Scotts during a dinner-party, to announce that Maitland was certainly Buchanan. In Scott's view, this diminished the damage: a rival poet under a false name could do little harm: all he wrote would be ascribed to spite. But though Gabriel pretended to be rather amused than hurt, he was making 'rhymes without end on author and publisher'.[26]

> As a critic, the poet Buchanan
> Thinks Pseudo much safer than Anon
> Into Maitland he's shrunk
> Yet the smell of the skunk
> Guides the shuddering nose to Buchanan.

This was one of the more printable. 'My brother was impulsive and outspoken,' William wrote later, 'and among friends frequently more vociferous than polite manners prescribed.'[27]

He began an angry, mocking riposte entitled *The Stealthy School of Criticism. A letter to Robert Buchanan Esq (alias Thomas Maitland)*. Would Ellis kindly send it *'at once today'* to the printer, and get a proof *'by tomorrow.'* Once printed, they could discuss publication. He read the text to friends, explaining it was 'pure banter and satire' chiefly designed to humiliate the author. With his usual wisdom, William counselled against responding at all. Characteristically, Swinburne was in favour, and at once began a counterblast of his own.

Though the *Contemporary*'s editor told Simeon Solomon that Maitland was not Buchanan, by mid-November the culprit was finally confirmed. Opinion was still divided over the response. Colvin spoke of composing a rebuttal. Fellow poet G. A. Simcox proposed a counter-article signed 'Thomas Maitland' – which tickled Rossetti until he realised that the piece would be credited to him. Frederick Locker, author of *London Lyrics*, reported that Tennyson said that Rossetti's sonnets were among the finest in the language. (Conversely, Buchanan himself claimed to have heard the Laureate name *Nuptial Sleep* as 'the filthiest thing he had ever read'.[28])

So the affair simmered until, prompted by a gossip line in the *Athenaeum*, Rossetti offered the paper 'the more serious portion' of *The Stealthy School*, which appeared on 16 December. As 'the individual chiefly attacked', he wished to make a 'specific denial to specific charges' which if unrefuted might continue to circulate to his disavantage.

Firstly, the accusation of animalism. *Nuptial Sleep* was but one small segment of a longer poem, *The House of Life*, throughout which 'all the passionate and just delights of the body are declared ... to be as naught if not ennobled by the concurrence of the soul'. Other allegedly 'sensual' phrases were also quoted entirely out of context, including *Willowwood*'s lips bubbling with brimming kisses, to which Buchanan had taken great offence. The sonnet was not literal, but 'describes a dream or trance of divided love momentarily re-united by the longing fancy'. *Jenny*, which Buchanan claimed was based on his own *Artist and Model*, had in fact been written 'some thirteen years ago', and anyway Rossetti had never read Buchanan's poem. His own was not sensual but dramatic, told from within the mind of the speaker – a 'young and thoughtful man of the world' – reflecting on a social and moral issue.[29]

So much for content. On the Aesthetic prong of Buchanan's critique, that the Fleshly poets placed form above thought and sound above sense, Rossetti strongly demurred. His themes were as serious as Shakespeare's – love turned to hatred, lost ideals, unjust exile, the complex analysis of passion and feeling. The charge of 'creating form for its own sake' was patently unfair.

But after this reasoned, if inadequate, response (several of Buchanan's palpable hits went unanswered) the tone of Rossetti's piece altered, as he plunged into the pseudonymity of 'this particular Mr Robert-Thomas', who from behind a mask had the gall to charge another with insincerity – 'while every word on his own tongue is covert rancour, and every stroke from his pen perversion of truth'. Such were the lengths to which 'a fretful poet-critic' would carry personal grudges. 'Thresh and riddle and winnow it as you may – let it fly in shreds to the four winds – falsehood only will be that which flies and that which stays. And thus the sheath of deceit which this pseudonymous undertaking presents at the outset insures in fact what will be found to be its real character to the core.'

Ironically, the same issue of the *Athenaeum* carried a letter from Buchanan blaming Strahan for the pseudonym. He promised to reissue his essay under his own name, 'with many additions'.

Rossetti sprang back in attack, with parodic verses on a two-faced 'Scotch Bard and English Reviewer'. A good hit, in William's view. And when Colvin proved less than eager to pen a rebuttal on his behalf, Gabriel revived the idea of issuing *The Stealthy School* in full, as a pamphlet. Ellis panicked, foreseeing writs.

A fine literary sparring-match was in progress. Seen in retrospect, however, the incoherent syntax towards the close of Rossetti's article was a warning sign. And there is other indirect evidence of a change towards the turn of the year. In the following six months, he wrote far fewer letters than was customary. He brooded more and in January, when Dr Hake called, he was 'sulky' to the point of rudeness. Oh, he apologised, it was because he had 'just scratched out a hand in the picture for the third time'. A little while later, he confided in William about the child heard whimpering in the

corridor, two years past, refusing to contemplate a more rational explanation. His stillborn daughter's tenth anniversary was approaching.

Now that Dunn was no longer living at Tudor House, Rossetti was also
alarmed to calculate that household bills topped a thousand pounds a year –
an astonishing amount for a single man who kept no carriage; Emma should
henceforth have five pounds a week to pay all tradesmen. Later it was
discovered that orders for wine and spirits were so frequent that she and
Allan were thought to be selling as well as drinking it. 'The bill shows 2
dozen Cognac sent on 1 January 1872, and a third dozen on 19 February!!'
noted William in dismay, fielding a demand for £163 17s.[30] Meanwhile, large
orders for colours, brushes and canvases mounted in Roberson's ledger; in
April, Rossetti paid fifty pounds towards his outstanding account.

Yet in other respects, he seemed well. On 21 February, he hosted a dinner
for Brown, Leyland and the Whistler brothers, when he unveiled *Veronica
Veronese* and *The Bower Meadow*, and spoke positively of 'going to Italy
soon', to paint. A week later he was at one of Brown's parties, where
William produced a shard of Shelley's blackened skull, plucked from the
beach-side pyre. Sharing William's passion, poetess Mathilde Blind kissed it
exultantly. Swinburne took evasive action. Gabriel passed it off jokingly,
but was impressed.

When the heavyweight *Quarterly Review* contained another negative
account of his 'endeavours to attach a spiritual meaning to the animal
passions', Rossetti claimed to laugh, telling Hake he feared his letter to the
Athenaeum had given friends 'quite a false idea of the effect which adverse
criticism has on me [and] a mis-apprehension as to the importance I attach
to such things'. Nor did he respond to the *Saturday*'s view that the 'spirit of
coterie' was most damaging, and that, whatever the merits of the squabble,
Rossetti was ill-served if his personal friends wrote all the reviews; Harry
Forman, who had lodged a zealous defence in *Tinsley's*, was 'that worst of
enemies, your worshipper'.[31]

Meanwhile, Buchanan was busy, with other barbs. In March he inserted
into an article on Tennyson a glancing reference to the Fleshly School as
imitators of George Sand, Gautier and Baudelaire, and a jibe against
Rossetti as 'Euphues come again . . . in the shape of an amatory foreigner, ill
acquainted with English'. There followed 'Criticism as one of the Fine
Arts', with another side-swipe at the Mutual Admiration School of
'sensualists and spooneys'.[32] The whole affair continued to divert literary
London.

Buchanan's expanded pamphlet was announced for mid-May. While
Colvin promised to ensure it was rubbished in the *Athenaeum*, *Saturday
Review*, *Daily News*, *Fortnightly* and *Pall Mall Gazette*, so that there 'shall
not be a whole bone left' in Buchanan's shin, Rossetti was growing seedy

and insomniac again. Alarmingly, he coughed blood on a couple of occasions. Inauspiciously, the long-heralded assault coincided with his birthday, 12 May, when *The Fleshly School of Poetry and Other Phenomena of the Day* by Robert Buchanan was issued by Strahan & Co. of 56 Ludgate Hill.

Now divided into seven sections, its new remit covered general indecency, in risqué magazines, popular songs, photographs and the contemporary cult of the female Leg – code for sexual licence. Having recently returned to London from the west of Scotland, Buchanan claimed to be shocked by the proliferation of lewdness. 'Open the last new poem,' he wrote; its title would almost certainly be 'Leg is Enough'. (A prescient joke against Morris's next publication, which was to be entitled *Love is Enough*.) The source of this metropolitan infection were the vulgar debauchees and 'free lovers' among the literary and artistic sophisticates of the day, who smiled at conventional morality – a bohemian *demi-monde* of 'men and women of indolent habits and aesthetic tastes' who were guided by neither religion nor conscience. 'Ingenious almost to diablerie, they will prove to you by critical theory that art is simply the method of getting most sweets out of one's living sensations . . .' Beginning with the minor poets of Dante's era, a sensuous 'Italian disease' had infected verse down the ages, its worst exemplar being Charles Baudelaire (quoted at length with lubricious relish) from whom the Fleshly School learned blasphemy and perversion. Now there was 'running rampant in English society a certain atrocious form of vice, a monster with two heads – one of which is called Adultery, the other Dipsomania – and these two heads, blind to all else in the world, leer and ogle at each other'.

'The Italian Falsetto Singers and their Imitators' was one provocative heading. Another was 'Pearls from the Amatory Poets', consisting of liberal examples of sexual imagery from Donne, Crashaw, Swinburne and Rossetti. Could anything be worse than DGR's vile comparison in *Love's Redemption* of the sexual act with the sacrament of bread and wine? It was no defence of *Eden Bower* to say that a snake's embrace was described; all lovers in the Fleshly School were 'invariably snake-like in their eternal wriggling, lipping, munching, slavering'. In *Troy Town*, Paris was disgustingly at risk of being suckled by Helen, with her 'breasts meet for his mouth'. *A Last Confession* was a monologue spoken by a murderous Italian madman.

The House of Life, far from being a profound meditation, was 'flooded with sensualism . . . a very hotbed of nasty phrases' (quotations ad nauseam); 'the sort of house meant should be nameless but is probably the identical one where the writer found "Jenny" ' – that is a brothel. Most deplorably, 'Mr Rossetti, in his worst poems, explains that he is speaking dramatically in the character of a *husband* addressing his *wife*. Animalism is animalism, nevertheless, whether licensed or not; and, indeed, one might tolerate the language of lust more readily on the lips of a lover addressing a mistress than on the lips of a husband virtually (in these so-called "Nuptial" Sonnets) wheeling his nuptial couch out into the public streets.'

As to the attacks upon himself, wrote Buchanan, they were 'the inventions of cowards, too spoilt with flattery to bear criticism, and too querulous and humorsome to perceive the real issues of the case'. All the hubbub about anonymity was a vulgar farce, got up to divert attention.

By the following weekend, the literary row reached the halfpenny papers, the tabloids of the time. In a front-page article called 'Fleshing the Fleshly', the *Echo* outlined the gross offensiveness of Buchanan's criticism. If sensual, Mr Rossetti's poems became 'absolutely filthy' in Buchanan's handling; the remark about wheeling his marriage-bed into the street was quite unrepeatable. Indeed, if they bore tamely the insults hurled at their heads, the Fleshly poets must as alleged be utterly effete – 'the veriest aesthericised simulacra of humanity'.[33]

'You may be sure that these monstrous libels – both the pamphlet and its press results – cause me great pain,' Rossetti told Joseph Knight ten days later, adding that he had laid aside a denunciatory reply, having no wish to become involved in 'insult and violence'.[34] But his resolve proved weak and one evening at Scott's he was greatly agitated as how best to respond. Then, at the end of May, the *Saturday* joined the fray. If Buchanan was offensive, so were the so-called Fleshly poets, with their 'utter unmanliness', their 'sickly self-consciousness, their emasculated delight in brooding over and toying with matters that healthy manly men put out of their thoughts . . . by a natural and wholesome instinct . . .'[35]

Never mind unmanly. Rossetti was unmanned. His fair fame as an artist was being destroyed. He would be deemed craven as well as vicious if he did not challenge the libellers. The articles in his defence only served to blazon the 'fleshly' epithet more boldly. Like a personified rumour, it would snake and susurrate its way round town, too sly to be scotched. Emphatic denial was taken as a sure sign of guilt. Stigmatised as a sensualist, he would lose all reputation, respect, patrons. No husband or father would allow a respectable wife or daughter to visit him, even chaperoned. Worse, he would be a laughing-stock in public and private – the butt of lazy sneers, the source of cheap jokes. His honour was destroyed.

The next day, Gabriel was deranged. On Saturday 1 June, he called on William in high agitation, insisting on unmistakable evidence of a hostile conspiracy against him, of which the latest attacks in the *Echo* and *Saturday*

Review were but the most recent. His work was assailed, his name blackened, his reputation destroyed. He would be hounded out of society. He was spied on, abused on all sides by friends as well as strangers. Soon, his enemies would come for him physically. His life was in danger.

Charged with cowardice, should he not challenge his accuser to a duel? But he could not fight, 'he had no manhood, he would have to die in shame'.[36]

Dismayed, William hustled his brother straight back to Cheyne Walk, scribbling a fib to their mother. Gabriel was peremptory. William must not leave him alone, at the mercy of his enemies. Everywhere, they were catcalling and whispering insults; could his brother not hear their voices? With despair, over the next few hours William perceived that his brother was insane, 'in the ordinary sense of that term'. He went along to no. 92, to get Scott.

Through Sunday, Gabriel remained in the grips of mania. Arriving at Tudor House with the outstanding 350 guineas for *The Bower Meadow*, Pilgeram's partner was assailed by the artist's assertions that 'all sorts of people' were trying to defraud and destroy him. William long remembered Mr Lefevre staring in surprise when Gabriel proposed the contract be cancelled.

On Monday, William had to attend to his duties at the Revenue Office. Scott, Dunn and Fanny kept Gabriel company. In the early evening, they tried table-turning, presumably for distraction. The table moved, and some messages came. It was Lizzie, as usual. She was happy, and still loved Gabriel. To check her identity, she was asked the name of her young brother and correctly gave his initials as H. S., which only Gabriel knew. After the seance, he went off to Brown's, with William; in his agitation, he could neither rest nor sleep.

At Euston Square, there were already grave anxieties, for Christina's condition, at length diagnosed as thyroid malfunction, left her in need of constant attendance. Although Jenner said the disease was not fatal, the strain on her heart was beginning to tell. William therefore told their mother merely that Gabriel was 'hippish' and might go to stay with Dr Hake at Roehampton, for fresher air.

To combat the delusive convictions of conspiracy, Brown proposed proofs of public esteem from influential friends like Tennyson and Browning. Two days later, an affectionately inscribed presentation copy of Browning's new book, *Fifine at the Fair*, arrived. At first, Gabriel was 'touched even to tears' at this evidence of support against the legions. 'My dear Browning, Thanks once more for a new book bearing your name loved as of old,' he replied by return, acknowledging also the 'warm expression of regard at this moment'.[37]

But the thanks were premature. As he began to read, the text turned hostile, full of allusions to himself, his works, his life. At the end, especially, was 'a spiteful reference to something which had occurred, or might be alleged to have occurred, at his house'. The widowed narrator, who has loved his wife spiritually and Fifine carnally, is visited by his wife's ghost:

> When, in a moment, just a knock, call, cry,
> Half a pang and all a rapture, there again were we! –
> 'What, and is it really you again?' quoth I:
> 'I again, what else did you expect?' quoth She.
> . . .
> 'If you knew but how I dwelt down here!' quoth I:
> 'And was I so better off up there?' quoth She.

Browning had always deplored attempts to communicate with the dead. What was implied here? All of sudden, 'Browning was his greatest enemy, determined to hunt him to death.' A moment more, and Gabriel relented, tearfully affectionate again. Then the delusion returned: Browning was a leading figure in the conspiracy. He threw the book towards the fire and could not be persuaded to touch it again. Miserable beyond measure, William abandoned the daily diary he had kept for years past.

On Thursday, Brown arranged for Dunn to go 'for a *very long walk* with DGR to-night', promising that either he or William would sleep at Tudor House. He proposed they all take turns with this routine and also enlist Arthur Hughes. But the next development was decisive, for to their dismay Gabriel 'declared the walls to be mined and perforated by spies, and that all he did and said was known to the conspirators'. Whatever the others protested, he knew he was surrounded; his persecutors were drawing near.

At last, Scott and Brown understood what William already knew: DGR was without doubt deranged. On Friday 7 June they therefore consulted with Doctors Hake and Marshall, both of whom Rossetti regarded as friends. Marshall brought along Henry Maudsley, distinguished mad doctor. After talking with the patient, it was settled that he should accept Hake's invitation to Roehampton.

But immediately the medical men were gone, Gabriel swore they too were in the conspiracy, and he would not go. A 'long and troublesome' discussion followed before he was finally persuaded into the cab, assisted by Hake's son George. William went too, in acute distress. During the dismal journey Gabriel heard a bell being rung on the roof of the cab, inaudible to his companions, about which he tartly remonstrated with the driver.

They had not reckoned on its being Whitsun weekend. On Saturday, far from being quiet, Roehampton was filled with holiday-makers and fair-folk. The road streamed with carriages and caravans. Taken for a calming stroll, Gabriel saw at once that this was a hostile demonstration, got up to revile him. A banner carried on a pair of high poles was a gibbet to be set up in Richmond Park, for him to be hanged. He made to attack the bearers, chasing the vehicles, shouting at their occupants. His companions forced him back into the house.

He and William stayed up late, talking on 'various family matters'. But even in bed there was no escape from persecutors. Twice, a voice called out to him, with 'a term of gross and unbearable obloquy' which even after twenty years William would not write down.

Unbeknownst to the others, Gabriel had a bottle of laudanum, which he had never before used. But now he wanted to die, like Lizzie. He drank the whole phial and fell into unconsciousness. On the Sunday, Hake let him sleep, hopeful that the crisis was over, raising the alarm only at four in the afternoon when Rossetti could not be woken and looked as if he had had a stroke. A local doctor confirmed the diagnosis. If he survived at all, his brain would be irreparably damaged.

Rossetti did not want to survive. William sped back to London to bring his mother and sister Maria to the deathbed, calling also on Brown, who undertook to collect John Marshall. When they reached Roehampton again, Gabriel was still unconscious, but breathing in ammonia from a bottle held by Hake, who had found the laudanum container and administered a traditional antidote. Marshall chose strong black coffee and vigorous massage to stimulate circulation. Around noon on Monday Gabriel regained consciousness, having been comatose for thirty-six hours. One leg seemed paralysed.

Sadly, as he woke his delusive fantasies resurfaced. No longer violently excited, he was sunk in gloom. 'By the evening of Tuesday things seemed in this respect worse than ever,' William recalled later.

What was to be done? Following prevailing wisdom, Marshall counselled against familiar companions and surroundings. Hake commended a private asylum, with trained staff. William saw no other choice; Maria and their mother concurred, aware that such a step might effectively end Gabriel's career. Brown, however, arriving the next day, offered to care for Gabriel himself, no doubt recalling the support provided by this 'friend of friends' in his own depressive episodes. That evening they returned to Cheyne Walk. Emma the housekeeper went running along to summon Scott, saying Mr Rossetti was back again with Mr Brown and Mr George Hake, and just the same as he was on leaving.

Brown's determination to keep him out of an asylum was most noble, 'and if the move is successful we must honour him for it', Scott told Alice.

The delusions seemed to be diminishing, although when on 14 June Gabriel asked everyone to acknowledge how much quieter the house was tonight, his own inference was merely that the spies had left off eavesdropping.

Informed of the catastrophe, Jane now came to Cheyne Walk, with 'her more than amiable husband'. Even more generously, Morris offered to take a turn at caring for Gabriel. Scott, who saw Rossetti's passion for 'Mrs M' as a major cause of the trouble, was thankful that she had not rushed hysterically to Roehampton. Preparing for another summer at Kelmscott, Janey was remarkably self-controlled; after seeing Gabriel, she wrote a short note saying she hoped he would call before he went away. Her letter, Gabriel noted confidentially, was clearly a forgery . . .

At Tudor House Fanny was 'in and out constantly' for a few days. Then Brown took Gabriel off to Fitzroy Square. Powers of attorney were entrusted to him and William, who was forbidden to see his brother but preoccupied with the practical consequences. As a precaution, *Dante's Dream*, which legally belonged to Graham, was moved to Scott's studio, lest bailiffs attempt to seize any assets on behalf of creditors.

Graham provided the first solution to finding a retreat, where Rossetti might rest and recover without recourse to an asylum. Urrard House, his Scottish country home in Perthshire, was available until the end of the London season. So on the evening of 20 June Brown, George Hake and Allan McClounie escorted Rossetti on the long journey north to Pitlochry in a reserved rail carriage. The next day, he wrote to his mother in terms that must have been mightily, if misleadingly, reassuring. 'We got here to-day at 11, after 14 or 15 hours' hard travelling, but in a most luxurious way such as I could hardly have imagined,' he told her. 'An immense deal has been done by Mr Graham to smooth away difficulties, and his kindness throughout has been excessive. What to say of Brown's brotherly lovingness to me I do not know – even from him I could hardly have supposed such love and long patience possible.' Urrard House, he added, was on the site of the battle at which 'Bonny Dundee', first viscount and Jacobite hero, was killed; 'in the garden a mound marks the spot where he fell by a bullet after reaching his own door.'[38]

Though he confessed to being 'no correspondent just now', the letter showed no sign of derangement. After a week, George Hake, who was to be Rossetti's most constant companion in the months to come, sent his first report to William. 'The delusions I am sorry to tell you still continue but in a modified form,' he wrote, adding that occasionally Gabriel threw off gloominess and talked of people and books with 'all his old brilliancy'. But he could not draw, and was convinced there was no hope of recovery – 'in fact he gets angry if we tell him he is better'.[39] Arriving to relieve Brown, Scott's impression was pessimistic. 'He will simply sit and listen and think of things that he does not dare to speak of,' he told Alice. 'He breathes a little heavy and his hand shakes a little, so that if we could get him to try painting the result might be a disaster.' Moreover, 'his delusions about everything (and everybody except us) being in a conspiracy against him continue, only he conceals it better . . . All the birds even on the trees are villains making cat-calls.'

Subject to hallucinatory voices and unremitting interior torments that misconstrued external events, Gabriel was most wretched. Briefly, he could converse normally, and even write an occasional letter that betrayed no madness. But he could do nothing sustainedly, not even read with any degree of concentration. He was anxious, irritable, stubborn, restless, finding endless objections to every course proposed. In addition, his hip joint remained stiff, so he required a stick, and the swollen hydrocele made sitting uncomfortable. At night, his fear-filled thoughts allowed no rest and the only respite came from chloral, washed down with alcohol, bringing a few hours' oblivion. Then the terrors returned.

'*Nel mezzo del cammin di nostra vita*': Rossetti found himself like Dante, in a dark wood, descending into hell. 'It was lamentable to see the downfall, like the fall of a great Colossus, a great mountain,' Burne-Jones recalled sadly. 'Down he went. We *all* suffer for it.'[40]

CHAPTER TWENTY-THREE

Recovery

Lying in the picturesque Pass of Killiecrankie just below Blair Atholl, Urrard House was less than a mile from the nearby station, but surrounded by scenic gorges, waterfalls, glens, and ruined castles. In another life Rossetti might have enjoyed drives and short walks as at Penkill. But he could not respond, and in any case within a week of arrival they had to leave, since Graham's family were coming. So on 28 June the ill-assorted male group – Madox Brown, George Hake, alcoholic Allan and Rossetti in an invalid carriage – removed to Stobhall, a fishing lodge high above the Tay between Dunkeld and Scone. Also leased by Graham, primarily for the salmon season, Stobhall was an ancient Jacobite pele tower and courtyard, with modern living quarters and a charming old topiary garden of yews and hollies. It too had historic associations, lying midway between Birnam Wood and Dunsinane. Again, a perfect location, in other circumstances.

Scott's first act was to attempt to stop Gabriel taking whisky as well as chloral. A 'scene of fury' ensued, Rossetti declaring that if they took away his sleep he would leap from the window – fifty feet into the river. Scott then 'hinted pretty plainly' that if he did not take friends' advice he would soon have to obey doctors. 'He fully understood what was implied,' reported George, 'but told us it would be very difficult to prove him mad!'[1]

Young George was personable, good-natured and remarkably obliging, given the exacting behaviour of Mr Rossetti, his elder by twenty years. The second of Dr Hake's five sons, he was twenty-five and 'between terms' at Oxford, having not yet fixed upon a career. More an athlete than a scholar, he liked fishing and shooting, for which Perthshire was ideal, and was sufficiently easy-going not to chafe at the restrictions involved in attending an invalid. Indeed, Rossetti soon became attached to George, who slept in his room and had responsibility for doling out the nightly measures. Despite his youth, he was also charged with ordering supplies and keeping accounts, for William to pay on Gabriel's behalf. He proved reliable and responsive, his equable temperament no doubt helping to calm one whose mind alternated between turmoil and despair. In short, George was a godsend.

In the first week at Stobhall, his report was hardly encouraging. Rossetti was convinced the place was surrounded by boys, whistling and signalling like birds, and that indoors the white-painted wainscot was hollow, concealing spies listening through small holes. When George obtained a day's fishing permit, Gabriel grew convinced he had been 'decoyed away' so there would now be one less friend with him, and insisted on going with Scott to find him. Most graphic of all were the glimpses of paranoia. 'If we start a rabbit (you know how they lie in the grass) or if a passing countryman civilly bids us "Good night" or even a watchdog barking as we pass – all are studied insults,' George told William on 11 July. Down on the Tay they saw men seine fishing, starting out from the bank with a large net to form a great arc before landing downstream and slowly pulling the net in from each end. 'You see that?' said Rossetti. 'It is an allegory of my state. My persecutors are gradually narrowing the net round me until at last it will be drawn tight . . .'

Allan, who was neither fit nor sober, was sent back to London. Then, when letters continued to arrive from Emma, Gabriel wanted to open them, convinced both correspondents were 'leagued with his enemies'. These included Swinburne, who as it happened was imminently due in Perthshire, on holiday with Benjamin Jowett and others. There was every possibility he would seek out Gabriel, and William wrote hastily to deter him. Though hurt – it was a grief to be prevented from showing the same affection as other friends – Swinburne agreed to avoid a meeting, and never in fact saw Gabriel again, nor understood exactly why.[2]

Perhaps Rossetti had heard (but how? – his mail was carefully censored) of 'somebody, a friend of somebody else, being in the Solferino restaurant and hearing Sandys and Swinburne going over the whole matter at one of the tables', as Dunn reported to William.[3] Certainly, he was already out of patience with Algernon's intemperance and may have come to regard him as the poisonous cause of the whole catastrophe, encouraging both indecency and unwise self-defence; or perhaps he simply knew that close association with such a friend had fatally injured his reputation. Purporting to attack the whole Fleshly School, Buchanan had bestowed all its faults on *Poems*. But, as with Browning, there was no rational explanation, or hope of dislodging Gabriel's *idées fixes*. In his mind, both men were now confirmed adversaries.

'What is to be the end of all this, Scott, staying here this way?' he asked mournfully. 'It is all the same – Cheyne Walk, Roehampton, at Brown's, Urrard and here, they are always round me.' The whole scheme was drawing closer, and, when ripe, he would be murdered.

But he was not utterly unhinged, dealing as best he could with his financial affairs by agreeing to the sale of major assets in order to create a fund. Howell offered to raise £550 or £600 for the porcelain. With thanks for his 'friendly letter', Rossetti replied that he needed at least £700,[4] and in the event, Murray Marks offered £650, plus £100 for the drawing called *Silence*.

Gabriel's first consideration was to secure Fanny's future, for without his protection she and her possessions were at risk from those to whom her long-estranged husband was in debt. So one of his first acts was to assign to William 'the furniture (all of which belongs to myself) now at the house rented by me at No. 36 Royal Avenue, Chelsea'. But how to secure her the lease? 'The house business is a great difficulty to me to settle – in fact not possible,' he wrote on 1 July, suggesting William consult Matthias Boyce, George's lawyer brother. If they could resolve things, poor Fanny would be greatly relieved. He was surprised to hear she had been given no news. 'Can you not let her know what is doing about the house and furniture and try to soothe her great anxiety a little?' he asked Brown. 'Heaven knows I would *wish* to do something decided at once, but can it be done unless more money is raised?' To Fanny herself he insisted – rightly or wrongly – that neither William nor Brown was ill-disposed towards her; 'and as for myself, you are the only person whom it is my duty to provide for, and you may be sure I should do my utmost as long as there was a breath in my body or a penny in my purse.'[5]

In London, William met the Chelsea bills as they came in. Checking where he could, he asked Webb if the builder's account for studio alterations was in order. Should Allan and Emma be discharged, or kept on board wages? They would gossip if given the least grievance. And urging Howell to 'say nothing to anybody', he inquired after Gabriel's state at Speke. 'Of course I know that he was madly in love, and can believe in anything in the way of hypochondria on that account,' he wrote. 'But had he any and what sort of positive hallucinations?' It appears that Howell's answer was negative, though to William, as to Scott, Gabriel's passion for Jane was now viewed as an ominous herald of the greater malady. Scott also recalled the chaffinch at Penkill, unhesitatingly identified as Lizzie's soul. In retrospect, there had been many aberrant signs.

At home, William was sunk in silent gloom. Christina, however, appeared to have turned the corner, her condition stabilised during a recuperative month in Hampstead. Once more able to walk, she and Frances Rossetti went to stay at the farmhouse near Scalands, through Barbara Bodichon's generous agency. Before they left, William had a long talk with his mother and John Marshall, who still advised placing Gabriel under professional supervision, for current medical thought strongly advocated separation from family and friends. Graham recommended the Highland Asylum. William's idea of Penkill was strenuously opposed by Scott, fearing the burden on himself and Alice. How about Kelmscott? It was secluded and easier for friends to reach. 'The question seems to be now as to who Gabriel would endure about him,' wrote Jane, who had been asked not to communicate directly. Could Scott find out who he would like? for all friends seemed ready to volunteer. As to 'the possibility of his using the house at Kelmscott', she was not hopeful; 'he has said to me so often he never could go there again, that I doubt if he could be persuaded to think of it now,' she wrote; moreover, she suspected he would not care to be in Morris's company. For the present, surely 'the longer he can stay in that northern air the better it will be for him'.

William's next idea of a long Continental trip was quite impracticable. 'If he shows such manifest reluctance to walk beyond these grounds even when he has my protection (I use his own expression) could he be induced to brave the inconveniences of travel?' wrote George incredulously. Brown's suggestion of new treatment involving a shower bath was equally futile, replied Scott; Gabriel was 'a man under insane delusions, but neither imbecile nor violent'.[6] One evening, however, Rossetti was violently disturbed, demanding to be taken away from 'all this'. Other days he was better, acknowledging that his ideas might be delusions – or more likely his enemies had tired of their persecution. 'Sometimes he speaks and acts so as to make it difficult to resist the hope that the darkness has left him,' Scott told Alice; 'then by and bye the old horror of his delusions is confided to us by him just as bad or worse than ever ...'

A small crisis erupted when, having completed his promised fortnight, Scott left and Dunn declined to take his place. 'Much excited', Gabriel asked instead for Stillman, or Howell, or Dr Hake. The last obliged, arriving the day after Scott departed, and was favourably impressed, seeing signs of improvement invisible to others. Rossetti, in his view, was now chiefly depressed and hypochondriacal, and certainly too sane for anything to be done without his consent. 'This is a cheering account,' wrote George to Scott, 'which for the present keep to yourselves at Penkill as we do not wish to buoy them up too suddenly in London.'

Pleased to see Dr Hake, Rossetti was ready to accept his advice on everything except soporifics. On account of the hydrocele, he spent the mornings in bed, dozing. 'When he gets up he is disinclined to converse, and seems hipped so we say little or nothing,' Hake reported to William. In late afternoon he took a walk, had supper, and then grew chatty on a glass of whisky. He now liked being read to (except from his own works), and even looked at the newspaper. 'Sometimes no one could say there was anything wrong about him', and one night he even remarked, with something of his old spirit, that if there were any pretty peasant girls about he would paint them. This was the first sign of returning vitality.

But soon they had to leave Stobhall too. Hake suspected local gossip. 'I cannot but infer that Allen is a blab and that he spread the report at Stobhall that his master was insane,' he wrote, rather unfairly; 'and I am sure we got hustled out, prematurely, in consequence.' Graham sent a list of places available to let in Perthshire. George set off south-eastwards, searching in and around St Andrews. His father followed, and then turned towards Crieff, introduced himself to the local doctor, and thereby found a comfortable farmhouse at Trowan. On 26 July the trio accomplished an impressive feat, going via the George Hotel in Perth, 'through the midst of people and noise' without mishap.

Trowan offered good walks, seclusion, and Mrs Stewart, 'lady-farmer' and excellent landlady. The house was conveniently arranged, the cooking plain but good and enlivened by the hampers of game – grouse, hare, partridge – sent by Graham. The place was more beautiful and breezy than Urrard or Stobhall, Rossetti told Brown, and its independence from patronage was a great improvement. They settled into a regular routine of Dr Hake's devising and though at first Rossetti took little interest in the surroundings, after a time he began to enjoy the local walks, particularly that immediately behind the house, where a conical hill is surmounted by a memorial to General Sir David Baird, hero of the Siege of Seringapatam. With a gentle gradient, the spiral path, starting in woods, 'sometimes emerges on an unscreened platform commanding wide prospects hemmed in by the hills, then again passes into woodland, and so on; till at last one finds one has unwittingly reached some eminence, which, seen from below, would have seemed a task not to be attempted.'

'A stranger looking at him now would say he was a valetudinarian, or perhaps a *malade imaginaire*,' Hake reported of his patient on 2 August, adding that a week might pass without any reference to delusions. Towards 'outsiders and menials' his conduct was quite normal, and no one at Trowan suspected madness. On the contrary, they might wonder why he shrank from social interaction. A mere two months since the onset of the illness, the situation at last began to look favourable. For the sake of continued calm, however, the good doctor discouraged letters, suggesting instead a sort of health bulletin, saying Rossetti was temporarily forbidden to work. The idea of moving him to Dieppe, out of creditors' reach – the cause of William's greatest anxiety – was unnecessary, since Scotland was also beyond English legal jurisdiction, and Trowan a great deal quieter than Dieppe. 'When R. is well he will set all right himself,' Hake continued; 'any day he may take to work again and that without surprising us any more than his every day increasing interest in reading has done.'

Word came that Dunn was to finish certain chalk drawings for patrons. That would never do, Rossetti protested. 'I am not attending to these things now,' he said firmly; 'when I go back I can get better bargains.' At last, he too contemplated recovery.

The Hakes, however, remained concerned about 'the female complication', on which they were only partly informed. On 10 August, George promised Scott 'all the latest news about DGR and also of JM and Alexa whoever she is! We send the letters back to Brown unopened; but ask to be let into the secret.' The mystery of Alexa was soon solved, but the misapprehension underlines the general conviction that Rossetti's obsession with Janey was the cause of his collapse. When she wrote, requesting news and saying she might be in Scotland at the end of the month, the visit was vetoed and Rossetti was not told. But on 12 August he wrote to Jane directly, for the first time since his breakdown, in a long letter that does not survive. Subsequently, he slept poorly and woke in a very blue mood, talking again of the conspiracy. 'In consequence our bulletin today is not quite so good,' reported George, blaming the same 'disturbing cause'.

Dr Hake pondered whether to mail the letter, which finally went, with a covering note from himself (copied to William for information) asking Jane to let them know if it showed any sign of madness, and telling her to be 'very guarded' and cheering in her reply, not noticing in the slightest degree his delusion if he has manifested any ...' Happily, Jane reported that the letter showed 'no sign whatever of his late distressing illness', adding that she had received in the past many letters 'of a far more depressing kind'.'

He had recovered before, from disturbed vision and confusion in the head. 'We are all hoping that his mind may have begun to clear to some considerable extent before he bends his steps homewards,' wrote William to Scott, cautiously.

Now Gabriel began to open his own letters. He gave permission for his work to be included in *The Treasury of English Song*, and for a German translation of *The Blessed Damozel*. He instructed Dunn to forward the replica *Beata Beatrix* canvas, for which Graham had advanced £900. By the third week of August, improvement was unmistakable. Progress was as rapid as a revolution, wrote Hake, almost euphorically. 'Yesterday he looked over all his paints, brushes etc, and wrote [Dunn] a long letter desiring him to supply deficiencies. He has now got into regular correspondence with his brother, sister Christina, & Mrs Morris. To all outward appearance he is well – and who can be more than that? His mind is turned inside out as to the external world. Everything interests him in the old way, the scenery – newspapers, books, conversation ...' There could be no doubt that he would work as well as ever, and that the morbid delusions were banished for good.

Though it was in Hake's professional interest to stress the positive, it is clear that the acute phase of Rossetti's malady was subsiding. 'I fully expect to see him quite well by the end of September,' added George, telling William candidly that he had not originally shared his father's optimism. Naturally, there were qualifications. Rossetti was still occasionally 'explosive' and less cheerful than the Hakes, sometimes referring glumly to what was evidently now established as his 'flourishing condition', not perceived as such by the sufferer. 'I manage to go out daily, but my lameness and all else is just the same as ever,' he told William. 'I thought I would write, but, as you see, have nothing to say.'

Brown strongly advised leaving Cheyne Walk, telling William 'that costly and gloomy establishment' should be broken up. 'You are always in extremes,' Gabriel replied. 'Lately you talked of my garden at Chelsea as a paradise, and the house is undoubtedly very superior to any other I know, particularly now the studio has been so laboriously constructed.' He could not yet decide whether to return, 'but assuredly the few pounds expense which some delay involves are not to be weighed against so rash a precipitation. To settle in some mean and confined quarters is impossible to me.' This was the old Gabriel, not lost but briefly occluded. A long letter to William expanded the arguments, following instructions to delay payments to tradesmen as usual and instead settle Fanny's maintenance with the money in hand. Moreover, if Dunn came to Scotland, Tudor House should not be left with only the servants, so he wrote to Fanny to lock the studio and keep the key.

William sent hopeful, if somewhat misleading bulletins to friends. 'I am so glad to know that Gabriel is in good health again,' replied Whistler on 2 September. 'I supposed by this he must be nearly well and will soon return to Chelsea ... When you write, give him my love ...'[8]

Rossetti sent orders to Roberson's, and before Hake left made crayon portraits of both father and son, as a thank-you and sign of recovery. The lines were soft and less forceful, but displayed no debility of eye or hand. And at Graham's suggestion he drew a predella for the *Beatrix*, showing her meeting with Dante in Paradise. 'Look at me well: I am indeed Beatrice,' she says, lifting her veil. It was his motif, his talisman, dating from the days of the PRB, when he had first drawn the *Salutation* diptych. He had since made a watercolour for Boyce, painted the scene on the Red House settle, and repeated the watercolour for Lady Ashburton. Shaped to fit the predella, his new design showed Dante kneeling, arms outstretched, but gazing down, as if he cannot see Beatrice. She, looking more like Lizzie than ever, leans forward anxiously, both hands to her veil. They are meeting, but

forever apart. '*Guardami ben, ben son, ben son Beatrice*' runs the
inscription. He gave the drawing to George. It was the first real evidence of
recovery.

Feeling altogether fitter, he arranged for a routine draining of the
cumbersome hydrocele. 'Within the last week or so, I have rather decidedly
rallied in some respects as regards health and spirits,' he then told William,
adding that he was therefore preparing to leave Trowan. 'Wherever I can be
at peace there I shall assuredly work; but all, I now find by experience,
depends primarily on my not being deprived of the prospect of the society
of the one necessary person.' So he was going to Kelmscott.

William may have sighed, seeing Janey – 'the one necessary person' – as
cause not cure. But Rossetti had reason. In 1870, his disturbed vision had
vanished at Scalands when Janey arrived, and the following year the weeks
in Oxfordshire had proved equally restorative. At his worst moments, he
could not bear to be with her, but now he was getting better, her presence
was imperative. On 24 September he and George began the journey south,
stopping only for a family reunion of a few hours at Euston Square. The
following day Janey greeted him at Kelmscott.

The nightmare was over. 'All this past cursed state of things began on my
birthday,' he wrote to William. 'May the spell be removed now that yours is
past!'

'That Gabriel *was* mad is but too true; no one knows it better than myself,'
recalled Janey, sadly.[9] But why, at the age of forty-four, had a successful
man, in the prime of his career, with an acclaimed book of poems and a
major picture ready for exhibition, succumbed to acute delusional mania,
and tried to kill himself?

It was hard for William, looking back, to understand how such an
essentially minor matter as a venomous review could have such a
devastating effect on 'a person so self-reliant in essentials as Rossetti – one
who all his life had been doing so many things just as he chose, and because
he so chose, and whether other people liked them or not'. Nevertheless, 'it
is a simple fact that, from the time when the pamphlet had begun to work
into the inner tissue of his feelings, Dante Rossetti was a changed man, and
so continued till the close of his life'.[10]

Gabriel had never been timid: why should Buchanan's pamphlet provoke
distress, let alone delusions? What filled the walls with listening spies,
turned old friends into enemies, made a voice call out unspeakable names,
transformed poles into a gibbet? A gross libel may provoke anger, but
should not cause derangement. Rossetti told himself so in the miniature
notebook where he jotted down lists, addresses, quotations. 'In receiving an

unjust insult, remember that you can afford to despise it, while he who has been guilty of it can only despise himself,' he wrote; 'thus the advantage is yours.'[11]

At this distance, only suggestions and connections can be made to account for his catastrophic collapse. Although more common in young men, breakdowns with paranoid symptoms, obsessional thoughts and hallucinatory voices are not unknown in mid-life. Often triggered by a slight event and exacerbated by drugs taken in the desperate search for respite, the crash from minor to major disorder typically coincides with interior stresses and unresolved conflicts. Objective and subjective assessments become grossly misaligned, intolerable oppositional pressures on the sense of self lead to sudden fracture. Somehow, the mind fissures, creating erroneous inner perceptions with all the force of external, verifiable reality.

It is said that late-onset breakdowns are more common in those with high degrees of narcissism, as the sense of mortality and failure impends in middle life. Certainly Rossetti was self-absorbed, though not therefore unself-critical, and in any case collapse coincided with a peak of success. But in several ways he was more vulnerable than William could perceive, accustomed as he was to Gabriel's self-confident pride.

Tracing the course of Rossetti's breakdown, one may infer from his reaction that the real power of the *Fleshly* attack lay in its accuracy. Many of the poems were indeed sensual, speaking in an open if flowery manner of indecent matters – unnatural connection between woman and snake, or natural coition between man and woman. The *Fleshly* charges might be exaggerated, but identified a strand which Rossetti himself had anticipated would cause trouble; despite their Aesthetic tone, *Troy Town*, *Eden Bower* and many of the sonnets were erotic in intent.

Posing as an idealist, he had written as a sensualist. It was an appellation he could not accept; yet, protest as he might, it could not be refuted. He had betrayed his own high principles. In painting, he had come to accept this, as the inevitable result of depending on the market. In *Hand and Soul*, Chiaro dell'Erma had determined to remain true to his inner vision. But the wish to succeed had made his author more worldly. He had 'often said' that to be dependent on patrons was like being a whore. He claimed his poetry had remained 'unprostituted' but in actuality it was shown to be impure – a far worse accusation.

A bad error of judgement had led him to change the title of *Placatâ Venere* to *Nuptial Sleep*, when the word 'nuptial' meant 'marital'. Rossetti was known to be a widower, so to publish a poem describing sexual intercourse under this title was horrifyingly disrespectful to his wife's memory. When he republished *The House of Life*, this sonnet was omitted.

The second prong of the attack that had all but unmanned him were the charges of cowardice and effeminacy. The Fleshly writers, wrote Buchanan, were 'too spoilt with flattery to bear criticism' – a palpable hit, unmistakably directed, given Rossetti's careful orchestration of reviews; moreover, they were promoters of an affected style that threatened to corrupt and emasculate the rising generation. This 'plague from Italy and France' was a 'school of falsettoes innumerable – false love, false picture, false patriotism, false religion, false life, false death', all disguised in 'the poisoned chalice of a false style'. To support the subtext without risk of libel, the work of Simeon Solomon, like Swinburne known or suspected of homosexuality, was here adduced. There was 'nothing virile, nothing tender, nothing completely sane' in Mr Rossetti's verses; *Jenny* was the work of 'an emasculated Mr Browning'; the entire school was effeminately engaged in contemplating their own images, and wholly lacking in healthy, male, English vigour.

When the *Saturday Review* had repeated these themes, Rossetti's sanity snapped. But the charge of cowardice was hardest to bear. Since schooldays, Gabriel had believed himself to lack physical courage. A true man, as everyone knew, was ready to fight for his honour and knock down any insulting fellow – as Whistler had shown on several occasions. At the same time, a true man bore criticism stoically, silently. According to Carlyle, if any poet could really be killed off by a review, the sooner he was so dispatched the better. But Rossetti had found this a double bind: to defend himself or ignore all slings and arrows had only opened the way to further calumny. Protest and denial had encouraged renewed assault.

Buchanan's charges thus hit home. Both his artistic integrity and his masculinity were assailed, with additional blows at his national origin (so much for his adoption of bulldog patriotism). At a deep level, self-belief – which, as William observed, seemed so secure – was fatally destabilised.

He was vulnerable in another sense, too, for all too clearly his collapse brought others to mind, confirming the traditional view of inherited insanity. John Polidori, the uncle he had never known, manifested similar symptoms of derangement before killing himself with prussic acid. His own father Don Gabriele suffered a comparable breakdown when his life's work was assailed and his reputation as a scholar crumbled. His vision too had become disturbed as he responded paranoically to criticism and grew convinced his enemies were closing in, before descending into pathetic, petulant invalidism.

Today, such afflictions are known as schizo-affective disorders and believed to have a genetic component, through studies that reveal correlated symptoms, most commonly in families with especially creative members.[12] Suggestive rather than conclusive, such studies indicate a predisposition to minor and major breakdown encompassing emotional volatility coupled with high levels of intellectual or artistic talent. In Rossetti's case, such an inheritance came from both sides of the family.

In this context, the frantic early efforts to prevent Buchanan reviewing *Poems* were warning symptoms of the malady, whereby a conviction of external hostility assumes irrational proportions, crystallising around a legitimate suspect but magnifying him to demonological size. Typically, in paranoia this figure multiplies, aggregating others into a hostile camp; then, the adversaries are not only in league, but constantly watching, plotting. The irrational self becomes obsessed with the idea that even strangers in the street (especially strangers in the street) are watching, mocking, threatening.

For Rossetti, the world was henceforth divided into friends and foes, whom it became imperative to identify. 'What man is not jealous in bestowing the name of friend?' begins one notebook jotting. 'In like manner that of foe should not be lightly yielded, but should demand some worthiness in its recipient: a dog can be but a dog. "For enemies thine enemies tell o'er / But dogs for what a dog is and no more." '[13]

With hindsight, his lifelong moodiness, tending to swing from geniality to glumness and grow intolerant and irritable when opposed, signalled a temperamental disposition that had steadily become disabling and erupted dramatically in 1872. But if partly inherited, Rossetti's vulnerability and internal conflicts were surely aggravated by his relationship with Jane, which his adversary also assailed.

'There are certain passionate phases of the soul when to know one thing true and to believe it are found two separate things,' he scribbled in one of his notebooks. For a long while, he had protested – and believed – that his love for Janey was pure, idealised, unimpeachable; she was too beautiful and too good not to be loved. And for a long while the adoration had indeed been ideal, whatever the world thought. But at some stage, the illusion had broken. It might not be possible to tell the beloved's body from her soul, or their love from God, but in plain terms, it was an adulterous affair. He was in love with – and by 1871 living at Kelmscott with – another man's wife.

Though always sensitive to criticism, he had previously affected to disregard the opinions of others. But he had always sought eminence with a carefully cultivated if negligently worn sense of celebrity. Indeed, he dreaded the fickleness of fame, the loss of limelight, even while he naturally shrank from personal exposure. Yet, by casting his sonnets in the first person, he had laid himself open. 'Shall I sonnet-sing you about myself?' asked Browning four years later in a poem called *House* that seems unmistakably to comment on Rossetti's sequence, comparing self-exposure in verse to an earthquake that rips the front off dwellings, revealing all domestic secrets.

It was public knowledge that Mr Rossetti's wife had died tragically. In literary-artistic circles it was also known – who could tell how widely? – that her coffin had been disinterred to retrieve the very poems under attack. Moreover, his pictures and verses proclaimed him a lover of female beauty, while his passion for Mrs Morris was near-public. Thanks to Buchanan's moral peroration, he now guessed how his private life was gossiped about, for the *Fleshly* pamphlet had invoked the 'free lover' scornful of continence and conventional virtue, joked knowingly that the next volume of verse would be called 'Leg is Enough' and – worst of all in an essay attacking poets by name – personified contemporary vice as a two-headed monster: Adultery twinned with Dipsomania. Swinburne was certainly the latter, and Rossetti was his Fleshly brother. Did all London know of their affairs? There was good reason to fear Rumour because, as with the eroticism of his art, the immorality of his private life was true.

Moreover, while he might ignore the charge as regards his own reputation, the world would also blame him for ruining Jane's. An adulterous woman, living openly with another man, was cast out of many social circles, as others besides the guiltless George Eliot knew only too well. Gabriel could offer Jane no protection from this danger – except that of renunciation – which itself would underscore the illicit nature of their relationship. Again, he was double-bound, unable either to fulfil his love or withdraw it. Small wonder he felt ambivalent towards Kelmscott. The immediate effect of his breakdown, it may be noted, was to prevent him spending another summer there in secluded intimacy with Jane.

Then there were issues of masculine self-esteem. It was not honourable to seduce the wife of one's friend, disciple, business partner. Topsy's forbearance only made the betrayal worse.

Nor was it the only betrayal. In his poems, and in his heart, Gabriel had not experienced awakening love for Jane as a betrayal of Lizzie. But his continued evocation of Lizzie's unquiet spirit was a desperate show of doubt: the deeper his love for Jane, the more insistently he wanted to hear Lizzie say she was happy. He had of course betrayed her before – when he had flirted with Annie, and when he had left her in Matlock and taken up with Fanny, in an unequivocal gesture of rejection. The public celebration of his passion for Jane could well appear further evidence of inconstancy. Given Jane's reciprocal love, however, Rossetti could not be ashamed without also shaming her. The conflict between love and honour was acute, and his self-image as a man as well as an artist was fatally twisted as he had to confront his failure to live up to the standards required.

Betrayal, immorality, sensuality, impurity in word and deed: these were harsh charges. All his life, Rossetti had held to principles learnt at his mother's knee. 'Your first inculcations on many points are still the standard of criticism with me,' he would write a few years later; 'and I am often conscious of being influenced correctly by those early-imbibed and still valuable impressions.'[14] He had not always followed them, but her precepts were still believed in: honesty, integrity, loyalty, honour in word and action. Nothing mean, unclean, self-serving, venal. Raised on Watts's *Divine and Moral Songs*, Rossetti had outgrown his childhood belief in sin without exorcising its power. Retribution followed wrongdoing; redemption came through remorse and penance.

Other ancient derelictions were recurring presences. Towards the end of his life Rossetti spoke with anguish of the disrespect that had angered his father, and of his urgent, unrealisable wish for forgiveness. 'I can make nothing of Christianity,' he told Scott, 'but I only want a confessor to give me absolution for my sins.' The voices Rossetti heard, in the street, on the shores of a loch, behind the wainscot, were internally generated. Unlike Blake's, they were malign, accusatory. If such symptoms can be rationally deciphered, they would seem a projection of fears based on the appropriate punishment for his wrongful deeds and desires.

Moreover, his conviction that enemies intended not merely to hound but also to kill him, that a bell was ringing for his arrest and a gibbet being built for his execution, suggests a projection of severe guilt, that he was unworthy of life. The term of unprintable obloquy he heard inside his head on that first, terrible weekend must have been one for which death was an appropriate penalty. Unable to offer a defence, he swallowed the laudanum. 'Murderer' seems the worst word of abuse, but William had little reason to call this unrepeatable, since his brother had killed no one. 'Traitor', 'liar' and especially 'adulterer' are equal possibilities.

Towards the end of his life, Rossetti spoke, rather elliptically, of blaming himself, not for Lizzie's death, but for the lack of affection that had prompted her overdose; perhaps, too, he felt obscurely responsible for the loss of their daughter. He also regretted the exhumation, done for the sake of literary ambition. It was as if the Faustian day of reckoning had arrived, with a net like that of the Seine fishermen being drawn around him, and curses no one else could hear, which he could only make sense of as an invisible conspiracy. In *Rose Mary*, the evil spirits of the beryl-stone threaten the transgressor with an eternity spinning in hell, like the *Inferno's* adulterous lovers Paolo and Francesca.

As with his namesake, it was ten years since the death of Rossetti's first beloved. In the *Purgatorio*, Beatrice reappears to Dante, rebuking his derelictions and inconstancies. Overwhelmed by guilt and failure, he snaps like a crossbow under pressure, and is then re-baptized into grace, joining the four Virtues. No such epiphany awaited Gabriel, but the acute phase of his breakdown was succeeded by a gradual recovery that suggests inner healing.

As the doctors had hoped, rest and seclusion in Scotland were recuperative, and friends may have credited Rossetti with virtually miraculous powers of recovery, seeing how speedily he resumed painting, with a professionalism that belied the weeks of incapacity. On the eve of departure from Trowan, he learnt that Pilgeram had sold *The Bower Meadow* to Dunlop for just under a thousand pounds. 'So if my foes as well as my friends will buy, I hope the dealers will take some more,' he told Brown. 'I trust when at Kelmscott to do a good stroke of work, and purpose carrying on two pictures from Janey if she is well enough to sit as I hope. One to be the lady seated in a tree with a book in her lap, and the other a full-length *Pandora*.' Would Brown inquire whether Leathart was interested?[15] Either picture should be worth at least a thousand guineas. Already, his brain was again full of pictorial ideas. In Scotland, he and the Hakes had been reading Merivale's history of the Roman Empire, and as his recovery progressed, he found several subjects for pictures, well aware of the growing popularity of neo-classical themes in the current art market.

Safely installed at Kelmscott, his first letter contained heartfelt thanks to Brown. 'Here I am, as well as ever I was in my life, which is perhaps a pretty good reason for coming here,' he wrote. 'The better I am, the more intensely I feel your friendship in word and deed. I need not doubt that you have pardoned any feeble petulance of my late ailing condition.' And gratitude to his brother was equally deep. 'I know well how much you have suffered on my account; indeed perhaps your suffering may have been more acute than my own dull nerveless state during the past months,' he wrote. 'Your love, dear William, is not less returned by me than it is sweet to me, and that is saying all.'[16]

'I am determined now to make every effort not to go under again, and feel at this moment as if such a thing were impossible,' he added. Indeed, he was well enough to resume control of his finances, and safely negotiate an untimely annoyance, as when he found that the bank had cashed a forged cheque. On inquiry, he recognised the hand as that of Elizabeth Rovedino, the daughter of a music teacher long ago known to the Rossettis, who, having previously asked for money, had now copied his signature on a cheque for £47 15s. The Union Bank ought to have shown more vigilance, in his view, and refund the money. He would not contemplate prosecution, and asked good Dr Hake to call on the bank manager on his behalf. Hake consulted a legal friend, who advised that the only way to avoid the publicity of prosecution was to forgo a refund. 'My dear Sir, It is of all things my wish to do nothing whatever in this matter – above all not to appear personally,' Rossetti replied during his brief stopover in London, requesting Mr Watts to speak to the bank instead. And thus not only was the affair dealt with, but a new friend moved into Gabriel's orbit.

Theodore Watts was aged forty, going on seventy, with a solicitor's habit of seeing worst-case scenarios, a liking for literature and an unexpectedly Romantic passion for gipsies. William, who met him for the first time on 21 September, later described him as 'the steadfast and most assiduous of friends', although over the years Watts's conduct was often irritating. In time, he also proved useful to Swinburne, rescuing him in 1879 from near-fatal alcoholism by taking him to live in Putney.

Other practical matters were attended to in the first few days at Kelmscott – fire insurance for Tudor House, Marshall's fees for medical attendance, board wages for Emma and the ailing Allan. Gabriel renewed his share of the Manor's lease, and wrote to Fanny about 'an immense quantity' of green velvet rolled up somewhere at Chelsea, wherewith to make winter curtains. He decided not to repurchase the Tudor House china, confident that Murray Marks could find him new pieces when required. 'I'll hope to see you here as soon as you like,' he told William on 6 October, conscious that his troubles had cancelled his brother's summer vacation.[17] George would meet the train, Janey joined warmly in the invitation, 'and so would Top if here'. And could William bring him another coat, and his wideawake hat? He was settling in for a long stay.

At Kelmscott, William found Gabriel 'apparently just as he used to be before his attack' and free of delusions. Outwardly, the household was the same peaceful Paradise as before, with ripe fruit in the orchard and autumn yellows tingeing the elms. Janey and her girls had been here all summer, and they were extending the last weeks as long as possible. George's advent was the greatest bonus, for he proved endlessly helpful, carrying messages to Lechlade and Faringdon, going fishing with Morris, who came for short weekends, and amusing Jenny and May with a daily programme of punting, pony rides and ginger beer, like a wondrously amiable elder brother. 'George keeps everything going, and I am convinced makes life smoother to all inhabitants of Kelmscott Manor House than they ever found it before,' William told Dr Hake.[18]

He himself attempted to talk to Gabriel 'on a certain serious subject', namely Jane. But Gabriel would not be drawn. 'He utterly scouted the idea that this matter had had anything whatever to do with his recent gloomy frame of mind, and only regretted he had not at an earlier date in his convalescence come to Kelmscott.' Subconsciously, perhaps, the decision to return to the Manor also marked a determination to demonstrate that their relationship was honourable.

As for Jane, she kept her own counsel as usual; or at least did not confide it to correspondence. A year before, she and Gabriel had been lingering in the country after an idyllic lovers' summer, postponing the return to the smoky city. Now, whatever her dreams had been, all was altered. Gabriel was the invalid, and there was no realistic prospect of life together. His breakdown had yoked her anew to Topsy. Moreover, this year her husband had come to love the Manor, as he knew he would: to Morris, buildings were objects of intense longing, and he once described to Jane how revisiting an ancient mansion in Kent made his stomach turn over 'with desire of an old house'.[19]

'Time has tossed all of us about and made us play other parts than we set out upon,' wrote Webb to Jane this autumn. 'I see that you play yours well and truly under the changes and I feel deeply sympathetic on that account.'[20]

Striving hard to feel sympathy, Morris could only be crabby. When he next came to Kelmscott, for a wet and windy weekend, William was there – whether in his bed or not is unclear, though in inviting his brother Gabriel had certainly offered him Morris's room. And Morris did not like WMR. 'Lord how dull the evenings were! with William Rossetti also to help us,' he groaned on 24 October.[21] Later, when told how Gabriel mocked the story of Sigurd, asking who could take serious interest in someone who was supposedly brother to a dragon, Morris retorted explosively that a dragon for a brother was better than a bloody fool.

No, they had not quarrelled, Morris assured Aglaia Coronio in November, during a fit of 'mulligrubs' or blue devils. 'One thing wanting ought not to go for so much: nor indeed does it spoil my enjoyment of life always,' he wrote; 'often in my better moods I wonder what it is in me that throws me into such rage and despair at other times.' Then he confessed: 'another quite selfish business is that Rossetti has set himself down at Kelmscott as if he never meant to go away; and not only does that keep me away from that harbour of refuge (because it is really a farce our meeting when we can help it) but also he has all sorts of ways so unsympathetic with the sweet simple old place, that I feel his presence there as a kind of slur on it: this is very unreasonable though when one thinks why one took the place, and how this year it has really answered that purpose: nor do I think I should feel this about it if he had not been so unromantically discontented with it and the whole thing which made me very angry and disappointed.'[22]

Morris's irritation attested to Rossetti's recovery: previously his querulous discontent had been a symptom of sickness. But Gabriel was by no means fully restored. His hatred of Browning had not diminished, and others like Rose ('a blackguard and no friend to me') had joined the 'enemy' ranks. Hake was warned that there was still such 'a dead set' being made against him, by others besides Buchanan, that any connection with his name would assuredly arouse 'a swarm of malignity' against Hake's new book. Then, on hearing from Dunn that a cook temporarily employed at Cheyne Walk had pawned several items before departing, Gabriel grew not only angry but suspicious, saying she had been introduced by spies, to make prearranged signals from within the house ...

Promising to return after Christmas, Jane took the girls back to London, where at year's end the Morrises were due to make room at Queen Square for the business, moving to a new home near or beyond the Joneses in Fulham. Before she left, Gabriel asked her to pose for a full-length Proserpine or Persephone, who spends half the year in Hades, as wife to Pluto. The subject had been composed a year past, during the first summer among the flower meadows of Kelmscott, anticipative of Jane's winter return to the dark underworld of London with a husband she had not chosen. It now bore complex layers of symbolism, for Gabriel had signally failed to rescue her from this fate, and was himself now often as gloomy as Dis.[23] His own mood seems expressed through Proserpine's. '*Oimè per te, Proserpina infelice!*' he wrote in a sonnet, in Italian, sent for William 'to pick holes in' on 7 November. Alas unhappy indeed, for the absolute distance separating past from present, as great as that between joy and sorrow:

> Afar away the light that brings cold cheer
>   Unto this wall, – one instant and no more
>   Admitted at my distant palace-door.
> Afar the flowers of Enna from this drear
> Dire fruit, which, tasted once, must thrall me here.
>   Afar those skies from this Tartarean grey
>   That chills me: and afar, how far away,
> The nights that shall be from the days that were.
> Afar from mine own self I seem, and wing
>   Strange ways in thought, and listen for a sign:
>   And still some heart unto some soul doth pine,
> (Whose sounds mine inner sense is fain to bring,
> Continually together murmuring,) –
>   'Woe's me for thee, unhappy Proserpine!'

'*Lungi da me mi sento ...*' 'Afar from mine own self.' Time had indeed made them play other parts.

Taking his motif from Lemprière's classical dictionary, Rossetti related how, when Ceres persuaded Jupiter to restore her daughter to the upper earth, he consented on condition that Proserpine had eaten none of the fruits of Hades. Alas, 'she had eaten one grain of a pomegranate, and this enchained her to a new empire and destiny. She is represented in a gloomy corridor of her palace, with the fatal fruit in her hand. As she passes, a gleam strikes on the wall behind her from some inlet suddenly opened, and admitting for a moment the light of the upper world; and she glances furtively towards it, immersed in thought. The incense-burner stands beside her as the attribute of the goddess. The ivy branch in the background ... may be taken as a symbol of clinging memory.'[24]

By the New Year, he had begun and abandoned three Proserpines, before getting the fourth right. Though the later history of the painting is confused, he was not mistaken in saying that his work was now as good as it had ever been, and contradicts the often-voiced view that both his pictorial and poetic powers failed with his illness. For *Proserpine* is a compelling, haunting image, much admired for its Symbolist power. Its forms and lines have greater gravity than any previous works, and are replete with sombre feeling. The figure's full lips, flowing hair and intense gaze, according to a recent commentator, create a mood of heavy sensuality, heightened by the shape and glistening blood-red flesh in the cleft of the ripe pomegranate she holds, and the burning incense below.[25] To many, this is Rossetti's greatest work, with all the iconic quality Pater had ascribed to the *Mona Lisa*.

For Gabriel himself, Kelmscott was like light from the upper air, compared to the hell of preceding weeks. And he was vigorously back at the easel. To ensure that his reputation did not suffer from rumours as to his mental state, a swift resumption of professional practice was required. Between September and Christmas he ordered four new canvases, brushes, paints and a painting case, to be sent from London. He had a verbal agreement with Leyland, who was furnishing a new London house with excessive grandeur, for one large and six small pictures, to hang round the drawing and music rooms. Currently, the large one was to be *The Ship of Love*, the six others to complement *Veronica Veronese*. Leyland never bought for love, said Howell acutely, only to fill particular spaces. As he was by far the richest patron, this was not to be argued with.

In addition, Rossetti asked to be sent all the 'old drawings' in the studio that could be worked up and offered for sale. 'There is a very large value lying idle there, which might bring in good money now; whereas, if one waits till a moment when one needs money in a hurry, the only result is that all those who call themselves one's best friends gather round one to try and get one's best things for as few shillings as they can manage to get them for,' he told Fanny. 'When I needed money in the summer, not one friend who had capital came forward to offer to lend me any, though I would have done in a like case not only for my intimate friends but for any friend who needed it. All they did was to stand aloof while I sold my property much under its value. Therefore the best thing I can do is to turn everything that will sell into money while they know they must give the full value.'[26]

Though this account was partial, like many who recover from serious illness, Rossetti reflected on past friendship and future needs.

If, as was urged on him from all sides, he would henceforth live in the country, he would need a London agent who would take works on a regular basis but also allow him to sell direct to private clients. Price levels should be controlled, comparable and confidential.

Though not the most suitable dealer, Howell was available and willing, and since the abrupt termination of his employment with Ruskin had been dealing in the decorative arts. He had a wide network of contacts, a discreet as well as a blabbing tongue, and a congenial personality. Rossetti had never suffered personally from his slipperiness. 'I would of course try to make the prices lower to you than to a person who meant to keep the pictures, but still they would be high priced works,' Gabriel told him, in the first week at Kelmscott. 'Is there a chance of any of them suiting you and of the tin coming to me by instalments whenever I may need it . . . ? I had rather deal with you than with Pilgeram & Co. if feasible.'[27]

Howell agreed 'with alacrity', on condition that the dealership was exclusive. He would take *Proserpine* for 550 guineas, paying half the sum at once and the balance on delivery. 'I must impress on you the absolute necessity of early deliveries,' he wrote on 30 October. 'I am anxious to make as important a market for your work (for both our sakes) as I can, but in order to do this with success you must in turn do your best to aid and encourage me.' The funds, he added, came from his partner, their old friend the photographer Parsons, who had 'a rich capitalist' backer.[28]

It sounded businesslike enough. 'Our bargain being concluded, there is no time like the present,' returned Rossetti the next day, 'and I will be obliged for your cheque by return – viz.: £288.15/–'. *Proserpine* had been restarted on a larger canvas, and would now measure 43 by 21 inches. The first version, where head and shoulders were almost finished, would be cut down and priced at 200 guineas. He was also working on a drawing of little May holding a pansy, which was quite as full of colour as a painting; Foord & Dickinson were making a frame. Size 28³/₄ by 19 inches, price 100 guineas to Howell, 150 to anyone else.

'I think with Charley's help I shall drive a flourishing trade without the insufferable bore of writing myself to people offering pictures I cannot show them,' Gabriel told Kate a little while later. Between Howell's sharp practice and Rossetti's partly dilatory habits, it is hard to determine how businesslike their arrangement actually was, or indeed to track the history of several of the pictures recorded in the correspondence. Potentially, however, the connection was mutually rewarding. 'As a salesman – with his open manner, his winning address, and his exhaustless gift of amusing talk, not innocent of high colouring and of actual *blague* – Howell was unsurpassable,' wrote William in later years; 'and he achieved for Rossetti, with ease and also with much ingenious planning, many a stroke of most excellent professional business.'[29] Gabriel 'though in some ways extremely heedless and lax in spending money, was always keenly alive to his own interests in acquiring it, and not at all the man to be long hoodwinked by anybody', he added, and as his brother had never complained, William inferred that Howell did not line his pockets at Gabriel's expense. Gabriel indeed confirmed that he had not the least suspicion of false dealing.

His next thought was of the long-projected, oft-postponed exhibition. Thanking Parsons for the first *Proserpine* payment, he stressed the need for purchasers to guarantee that pictures would not be lent when required. He sent draft wording for printed labels to be stuck to the back of pictures, in accordance with exhibition practice, and on 11 November asked Howell specifically about 'getting up a collection of some dozen or so of my latest and best things' for exhibition in the spring. 'What is your opinion about this? Gambart some 5 or 6 months ago pressed me very much about it, together with engraving the large picture, but I don't want to do it with him. One leading question is, what *good* gallery could one get?'

Howell's reply was quick and entrepreneurial. 'We will undertake the exhibition with pleasure,' he wrote. 'The best room in London is the new British Institution in Bond Street and this I can get, only the rent is very high, but that should not be considered in the *least*. It would be better to have it when everyone is in town, but when *nothing else is going* in order to concentrate all attention on our exhibition[,] then again we must make friends with the press and give a dinner or two and thus secure the most we can good and indifferent. This should be done entirely by myself, you helping me only on the sly as far as a few friends are concerned. For the monthly periodicals we could go on preparing notes on the pictures which would help – Swinburne and "such like". Then have a very swell private view and invite every nob in the kingdom.'

Fashionable Bond Street, discreet dinners for critics, a private view full of nobs, and Swinburne as chief cheer-leader? Rossetti's recovery was not so advanced as this, and there the matter rested, although at Christmas Gabriel was still talking of showing *Dante's Dream* and other pictures in the spring, telling his mother he could get things organised in London without being present. Howell remained keen, but Graham urged caution, apprehensive of the consequences.

For years now Rossetti had failed annually to exhibit 'next spring'. But his willingness even to contemplate presenting work to the public suggests a remarkable recovery of nervous stability. As, too, does his correspondence over subsequent months with Howell, who grew increasingly evasive in all dealings. Surprisingly, Rossetti remained friendly, equable – if sometimes rhetorically irascible – and quite unparanoid.

In December, the weather worsened and the winter waters rose, turning the roads around Kelmscott into causeways. A fierce gale uprooted six trees near the Manor. Gabriel stopped shaving altogether. He acquired a sheepdog, named Turvy. He moved from the draughty studio to the room beneath, sealing up the windows. 'If you saw the place, you'd soon see one good reason for staying here even in winter, as it still looks more beautiful than other places,' he wrote when Brown commended a new residence in London. Nor was he tempted by Scalands, which Barbara again offered, for six months. 'I have a complete artistic "plant" here now,' he explained, adding, 'I should not think in any case of losing my hold on this place, and finding someone else installed in my rooms.'[30]

So Morris was right: Gabriel did not mean to leave, lest his position at Kelmscott be usurped. There was not room for both men, figuratively speaking, and the sexual rivalry was displaced into a submerged struggle for mastery of the Manor. Morris, incidentally, detested dogs.

Jane had left a servant named Mary to cook and house-keep. George remained an invaluable companion, showing little real desire to return to his studies, or to any of the occupations his father suggested. A pony trap was procured, making it easier to fetch supplies and visitors. Both Scott and Dr Hake came for a few days, and Rossetti repeatedly urged Brown to join him, before or over Christmas. Unable to contemplate the season without a family gathering, he went to London for a short visit, finding Christina still forbidden to climb stairs but able to walk to church, and on Boxing Day he returned to Chelsea for the first time in six months. Brown, Dunn, Howell and Stillman came to dine. He saw Fanny, whose 'incubus' of a husband had recently died, and could therefore no longer lay claim to any assets. Gabriel promised to provide a nest egg, and asked Howell to dispose advantageously of any drawings she wished to sell. He met Theodore Watts for the first time. Graham also called, enabling Gabriel to express in person both his gratitude for the Perthshire respite and his sympathy with Graham's own vale of sorrows – the death of his teenage son in the autumn. Three years before, Rossetti had drawn a life-size head of young Willie, and bereavement formed an additional bond between painter and patron.

Graham was a reserved personality, who valued Rossetti's friendship in ways he could not easily describe. Heir to a comfortable fortune from port wine and cotton, he had represented the family interests in Portugal and India and since 1865 had been MP for rapidly growing industrial and mercantile Glasgow, though his heart was in neither business nor politics. He bought more pictures than he could house, chiefly early Italian and the latest works from Burne-Jones, Rossetti, Millais, Legros, Fred Walker. But no pictures could compensate for a dead son. He said Gabriel was looking ten years younger than when last seen, before the breakdown. All credit to country air and quietness.

On 27 December Gabriel dined as of old with the Scotts (Alice detested his new beard) and the next day he went back to Kelmscott, fixing no date for a return. On New Year's Eve William saw the old year out at Tudor House, with Dunn for sole companion, commenting briefly that it was 'the most painful year I have ever passed'. Had Gabriel heard, he would doubtless have agreed – as also with the observation that 1872 was however 'much less black at its close' than it had been in midsummer.

At the Manor, two more dogs joined Turvy: a deerhound-collie cross called Bess, acquired by George from Scotland, and George's own black-and-tan terrier who rejoiced in the name of Dizzy, 'after a celebrated politician'. On New Year's Day, they were visited by carol-singing children. But the modern world was encroaching. The railway had reached Lechlade, and the beetroot-processing factory upriver had acquired a horrible steam-whistle to summon the workers seven times a day, starting at 5 a.m. George graduated from fishing to wildfowling. 'Several of his moorhens have already cried "How long O Lord?" on our dinner table,' Gabriel told Dr Hake in February, joking that when quadrupeds began to fall he would furnish himself with a pocket pistol in self-defence against the escalation of murder. Soon, a jet-black retriever named Nero joined the household, and a long-haired terrier named Jemmy. The result of these additions, as Gabriel told his mother, was that Dizzy yapped inquiringly at George's heels, 'as much as to say "What, more dogs! Explain!" '[31]

Out for a snowy walk, Dizzy nearly drowned in an ice-filled ditch. Retracing his steps, Rossetti found the submerged dog with forepaws on a ledge of snow, like an Elizabethan portrait, whom he hooked out with his umbrella. The walk was an hour's daily trudge, 'straight as the crow flies to a certain point through the fields, regardless of their owners' rights', as Brown later wrote; 'and then home again, at a rapid pace as though it were a penance.'[32]

Snowdrops surfaced all over the garden. 'I am painting some today,' Gabriel told Fanny, sending a small bunch. The cut-down *Proserpine* was adorned with a snowdrop bouquet, and renamed *Blanzifiore*.[33] Then 'the loveliest thing' appeared in the field – a breeding-fold made of hurdles and thatched with straw, hard against a hollowed-out haystack in which the shepherd slept while his flock of thirty ewes produced their lambs. Like the box-tree armchairs, the thatched sheepfold took Gabriel's fancy. Really, Brown should come and incorporate it into a painting. 'You could stow your belongings in the haystack,' he wrote persuasively. 'If I were doing it, I should put a Christ walking up and down the centre of it.'[34]

It was a long time since he had had such a devotional idea for a painting. An almost Wordsworthian sonnet followed:

> Soft-littered is the new year's lambing-fold,
>   And in the hollowed haystack at its side
>   The shepherd lies o' nights now, wakeful-eyed
> At the ewes' travailing call through the dark cold.

'How large that thrush looks on the bare thorn-tree!' he would remark later, observing the wintry garden. Even the river-edges began to freeze, each tall reed circled by a clinging diamond of ice.

CHAPTER TWENTY-FOUR

Respite

Earlier in the winter, the old grievance against Ruskin, who since 1870 had occupied the equivalent chair at Oxford, spurred Madox Brown to apply for the Slade Professorship of Fine Art at Cambridge University. It was a chimerical hope, for Brown had no qualifications or ability as lecturer, and had opposed the establishment of the Slade School in London – directed by Ned's brother-in-law Edward Poynter – on the grounds that art practice did not belong in a university setting. But by the same token he felt strongly that practising artists rather than scholars should speak on art. Gabriel did not hesitate to lend his support. 'One thing *va sans dire* – that, whether in doing or not doing, I am at your disposal to command,' he wrote on 3 December, before adding that he feared Brown was 'too good' for the post, and that 'something that shall fall more or less into the routine of Cambridge Lectures' is what the electors wished for. A testimonial from Ruskin was out of the question, but Poynter might agree. Of course Gabriel would canvass all influential acquaintance.

He therefore wrote to Bruce (now Lord Aberdare) and the Cowper-Temples, offering also to approach Lady Ashburton, F. W. Burton, Theodore Martin, and even Monckton Milnes (now Lord Houghton) 'though he's a frightful old humbug'. Half-suspecting that the application was motivated by financial need – at fifty-two, Brown was as far from assured success as ever – he offered a loan, or a gift. 'Are you crippled for tin at all at this moment?' he asked. 'I have much more than usual and am besides earning rapidly.'[1] Brown was proud, but seems to have accepted fifty pounds. The old quotation was never so apt: 'There's that betwixt us been, which men remember ... till all's forgot.'

When Brown's printed Address setting forth his ideas on Professing Fine Art arrived, however, Gabriel was dismayed by its verbal errors and vile punctuation. But in commenting on Brown's historical outline, he incidentally revealed some views of his own. Surely it was nonsense to say that Hogarth had revived painting? 'I have seen Watteaus which might be Hogarths only drawn with more style,' he wrote; 'indeed Watteau is more absolutely a colourist than Hogarth and I suppose was still living or only lately dead when H. began to paint.'

Be that as it may, Sidney Colvin got the Slade chair. 'I've seen the bad news in print,' Rossetti told Brown. 'Well, I suppose the only thing to say is *Pazienza*!' A fellow of 'Trin:Camb' was obviously the preferred candidate, doubtless preselected; no discredit to Brown.[2]

In January 1873, Morris came to Kelmscott with Janey, who stayed on for a fortnight, while their new home in west London was being got ready. Rossetti undertook to design stationery for each address, decorated with her personal emblem, the heartsease. But the result was coarse and heavy. Some of the flowers looked more like forget-me-nots, he complained to Howell, intermediary with the die-maker, and the gold printing was too loud. To Jane, silver looked like wedding stationery and though Gabriel endeavoured to improve the die and try various inks, in the end the decorative device proved too difficult to achieve. A proof sample survives among Howell's papers, showing 'JANE' garlanded by leaves and flower-heads.

She also received gifts of jewellery, for herself and the girls; and a watch, to replace one lost. But these would seem to have been thank-yous rather than love-tokens. For in his correspondence with Howell, Gabriel now began to use slightly disrespectful nicknames for his once and true beloved. 'Two things are wanted for the Moocow in its new house,' he wrote on 9 January. 'It is going to make its bedroom half into a sitting room, and so a screen is needed to divide it.' Then he was anxious that the watches be delivered before the next visit of 'the Inspecting Committee of One'.[3] His sense of worship seemed to be ebbing.

Meanwhile, Fanny was not forgotten, receiving regular gifts of money – sending twenty pounds for her birthday in January, Gabriel calculated she should soon have saved at least £150 – and instructions, including a demand that she return an important piece of Nankin china, 'borrowed' from Tudor House and now required for a picture. 'Hullo Elephant!' he wrote. 'Just you find that pot! Do you think I don't know that you've wrapped your trunk round it and dug a hole for it in the garden? Just you find it, for I can't do without it.' A wonderfully elaborate drawing of an elephant wielding a spade followed.[4]

From a distance, he noted the opening of the Bethnal Green Museum with pictures from the Wallace Collection, a disastrous fire at Bath House, whose important paintings he itemised to William (including a large Rubens, 'almost the finest I ever saw' and 'a noble Velazquez of the Boar-hunt order') and the proposal to erect a statue to their father in his Italian birthplace. As in previous years, he had weak, recurrent impulses towards travelling thither himself. Apart from the risk of welcoming ovations, he told William, he would be tempted to visit Vasto, while preferring to seek out the 'very quietest and most Italian places' that could be found. Of course, it was all a fantasy, amid the sunless Oxfordshire water-meadows.

The winter nights were long and books seldom too big. He read *Salammbô*, judging its horrors symptomatic of a country on the brink of disaster such as had afflicted the Second Empire. 'It seems the work of a nation from which mercy had been cast out, and which was destined to find none,' he told William, while none the less requesting Flaubert's latest title. By contrast, Cellini's boastful autobiography was gloriously diverting; the sculptor's scorn for every mortal except himself and Michelangelo was 'Titanic or Topsaic'.[5]

Michelangelo suggested a new translation project to occupy the evenings, a sequel to *Early Italian Poets*. 'Michelangelo stands about alone as a good Italian poet after Dante etc, unless we except Poliziano,' Gabriel told William. 'I shall get about it at leisure when feasible.'[6] First, however, came the reissued anthology, now retitled *Dante and his Circle* and rearranged so that the *Vita Nuova* and Dante's contemporaries featured more prominently than the earlier poets. One *canzone* was added, from a 'very old portfolio' of manuscripts lying in a bottom drawer at Chelsea, but generally Rossetti resisted the temptation to rework the whole collection. He retained the original preface, and some errors of translation, despite William's corrections, but added a new foreword and dedication, to Frances Rossetti – appropriately, since the book was in homage to his Anglo-Italian heritage.

Repeatedly summoned, at the end of February 'Howell did bestride the telegraph wires like a broomstick and got here at last, after which he whirled us for 3 days in a tornado of lies, and was off again, probably on his ways to the Walpurgisnacht', Rossetti wrote Brown. 'Three A.M. gave way to 5 A.M. as bedtime before the house was clear of him, and reputations fell thicker than the trees in the last great gale.'[7] To his friends' astonishment, Howell had been elected to the Fulham School Board, charged under the new Education Act with providing universal schooling, and his accounts of councillors and clergymen debating whether to charge illegitimate children 1d or 2d a week, and how to prevent parents from all London – nay, all England – sending their infants to Fulham were full of inimitable flourish.

As the days lengthened, Rossetti noted the signs of spring:

> The young rooks cheep 'mid the thick caw o' the old:
> And near unpeopled stream-sides, on the ground,
> By her Spring cry the moorhen's nest is found,
> Where the drained flood-lands flaunt their marigold.

He began to plan his next picture, showing Desdemona singing the willow-song, which was apt to his surroundings. 'This would form a splendid centre for other musical pictures in your drawing rooms,' he told Leyland. 'Shall I view the matter in this way for you?'[8] The shipowner did not bite, but there was plenty to be proceeding with. He needed a larger studio. By the gardener's cottage was a 'jolly old barn', adjoining the Manor's walled garden, 'very large and quite well adapted to the purpose', he wrote,[9] wondering whether to employ a local or a London builder.

Janey came briefly in March, and was due again at Easter, in what seems to have been an agreement to ensure his well-being. But these visits only partially solved the problem of models. As a stopgap, village girl Annie Cumley, who helped in the house, was asked to pose, wearing a servant's snood and raising a jar of flowers to the Green Room mantelpiece. Dunn promised to bring down 'a gipsy model', who may have been Kiomi but in any case failed to materialise, and then procured 'a singular housemaid of advanced ideas', who was willing to pose nude.

Presumably taken by the village to be Dunn's wife or at least companion, this unidentified young woman stayed for four or five days, and sat first for Rossetti to repaint the head in Leyland's *Loving Cup* and then 'naked and almost to the knees' for various studies,[10] including the figure of a Siren, which was the latest effort towards the 'series of musical pictures' commissioned by Leyland. Linked to his own 'Doom of the Sirens' – the projected operatic libretto, in which the hero resists the temptations of wealth and glory but succumbs to passion – Rossetti placed his naked Ligeia before an ocean background, fingering 'an extraordinary lute' (in fact an Indian sarinda) with hollowed-out sections that mirror the roundness of her breasts, almost as if echoing the motif of *Troy Town*. But this Siren is less a classical figure than a female personification *tout court*, bearing the same name as Poe's allegory of Music, who uses the beauty of music to entrance and destroy men, and as such a symbolic depiction also of the sensual force of physical and aesthetic beauty in the Swinburnian or Paterian mode. The motif is similar to that of the *Veronica*, and had Rossetti painted *Ligeia Siren* for Leyland they would have formed a complementary pair, one draped and the other nude.

As it was, the advanced housemaid could only stay for a week, and neither Leyland nor Graham wanted the picture, even after the 'unpopular central detail' of her pubic region was masked by strands of flying drapery. To be more precise, Graham wanted it, but deferred to his wife, and refusal followed. Before this, however, Gabriel was greatly pleased with the work, planning to paint it at once in oils. Again he appears to have been stimulated by others' success, for Poynter, Leighton and Watts were currently exhibiting nudes with classical names. Poynter's *Siren* of 1864 was an evident prototype, with her ancient Egyptian harp, while Watts's *Three*

Graces, a work long in progress, had been recently described in the press. As this element in the artistic repertoire increased, a 'moral revival' emerged in sections of public opinion, loudly denouncing lewdness in art. This had of course contributed to the outcry over *Poems*, and to the difficulties Rossetti now encountered. To keep in the artistic vanguard, nudes were *de rigueur*, while to sell to private patrons with wives and daughters, draped figures were both decent and prudent.

So the next projected 'music' figure was clothed. Like Dunn, Alexa was still receiving a regular retainer, formally resumed when Gabriel left Scotland. She was escorted by Harry to Kelmscott, where she sat for new studies holding a 'queer old harp' from the stock of studio props, which looks something like a zither, held upright. 'I have got those two instruments you bought me,' Rossetti told Howell. 'Dunn has strung them and I am going soon to paint 2 pictures from Miss Wilding with them.'

Like *Ligeia Siren*, the finely finished drawing of *La Ghirlandata* was 'a stunning study'. It would be 'the greenest picture in the world', he explained, 'the principal figure being draped in green and completely surrounded in glowing green foliage'.[11] The garland of the title was made of roses and honeysuckle, his favourite flowers, but the auburn-haired figure floats as if garlanded in leaves, attended by angels. The hues are bright, even gaudy, but at the foot are blue flowers meant for the poisonous monkshood, adding an ominous note.

Janey's Easter visit was deferred, but Hueffer and Watts came for the weekend. Then late on the Sunday Gabriel made a flying visit to London. He saw Howell on business matters, called on Scott and the Browns, and invited Boyce, Fanny, Howell and William to dine at Chelsea. 'He was looking extraordinarily well and stout, and younger than a year or two ago,' Boyce recorded, not having seen him since the breakdown.[12]

There was a good deal of London gossip. Some weeks before, Simeon Solomon had been arrested (again) for homosexual indecency; was he still in gaol, or in an asylum for those of 'unsound mind'? Sandys' lover Mary Clive was about to make her acting debut on the West End stage, with loud attendant publicity. Cathy and Franz Hueffer had a son, little Fordie, the Browns' first grandchild. Marie Stillman's picture was accepted at the Academy, Lucy Brown's was not. William was going to Italy with the Scotts and Alice.

Back at Kelmscott, Janey and the children arrived in May, together with the cuckoo. Marsh marigolds filled the field ditches, and the orchard was awash with apple blossom. Gabriel completed his sonnet on spring, stimulated by the *Athenaeum*'s request for a contribution but sending instead *Sunset Wings*, about the starlings. And so, though as usual he forgot his mother's birthday on 27 April, his own on the foreboding anniversary of the *Fleshly* pamphlet passed without incident – except that, during his daily walk, a plank bridge broke beneath his weight and nearly dropped him in the water. His belly was now enormous, he told Brown.

At the last minute Lucy Brown accompanied William and the Scotts to Italy. At Basle on the return journey, William proposed. 'You know the extreme regard in which I (as also you and all of us) have always held Lucy,' he told his mother on their return; 'and while abroad I soon began to feel that she is too dear to me to allow of my ever parting from her again if I can help.'[13] Lucy accepted, in despite of the 'serious discrepancy of age', for at forty-three, William was thirteen years older.

Both families were astonished and delighted. Since the end of his engagement to Henrietta Rintoul in 1860, William had been a confirmed bachelor, dividing his life between the domestic comforts of Euston Square and the masculine freedoms of Cheyne Walk. Since Gabriel's collapse he had been deeply depressed and silent. Now there was cause for rejoicing. Frances and Christina Rossetti were at Kelmscott when his letter arrived. 'My dear Lucy, I should like to be a dozen years younger and worthier every way of becoming your sister,' wrote Christina. 'I hope William will be all you desire ... may love, peace and happiness be yours and his ...'[14]

They had known Lucy well since 1855 when she had been Maria's pupil. William was not the first of her admirers, but his artistic interests and political radicalism chimed with hers, and she agreed to share the house at Euston Square rather than evict his mother and sisters, so the omens were good. 'No more welcome news could have reached me than that of your engagement,' Gabriel told her, adding his own tribute to William. 'What return can I ever make now for all that my dear brother gave me so freely in early days, at a time when it is still a mystery to me how he could manage to give at all? To him and to your father I owe more in life than to any other man whatever; and your marriage with William will cement still further my closest and almost my only remaining ties of family and friendship.'[15]

It was no exaggeration, although at the same time he indulged in a joke at his brother's expense. William had a way, when a picture or poem was criticised, of insisting that no work was without its merits, and of indicating warm approval with the temperate judgement that he 'liked it pretty well'. Therefore, teased Gabriel with a little rhyme, his brother must have reasoned thus: 'My name begins with W, And hers begins with L. She's not without her merits, and I like her pretty well.'[16]

As the Manor welcomed a steady stream of summer guests, the nightmare June of the previous year might have belonged to another life. Hake and Watts came for a fortnight, briefly joined by Morris for a day's fishing. What was Morris like? asked Watts before he arrived. 'You know the portraits of Francis I,' replied Rossetti. 'Well . . . soften down the nose a bit and give him the rose-bloom colour of an English farmer, and there you have him.' But he warned Watts to expect brusqueness: 'He is a wonderfully stand-off chap and generally manages to take against people.'

Morris arrived from the station riding Mouse the Icelandic pony. 'H'm!' he said to Gabriel. 'I thought you were alone.' Courtesy prevailed, however, and Watts was invited to join the fishing party. Forewarned, he kept off literary topics, chatting instead about his own boyish pursuits. Morris absorbed himself in baits, lines, floats, bream, roach and gudgeon. Eventually he asked: 'How old were you when you used to fish in the Ouse?' Ten or twelve, replied Watts. 'And when you got a bite, were you as excited as I am when I see my float bob?' 'No.' 'I thought not.'[17]

The next visitors were the Browns, followed by Gabriel's mother and Christina, for three weeks, overlapping with the Browns' return. Suddenly, all bedrooms were in use, and scheduling became necessary, especially as Alexa was again available to sit. She came on 27 June, together with Howell for an overnight stay. Here we are, wrote Christina to Amelia Heimann, 'in a pretty old house, in a charming garden, in a green and flowery world (a *rainy* world too, this morning) hard by a river.' They breakfasted at ten, and dined at eight, with bread and butter for lunch '(though I don't think Gabriel takes a morsel)' and spent the days at leisure in the house and garden, with an occasional excursion on the river. A beautiful Proserpine was in the studio: 'In her hand is the fatal pomegranate, and in her face the expression of the irretrievable.' Seldom condescending to amuse his guests personally, Gabriel stuck to his drawing board and easel, but in the evenings they played whist, and sometimes Emma Brown sang (Gabriel called her 'the Warbler').[18]

'My mother and sister leave here Wednesday,' he told Dunn on 11 July. 'Christina has benefited surprisingly and both enjoyed themselves very much indeed. Alice W. has also shown more faculty for enjoyment than I ever saw her display before.' He had been anxious, for models seldom mixed socially with artists' families. Miss Wilding was 'quite ladylike' but neither gifted nor amusing, he explained anxiously in advance. 'Thus she might bore you at meals and suchlike (for one cannot put her in a cupboard) . . .'[19] But it was his own problem. Alexa's willingness to please charmed Mrs and Miss Rossetti, while their presence no doubt enlivened the visit for her, whom Gabriel might well have preferred to shut in a cupboard. All three women left on 14 July, for Janey and the girls were due to return for their now customary long summer. Topsy himself was already en route again for Iceland. With good grace, Gabriel restored the ground-floor studio to its original state as 'a nice airy drawing room' with chintz curtains, re-establishing himself in the tapestry room above, with the east window reopened.

The Morris girls delighted in their holiday paradise once more. May even persuaded Mr Rossetti to push their swing, in default of George, who was in Oxford having a lump on his neck removed. She also served again as his model, sitting for angels' heads in *La Ghirlandata*. Flatteringly, he treated her as a young woman. 'One day he seriously inquired which I thought the uglier of two ladies of our acquaintance,' she recalled. 'I considered the matter very gravely, and proceeded to give my verdict, explaining the why of it. With equal gravity he said, "I think you are right," and we discussed the points of the ladies.' When the conversation was innocently reported to Jane, however, her comment was severe. 'That was very, very naughty of Mr Rossetti,' she told May.[20]

Out of May's hearing, Gabriel asked if he might adopt her. The idea was crazy, as he surely knew and Jane surely said, if with sympathy. But May's response when she learnt of this request is an index of Gabriel's charm to sitters old and young. 'Oh, mother, why didn't you agree?' she wailed.

As well as other works in hand, he had a commission from William Graham for a *Blessed Damozel* from his own poem. The first effort did not come right, but on the cut-down canvas he painted in Alexa's head, with stars in her hair, and her hand holding yellow irises, perhaps taken from the river-bank, in lieu of lilies. Did he remember digging up yellow flags with Lizzie in Somerset, to carry back to Chatham Place?

Back in London, Alexa boasted that Mr Rossetti was so pleased with his pictures of her that he gave her handsome presents in addition to the retainer. She also asserted that Fanny could expect no further support. On both counts, Fanny was angry and upset. How stupid of Miss W. to repeat such a pack of nonsense, wherever she might have heard it, replied Gabriel, soothingly; Fanny should know he would never neglect or forget his good and dear old friend. He sent another small cheque and a drawing of an Elephant adding to its hoard. But Fanny was neglected, and knew it. She wanted to visit, but Gabriel resolutely refused to invite her to Kelmscott, either because Jane forbade it, or because he feared the inevitable village gossip. 'Please don't ever press the matter again, as it is very distressing to me to refuse,' he replied in September; 'but as long as I remain here it is out of the question.'[21] Late in life, Fanny was still resentful of Jane – although to his 'dear Fan' Gabriel's tone remained more tender than to anyone else. 'Believe me ever your affectionate R', he wrote, the initial standing not for his surname but for 'Rhinoceros', a fit, if sometimes brutish, companion for his Elephant. And Fanny was needed to keep an eye on Tudor House, where the now-widowed Emma McClounie had been given notice for continuing to entertain male visitors, and a new housekeeper employed.

'I am embedded in work such as it is, and find it more difficult daily to get *to* London just as I used to find it impossible to get *out of* it,' Rossetti told Sandys on 20 July. 'From no source could encouraging words be more welcome than from you . . .' Largely at Howell's urging, he had repaired the rupture, after Mary Clive's West End debut had ended in illness. 'I do think you are at all times the unluckiest fellow in the world,' he added, tactfully downplaying his own recovery. 'I myself never expect to get beyond the hand-to-mouth phase of professional life now.' Then he quoted his father's proverb, translating its final couplet to read 'if you're owing at forty / you always will owe'. Alas, he continued, 'I am forty-five and owing! To say nothing of knowing no more than at 20 and certainly doing no more than at 30.' This was generous self-denigration, for the lines were more strikingly apposite to Sandys. Gabriel may have been deceived, but he saw Fred as a serious fellow artist, striving like himself for excellence.

Since painting *Dante's Dream*, he went on, 'I feel for the first time in my life something like a sense of *style* in my work, a quality quite deficient before with me, while with you it always seemed the first of natural instincts. The fact is, to paint even one big picture is one's best chance of improvement . . .'[22]

When he was 'mad', Rossetti could not paint, but this letter shows how the breakdown only temporarily affected his career. The 'style' he referrred to meant something akin to visible ease and accomplishment – as in a stylish picture – for which he had long struggled, despite his wealth of conceptual 'invention'. (Sandys, by contrast, had effortless skill, and no intellectual capacity.) Notwithstanding his mental troubles, his grasp and reach were coming closer together. Although there is no great distinction to be observed between the comparable works of the middle 1860s such as *Sibylla Palmifera* or *Mariana* and those of the early 1870s like *Proserpine* and *La Ghirlandata*, and many later works were based on earlier designs and beginnings, the later pictures do possess greater assurance, and include fewer pot-boilers. Not all are masterpieces, but it is as if Rossetti worked with greater concentration, perfecting his mature manner.

Through 1873 he painted steadily and well – and almost entirely without assistance, with several works in hand at the same time, to minimise delays while paints and glazes were drying. In June, after final varnishing, *Proserpine* was dispatched to Parsons, who sent payment at once. By this date Rossetti was at work on a slightly larger version – here designated *Proserpine 2* for convenience – which had additional ivy leaves in the background. Painted 'very rapidly' over a fortnight, it was offered by Howell to Graham on 2 July, for 800 guineas. At about the same time, the finished *Siren* went with Howell to London, together with the 'stunning study' for *La Ghirlandata* that contained the two angels drawn from May and was intended for Leyland, as companion to *Veronica*. Thanks to Alexa's visit to the Manor, the central head was already on the canvas, but perversely Leyland declined outright. 'Damn this stay at Kelmscott, one cannot see his work, and I am not going to buy pictures without first seeing them,' he said, adding that Rossetti knew perfectly well that he wanted only single heads, to run round the room like musical notes; moreover, other commissions were as yet undelivered.[23] Graham's patronage was ruled by his heart, but Leyland had a hard head for business.

Graham declined *Proserpine 2*, as too sad. 'Mrs Morris's face and the deep earnest expression of it, always brings me to all my sorrow, I cannot help it,' he told Howell, alluding to his recent bereavement. 'I could not look at the picture without such emotion.' Promptly, Howell produced the *Ghirlandata* design, asking 1,000 guineas for the finished work. Graham brightened, but still demurred. 'Well, Howell, you know I really do want Rossetti's pictures but I really cannot afford to pay his prices,' he replied, not liking to haggle. 'If I was to say I can at times afford only say £700 when he wants £1,000 he would not believe me, and might take it as a simple excuse [and] I would be more than pained,' he explained. 'I have already lost two or three things of his through being unable to reach the price, and lately I found that the only way I had was to decline buying on the ground of being already full . . .'[24]

In the event, however, Rossetti willingly agreed to take 800 guineas for *Ghirlandata*. 'I am glad he is to have it as he is the only buyer I have who is worth a damn,' he told Dunn, not unfairly. Payment arrived on 11 July – a token of Graham's generous nature, for much remained to be done. The drapery in particular caused delays as passages were scraped out and repainted, but it was dispatched to Scotland on 3 October – just over a year since Rossetti had himself left Perthshire doubtful he would ever paint again.[25]

Meanwhile, Leyland had seen and admired *Proserpine 1* in Parsons' shop. It was splendid, he told Howell; what was Rossetti's lowest price?

Oh, replied Howell, don't buy that one: Gabriel is doing a second, far better version. Leyland was tempted, and offered as part-payment to return the watercolour *Lucrezia* acquired in 1868, and transfer the advance on *La Pia* to the new work. But Rossetti wanted money upfront, and did not wish to take back *Lucrezia*. He told Howell to counter-offer *Proserpine 2* for 400 guineas cash plus £400 remission of debt. And there negotiations hung fire, for Howell was otherwise occupied, Leyland a determined bargainer, and Rossetti reluctant to proceed while *Proserpine 1* remained unsold. But when in September, Parsons asked him to take back the first version, *Proserpine 2* ('vastly superior') was newly offered to Leyland for 400 guineas cash, plus *Lucrezia* and remission of 280 guineas advance, together with first refusal on yet another proposed work, *Dîs Manibus*, showing a white-clad Roman widow mourning by a white marble tomb. All would combine to beautiful effect, and the feeling would be 'as beautiful and elevated' as any he had produced. Tempted, Leyland agreed to take the new subject if he liked the cartoon, but pointed out that he had already paid 1,050 guineas towards *Pia* and *Aspecta Medusa* without having received either. However, he now regretted rejecting the *Ghirlandata*, and therefore suggested taking *Proserpine 2* for 800 guineas, set against *Lucrezia* and £350, one-third of the advances already paid. Another £350 would stand towards the Roman Widow, and the third towards the *Pia* or an alternative work. But he wished they could talk face to face. He was gravely disappointed at the non-delivery of so many promised works.[26]

Eventually, it was settled – *Proserpine 2* in exchange for *Lucrezia* and 400 guineas cash, leaving advances of £748 to be divided equally against *Dîs Manibus*, *La Pia* and a further subject to be decided. At the end of November, £200 arrived, and work on *Proserpine 2* proceeded, the Italian text of the picture's sonnet being added to the image. But then there was another hitch, when the canvas support was found to be rucked, right across the face, when viewed obliquely. Rossetti summoned Henry Merritt, the best picture restorer in London, and at the same time began a third version – *Proserpine 3* – in case the canvas could not be unwrinkled. It went off to Liverpool on 22 December.

Then there was a further disaster, when frame and glass were smashed in transit. Promptly, the picture returned to Kelmscott in New Year 1874, together with a cheque for 400 guineas – £240 for *Proserpine* and £200 advance on *Dîs Manibus*, which was said to be 'now well in hand'. It was swiftly reframed, but as *Proserpine 2*, after some mishaps of its own, returned from Merritt new-lined and 'vastly improved', this version was now reallocated to Leyland and delivered by George to his London house on 25 February.[27]

By this date, the large *Dante's Dream* had returned to Cheyne Walk, on the understanding that Rossetti would produce a smaller replica, and sell the original, for which Howell received a conditional offer from L.R.Valpy, a mild-mannered, art-loving lawyer with a practice in Lincoln's Inn Fields. From Scott, Rossetti heard a rumour that the great arms magnate Sir William Armstrong wanted one of his pictures for Cragside, his new house in Northumberland. If true, Armstrong was one of the few patrons who could easily afford the original *Dante's Dream*, and the sale would do much for Rossetti's reputation. But a bird in the hand ... Valpy's offer was accepted.[28]

Happily, Graham was in raptures over *Ghirlandata*, whose bright tones gave no hint of melancholy. He inquired after a companion, the ideal head of 'a fair beautiful woman', fit for a lady's boudoir. Annie Cumley with the marigolds was offered as *The Bower Maiden* for 650 guineas. But on delivery Graham was disappointed: he had ordered an ideal head, not a pretty country lass. *Tant pis*, was the artist's immediate response. 'He wanted a "bright cheerful" picture and I gave him one, but cannot make bright cheerful ideals,' he told Howell, hoping Graham could be persuaded. 'It is really good work, but realistic.'

Nevertheless, satisfied clients were to be preferred. However, his year's hard work and earnings enabled him to refund Parsons for *Proserpine 1*, plus interest – a total of £604. To prevent future misunderstandings, he also wrote to Leyland explaining the existence of the two other versions. Moving his studio once more to the ground floor, he then intended to work on *Dis Manibus*, to forestall future complaints. However, as Alexa could not come immediately, he turned instead to *Rosa Triplex*, a head in three poses designed in the mid-1860s. Dunn sent the sketches from Chelsea, Jane made a dress of crimson silk, and May modelled 'charmingly' for the features.

But he had been working at Kelmscott for nearly eighteen months, and all the selling had been done by himself, to existing buyers. 'I am still wanting a dealer ready to *take and pay for* whatever I could let him have and dispose of it in his own way afterwards,' he told Howell in April. He had *Lucrezia*, two *Proserpines*, and a *Blessed Damozel* head available for cash, but he refused to let Howell have them on commission, for despite repeated claims, neither he nor Parsons had found any new clients. Clearly Charley's vaunted skills as salesman were vastly overrated. He also ducked and dived, borrowed and lent (most of the former), promised, repromised, excused and evaded. He lived on credit and a complex web of continually circulating debts; Gabriel was surely not the only friend pressed to guarantee bills and loans as they were renewed. And inexcusably for a dealer, he frequently failed to communicate, or vanished for days without trace. (One explanation surfaced when from a hotel he mailed a photo of himself embracing a woman not his wife, saying that 'when the coast was quite clear' he would bring her to Kelmscott for Gabriel to draw; at the moment she was weak, having just lost a baby. 'Pardon my ways, but the Devil never does leave me alone.' A month later, Brown sent news of a whole 'supplementary family' belonging to Charley.)

Still half-trusting his good intentions, in April 1874 Gabriel abandoned the pretence that Howell was any sort of dealer. There had simply been too many irritating incidents, including a row with Fanny, whom Howell had never paid for drawings he sold on her behalf, and the sale of one of these to Graham against Rossetti's express instruction. Most serious was the failure to honour a bill when due, so that the bailiffs threatened to distrain goods from Tudor House. And his dealings over *Dante's Dream* were quite murky; what exactly was the position with Valpy? 'You see I have spoken quite plainly on these points,' Gabriel wrote; but protestations of affection had no value, only deeds of friendship. 'You may answer that I have *done nothing*,' protested Howell, hurt. '*Quite true*, but I have tried damned hard.'

There was no quarrel – there were outstanding drawings and photo-graphic plates to be accounted for – but like others Rossetti had learnt the inevitable lesson of dealing with Howell. 'I have only to say that I consider you, after some 9 or 10 years' intercourse, a very good-natured fellow and a d—d bad man of business,' he wrote, more in sorrow than anger, at the end of the year.

When William had announced his forthcoming marriage, Maria decided to join the All Saints' Sisters of the Poor. She had been drawn to the religious life since the age of eighteen, and had long worked as a lay member of the All Saints' community. Now, with housekeeping responsibilities trans-ferred to Lucy, and their mother's blessing, she at last fulfilled her vocation, and entered her noviciate on 11 September, one professed aim being to secure the salvation of her faithless brothers through prayer and sacrifice. Convinced of the reality of heaven, and certain of the doctrines on unbelief, she feared that while hell was as yet unknowable, it was undoubtedly their destination.

'I know, my dear Maggie, that your longing is to die to the world, and to live to Christ: to suffer, work, love, and be saved by love,' wrote William, lovingly and tactfully. 'There are other ideals than this, but not greater ideals ... May you find the peace that passeth all understanding, and be an example of attainment to all others.'[29] For his part, Gabriel regretted Maria's decision, above all deploring the narrowing of interests – as he saw it – for one whose intellectual gifts he had always admired. 'My eldest sister is turned what is called Sister of Mercy – one of those old things whom you see going about in a sort of coal-scuttle and umbrella costume,' he told Fanny. 'However I believe it is really her sincere desire, so perhaps it is for the best.' Selfishly, however, the depletion of the family circle most concerned him. 'She will indeed be a great loss, being much the healthiest in mind and cheeriest of us all, except yourself,' he wrote his mother on the morrow of Maria's profession. 'I suppose of course she will appear duly at our Christmas gathering, will she not?'[30]

Recently, he had seen his sister only once or twice a year, but having thus relied on her permanent presence, felt any change at Euston Square keenly. So, though startled by her full 'canonicals', he was relieved to find her 'as cheerful as possible' at New Year, when she paid her first home visit. Maria, who tried to explain that the religious life meant no substantive separation for her, might also have pointed out how seldom Gabriel had made any effort to be with her. For all his protestations, Gabriel's affection for his family was often honoured in the breach.

He had in fact little in common with either sister, despite Maria's exposition of Dante or Christina's poetry. Now Maria had relinquished scholarship, and Christina had turned to religious works. In April 1874 she published a devotional calendar, entitled *Annus Domini*, and sent Gabriel a copy, trusting it would not displease. Having looked through the little book he wrote an appreciative word on its 'fervent and beautiful' prayers, for which Christina thanked him, none the less disappointed that he had ignored the single poem in the volume. Of course, he hastened to add, it was 'most excellent', like all her religious poetry. He was only being polite, although the poem's opening appeal might have chimed with his own insomniac despair:

> How can it need
> So agonised an effort and a strain
> To make Thy face of mercy shine again?

In all sorts of ways, Gabriel had pitied his sisters' uneventful, unfulfilled lives, knowing how lively and ambitious each had been in childhood. He could not think that to become a middle-aged nun in a coal-scuttle bonnet was any kind of goal. Yet their faith offered what he still lacked: hope and peace of mind.

'From child to youth; from youth to arduous man; / From lethargy to fever of the heart ...' began a sonnet written during these months at Kelmscott:

> Alas, the soul! – how soon must she
> Accept her primal immortality –
> The flesh resume its dust whence it began?

Mortality was much on his mind, and the imagery invokes traditional motifs of eternal rest.

As regards William, Gabriel was genuinely pleased that marriage to Lucy promised to break his brother's rather 'fossilized habit of life', and endeavoured to assist with furniture from Chelsea for their new quarters on the upper floors of Euston Square. He himself was in no hurry to return to London, though as Janey's health was poor he was twice on the point of leaving when deterred by telegrams. Over Christmas he remained ten days in London, giving her a copy of Robert Burton's *Anatomy of Melancholy*, inscribed with a portrait in the manner of a gift-tag, and nearly missed his train back to Kelmscott through staying too long at her new home in Chiswick.

A month later, Jenny and May were at the Manor, recovering from measles. (Don't tell Fanny, he warned Dunn.) He and the girls teased poor Dizzy, asleep on the hearthrug, by shrieking into each ear simultaneously, while 'beating a tattoo' on his head. 'The instant result was that he turned round howling and bit me (fortunately not Jenny) at which I am not surprised,' Gabriel reported. 'At present I am going about with a black patch over my nose.'[31]

When Jane took Jenny back to London, May stayed behind 'to be painted'. Alexa and Dunn were also there, and May recalled an afternoon spent snowballing in the garden, followed by a boisterous game of hide-and-seek through the darkened, rambling house while Gabriel sat by the fire, feeling elderly; returning to base, May found him sunk in solitary gloom. Katie Adams, another of May's playmates, recalled a game called 'running away from Mr Rossetti'. Before dusk each day, he set off for a melancholy walk across the fields and ditches. 'I can see the rather broad figure tramping away doggedly over the flat green meadows,' May recalled; 'I can see him returning after dark with a burden of weariness upon him – even the young child in pauses of happy playhours felt the loneliness of it.'[32]

He was however well enough to attend William's wedding breakfast on 31 March, tastelessly joking to their mother that it was perilously close to All Fools' Day. But he excused himself from the larger party hosted by the Browns the previous evening, telling his brother frankly that 'every bore I know and don't know would swoop down on me after these two years' absence, and I am not equal to it'. More than bores, he feared meeting Swinburne, for whose 'abominable ways' he had no tolerance whatsoever.[33] Morris also growled at having to attend the wedding of 'two old boobies', when he neither cared for nor they for him.[34] Writing shakily in pencil to thank Lucy, Jane was more gracious; they would be at the breakfast. Partly to see her, Gabriel came up a week early. On 22 March, when Boyce called on Morris, Gabriel also arrived, presumably to take tea.

'Janey told me last night that you are in town for a few days. I should like to see you,' wrote Ned. He had seen and admired *Proserpine* at Leyland's. 'It drew me out of myself and my wretched affairs . . .' Rossetti might have reciprocated by going to see *Le Chant d'Amour* or *Laus Veneris*, Burne-Jones's latest commissions from good William Graham. But though Ned's approval was 'very very precious' to him, Gabriel had lost interest in his friend's work, and was anyway soon back at Kelmscott. He did, however, quietly manage to see Hunt's large, controversial picture, *The Shadow of*

Death, for which Agnew had paid 5,000 guineas and which was now on offer for 10,000 guineas. He may have heard – via Brown, who invited Hunt to the larger wedding party – that, like Ned, his old PR Brother admired his latest works, for in April Hunt commented on their excellence, having presumably also seen *Proserpine*.[35]

Another event brought back former days, for *Ecce Ancilla* was up for auction, being sold by the hated Heugh. To avoid humiliation Gabriel asked Marks to bid up to £350, and was relieved when it was knocked down to Agnews for 370 guineas. At his request, it was then offered to the blessed Graham, who boggled, but bought, for 400 guineas. When it came to Kelmscott for refreshment, he was moved. 'Alas! in some of the highest respects I have hardly done anything else so good,' he told Brown. Despite faults and quaintness, it really had 'inspiration, of the kind infectious to those born to feel it'.[36]

It was a quarter of a century since the days of the PRB and Paris with Hunt. Fusing the real with the symbolic, Hunt was still faithful to that inspiration, unembarrassed by religious themes. But for Rossetti it was as in another life.

In April Nolly Brown came to Kelmscott, with Hueffer. Gabriel was bearish, angrily anxious when Nolly stayed out late, and dogmatic about literature. He had not been well, he confided to Leyland. And soon after his birthday, just before the second anniversary of his breakdown, a trailing postscript tò Brown confirmed the worst. 'I am in a state of great despondency of low spirits,' he wrote. 'I can hardly make myself work and all ...'[37] In June he rallied sufficiently to entertain William and Lucy, returned from honeymoon, as well as the Browns and Watts, and also to invite Graham, Sandys and Leyland (separately). But the respite was over; the demons were returning. Walking on the river-bank, he passed some local anglers and, as by the Tay, he heard insults. Angrily, he rounded on them, full of abuse and challenge. George intervened, but the damage was done, as accounts of the outburst began to circulate in the village. Immediately after Leyland's visit he left Kelmscott hurriedly, saying he was unexpectedly called to London, but did not want to see anyone.

There had been intermittent symptoms. From the earliest weeks at Kelmscott, he had urged correspondents to seal their letters, which were liable to be opened by spies. As the quarterlies did not reach Kelmscott, 'the dirt of dogs is quite out of sight and scent', but critics remained enemies: he feared that a sonnet in his honour by Edmund Gosse would blight the chances of the volume that contained it, by setting 'all Dogdom' at its heels. But without evident strain he had survived the publication of *Dante and his Circle* and the German publication of his *Poems*, though admittedly reading no reviews. 'Don't send me any notices of the book when it appears, good or bad,' he told Hueffer.[38]

But the key factor in maintaining equilibrium (as he believed) was Janey's presence, which was withdrawn in midsummer. Morris had acted, announcing at Easter that he would relinquish the joint tenancy on 25 June. 'As to the future . . . I will ask you to look upon me as off my share,' he wrote, 'since you have fairly taken to living at Kelmscott, which I suppose neither of us thought the other would do when we first began the joint possession of the house.'[39] This was true: Rossetti's permanent occupation of the Manor precluded Morris from enjoying it too. He also pleaded poverty, since his investment income from mining shares had virtually ceased, and he was working hard to increase the Firm's business. But the chief reason was no doubt propriety, arising from the girls' post-measles visit in the spring. Although 'not beyond a romp', at thirteen and twelve Jenny and May were growing up. George Hake and his brothers, who also visited the Manor, were young unmarried men. Mr Rossetti was a queer cove, and some of his visitors were questionable. Last autumn the arrival of two models hired by Dunn had provoked a warning letter from the local parson 'on the subject of the nude'. It was hardly right that May should have stayed on unchaperoned, 'to be painted'.

Gabriel had paid a short spring visit to London, primarily to see Janey, and after various postponements, she came to the Manor for a final week at Whitsun. They appear to have been alone, for George was in Oxford. Rossetti had planned to renew the lease for a further seven years, and convert the roadside barn into a studio. But without the fiction of a shared tenancy, Janey could not be there. In July she and Morris were going to Belgium, retracing their honeymoon visit *en famille*. Time had indeed tossed them all about, in Webb's words; but Topsy and Jane now seemed to have resumed their original roles. When she left, Rossetti's spirits crashed, and following the river-bank incident, he fled to London.

Kelmscott never saw him again. Without the presence, or at least the promise, of the 'one necessary person', it was no longer a haven.

Some months later, resurrecting the 'Beryl-Song's' original burden, he used its images for a lament, in which separation was equated with death:

> Leaves and rain and the days of the year,
> (*Water-willow and wellaway*)
>
> All these fall, and my soul gives ear,
> And she is hence who once was here.
> (*With a wind blown night and day*) . . .

Parted Presence was equally eloquent:

> Your eyes are afar to-day,
>   Yet, love, look now in mine eyes.
>   Two hearts sent forth may despise
> All dead things by the way.
> All between is decay,
>   Dead hours and this hour that dies
>   O love, look deep in mine eyes!
>
> Your hands to-day are not here,
>   Yet lay them, love, in my hands.
>   The hourglass sheds its sands
> All day for the dead hours' bier;
> But now, as two hearts draw near,
>   This hour like a flower expands.
>   O love, your hands in my hands!

The threatened crisis was averted, however, and indeed in London Rossetti saw Jane as often as in the country; soon after her return from Belgium she was with him for a whole day, sitting for studies.

Another good reason for returning to Cheyne Walk was the replica *Dante's Dream* for Graham, as it was quite impractical to move the large canvas elsewhere. And though William reported that his brother's spirits were 'not exactly what I would wish them', once in the studio Gabriel set to work vigorously. He completed an elegant chalk portrait of Lucy to commemorate her wedding, and sold *Rosa Triplex* to Frederick Craven. By early September *Dante's Dream* was well under way, and Cowper-Temple had fallen in love with the gilded *Damozel* holding yellow lilies, paying over 250 guineas. *Dîs Manibus* was virtually finished, and an oil version of *The Damsel of the Sanc Grael* was rapidly painted and sold to Rae for 450 guineas.

His next project, he told Hake, was 'a good-sized Titianesque subject – a girl washing her hands with two attendant Cupids' called *La Bella Mano*, which would concentrate on flesh tones and painterly qualities. Next would come the full-length *Pandora*, for which Janey would sit when well. Both form and drapery were to be fully rendered, and the whole as monumental as he could make it.

Tentatively, he also resumed a social life. Hearing of his advent, Whistler swept Gabriel off to his first solo show, and no doubt to exchange gossip about Leyland, major patron to both artists. Then Rossetti hosted a family gathering at Chelsea, including the aunts, and hired a new cook and housemaid. He welcomed Louisa Ashburton to his studio, and agreed to draw her daughter's portrait. Often, he was fully occupied, the door closed to casual visitors. Never bring strangers, Howell was warned. Chloral was still a necessity, but there were few overt signs of paranoia.

Indeed, it was Brown who was most suspicious this autumn, over Morris's decision to restructure the Firm. For long the managing director, he now wanted sole control; the business needed to expand, but capital was limited and the partnership structure unwieldy. Distributed profits were modest, so the partners, who had invested nominally, earned little, while being severally and generally liable for the company's debts. By contrast, Morris was dependent on the Firm, his salary of £1,000 p.a. being now his only income. By August, new articles of association were in preparation. In October, Morris, Marshall, Faulkner & Co. was reborn as Morris & Co.[40]

Rossetti agreed that the decision appeared 'sudden and arbitrary', but his inclination was 'to put Top pretty well in possession', as requested. Madox Brown and P. P. Marshall resisted, and a partners' meeting was called. Attempting to mediate, Rossetti argued:

> If in 1861 we had been asked as a firm: 'Do you think your managing member ought, in 1874, to command an income of £1000?' we should have said Yes. And if the question had followed 'Do you think it would be otherwise worth his while to take up the position?' we should have said No.
>
> If we had further been then asked: 'Do you think that each member ought in 1874 to be receiving a dividend from the firm at the same time that the manager is satisfied as to salary and a sufficient sum kept in hand to carry on the works?' we should have said Yes. And had it further been asked: 'Do you think it worth beginning in 1861 if no such result will be obtainable in 1874?' we should have said No.

So, he concluded, since dividends could not be assured without risks greater than the partners would underwrite, they should dissolve. Moreover, 'if Morris had come to us in a friendly spirit of appeal and said, "The business will only yield a fair income for one man and no more – ought not that man to be myself who have no other resources?", we as friends might probably on consideration have answered Yes.' Could not matters be sorted out through a confidential meeting between himself, Morris and Brown?[41]

Brown countered that the Firm's reputation had been built by the partners, as artists and designers. But as neither he nor Gabriel attended the meeting when the others unanimously agreed to dissolve the partnership and appoint assessors to value the business, a further meeting had to be scheduled. Forwarding the resolution, Morris requested his formal approval, not doubting he would 'support this peaceful way of settling matters', which was indeed the only way out of the deadlock. Replying, Rossetti 'of course' raised no objection, saw no point in attending the meeting – and had been experimenting with a new colourway for the 'marigold' wallpaper design. Relations clearly remained friendly.

In the event, while Burne-Jones, Philip Webb and Charley Faulkner freely made over their shares to Topsy, Brown and Marshall held out for compensation, asking Watts to represent them. The sum eventually agreed was £1,000 each – a good deal to pay for 'sheer nothing', as Morris grumbled, having to find it. Rossetti's position was ticklish; for Brown had lifelong claim to his loyalty. Moreover, he knew Brown regarded Morris's salary as an income he himself could never command. But at the same time, Rossetti did not want to take Topsy's money. His solution was to give his share to Jane. 'I have no objections,' replied Morris, 'but we must settle how the thing can be done, as the money must be vested in trustees.' As a married woman, any capital Jane acquired became her husband's property, unless placed in an independent fund. To circumvent this, Rossetti placed his thousand pounds on deposit at Watts's bank, making the interest available to Jane and thus giving her a small but symbolic degree of economic freedom. However, as he also often 'borrowed' the money when in need of tin himself, it is not clear how much use Jane made of the gift.[42]

And so the Firm was undone. Brown swore never to speak to Morris again, and cast Burne-Jones into the same camp. Webb stuck loyally to Topsy and Ned. The years of good fellowship closed as 'the circle' divided. Rossetti, now even more firmly linked to Brown by intermarriage, was equally closely tied to Jane by love. He had ended many friendships in his time, but this was none of his doing.

It was all the more tragic because, while the Firm's meetings were taking place, nineteen-year-old Nolly Brown was dying of septicaemia. Sick for seven weeks and delirious towards the end, he died on 5 November. Brown's heart was broken, for Nolly had been his pride and joy – the son whose genius in art and literature would compensate for his father's struggles. Already, the lad had exhibited at the Royal Academy, and published a dramatic novel (whose hero Gabriel Denver shared Rossetti's name and Howell's ancestry). To lose him now was too cruel.

'How shall any friend of yours attempt to comfort you at such a moment?' wrote Gabriel. 'Your son, with such a beginning, would probably – most probably – have proved the first imaginative writer of his time.' The hyperbole was excusable, in the circumstances. 'My dear Friend, may you find help in yourself, for elsewhere it is vain to seek it.'

'It is always Gabriel who speaks the right word,' commented Brown,[43] who nevertheless immediately feared Rossetti would not come to the funeral because Swinburne and Hunt were invited. Of course he would attend, replied Gabriel instantly; 'and of course, at such a moment, could have no shadow of personal feeling as to who else may be present.'[44]

Beyond this, his presence at the cemetery on 12 November was testimony to self-possession, for as far as possible he had always avoided funerals, and since his breakdown had conceived a morbid dread – his own perception – of such semi-public gatherings. Before standing at the graveside, he drafted a memorial sonnet to Nolly, in which the sestet invoked general consolation. 'A mist has risen: we see the youth no more,' he wrote: 'Does *he* see on and strive on?' Would his young hand be there to help them up death's shore? Or, 'echoing the No More with Nevermore, / Must Night be ours and his?'

'We hope:' this concluded wishfully, for as in *The Cloud Confines*, his Arnoldian attempt at philosophic inquiry, Rossetti still trusted in the after-life, however it might be. But stoic Brown did not. 'My wife and I have bid goodbye to our Son forever,' he wrote candidly some months later of the well-meaning obituary verses. 'After the glorious prospects we had of his career with us here on earth, I am not to be put off with such inane twaddle as the idea of meeting him again, and talking over what we lost on earth, as a couple of absurd vapours.'[45]

While working on the Titianesque *Bella Mano* – a bright, optimistic picture, full of warmth and light to please the patrons – Nolly's death weighed on Rossetti's soul. Early death was the hardest of all impenetrable dooms, he wrote later. Less than a year past, Nolly had spent ten days at Kelmscott – the only time Gabriel had been thus in his company – when his boyish carelessness had caused annoyance, and maybe also memories, for at nineteen Nolly was younger than Gabriel himself at the time of the PRB and *The Germ*. What if his own youthful promise had been so snuffed out?

'I have been finishing the Sphinx design I spoke of,' he told Janey in March. 'The idea is that of Man questioning the Unknown.' A visual version of *The Cloud Confines*, this invoked the human 'eyes fixed ever in vain / On the pitiless eyes of Fate'. By dim moonlight, a man gazes fiercely into the blank eyes of a sphinx, while at his feet a boy falls backwards. It depicted the Sphinx and Her Questioners.

Traditionally, the answer to the Sphinx's question is the three ages of Man. Here, they are her supplicants, demanding responses to unanswerable questions, for in working up the composition, Rossetti added the figure of an old man, in direct homage to Ingres's renowned *Oedipus and the Sphinx*, which he had seen in 1849. The complete design for *The Question* therefore depicts Youth, Manhood and Old Age vainly interrogating the statue, which stares blindly and unrelentingly into space. In due course he gave a full narrative background to Fred Stephens, hoping publicity would attract a buyer. 'The subject represents three Greek pilgrims,' he explained. 'In the distance, between sharp rocks on either side, in a difficult creek of the sea, is seen the ship which has brought them from afar to the nearest navigable point, & thence they have clambered over the crags to the elevated rocky platform on which the Sphinx is enthroned in motionless mystery, her bosom jutting out between the gaunt limbs of a rifted laurel-tree, & her lion-claws planted against them. The youth, about to put his question, falls in sudden swoon from the toils of the journey & the over-mastering emotion; the man leans forward over his falling body and peers into the eyes of the sphinx to read her answer; but those eyes are turned upward and fixed without response on the unseen sky which is out of the picture & only shows in the locked bay of quivering sea a cold reflection of the moon. Meanwhile the old man is seen still labouring upwards and about in his turn to set foot on the platform, eager to the last for that secret which is never to be known . . .'[46]

'It is said that in this conception of Youth dying on the threshold of knowledge, Rossetti wished to symbolise the untimely death of the brilliantly gifted son of Madox Brown,' wrote the *Art Journal* thirty years later. This is too literal, but has resonance in relation to the hard, inexplicable riddle of youthful death. Pictorially, *The Question* anticipates Symbolist works of the late 1880s and 1890s: Moreau's *Oedipe Voyageur*, Toroop's *Fatalism*, Khnopff's *Les Caresses*, and a host of works depicting Sleep, Death and Oblivion. The theme spread through Europe, to signify the menace and mystery of Fate in a faithless age, which by deriving from antiquity also invoked eternity. Within British art, Rossetti's work is closest in conception to Watts's famous *Love and Death*, where a winged boy is pushed back through a doorway by the shrouded, implacable figure of Death, 'to suggest the passionate though unavailing struggle to avert the inevitable'. First shown in 1870, this is likely to have been at least at the back of Rossetti's mind.

As in many Symbolist works, however, the visual rhetoric in *The Question* is too histrionic. Listlessly clasping a long-shafted arrow, the naked youth holds an impossible posture. The man, wearing only a wide-brimmed helmet, presses his face myopically into the Sphinx's. Behind, the grandfather, whose full beard covers his nudity, clambers over the cliff-edge to witness a very peculiar encounter. What kind of bathing party is this?

Rossetti recognised that the composition was too dark and too strange – 'all men and a Sphinx!' – to please a patron. Moonlight scenes were always problematic, he explained to Jane, while a picture without women would never sell.[47] As he foresaw, no one came forward with a commission. Perhaps however this was in truth a private image, meant for himself and Brown. It was a time of endings – at Kelmscott, in the Firm, and family life as it had been known both in Euston and Fitzroy Squares.

CHAPTER TWENTY-FIVE

Decline

'DGR was not a happy man, being too self-centred,' observed Morris after Rossetti's death.[1] Perhaps it were truer to say that inner agitation made his subjective state a pressing, daily matter. Sometimes he felt better, often worse: his spirits fluctuated at what seemed their own will, and the more he was exhorted to 'pull himself together' the less possible this became. Steadily, in the years after leaving Kelmscott, Rossetti's sphere contracted, mentally and physically. Alienated or sorrowful, family and friends felt unable to assist. The everyday dynamism of his life virtually vanished under a welter of anxieties and depressions, and though the 1960s edition of his correspondence contains over a thousand letters written in the seven years from 1875, they chronicle morbid apprehensions and unrealised hopes more than achievements or pleasures.

Between times however came periods of remission; he had, after all, recovered before, and not all was gloom. Indeed, for most of this time, he held himself to the easel, as if conscious that to abandon art meant the end of meaningful life. In 1877 he vigorously contested Fred Shields's argument that chloral was deleterious to his painting. 'I have, as an artist should, made solid progress in the merit of my work, such as it is, and this chiefly within the last five years,' he wrote; 'and produced, I will venture to say, at least a dozen works (among those covering the time) which are unquestionably the best I ever did.' If it was held that his art was adversely influenced by 'the eternal drug', this came from preconceptions rather than anything 'provable from the work itself'.[2]

It was a robust and reliable defence. Rossetti's art did not deteriorate in his last years, whatever the critical views on its specific qualities. When able to work, he produced large pictures with powerful presence, comfortably ranking alongside those of his coevals Watts, Leighton and Burne-Jones. During the past century, they have not always been in critical favour, but they are distinctive and worthy of their place in the history of late-Romantic European art.

He himself counted *Proserpine* and *Dîs Manibus* among the 'best works' of his career, together with *La Bella Mano*. Completed in 1875–7, this last is a mannered but attractive depiction of a woman rinsing her hands in a scalloped basin, attended by two girls with red angelic wings. A large canvas with life-sized figures, it was bought by Murray Marks for 1,000 guineas and sold on to Ellis. Marks claimed to have gone to great trouble to find mauve irises and red tulips at Covent Garden market of the exact shade specified by the artist and to have supplied also the circular mirror and toilet castor, but perhaps saw no further than the profusion of accessories. In effect, the work is a study in reds and golds, offset by white drapery and dark panelling. Circular and rounded shapes create a visual rhythm more complex than usual in Rossetti's work, and though the *toilette* subject appears (and partly is) a trivial one, its aesthetic and symbolic aspects hold greater depth of meaning than is at first perceived. With visual metonymy, the 'lovely hand' of the title stands for erotic female beauty combined with purity – as in the red/white colour balance – to form a pictorial hymn to a Marian Venus. One attendant prepares to dry her white hands, the other to adorn them with silver and gold: chastity combines with sensuous allure. The shell-shaped bowl invokes the sea-birth of Venus, while the white towel and brass urn, whose shapes echo those of the lady's figure, are deployed as central features rather than signature accessories in yet another homage to Dürer's *Birth of the Virgin*.[3]

Perhaps Rossetti himself could not have explained the emotional significance of these mundane objects, repeatedly borrowed; they seem to speak of the tension between actual and ideal constantly negotiated by means of representation in visual art, and here elevate *La Bella Mano* above its boudoir subject, as do the angelic attendants. Despite the vivid image, this is not a depiction, but an extended metaphor. Or rather, as in metaphor, it brings two worlds together. Behind the lady's head, the mirror forms an aureole, yet contains the reflection of a real room. She looks out, but not at the viewer, seeming lost in reverie, while her attendants' half-linked gazes underline the arrested moment. In the foreground a tub holds a small lemon tree, and at some stage the canvas was lengthened to increase the viewer's distance from the scene. All suggests conceptual thought and development. And, as was now Rossetti's regular practice, a sonnet was penned to explain the theme.

> Go shine among thy sisterly sweet band;
> In maiden-minded converse delicately
> Ever more white and soft; until thou be,
> O hand! heart-handsel'd in a lover's hand.

Naturally though less obviously than the poem, the picture also implies a lover. The viewer stands in his place, watching the lady adorn herself to receive him. Above her fetishised fingers, the phallic spout of the urn hangs towards the vaginal bracelets and rings, forming the central motif of the canvas cradled between the three figures and Venus's scalloped bowl.

One may not much like such images. But, whatever else had happened to his mind, Rossetti's artistic ideas, compositional intuition and colour sense were as strong as ever. And as if to demonstrate his continuing presence in the world of art, his sonnets for both this picture and for *Proserpine* were published in the *Athenaeum* in August 1875. Otherwise, he told Alice, 'poetry seems to have fled from me; and indeed it has no such nourishing savour about it as painting can boast'.[4] Thus, late in the day, he found the technical challenges rewarding, and perhaps proved art was his true métier after all.

His next subject was an older, antecedent Venus, whose legends he found in Lemprière's dictionary. *Astarte Syriaca*, the ancient Assyrian goddess, combines the aspect of a chthonic deity with the classical Pudica pose, wearing metallic girdles beneath the bust and round the hips, symbolic of the union of heaven and earth. Behind her rise two muscular messengers bearing torches, staring fixedly upwards, silhouetted against a sun and cresent moon that evoke 'inexplicable cosmic forces', and once more forming a triangular group. Astarte herself is monumental, larger than life-size, minatory. Mannerist in style, the picture is also Symbolist in conception and colour, built on a dark palette in which green drapery and shadowy flesh-tones dominate, with strangely illuminated chiaroscuro effects. Owing something to Leighton's forbidding, full-length *Clytemnestra* of 1874, it is also a tribute to Michelangelo, the giant of Renaissance art, whose work Rossetti increasingly admired and whose head studies of Vittoria Colonna he claimed were veritable portraits of Janey, his own model and muse.[5] Jane's dark complexion also fitted the conception of a Syrian deity.

The focus is on Astarte's face, with its large, 'glowing, mysterious and steadfast eyes' that both engage and look beyond the viewer, and her 'ascendant masses of bronze-black hair'. She is no coy, youthful Venus, but an awesome archaic presence, allusive of prehistoric rites – 'amulet, talisman, and oracle', in the words of her accompanying sonnet – more malevolent than sexual. Indeed, to her first owner, the concept brought to mind the woman arrayed in purple riding on the Beast of the Apocalypse, with 'Mystery, Babylon the Great, the Mother of Harlots and Abominations of the Earth' inscribed on her forehead. As he noted, Babylon was of course 'Syriaca' or Assyrian. Seeing it for the first time, William was reminded, despite the disparity of scale, of Blake.[6]

Astarte's owner was Clarence Fry, proprietor of a successful photographic business in Baker Street, who had just bought Hubert Herkomer's

Chelsea Pensioners – star of the 1875 Academy. For the first and probably only time, Howell made the introduction, taking a ten per cent commission on the sale, to be paid partly in art. Insisting it was his most important composition to date, Rossetti priced the work at 2,000 guineas, and in October received £500 on account.

Before Fry's advent, he had offered the commission to Leyland, alongside a design of Orpheus and Eurydice, thematically reminiscent of *Proserpine*. Leyland wanted neither subject, but instead selected a companion to his green *Veronica*, showing 'a damsel with a dulcimer' from Coleridge's *Kubla Khan*, in creams and pinks. This was a bright, light painting, Rossetti promised, 'as brilliant as anything I have done or can do' and showed Alexa as an improbably fair Abyssinian maid playing her music in 'passionate absorption' amid tree branches. Above, a dove 'hearkens to the magic lay', thus complementing *Veronica*, in which the musician listens to the bird.[7] This was an attractive conceit, and easily within Rossetti's current capabilities. The figure was well advanced by August, when he received £200 towards the purchase price of 800 guineas. When the next instalment was requested a month later, drapery and flowers were finished and the work only waited on a satisfactory stuffed seagull from which to paint the bird. Distanced from its source, the damsel became a siren and the title *The Sea-spell*, in due course with its own sonnet.

Given the ambition and assurance of these 1875 works, together with *The Blessed Damozel* long-promised to Graham and now under way, Rossetti's nervous worries in daily life strike a pathetic note. Missing Kelmscott, from early summer he sought a season's tenancy near some resort, where 'the Divine One and her offspring' might visit. Watts and the Hakes started house-hunting, and Christina sent details of a house near Bristol, where she was visiting Maria. 'I suppose I *shall* get away – in winter!' Gabriel joked all too truly to his mother at the end of August.[8]

There were additional pressures. The Tudor House lease was due to expire and the Cadogan estate wished to inspect its condition; during the surveyor's visit, Rossetti proposed to hide first in the bedroom and then in the studio. Then he was named as a potential witness in a libel case brought by Buchanan against Swinburne, on account of a new squib, while simultaneously subpoenaed in a claim against Howell, who owed £40 for costumes ordered on Rossetti's behalf. He would rather pay the money himself than give evidence in court, Gabriel declared, hastily renting and removing in mid-October to a house at Bognor Regis, with George and the Cheyne Walk servants.

Aldwick Lodge was a large, characterless mansion in its own secluded grounds close to the sea, the other side of Bognor to Felpham, where Blake stayed in oddly comparable circumstances. Gabriel sent an amusing account of Dizzy's behaviour on the beach, shaking a hank of seaweed like a rat and barking indignantly at the aggressive waves. Fanny and Dunn were left in charge at Chelsea, the latter receiving a stream of instructions, to send canvases, cartoons, easels, draperies, photos, studio props and notebooks. 'All must come,' Rossetti wrote at the end of one list, only to apologise the following day for impatience.

He feared isolation, for it was the wrong season for Jane, whose daughters were now at school. Would Watts come down? And his mother and Christina, with or without the 'other household of Euston Square' – where William and Lucy were the proud parents of their first child, one-month-old Olivia, named partly for poor Nolly. (She should be called Olive, wrote her uncle ungraciously; it was much prettier.') But when they proposed to come, he took fright, insisting there was not room for baby or nurse. It was symptomatic, for while he had welcomed Lucy's advent, neither he nor Christina could adjust to the reality, as Lucy entered her role as wife, mother and hostess with gusto. Distrustful as he was of unplanned encounters, Gabriel feared meeting her guests when visiting his mother, and was no doubt relieved when Frances and Christina decided to split the joint household, and live instead with the aunts.

His mother and sister came to Bognor in November, after Maria made her formal profession. 'Poor Maggie is parting with her grey hair next Saturday and annexing the kingdom of Heaven for good,' Gabriel told Alice.[10] On 13 November, there was a great gale that uprooted a fine elm, central feature of Aldwick's lawn. Superstitiously, Rossetti recalled similar events at Chelsea and Kelmscott.

Alexa came briefly to sit for the *Damozel*, followed by Jane on 24 November, for *Astarte*. Privately, she hated the first version of the painting, later describing it as 'my old abomination'.[11] She stayed a fortnight and found the sittings arduous. Gabriel claimed the climate was invigorating, but Bognor was cold, the house gloomy and conversation slow. He roused himself sufficiently to look through the new edition of Christina's poems, praising several new pieces, but frankly dispraising those in which he discerned 'a real taint ... of modern vicious style' and telling her to expunge such elements from her verse. All dealt with unidealised subjects in a partly 'strong-minded' manner, and he was angry that she had after all included *The Lowest Room*, 'that vile trashy poem' he thought fit only for lavatory paper.'[12] So had his sympathies shrunk.

His petulance and irritability worsened, as did his demands. Afraid of a lonely Christmas, he urged his mother, sister and aunts to come to Bognor (and refused to understand why Maria could not join them) together with Dr Hake, two of George's brothers and the faithful Watts. A dismal time was had by all, for the cook was unequal to the task and their host in inhospitable mood. Dissatisfied, indecisive, fault-finding, silent, he needed constant cajoling. In the afternoons, he took what Dr Hake described as a violent walk along the 'penal shore' of boulders and shingle, crunching and stamping as if doing penance. Sadly, Hake also saw that Rossetti was again 'much unstrung'; and before the festive season was over he drove his guests away. Christmas was a great failure, Gabriel told Fanny, blaming the servants.[13]

In the New Year of 1876, reading a new Life and Letters of Benjamin Robert Haydon, he was struck by a fine declaration by Keats: 'I value more the privilege of seeing great things in loneliness than the fame of a prophet.' But Haydon's suicide thirty years before had been very terrible; as Gabriel noted to his mother, 'It seems that poor Mary Haydon we used to know was the first to enter the studio and find her father's dead body.'[14] His own thoughts frequently ran in a similar direction. He would like William to know how things stood, he told Watts gloomily in June. 'How long he may have a brother . . . is not easy to judge.'

Returning to Bognor for a short while, Jane acknowledged the inevitable and decided she could no longer visit. 'When I found that he was ruining himself with chloral and that I could do nothing to prevent it I left off going to him – and on account of the children,' she explained later, adding sadly that 'all were devoted to him who knew him – he was unlike all other men'.[15] They continued to correspond, but the intimacy was over.

Soon after her departure, Gabriel drafted a memo telling George what was to be done in the event of his death. 'If I die suddenly at any moment, it is my special last wish that my remains may be burnt,' he wrote. 'Let no cast be taken on any account of my face or head and let no one come near my body except in your presence or in that of my brother. Let me not on any account be buried at Highgate, but my remains burnt as I say . . .'

His will was in a sealed packet in the carved wardrobe in the studio at Chelsea, he continued (later, he would tell William he had made no will). In the same drawer '(or else in the iron safe, but I fear they were never put there)' were letters in sealed packets, which must be carefully burnt at once, together with other letters in the drawer of the bookcase and in his black portmanteau. When this was done, the writer of the letters was to be informed.[16] Without doubt, the writer was Janey, who must have requested such a promise when coming to her sad conclusion that Gabriel could no longer be helped, and may well have feared he would die suddenly, by his own hand. Fanny had keys to many doors and cupboards in Cheyne Walk.

Another symptom of his nervous state was constant fear of imminent penury. Paying bills at a distance, via Dunn, it was admittedly difficult to keep in full control, especially over items such as those from Liberty's Oriental emporium, which could be taken on approval. Would his mother believe that he was always hard pressed to find fifty pounds, though his bank book showed receipts totalling £3,725 in the past twenty-four months? he asked in April. Maybe this was true, but one suspects a simple neurotic delusion, impervious to evidence. Like his father, he saw shame and destitution fast approaching.

In London, Watts continued to negotiate with the Cadogan estate, who submitted a repair bill of £1,000, suggesting also that the house be vacated before the lease terminated in 1878, there being plans to build on part of the garden. Howell continued to cause problems, attempting sharp practice with Fry and succeeding with Valpy, by bounced cheques and sale of works he did not own. No doubt neither would press charges, Gabriel commented; else Charles might end in gaol for fraud, 'like his last friend Hogg'.[17] In fact Fry proved tougher than Valpy, declaring that he would see Howell bankrupted. By midsummer, Rossetti decided to sever all relations with the notorious *blagueur*.

As soon as the Buchanan libel case was over, and he had escaped subpoena, Rossetti returned to London. Just before leaving Bognor he finally got over to Felpham, glimpsing Blake's cottage. He was coming back, he told Dunn; but no one must know. It was *most necessary* that all letters be sealed. The studio must be soundproofed, to prevent neighbours from spying. He must retrench, but what to do with everything in Cheyne Walk? and where to find a country home? He knew how bad his condition was. 'When you were here last I must have tried your patience in various ways,' he told Watts with understatement. 'The fact is that I have now got so completely out of health that I need more indulgence from my friends than I have any right to expect ...'[18]

Yet, the painting continued. *The Blessed Damozel* progressed, slowly but satisfactorily. After a false beginning, *Astarte* came together too, on a slightly larger scale. By spring it was well in hand, and moreover the abortive canvas would be developed, either as Hero watching for Leander, or a personification of Memory, *La Ricordanza*, with her lamp.

Graham, jocularly anticipating 'a grove of new work' when Rossetti returned to town, received a long and confident reply, acknowledging that besides the *Damozel*, commissions were still outstanding on *Found*, *The Ship of Love* and the smaller *Dante's Dream*. However, five pictures had been delivered in the last few years: *Mariana*, *Beatrice*, *Ghirlandata*, *The Bower Maiden* and the large *Dante's Dream*, together with various studies and revisions to previous works. He had also delivered three pictures for Leyland in the same period. 'Thank you for your inquiries after my health, which does not prevent my work from improving as yet, and that is all the function I claim from it.'[19] A reasonable comment, at odds with actuality yet not contradicted by the schedule of work.

Back in Chelsea, he departed again almost immediately for the Cowper-Temples' country house, Broadlands, in Hampshire. Currently, they were hosting a religious conference in the spacious grounds, with guests of both sexes, 'all on the parsonical tack', and though George reported that at the outset of the visit Gabriel kept reclusively apart (even changing rooms once in the middle of the night, unable to sleep) by the end of a month he was cheerfully mixing with other guests, and charming them in familiar manner. Mrs Temple was womanly goodness itself, and the family governess was a welcome old friend, none other than poor Alex Munro's sister Annie. It was very hot. 'As I write my bottom scorches my chair and my chair my bottom,' he told Watts.[20]

The local vicar's infant son was procured to model for a cherub in *The Blessed Damozel* (succeeding a workhouse baby who did not suit) and in addition fellow guest Georgina Sumner proved so handsome and gracious that she too must be painted, as a Roman noblewoman. Back in London in September, she came several times to the studio. Tall and dignified, Mrs Sumner represented the kind of mature beauty that now attracted him in women – perhaps also because she in turn was much smitten by Mr Rossetti's attentions, and touched by his plight. Flashes of the old charisma were visible, and, as with Mrs Cowper-Temple, the notion of ministering to a fallen genius may have appealed.

Once more in remission, Rossetti lost various plaguey aches and pains. He arranged more sittings for Janey, and for Marie Stillman, whom he cast as Fiammetta, Boccaccio's beloved. Marie's step-daughter Lisa recalled Mr Rossetti's regal carriage, portly body, light footstep and melodrious voice. He travelled across town to visit his mother, who this month moved to a house in Torrington Square, still in Bloomsbury. He went with Marshall to consult Jenner, who prescribed the 'awful ordeal' of two nights without chloral. He tried hypnosis, which to his surprise helped physically, though it did not secure sleep. But then his own concerns were overshadowed by those of his sister Maria, who was dying of an abdominal cancer in the All Saints infirmary.

How terrible to think of 'that bright mind and those ardently acquired stores of knowledge now prisoned in so frail and perishing a frame,' he told their mother, after his second visit. 'How sweet and true a life, and how pure a death, hopeful and confiding in every last instant!'[21] Speaking so surely of being about to meet her Lord in person, Maria seemed already past the threshold of heaven.

In infancy, Maria had been violently jealous of Gabriel's gifts and privileges. In adulthood, they had few shared interests, and there is no evidence of closeness, though the family affection that bound the Rossettis never faded. He was aware of her prayers for his conversion, and indeed partly envied her fervour. While at Broadlands he had read Christina's poetry with Mrs Cowper and Mrs Sumner, gratified to find they esteemed it highly, and had proffered his own *Cloud Confines* as an account of his shadowy beliefs but, as with Nolly, Maria's untimely death did not encourage ideas of divine beneficence. At her funeral in Brompton Cemetery, he was grateful for the silent support of Fred Shields, whose devotionalism matched Maria's, but himself seemed veritably geriatric, at only forty-eight. He joined the family party for a sombre Christmas, on condition no one else was invited. Perhaps Lucy was more subdued than usual, for she was two months from her second confinement. On 2 January all met again at his mother's house, which now Maria would never visit.

Then, after endless bickerings and abuse, faithful George Hake, who had served four years as effective 'minder', decided to leave. The immediate cause was his late homecoming one evening, when Gabriel told him to go, at once. Dismayed, William and Christina, who knew George's value and what he had endured from Gabriel's preremptory temper, sent him their warm thanks. It was in truth no life for an active, educated young man, and George had been accused too often to accept further apologies, though perhaps also meriting Gabriel's complaints of sluggish neglect and occasional surliness. George himself blamed Fanny, which perhaps indicates bad conscience. 'That woman has been planning the whole thing for the last month or two,' he told his father; 'and has gained such an ascendancy over DGR that he is really not accountable for his action.'[22] Subsequently there were arguments over books and other items that left Tudor House with George, including Rossetti's funeral instructions. In due course Harry Dunn, who had a drink problem, moved back to Cheyne Walk, with Fanny also on hand when required. But on 3 February, when William called, no one answered his knock. Servants were hard to obtain, and even harder to retain.

Increasingly, friends and family identified chloral as cause of all ailments. Gabriel agreed, in principle, to diminish and then relinquish the dosage; in practice, without chloral he was condemned to the unendurable hell of sleeplessness. Moreover, the cold turkey of withdrawal brought no apparent benefit. Over the months, as well as mesmerism, he tried other remedies including beer, galvanism and vigorous late-night exercise, all without success. 'Trivial experiments may be made by a person who has not got used to stronger remedies, but of course not by a person who has,' he explained to his mother,[23] while at the same time demanding instant results from the alternatives proposed. Other drugs he resisted, saying bromide was very lowering, and morphia even more addictive than chloral.

It is hard to judge how deleterious the drug was. Jenner recommended a maximum dose of 20 grains per night, while Marshall sanctioned 46. But Gabriel's doses were not uniform and during a bad spell in 1877 he was taking 180 grains, coloured with purple amaranth and flavoured to make it more palatable. Lacking George, he sent Fanny to collect supplies, or her lodger John Schott, who with wife and sons was now occupying rooms at Royal Avenue. In May 1877 the pharmacy sent a worried note, 'rather alarmed at the quantity of "Chloral" taken by Mr Rossetti' and begging to know that such amounts were medically sanctioned. By spring 1878 Dunn said the measure was down to 50 grains, though it soon rose again to 90 and above. In 1879, Messrs Bell again protested, saying henceforth they would supply only one bottle a day. Not outwitted, Rossetti promptly ordered more from another firm.[24]

The chronic dependency must have been harmful, and even in respect of restful sleep achieved little, although the fluctuations in his condition appear largely independent of his chemical intake, which indeed rose and fell according to other symptoms. Undoubtedly however it worsened his problems, being physically damaging, and there is no question that in these years Rossetti was fatally abusing his body. William held that, having been almost teetotal up to the age of forty, his brother's later habit of gulping down stiff doses of raw whisky to accompany the chloral was 'quite as ruinous to his constitution' as the drug itself,[25] though it is also true that without chloral, Gabriel would have been literally suicidal.

Following the completion of *Astarte* in spring 1877, his condition deteriorated due to a combination of factors. The voices and delusions reappeared so that he became beset with imagined threats, discerned in the song of a thrush. Noise from neighbouring houses led him to order false walls to be inserted in the studio, as previously planned; earlier the front-door locks had been replaced owing to suspicions of theft. At the same time he was troubled by physical pains, for the swollen hydrocele had become filled with blood. In June Marshall performed emergency surgery and hired a nurse. The operation was clearly more serious than before, perhaps involving removal of scrotum and testicles, and for two months Rossetti remained bedridden, too shaky to walk and with a tremor that prevented all painting, drawing, writing. Marshall held that chloral was retarding recovery and early in August insisted Rossetti must go to the seaside and relinquish the drug. But how could this be accomplished, without George? Lovingly, Frances Rossetti and Christina volunteered to sacrifice their own holiday and keep Gabriel company as long as required. William gave his brother a serious warning about obeying medical advice, to which Gabriel listened sullenly. A frustrating night and day of agitation, 'cross-purposes, false starts and graver tribulations' followed, during which Gabriel (assisted by Fanny, who resented the employment of a nurse) obstructed 'all rational projects for his welfare', and refused to move. In the end, William and Dunn got him to Fitzroy Square, whence Brown took him to Herne Bay on the Kent coast, with the nurse in attendance. It was a struggle, since Rossetti insisted on taking everything, including a special mattress for the bed, without which he could not sleep. Refusing the first lodgings, he eventually settled in a more secluded house at Hunter's Forestall, where his mother and sister joined him for what proved a twelve-week convalescence. To add to his miseries, he contracted shingles.

Deeply depressed and physically inert, he foresaw an entirely invalided future, and warned Fanny that he could not henceforth be relied on. In response, she sent a demand for money and returned her Cheyne Walk keys. This left the servants unsupervised, for Dunn was away. Oh, he was much too ill to be receiving angry reproaches, Rossetti replied. 'If I recover the use of my hands, you will be my first care as always. If not, I shall myself be living on charity.'

'You surely cannot be angry with me for doing what I have done after receiving such a letter from you telling me I must forget you and get my own living,' Fanny replied, taking the opportunity to complain that Dunn rejoiced in her downfall; 'but your letters led me to suppose you were tired of me, you shall never say I forsook you although I felt it very much when another woman was put in my place and that is the way I was treated for taking your part. I hope I shall see you again and be with you as before but I never wish to meet any of your friends after the cruel way in which I have been treated.'[26] Precipitately, with funds provided by Schott, she took the lease of a small hotel in St James's, declaring this better than letting out lodgings.

'My dear Fan, Your letter has upset me extremely,' Gabriel replied, forbearingly affectionate. 'To be uncertain of your whereabouts and well-being is greatly to add to my anxieties.' At times her presence was essential, he told Watts. Demanding as she might be, alone in his circle she did not lecture on chloral.

Again, the tranquillity and care were beneficial: under the restorative regime at Herne Bay, his ailments subsided. After six weeks the chloral dose was down to 30–40 grains and his hands were steady, leading to chalk portraits of his mother and sister that were as accomplished as any he had produced, although most gloomy in mood and the reverse of flattering. He had feared he would never work again. But the episode had its costs, for William's patience was sorely tried by Gabriel's apparent refusal to exercise any will-power, while for the first time ever Brown's affection was withdrawn. Requested to escort Gabriel back to London, he wrote what was received as an 'absurd letter' on the 'eternal question', saying he would only help if the chloral were stopped; to come to Kent otherwise would condone its use. 'My dear Brown,' replied Rossetti, 'I cannot see what you would sanction by your presence except the fact that we are old friends and like to see each other. Surely you cannot be responsible for what I alone must do or leave undone as I please.'[27] But Brown was unmoved and at last estranged, after thirty years' unconditional affection.

'Chloral is like ardent spirits, utterly besotting and cheating its poor victim with the same delusion that the sufferings can be cured only by their cause,' wrote Shields, truly but melodramatically. If Gabriel returned to Chelsea with his habit unbroken, 'then farewell to his great mind. He trembles on the verge of lunacy now from its effects.'[28]

His mother and sister forbore to lecture. Gabriel was grateful, writing later that his recovery was due in large part to their care. In his worst moments, however, he claimed they were trying to convert him. Would this matter? wondered William, in his own worst moments; perhaps religion would assist Gabriel after all. A few months hence, his brother would tell young William Sharp that he could conceive of no higher ideal than Christ; moreover, 'to write anything lowering that ideal in many minds would be very rash'.[29] If he said the same to Christina, she must have rejoiced devoutly. More likely, he simply scowled.

Gabriel reached London in time to see Janey before she left for Italy. She had troubles of her own, for her elder daughter had developed epilepsy. Now sixteen, Jenny had been forceful, bright, intellectually inclined, looking forward to becoming one of the first generation of female graduates. Epilepsy destroyed that future, and the whole Morris family was afflicted. With gratitude, Jane accepted an invitation to take both daughters to the Riviera, to spend the winter in company with Rosalind Howard, wife of the Earl of Carlisle, and her large brood. Once, she had dreamed of being in Italy with Gabriel.

The house question remained worrisome, for no suitable new home had been found. Fanny was involved in viewing prospective properties, and Rossetti went to inspect the most eligible – an old mansion at Percy Cross in Fulham and a large house called The Retreat facing the river at Hammersmith, soon to be vacated by the family of George Macdonald, author of *The Princess and the Goblin*. It was commodious, but liable to flooding, he reported, with basement kitchens so dark that no servants would stay. Eventually Watts agreed a new lease for Tudor House, at a higher ground rent and on condition that when required for building, a large area of the garden would be lost. By this time the menagerie was no more – indeed, the animals must all have been disposed of before Rossetti settled at Kelmscott – and the garden was completely overgrown (one of the Cadogan complaints: from Bognor, Rossetti had ordered Dunn to see to this). So by midsummer 1878, the threat of having to move evaporated. Somewhat ironically, the following winter, while Jane was again in Italy, Morris leased The Retreat. Thinking the name suggested a private asylum, he rechristened it Kelmscott House.

Briefly, before leaving at Christmas to join her husband in Italy, Marie Stillman came to Chelsea for a few sittings. 'All my models of any value, to wit two only ... are leaving me in the lurch,' Rossetti lamented to Jane. Numerous drawings of Jane were still displayed in the studio, alongside uncommissioned subjects. Encouragingly, a new client appeared in the shape of William Turner, a young cotton manufacturer introduced by Shields, who though not as rich as Leyland or Graham was a genuine collector. In December Turner agreed to purchase *The Vision of Fiammetta*, for which Marie was the model, together with *Proserpine 1* and the old *Water Willow*, Jane's favourite. She would be glad and sorry to hear this, Rossetti wrote; in present circumstances the promise of 1,500 guineas for all three pictures allowed for no haggling. It was important, too, to get pictures into Manchester, 'where the principal buyers are'.[30] He told the widowed Madame Maenza, whom he was now assisting financially, that he had lost five months through illness, but assured Leyland that he was once again 'in good working order'.

By March 1878, *Fiammetta* was well progressed, and would be finished 'before it can say Jack Robinson or Giovanni Boccaccio', he joked (Fiammetta being Boccaccio's *innamorata*). Graham's *Blessed Damozel*, now to have a predella showing the yearning lover, was also nearly finished, and looking very brilliant. In addition, an existing study of Jane was worked up in watercolour and called *Bruna Brunelleschi*, in oblique reference to Michelangelo's Vittoria Colonna, whose colouring Jane shared, and sold to the faithful Valpy.

Though Gabriel called it *'a ripper'*, William did not rate *Fiammetta* among the best products; it was painted with much brilliancy but little grace, he told Lucy.[31] Probably the brilliance was to blame, for filling the space around the red-gowned figure with red-and-white apple blossom made the tones too hot, the shapes too spotty and the whole too loud. The artist, in fact, had been responding to criticism, for the judgement among his peers and patrons was that depression, or drugs, or both, gave his works a dark, melancholy cast. Not true, Rossetti protested to Shields; but *Astarte* was demonstrably dark – Brown said his colour sense was waning – and *Fiammetta* was evidently intended to contrast.

When painting, however slowly, he was better; as he confessed, it was 'pure purgatory' for him to be without work in hand, as long ago he had discovered when chasing away moodiness. Of course, when he was better, he could paint; the relation was reciprocal. Through 1878, he remained relatively healthy in mind and body. Looking back at this period of his brother's life, William disputed that it was unrelieved decline. Gabriel jogged along, he wrote, 'more than sufficiently depressed in his own mind and feelings, but cheered by friendly conversation and attentions, and always (it must be remembered) as diligent in his art-work as he had ever been'.[32]

In the *Fortnightly*, Walter Pater had published his declaration of Aesthetic principles in 'The School of Giorgione', arguing that criticism should discuss the arts in terms of their successful interpenetration of content and form, realised completely only in music, to whose qualities other arts aspired. Visual art, he wrote, must first of all delight the senses as directly and sensuously as a fragment of Venetian glass. 'In its primary aspect, a great picture has no more definite message for us than an accidental play of sunlight and shadow for a moment, on one's wall or floor, is indeed a space of such falling light, caught as the colours are caught in an Eastern carpet, but refined upon and dealt with more subtly and exquisitely than by nature itself.'[33] The essay had many incidental references to delight Rossetti – to Sordello, Titian, Blake, Legros – and two that would gratify: a note on the song in *Measure for Measure*, which he had taken for his subject in *Mariana*, and an allusion to himself – the poet whose 'own painted work comes often to mind' in relation to the idylls of Giorgione. It is not known which works Pater had in mind, but he may have seen *The Bower Meadow* – the most 'idyllic' of Rossetti's pictures – on view at Pilgerams in 1872.

In the past couple of years, Aesthetic art had acquired its own showcase at the Grosvenor Gallery, founded by Sir Coutts Lindsay and his wealthy, talented wife Blanche. Exhibition was by invitation; famously it made Burne-Jones's reputation, providing much-needed exposure and criticism, and many friends hoped Rossetti would also be persuaded. While at Bognor he was approached, and when back in London, he consulted both Burne-Jones and Madox Brown. When the Grosvenor's organiser Charles Hallé renewed the subject in January 1877, however, he formally declined. At the same time extracting a promise that works would not be exhibited without his consent, he declared that the refusal was based 'simply [on] that lifelong feeling of dissatisfaction which I have experienced from the disparity of aim and attainment'.[34]

This was a blow to the Grosvenor, whose success was to be partly based on exclusivity. Then, two months before the opening in May 1877 – boldly chosen to chime with the RA – a paragraph of art gossip in *The Times* stated that 'Mr Dante Rossetti, though cordially sympathising with Sir Coutts Lindsay, is prevented by ill-health from undertaking any work for this year ...' Though certainly ill, Mr Dante Rossetti was enraged: to advertise an artist's incapacity was to kill his sales. This was not his reason for absence, he reproved the paper, insisting that his letter to Hallé be printed in confirmation. 'I never painted in the same space of time so many pictures of the same size and study as within the last few years and up to this writing,' he asserted, anger fuelled by finding that Fry had been willing to lend *Astarte*. Not surprisingly, such apprehension of conspiracy coincided with the songbirds' resumption of delusory messages, and eavesdropping spies in the next-door houses.[35]

To Janey he more candidly confessed that the prospect of 'public failure' at his advanced age was too powerful. All suggests he was permanently scarred by the *Fleshly* affair. Against his wishes, Graham's uncle sent his *Pandora* to a loan exhibition in Glasgow, but rather surprisingly two years later Rossetti allowed Turner's *Proserpine* to go to an 'Art Treasures' show in Manchester, for the benevolent purpose of raising funds for the city's Art School.[36]

A year later, Sir Coutts asked again, saying Grosvenor space would be reserved. Again Mr Rossetti declined, while nevertheless admitting – to Janey at least – that he still yearned to 'come out somewhere and somehow'. *The Blessed Damozel* looked very well now it was finished. From Oneglia, Jane encouraged the idea, believing that public acclaim would be beneficial. 'I assure you I have thought very seriously as to exhibiting this year and your urging me is of course the strongest incentive,' Rossetti replied, nevertheless repeating his refusal.[37] Towards the end of the year, he no doubt congratulated himself on withstanding Lindsay's pressure, when Whistler brought his notorious libel case against Ruskin for abusing his falling rocket, the *Nocturne in Black and Gold*, shown at the Grosvenor Gallery in 1877; suppose some hostile critic had similarly mocked *Astarte*? Whistler won the case, but received no damages or costs, and was bankrupted. 'Alas for Jimmy Whistler! what harbour of refuge now, unless to turn Fire-King at Cremorne? – and Cremorne itself is no more!' wrote Gabriel, roused to an apt flight of fancy. 'A nocturne andante in the direction of the Sandwich Islands, or some country where tattooing is the national School of Art, can now alone avert the long-impending Arrangement in Black on White.'[38]

So neither wit nor humour had entirely deserted him. When Jane returned from Italy in early summer 1878, she postponed coming to see him, on the grounds that recurrent fever had left her looking like a scarecrow. Please, he protested, she should never call herself that; he might as well sign himself 'Paint-rag' or 'Dish-clout'. Once, she had been 'famed for her beauty' and he for painting her. Now he was fifty, and she just thirty-eight, but sorrows made them feel they were tottering towards the tomb. He was upset, too, that she should even imply that her altered looks would affect his desire to see her. The suggestion was an outrage to his deep regard for her, he protested – a feeling far deeper than he had ever felt towards any other living creature. Oh, she had never believed him, but it was truth. 'Would that circumstances had given me the power to prove this: for proved it *wd* have been,' he wrote. 'And *now* you do not believe it.' Please would she come the very first day she could, to see *Fiammetta* and the *Damozel*.[39]

The 'eternal *Blessed Damozel*' was finally shown to Graham, if not delivered. Seven years' gestation had resulted in an ambitious canvas. The half-length figure of the beloved, leaning against the bar of heaven with seven stars in her hair, was placed above three angelic heads reminiscent of Raphael's putti and in front of a background sequence of embracing lovers derived from Botticelli's *Mystic Nativity*, each couple in a different action. In the predella, the bereaved lover stretches out on the ground, gazing upward. The lines are lyrical and the tones both deep and brilliant, dark greens harmonising with dusky pinks and browns. Special care was given to the final glazing, so that the Damozel is softly highlighted, the other figures gently backlit in half-shadow, to lift them a little forward. Not surprisingly, the feeling of the picture echoes that of *Beata Beatrix*. A replica was under way.

To the outside world, Rossetti was not the fallen colossus of later legend, but an artist of still surpassing power – if one could but see his pictures. Offering the only window, Fred Stephens continued to write regularly on 'Mr Rossetti's New Pictures', describing *Astarte*, *The Blessed Damozel* and *The Sea-spell* in April 1877, and *Fiammetta* in October 1878. The following year, when F. S. Ellis re-emerged as a buyer, commissioning a half-length subject based on Janey as Dante's *Donna della Finestra*, he was informed that the picture would in due course be reviewed in the *Athenaeum*, as usual. With such a mouthpiece, who needed the Grosvenor Gallery?

And indeed Rossetti took some steps to circulate his work more widely, via autotype reproductions published by a Manchester company with which Shields was connected. The idea was a sequence of drawings, mostly in crayon, which would look well in monochrome, through a process that allowed for retouching at proof stage until the effect was as good as it could feasibly be. As so often with reproductions, this proved less simple in practice, and Rossetti was always a perfectionist. One autotype was a profile head of Janey drawn in 1871; hunting for a good title, he first proposed 'Twilight', then hit more happily on *Perlascura*, a Dantesque appellation signifying dark pearl. The second subject was *Silence*, a half-length from 1870, also from Janey. 'Silence holds in one hand a branch of peach, the symbol used by the ancients; its fruit being held to resemble the human heart and its leaf the human tongue,' he explained to the sitter. 'With the other hand she draws together the veil enclosing the shrine in which she sits.' The dates should be taken off the negatives, he told Shields. 'There is no objection to their being supposed more recent works of mine, but rather the contrary, and I should prefer it.'[40]

Given this modest attempt at reaching a wider public, it was alarming when the Hon. Percy Wyndham, a rising politician and friend of Burne-Jones, purchased a chalk drawing by Rossetti that the artist did not recognise. It bore 'a colourable imitation' of his monogram, and the date 1876. 'I saw it at once to be spurious,' he wrote when the forgery was brought for verification, drafting a press announcement to warn other buyers. Widely supposed to be the work of Rosa Corder, Howell's partner in several senses, the drawing was one of several which seemed to have been pledged for money – the shop offering them for sale being an up-market pawnbroker. He must issue a denial, Rossetti told Shields, the prices charged were so low they would ruin his market.[41]

In these years Shields was a frequent visitor and correspondent, who like Smetham before him valued Rossetti's sympathetic interest in his own endeavours and repaid it with devoted, if nervous, loyalty; he too suffered from depression. When in London he was often invited to work at Cheyne Walk, and in return undertook various services, of which as the months progressed the most important was simply his company, on those evenings when Gabriel was otherwise alone. Dozens of notes survive from these later years, summoning Shields to paint and/or dine, and requesting assistance with artistic and non-artistic matters. He bought pigments and accessories, helped set the lay-figure, shared models, lent his wife's shawls for drapery, hunted for source materials, advised on servants, procured flowers and foliage, and also visited the theatre – a penance for such a puritan – when *Punch* reported that 'DGR' featured in a London play ridiculing the Aesthetic School, and again when Bunthorne in *Patience* was described as a Fleshly Poet. According to Shields, neither was the personalised attack that Gabriel feared.

Another loyal acquaintance was William Davies, a friend of Smetham and modest painter and poet, who also suffered from the 'Black Visitant'. Poor Smetham himself was now lost to dementia, sunk in catatonic immobility interrupted only by occasional violence. On learning this, Gabriel offered to act as his agent, taking dozens of the small, Blakean paintings to press upon his own patrons for sums up to £75. The Cowper-Temples proved charitable, as did Judge Lushington, in memory of the old days at the Working Men's College, where Smetham had started. Even 'graceless

Graham' was reluctantly induced to part with £25 when Rossetti knocked fifty pounds off the price of the *Damozel's* predella.[42] Sarah Smetham was lastingly grateful.

Constantine Ionides declined to assist, but when brought to Cheyne Walk by his sister Aglaia expressed a wish to play patron once more. One of the old drawings of Janey, seated in a tree with a book, caught his fancy. 'It is a pleasure to me to think that luck generally comes through the drawings of your dear face,' Gabriel informed the model jubilantly. The price of 700 guineas was 'very convenient to turn round upon. I think of calling the picture Vanna Primavera, making the tree a spring sycamore.'[43] Derived from Giovanna, 'Vanna' is the Italian equivalent of 'Janey' – as no doubt she knew – so that the title may be read as 'Janey in Springtime'. In the event, however, the study in greens was called *The Day Dream*, evocative and loosely allusive to Tennyson's poem of the same name, on the Sleeping Beauty. Critical of *Astarte* and *Fiammetta*, William placed both *Day Dream* and *Donna della Finestra* among Gabriel's finest pictures, especially after the former's head was repainted with softer shading and a sweeter expression.

Jane's loyalty was greatly valued. Compared with 'those who made apes of themselves and kissed my hands with insane obeisance in early days' but now ignored him, she was 'always faithful and always will be'. And when his spirits rose, the letters to Janey grew longer and livelier. Among the recurrent jokes was his prediction that Topsy, with his growing involvement in public affairs, would soon become a politician – the MP for Lechlade, perhaps. 'It seems they have been smashing Gladstone's windows,' Gabriel wrote in the winter of 1877, when jingoistic demands for British intervention in the war between Russia and Turkey was at its height; 'if you were in town, perhaps the air would come in without your throwing the windows open, considering Top's political bias ... my dear Janey, depend on it, [he] will be in parliament next change.'[44] He was half right: soon Morris was in the thick of public affairs, with a range of urgent causes from the prevention of war to the protection of ancient buildings from ecclesiastical 'restorers' (he invited Gabriel to add his name to both campaigns in vain, although amusingly one newspaper listed Rossetti as those on the platform at a public meeting of the Eastern Question Association, alongside Morris and Cowper-Temple). Thence he turned to national politics – but in the Socialist rather than the Liberal cause, firmly opposed to the sham democracy of bourgeois elections. The best use for the Houses of Parliament, in his view, was as a dung market. Gabriel, who boasted he had never read a parliamentary debate in his life, would doubtless have agreed.

To assuage lingering jealousy, soon after Janey's return from Italy in 1878, he wrote a last dramatic squib, entitled *The Death of Topsy*. This new burlesque took its motif from the startling circumstance that George Wardle, long-time Firm manager, was married to the erstwhile Madeline Smith, the 'stunner' who in 1857 had escaped the gallows after poisoning her young lover. As with his own affairs, tangential events in Rossetti's life had a curious tendency to imitate fiction: now with witty, transparent wishfulness he imagined Madeline Wardle lacing Topsy's coffee with arsenic, in order to oust him from the business. Following his dramatic decease, Topsy reappears at a seance, to the disgust of the medium, who declares him a very low-class spirit, owing to his profane language.[45] William declared this a piece of 'rollicking fun' but in truth the satire is a trifle tired. As he moved further into public life, growing in stature and significance, Morris was less and less a figure of mockery – while Rossetti's decline offered a poignant contrast. Later, Morris himself wrote a political satire called *The Tables Turned*, which had nothing to do with Rossetti, apart from being an apt title for their final relationship.

With her husband, Jane also began to follow public affairs, teasing Rossetti for his increasingly conservative opinions. 'You don't really think I'm a Tory?' he protested on one occasion, perhaps for her sake trying to raise an interest in politics. A few months later, he informed his mother that economic recession was over: trade in cotton, iron, copper and coal were all improving. 'You may perhaps think this report not much in my line,' he observed, 'but I view it as vitally bound up with the picture-market.'[46]

Despite, or because of, his reclusive habits, his fame was spreading; many strangers were now aware of the seldom-seen poet and painter who lived in the large neglected house along Cheyne Walk. One June morning in 1878, a tubercular young Oxford graduate named Hardinge, who had long worshipped at the shrine of Rossetti, was introduced by Louisa Ashburton. They saw first the Botticelli portrait of Smeralda Bandinelli, which Rossetti boasted of buying from Christie's for £20, and a Dutch genre painting. Then DGR appeared. 'Face handsome and sanguine: red lips and cheeks, grey eyes very clear ... Dress very slovenly, an old frock coat, check trousers, or shepherd's plaid, white cotton socks, low black shoes.' He kept brushes in the pockets of his long coat, and led the way to the studio, where Hardinge immediately glimpsed a *Proserpine*. It was 'as if I were entering a room full of people I had never seen but whom I recognised at once,' he wrote later. 'The well-known Rossetti type seemed all around one.'[47]

They saw *The Blessed Damozel* and Rossetti was pleased when Hardinge asked where was the seventh star? (Round the back, came the laughing reply.) Then came *Fiammetta*, which was currently sprinkled with blue pimpernels rather than Boccaccio's 'vermeil flowers'. Discerning from the aggressive response to one or two ingenuous remarks that Mr Rossetti did not welcome criticism, Hardinge kept quiet until the *Proserpine* was displayed, when he disclosed that the cut-down head with snowdrops was owned by the mother of a college friend. Rossetti flatly denied any such picture existed, and hearing that it was purchased through Howell declared it and three drawings from the same source to be forgeries (a statement retracted when the works were sent for verification). Over the fireplace was a study of Janey for the *Day Dream*, only the head in colour; it would be painted, Rossetti said, 'all in greens and greys'.

Finally, in the centre of the room was *Dante's Dream*. The artist read his printed description and graciously signed a copy for Hardinge. 'It was precisely at this moment that Rossetti was most bright and humorous,' he recalled. Ruskin's name came up. 'I have not seen him for twenty years, and he has forgotten me; I had nearly forgotten him,' remarked Rossetti, adding that Ruskin often spoke too strongly. In respect of the libel case, it was a pity that instead of calling Whistler an impostor Ruskin had not said he could paint 'a good deal better than in these sketches.' Rossetti's own view was that when Whistler did such daubs, he was 'an amateur', but that he could really paint. As the visitors left, Hardinge explained that he could not climb stairs, and rarely left home. Rossetti was sympathetic – and even more so when Hardinge alluded to the soothing effect of 30 grains of chloral . . . 'He stood on the steps of the old red house and waved his hands as we drove off.'

In Hardinge's recollection, this was Rossetti at his most natural, happy and radiant. By early 1879, however, personal depression again set in, exacerbated by dark days and increasing isolation. Months passed between William's visits; he had a growing family and new pleasures as guest and host, for Lucy cultivated radical, literary friends. Good Dr Hake, determined not to quarrel over Rossetti's treatment of George, found his friendly approaches courteously rebuffed. For old times' sake, Burne-Jones and Arthur Hughes continued to call occasionally, receiving a contradictory welcome. On the one hand, Rossetti was pleased; on the other, he complained of those who paid visits just once or twice a year. It was grievous, recalled Ned, going to the dark, neglected house to sit with Gabriel for the evening amid oil-lamps and old unsilvered mirrors, and then creep away in low spirits oneself.

He grew ever more corpulent – a sketch by Brown in August 1879 shows him with a belly like a beach-ball, lying on the sofa with his feet characteristically higher than his head. The following autumn was extremely gloomy, when Rossetti felt more than usually unwell and especially lonely. His requests for company became urgent: on one occasion he implored William to call if only for an hour, writing pathetically: 'I am at present as ill as ever I was in my life, and really don't know how it may end.'[48] On 13 October he overdosed on chloral, and John Marshall was summoned (it was now that Messrs Bell restricted the chloral supply). Anxiously, his mother and sister came to Chelsea two mornings in a row, to be of such assistance as they could. Sometimes he prevailed upon Fanny to stay overnight, sending a note to tell the now-widowed John Schott why she would not be returning. A short while later Fanny married Schott, presumably to secure her future, while remaining close to Rossetti. She kept scores of his scribbled notes, which contain equal measures of humour and pathos. 'Dear Good Elephant,' begins one such. 'An old Rhinoceros was nasty last night, & his horn is wet with tears which he has shed on the subject. He wants a good Elephant to come down as soon as possible, & he will give it something to amuse it.' But on other occasions, the message was more melancholy. 'Good Elephant. Do come down. Old Rhinoceros is unhappy. P. S. Tiddy cheque.' And sometimes the scrawl was half-illegible, even the long-running nicknames abandoned. 'My dear Fan, You know I have not written very many letters written [sic],' began one, sent in sickness; '– but the idea that I may not be seeing your kind face tonight makes me so sincerely miserable that I cannot but sit down to write this. Do come to dinner. Do pray come at once. What I said and did has not satisfied . . . Your loving R.'[49]

Of all those who had loved Gabriel, in his times of most need Fanny proved the most faithful, if not the wisest.

CHAPTER TWENTY-SIX

The End

Yet again he rallied, and towards the close of 1879 resumed writing poetry, which was somewhat unexpected. After the great perturbation associated with the volume of 1870, he had forsaken virtually all verse apart from sonnets to accompany paintings. Once again the impulse stirred, however; returning to his 'old and grisly' ballad of *Sister Helen*, now thirty years old, he added an entirely new incident which set the narrative on the morrow of the faithless lover's marriage and thus made Helen 'more human' – a wronged woman rather than a wicked witch. He also went back to *Rose Mary*, composing three 'Beryl-Songs' to stand between the sections and overcome William's objection to the arbitrary plot. And he turned to his notebook drafts, resurrecting unused pieces to complete some verses from 1871 with a sequence of homilectic observations, on flattery, friendship, aspiration, failure, memory, and trustful faith in the goodness of all things. Renamed *Soothsay* – signifying truth-telling rather than prediction – this has a melancholy quality when set beside the evident despairs of his life at this point. 'Strive that thy works prove equal: lest / That work which thou hast done the best / Should come to be . . . / hateful and abhorr'd' reads one injunction. 'Yet woe to thee if once thou yield / Unto the act of doing nought!' is another. 'How callous seems beyond revoke / The clock with its last listless stroke!'

All his life he kept ambitious intentions in view, lest his days should end with nothing to show for his talents. It was now too late, and the verses were valedictory.

> In the life-drama's stern cue-call,
> A friend's a part well-prized by all:
> And if thou meet an enemy,
> What art thou that none such should be?
> Even so: but if the two parts run
> Into each other and grow one,
> Then comes the curtain's cue to fall.

Such retrospective versifying chimed with his implicit conviction that, though he was only just over fifty, life was foreclosing. He may implicitly have compared his position with that of Swinburne, now deaf, docile, half-amnesiac, living as a virtual invalid with Watts in Putney. There was no direct communication, but Watts remained a regular visitor to Tudor House, and was moreover carving out a minor literary career for himself. He had a commission for an edition of poems by Thomas Chatterton, the marvellous boy whose fake medieval writings by invented authors Rowley and others were all too speedily succeeded by his suicide at the age of eighteen.

This led Rossetti back to Chatterton, and thence to Keats, who had dedicated *Endymion* to Chatterton's memory, and so to more sonneteering. *Ardour and Memory*, invoking red-tinted rose leaves in autumn as a figure for the remembered joys of spring, appeared at Christmas, followed by a gradual resumption of the *House of Life* scheme. 'With me, sonnets mean insomnia,' he told Christina gloomily;[1] but if devised chiefly to occupy wakeful hours, the impulse brought some consolations. Others encouraged it as a hopeful development, not sharing Gabriel's own assessment of his parlous state. Lacking interest in pictorial art, Watts was especially supportive, offering comments and suggestions to sustain Rossetti through solitary hours. At year's end William first recorded the idea of a new volume. As well as *Rose Mary*, *The Cloud Confines* and other lyrics, Gabriel already possessed some thirty new sonnets for *The House of Life* written mainly in the first, idyllic summer at Kelmscott. By mid-1880 he had nearly enough for the full *House of Life* sequence.

Composition was stimulated by old and new acquaintances, who supplied life-sustaining attention (and some flattery) in these closing years. The old friends included Philip Marston and William Davies, while the first of the new young fans was William Sharp, a young Scot who like many before and since moved to London with his sights on a literary career, and in due course created one for a wholly fictitious Highland writer called Fiona Macleod. At this period he wrote popular stories and edited cheap anthologies, and came with an introduction from Noel Paton, whom Rossetti had known in the early 1850s. At Tudor House, the servant said Mr Rossetti received no one, but eventually Sharp was admitted. What did he want? Only to shake hands with you before you die! 'Well,' came the response, 'I am in no immediate danger of dying, but you may shake hands if you wish.'[2]

In the studio, Sharp was shown *La Donna della Finestra* and the reduced *Dante's Dream*, with its predella panels showing Dante asleep and waking. As he gazed, Rossetti read from the *Vita Nuova*. 'He told me to come again to talk with him,' Sharp recalled. 'I went out in a dream.' Four months later, in January 1880, the promised invitation came. This time Rossetti read from his own poems. 'I have never heard such a beautiful reader of verse as yourself, and if I had not felt – well, shy – I should have asked you to go on reading,' confessed Sharp the next day. Enclosing his own verses, he added flatteringly that 'the "Dancer" is modelled on your beautiful "Card-Dealer" '.

The second young admirer was Thomas Hall Caine, an architect's clerk in Liverpool with dreams of a more glamorous career, who got to know Rossetti initially through correspondence. Holidaying in Cumbria in the summer of 1878, he met a figure from the Pre-Raphaelite past in the shape of Philip James Bailey, author of *Festus*. Bailey spoke of DGR in the days of the PRB, lamenting his decision to relinquish poetry in favour of painting. Caine, who had only vaguely heard such names, promptly bought a copy of *Poems* and in the autumn delivered a local reading-circle lecture on 'this single precious volume', full of music and magic, sweetness and force, ardency and harmony.

Two more lectures followed and in summer 1879 Caine sent a printed copy of the third. 'You say you are grateful to me: my response is, I am grateful to you, for you have spoken up heartily and unfalteringly for the work you love,' replied Rossetti, graciously. Even while cautioning himself against flattery in *Soothsay* he succumbed, initiating a warm correspondence, 'thankful to anyone who will give me a little praise'.[3]

During the early part of 1880 the main topic of their letters concerned the question of 'Politics and Art' – the subject of one of Caine's lectures. Vigorously, Rossetti insisted on his 'utter aloofness' from politics, despite an occasional sonnet on current events, and on the undesirability of any artist becoming actively involved in such affairs. Citing Coleridge, Cellini and David, he also invoked Henri Regnault, the French artist killed in the last *sortie* while Paris was under Prussian siege. All honour to his patriotic ardour, yet what a loss to art – especially when compared with those who had sought sanctuary in Britain and were now still contributing to the cause of art, as they had been born to do. He demurred however when Caine implied, apropos the publication of *Early Italian Poets*, that Rossetti himself thought rescuing the works of Cecco Angiolieri of more importance than the struggle for Italy's unification. Since he could do nothing personally to advance the latter, he wrote, the reputation of her early literature was a small but worthy cause.

Caine meanwhile proposed an anthology of sonnets, aspiring to solicit new pieces from well-known poets. Disabusing him of this hope – poets of note would always keep new poems for their next collection – Rossetti assumed the role of literary mentor, offering Caine his views on Keats, Coleridge, Milton, Shakespeare, Wordsworth and the rest, and drawing his attention to the unfamiliar and disregarded: Donne ('hardly an English poet better worth a thorough knowledge in spite of his provoking conceits'); Chatterton ('in the very first rank'); John Clare, Fanny Kemble, Charles Wells, Ebenezer Jones, William Davies, William Bell Scott, Nolly Brown, Philip Marston and Alice Meynell ('sister of Eliz. Thompson the painter'). He took the opportunity to commend Richard Dixon, the college friend of Ned and Topsy at Oxford whose life had passed in clerical obscurity, and wrote with serious praise of Christina, as one who had proved her 'poetic importance'. In a varied body of work, he told Caine, her verse commanded a quality he would have been proud to call his own.[4]

With callow, under-educated enthusiasm, and support from Watts, Caine dared assert that the more 'correct' and sophisticated the form the better the sonnet. Octaves and sestets were not the main point, advised Rossetti, proffering a few words of basic wisdom. If too loose, the English sonnet became a bastard madrigal, but if too formally rigid, it turned into a shibboleth; the only things that mattered were 'the brains and the music', he wrote. 'Conception, my boy, *fundamental brainwork*, that is what makes the difference in all art. Work your metal as much as you like, but first take care that it is gold and worth working.'

However, when Dixon presumed to commend the sonnets of his friend the Rev. Gerard Manley Hopkins to Caine, Rossetti rejected them out of hand – thus missing the true metal of poems like *Spring*, *The Windhover* and *God's Grandeur*, and perhaps the chance of lengthening their author's life through a smidgen of recognition. In the event, Hopkins survived less than a decade, and his poems waited another generation to be published, by Robert Bridges whose own poetic reputation has been eclipsed by that of his friend. Coincidentally, this season Dixon brought Bridges to Cheyne Walk, rather to Gabriel's disgust, since he did not relish unknown visitors, although if Bridges had been as ingratiating as Sharp he might have been welcome. 'I am quite sure Rossetti's sonnets bore me profoundly,' he told Dixon a decade later; 'I doubt whether you could read them now without being of my opinion that they are sensuality affected to dullness ...'[5]

Towards the young men's own efforts, Rossetti was courteously brutal. Sharp's adjectives were too crowded, he wrote, and 'there are continual assonances of *ings*, *ants*, *ows* etc., midway in the lines'. Caine's literary style was pretentious, with long and ugly words like 'mythopoeic' and 'anthropomorphic'; in prose 'simple English' was a resource not to be ignored. Moreover, neither Sharp nor Caine showed aptitude for the 'condensed and emphatic form' that was the sonnet. Of course, he added, to soften the blow, 'there is no need that every gifted writer should take the path of poetry – still less that of sonneteering'. Despite the warning, he received from Sharp a fulsome, ill-wrought tribute:

So thou, Rossetti, know'st thy Autumn crown'd
With the full fruit, and makest many a mate
Grow great with spoils in steps of thy feet found;
Yet farest thou best; well may'st thou choose to wait;
For lo, strong toiler, thou com'st last tho' late
Laden with golden treasure to the ground.

Such applause rekindled his own poetic fire; once again in letters and in person Rossetti revived the genial self that had charmed Marston, O'Shaughnessy and Payne. Caine, he discovered, was but twenty-seven, on the threshold of creative life – indeed, born at the very time he himself had chosen painting instead of poetry as a livelihood. By a neat correspondence, their birthdays were two days apart. 'I myself was born on Old May Day ... in the year after that in which Blake died,' he wrote, as if establishing a dynasty.

Returning to the archaic themes of his youth, he took up an old ballad subject: the shipwreck of Henry I's son and daughter in 1120. Narrated by the sole survivor, *The White Ship* was composed in couplets and triplets separated by the favourite Rossettian device of an incantatory burden, and is a vigorous, effective piece of Victorian balladry, indebted like most of the genre to *The Rime of the Ancient Mariner*, albeit also imbued with the spirit of Hemans's *Casabianca*. In *The White Ship*, Prince Henry redeems his lawless youth by sacrificing his life in a vain attempt to save his sister. Such subjects were very wholesome, commented Christina warmly. 'I am so glad you have written this fine piece, one really worth writing.' Later she added: 'I wish you would write more such, and on such subjects: surely they are well worth celebrating, and they leave no sting behind.'

Not so long before, Gabriel had been giving, not receiving, poetic advice from his sister. He suspected her motive in commending wholesome subjects, but was mistaken. No, she replied firmly, 'I was not thinking of arousing envy and spite – but rather of one's own responsibility in use of an influential talent.' He was duly rebuked.[6]

Currently, Christina was actively 'sonneteering' on her own account, producing two extended sequences, *Monna Innominata* and *Sonnets of Later Life*, and hoping before long to publish a new volume. She and Gabriel had recently collaborated on a present for their now-venerable mother's eightieth birthday (she being as old as the century) in the shape of a new-issued sonnet anthology edited by David Main, to accompany which both contributed their own. The idea came from Christina, who for three years past had written her mother a Valentine poem; maybe she hoped for a birthday verse from her brother. Instead, his was an impersonal sonnet on the subject of the sonnet – 'a moment's monument – memorial from the soul's eternity' – a coin whose face reveals the soul:

> Whether for tribute to the august appeals
>   Of life, or dower in Love's high retinue,
>   It serve; or, 'mid the dark wharf's cavernous breath
>   In Charon's palm it pay the toll to Death.

Reading this over, he worried that the final image was too funereal. He was right, though Frances Rossetti had long since been glad to receive any intimation of creative energy rather than mental gloom. Inscribed 'DG Rossetti pro Matre fecit', the Paterian sonnet was enclosed within an allusive, figurative design, showing the floating figure of a female spirit, crowned with bays, holding a lyre and touching an hourglass. Roundels encompass a butterfly – emblem of the soul – with Alpha and Omega, signifying eternity. Of Christian symbolism there is nothing.

Christina's own poem was simpler, sweeter and more personal. 'Sonnets are full of love,' she began:

> And so because you love me, and because
>   I love you, Mother, I have woven a wreath
>   Of rhymes wherewith to crown your honoured name ...

The parallel efforts were a faint echo of the *bouts-rimés* of so long ago, in which both Gabriel and Christina had excelled. And as before, the exercise was stimulating.

If Frances Rossetti lamented the outcome of a life for which she had nurtured such high hopes of artistic genius and immortality, she kept silent. But it was sad in old age to have an adult son incapacitated in so many ways rather than taking his rightful place on the national stage. She had wanted a renowned poet, or painter, or scholar, who might have been a professor, Academician or Laureate. Less fundamentalist than her daughters in matters of religion, she still trusted in God's eventual mercy towards his soul, but now doubted he would attain joy on earth.

Meeting Rossetti for the first time in autumn 1880, Caine observed his corpulent body, 'full round face deathly pale, large black eyes, massive forehead, thinning hair and grey-streaked beard'. His gait was 'painfully weak and shaky and the whole outward seeming is that of man grown old long ages before his due time'.[7] In conversation his voice was thin and fretful; only when reading aloud did the sonorous tones return.

This year, Anne Gilchrist, invited to update her husband's biography of Blake for a reprint, appealed for renewed support. In the twenty years since Gabriel had collaborated on the first version, Blake's reputation had been transformed, not least owing to their work. He assisted in the revision diligently, sending omissions, errors and suggestions, acknowledging the contributions of others – notably Smetham, whose essay on Blake was included in the reprint – and admitting his own mistaken emendations without wishing to replace them. Looking back, he was satisfied at the service rendered to Blake, from whom however he felt now rather distant. He declined to take any part in the proof-reading but actively helped Watts on the new edition of Chatterton, with whom he expressed equal affinity, as also with Christopher Smart, author of the ecstatic, mystical *Song to David*. Smart, Chatterton, Blake, Rossetti: a line of English poets in whom genius was to madness near allied, in the common misquotation.[8]

Meanwhile, in painting he had run into difficulties with Graham, who wanted no more pictures and would agree to take only the long-commissioned *Found*. Watts advised enforcing the contract also for *The Ship of Love*, which Rossetti would have preferred to paint, having perceived what he saw as direct borrowings from his own work in Burne-Jones's *Golden Stairs* – star of this year's Grosvenor Gallery.[9] But the ever-faithful Graham refused, so Rossetti returned to *Found* and to *La Pia*, and also took up a full-size study of Janey, now making it represent Beatrice walking in a Florentine street watched by Dante, in yet another reworking of the *Salutation*. From Italy, Fairfax Murray sent contemporary photos, showing medieval streets and buildings.

By the end of the year, Ionides's *The Day Dream* was almost ready, as was Leyland's long-awaited *La Pia*. Moreover, Graham's replica of *Dante's Dream* was finished and mounted in its tripartite frame. With deep, glowing colour and perspective depth, the forms are mannered but firm, belying any suggestion that his brushwork was failing, while the predella panels balance and support the main image in a satisfying whole. *The Day Dream*, too, is effectively wrought, although *La Pia* appears to lack the finishing glazes with which Rossetti's compositions are characteristically pulled together. The demand for his work was diminishing, he lamented to William, as old patrons dropped off and trade cycles deterred others. Although still more than sufficient for his needs, at over £1,000 his earnings in 1879 were less than in previous years. Good old Valpy, who had neither the money nor the room to house it, returned the large *Dante's Dream*, and Alecco Ionides had just declined to buy *The Blessed Damozel*, even for the bargain price of £500. William was inclined to blame the recession, noting that picture-selling had for many months been very dull with most artists, but Watts proffered an additional explanation, alleging general objections to Rossetti's style – the exaggerated, 'almost mulatto', mouths and 'tumid' throats, suggestive of goitre.[10]

If his hallmarks were out of favour, sales would inevitably decline. And though the picture market picked up over the next half-year, poetic stock was rising faster. In August, for example, a writer in the *Contemporary Review* named Rossetti the leading sonneteer of the age. What a gratifying ray of generous recognition, he told Caine, all the more welcome from the very journal which had launched the original attack.[11]

So, although at the end of the year William again found his brother in a very depressed state, once more prone to 'fanciful impressions' of the fictive variety, he was also actively preparing a new collection. On 25 November, Ellis called to discuss publication. 'I am really going to get a new volume out to be called *Poems Old and New*,' Gabriel told Janey, who was going again to Italy; 'but do not talk about it in the least, or there will be gossip paragraphs prematurely.' (One wonders he could even mention this prospect, after the experience of 1871–2) 'Perhaps I told you that the *House of Life* now numbers 100 sonnets, and that I have forty-five besides as an extra series.'[12]

Displaying his old imperiousness, he had Watts composing too, and in New Year 1881 proposed that William write 'a century of sonnets' dealing with the public events of his lifetime. Having last written verse in the far-off days of *The Germ*, William was gratified by the idea, immediately discerning a unique combination of literature and contemporary history, seen in radical perspective. He set to, producing in short order two score 'Democratic Sonnets'. At first all was well received, Gabriel writing appreciatively of the first tribute to Garibaldi and even joking that William might yet prove 'the family bard'. Praise for those on Mazzini, Corn-Law repeal and the annexation of the Transvaal followed. But alarm arose with 'Tyrannicide', 'Fenianism' and 'other incendiary subjects'. Supported by the conservative Watts, Gabriel wrote urgently to Lucy in April (ignoring her imminent fourth confinement) arguing that the whole project was danger-ous, to William's career in the Civil Service and his family's livelihood. Indeed, 'the very title *Democratic Sonnets* seems to me most objectionable when coming from one who depends on the Government for his bread ...' he wrote.[13]

Stuff, replied William, only more courteously. 'This is a country in which political and religious opinions are free, and in this very Office men of all shades of opinion are to be found.' In Gladstone, John Forster, Henry Fawcett, John Bright, Joseph Chamberlain and Charles Dilke, the current government held several determined democrats. Even as a professed republican, his job was nowise at risk; further, 'any idea of my undertaking to write verse about the public events of my own time, and yet failing to show that I sympathise with foreign republics, and detest oppression, retrogression, and obscurantism, whether abroad or at home, must be nugatory. To set me going is to set me going on my own path.'[14]

Of course, it had been Gabriel's idea in the first place. But he had envisaged a sequence 'in exalted and poetic strain' rather than the frank and sardonic manner favoured by William. The response was a blow, and though William resolved to complete his hundred sonnets 'in my own way and not in other people's', his appetite for the project waned. This was not the only event, but a worm had turned. Increasingly William grew exasperated with Gabriel's vagaries, anxieties, self-pity, and lack of interest in his nieces and nephew. When this spring Lucy gave birth to twins, their uncle Gabriel expressed only astonishment. Swinburne, by contrast, sent a long, lyrical effusion, whose sentiment William welcomed while judging the verse feeble and facile.

Of course Gabriel, who had never liked babies, was hardly going to change now, though he once expressed regret, telling Lucy that he must seem as bad an uncle as that of the Babes in the Wood.[15] In his heart he loved Olive and her siblings, he protested, and 'look forward to their future with as true an interest as any one', but he seldom saw them, and though in a sombre and often tedious echo of past times William dutifully spent every Monday evening at Chelsea, his affection was chastened. His political poems, however, appear to have influenced Gabriel's, for it was during this season that, having composed his own sonnet on the last surviving sailors from the Battle of Trafalgar in 1805 – an event etched on every Victorian schoolboy's heart – he also wrote on the erection of 'Cleopatra's Needle' on the Thames Embankment, and a tribute to Alexander II of Russia, liberator of the serfs, who had just been assassinated. Projected to follow was an even unlikelier subject, a ballad on the death of Abraham Lincoln, to include the story of John Brown;[16] it is as if to mitigate his failure to support William, Gabriel proposed a radical sequence of his own. Unfortunately, as poetry, DGR's political sonnets are no better than WMR's.

As yet the projected new volume-lacked 'bulk'. There was of course the long-unfinished *Bride's Chamber*, never yet printed. Instead, for another narrative he chose a popular subject from Scottish history, the murder of James I in 1437. Begun in December 1880, this was completed by the following March.

Though with national partiality William Sharp ranked it Rossetti's best poem, *The King's Tragedy* is seldom discussed critically. Compared to *Jenny, The Stream's Secret, Dante at Verona* or even *The Blessed Damozel*, it appears slight, a simple ballad rendering of historical sources in dramatic manner, in the long shadow that Sir Walter Scott cast over the nineteenth century. Its story of James, killed by nobles in the Charterhouse at Perth, is taken from a fifteenth-century prose chronicle entitled *The Dethe of the King of Scotis*. There are supernatural touches, and as narrator Rossetti cast Catherine Douglas, the Queen's waiting-woman, traditionally famous as 'Kate Barlass' for holding the door against the assassins with her own arm.[17]

Poet as well as king, James I was author of *The Kingis Quair*, a Chaucerian romance in rime royal celebrating his courtship of Lady Jane Beaufort. At Penkill, Scott had chosen to decorate the walls of the wide tower staircase with scenes from the poem. 'After that,' wrote William, 'the virtues of the King in vindicating the common people against oppression, and his interesting combination of poetry with kingship, took a strong hold on my brother's feelings.' One of his projected titles was 'Queen Jane's Poet', and one may easily imagine how Rossetti responded imaginatively to a royal author inspired by love for his Queen Jane, especially since it was at Penkill that Gabriel's passion for his own Jane first found full expression.[18] Then, in 1872, he had found himself in James's county of Perthshire, staying at fortified Stobhall, not far from the place of the King's death.

Into his own poem he incorporated some of James's archaic verses, cavalierly altering their metre to fit his own. The song was 'long, and richly stored', says the narrator. But doom portends: King and Queen have encountered a soothsaying woman or witch, and this very night Sir Robert Graeme and his henchmen will carry out their murderous deed. *The Kingis Quair* has foreboding visions of the 'ugly pit as deep as hell' that lies beneath the wheel of Fortune, which is the pit of Acheron, but also the privy in which James hides as his attackers break Kate Barlass's arm and the door. In Rossetti's poem fearful combat ensues, between naked king and knife-wielding assassins out of *Macbeth*.

Vigorous, vivid and direct, thematically and to some extent poetically, *The King's Tragedy* returned to childhood days in the family parlour, play-acting Shakespeare's bloodiest scenes and episodes from *Ivanhoe* or *Marmion*. It harks back to *Sir Hugh the Heron*, Rossetti's earliest poem, although once again the main model is Coleridge. Emotionally, the focus is on an isolated hero at bay before enemies, but owing to the demands of the action the sense of identification is faint. Only the conclusion, which recounts Queen Jane's vigil over James's body while his assassins are hunted down, gives a glimpse of the violent fantasies that may have been personally as well as poetically roused during the sleepless nights when the piece was written:

> And now of their dooms dread tidings came,
>   And of torments fierce and dire;
> And nought she spake, – she had ceased to speak, –
>   But her eyes were a soul on fire . . .

> And then she said, – 'My King, they are dead!'
>   And she knelt on the chapel-floor,
> And whispered low with a strange proud smile, –
>   'James, James, they suffered more!'

He was getting into his stride. The next subject was to be Joan of Arc. After that, the death of President Lincoln. And the flight of Alexander III of Scotland, suggested by Sharp.

Why was Rossetti not some exiled king, so they might restore him to his throne? lamented Philip Marston. As Gabriel told William Davies on 16 March, verse kept him going. 'I shall not sink, I trust, so long as the poetic life well up in me at intervals,' he wrote, 'and so long as my painting still interests me and still staves off the horror (against which I am not proof) of inability to meet indebtedness.' Instead of one volume, he now planned to issue two: a reprint of *Poems* of 1870 and a collection of new pieces to be called *Ballads and Sonnets*, to include the full *House of Life*. The title was conscious homage to the Laureate's latest volume, *Poems and Ballads*, in which Rossetti particularly admired *Rizpah*. 'The only man who has husbanded his forces rightly and whom you can never open at the wrong page, is Tennyson,' he declared. 'He has written as much as any poet ought now to write in a long lifetime after all foregone poetry. Self-scrutiny and self-repression will bear a very large part in the poetic "survival of the fittest".'[19]

Despite disavowals ('Even if I did not paint, I should never be a redundant poet') he himself hardly now practised self-suppression. To fill the space left by *The House of Life* in the reissued *Poems*, he decided to include *The Bride's Chamber*, renamed *The Bride's Prelude*, and labelled it Part I of a longer work. In Part II, he informed Caine, the passionate frailty of Aloyse's first love would be followed by 'a true and noble love', rendered calamitous by her seducer and fully justifying her fearful horror on the bridal morning. And, he added rather wearily, 'the poem wd. gain so greatly by this sequel that I suppose I must set to and finish it one day ...'

Both volumes were ready for publication in late spring. *Ballads and Sonnets* led with *Rose Mary*, *The White Ship* and *The King's Tragedy*. Then came the hundred sonnets of *The House of Life*, newly divided into two sections: 'Youth and Change' and 'Change and Fate'. Odes and lyrics followed, opening with *Soothsay* and closing with *The Cloud Confines*, and the volume ended with assorted sonnets, on pictures, poets and historical events (*The Last Three from Trafalgar*, *Czar Alexander the Second*, etc.). With half-titles and over-generous line-spacing, it filled an octavo volume of 332 pages.

Silently, *Nuptial Sleep* was deleted from *The House of Life*. Writing from

inside knowledge a year later, Sharp explained that 'to the last' Rossetti
continued to deny any taint of 'animalism' in his poems and that 'personally
speaking' he would never have withdrawn the contentious item, but for the
fact that its forceful realism caused 'misunderstanding' among unsophisti-
cated readers. He added that when it was suggested (by Watts or Caine)
that the sonnet be redrafted with a different, central metaphor, he refused,
believing it should be simply cancelled verse.[20] This was fair enough, though
the explanation is specious. The sonnet was suppressed either because it had
been singled out for attack, or because its author now recognised its grossly
sensual nature. By the same token, he drastically revised the key figure of
Love's Redemption, substituting pagan imagery for that of the Christian
sacrament of body and blood, and renamed it *Love's Testament* – a change
that demonstrates he was not opposed to altering a metaphor on principle,
and also that he feared further accusations of indecent blasphemy.

Sharp claimed the sequence was really 'the House of Love', recording the
experiences of 'a poet-soul' whose 'genius lived and had its being in the
shadow of Love'. While Rossetti resisted the notion that love was his only
theme, as finally presented to the world his sonnet sequence is indeed like
Dante's in this regard – largely if not wholly so concerned. As was fitting:
from its earliest origins in Italian and Provençal the form was used for
courtly love-verse. And thus, Rossetti completed his latest version of, and
tribute to, the *Vita Nuova* of his namesake, which he had first adopted as
his life's text while studying at Sass's.

Coincidentally, his final painting of Beatrice's *Salutation* echoed one of
his earliest themes, first identified with Lizzie and now a silent salute to
Jane. *Ut pictura poesis.*

Among the last of his poems were two final tributes to Lizzie, however.
'Ah! dear one, we were young so long, / It seemed that youth would never
go,' he wrote, looking back thirty years and linking his lost beloved to the
springs of his poetry. 'Ah! then was it all Spring weather? / Nay, but we
were young and together.' Now, he had been 'old so long', and she so long
dead that it was doubtful whether any art could still warm their hearts. But
how long until they met again 'Where hours may never lose their song'?

> Alas, so long!
> Ah! shall it be then Spring weather,
> And ah! shall we be young together?

In *Spheral Change*, identified by William as the last poetic composition
of all, Gabriel wrote of the new 'shadow of death' where he watched all
those who had gone before:

> If only one might speak! – the one
>> Who never waits till I come near;
> But always seated all alone
>> As listening the sunken air,
>> Is gone before I come to her.

Indirectly, he recalled the painful days around their marriage, when Lizzie had hovered between life and death:

> O dearest! while we lived and died
>> A living death in every day,
> Some hours we still were side by side,
>> When where I was you too might stay
>> And rest and need not go away.

> O nearest, furthest! Can there be
>> At length some hard-earned heart-won home,
> Where, – exile changed for sanctuary, –
>> Our lot may fill indeed its sum,
>> And you may wait and I may come?

In art, his final success was also identified with Dante. Towards the end of 1880, Caine wrote to say that Liverpool's new municipal art gallery was interested in purchasing one of Rossetti's works. The most available, and most obviously suitable as 'a gallery picture', was the great *Dante's Dream*, returned by Valpy, which seemed otherwise destined never to leave the studio. He would gladly welcome Alderman Samuelson, Rossetti wrote on 14 December, with a full account of the picture, its price (still 1,500 guineas) and its frame ('cost over £100'), adding that he had yet plans to repaint some passages of drapery.

In all, the negotiations took nine months, largely because the city's Arts and Exhibitions Subcommittee could not buy without seeing the picture, while Rossetti never sent works 'on approval'. When in March Samuelson was in London, all seemed about to progress until Rossetti learnt that he was accompanied by councillor Rathbone, a key figure in Liverpool's patronage of the arts but unhappily a man who had criticised Caine's original lecture defending DGR's sensuous poetry. Or so Caine said, perhaps having exaggerated in order to ingratiate himself, for Rathbone was not evidently ill-disposed towards Rossetti, and certainly saw himself as an admirer of the Pre-Raphaelite school. Peremptorily, Gabriel cancelled the proposed call, saying he would rather not sell than have 'enemies shot into my house in the guise of friends'. The difficulty was smoothed over, however, when Samuelson brought another colleague, and told Rossetti that they hoped to see the picture in the art gallery's autumn exhibition. By June, Beatrice's hair had been changed from dark to golden, but although it was soon ready for delivery, anxiety and hesitation set in. Rossetti first asked for a written guarantee that the sale would proceed, and then suggested that exhibition be delayed till next year. As always, he felt full perfection lay just out of reach.

Rathbone sent such cordial assurances that Rossetti was shamed into agreeing he might see the picture, finding him 'quite civil' and no enemy after all. A week later, however, Samuelson explained that *Dante's Dream* would be exhibited before purchase was completed. 'This I should not think of for a moment,' Rossetti told Caine, adding that the hated 'Ratsbane' was a plainly a liar. Eventually, he calmed down, agreeing to release the painting and apologising for his hastiness; eventually a finesse ensured that the work was officially sold before it proceeded north. Fred Stephens announced its first public appearance, and on 23 August the Arts and Exhibitions Subcommittee ratified its purchase.[21]

Then, as the new volume of poems approached publication, anxiety arose from another direction when Janey intervened, fearful of renewed accusations that might threaten his equilibrium or her reputation. Her letter does not survive, nor was Gabriel's reply sent, but his draft is poignant. 'Unless you think me quite without feeling, you must know what I feel on reading the first of all your letters that had any bitterness for me,' he began, going on to assure her that there was no risk. Watts was confident that critical hostility was a thing of the past. But, he continued, he could not bear to think Jane might be upset or angry. 'Every new piece that is not quite colourless will be withdrawn and the book postponed,' he promised. He drafted a disclaimer, 'To the reader of the "House of Life"', which began 'the "Life" involved is neither my life nor your life, but life representative . . .' Then he tried again, saying 'to speak in the first person is often to speak most vividly' but that the emotionally loaded poems were not confessional. 'Whether the recorded moment exist in the region of fact or of thought is a question indifferent to the Muse, so long only as her touch can quicken it.'[22] As an aesthetic declaration, this was unexceptionable: only the naive took all verse to be personal. But it also betrayed anxiety, drawing attention to the very interpretation it aimed to refute.

Publication was delayed until the autumn, but it does not appear that any poems were dropped, and it is likely that Gabriel misinterpreted Jane's anxieties. She still came to Tudor House occasionally, to sit and perhaps cheer him a little. But this August she cancelled a date when leaving for Kelmscott. 'You say "on reading your letter I see" etc. Then did my poor letter remain unread till now?' he wailed. 'I have not the least claim on your consideration; but if you withdraw it, it is the only one of many withdrawals which will go to my heart ... If you read this letter, do not answer harshly, for I cannot bear it.'[23] Jane replied soothingly, and indeed came for what proved a final visit in early September, when he drew her hands for the figure of Desdemona, which he now planned to paint.

By this date young Caine had moved to London as new 'housemate' in Cheyne Walk, receiving board and lodging in exchange for company and occasional errands. In his own account of these months, he represented himself as an innocent provincial lad, overawed by his illustrious new acquaintance. In fact, he was a regular visitor to London and already a good friend to Rossetti's new neighbour at no. 27, Bram Stoker. Currently manager of the Lyceum Theatre for Henry Irving and in due course creator of Count Dracula, Stoker would form a curious Gothick link with uncle John Polidori.

This summer, the Cadogan estate exercised its right to begin building a mansion block on the rear of the garden. At no. 19 Anna Mary Watts lamented the loss of the tall elms. 'Several of the elm trees fell today, and Mrs W. is doubtless a weeping willow,' Gabriel joked, more distressed by the noise than the lack of amenity, having largely abandoned the garden to its own devices. But the work was disturbing, and mindful of the season, in late summer he arranged to transport himself, his painting equipment and his mattress to St John's Vale near Keswick in Cumberland, Caine's favoured haunt. They travelled by special carriage, Fanny coming too at the last minute. Either she wanted to keep an eye on Caine, or Mr Rhinoceros needed her familiar presence.

They arrived at Fisher Place, a farmhouse not unlike that at Trowan, at the northern end of Thirlmere, on 20 September. 'The scenery is grand in the extreme – mountains rising on all hands,' Gabriel told his mother. On the first fine day the ill-assorted trio successfully climbed a nearby hill named Great Howe, an ascent of over 400 feet, each placing a stone on the summit cairn. Coming down there was much hilarity when Rossetti elected to descend 'on a natural basis broader and also in such a case more rapid than the feet – i.e. sitting down' – at which Fanny 'lay down and roared' in paroxysms of laughter which themselves left Caine helpless with mirth.[24] So invigorating was the experience that in the evening Gabriel set up his easel with the *Proserpine* replica Valpy had chosen in place of *Dante's Dream*. But the improvement was short-lived – in his notebook he wrote of 'plaintive days that haunt the haggard hills with bleak unspoken woe' – and though to Watts he claimed to have reduced the chloral with Fanny's assistance, Caine told a different tale. To prevent the consumption of more than one phial a night he entered into a small subterfuge, which backfired when – as he alleged – Fanny disclosed the ruse and thus led Gabriel to suspect Caine of doctoring every dose.

Caine also claimed that Fanny went to Cumbria with the aim of getting

Gabriel to make his will in her favour, and left when this plan failed.[25] Or so Gabriel told him; relations between the three were not easy. While they were away, the new books were published, though Gabriel took no visible interest in the reviews and indeed absence from London at this moment may have provided the true motive for the trip. After a month, as winter was setting in and Caine spent a day and night each week lecturing in Liverpool, Rossetti decided to go home. On the long journey he sat up in his greatcoat, despite the special sleeping-car, and according to Caine talked disconsolately all night of his remorse at opening Lizzie's grave, of his self-blame regarding her death, and of finding her farewell note.[26]

Back in Cheyne Walk, he was in William's view again 'much unstrung' both physically and mentally, while Scott was upset to find him 'emaciated and worn out', lying half-dressed on the sofa, coughing and sweating, with only Fanny in attendance.[27] He protested that he was dying. On John Marshall's instruction, a nurse was hired and to other friends' relief Fanny was banished, for on return from Cumbria she spread or supported slanders to the effect that Watts was fleecing, or at least defrauding, Rossetti. Informed of the allegations, Watts threatened to sue for libel, and Fanny was excluded from the house. 'Dear F,' Gabriel wrote in his last letter; 'such difficulties are now arising with my family that it will be impossible for me to see you here till I write again.'[28]

Thus, though the autumn of 1881 saw two signal successes – the publication of his new volume of verse and the sale of his largest picture to the most prestigious public collection that bought contemporary work – yet as William observed, 'no scintilla of pleasure or cheerfulness seemed to come from this double achievement; the curtains were drawn round his innermost self and the dusk ... was fast darkening into night.'[29] It appeared he was heading for another breakdown, with disordered thoughts and terrible nights. Most strikingly, he was haunted by apprehensions of sin and guilt from years long past: not merely Lizzie's suicide, but the old incident from his adolescence, when he had been insolent and disrespectful towards his father. He spoke of this – thirty-five years on – in terms of anguished remorse, as a deed for which he desperately sought absolution. William, who had already noted that Gabriel was now 'fully re-convinced' of the immortality of the soul, dutifully passed this on to their sister. 'No wonder that in weakness and suffering such a reminiscence haunts weary days and sleepless hours of double darkness,' commented Christina feelingly when reminded of the ancient misconduct;[30] she too knew the depths of depressive self-blame, when inner demons magnified faults to terrifying proportions. A day or so later she wrote to share with Gabriel her own experience of formal confession, hoping he might see a sympathetic clergyman. No, Gabriel responded, he did not seek spiritual counsel, only forgiveness of his sins. As he approached the next life, his soul was sorely troubled. Though we should not take this as objective proof of wrong-doing, he had never made peace with his father.

On 11 December, Rossetti suffered a mild stroke, which left his sight dim and his left side paralysed. Summoned at ten in the evening, John Marshall thought the malady imaginary, or at least aggravated by melancholy. In addition to the nurse, however, he got a young medical man, nephew to the eminent Henry Maudsley, to give the patient daily injections of morphia in place of chloral, and reduce the whisky. The immediate result was four days of delirium: 'painful opium dreams' while dozing, distressing illusions while awake – replying to non-existent questions, seeing non-existent books – and mental confusion, as when he failed to recognise Shields, or babbled in a mixture of English and Italian, as if returning to childhood.[31] When the morphine was reduced most of these symptoms disappeared, but the weakness and fretful temper remained. Young Dr Maudsley was however convinced he could recover, if he had the will, and urged him to set his palette as usual, in readiness for the day's work.

But Rossetti knew better. He was surely dying, he told Scott again on 17 January, insisting also that the chloral did not cause his delusions: for the slanders had begun at Penkill, before he discovered the drug, when the children at the toll-house had called him 'foul names'.[32] This, he claimed, was early, unmistakable proof of the great conspiracy.

'Pray do not ascribe all his doings and non-doings to foundationless fidgetiness, poor dear fellow,' wrote Christina to William, whose sympathy was exhausted. 'Don't you think neither you nor I can quite appreciate all he is undergoing at present, what between wrecked health at least in some measure, nerves which appear to falsify facts, and most anxious money-matters?' If it was difficult dealing with him, what must it be like to *be* Gabriel? 'And he in so many ways the head of our family – it doubles the pity.'[33]

The next plan was another seaside sojourn. His old friend John Seddon was currently involved in the development of Birchington, a village on the north Kent coast, and on 4 February Rossetti travelled thither, accompanied by Caine, nurse Mrs Abrey and Caine's young sister Lily, age twelve. Installed in a large, well-appointed bungalow designed by Seddon to attract well-to-do holiday-makers, they might have been at the North Pole for all the interest Gabriel took in the location. There was indeed only the North Sea between the Pole and windswept Westcliff bungalow, built as it was on the unsheltered cliff-top. His mother and sister arrived at the beginning of March, to provide more anxious attendance.

Alone with Caine, Gabriel asked if he had heard from Fanny. No, was the reply. Would they tell him if she wrote? Assuredly, said Caine, though the suspicion was surely justified; no one wanted her to know his address. Other faithful friends, including Leyland, came to visit. Sharp recalled one short walk to the cliffs on a warm day, when Rossetti's dejection lifted momentarily. Even Howell put in a final appearance, raising Gabriel's spirits with outrageous tales about all and sundry. Rossetti responded with a joke about a dying man. 'Why did Christ die?' asked the vicar at the deathbed. 'Oh, sir, this is no time for conundrums!' came the reply. A similar impulse prompted Gabriel to return to one of his very oldest poems, *The Dutchman's Wager*, about a smoking duel with the devil, dating from long-ago evenings with Major Campbell. Under its new title, *Jan van Hunks*, this mock-solemn ballad grew to forty-four stanzas and a remarkably good poem, full of grim humour according to a recent critic, whereby the reader can enjoy both Van Hunks's misanthropy and his impending fate.[34] The manuscript was sent to Watts, together with two sonnets for the unpainted Sphinx design *The Question*, which Watts proposed to publish.

If Rossetti's Faustian preoccupation with the Evil Spirit was concluded in the comic ballad, the sonnets voiced his final conviction of the unknowable mystery of existence beyond death:

> Oh! and what answer? From the sad sea brim
>   The eyes o' the Sphinx stare through the midnight spell,
>   Unwavering – man's eternal quest to quell:
> While round the rock-steps of her throne doth swim
> Through the wind-serried wave the moon's faint rim,
>   Sole answer from the heaven invisible.

They were truly fine compositions, remarked William, which did not support the local doctor's diagnosis of neural deterioration whereby the paralysis was a delusion caused by damage to the brain. But in fact Rossetti was suffering both from the effects of his stroke and from kidney failure. He made no progress, until his daily companions were forced to concede that some as yet unidentified condition prevented recovery (nurse Abrey suggested liver damage) and so it proved. 'Pray do not doubt the reality of poor dear Gabriel's illness,' Christina wrote firmly to William on 14 March.[35] He grew steadily worse.

On 1 April, William found Gabriel tottering, half-blind and in considerable pain. Summoned again, he returned with Watts a week later on Good Friday, and wrote the next morning to tell Lucy that his brother was 'still dying – not dead', and was expected to sink gradually. Persuaded to sign a cheque to meet posthumous expenses, Gabriel revealed that it was his intention to leave no will, so that half his property would go to his mother and half to his brother and sister. Learning that a will had once been made leaving everything to Lizzie, Watts advised signing a revocation, which grew into a new document – 'the last will and Testament of Gabriel Charles Dante Rossetti'. Christina vehemently refused her formal naming as beneficiary, so in the end the two legatees were Gabriel's mother and brother. Nine friends – Madox Brown, Bell Scott, Burne-Jones, Leyland, Graham, Valpy, Watts, Caine and (perhaps at Watts's suggestion) Swinburne – were to select a small drawing or item as a memento, while 'three of the largest and best chalk drawings for the subjects for which she sat' together with the profile head 'now hanging over the mantelpiece in the studio' were specifically bequeathed 'to my friend Mrs William Morris of Kelmscott House Hammersmith'.

Shields came, and John Marshall, who applied anti-uraemia remedies in a last effort, which resulted in a slight improvement during Easter Sunday. But twice during the day, showing no distress, Rossetti said, 'I believe I shall die tonight,' and shortly after nine in the evening he cried out loudly, suffered a convulsive fit, and died within a few minutes. He was a month short of his fifty-fourth birthday.

It was sorrowful, William told Scott, but better than a lingering end with loss of all powers. He asked Shields to draw a final portrait, and arranged for a memorial cast to be taken of Gabriel's head and hand – a common Victorian tribute to genius. It must be assumed that Rossetti's instructions to the contrary, as well as his vehement request that his body be not buried but burnt, were lying *perdu* at Cheyne Walk, for they had been given to and returned by George Hake, and not necessarily disclosed to William. In any case, the Rossetti women had a pious fear of cremation. 'For more than one reason' those present determined the burial should be at Birchington, endeavouring also to keep the news from the press, so that only invited friends attend the funeral. When Fanny wrote to beg a last look, William delayed replying until the morning of the interment, when the coffin was already closed.

That afternoon, 14 April 1882, in the little parish churchyard Frances Rossetti, William and Christina were joined by Lucy and good aunt Charlotte, who had so assisted Gabriel's early career. Old friends included Boyce, Fred Stephens, John Seddon and Vernon Lushington. Madox Brown was working in Manchester, Burne-Jones turned back at the station, too unwell to travel, Scott had a leg injury. Patrons were represented by Leyland, Graham, Aldam Heaton and Murray Marks, and newer friends by Hueffer, Shields, Watts, Caine, blind Philip Marston and Sharp, who placed a sonnet in the coffin. The burial service was read by the Birchington rector, reported Lushington to Scott,[36]

> then we all looked into the resting place of our friend and thought and felt our last farewells – many flowers, azaleas and primroses were thrown in ... Sad it was, very sad, but simple and full of feeling ... Dear Gabriel, I shall not forget him.

Epilogue

'Remember, my dearly loved son, that from your earliest years, you made us conceive the brightest hopes that you would become a great painter,' wrote Rossetti's father in 1853. If posterity has so far withheld that accolade (in a century that so rapidly chose to elevate Impressionist and Modern painters above those of the Victorian and Symbolist eras) Dante Gabriel Rossetti assuredly succeeded in creating a distinctive, influential and enduring presence in the art of his time.

His œuvre contains over three hundred subject pictures, with their attendant studies and revisions, plus a similar number of portrait drawings, and at least another three hundred designs for unexecuted works. For a working life of nearly thirty-five years – from which two or three years of severe illness should be subtracted – this represents a sustained output.

Like the best artists, his work passed through different phases, as he explored different means to realise his visual ideas, always however retaining an umistakably 'Rossettian' idiom or signature. Thus his style modulated from what may be termed the poetic realism of early Pre-Raphaelitism, through the imaginative patterning of 'mystical medievalism', to the symbolic idealism of his later works. At any moment his approach could be aesthetically innovative – as with *Ecce Ancilla*, or the 'chivalric' watercolours, or *Bocca Baciata*. At other times the work was uneven, or repetitive, yet as an artist Rossetti never became complacent, always striving towards higher conceptual and technical command. His range of subjects – figure groups drawn from literature and religion – tended to remain constant, although in later years it narrowed to feature single female figures most prominently.

For most of the twentieth century, his generation and style were quite out of favour. Latterly, the popular appeal of Pre-Raphaelitism may ironically be one reason why his work as yet lacks full scholarly esteem as important and influential – for it seems to me that his originality and impact on British and European painting are currently under-explored and underestimated.

In poetry, his published works fill 300 pages, with in addition 240 translated Italian poems and the *Vita Nuova*. His original pieces range from the simple narrative ballad, through the dramatic monologue, Miltonic ode and short lyric, to ornate sonnets in which intricate conceits are used to convey abstract ideas. Though expressive, in his own words, of 'the *dramatis personae* of the soul', both pictorial and poetic works are carefully crafted by and conceptually distanced from their author. The most original and successful poems – both in intrinsic terms and in relation to their critical after-life – are undoubtedly the precocious *Blessed Damozel* and the verbally vigorous, finely nuanced *Jenny*, with its topical intervention into the social issues of the day. Like those of Shakespeare and Donne, the dense, often riddling sonnets can be intriguing or irritating according to taste.

As in art, so in literature. Here, too, Rossetti's undoubted influence on writers as varied as Swinburne, Hopkins and Yeats – to say nothing of lesser lights in the late-Victorian poetic firmament – was denied and then erased by the critical dominance of Modernism in the twentieth century; this process being orchestrated by T. S. Eliot and his followers, especially during the 'anti-Victorian' atmosphere that followed World War I. Once quite widely read, his poetry has also fallen from popular favour. Only lately have critics, overcoming inherited prejudices, returned analytically to include and assess Rossetti's position in the nineteenth-century canon with due historical impartiality.

Rossetti's other significant interventions have also been generally under-valued. He was, for example, more than half-responsible for establishing the reputations of both Blake and Dante in Britain – the latter as much through painting as poetry – and he also played a vital role in drawing attention to early Italian art and literature, of the pre-Raphael and pre-Dantean periods respectively. Further efforts to rescue neglected writers and painters, mainly of his own time, were however largely in vain; for it cannot be said that all Rossetti's ducklings proved to be swans.

As regards his own achievements, in both poetry and painting his reputation has been erratic, and dispassionate responses remain rare, for at any moment readers and viewers – whether general or 'expert' – will simultaneously regard his works as beautiful or repellent, artistic successes or grotesque failures.

His personality and behaviour are similarly viewed, often with a strength of feeling that is surprising in relation to one who died over a century ago, in an age very distant from ours. A hundred years ago, H. C. Marillier, compiler of the first full account of his art, complained that it had become the fashion to decry Rossetti, and paint him as sordid, self-indulgent, mean and querulous, so that stories of his egotism, shabby conduct towards patrons and ungoverned temper were 'reeled off with a sort of zest'.[1] By

1948, the centenary of the PRB, Rossetti's last years were commonly described, according to his great-niece, as those of a 'drug-sodden and degenerate wretch, bankrupt in character and reputation, who led a ghastly posthumous existence behind closed doors in Cheyne Walk, abandoned by all decent-minded people'.[2] Such views remain current: to the biographer it sometimes seems as if the polarised responses of Rossetti's contemporaries and successors are still actively replayed. Which makes it equally surprising that so few studies of his life have been published and broadcast since the last major biography appeared in 1949. Again, it seems to me that there is great scope for further analysis and appraisal and that the present book will have succeeded if it allows for a clearer, less prejudiced view of its subject, while recognising all his complexities of character and attainment.

The story of his posthumous reputation also remains to be written in detail. Owing to his sad final years, the response to Rossetti's death by his closest friends was mixed and muted. 'So at last, rather suddenly, the long nightmare of the later years of our dear friend DGR has quieted down into the everlasting sleep,' wrote Scott to Swinburne.[3] By contrast Burne-Jones elected to recall only happier memories, telling Leyland that '[t]hese last sad years seem rolled away and I see only the brightness of the old time'.[4] To Brown it was 'like part of one's life torn away'. 'I had known him without a break since '48,' he told Watts. 'All day the memories of 10, 20, or 30 years past away [sic] have been "crowding up" (as he beautifully writes the waters did round the White Ship) in my memory.'[5]

Swinburne wrote a typically grandiloquent sonnet, hailing 'a light more bright than ever bathed the skies' and 'the soul most radiant once in all the world'. Christina wrote a plainer poem, about her brother's grave on a low hill near a seaweedy coast, although when later prevailed upon to contribute her memories to a literary magazine, she also preferred cheerful recollections of Tudor House. 'Gloom and eccentricity such as have been alleged were at any rate not the sole characteristics of Dante Gabriel Rossetti,' she wrote: 'when he chose he became the sunshine of his circle, and he frequently chose so to be. His ready wit and fun amused us; his good nature and kindness of heart endeared him to us.'[6]

William, who had perhaps suffered most from his brother's decline, could only feel 'a real sense of relief which one does not talk of much, but which one is not at all ashamed of – namely the feeling that it really was an alternative between loss of life and gradually increasingly and finally perhaps total loss of working power, perhaps even of deforce [sic] of mind'.[7] To her own surprise, Janey was badly affected. 'The effect on me at the sudden news of Gabriel's death was quite unlooked for,' she wrote in a shaky, invalid hand, explaining that while she had regarded him 'as one dead many years ago' and had expected to feel only relief when he finally ceased to suffer, the brevity of his final decline came as a terrible shock.[8]

'One of the most rarely gifted men of our time has just died', wrote Watts in an obituary notice for the *Athenaeum*, choosing his words carefully but going on to assert that, 'wonderful as an artist and a poet', Rossetti was 'still more wonderful as a man'.[9] At the Royal Academy banquet a fortnight later, the president, now Sir Frederic Leighton, paid his own tribute to an artistic peer and rival, as one who 'at one period of his life wielded a considerable influence in the world of Art and Poetry'. Rossetti was both painter and poet, he added: 'a mystic by temperament and right of birth, and steeped in the Italian literature of the mystic age, his works in either art are filled with a peculiar fascination and fervour, which attracted to him from those who enjoyed his intimacy a rare degree of admiring devotion.'[10]

In May the Royal Scottish Academy – presumably in the words of his old acquaintance Noel Paton – also registered the passing of one 'whose many-sided and original genius and high accomplishment, not only as a painter but as a poet also, have shed a lustre on the artistic profession'. Owing to his aversion to exhibition, the tribute continued, Rossetti's 'thoughtful and imaginative pictures are but little known to the general public; but his influence on contemporary English art has confessedly been very great, while that of his poetry has been more markedly and widely felt. Probably few artists of more distinct individuality and intellectual force ever appeared; and his removal in the full maturity of his power cannot but be regarded as a heavy loss to art and literature.'[11]

One immediate consequence of Rossetti's death was that the amounts advanced for various commissions that would now never be delivered fell due to his estate. Of these, the largest was that for around £2,250 owed to Valpy. On 5 July, the contents of Cheyne Walk – excluding works of art – were auctioned at a dismal house sale where everything from valuable antique furniture to worthless scullery pails was ticketed and picked over. The proceeds amounted to nearly £3,000. The ragged drawing-room curtains fetched an astonishing £35, while the precious Blake notebook, which had originally cost ten shillings, realised only 105 guineas.

In his speech Leighton had pronounced that 'such a man should not leave the world unnoticed'. Obtaining the family's approval, William Sharp began a critical record of Rossetti's works, while Hall Caine prepared his recollections of what he liked to claim was his intimacy with the great man during the final days. Both books appeared in autumn 1882. As Christina told George Hake, Caine's was essentially the portrait of a wreck.[12] With more decorous eulogism, Sharp opined that Dante Gabriel Rossetti 'held and will continue to hold a unique position' and that 'literature and art have both been enriched with the creations of a master'. Presciently, however, he hinted at future divisions of opinion, saying that 'those whose attention is specially given to literature regard him as one of the truest and most remarkable poets of his time ... while those whose studies or taste concern the art of painting consider him even greater as an artist than as a poet'.[13]

At Leyland's suggestion, Leighton arranged for a retrospective exhibition of Rossetti's works at the Royal Academy. And do you think such an exhibition will do Rossetti's reputation any good? a smirking Academician asked Holman Hunt. 'Not it. It will rather ruin it altogether.'[14] But at the end of the year, a total of 84 works were duly displayed in a limited space at the RA Winter Exhibition alongside those of Blake's friend John Linnell, who also died in 1882, in his ninetieth year.[15] Simultaneously, 153 works were exhibited at the Burlington Fine Arts Club, with a catalogue compiled by H. V. Tebbs. These two 'official' shows were complemented by a small one held in Bond Street premises hired by John Schott, where various works and photographs belonging to Fanny were displayed.

The public response to this first appearance of pictures long unseen was mixed. Some spectators like Elizabeth Eastlake, widow of the artist, were heartily repelled by the goitrous necks and soulful expressions of the late female figures. The *Times*'s critic offered a more measured response, only gently regretting that in the later part of his career Rossetti had 'concentrated all his energy on the development of a type of female beauty which in the history of art will remained identified with his name' but of whose pictorial values and poetic sigificance 'very different opinions are naturally entertained'.[16]

On 12 May 1883 – which would have been Rossetti's fifty-fifth birthday – the 'studio sale' of over two hundred works – mainly drawings, sketches and studies – opened at Christie's auction rooms. The third and last oil replica of *Beata Beatrix* was sold for 630 guineas; the never-finished *Ship of Love* for £126; a finely detailed study of Janey, done in Oxford in 1858, for £24 2s; and the *Last Judgement* stained-glass designs for 12 guineas. The sale raised a total of £2,570 – less than William had hoped but more than the probate valuation. The final sum credited to the estate was £7,210, with debts of £2,700.

A century later, in 1987, the *Proserpine* begun for Leyland and then sold to W. A. Turner was resold at auction for £1.4 million. Such a sum would have mightily impressed the artist who when all was said and done had no very inflated notion of his own capacity, notwithstanding an 'extreme longing', such as possessed his youthful hero Chiaro dell'Erma, that his works should be found good. Such idealistic hopes and dreams can perhaps never be realised; as Rossetti explained in relation to the Grosvenor Gallery, he had a 'lifelong feeling of dissatisfaction at the disparity of aim and attainment', and he would surely have agreed with Whistler[17] that, despite his desires and ambitions, he had finally failed in both poetry and painting, at least in so far as his reach ultimately exceeded his grasp. Many great artists share this feeling: whatever his undoubted egotism and self-absorption, Rossetti was never smugly self-satisfied, and in his best moments had a balanced vision of life's limitations. His epitaph may be taken from his own lines at the end of his poem *Soothsay*:

> As in a gravegarth, count to see
> The monuments of memory.
> Be this thy soul's appointed scope: –
> Gaze onward without claim to hope,
> Nor, gazing backward, court regret.

Notes and References

References to each chapter are given in abbreviated form: for full details, see Bibliography. In addition, certain abbreviations are found within the Notes; these are listed alphabetically below.

ABBREVIATIONS

AB   Alice Boyd
ACS   Algernon Charles Swinburne
AFS   Anthony Frederick Sandys
AH   Arthur Hughes
CAH   Charles Augustus Howell
CEN   Charles Eliot Norton
CFM   Charles Fairfax Murray
CGR   Christina G. Rossetti
DGR   Dante Gabriel Rossetti
EBJ   Edward Burne-Jones
EES   Elizabeth E. Siddal
EH   Ellen Heaton
FC   Fanny Cornforth
FGS   Frederic George Stephens
FLR   Frances L. Rossetti
FMB   Ford Madox Brown
FRL   Frederick R. Leyland
FSE   Frederick S. Ellis
GBJ   Georgiana Burne-Jones
GFW   George Frederic Watts
GGH   George Gordon Hake
GM   George Meredith
GPB   George Price Boyce
HAB   Henry Austin Bruce
HTD   Henry Treffry Dunn
HTW   Henry Tanworth Wells
JEM   John Everett Millais
JL   James Leathart

JM   Jane Morris
JMW   James MacNeil Whistler
JR   John Ruskin
MFR   Maria F. Rossetti
MMF & Co Morris, Marshall, Faulkner & Co.
MZ   Maria Zambaco
PJT   Pauline J. Trevelyan
PPM   P. P. Marshall
PW   Philip Webb
RB   Robert Browning
RH   Ruth Herbert
RWB   Robert W. Buchanan
TEP   Thomas E. Plint
TGH   Thomas Gordon Hake
THC   T. Hall Caine
TW   Thomas Woolner
TWD   Theodore Watts Dunton
WA   William Allingham
WBS   William Bell Scott
WG   William Graham
WHH   William Holman Hunt
WJK   Walter J. Knewstub
WM   William Morris
WMR   William Michael Rossetti
WSB   Wilfrid S. Blunt
WT   Warrington Taylor

CHAPTER I: BOYHOOD

1 See *EIPs*, preface.
2 WHH, I, 154–5.
3 See Macdonald 1991, 238.
4 DW 1340.
5 See WA Diary, 15 Oct. 1867; and Philip Marston, quoted OD 642.
6 See Baum 1931, 34.
7 See *VP* 20 1982, 239.
8 *FLM*, I, 66. For *The Castle Spectre*, see VS 2 where inscribed 'Gabriel' and '1836' on verso; and WEF 1991, 74, where verso inscription 'Castle Spectre / Osmond and Kenrick / Gabriel. Oct. 1836' is said to be in DGR's hand, though this seems improbable. The latter is also inscribed recto 'Gabriel 1834' in what seems FLR's hand and the scene includes two plinths clearly labelled by the artist 'Kenric' and 'Regenard' which appear to name the combatants. I conjecture that both works date from 1835, following DGR's purchase of a paintbox, and were probably copies.
9 Baum 1931, 35.
10 See *FLM*, I, 66; Waller 129; DW 2; also *FLM*, I, 59; DGR notebook annotated by FLR contains copy drawings of Buckingham and Catesby, Falstaff and Prince Hal, Macbeth and Siward, Casca stabbing Caesar.
11 See DGR to CFM, 13 Apr. 1880, UT; *FLM*, I, 74; Marillier 1899.
12 See *PWs* 1891, xxviii; DGR to CFM, 2 May 1880, UT; *FLM*, I, 80.
13 *FLM*, I, 85.
14 Peattie 1990, 198; for drawings, see VS 3; WEF 1991, 77 and 82 s & d May and July, 1840; Rosenbach Library, Philadelphia; *FLM*, I, 86–7; VS, 7 and 7a.
15 For *The Cavalier*, see DW 7; WEF 1991, 86; a careful duplicate was also made. For *Front-de-Bœuf*, see WEF 1991, 77; Browne 1994, 111.
16 DW 11; *FLM*, I, 85; *PDL*, 11; WEF 1991, 83. Two MS copies of the text survive, in Duke University (with accompanying letter) and at Rosenbach Foundation (in hand of FLR or MFR); it was published by B. F. Fisher in *English Language Notes*, vol. 92, Dec. 1971, 121–9. WMR suggested that poem and illustration were sent to *Smallwood's Magazine*, where Prof. Rossetti occasionally published verses, though as *Smallwood's* did not carry illustrations, it perhaps also went elsewhere – possibly to the *Illuminated Magazine*. The outline drawing (WEF 1991, 83) looks like a copy or even tracing, and was based on a lithograph illustrating The Rape of the Sabines, done by the Rossetti family friend Filippo Pistrucci. To THC, 1 Apr. 1880, DGR described *Smallwood's* as 'a short-lived monthly thing' to which his father contributed Italian verses, and where he read a continuation of Coleridge's *Christabel* 'long before I saw the original, and was all agog to see it for years'.

17 Ruskin CW, vol. 3, 286.
18 WHH, I, 34.
19 Quoted Wood 1904, 23–4.
20 For this section, see DW 13 and 14.
21 See *FLM*, I, 103; DW 14.
22 *PDL*, pp. 38–40.
23 DW 14; *FLM*, I, 93.
24 *PWs* 1891, xxi.
25 DW 17.
26 DW 17.
27 WHH 1890, 526–7; WHH 1905, II, 357. WHH first told the story in 1883, as an event that occurred before he knew DGR; see also *Athenaeum*, 15 Sep. 1894, 360, for review that must be by WHH. WMR did not recall the incident with clarity; nor is it likely that the telegraph position would have been offered to anyone older than DGR was in 1844.
28 DW 18.
29 VS 12–15, 615–19; WEF 1991, 34–5 (where 'Turkish dancers' are evidently a French couple).
30 See DW 23; *Works* 1911, for *Lenore* and *Henry the Leper*; *FLM*, I, 104, says *Nibelungenlied* was begun in Oct. 1845 and no MS survives.
31 See *FLM*, I, 105; Arnold 1923, 214; *EIPs*, preface; Wood 1904, 23. As regards sources, according to DGR, he did not read Nannucci, *Manuale della Letteratura del primo Secolo* (Florence, 1843) until a decade later.
32 RA Register gives DGR's admission as December 1845, but see *FLM*, I, 91–2 where WMR says DGR was at Cary's until July 1846. WHH, I, 56, says DGR was accepted as a probationer at the same time as himself (Dec. 1844) but as he then went abroad he did not complete his three probationary drawings in the term allotted so was permitted an extension. Wood 1904, 30, gives the date of DGR's application to the RA as end 1845, from information by J. A. Vinter who was himself however admitted to the RA Schools in Dec. 1844, apparently alongside DGR. If Dec. 1844 is the correct date, had DGR not caught smallpox, he would have started as a probationer in Jan. 1845 and after the formal exam six months later become a full Student. If he became a full Student in July 1846, the probationary period must have begun in Dec. 1845. It may be that his drawings were rejected by the examiners in Dec. 1844 and that this failure was obscured by illness and absence abroad, so that only in Dec. 1845 was his work deemed satisfactory. Stephens 1894, 9–10, correctly states that DGR was admitted as full Student in July 1846, but conflates this with his arrival as probationer, aged 'nearly eighteen'. (By July 1846 DGR was over eighteen.) The accounts cannot be fully reconciled, but it would appear that DGR first entered the Schools at the end of 1845.
33 Stephens 1894, 10; the 'fellow student' may be himself, or WHH, or Vinter.

CHAPTER 2: STUDENTHOOD

1 See evidence by GFW, JEM and WHH to Royal Commission on the Royal Academy, 1863, # 3111, 3115, 3028.

2 VS 434; *AJ*, 1884, 149; *FLM*, I, 110–11.

3 See Baum 1931, 17–25, for details of the MS entitled *The Dutchman's Wager*, an early version of the ballad revised in 1882 as *Jan van Hunks*. DGR found the theme in *Tales of Chivalry* (*FLM*, I, 108) not in Campbell.

4 See Caine 1882, 284. On the date of *Blessed Damozel*: WMR stated it was written in DGR's 'nineteenth year' (*FLM*, I, 107) and 'before he was nineteen years of age's (*Works* 1911, 647), i.e. before 12 May 1847. In 1880 DGR told THC of 'the "Blessed Damozel" which I wrote (and have altered little since) when I was 18'. THC however described it as 'this little work of his twentieth year' (Caine 1882, 20), which rather suggests he knew or suspected DGR should have said it was written when he was nineteen, i.e. before 12 May 1848. This is the date assigned it by Sharp 1882, 338. To FLR in 1873, D.G.R. wrote of a *Blessed Damozel* text from the *Hodge Podge* family magazine, but this would date the piece to 1843–4. One MS version, five stanzas shorter than the *Germ* version, is entitled 'The Blessed Damsel' and initialled 'D.G.R 1847' (JPM). This MS is thought to be an autograph copy given to the Brownings around 1855 and assumed to have been copied then (in 1847 DGR did not sign his name in this form) with the original date given. It is possible however that the MS is of earlier date, with the date added in 1855. In some ways it seems to be so, being shorter than the published version (according to WMR 'four stanzas' were added to the text before printing in *The Germ*). The MS version has been described as a retrospectively-dated fabrication designed to support the notion of precocious composition (see Stanford 1931, 471) but I incline to view it as an authentically early version, either taken or copied from an early notebook. This is partly because 'blessed damsel' is in direct imitation of Poe's 'sainted maiden' whereas the archaic 'damozel' (used by Spenser in *The Faerie Queene*) looks like one of the obsolete terms DGR reported finding in the BM while 'reading up all manner of old romaunts to pitch upon stunning words for poetry' in Sep. 1849 (DW 43) prior to redrafting the poem for *The Germ*. It seems unlikely that if 'fabricating' a MS version later he would omit existing stanzas, or fail to use the word which had been responsible for a good deal of the poem's renown after 1850; but it is plausible that he sent the original text to the Brownings. Whatever the MS status, however, I see no sound reason for doubting 1847 as the date of the original composition. To DGR on 31 Mar. 1848 Leigh Hunt referred to the 'Dantesque heavens' in his original verses (*FLM*, I, 123) which

seems to indicate the *Blessed Damozel* and suggests the piece was in its first complete draft by Jan. 1848.

5 DW 39.

6 *Works* 1911, 240; see also *Works* 1911, 663; DW 1340.

7 Bailey endpapers, 2nd edn *Festus*, 1845 (it is possible Gilfillan intended irony); *FLM*, I, 89.

8 Robinson, 1882, 696.

9 WHH 1905, I, 168–9.

10 Ibid.; see also DGR's letters in later life, including one from William Davies in Dec. 1880, Lasner.

11 For DGR and Holst, see Browne 1994.

12 Reynolds, *Discourses*, 1975 edn, 111–13.

13 *FLM*, I, 109; on the flyleaf DGR wrote: 'I purchased this original MS of Palmer, an attendant in the Antique Gallery at the British Museum on the 30th April 1847. Palmer knew Blake personally and it was from the artist's wife that he had the present MS which he sold me for 10s … D.G.C.R.' (see Erdman 1973).

14 Sharp 1912, 73.

15 The copy of *Verses* with DGR's portrait of CGR is now in UT; VS 421, a duplicate version in V&A, inscribed to Amelia Heimann, is said to have been drawn at 57 Gordon Square, the Heimann home. The UT copy contains illustrations to *The Dream*, *The Ruined Cross* and *Tasso and Leonora*, while *FLM*, i, 99, mentions also *Lady Isabella*.

16 CGR to unidentified correspondent, 23 [Jan.] 1888, PUL.

17 See *VP* 20, 1982, for full text of Stanhope elegy; the quatrain on Louis Philippe is in LC.

18 RB to DGR, 10 Nov. 1847, Lasner; Sharp 1882, 65–66. RB's letter is so courteous that possibly he thought he was replying to Prof. Rossetti.

19 *SR*, 1906, I, 167, and CGR *FL*, 102; Birkbeck Hill 1897, 50.

20 *FLM*, I, 99; see Luke 4:8; VS 37; Grieve 1973(a), pl. 5.

21 DW 28.

22 *Academy*, 6 May 82, 323.

23 *FLM*, I, 99; see also *AJ*, 1884.

24 Arnold 1923, 211–14.

25 *FLM*, I, 123.

26 DW 32.

27 See R. G. Howarth, *N&Q*, 10 July 1937, 20–1, where likely source in Memoirs of Harriette Wilson (1825) is suggested.

28 DW 29.

29 DW 30.

30 FMB, 25 Mar. 1848

31 Frith 1888, 50.

32 Marillier 1899, 22.

33 Baum 1931, 7.

34 See Newman and Watkinson, 1991, 34 and 201; Caine 1928 19; HTW to FGS, 29 Jan. 1897, Bod. MS. HTW lived near Gloucester Gate, Regent's Park; in 1897 he still possessed a half-finished nude study by DGR of a model calling herself Mrs De Banks.

35 MS of 'At the Sun-rise' in UT, apparently containing original text, with later emendations.
36 *Works* 1911, 673.
37 DW 1420.
38 See Caine, 2000 [25 Feb. and 28 Mar. 1880].

CHAPTER 3: BROTHERHOOD

1 WHH 1905, I, 107.
2 WHH 1905, 1905, I, 144.
3 DW 91.
4 WHH 1905, I, 102; *PRBJ*, 109; for HBs, see TG 1984, 14.
5 DW 28.
6 For *Hyperion*, see Bennett 1969, no. 95; WHH 1913, I, 69; for *La Belle Dame*, see *PRBJ*, 108 (drawing itself dated Apr. 1848); VS 32.
7 WHH 1905, I, 103.
8 For Cyclographic criticisms, see *PRBJ*, 1975, 109–112. Delacroix' *Faust* lithograph shows the Evil Spirit tapping Margaret on the shoulder; Scheffer's 1832 picture shows her kneeling in church.
9 For WHH, see Bennett 1969, nos. 96, 97, 98 and 100; also Grieve in Parris 1984, 24, for 'The Pilgrim's Return' to an unidentified text; for JEM's *Ferdinand*, see Bennett 1988, no. 10364; for Isabella subjects, see Wood 1904, 60; for JEM's *Lovers*, TG 1984, 158, s & d 1848 (see Wildman 1995, 12, where it can be seen that the inscription and PRB monogram were added later in a different ink); *Lorenzo and Isabella* study in Millais 1979, 34, and Parris 1984, pl. 5; for WHH, *Brothers watching Lorenzo*, see TG 1984, 163.
10 DW 38; TG 1984, 15, states that the picture was composed in early summer 1848; the subject may also relate to Dyce's *Virgin and Child*, bought by the Queen from the RA.
11 WHH 1890, 526; see also Prinsep 1902, 283, for a slightly different text, presumably from a verbal account by WHH.
12 DW 35.
13 List of Immortals in WHH 1905, I, 159; the whole owes something to FMB's secular altarpiece *The Seeds and Fruits of English Poetry*, which placed Chaucer in the centre of a pantheon: see TG 1984, 6.
14 DW 35.
15 DW 37; first meeting of literary club scheduled for 14 Aug. 1848 – see Peattie 1990, 3, and DGR to WHH (ASU) where it is said to clash with 'Somerset House Sketching Club', which may have been rival to the Cyclographic.
16 *Athenaeum*, 23 Oct. 1852, 1147; see also Browne 1994, no. 74, and Gilchrist 1863, II, 380. Normally Holst's work hung in Thirlestaine House, Cheltenham, where it is clearly seen in a watercolour of the Picture Gallery dated 1846–7 (Browne, fig. 25). Unless DGR went to Cheltenham, perhaps

on an unrecorded visit to his uncle Henry, the canvas must have been in London in 1847–8.
17 DW 37.
18 WHH 1905, I, 153.
19 See Landow 1976–7, 103; *Works* 1911, 661.
20 DW 38.
21 DW 27 from WBS, I, 243, where dated 15 Nov. 1847, and said to have accompanied 'Songs of the Art Catholic'. My view is that whatever the date of the letter, 'Songs of the Art Catholic' are likely to have been sent in Nov. 1848, a date supported by WBS's claim (WBS, I, 248–9) that soon afterwards he was in London for Christmas and saw DGR at work on *The Girlhood* in Cleveland Street, which can only have happened in Dec. 1848. I incline to date both letter and Songs to 15 Nov. 1848. DGR would have seen WBS's *King Arthur carried to the Land of Enchantment* at the 1847 RA.
22 DW 37.
23 *New Monthly Belle Assemblée*, Sep. 1848, 140–2. See also David Bentley in *VP* 12, 321. *My Sister's Sleep* is always dated as having been written in 1847, on DGR's authority in a note to *Poems* 1870, 169, stating 'written in 1847, printed in a periodical [*The Germ*] at the outset of 1850'. But his statement to WHH around Aug./Sep. 1848 (DW 37) that it was 'one of the last things I have written' suggests otherwise, as does the theme which is in keeping with the Anglo-Catholic symbolism of *The Girlhood of Mary Virgin*. If, as is likely, *My Sister's Sleep* was one of the 'Songs of the Art Catholic', then WBS's visit to Cleveland Street also supports this dating.
24 See Caine 1882, 170; DW 2189.
25 Sharp 1912, 11.
26 *Works* 1911, 296. Originally DGR's father had wished to christen his firstborn son 'Dante Charles Rossetti' and sometimes referred to him in infancy as 'our little Dante', though by 1840 'Gabriel' was always used: see Purves 1931.
27 DW 40.
28 WHH 1905, I, 152.
29 *FLM*, I, 126.
30 *Pall Mall Gazette*, 10 Sep. 1886, 6; *FLM*, I, 135.
31 No contemporary or consequent record of the exact date and place of the PRB's founding survives. September 1848, the date usually given, is evidently too early, for in DW 40 to TW, DGR signed himself 'your sincere friend', rather than 'your PR Brother', as became customary, while 'PRB' initials on drawings from 1848 were added at a later date. The words 'our first anniversary meeting' (*PRBJ*, Jan. 1850) surely mean what they say.
32 Quoted *FLM*, I, 129; DW 1420; see also WHH to JEM, 28 Mar. 1895, JPM.
33 *FLM*, I, 128.
34 See WHH 1905, I, 256.
35 *FLM*, I, 133.
36 WHH 1905, I, 91.

37 *Germ*, ii, 61–4.
38 WHH 1890, 527.
39 WHH 1905, I, 164.
40 *FLM*, I, 145.
41 *FLM*, I, 147.
42 DW 41.
43 *PRBJ*, 15 May 1849.
44 See *PRBJ*, May 1849; *SR*, I, 151; *Pall Mall Gazette*, 8/10 Sep. 1886.

CHAPTER 4: YOUNG PAINTERS OF ENGLAND

1 See DW 41; *PRBJ* 14 Aug. 1849 and 27 May 1849 (which quotes one of the Dickinson brothers as saying: 'When Cottingham first mentioned to him his intention of buying Gabriel's picture, he descanted glowingly on his genius' and expressed his horror at 'having found him in a garret'). Cottingham did not buy the picture and 'his transactions with the PRB were considered anything but satisfactory' (*PDL*, 210). WHH, I, 179–81, outlines his own relations with Cottingham and the extant portions of the *PRBJ* contain details of TW's experience. 'I never liked the look of the fellow,' wrote JEM to WHH about Cottingham; 'he was *sloshy* and behaved so at first with Gabriel about his picture' (quoted *PRBJ*, 188 n.16.2). It seems plausible that the extensive mutilation of *PRBJ* entries for June 1849 relates to Cottingham's conduct over *The Girlhood*.
2 *PRBJ*, 22 July. 1849; *Germ*, 1901, 10–11. 'He appears to have been going on in his usual style up to the very last,' DGR noted when North's suicide was reported in 1854, with an advertisement for a new comic paper lying on his table, jokingly requesting agents in New Zealand, Australia, Polynesia, etc. 'NB. No cannibals need apply.' (DW 196)
3 In *Idle Blessedness*, the text printed by WMR gives 'lounge at shuffle' which has been queried by critics; I suspect that the true reading should be 'lounge or shuffle'. 'Bride-chamber Talk' was lengthened and renamed *The Bride's Prelude*, with the sisters' names as Amelotte and Aloÿse. 'The Scrip and Staff' was retitled *The Staff and Scrip*.
4 WHH, I, 185.
5 DW 47.
6 WHH, I, 186.
7 DW 47.
8 DW 48.
9 DW 49; WHH, I, 193.
10 DW 50.
11 DW 50.
12 *FLM*, I, 71.
13 *PRBJ*, 6 Nov. 1849.
14 In *Works* 1911, 674, the poem is dated 1851. When first printed in 1895, it was dated 20 Jan. 1850 (St Agnes' Eve) and said to have been sent to CGR, 'then in Brighton'. In fact CGR was at Longleat.

By Jan. 1851, DGR had left the studio above the 'hop-shop' and Collinson had left the PRB.
15 *PRBJ*, 25 Nov. 1850.
16 Jameson 1848, 3rd edn 1857, I, 126; Bryson 1976, 14.
17 TG 1984, 22; Faxon 1989, 55; Grieve 1976, II, 21. Especial thanks to Christie Arno for art historical and iconographic guidance.
18 *PRBJ*, 28 Dec. 1848.
19 *Works* 1911, 680.
20 See Allen 1997, 84; see also Grylls, 1964, 32.
21 Robinson 1882, 696.
22 *PRBJ*, Feb. 1850
23 *Love's Mirror*, or *Parable of Love*, VS 668, is conjecturally identified as an illustration for *Hand and Soul*, but the subject fits, and the titles attached to the drawing are not otherwise explained. In *PRBJ*, 13 Mar. 1850, DGR is said to be planning 'as his subject the painting by Chiaro of his own soul, from the "Hand and Soul" which appeared in No. 1. Of this he had thought before as a frontispiece to the volume – if one were ever to be completed.' On 15 Apr. 1850, DGR and FMB 'spent the evening together on the designs for their respective etchings.' 21 Mar.: 'Gabriel [finished today] his [design] of Chiaro's painting.' 23 Apr.: '[Gabriel] has begun his etching.' 26 Apr.: 'Gabriel ... continued to work on [his] etching.' 28 Apr.: 'Brown had his proof taken, which he sent in the evening, together with the plate, to Tupper's. Gabriel's also was taken, but disgusted him; whereat he tore up the impression, and scratched the plate over.'
24 See WHH, II, 300.
25 *Athenaeum*, 20 Apr. 1850, 524; OD, 101.
26 Dobbs 1977, 72.
27 For PRB reception in 1850, see *Illus. London News*, 4 May 1850; JGM, I, 75–6; *Athenaeum*, 1 Jun. 1850, 590–91. Meeting JEM a few months later, Stone repeated his opinion of the 'ignorant' young men, 'imagining they are going to do something new'. No doubt the PRB thought poorly of his own productions, he added. JEM could only agree (see *PRBJ*, 21 Jul. 50 and 30 Nov. 1850).
28 See *PRB*; June 1850; see also Bod.MSS. don.e.78.
29 *PRBJ*; DGR to WHH, c. May–Jun. 1850, ASU.
30 WA Diary, 91.
31 WA Diary, 59.
32 *SR*, I, 163–4; WHH, I, 231; Crowe 1895, 43–4; Worth 1964, 39; FMB, 10 Mar. 1855; DGR to WHH, ASU.
33 Dobbs 1977, 72.
34 *Apollo*, 1967, 380.
35 DW 51 (which must date from summer 1850), 56, 57; VS 229; DW 59.
36 DW 58, 59; WHH, I, 237; *PRBJ*, 5 Nov. 1850; JEM to WHH, 8 Nov. 1850, quoted Lutyens 1967(b), 380; for DGR to JEM, see DW 193 (from Sevenoaks) where wrongly dated Dec. 1854 instead of Oct. 1850.

37 DW 193.

38 *PRBJ*, 7 Nov. 50.

39 *PRBJ*, 7 Dec. 1850; DGR to FGS, Bod.MS. don.e.75, dated in pencil '24.1.50' but must be 24 Dec. 1850 as 'much hurried by preparations for removal'. See also DGR to WHH, 31 Dec. 1850, ASU, where gathering at FGS deferred to 2 Jan. 1851.

CHAPTER 5: RUN TO ME, DELIA

1 Peattie 1990, 19; WHH, I, 241–5; OD, 104–6; Peattie tentatively identifies the cabinet picture as VS 48, which bears the date 1851 and was originally titled 'To caper nimbly ...' But this is neither a genre subject nor an oil painting, and the work is more likely to have been that now known as *The Two Mothers* (VS 44), said to be cut down from *Kate the Queen*. VS 103 illustrating Longfellow presumably dates from this period.

2 *FLM*, I, 168, which suggests this as the date for DGR's unwilling application for work as a telegraph operator, although at twenty-two he was rather old for such employment and in any case WHH mentions this as having taken place before he met DGR; OD 107; DW 63; Roberson's Archive shows that DGR gave his address as Red Lion Square.

3 OD 107; Peattie 1990, 21; *Spectator*, 19 Apr. 1851; DW 63.

4 See WHH, 30 Apr. 1851 in *Letters to WA* 1911, 210; JGM, I, 101; *Works* 1911, 577–81; *PRBJ*, 16 May 1851.

5 *PRBJ*, 2 May 1851; *Times*, 7 May 1851; WHH, I, 249–51 where *Athenaeum* review quoted. Quotations in the following paragraphs are also from *PRBJ* and WHH 1905, I; see also Dobbs 1977, 81; DW 70.

6 DW 69 where the mutual acquaintance is identified as the American writer Buchanan Read; JGM Diary, 25 Oct. 1851, quoted JGM, I, 128; JEM to WHH, 25 Oct. 1852 and 11 Sep. 1854, BL RP 565.

7 DGR to WHH quoted Dobbs 1977, 80–1, where dated May 1851; but it was Oct. 1851 when WHH and JEM received the letter from Thomas Combe urging them to paint in biblical lands.

8 Quoted Worth 1964, 113.

9 DW 57; WHH to JLT, Sep. 1850, sold Sotheby's, 5/6 July 1971, lot 751. From 17 Newman Street, DGR asked WHH for the addresses of professional models named Child and Miss Gregson, and it may be he contacted EES the same way. For *To Caper Nimbly*, see VS 48 in original form; for *Return of Tibullus*, see VS 62; DW 67; *Works* 1911, 605–6. In Dec. 1851 DGR bought more canvas, paints and brushes at a total cost, with hire of lay-figure, of £2 16s.2d.

10 *FLM*, I, 171; BL RP 3731 (v); FMB, 10 Mar. 1855; DW 57; *Works* 1911, 666, where image in *The Mirror* is elucidated.

11 Peattie 1990, 25; for EES, see also WA Diary; *FLM*, I, 173; Marsh 1985 and Marsh 1989.

12 *PRBJ*, January 1853; Harrison, 41 and 42.

13 For Hermitage, see Howitt 1889, 212; TW, 53. For pictures there, see VS 51 (given to Bateman in May 1852); Grieve 1978, 17; VS 50, where dated 1851, but in DW 91 DGR refers to it as 'one which you may remember my making at Highgate'.

14 WBS, I, 316.

15 For TW's departure and correspondence, see DW 75, 91, 104, 128, 134; TW 18, 22, 23, 34, 37, 60, 61; WBS, I, 305–6.

16 For portraits, see DW 104; VS 341 (where inscription 'to Thomas Woolner, Edward Bateman, Bernhard Smith' is said not to be in DGR's hand); TG 1984, 183, 184; Ormond 1967, 26; TW 62–3, where portrait of WMR, not listed in VS, is reproduced and said to have been sold at Sotheby's after the death of TW's wife in 1912. See also Peattie 1990, 378; *DGR Letters to WA* 1897, 26.

17 DW 77. For Hannay's fiancée, see DW 88, 91.

18 For Chatham Place, see DW 76, 80 (which must be earlier than DW 76), 82, 84, 91; DGR to FGS, 21 Jan. 1853, Bod. MS. AH described the apartment as overlooking the Fleet Ditch.

19 GPB, 30 Dec. 1852, 6 Jan. 1853; *Pall Mall Gazette*, 5 May 1886, 4.

20 See Peattie 1990, 27, nn. 1–2; WHH to FMB, 18 Nov. 1852, NAL; DGR to WHH, 25 Nov. 1852, ASU.

21 DW 86; third exhibit identified as *Rossovestita* (VS 45) owned by FMB, but this would seem an unlikely item to exhibit. DGR to GPB, 12 Nov. 1852 (BL RP 4540, ii) shows he also wished to exhibit a work owned by GPB; if three works were hung, the third must have been *To Caper Nimbly*, but to TW DGR mentions only 'two exhibited'.

CHAPTER 6: ART, FRIENDSHIP AND LOVE

1 Correspondence between MacCracken and FMB is in NAL.

2 Collins 1848, I, 345; see also Macleod 1996, 48.

3 See Watkinson, *JPRS*, Nov. 1983, 137–8.

4 DW 91, 104.

5 *PDL*, 4; DW 95, 104; Peattie 1990, 31.

6 WHH 1890, 527; WHH, I, 252.

7 DW 119, 104; *Works* 1911, 271, 675.

8 Lee 1955, 216. For DGR's sketch of Anna Howitt, see WEF 1991, 46.

9 Peattie 1990, 29; DW 93, 94, 97, 104.

10 See VS 48; Grieve 1978, 20; DW 125, 129, 152; see also WHH 1890, 527.

11 DW 172.

12 DW 108; *FLM*, II, 111.

13 For visit to Newcastle, etc., see DW 113, 115, 117, 144; Grieve 1978, 62, 64. According to WBS, I,

290, the pair of sonnets entitled *The Church-Porches* were copied out by him for submission to a magazine issuing from Durham University, which promptly folded. WBS's watercolour of Hexham Market Place is now in Laing Art Gallery, Newcastle.

14 For Rosabell, etc., see WBS, I, 287–9; DW 116.

15 For visit to Warwickshire, see DW 117, 123, 144, 180, 187; WBS, I, 291 erroneously states that he and DGR parted at Wetheral.

16 WBS, I, 291; WHH, I, 149; DW 1650.

17 Muller 1856, 59.

18 *Letters to WA* 1911, 225–6.

19 On DGR's faith, see DW 654; FLM, I, 407; DW 1025; WMR 1889, I, 408; DGR's mother prayed for her sons to be 'brought to Confirmation and to Spiritual Communion' with God – see Rota 1973, lot 37.

20 WBS, I, 293.

21 DW 115; DW 99 (in which DGR writes of 'dear G's drawings') was dated 29 Jan. 1853 by WMR in *PDL*, 31–2, but is headed 'Albany Street', an address the Rossettis did not then occupy, and therefore probably belongs to May 1854, when the Photographic Exhibition referred to was open. However, when the exhibition closed, EES was in Hastings, so conclusive dating remains problematic.

22 See VS 459, 460, 691 (dated by Grieve to 1852); Marsh 1985, 36; Marsh 1989.

23 FLM, I, 177. For EES's version of events, see Marsh 1989(b), ch. 13.

24 DW 122.

25 FLM, I, 174.

26 DW 177.

27 See TG 1984, no. 58; Landow 1983–4, 151–2.

28 See Landow 1983–4, 119; WHH, I, 365.

29 DW 134, 144.

30 DW 138.

31 DW 144, 142; see also DW 148, 153.

32 Walpole Society 1972–4, 53.

33 DW 149.

34 For story of JEM and the Ruskins, see James 1947 and Lutyens 1967(a).

CHAPTER 7: MANY CAPITAL PLANS

1 DW 179, 99 (see ch. 6, n. 21).

2 DW 131.

3 See Hirsch 1998, 50; BRP Papers.

4 Ibid.

5 GPB, 8 Apr. 1854; Peattie 1990, 33; DW 157; see also GPB, 13/21 Apr. 1854.

6 DW 162.

7 DW 166; thanks to Jenny Ridd and Peter Marsden for sharing their research into 5 High Street, Hastings. For more on EES's visit to Hastings, see Hirsch 1998.

8 Hirsch 1998, 51.

9 DW 168; FMB, 7 Oct. 1854.

10 Walpole Society 1972–4, 14–16.

11 DW 174.

12 DW 169, 174.

13 Allingham 1888, 194.

14 *Works* 1911, 616.

15 See VS 65; DW 180; Lasner 1990, 93; DW 172; see also DW 180, written 22 or 29 Aug. in response to texts sent by WA before 15 Aug. For more on *Maids of Elfen-Mere*, see Grieve 1978, figs 61 and 60 (VS 67A is Grieve's 61). VS 67 (from Marillier 1899, 44) describes an unlocated version showing the youth at a table facing a vision of four maidens: this may in fact refer to VS 19B, one of the *Raven* designs with such components (which coincidentally belonged to WA) as it is unlikely that any illustration to the *Maids of Elfen-Mere* would contain four elf-maidens. For Fates, see VS 589, which echoes an image of the Parcae in Cartari's *Imagine de idei de gli Antiche*, Venice, 1571, a later edition of which DGR owned. Literary and pictorial sources are discussed in Life 1982; VP 20, 1982, 65ff.

16 For printing history of the woodblock, see Dalziel 1901, 86; *DGR Letters to WA*, 1897, 112; DW 198, 199.

17 'Some like Rossetti's best of all,' wrote WA to AH; see Lasner 1990 and Life 1982, cited n.15 above.

18 *Letters to WA*, 1911, 59.

19 DW 180, 17.

20 DW 187, 190.

21 DW 195.

22 DW 204, 227.

23 Ruskin CW vol. 12, 162.

24 For the history of *Found*, first, see reference to an unspecified 'great modern work' (DW 110); then 'the town subject' to MacCracken in May/Jun. 1853, to WMR (DW 147) and to WBS Aug. 1853. VS App. 4 (Grieve 1976, fig. 3) may be correctly identified as a first sketch for *Found* or may be an idea towards *Mary Anne* illustration (idea rejected by WBS because it was drawn as for a book page, then transferred to the 'town picture'. VS 64B, a very careful and complete design (with some later alterations to calf and cart), must have been done by Sep. 1853, as on 30 Sep. 1853 DGR wrote to his mother: 'I shall be wanting to paint a brick wall and a white heifer tied to a cart going to market' (DW 125).

25 DW 176.

26 *Times*, 25 May 1854.

27 RRP, 4.

28 See JEM, May/Jun. 1853, quoted Ironside and Gere 1948, 41, and TG 1984, 190.

29 DW 180; see also Hirsch 1998, 47–8, for Folio Club.

30 DW 180.

31 FMB, 3 Nov. 1854.

32 DW 182, 183; in DW 182 DGR wrote of a still outstanding loan from his aunt for £12 received 'last year'. At £60 p.a. the monthly rent on

Chatham Place would be £5, though it is unclear how much of this was being paid by WMR.

33 FMB, 5 Sep. 1854 and 7 Oct. 1854; DW 186. For the rest of DGR's visit to Finchley, see FMB.

34 DW 187; FMB, 9 Dec. 1854; the picture is now ascribed to Memling and its similarities with *Found* are not evident, but this is immaterial to the idea of an omen, which was perhaps augmented by the fact that DGR's own picture seems to have been on panel, not canvas (see VS 64M and VS 64Q now reunited); Grieve 1976, fig. 4; TG 1984, 63.

35 DW 191.

36 See TG 1984, 196; Grieve 1976.

37 DW 2042; WHH 1913, II, 1–2.

CHAPTER 8: RUSKIN AND BROWNING

1 Surtees 1979, 88.

2 For material on the Working Men's College and DGR's association with it, see Lowes Dickinson, 'Art Teaching in the College in its Early Days I', and J. P. Elmslie, 'Art Teaching in the College in its Early Days II', in Davies 1904; Sulman 1897, 547ff. For George Campfield's recollections, see *Pall Mall Gazette*, 28 Nov. 1888, 3.

3 DW 190, 196; *RRP*, no. 15; WHH 1913, II, 1.

4 Sulman 1897, 549. Sulman believed that *Carlisle Wall* was painted on this occasion, but as the watercolour was executed in 1853 in Newcastle it seems probable that DGR made a copy to demonstrate technique, though no replica is now known to exist. Later critics have pondered on his medium at this period, suggesting the use of gum thickener, as in gouache.

5 *SR*, I, 177.

6 JR, 'On the Nature of Gothic', Ruskin CW, vol. 10, 184ff.

7 WA Diary, 18 Sep. 1867, 163.

8 DW 177; previously Alexander Macmillan had expressed interest, through WMR.

9 DW 202.

10 DW 202; FMB, 13 Apr. 1855.

11 For correspondence with JR, see *RRP* and Ruskin CW, though the datings are very uncertain. JR's views on male and female duties are in *Sesame and Lilies*, 1865.

12 *FLM*, I, 180–2.

13 DW 204; JR, *Academy Notes*, 1855.

14 In the event JR kept *Lute Player*, sending Acland instead a study for the *Passover*; see DGR to Acland, Bod.MS.Acland.

15 FMB, 14 Jul. 1855, 19 Mar. 1856; DW 217.

16 FMB, 16 Aug. 1855, 15 Sep. 1855.

17 DW 221, 222; Peattie 1990, 41.

18 DW 227, 254; Sulman 1897, 550; see also VS 275.

19 DW 227.

20 See BL RP 382; Surtees, 1972; DW 227; Peattie 1990, 41.

21 WMR 1867, 108–9; also WMR's copy of the

Exposition Catalogue in Beinecke Rare Books Library, Yale.

22 See entries for 17 and 30 Jun. 1855, Delacroix 1895; DW 227 n.3; Chesneau 1885, 168–9; 'French Criticism of British Art', *Art Journal*, 1855, 251.

23 WBS, II, 30.

24 For correspondence with JR, see *RRP*; also DW 207; VS 74; Ruskin CW vol. 36, 227, 229; Troxell 1937, 28–9. JR's letter on the *Nativity* (*RRP*, 48) must antedate DW 207, as in the latter DGR says he will do another for JR and sell the first to someone else. However, he must instead have worked further on the existing drawing, for in *RRP* (p. 113) JR says, '*Nativity* is much mended; many thanks.' As there is no recorded location for this *Nativity* (VS 71) yet JR's description tallies so well with the watercolour study for *The Seed of David* (VS 105B central panel), I believe this is in fact the missing *Nativity*, reused when the Llandaff commission was received, and adapted into an *Adoration*. If so, JR must have handed the drawing back to DGR in April 1856. Its existence would have helped DGR complete the whole three-part study for the Llandaff altarpiece in record time; see below. When completing the full-size work, the main alterations made by DGR were in the positions of the Virgin, Shepherd and King, in line with JR's comments.

25 See Ruskin 1856, III and IV, # 135–9.

26 See VS 81.

27 DW 256.

28 See Robinson 1882, 696; Gerard's *Herball*, 1597 edn, bk 2, ch. 132 (though this illustration does not relate to the poem); Ruskin CW, vol.5, 209; DW 653.

29 DW 229.

30 FMB, 27 Jan. 1856. DGR's chivalric subject is believed to be the first version of VS 99, but is otherwise unidentified.

CHAPTER 9: MORRIS AND BURNE-JONES

1 GBJ, I, 129; EBJ must already have known Lushington, who contributed to the *O&C*.

2 DW 234; GBJ, I, 130; *O&C*, Jan. 1856; GBJ, I, 121. EBJ later stated that DGR knew more than one of WM's poems at this first meeting; as only *Winter Weather* had been published, he may have conflated more than one meeting.

3 Harrison 1999, 81; GBJ, I, 139.

4 FMB, 19 May 1854; DW 240.

5 DW 196; WHH 1913, II, 1–2.

6 For London Institution, Finsbury Circus, see Surtees, 1972, 184; *RRP*, pp. 109–10; Ruskin CW, vol. 36, 227, where dated ?Oct.55 but must in fact be c.March 1856, see Peattie 1990, 41. For DGR's letters to Ellen Heaton, see BL RP 382.

7 See Rose 1981, 102; FMB, 19 Feb. 1856, 3 Mar. 1856; Surtees 1997.

8 For FMB and FGS to WHH, see DHH 1969, 152–3.

9 See DW 234; information and correspondence relating to *The Seed of David* (here and in later chapters) is from Llandaff Chapter Act Books and Henry Austin Bruce Papers, Glamorgan County Record Office. My thanks to both Nevil James, Llandaff Cathedral Hon. Archivist, and the staff of Glamorgan CRO.

10 DW 234, 240; *RRP*, pp. 107–8; Peattie 1990, 41; FMB, 24 Apr. 1856. In spring 1856, full-size tracings of frescoes by Giotto, Piero della Francesca and Gozzoli were on display at the Crystal Palace, with coloured chromolithographs. 'Together they have given one one's first real chance of forming a congruous idea of early art without going there,' wrote DGR.

11 Llandaff MSS; *RP*, pp. 50–1; Street 1858, 239. Paired images of David are uncommon in European art. David advancing on Goliath may have been suggested by Gozzoli's rendering of the story in the Camposanto frescoes at Pisa; see DW 240. Other representations of David as a youth known to DGR include Michelangelo's *David and Goliath* in the Sistine Chapel – a very different conception – and Donatello's two sculptured Davids in the Bargello, Florence. BL MSS.Harl.4804, f. 4, has David Harping in historiated capital B. The coincidence of the name, between the Hebrew David and the patron saint of Wales, seems an unintentional holy pun on DGR's part. Llandaff is not connected or dedicated to St David. *The Seed of David*, however, might be thought by some to refer both to the Son of God and to the Church in Wales. See also JR on David and Titian's *Adoration*, in Ruskin 1856, IV, ch. 4 # 22 and ch. 7 # 2/3.

12 Bruce 1902, I, 23–4.

13 See Faxon 1989, 120–1, 232 n.12. For a more traditional working, see Thomas Gambier Parry's *Adoration of Our Lord on Earth* on the roof at Ely Cathedral completed in 1863, showing Madonna and Child flanked by Kings and Shepherds on either hand. Botticelli's *Mystic Nativity* of 1500, now in the National Gallery, which also has Shepherds and Kings led to worship by angels, was not seen by DGR until 1868, though it is possible he already knew the subject.

14 DW 240; FMB, 11 Apr. 1856.

15 See FMB, 20 Apr. 1856.

16 See FMB, Jul. 1856.

17 Horner 1933, 21; another version involves only one book.

18 See Horner 1933; Fitzgerald 1975, 49; GBJ, I, 136, 141; Baldwin 1960, 52; Caine 1908, 39 (where the college friend is R. W. Dixon).

19 GBJ, I, 149.

20 Horner 1933, 15, Kelvin, I, 17.

21 DW 254, 255, 262; WBS, II, 37; *EBJ* 1998, 42.

22 *The Crayon* (New York), Apr. 1858, 95.

23 See DW 254; VS 110; BL RP 382; FMB, 9/12 Nov.

1856, where it is suggested that the oil could have been *Found*, despite the fact that by the following year Leathart was the potential purchaser. DGR's dealings with TEP are unclear, but as far as is known TEP acquired no large oil from him; I therefore incline to think that this commission was for a Mary Magdalene of some kind. DGR had the subject in mind as early as 1853; he delivered a watercolour (VS 88) to W. Marshall in 1857, and the elaborate ink (VS 109) completed in 1857 was in TEP's possession in 1860. A number of oil versions replicate the ink drawing (VS 109 R1, R2); that promised to TEP perhaps remained unfinished at the time of his death. See also *Letters to WA* 1911, 289.

24 Quoted Vanderbilt 1959, 55; DW 246.

25 FMB, 8 Sep. 1856; *Daily News*, 9 Sep. 1856; Surtees 1972, 195 n.4; FMB, 17 May 1856; Mackail 1899, 109; DW 228; JGM, 1899, I, 52.

26 DW 254.

27 FMB, 8 Oct. 1856, 16 Mar. 1857; DGR received advance payment from TEP Nov. 1856; see also DW 254.

28 *FLM*, I, 93 (where remark dated 'towards 1857').

29 DW 245; Freemantle 1901, xxi; DW 247. For an account of DGR's career in illustration and book design, see WEF 1996.

30 *O&C*, Aug 1856; *Prose and Poetry by William Morris*, OUP, 1913, 632; see also Goldman 1994, pl. 9.

31 *EBJ* 1973, 61; GBJ, I, 195.

32 Quoted Lutyens 1975, xxi.

33 FMB, 9/12 Nov. 1856; DW 252; GBJ I, 157. For *St Cecilia* watercolour, see BL RP 382 and VS 83 R1. A month later TEP changed his mind, asking instead for a *Blessed Damozel*.

34 *AJ*, Jul. 1857, 231; see also 'Nuremberg' in WEF 1991, 71a, which almost certainly dates from 1856 and is drawn on the wood, with the title and a line of verse on the side reading 'Lived and designed Albrecht Dürer, Evangelist of Art'. For Longfellow, see WHH 1905, II, 253; it is possible that DGR's design for 'The Skeleton in Armour' (VS 103) also belongs to this period.

35 *Letters to WA* 1911, 65; Freemantle 1901, 101; DW 251, 252, 254, 262; the famous verse is 'O woodman spare that tree' by G. P. Morris.

36 See Joseph Pennell, preface to Freemantle, 1901, xiv; *Pocket Cathedrals: Pre-Raphaelite Book Illustration*, exhibition catalogue, Yale Center for British Art, 1991. For other Moxon engravings, see DW 251, 254, 257, 258; *Galahad* proof sheet in Lilly Library, University of Indiana at Bloomington; and see Marsh 1989(a), 13–14. For *Lady of Shalott*, see Freemantle 1901 and corrected proof on display at Fitzwilliam Museum, 1996, showing shadow removed from the face of the Lady. For JEM, see Freemantle 1901, xxiii. Hunt's images were cut by J. Thompson and T. Williams as well as Dalziel but it is not known which had to be recut; see also Marsh, 1989(a), 13–14. Delay

was also caused by the illness of the engraver W. J. Linton at end of 1856.

37 DW 254.

38 GBJ, I, 147; Mackail 1899, 113; Christie's sale, London, 29 Oct. 1997, lots 20–21; VS 116 and 117; also V&A 1996, J6 a–d, where panel motifs correspond with DGR's other works.

39 Stephens 1894, 110–11; GBJ, I, 149; Smetham and Davies 1892, 102.

40 Macdonald 1919, 67.

41 *RRP*, no. 78.

42 GBJ, I, 150.

CHAPTER 10: AN OLD SONG ENDED

1 DW 263.

2 DW 264.

3 FMB, 16 Mar. 1856 (actually 14 Mar.).

4 FMB, 16–19 Mar. 1856.

5 DW 267; this is the probable date when the Llandaff commission was confirmed with £100 advance.

6 Smetham and Davies 1892, 102.

7 *Atlantic Monthly*, Nov. 1857, 45.

8 Ruskin CW, vol. 36, 272.

9 Other exhibitors listed as Campbell, Bond, Arthur Lewis, J. D. Watson, Wolf.

10 *Athenaeum*, 11 Jul. 1857; *Saturday Review*, 14 Jul. 1857.

11 See Sotheby's sale, 11 Nov. 1998, lot 1.

12 Ruskin 1857 (see Everyman edn, 1906, 247).

13 See Casteras 1990, 28; according to Norton, the MS was recovered eight months later, the trunk in which it was packed, along with other contributions, having lain *perdu* in a Liverpool hotel.

14 DW 271; GBJ, I, 158. For proposal to illustrate *Stories after Nature*, see Wells 1891, where Linton says he lent the original edition to DGR.

15 DW 274.

16 Prinsep 1902, quoted GBJ, I, 159, 161–2; Kelvin, I, 19.

17 Pollen 1912, 270; Mackail 1899, I, 120–1; GBJ, I, 162–7.

18 DW 276; and see R. W. Dixon in Mackail Notebooks, WMG.

19 Prinsep 1902; Birkbeck Hill 1897, 72.

20 *Works* 1911, 587, 681; DW 289; GBJ, I, 164.

21 See Girouard 1981, 81; Pointon 1979, 104–8, 177; Poulson 1999, ch. 3.

22 *Letters to WA* 1897, 144.

23 VS 363; possibly the inscription was added later, as in 1857 DGR was not to know this was his first drawing of JM; see also BL Ashley 1410(i).

24 See WHH to Emily Patmore, 28 Oct. 1857 (with thanks to Tim McGee); Mackail 1899, I, 126–7; GBJ, I, 168. When Smetham went to Oxford early in 1858, he was told DGR had been away eight weeks.

25 See DW 278, 279, 280; Grylls 1964, pl. 10; TEP

agreed to pay 55 gs for *St George* and 40 gs for *Hamlet and Ophelia*.

26 GBJ, I, 176–7.

27 DW 289, 422.

28 Quoted Harrison and Waters 1989, 29.

29 Lang 1959, I, 18.

30 EBJ MSS, Fitzwilliam

31 See Patmore to DGR, 19 May 1858, UT; DW 289; WEF 1961, 195.

32 DW 422, 1953, 289, 285. EES stayed on at Lime Tree View after DGR left. Later DGR sent money when Mr Cartledge, the boarding-house keeper, fell on hard times (FLM, II, 147). The poems by DGR quoted here are ascribed to this period by WMR and can thus be linked to his estrangement from EES; the date of her verses is not known for certain.

33 *DGR Letters to WA* 1897, 243; DW 289, 293 (which must date from 1859), 313; letters to Macmillan, Berg Collection, NYPL.

34 DGR to Brough, see *N&Q*, 1991, 321; DW 289.

35 See Chapman 1945, 153; JR to WM, 27 Jun. 1858, BL RP 2917.

CHAPTER 11: PLACATÂ VENERE

1 See Surtees 1997, 35, 28. Tom Taylor made the introduction.

2 Ruskin CW vol. 36, 302; GBJ, I, 187.

3 GBJ, I, 169, where these words are attributed to an unnamed 'lady whom I had not seen for many years and who had been in her youth an object of wild enthusiasm and admiration to Rossetti, Morris and Edward' and to whom GBJ had spoken 'quite lately' of old times. A few pages later, GBJ relates how one day in (apparently) the 1890s, RH drove from Brighton to see EBJ at Rottingdean and 'shook hands across the gulf of time'. The identification is conjectural, but supported by Surtees 1997, 42. The drawing of RH feeding a cage-bird is inscribed 25 June 1858 by DGR and described by Georgina Trehearne (Surtees 1997, 42–4) as 'a sketch drawn at Little Holland Hse by Rossetti – Reminiscence of Miss Herbert an actress all the Pre-Raffaelites were in love with'. I do not think the event took place at Little Holland House since the bullfinch is evidently RH's own, and the drawing is explicitly said to be 'a reminiscence'. In DGR's poem *Beauty and the Bird*, the final phrase is 'I heard the throng / Of inner voices praise her golden head'. RH sat again in the autumn, for drawings dated 20 Sep. and Dec. 1856. NB her stage name was Louisa Herbert, but to DGR and his circle she was always Ruth.

4 Surtees 1997, 45; VS 599; *N&Q*, 1991, 321.

5 See DGR to Macmillan, 21 Jul. 1858, Berg; DGR to F. J. Furnivall, 16 Jul. 1858, UT. In August the Rossetti family thought he was at Matlock: see Harrison, I, 97.

6 See Trevelyan 1978, 141 (the picture was already promised to Ellen Heaton); VS 110. For Solomon's view, see GPB, 3 Jan. 1859.

7 See Trevelyan 1978, 145; PJT's reference was to *The Blue Closet* and *The Tune of Seven Towers*.

8 For *Christmas Carol*, see VS 109; WBS to WMR, 5 Sep. 1858, Peattie 1990, 49 n.2; for *Mary Magdalene at the Door*, see VS 109, from *Pall Mall Budget*, 22 Jan. 1891, 14. For the 'strapping Scandinavian', see Rooke MSS, 433; G. A. Sala identified her as the real-life inspiration for *Jenny*; it is possible she was Mrs Beyer, otherwise identified as German, of whom two portrait studies survive (VS 266 and 267) and a Dodgson photo from 1863 (UT).

9 For Hogarth Club, see Cherry 1980; Peattie 1990, 62; GPB, 4 May 1858; see also Octavia Hill on 7 Feb. 1859, quoted in Maurice 1913, 129.

10 Prinsep 1902, 283; oddly enough, *Mary in the House of St John* is a sunset picture: the recollection may not be precise.

11 AH to WA, 5 Dec. 1859, in *Letters to WA* 1911. But is this date correct? In Dec. 1858 DGR was working on the Llandaff triptych and *Mary Magdalene*. AH goes on to say that the Hogarth viewing cards had just been issued but there was nothing much to see except a drawing by DGR and sketches by EBJ. In Dec. 1858 the Hogarth Club was approaching its first proper show, which was then delayed for various reasons (see Cherry 1980, 238 n.27). On Christmas Day, DGR told FMB he had only *The House of St John* to send (which accords with AH's wording) but two days later he borrowed *To Caper Nimbly* from GPB, to convert it into a Borgia subject, which was on view by 3 Jan. 1859, with *House of St John* and a third work, which must have been his watercolour *Annunciation* (VS 69; TG 1984, 212), also borrowed back from GPB; in addition he was promising *David Rex*. By contrast, the following year's winter show opened on 1 Feb. 1860, when DGR showed a striking oil. Furthermore, AH's letter says DGR was just beginning the Llandaff triptych, which is true of Dec. 1858 as well as Dec. 1859. In Dec. 1859 he was not at work on *Mary Magdalene* because TEP cancelled or postponed this commission in June (see DW 306).

12 See Watkinson 1983; also GPB, 24 Mar. 1859, when DGR went to Zoo to draw fawn.

13 Stirling 1926, 164–5; Lang 1959, I, 19.

14 FMB, 27 Apr. 1856; GBJ, I, 105; see also Peters 1991, 194, 435–6.

15 *Works* 1911, 618.

16 Hudson 1972, 119.

17 Prinsep 1902, 282.

18 For FC, see Baum 1940, 4; ACS, 27 Nov. 1886, PUL; GPB, 15–16 Dec. 1858; Elzea 1980, 95. FMB Diary, Jan. 1858, records a visit to EBJ and DGR and 'Fanny their model' at Red Lion Square. If this was FC, she met DGR at an earlier date than I suggest. But FMB's grasp of proper

names was notoriously weak, and 'Fanny' was popular at this date. DGR was away from London for most of the period July 1857–May 1858, and evidence of FC in his art begins only at the end of 1858. In 1895 FC's stepson replied on her behalf to Samuel Bancroft, saying her maiden name was Cox, she had married Mr Hughes and when she first set up as a model had assumed 'an art-name' which was that of Hughes's mother. To the same correspondent FC fixed the date of her meeting DGR as 1859, about a year before she married Hughes; but *viva voce* she told Bancroft and CFM that it was at the time of the Crimea Victory celebration, which was 1856. The true year does seem to be 1858.

19 *Placatâ Venere* was retitled *Nuptial Sleep* in 1869; the text here comes from MS version under the original title, on the verso of which is a preliminary sketch for the figure of Hector in *Cassandra* (VS 127) conceived 1860–1. In *Works* 1911, WMR dated the sonnet's composition to 1869, but his own correspondence that year (Peattie 1990, 161, 162, 166) shows that it was a text he already knew (e.g., ' "chirped" I personally have always had a certain antipathy to ... I regard it as Leigh Huntish – or perhaps more rightly Browningish'). There is no way of ascertaining when it was first drafted but insofar as it is a graphic account of coition it seems plausible to ascribe it to 1859, alongside *On the French Liberation*, whose date is secure. It is possible that *Placatâ Venere* was written later, during DGR's marriage; but the title, which WMR thought even more indelicate than the sonnet itself, does not exactly suggest conjugal joys, while neither tenor nor imagery accord with the poems written in 1869–70. The emendations on the MS copy of *Placatâ Venere* suggest it was written out for inclusion in *Poems* 1870 and revised before the title-change.

20 See GPB, 87 n.7; in Prinsep 1892, Val Prinsep mentions his studio in Serle Street; VS 107, 112, 116, 64n; late in life FC claimed that the first picture she posed for was the *Beatrice Salutation* diptych, painted on the settle doors in June 1859, six months before she is first mentioned by GPB.

21 Hudson 1972, 28.

22 DW 353.

23 *Letters to Charles Eliot Norton*, 1905, I, 67; see also Ruskin 1856, IV, ch. 1 # 13.

24 *RRP*, 234; JR did offer to recommend *Love's Nocturn* and *A Portrait*, but DGR declined to allow this.

25 See 25 Oct. 1859, Whitehill 1932, 38; for JR, see BL RP 2917.

26 For *Bocca Baciata*, see VS 114, 283; *Peter Bell the Third*, XIV; Fitzwilliam MSS 'Three Songs'; *FLM*, I, 203.

27 *Athenaeum*, 1859, 618; *Times*, 10 May 1859.

28 See VS 114; GPB, 88 n. 16; Faxon 1989, 233 n.7, on survival of both oil versions, though only one

known to VS; see also TG 1997, 2; DGR to GPB, 16 Oct. 1859, UT.

29 GPB, 15 Oct. 1859, 22/28 Dec. 1859; see also DGR to GPB, 28 Feb. 1860, Ogden MSS, UCL.

30 Skelton 1895, 77.

31 DW 381; GPB, 20 Feb. 1860; Horner 1933, 16; Smetham and Davies 1892, 97.

32 For responses to *Bocca Baciata*, see VS 114; Marsh 1985, 158.

33 DW 319.

34 Faxon 1989, 148; DW 335; WHH, II, 143; TG 1997, 2.

CHAPTER 12: MARRIAGE

1 DW 323, 324, 325; Peattie 1990, 71.

2 ACS later wrote of DGR's difficulty in resolving the plot 'in the old days at Chatham Place' – see MS note dated 27 Nov. 1886, PUL. For WMR on link with *How They Met*, see *Works* 1911, 647.

3 DW 329.

4 Sharp 1882, 139.

5 *DGR Letters to WA*, 1897, 226.

6 DW 331, 333.

7 GBJ, I, 207–8.

8 GBJ, I, 220; for portraits, see VS 276 and 274; the latter is dated 'Nov. 1860' and when giving it to the sitter's daughter in 1872, DGR wrote: 'I well remember making it one pleasant [summer] (Can't be sure of the season) day at Hampstead, in a lodging we had there all the time I was married' (DW 1290). But no other evidence suggests that Spring Cottage was retained.

9 See Friends of Llandaff Cathedral Annual Report 43, 13; Aberdare Papers.

10 Stirling 1926, 274.

11 Bradley and Ousby 1987, 24.

12 *RRP*, 27.

13 DW 345.

14 See DGR to GPB, 12, and 16 Sep 1860, UCL; DW 343. The head for which Gambart offered £50 must be that with honeysuckles mentioned to GPB, though as Gambart did not take it, this cannot be ascertained. It would appear that the work remained with DGR, until being offered to TEP's estate at the end of 1861 as *Burd Alane* (VS 144) which has the head and shoulders of a female figure (for whom the model may have been Mrs Beyer) with a foreground parapet and background filled with honeysuckles (see *Burlington Magazine*, Dec. 1970). This confirms the comparison with *Bocca Baciata* made by DGR to GPB and though doubts have been expressed as to *Burd Alane*'s authenticity, the correspondence indicates that it is indeed by DGR. For Gillum, see Nikolaus Pevsner, 'Colonel Gillum and the Pre-Raphaelites', *Burlington Magazine*, Mar. 1953, 78–81; and Macleod 1996, 422. There is some confusion over Gillum's military rank, probably occasioned by the fact that his nephew, also

William Gillum, became a colonel whereas the artists' patron and associate was Major; see, for example, GPB, 12 Mar. 1860, when Major Gillum was among those attending a life class at the Hogarth Club.

15 Bradley and Ousby 1987, no 24.

16 See DGR to J. M. Boyce Wells, 2 Jan. 1861, with thanks to descendants of the Wells family. DGR's posthumous portrait drawing of Joanna Wells, dated 16 Jul. 1861, was destroyed in World War II.

17 VS 121; the subject is linked to *St Agnes of Intercession*.

18 DW 422.

19 DW 348, 352; see also Harrison, I, 124.

20 GBJ, I, 213; Horner 1933, 13; DW 363, 422.

21 Mackail 1899, I, 160; Friswell, 1898, 266–7.

22 GBJ, I, 217, 214; see also EBJ to Frances Horner, Fitzwilliam MSS.

23 DW 363.

24 See Whitworth 1986, 128.

25 DW 345.

26 DW 359, 363.

27 *Letters to WA*, 1911, 272.

28 Ellis 1923, 78; VS 125.

29 DW 335.

30 DW 364.

31 DW 360 (redated 8 Feb. 1861 by WEF.)

32 See Hudson 1972, 24 Feb. 1861; DW 364, which must therefore be redated 25 Feb. 1861.

33 DW 367, 368, 369, 370, 371, 372; also GBJ, I, 222.

34 DW 385.

35 DW 378.

36 Meredith 1970, I, 101.

37 DGR's correspondence with Macmillan is partly in Packer 1963, and partly in NYPL.

38 For Leathart, see correspondence in NAL; DW 387; for watercolour *Dr Johnson*, see DW 386, although this does not seem to be one of the three pictures DGR owed TEP's estate as mentioned in DW 393, none of which was far advanced, whereas *Dr Johnson* was finished by 11 July (DW 387). Whether any payment was made is unclear, but the work was among those auctioned at the TEP sale in March 1862, so it was perhaps accepted by the executors in lieu of another commission. For J. A. Rose, see GPB, 4 May 1861. That *Regina Cordium* went to Gambart is based on DGR to EH, 26 Dec. 1861, which in the context of the TEP estate refers to 'my little picture' sold to Gambart, thence to White and thence to John Miller. DW 428 states that Gambart offered to get *Regina Cordium* withdrawn from the TEP sale (presumably on the grounds that it depicted the recently-bereaved artist's wife); DGR preferred that John Miller do this, rather than Gambart. Annotating this letter, DW claimed that Miller was selling not buying the picture, but Miller's collection was not auctioned in spring 1862, whereas TEP's was; all this

remains unclear, unless Miller put work into the TEP sale.

39 DW 393, 389 (which cannot be 11 July as this was some time after TEP's death). TEP had bought prodigiously: 400 gs for FMB's *Work*, 350 gs for EBJ's *Blessed Damozel*, 1,000 gs for JEM's *Black Brunswicker*, 3,000–4,000 gs for WHH's *The Finding of the Saviour* from Gambart, 400 gs for Brett's *Warwick Castle* – see Macleod 1996, 184–5. WM suggested negotiation through MMF & Co. (see DW 388). Partly through the Firm, EBJ negotiated with Bodley to offer his *Adoration* to the TEP estate in place of the unpainted *Damozel*, and produce a new one for the Brighton church (see GBJ, I, 223–4). On 15 Aug. WMR called on Gambart on behalf of WBS, who was also owing.

40 See correspondence with Leathart, summer 1861, NAL; DW 393.

41 *RRP*, 288.

42 See Maas 1975, 141; Fitzwilliam MSS; VS 142.

43 Hudson 1972, 91; see also DW 396, 398.

44 DW 372; WBS to WMR, 17 Nov. 1861, DUL.

45 VS 129, 324; see also VS 323; *RRP*, 310; Sewter 1975, 421; WMG 1996, Stained Glass Exhibition no. 1.

46 DW 409, 408; Ellis 1923, 80.

CHAPTER 13: LOSS

1 See Mackail Notebooks, WMG; DW 422, 363.

2 WMG; V&A 1996, L1a (the original design shows four variant colours for the ground: green, brick, blue and dark grey) L3, and p. 206.

3 *Athenaeum*, 10 Oct. 1896.

4 Mackail 1899, I, 150–1.

5 See DGR to GPB, 23 Jan. 1859, UCL; Campfield also listed as assistant tutor at WMC in 1859, presumably taking DGR's class when necessary.

6 See Harvey and Press 1991, 43; VS 142; DW 387.

7 *RRP* p. 310

8 DW 422.

9 DW 412; VS 133–9.

10 V&A 1996, J.14; see also H.16–17. For 1862 exhibition and reviews, see Whitworth 1986, 86–99.

11 For DGR's stained glass designs, see Sewter 1975; for *St George*, see Wildman 1995, 60–4; V&A 1996, H.15 where, following Marillier, the commission is ascribed to Dunlop. But the MMF minute book reads: 'Agreed that the design for Hastings's window be allotted as follows – 2 windows in dining room "Prison scene, Richard I" and "Henry V and his queen crowned" to Marshall at £3 each. 4 other lights (History of St George) in dining room at £5 a piece. Centre light of the 5-light bay window of drawing room (Genius of house) Rossetti's old design. 4 other lights – the calendar. In 3 light window of drawing room – "Sculpture", "Painting" and

"Music".' Hastings also ordered four glass panels showing poets: David, Homer, Dante and Chaucer; when were these done? A second version of St George (now Birmingham Museums and Art Gallery) was commissioned in 1872 by Joseph Pease of Hulton Hall, Guisborough.

12 V&A 1996, 139.

13 See correspondence in NYPL. Macmillan suggested a 'quaint initial ... of a goblin grinning at a sweet woman's face'; though not carried out, this idea bears some resemblance to the eventual frontispiece. The fate of the unused *Birthday* design is not known; it was perhaps destroyed. At some date DGR made a sketch for CGR's *A Triad*, presumably with illustration in mind: see VS 184, where this is linked with her second volume, *The Prince's Progress*, published in 1866. But *A Triad* is not in this or any subsequent volume, only in *Goblin Market and Other Poems*.

14 DGR to C. J. Faulkner, 9 Dec. 1861, WMG.

15 *Spectator*, 18 Jan. 1862; *Fraser's Magazine*, Feb. 1862; *Athenaeum*, 22 Feb. 1862; see also DGR to EH, BL RP 382.

16 HRA 1954, 79; Belford 1990, 49.

17 For ACS, see Marsh 1989(b), 66; for *Laird o' Waristoun*, see VP 1978, 229ff.

18 GBJ, I, 237; inquest report by coroner William Payne, dated 12 Feb. 1862, reprinted in Hunt 1932, 329–33; see also Charles Ricketts in *Observer*, 14 Oct. 1928, and all other accounts of EES's death and inquest recorded in Marsh 1985 and Marsh 1989(b). ACS told his mother that 'the worst verdict of all' (presumably suicide) was avoided, as there had been 'no difficulty in proving that the balance of her mind was disturbed'. This does not appear in the inquest report, but may have been verbally mentioned by the coroner.

19 See Violet Hunt diary, 26 Dec. 1882, Cornell UL. But see also the tradition in the Hannay family, cited Grylls 1964, 202 n.69, that DGR blamed himself for the strength of the dose.

20 According to *Works* 1911, 663, the lines were written in 1848, but the MS with revisions now at UT dates from 1862/3.

21 OD, 310.

CHAPTER 14: TUDOR HOUSE

1 DW 424; FLM, I, 233; see also Dobbs 1977, 145. For Lucy Brown's recollection, see HRA 1954, 80, where speaker identified as Peter Paul Marshall.

2 Peattie 1990, 77; DW 428.

3 Prior to the sale, *Lancelot in the Queen's Chamber* was bought by Rose, who probably also helped negotiate over DGR's residual liability to the Plint estate, and *Hamlet and Ophelia* by Gillum. Leathart acquired *The Bower Garden*, probably at the sale. The two works shown at the

Royal Scottish Academy in summer 1862 were *Fair Rosamund* and *The Farmer's Daughter* (the last perhaps that now known as *Hanging the Mistletoe*, see *Antique Collector*, December 1972, front cover).

4 Hudson 1972, 127.

5 GPB, 21 Apr. 1862; see also Hudson 1972, 103.

6 DGR to GPB, UCL; Cline 1970, I, no. 16.

7 DW 420; Lang 1959, I, 34; for *Rubáiyát*, see *Times Lit. Supp.*, 10 Apr. 1959.

8 DW 456; for GPB visits, see 13 Nov. and 7 Dec. 1862.

9 For visit to Newcastle, see DGR to JL, 19 Jan. 1863, NAL; DGR to EH, 25 Jan. 1863, BL RP 382; DGR to WJK, UT; Peattie 1990, 84; VS 34 and 344; also Macleod 1996, 274–5, 440.

10 TW to DGR, 6 Dec. 1860, LC.

11 DW 397.

12 DW 415, 424.

13 Account based on DGR letters to Anne Gilchrist and his notes in *Life of Blake* as published. Anne Gilchrist did not welcome ACS's offers, distrusting both his morals and his sincerity (see Gilchrist 1887, 128 and 193).

14 DW 458 n. 3.

15 Macmillan 1908, 159.

16 See Erdman 1973, N21.

17 For GM, see Sencourt 1929, 133; *FLM*, I, 235–6; Lindsay 1956, 131–5; Pennell, 1911, 80.

18 For ACS, see Adams 1918, 139; BL Ashley 5753 f. 16; Lang 1959, IV, 240, where source is said to be J. H. Pollen; Trevelyan 1978, 193.

19 See Benson 1930, 272; GM to Maxse, 1862, Lindsay 1956, 131; DGR to AFS, 28 Dec. 1862, UT; Hudson 1972, 283.

20 See FMB to WHH, 13 Oct. 1862, in DHH 1969, 286–91; DW 453. The truth behind this so-called 'imbroglio' is hard to determine. If the claim about DGR is the same as 'that infernal lie' ACS heard in December 1859, then the tattle began circulating long before 1862. Amor 1989, 184–5, gives Annie Miller as the source. ACS was still denying it was him in 1865 (Lang 1959, I, 93).

21 DW 507.

22 DW 495.

23 WA Diary, 26 Jun. 1864.

24 Du Maurier 1951, 5.

25 To CAH, 23 Sep. 1865, UT; Pennell 1911, 100.

26 Ionides 1996, 10.

27 *Pall Mall Budget*, 15 Jan. 1891, 21; *Philological Quarterly*, 1969, 102ff. Alice Boyd was also present but not photographed. JR's boast was quoted by M. Bradford to M. A. Bell, 30 Jun. 1863. FC's recollection was related by Samuel Bancroft to Ellen Terry, 2 Feb. 1894, Delaware Art Museum.

28 VS 164; DW 1429.

29 See DW 508; *RP* pp. 31–8.

30 Lang 1959, I, 50.

31 DW 523.

32 GPB, 30 Apr. 1863, which could be the occasion

of Meredith's jesting at DGR's expense, for Leathart, Rose and Boyce were all buyers.

33 Ionides 1996, 54–5.

34 *FLM*, I, 251–4.

CHAPTER 15: POT-BOILERS AND PARIS

1 Trevelyan 1978, 193; DW 535.

2 WMR 1867, 259.

3 See Maas 1975, 166, 174.

4 19 May 1863, VS 168; however, it would appear that at this point, the work on offer was the oil head of Marie Ford subsequently converted into *The Beloved*: see VS 182.

5 DW 498; Maas facing p. 65.

6 For the photographed drawings, see Dodgson print collection, UT, and DGR to Dodgson, 21 Dec. 1863, NYU, on how 'the original' would be pleased with the photo of the Queen of Sheba. For 'Beatrice' and EH, see VS 168 and 182; also Ruskin CW, vol. 36, 457; on 23 Nov. 1863, JR called to make sure *Dante's Dream* had arrived safely. For *Mary Magdalene*, see Clabburn 1891, 14.

7 See DW 520; DGR to A. C. Ionides, 25 Jan. 1864, UT; GPB, 5 Feb. 1864; DW 527, 524.

8 Emily Seddon was sister to Tom and J. P. Seddon, and thus a very old acquaintance of DGR.

9 DGR wrote to Dunlop on 7 Aug. and 21 Sep. 1865; Dunlop also bought *First Madness of Ophelia* and a watercolour version of the *Annunciation* designed for Scarborough, which DGR made over to John Miller in respect of a debt and went, with Miller's permission, to Dunlop for 130 gs., see DW 538.

10 See Tokyo 1990, 26; VS 175 (s & d 1864); DW 529, 551, 552; J. A. Rose accounts in NYPL show that a cheque for £84 (80 gs) was cashed on 7 Sep. 1864; VS 170 (*Morning Music*); VS 174 (*Woman combing her Hair*, first owner shipowner John Bibby); VS 202 (*Aurora*, first owner F. W. Craven, delivery recorded June 1865, see DW 615); VS 180.

11 Trevelyan 1978, 203–4; DW 535.

12 Inquiry probably about *Greensleeves* (DW 517) which fetched £73 10s in the second Plint sale; and see Rose accounts in NYPL, though these do not seem to be complete.

13 Eight of eleven works bequeathed by Gillum to the BM came from DGR's studio sale.

14 Maas 1975, 174–5.

15 WEF 1982, xxiii.

16 Du Maurier 1951, 235.

17 DW 545; Macleod 1996, 454–5; DW 610; VS 167; also DGR to John Mitchell, 8 Jun. 1864, NSW.

18 WA Diary, 26 Jun. 1864; WMR in *AJ*, 1884, 167.

19 VS 173B; DW 553.

20 Baudelaire, 1964, 36.

21 See Smith 1996; and BN 1997, especially the

essays by Sylvie Aubenas, Xavier Demange and Philippe Comar.

22 See Lightbown 1978, II, nos. C11 and C12; both now believed to be workshop pieces; DGR letters to CFM c.1880, UT; *Works* 1911, 664.

23 *Athenaeum*, 21, Oct. 1865, 491.

24 DW 548.

25 DW 549; Packer 1965, 21.

26 See HRA 1949, 92.

27 Marillier 1899, 92.

28 DW 537, 547.

29 DW 563; for accounts of Paris in this era, see Maneglier 1990; also Friedrich 1992.

30 See Druick and Hoog 1983, 176; Pennell 1911, 91.

31 See Fantin-Latour to Legros, Nov. 1864, in Spencer 1991, 234.

32 DW 562; Spencer 1991, 234.

33 DW 562, 563; Spencer 1991, 234.

34 Druick and Hoog 1983, 99.

35 Spencer 1991, 234.

36 16 Nov. 1865, NMM.

37 Druick and Hoog 1983, 23.

38 '*J'ai voulu tout simplement puiser dans l'entière connaissance de la tradition le sentiment raisonné et indépendant de ma propre individualité*' – Gustave Courbet, in *PDL* 1900.

39 Spencer 1991, 234; Charles Baudelaire, 'Salon of 1845', reprinted in *Mirror of Art*, 1955, 29.

40 See letter to WBS, 2 Oct. 1864, PUL.

41 DW 562.

42 16/17 Nov. 1864, NMM.

43 For Manet's career at this date, see Cachin and Moffet 1983, 209.

44 Spencer 1991, 234.

45 *Athenaeum*, 21 Oct. 1865, 546.

CHAPTER 16: THE WORLD BEYOND

1 VS 182; FMB's correspondence with Rae is in NAL.

2 DGR's correspondence with the Raes is in NMM; the works listed are *The Tune of Seven Towers, Death of Breuse, The Blue Closet, Chapel before the Lists, Paolo and Francesca, The Damsel of the Sanct Grael* (all bought by WM 1856–7) plus *The Wedding of St George*, sold at the TEP sale in March 1862 and presumably bought by WM or MMF & Co., which handled the transaction with Rae; in addition, *Heart of the Night* was already owned by Rae. See also Dianne Macleod, 'The "identity" of PR Patrons', in Harding 1996; and Macleod 1996.

3 Lorimer 1978, 162. See also *RP*, p. 175.

4 See Jan Marsh, 'For the Wolf or for the Babe he is seeking to devour?' in Harding 1996; Adams 1918, 183.

5 DW 422.

6 *Athenaeum*, 21 Oct. 1865, 546.

7 See Rae to FGS, 11 Apr. 82. In turn the honour passed to the Tate Gallery, which eventually

acquired all the Raes' pictures. From their acquisitions, it would appear that the Raes were genuinely discerning and progressive in their tastes. When, later in 1866, DGR wrote that JMW's 'Japanese Lady' was for sale at the 'dirt cheap' price of 150 gs, Rae was sorely tempted. But economic recession coupled with the expense of furnishing yet another new house made him decline to indulge in further 'luxuries'. Of FMB's *The Coat of Many Colours* he wrote: 'In subdued splendour and subtlety of colour, in dramatic pose, in drawing and in composition, in short in everything that contributes to make a picture great I see absolutely nothing that could be amended, as far as my poor judgement gives me light. I trust and believe that it will be followed by a series of works equally great and I could also wish ... that you will not think anything worth painting except out of the Bible or Shakespeare: for I consider these are virtually virgin ground as regards art.'

8 See DW 668–73; Westwater 1984, 121. *The Beloved* was displayed at Cheyne Walk on 19–20 Feb. 1866 and at the Arundel Club 21–22 Feb. 1866. According to Westwater, citing the diary of Mrs Walter Bagehot, née Wilson, her sister visited DGR's studio on 20 Feb. with GFW; see also Barrington 1905, 2, where the year is erroneously given as 1868.

9 Harrison, I, 266; in *RP*, this letter is ascribed to Apr. 1865 but represents in my view CGR's response to DGR's first suggestions towards the *Prince's Progress* volume. The contents are not consistent with the discussion in March–April 1865, when selection was virtually complete; the address is not a mistake, Albany Street having been renumbered in Nov. 1864, but correct for earlier in that year, as is the black border, used in the weeks following Philip Polidori's death in Feb. 1864. No family death took place early in 1865 and CGR would not use mourning stationery without cause. Other correspondence with CGR at this date is from Harrison and *RP*.

10 See CGR *FL*; VS 601.

11 See Packer 1963, 33, and 34; and to Kate Faulkner, 27 Feb. 1865, WMG.

12 See Crump, 1979, I, 234; and CGR to unidentified correspondent 1888, PUL.

13 DW 1604.

14 Harrison I, 258.

15 *Athenaeum*, 18 Mar. 1865, 387; that DGR was responsible is indicated both by the wording and Harrison, I, 260.

16 Packer 1965, 42.

17 Harrison, I, 264, 269.

18 WA Diary, 9 Nov. 1866; DW 701; see also WEF 1991, no. 23.

19 Harrison, I, 253.

20 See Shonfield 1987, 112. This is similar to Violet Hunt's diary entry (see above, ch. 13, n.19) which may have derived from the same source.

21 GPB, 10 Feb. 1865.

22 FLM, I, 255.

23 WBS to AB, 3 Oct. 1865, WEF 1976, 92; for CGR's remarks on Davenports, see Harrison, I, 233.

24 DW 424; see also FLM, I, 408.

25 WEF 1976, 338.

26 VS 168.

27 DW 686.

28 VS 168.

29 Baldwin 1960, 99.

30 According to Philip Webb, DGR's was the casting vote – see PW letter, 21 May 1866, UT.

31 Holiday 1914, 76.

32 See Williamson 1909.

33 DW 611, 612, 613.

34 See Harrison, I, 322; Lang 1959, I, 72 n.1; Trevelyan 1978, 248–9.

35 See RP, pp 88–91; Ruskin CW, 38, 497 (yet in Oct. 1865 JR told CEN he had sat to DGR 'several times' so could this be 1866?).

36 For CAH, see Cline 1978.

CHAPTER 17: PROSPERITY

1 JM to S. C. Cockerell, 4 Apr. 1908, NAL; VS 370 is endorsed: 'one of the very best D. G. Rossetti ever did of me (about 1865) June 1: 1908'; see also DGR's letters to Rae in June 1865, where his model is described as 'a lady, wife of a friend of mine & the very Queen of Beauty'. The lady must be JM, but the proposed painting, referred to by Rae as 'the "Queen of Beauty" picture' is not identifiable with any extant work. Marillier 1899, 99, cites WMR as saying DGR relinquished this idea in favour of Palmifera. For JM's visit, see DW 504 (misdated, see V&A 1996 A14).

2 It is likely that DGR saw the Bernhardt photos in Paris.

3 See Speight 1962, 79.

4 VS 179; DW 615. DGR later explained his hostility to WHH in terms of the latter having disparaged his work to Craven, but WHH identified the culprit as TW: see WMR Diary 1880, 23 Sep. 20, 230.

5 DW 622, 627, 629, 634, 635.

6 DW 637.

7 VS 181; see DGR to Miller, 9 Oct. 1865, Fitzwilliam MSS; to Gambart 2 Nov. 1865, Berg.

8 DW 592.

9 Athenaeum 14, 21 Oct. 1865; see also 11 Nov. 65.

10 DW 651, 650; RP 109; Maas 1975, 186–8, notes the obscurity surrounding the facts of this rumour, which WMR could not dispel. It was later claimed that Gambart had sold the work to Agnews, for £500, and they in turn had sold on to Sam Mendel, the Manchester businessman whom DGR was told now owned it. As Maas notes, this is plausible, but Agnews have no record of such a deal in 1865. They bought the work in 1873,

however, perhaps from Mendel, and resold it to W. Graham for £1,150. It seems most likely that Gambart did originally sell to Mendel, for around £500, and that this was misreported to DGR by CAH, who claimed to have been told by someone who had heard the report at Gambart's – see Maas, 187–8.

11 See Cline 1978, 16; Dobbs 1977, 152–3; Bennett 1988, LL 3628.

12 RP 78; for more on Wilding, see VS 530; Pedrick 1964, 167; GPB, 3 Aug. 1866, 15 Aug 1867.

13 DW 674; Whistler 1878.

14 Casteras 1995, 49, 133; RP 108.

15 DW 653.

16 Casteras 1995, 82–3.

17 DW 654, 653.

18 Smetham and Davies 1892, 302.

19 Bod. MS. don.e.75.

20 GPB, 21 May 1866.

21 See Lang 1959, I, 89a, 91, 92, 93, 94, 109.

22 Athenaeum, 5 May 1866.

23 Letters to WA, 1911, 130; Works 1911, 241. DGR is also quoted as admiring Leighton's sense of duty but not his manners – see Carr 1908, 67. When in 1883 hasty hanging at the RA aroused spiteful gossip, Leighton angrily rejected the imputation that the exhibition to which he had devoted much care was a deliberate attempt to 'stab poor Rossetti in the back' – see Ormond 1975, 104. The charge came from Hueffer in The Times, perhaps prompted by FMB. WMR acquitted Leighton of any such motive.

24 Maas 1975, 198; for DGR's response to invitation, see letter to FGS, 7 May 1866, Bod. MS; Maas 1975, 190.

25 DW 682; for sketch, see VP 1982, no. 9 and WEF 1991, no. 67.

26 DW 690, 693.

27 DW 695.

28 DW 1406; DGR alerted Ralph Wornum, Keeper of the National Gallery, who 'for once admitted authenticity without hesitation' and secured the picture for the 1867 International Exhibition. Holbein's portrait of Lady Guilford is now in the Art Museum, St Louis, Miss.; the companion portrait belongs to the Royal Collection.

29 Fennell 1978, nos. 4 and 1, where payment in three instalments originally agreed; DGR to JS, 1 Aug. 1866, Casteras 1995, 156; HTD recalled an excursion with CAH and GPB to Ruskin's home in Denmark Hill, where white roses bloomed in profusion, which cannot have taken place before June 1867, although this is not mentioned in GPB.

30 WA Diary, 4 Sep. 1866; for Lady Lilith see VS 205; TG 1997, 6.

31 DW 992.

32 DW 686.

33 CGR 1892, 129.

34 Correspondence on both incidents, involving firstly Legros and then Seymour Haden, is in the database of the Whistler Study Centre, GUL. The

second assault, in April 1867 in Paris, was occasioned by the sudden death and hurried burial of Haden's colleague Dr Traer, whom DGR had met and liked in London. DGR and WMR jointly remonstrated with the Burlington Secretary in June 1867 and resigned in January 1868.

35 VS 195, 201; RP, p. 224, where 'the little oil-picture sold to Leyland, The Christmas Carol ... is now finished'; but see also GPB, 10 Feb. 1867, which seems to say that GPB was offered first refusal but FC claimed it as hers, and GPB, 10 Mar. 1867, where it was still in hand; this is not very easy to reconcile with WMR's statement that it was finished and sold to FRL by February. VS 195 does not list FRL among the owners, but states that by 1872 it was owned by Murray Marks. FRL did not part with his DGR works, so it would seem that DGR either substituted The Loving Cup or altered its title.

36 DW 710; see also DW 729. For price, see £325 in WMR 1889, 56, £235 in VS 62 R1. DGR recieved £65 on 15 Feb. 1867 and £50 on 25 Feb. 1867, so it would seem the agreed price was 300 gs in instalments. Craven was presumably shown the preliminary studies amongst many other items in DGR's portfolio.

37 See RP, 228, described by WMR as an 'old design of a woman having her hair combed out upwards; VS 170 R1 where it was said to have belonged to 'Prange' before Dunlop; this year DGR hoped to sell to Agnew, but was obliged to stay with Gambart: see DW 724.

38 Rothenstein 1965, 10–11; Pedrick 1964, 173. In 1873 DGR wrote of Knewstub having started the third of three watercolour replicas of The Loving Cup, VS 201 (DW 1305), which suggests he continued to give Knewstub work, since the oil Loving Cup was produced in 1867, the date also borne by one of the three replicas, attributed to HTD.

39 See correspondence with CFM, UT; Cline 1978, 27; Elzea 1980, no. 17, where CFM unsure by whom the replica had been begun. HTD first worked for DGR in mid-1867.

40 HTD said he first met DGR in June 1863, but this must be an error; his presence is first noted by WMR on 22 May 1867, as being employed to copy Beata Beatrix; WMR had met HTD previously at CAH's (see RP, p. 233). Cline 1978, 47, suggests that by August 1867 HTD had been at work for a few weeks; also Pedrick 1964, 46 and 53 (where, according to HTD, his first task was The Loving Cup, which is contradicted by WMR's Diary). CAH did not purloin VS 329, as HTD alleged, for it was sent by DGR to an artist's benefit sale in Manchester in 1871.

41 See Cline 1978, 47; nevertheless, in the autumn he asked after a boy that Henry Wallis had discovered in Devon. 'If you would like to see him I will send him up; his journey would cost about 15s,' wrote Wallis (6 Nov. 1867, UT), adding that the

lad had natural quickness but might not prove a Giotto.

42 DW 723, 724; RP, p. 172.

43 RP, nos. 148, 149 (misdated – should be 30 Jun. 1867).

44 JL quoted by Dianne Macleod in Watson 1997, 113.

CHAPTER 18: LA PIA

1 See DHH, 246–9.

2 WA Diary, 26 Nov. 1867; 2 Jul. 1867; Cline 40.

3 See Lamont 1912, 195; WMR Diary 1880, 1 March.

4 HRA 1949, 171. Letters from Marie's father to DGR in 1870–1 allude to earlier prospects of her marriage. Ionides 1927 quotes Marie, aged eighty-four, recalling her meeting with DGR, when she asked him to take her as a pupil; though this source says he did so, in fact DGR must have referred her to FMB.

5 RP, p. 223; Pedrick 1964, 87–8.

6 DW 727; Pedrick 1964, 107–8.

7 WA Diary, 15 Oct. 1867.

8 WA Diary, 30 Jul. 1866.

9 See Dunn 1984, 29; Cline 1978, 137; OD, 362. For DGR's diet, see RP, no. 120.

10 WA Diary, 11–20 Sep. 1867.

11 DW 743.

12 For DGR's relation with Matthews, see RP, nos. 166, 171, 172, 173, 174; and Macleod 1996; Matthews called at Chelsea, to seal the breach in earnest. But no new commission was discussed and when Halliday called later, he spoke of the brewer having 'no really convenient space' for a large picture, which confirmed DGR's view that an important sale would never result. Cline 1978, 56, implies however that DGR went to Essex on Saturday 7 Mar. 1868; see also RP, p. 281.

13 See RP, p. 296; Cline 1978, 56.

14 Bryson 1976, 1.

15 WEF 1976, 103.

16 See RP, pp. 298, 304; and DGR to Emily Tebbs, 20 Apr. 1868, UT.

17 VS 207; BL Ashley 1410.

18 James 1920, 18–19.

19 See Morris 1973, I, 44.

20 BM 1939-5-13-1(5); VS 609 where placed after 1871. But the signature, 'D. Gabriel R.' accords with that used by DGR in his letters to JM of 1868 only (see Bryson 1976, 3 and 4) while the titles humorously bestowed on WM are those apparently alluded to in Bryson 4 (7 May 1868) where DGR sends a message to 'the Bard and PJ (I will not indulge him with his favourite title in full)'. If this is correct, Bryson has misread 'PT' as 'PJ'.

21 Pennell 1911, 84; in DW 682.

22 Morris 1973, I, 76.

23 ACS essay, with WMR 1868.

24 Bryson 1976, 2; VS 213. On 20 Aug. 1868 DGR sent a message to JM saying he hoped she would soon be able to sit again, 'as I want awfully to begin Graham's big picture where she is to sit for Beatrice' (Cline 1978, 79). On 15 Sep., WMR recorded that DGR was painting at the blue drapery of a half-figure of Mrs Morris commissioned by Graham for £500 (RP, p. 328) which would seem to be the same picture. There is no record of another Beatrice being begun in 1868/9 and it appears the picture was renamed Mariana.

25 HRA 1954, 63; and see Cachin and Moffet 1983, 521.

26 See Cline 1978, 77, 79, 80; RP, p. 323.

27 DW 784.

28 See Cline 1978, 136.

29 Lago 1982, 49.

30 See Cline 1978, 83; Elzea 1980, no. 23.

31 See RP, p. 301; DW 767.

32 DW 786; also Cline 1978, 85.

33 Cline 1978, 85.

34 DW 788.

35 In the two House of Life sonnets that form Newborn Death. They were not written at Penkill but in London on 19 Dec. 1868 – see RP, p. 339. Likewise, The Love-letter though dating from 1870 is apt to 1868. For this period, see also WEF 1976, 105.

36 DW 790.

37 Cline 1978, 87.

38 See WEF 1976, 104; DW 794; FLM, I, 269; RP, p. 330.

39 For these episodes, see WEF 1971, 101.

40 DW 795, 796.

41 See WEF 1971, 101–2.

42 WEF 1976, 105.

43 ACS, 'Notes upon designs of the Old Masters at Florence', Fortnightly Review, July 1868, 39.

44 RP, pp. 204, 205.

45 Originally called 'Flammifera', Love's Redemption was retitled Love's Testament with amendments made after the Fleshly attack (see Sharp 1882, 413) to alter the motif of Christian eucharist to an indeterminate, pagan, ceremony. Original octave:

O thou who art Love's hour ecstatically
　Unto my lips dost evermore present
　The body and blood of Love in sacrament;
Whom I have neared and felt thy breath to be
The inmost incense of his sanctuary;
　Who without speech hast owned him, and intent
　Upon his will, thy life with mine hast blent,
And murmured o'er the cup, Remember me!

In the original arrangement, these sonnets were placed with others treating of love in the second half of the House of Life. In the version published in 1870 they moved up, so that the most carnal sequence comes first.

CHAPTER 19: LIFE-IN-LOVE

1 Fitzgerald 1975, 150; du Maurier 1951, 20; GBJ, I, 309.

2 Fitzgerald 1975, 127; DW 809, 810.

3 Bryson 1976, 3.

4 See NAL, MS. 86 SS 57.

5 DGR to JL, 28 May 1869, NAL.

6 Fitzgerald 1975, 122.

7 Kelvin, I, 77 (possibly in relation to same occasion as Kelvin, 78).

8 DW 826; Bryson 1976, 15.

9 RP, p. 336.

10 RP, p. 339; DW 801, where DGR acknowledged that the second sonnet seemed 'rather far-fetched and obscure', which would fit the address in Newborn Death to Life, 'the lady of all bliss', and the references to Love, Song and Art, who 'o'er the book of Nature mixed their breath / With neck-twined arms, as oft we watched them there.'

11 DW 826; ACS 1868, 17.

12 DW 792; Smetham's article was in London Quarterly Review.

13 Works 1911, 658.

14 RP, p. 393; DW 835.

15 DW 813.

16 RP, p. 393.

17 Sharp 1882, 410.

18 See J. H. Gardner's defence of DGR's poetic method in VP 1982, detailing the struggle to realise ideas in Newborn Death II.

19 DW 781, 842; Kelvin, I, 74; RP records the presence of WMR, FLR and MFR at St James's Hall but not DGR or CGR (who was not allowed out in the evenings).

20 DW 781, 835.

21 To JL, NAL.

22 DGR to RB, 19 Mar. 1869, Mills College; RB's reply RP, no. 222.

23 DW 801.

24 VS 611; NAL MSS 86 SS 57. See Jan Marsh, 'Rupes Topseia: a New Suggestion', William Morris Society Journal, 1998, 4–6. Rupes Topseia has previously been ascribed to c.1874 and the dissolution of MMF & Co. (see VS; V&A 1996, D6; MacCarthy 1995, 343) but the key figure of WT in the drawing has not been identified, nor its connection with his 'funny cartoon' reference. It gently mocks WT's hysterical allegations.

25 James 1974, I, 120; it is not known exactly when this visit took place: either March or early May; the portrait however was hanging at Queen Square on 9 Mar. 1869 when Henry James visited the Morrises – see James 1974, I, 92.

26 See WEF 1971, 102; JM to Sarah Norton, 13 Jul. 1869, Harvard.

27 OD, 401.

28 Bryson 1976, 5; see also GBJ, I, 297.

29 Bryson 1976, 10.

30 For DGR's letters to JM in Bad Ems, see Bryson 1976.

31 Kelvin, I, 82.

32 Bryson 1976, 5, 11.

33 Bryson 1976, 5, 8, 10.

34 Bryson 1976, 12; 1869 Proofs.

35 DW 803 (which must date from before 21 Dec. 1868, as it refers to *Ring and Book* and bill due on 21st Dec.); DW 847.

36 DW 851.

37 See Peattie 1990 and DW for long discussions of poetic texts.

38 Bryson 1976, 12.

39 OD 508; Bryson 1976, 12. *The Stream's Secret* was completed and largely written in Feb–Mar. 1870, but its inspiration was Penkill.

40 ACS 1868, 18.

41 WBS 1892, II, 111–12; WEF 1976, 106; Bryson 1976 13; see also *RP*, p. 407.

42 ACS 1868, 20.

43 DW 874.

44 *RP*, p. 408.

45 DW 871.

46 PRO, HO 46/042/7828 (letter dated 3 Sep. received 14 Sep. 1869); Troxell 1937, 119; PRO, HO 85/24, f.322 (signed 16 Sep., dispatched 17 Sep. 1869); see also DW 867, 872, 873. Though registered in HO archives, DGR's original letter to HAB does not survive there; said to be 'missing', it was presumably returned to HAB as a personal communication. DGR's letters of 16 Sep. 1869 introducing CAH to HAB seem to have been rendered redundant by HAB's action the same day.

47 DW 877, 883; see also VS 524 and letter to Tebbs, 9 Oct. 1869, UT.

48 WEF 1976, 105; *RP*, no. 253.

49 DW 883; for WMR's reply, see Peattie 1990, 169.

50 DW 892, with n.1; see also DW 893.

51 DW 886.

52 *RP*, p. 415; among the lines added to *A Last Confession* were the 50 Italian verses.

53 McGann 1999, 78–9.

54 DW 892.

CHAPTER 20: POEMS AND REVIEWS

1 See John Carter, *Times Lit. Supp.*, 17 Nov. 1972, 1040.

2 DW 928.

3 See Peattie 1990, 162; DW 861.

4 DW 929.

5 See DW 902.

6 DW 910 n. 1, 928, 929, 934, 936.

7 For *John of Tours* and *My Father's Close*, see Elzea 1980, 161. According to CFM, DGR's original title for the former was 'John of Harth'; DW 904.

8 DW 926, 923.

9 See *RP*, p. 417; DW 902.

10 DW 910, 941, 929.

11 DW 956.

12 DW 958, 959.

13 JM to Susan Norton, Dec. 1869, Harvard.

14 Bryson 1976, 13, 17.

15 DW 989, 911, 982.

16 James 1974, I, 116; Bryson 1976, 117.

17 Quoted Fitzgerald 1975, 125; Bryson 1976, 18. Four drawings of MZ by DGR exist, all dating from this period. Their exact history is partly obscure. One is known to have been still in DGR's studio in 1872 (DW 1239); one was given to MZ's mother (probably VS 541: see Fitzgerald 1975, 288); one was sent in 1878 from EBJ to MZ's mother, then in Corfu (Fitzgerald 1975, 288). Later, one was owned by Mrs Cassavetti's brother or nephew C. A. Ionides (VS 540) and two passed to the sitter's cousin, A. Cassavetti (VS 541 and 542).

18 Stillman 1901, 81.

19 DW 947; Michael Spartali urged DGR in Feb. and Mar. 1871 to persuade Marie against the marriage, though the engagement had been announced in Apr. 1870; see also DW 1067.

20 DW 946, 981, 997.

21 *RP*, no. 302.

22 My thanks to Pam Hirsch for information on the Scalands estate. Fir Bank, which belonged to Barbara Bodichon's brother Ben Leigh Smith, had been the usual summer residence of their aunt. JM arrived between 11 Apr. (when DGR wrote to CEN) and 14 Apr. (when DGR sent her kind remembrances to Barbara). DGR told WBS she was staying 'in another house, lent by Barbara's brother' (Weintraub 1978, 172). Morris 1973, I, 149, says JM was at 'Firbank, Robertsbridge, Mme Bodichon's house, where Rossetti was painting at the time', but DGR was not himself at Fir Bank. JM left with WM and DGR on 9 May (DW 1017, 1022).

23 DW 989.

24 DW 981, 1009, 1015.

25 See JM to WSB, 4 Jan. 1909, Faulkner 1981, 130; what appear to be surviving letters were entrusted to the safe-keeping of WSB, 12 Nov. 1892, and repossessed 14 Jan. 1909. In 1882, after DGR's death, JM panicked when she heard that letters of a revealing nature addressed to DGR were being offered for sale by FC, although this turned out to be a false alarm.

26 BL Ashley 1400.

27 Stillman, 1901, 81–2; *Works* 1911, 636.

28 Skelton 1895, 87; see also *Fraser's*, Feb. 1869.

29 DW 919, 905, 957.

30 Harrison, I, 158.

31 DW 919; one surviving letter from DGR to Dilke belies this, however, since it is a courteous regret at being unable to accept Dilke's invitation to breakfast, to meet Whitley Stokes. The excuse is contrived, but does continue with a warm offer to show Dilke and Stokes his latest picture (BL Add. 43909, f.267, bearing the pencilled date 1 Jun. 1872, which can hardly be correct). It is possible

that DGR believed he had incurred Dilke's displeasure by declining to vote in parliamentary elections: Chelsea was a key seat in the Liberal vs. Conservative contest and on at least one occasion the candidate solicited his vote; see Hepworth Dixon to DGR ('Dear Sir'), 29 Jun. 1868, UT.

32 For RWB, see Jay 1903; also Buchanan 1868, 291; ACS 1872; Cassidy 1952, 65ff.

33 *Athenaeum*, 4 Aug. 1866, 137–8; *Spectator*, 15 Sep. 1870; Peattie 1990, 95, 108; *FLM*, I, 295; *Athenaeum*, 29 Jan. 1870, 154. The detailed sequence is not quite clear: on 7 Oct. 1866 (Peattie 1990, 108), WMR suggested other names as author of the *Spectator* verses. Nor does he seem to have known that RWB was author of the *Athenaeum* review of ACS. So his sneer may not have been prompted by his ascription of *Spectator* verses to RWB, as claimed in *FLM*, I, 295, but simply by his already-existing 'abhorrence' for RWB, based on the 'much more than commensurate laudation' that RWB's poems had received (*FLM*, I, 295). However, WMR's over-reaction to the doggerel may indicate that he did indeed believe RWB was the author.

34 DW 921, 927, 923.

35 See DW 828, 829; and AFS, 10 May 1869, UT.

36 See DW 995, 982, 984, 993.

37 See DW 986, 984; Kelvin, I, 112, 111.

38 See MacCarthy, 1995, 100 (from Mackail 1899).

39 *Athenaeum*, 30 Apr. 1870, 573–4.

40 *Fraser's*, May 1870, 609 ff.

41 *Academy*, 14 May 1870, 199–20.

42 DW 1027, 1018, 1009.

43 *Fortnightly Review*, 30 Apr 1870, 551–79.

44 DW 1018, 1014.

45 Browning Letters, 137.

46 Pater 1889, 228.

CHAPTER 21: PAINTER AND POET

1 *RP*, no. 225, p. 339; DW 890.

2 DW 992.

3 DW 992; *Fortnightly Review*, May 1870, 577.

4 *Works* 1911, 651.

5 *Works* 1911, 620.

6 DW 1153; *Works* 1911, 651.

7 *Works* 1911, 655.

8 OD 378; *Works* 1911, 638.

9 DW 1060, 1085.

10 DW 1060, 1085; Wright 1919, 241.

11 DW 1297.

12 DW 1082. Another would-be bard who sent his poems was called J. Hedderly, for DGR's reply to whom see *N&Q* 5ep. 1991, 322.

13 DGR to FSE, 26 Feb. 1871, Northwestern Univ.

14 DW 1030, 881; retitled *Valdarno, or the Ordeal of Art Worship*, *Vates* was currently being reissued in serial form. Other letters to TGH are DW 1023, 1094, 1106; see also DGR on TGH's poems in *Works* 1911, 630.

15 See WMR, 11 May 1870, Bornand 1977, 7; DW 1004, 1024, 1008.

16 DW 1025; ACS to TWD, 1875, Lang 1959, II, no. 592.

17 Hudson 1972, 282–3; Bornand 1977, 17–18.

18 DW 1095; Peattie 1990, 192 n.5, 194; Bornand 1977, 20; DW 1064.

19 GFW portrait (now NMM) was done by end Jul. 1870 (see Bornand 1977, 20) but not finished to the satisfaction of either artist or sitter. Further projected sittings never took place, and eventually the portrait was given to FC.

20 WG to DGR, 15/17 Mar. 1869, UBC; see DW 1099; Bornand 1977, 40–1 where these works are listed as near completion in Jan. 1871. While DGR was at Scalands, CFM was engaged to lay in certain figures (and ordered supplies at Roberson's, to DGR's account) but it is not clear which works were involved.

21 DW 1066.

22 *Times*, 11 May 1928, 17; VS 81 R1.

23 DW 1065.

24 *Blackwood's*, Aug. 1870, 178.

25 DW 1068, 1075.

26 DGR to EBJ, n.d., UT.

27 DW 1067; see also VS 378–82.

28 DW 1082.

29 DW 1098.

30 VS 224.

31 DW 1099.

32 See DW 1121; Bornand 1977, 59, 61, 72, 118; DW 1118 where frame and 'last glazings' only remain to be done.

33 'Impressive as *Dante's Dream* may be, it is not to be classed on all grounds with Rossetti's finest work,' observed Marillier. 'Yet it has been the object of boundless admiration. It has even been said that if no other of Rossetti's works survived but this and the *Beata Beatrix*, they alone would be enough to insure him a place among the few great artists of the world.' (Marillier 1904, 115); see also Faxon 1989, 205; Grieve 1978, 27; Anderson 1994, 36.

34 DW 1104, 1116.

35 EBJ to George Howard, quoted MacCarthy 1995, 276–7, where CAH not WM must be the substance of this 'skirmish'.

36 Harrison, I, 452, with n.1.

37 VS 378–9, 381, 382, 383 (s & d 29 Nov. 1870); as JM spent Nov. 1870 with WM's mother and sister in Torquay, it may be that she came briefly to London, or that DGR made an otherwise undocumented visit to see her.

38 DW 1156; Mackail 1899, I, 225.

39 See DW 1131, 1133, 1140, 1156, 1185.

40 DW 1133, 1130.

41 The gossip came from Violet Hunt, who lived with FMB's grandson Ford Hueffer and in the 1930s claimed to have been told that either or both the Morris daughters were fathered by DGR. 'Mrs Dannreuther told me everybody knew it,

and this was the reason Morris went to Iceland,' she wrote, crediting another, unnamed, informant with the remark about rye furrows; see MSS by VH, sold at Christie's, 6 Nov. 1995, lot 11A. For GBJ's remark, see Preston 1953, 520.

42 Morris 1973, I, 220–9.

43 See DW 1152; Bryson 1976, 23; Elzea 1980, 25 and 112.

44 DW 1133; for fat toads, see Miller 1920, 141.

45 *Westminster Review*, Nov. 1868, 310.

46 See Wahl 1954; McGann 1999, 106.

47 DW 1152.

CHAPTER 22: CATASTROPHE

1 DW 1139.

2 Morris 1973, I, 230–1.

3 DW 1153.

4 Rooksby 1997, 176.

5 DW 1148, 1154, 1155.

6 John Brandon Jones, 'The Importance of Philip Webb', *William Morris and Kelmscott*, 1981, 92.

7 WMR 1886, I, 438; WMR Diary, 30 Oct. 1871; Bornand 1977, 121.

8 See DW 1143, 1171, 1172; Miller 1920, 140.

9 DW 1165, 1170; additional source is the tale of Fair Geraldine and the Earl of Surrey, which Lucy Madox Brown was currently using as a source for her painting *The Magic Mirror*.

10 Dunn, 1904, 62–3.

11 Woodring 1952, 205.

12 DW 1169; see also DW 1167, 1168, 1171; Bornand 1977, 121.

13 DW 1174, 1185.

14 Miller 1920, 138–41. Miller gave 28 September as the date of this memorable dinner-party; 1871 was the year of his visit to Britain, but DGR was not in London on 28 Sep. 1871. Although writing fifty years after the event, Miller's source is said to be his diary.

15 Colvin 1921, 62.

16 DW 1185.

17 WEF, 1971, 104; VS 393; Bornand 1977, 159; DGR's testimonial is dated 29 Apr. 1872, UT.

18 See DW 1185, 1187; Bornand 1977, 121; DGR to FGS, Bod.MSS.

19 See Bornand 1977, 122; OD 511 (though this cannot have been 'in the early days of the Brotherhood' when JEM had no such influence).

20 Fennell 1978, 36, 37; VS 228; TG 1997, 73.

21 'the marriage of the voices of nature and the soul – the dawn of a mystic creation.'

22 DW 1155.

23 Prinsep 1892, 250.

24 All quotations here from Buchanan 1871.

25 DW 1177.

26 DW 1178, 1180 (by mid-October, RWB was positively identified as the author by various

people, including James Knowles, editor of *Contemporary Review*); for a detailed narrative of events, see Murray 1982–3, 207–9.

27 *FLM*, I, 298.

28 Jay 1903, 162.

29 *Athenaeum*, 16 Dec. 1871, 792–4.

30 Peattie 1990, 224, 219.

31 DW 1205; *Saturday Review*, 24 Feb. 1872.

32 'Tennyson's Charm', *Saint Paul's*, Mar. 1872, item by 'Walter Hutcheson' (another pseudonym). *Saint Paul's*, Apr. 1872, both cited Murray 1982–3, 188–90; Bornand 1977, 193.

33 *Echo*, 18 May 1872, reprinted Murray 1982–3, 205–7. Joseph Knight told DGR he suspected RWB had written this review of his own pamphlet, but not all commentators have agreed. The style and tone of the *Echo* article have little in common so I am not persuaded, though DGR may have been.

34 See DGR to Knight, probably 27 May 1872, quoted Knight 1887, 141–2.

35 *Saturday Review*, 1 Jun. 72 (DGR saw the item on 30 or 31 May, as customarily weekend papers appeared on the Thursday evening or Friday before the masthead date).

36 For breakdown, see WEF 1971, *FLM*, I, 303–16; Weintraub 1978, 186–7.

37 See Grylls 1964, 149; FMB's letter to WBS 6 Jun. 1872 (mentioning DGR's wish to solicit a supportive letter from RB) and WBS to AB 8 Jun. 1872 (describing DGR's hostility to RB) may indicate that the reading of *Fifine* took place on 6 or 7 June.

38 DW 1212.

39 For GGH's and all other letters relating to DGR's time in Scotland, see WEF 1971.

40 Lago 1982, 46.

CHAPTER 23: RECOVERY

1 For these events, see sources cited in WEF 1971.

2 See Murray, 1982–3, 200–2; Rooksby 1997, 197–8; WBS to WMR, said to be dated 4 Jul. 1872, but not extant (see Lang 1959, I, xlv, and Murray 1982–3, 202 n.80). Murray believed that ACS's pamphlet 'Under the Microscope' was sent to DGR at the beginning of July. But no evidence exists and this is exactly what WMR, FMB, WBS, TGH and others aimed to prevent from causing further derangement.

3 Pedrick 1964, 116–17.

4 Cline 1978, 132; FRL also offered to purchase the china (see FMB to FRL, 2 Jul. 1872, LC MSS) but it is not clear whether DGR was informed of this.

5 See DGR to FMB, 6 Jul. 1872, HRA 1949, 222; DGR to FC, 11 Sep. 1872, Baum 1940, 38.

6 See WBS to FMB, 9 Jul. 1872, NAL.

7 JM to WMR, 15 Aug. 1872, Grylls 1964, 155.

8 JMW to WMR, 2 Sept. 1872, GUL.

9 See Marsh 1986, 107.

10 *FLM*, I, 307.

11 BL Ashley 1410/2.
12 See e.g. works by Gordon Claridge, including Claridge, Pryor and Watkins, *Sounds from the Bell-Jar*, 1990.
13 BL Ashley 1410/2.
14 DW 1650.
15 DW 1232. Without DGR's knowledge, John Graham had sent his half-length *Pandora* to the Glasgow Institute of Fine Arts Exhibition, 1872.
16 DW 1238, 1239.
17 DW 1248.
18 Peattie 1990, 233.
19 Kelvin, II, 32.
20 BL Add. 45342.
21 Kelvin, I, 173; for WM on WMR, see Mackail Notebook, I, f.100, WMG, anecdote supplied by William de Morgan.
22 Kelvin, I, 180.
23 VS 233A; TG 1997, 46, says in 1871 this was intended as an image of Eve, with apple, and DGR referred to a narrow upright drawing with apple in Cline 1978, 146, which is clearly the same picture.
24 VS 233.
25 TG 1997, 46; Cline 1978, 191; OD 549; and see below. DGR is said to have made, or begun, eight versions of *Proserpine*, of which only three finished works are now known (the third is a very late version, done 1881–2 for Valpy and now in Birmingham Museum and Art Gallery); the others are said to have been cut down, or overpainted, or lost.
26 DW 1295.
27 Correspondence with CAH is in Cline 1978.
28 Cline 1978, 149; however, this backer may have been a figment, as CAH claimed not to know his name, and blamed him for fomenting a dispute over a *Proserpine* DGR sent for sale that led to the end of Parsons' involvement (see *FLM*, I, 325). The cynical may suspect that CAH was playing both sides off against the middle and Parsons was one of the losers.
29 *FLM*, I, 324.
30 DW 1265.
31 DW 1280, 1307, 1325.
32 See DW 1314 n.1.
33 VS 227; another (unlocated) canvas was called 'Vanna Primavera' after Cavalcanti's mistress in Cline 1978, 193. A few weeks later, before the canvas went to CAH, a garland of primroses was added.
34 DW 1298.

CHAPTER 24: RESPITE

1 DW 1264, 1265, 1270.
2 DW 1281, 1292, 1298, 1301.
3 For all correspondence with CAH, see Cline 1978.
4 DW 1299. It would seem the pot was not purloined from Tudor House but removed for safe-keeping; DGR promised to return it to FC in due course, even though he had not formally made it her property.
5 DW 1282, 1297.
6 DW 1291.
7 DW 1311.
8 VS 254.
9 DW 1297.
10 She was model for the head in 'Leyland's picture' (Cline 1978, 205) which is not named but must, by elimination, be the 1867 *Loving Cup*, currently in DGR's possession and shortly returned to FRL. Stephen Wildman (Tokyo 1990, 76) suggests she also sat for a 'statuesque nude study' for *Madonna Pietra*, to which a generalised head of JM is added. Other possible studies include the nude *Loving Cup* in red chalks with head in reverse action (Tokyo 1990, 47) and unidentified female portraits dated 1873 such as VS 564 and 565, which have similar red hair to the *Loving Cup* study, that in VS 565 being somewhat like that of *Ligeia Siren*. See also DW 1313; Macleod 1982.
11 VS 232.
12 GPB, 16 Apr. 1873.
13 Peattie 1990, 237.
14 Harrison, I, 530.
15 DW 1403.
16 Quoted in Field 1920, 77.
17 *Athenaeum*, 10 Oct. 1896; the date of this encounter between WM and TWD is not precisely known; it may have taken place at Easter 1873, during TWD's short first visit to Kelmscott, rather than his longer visit in June.
18 Harrison, I, 527; DW 1372.
19 DW 1367, 1344.
20 Morris 1973, I, 230–1.
21 DW 1388, 1400.
22 DW 1381; see also DGR to AFS, 4 Sep. 1873, UT.
23 Reported by CAH in Cline 1978, 311.
24 Reported by CAH in Cline 1978, 257.
25 VS 232; DW 1415 (WG was at Strathallan Castle, near Crieff).
26 For negotations with FRL, see Fennell 1978.
27 *Proserpine 1*, the Parsons' version (VS 233), returned to Kelmscott with HTD on 4 March (Cline 1978, 348) and after being rejected by Murray Marks (Cline 1978, 352) appears to have been sold to W. A. Turner, who exhibited it in Manchester in 1878. *Proserpine 3* was presumably that completed for Valpy in 1882 (VS 233 R3) if the same as that begun while FRL's canvas was being relined; given DGR's state of health in autumn 1882 it seems improbable, though not impossible, that he could have undertaken the whole task of producing a replica of one of his best works while away from home, or that under such conditions the work would proceed 'fast and well', as he reported to JM on 4 Oct. 1881. But disentangling these histories has proved complex and uncertain.

28 With all the various negotiations, muddles sometimes occurred. In Dec. 1873, WG asked when
The Ship of Love would be finished. 'I didn't
know he considered it his,' DGR told FMB,
evidently almost as confused about his various
commissions as subsequent commentators. But as
the work was now 'disengaged' from FRL it was
available for WG, price 800 gs: see DW 1438.
While at Kelmscott, DGR also retouched *Fazio's
Mistress*, *The Beloved* and *Monna Vanna* for Rae.

29 Peattie 1990, 238.

30 DW 1399, 1398.

31 DW 1456.

32 Morris 1973, I, 230; see also Marianne Tidcombe,
Women Bookbinders 1880–1920, 1996.

33 DW 1458, 1465, 1470.

34 Kelvin, I, 230; JM to EMB, March 1874, UBC.

35 DGR to FRL, 3 Apr. 1874, Fennell 1978, 74; it is
possible that DGR saw WHH's picture in
Oxford, where it was on show after London: see
Bennett 1969, 46; also WHH to Tupper, 15 Apr.
1874, in Coombes 1986.

36 DW 1485.

37 DW 1490; for Oliver Madox Brown, see Ingram
1883, 147–159. DGR accused Nolly of damaging
the Manor's boat and leaving a precious book in
the rain. Then, hearing Nolly was short of cash, he
offered to buy WM's painting of JM as Iseult,
done in 1858 and left in FMB's studio, which WM
had said Nolly could have. DGR suggested it be
transferred secretly to Euston Square, for him to
collect later and where it remained until rediscovered around 1900.

38 DW 1430, 1432, 1427.

39 Kelvin, I, 233.

40 See Kelvin, I, 246 and 251 n.1, where the new
name is already in use on 13 Oct. 1874; the
identity of the two unnamed partners cited in
Kelvin, I, 246 is unlikely to be FMB and PPM as
suggested, since they resisted ejection; moreover,
PPM was operating as MMF & Co. from an
address in Fenchurch Street (see Kelvin, I, 252 n.1)
which was probably an additional reason for
restructuring; see also DW 1531 and 1532 (which
should probably be redated 15 Oct. 1874) where
DGR suggested appointing an accountant, presumably to assess the value of partners' shares.
For more on the Firm negotiations, see Kelvin, I,
252; and *N&Q*, July 1971, 225; undated letter
from DGR to TWD (LC) about a forthcoming
'conference' at WM's house and PPM's unauthorised trading at a 'City branch' of the business.

41 DW 1531.

42 Kelvin, I, 252; DGR to TWD 25 Mar. 1875, LC;
see also subsequent correspondence between
DGR and TWD. At the end of 1875, TWD
proposed reinvesting the capital: see DW 1644.

43 *FLM*, I, 345.

44 DW 1537.

45 DW 1678 n.3.

46 VS 241. *The Question* may also be indebted to

Gustave Moreau's *Oedipus and the Sphinx*, an
early Symbolist work which caused a sensation at
the 1864 Paris Salon. A second related subject is
Moreau's *Young Man and Death* of 1865, though
we have no information on DGR's knowledge of
the French artist.

47 DW 1555; Bryson 1976, 20.

CHAPTER 25: DECLINE

1 Reported by S. C. Cockerell, Mackail Notebook,
WMG.

2 DW 1824.

3 Originally, *La Bella Mano* was to have held a
single figure, with urn and basin. Then the
attendants were added, firstly conceived as winged
boys: 'Venus's cupids', see VS 240D for nude
study of male models; although dated 1877 in
conception this would seem the earlier idea,
supported by the sonnet composed in summer
1875.

4 DW 1585.

5 See Bryson 1976, 26 (in C19 Michelangelo's sitter/
beloved was popularly identified as Vittoria
Colonna); TG 1984, 45; FGS, 'Mr Rossetti's New
Pictures', *Athenaeum*, 14 Apr. 1877, 486.

6 DW 1764; *VP* 20, 1982, 219.

7 Fennell 1978, 89; VS 248.

8 To TWD, 1 Apr. 1875 and 6 Jul. 1875, LC; DW
1587.

9 DW 1636 (DGR visited Euston Square on 26 Sep.
1875, a few days after Olivia's birth).

10 DW 1612.

11 To TWD, 26 Apr. 1888, Symington Collection,
Leeds.

12 DW 1627, 1640.

13 Hake 1892, 229–30; DW 1647.

14 DW 1650.

15 Quoted Faulkner 1981, 30 (note these may not be
JM's exact words).

16 DW 1693; WMR Diary 1880, 31 May.

17 DW 1666.

18 DW 1704; see also DW 2241 where DGR says he
saw Blake's cottage in high summer. JMW painted
a Nocturne (Freer Art Gallery, Washington DC,
no. 06.103) at Bognor in 1875–6 and it is tempting
to speculate that he visited DGR there.

19 DW 1677.

20 For the visit to Broadlands, see DW 1714, 1715,
1716.

21 DW 1737.

22 BL Add. 49467.

23 DW 1874; see also DW 2162.

24 See Peattie 1990, 287; Delaware MSS; *FLM*, I, 343.

25 Peattie 1990, 406.

26 For this episode, see DW 1788, 1789, 1796; BL
Ashley 3854; Baum 1940, 94–5.

27 DW 1830.

28 FGS to TWD, n.d., NYPL.

29 DW 1915, 2168.

30 Bryson 1976, 23.
31 DW 1931; Peattie 1990, 291.
32 DW 1893; *FLM*, I, 362.
33 Pater 1877, vol. 28, 526–538.
34 DW 1746; DGR also raised some issues of principle in relation to Academicians, who already dominated exhibiting space, being invited to show at the Grosvenor Gallery.
35 DW 1746, 1767; *Times*, 12 Mar. 1877.
36 Bryson 1976, 27; DW 1674; VS 233.
37 Bryson 1976, 26, 27.
38 DW 1995.
39 Bryson 1976, 32.
40 VS 225, 214; for Shields, see Mills 1912.
41 DW 1931, 1932, 1933, 1934, 1942.
42 Bryson 1976, 27; DW 1947.
43 Bryson 1976, 80; VS 259; see also *VP* 20, 1982, 227–9, for progress with *Day Dream*.
44 Bryson 1976, 26.
45 BL Ashley 1412; for WMR's remark, see *VP* 20, 1982, 223.
46 DW 2134.
47 Hardinge 1890, 398ff.
48 DW 2123, 2124.
49 For notes to FC, see Baum 1940.

CHAPTER 26: THE END

1 DW 2390.
2 See Sharp 1910, 35ff.
3 For THC story, see Caine 1882, 1908, 1928; Allen 1997.
4 For DGR's letters to THC, see Allen 1997 and 2000; many are previously published in Caine 1882 and 1928.
5 Stanford 1984, I, 253.
6 CGR *FL*, 85 and 89.
7 See letter to Edward Dowden, Allen 1997, 93.
8 Dryden's actual words were 'great wits are sure to madness near alli'd'.
9 See WMR Diary 1880, 10 May, 228.
10 WMR Diary 1880, 23–30 Sep., 230.
11 Quoted Lewis 1982, 203.
12 WMR Diary 1880, 27 Dec., 232; DW 2362.
13 DW 2451.
14 Peattie 1990, 317, 313.
15 DW 2171.
16 See WMR Diary 1880, 28 Mar., 234.
17 For further information on sources, see Culler 1944, 427ff.
18 *Works* 1911, 660; DW 2432.
19 DW 2435; Lewis 1982, 207.
20 See Sharp 1882, 412–14, 418–19.

21 See VS 81; Bennett 1988, 176–7; Allen 2000. The correspondence does not give THC the key role in negotiations that he claimed, for clearly Samuelson and Rathbone were at pains to be conciliatory.
22 DW 2522; see also Lewis 1982 (for draft disclaimers).
23 Bryson 1976, 144.
24 DW 2558, 2562.
25 WEF 1976, 335 (on 28/29 Oct. 1881 WBS told AB that the Jermyn Street hotel had 'not succeeded' and FC was 'falling back on Gabriel').
26 THC 1928, 123–6.
27 WMR Diary 1880, 236; WEF 1976, 335.
28 DW 2599.
29 *FLM*, I, 375.
30 CGR *FL*, 103.
31 WMR Diary 1880, 236–7; Shonfield 1987, 115.
32 WEF 1976, 339 (where DGR tells WBS this on 13–14 Jan, 1881).
33 CGR *FL*, 106.
34 Boos 1976, 181–90.
35 CGR *FL*, 112.
36 OD, 670.

EPILOGUE

1 Marillier 1904, 150, commenting on Harry Quilter's *Preferences*, 1899.
2 HRA 1949, 253.
3 16 Apr. 1882, Ashley A 4999
4 12 Apr. 1882, LC
5 11 or 12 Apr. 1882, BL Add 70627.
6 *Literary Opinion*, 1892, 129
7 Peattie 1990, 336.
8 To Cormell Price, 28 Apr. 1882.
9 *Athenaeum*, 15 Apr. 1882.
10 Quoted Sharp 1882, 37.
11 Quoted Sharp 1882, 38.
12 Quoted Gaunt 1943, 262, from MSS in BL.
13 Sharp 1882, 2.
14 WHH to FMB, 10 Jul. 1882; Sotheby's sale, 18 Dec. 1995.
15 At first in one gallery and then in two, following complaints about the overcrowded hanging.
16 *Times*, 13 Jan. 1883, 4.
17 Hueffer 1902, 181. But according to the same source (FMB's notoriously unreliable grandson), Whistler on his deathbed opened an eye to silence disparagement, saying, 'You must not say anything against Rossetti. Rossetti was a king'; see Hueffer 1911, 30.

Bibliography

Citations to exhibition catalogues and editions of correspondence are by item number where available; other citations use page numbers.

Aberdare Papers: in Glamorgan CRO.
ACS 1868: A. C. Swinburne, 'Notes upon designs of the Old Masters at Florence', *Fortnightly Review*, July 1868.
ACS 1872: A. C. Swinburne, 'Under the Microscope' (1872), in C. K. Hyder, *Swinburne Replies*, Syracuse UP, 1966.
ACS 1925–27. *The Complete Works of ACS*, ed. E. Gosse and T. J. Wise, 20 vols.
Adams 1918: *The Education of Henry Adams*.
Adrian 1958: A. A. Adrian, 'The Browning–Rossetti Friendship: Some Unpublished Letters', *PMLA*, vol. 73.
AJ: Art Journal
Allen 1997: Vivien Allen, *Hall Caine: Portrait of a Victorian Romancer*.
Allen 2000: Vivien Allen, *The Letters of Dante Gabriel Rossetti and Hall Caine 1878–1881*, Sheffield.
Allingham 1855: William Allingham, *The Music Master and Other Poems*.
Allingham 1888: William Allingham, *Flower Pieces and Other Poems*.
Amor 1989: Anne Amor, *William Holman Hunt: the True Pre-Raphaelite*.
Anderson 1994: Gail Nina Anderson, *Heaven on Earth*, exhibition catalogue, Nottingham.
Apollo 1967: see Lutyens 1967.
Apollo 1973: see Grieve 1973, I.
Arnold 1923: W. H. Arnold, *Ventures in Book Collecting*.
ASU: Arizona State University MSS.
Atlantic Monthly: Vol. 1, C. E. Norton, 'The Art Treasures Exhibition', Nov. 1857.
Bailey: P. J. Bailey, *Festus*, 1839; expanded edn. 1845.
Baldwin 1960: A. W. Baldwin, *The Macdonald Sisters*.
Barrington 1905: Emilie Barrington, *G. F. Watts: Reminiscences*.

Baudelaire 1845: Charles Baudelaire, 'Salon of 1845', reprinted *Mirror of Art*, 1955.

Baudelaire 1964: Charles Baudelaire, *The Painter of Modern Life and other Essays*, ed. and trans. J. Mayne.

Baudelaire 1965: Charles Baudelaire, *Art in Paris*, trans. J. Mayne.

Baum 1931: DGR: *An Analytical List of Manuscripts in the Duke University Library*, ed. P. F. Baum, Duke UP.

Baum 1937: *"The Blessed Damozel" Unpublished Manuscript Texts and Collation*, ed. P. F. Baum, Raleigh, North Carolina.

Baum 1940: *D. G. Rossetti's Letters to Fanny Cornforth*, ed. Paull F. Baum, Baltimore.

Becker 1996: *Sir Lawrence Alma-Tadema*, exhibition catalogue, ed. Edwin Becker, Amsterdam.

Belford 1990: Barbara Belford, *Violet*, New York.

Benedetti 1984: Maria-Teresa Benedetti, *D. G. Rossetti*, Florence.

Bennett 1969: Mary Bennett, *William Holman Hunt*, exhibition catalogue, Liverpool.

Bennett 1988: Mary Bennett, *Artists of the Pre-Raphaelite Circle: The First Generation*, National Museums and Galleries on Merseyside; citations by reference number.

Benson 1904: A. C. Benson, *Rossetti*.

Benson 1930: E. F. Benson, *As We Were*.

Berg: Berg Collection, New York Public Library.

Birkbeck Hill 1897: *Letters of George Birkbeck Hill*.

BL: British Library MS Dept.

BM: British Museum Prints & Drawings Dept.

BN 1997: Bibliothèque nationale de France, *L'Art du nu au xix siècle: le photographe et son modèle*.

Bod.: Bodleian Library, Oxford, MS Dept.

Boos 1976: Florence Boos, *The Poetry of Dante Gabriel Rossetti: A Critical and Source Study*, The Hague.

Bornand 1977: *The Diary of W. M. Rossetti 1870–1873*, ed. Odette Bornand.

Bradley & Ousby 1987: *The Correspondence of John Ruskin and Charles Eliot Norton*, ed. J. L. Bradley and I. Ousby, Cambridge UP.

Browne 1994: Max Browne, *The Romantic Art of Theodor von Holst*.

Browning Letters: *The Letters of Robert Browning*, ed. T. L. Hood, 1933.

BRP Papers: Girton College, Cambridge, MS Archive.

Bruce 1902: *Letters of the Rt Hon. Henry Austin Bruce, Lord Aberdare*, 2 vols, privately printed, Oxford.

Bruce Papers: see Aberdare Papers, Glamorgan CRO.

Bryson 1976: *Dante Gabriel Rossetti and Jane Morris: Their Correspondence*, ed. John Bryson in association with Janet Camp Troxell, Oxford.

Buchanan 1866: R. W. Buchanan, *London Poems*.

Buchanan 1868: R. W. Buchanan, *David Gray & Other Essays*.

Buchanan 1871: [Thomas Maitland] 'The Fleshly School of Poetry', *Contemporary Review*, Oct. 1871.

Buchanan 1872: R. W. Buchanan, *The Fleshly School of Poetry, and Other Phenomena of the Day*.

Burd 1969: *The Winnington Letters of John Ruskin*, ed. van Akin Burd.

Burd 1973: ed. van Akin Burd, *The Ruskin Family Letters*, 2 vols. Cornell UP.

Burlington Fine Arts Club 1883: *Pictures, Drawings, Designs and Studies by the late Dante Gabriel Rossetti*, with introduction by H. Virtue Tebbs.

Cachin and Moffet: Françoise Cachin and C. S. Moffet, *Manet*, New York, 1983.

Caine 1882: T. H. Caine, *Recollections of Rossetti*.

Caine 1908: T. H. Caine, *My Story*.

Caine 1928: T. H. Caine, *Recollections of Rossetti* (revised version).

Carr 1908: J. Comyns Carr, *Some Eminent Victorians*.

Cassidy 1952: J. A. Cassidy, 'Robert Buchanan and the Fleshly Controversy', *PMLA*, Mar. 1952, 65ff.

Cassidy 1973: J. A. Cassidy, *Robert Buchanan*, Boston.

Casteras 1990: Susan P. Casteras, *English Pre-Raphaelitism and its Reception in America in the Nineteenth Century*, Associated UP.

Casteras 1991: *Pocket Cathedrals: Pre-Raphaelite Book Illustration*, exhibition catalogue ed. Susan P. Casteras, Yale Center for British Art.

Casteras 1995: Susan P. Casteras, *James Smetham: Artist, Author, Pre-Raphaelite Associate*, Aldershot.

Casteras and Denny 1996: *The Grosvenor Gallery: A Palace of Art in Victorian England*, ed. Susan P. Casteras and Colleen Denny, Yale UP.

CGR 1892: Christina G. Rossetti: 'The House of Dante Gabriel Rossetti', *Literary Opinion*, 129.

CGR FL: *The Family Letters of Christina Rossetti*, ed. W. M. Rossetti, 1908.

Chapman 1945: R. G. Chapman, *The Laurel and the Thorn: A Study of G. F. Watts*.

Cherry 1980: Deborah Cherry, 'The Hogarth Club 1858–1861', *Burlington Magazine*, vol. 122.

Chesneau 1864: Ernest Chesneau, *L'art et les artistes modernes en France et Angleterre*, Paris.

Chesneau 1885: Ernest Chesneau, *The English School of Painting*.

Christian 1973: John Christian, 'Early German Sources for Pre-Raphaelite Designs,' *Art Quarterly*, vol. 36

Clabburn 1891: H. J. Clabburn, 'Some Relics of Rossetti', *Pall Mall Budget*, 22 January 1891.

Cline 1970: *Letters of George Meredith*, ed. C. L. Cline.

Cline 1978: *The Owl and the Rossettis: Letters of Charles A Howell and Dante Gabriel, Christina and William Michael Rossetti*, ed. C. L. Cline, Pennsylvania State UP.

Collins 1848: Wilkie Collins, *Memoirs of the Life of William Collins RA*, 2 vols.

Colvin 1921: Sidney Colvin, *Memories and Notes*.

Coombes 1986: *A Pre-Raphaelite Friendship: the Correspondence of William Holman Hunt and John Lucas Tupper*, ed. James H. Coombes et al., Michigan UP.

Cooper 1970: R. M. Cooper, *Lost on Both Sides*.

Cornell: Cornell University Library MSS Dept.

Crowe 1895: Joseph Crowe, *Reminiscences*.

Crump 1979: *The Complete Poems of Christina G. Rossetti*, ed. Rebecca Crump, 3 vols, Louisiana State UP, 1979–1991.

Culler 1944: Dwight and Helen Culler, 'The Sources of "The King's Tragedy",' *Studies in Philology*, 41, 427ff.

Curle 1937: *Browning's Letters to Julia Wedgwood*, ed. R. Curle.

Daly 1989: Gay Daly, *Pre-Raphaelites in Love*.

Dalziel 1901: *The Brothers Dalziel, A Record of Fifty Years' Work, 1840–1890*.

Davies 1904: *The Working Men's College 1854–1904*, ed. J. L. Davies.

de Vos 1994: Dirk de Vos, *Hans Memling: The Complete Works*.

Delacroix 1895: *Journal of Eugene Delacroix*.

Delaware: Delaware Art Museum Library.

DGR Letters to Alice Boyd, *Fortnightly Review*, 1928.

DGR Letters to WA 1897: *Letters of Dante Gabriel Rossetti to William Allingham 1854–1870*, ed. G. B. Hill.

DHH: Diana Holman Hunt, *My Grandfather, His Wives and Loves*, 1969.

Dobbs 1977: Brian and Judy Dobbs, *Rossetti: An Alien Victorian*.

Druick and Hoog: D. Druick and M. Hoog, *Fantin-Latour*, Ottawa 1983.

du Maurier 1951: Daphne du Maurier, *The Young George du Maurier*.

DUL: Durham University Library MSS.

Dunn 1904: H. Treffry Dunn, *Recollections of Dante Gabriel Rossetti and his Circle*.

Dunn 1984: H. Treffry Dunn, *Recollections of Dante Gabriel Rossetti*, ed. R. Mander.

DW: *The Letters of Dante Gabriel Rossetti*, ed. O. Doughty and J. R. Wahl, 4 vols, 1965–1967.

EBJ 1973: *Burne-Jones*, exhibition catalogue by John Christian.

EBJ 1998: *Edward Burne-Jones, Victorian Artist-Dreamer*, exhibition catalogue by Stephen Wildman and John Christian, Metropolitan Museum of Art, New York.

EIPs: *Early Italian Poets from Ciullo d'Alcamo to Dante Alighieri*, reissued as *Dante and His Circle*, 1874.

Ellis 1919: S. M. Ellis, *George Meredith*.

Ellis 1923: S. M. Ellis, *William Hardman: A Mid-Victorian Pepys*.

Elzea 1980: *Correspondence between Samuel Bancroft Jnr and Charles Fairfax Murray 1892–1916*, ed. Rowland Elzea, Delaware Art Museum, Wilmington.

Erdman 1973: *The Notebook of William Blake*, ed. D. V. Erdman, Oxford.

Faulkner 1981: *Jane Morris to Wilfrid Scawen Blunt*, ed. Peter Faulkner, Exeter UP.

Faxon 1989: Alicia Craig Faxon, *Dante Gabriel Rossetti*, Oxford.

Faxon 1992: Alicia Craig Faxon, 'D. G. Rossetti's Use of Photography', *History of Photography*, vol.16.

Fennell 1978: *The Rossetti-Leyland Letters: the Correspondence of an Artist and his Patron*, ed. Francis L. Fennell, Ohio UP.

Fennell 1982: Francis Fennell, *Dante Gabriel Rossetti: an Annotated Bibliography*, New York.

Field 1920: J. Osgood Field, *Things I Shouldn't Tell*, 77.

Fisher 1973: B. J. Fisher, 'Laird of Waristoun . . .' *Victorian Poetry*, vol. II.

Fitzgerald 1975: Penelope Fitzgerald, *Edward Burne-Jones*.

Fitzwilliam: Fitzwilliam Museum, Cambridge, MSS Dept.

Fleming 1998: G. H. Fleming, *John Everett Millais A Biography*.

FLM: *Dante Gabriel Rossetti: His Family-Letters with a Memoir* by W. M. Rossetti, 2 vols, 1895.

FMB: *The Diary of Ford Madox Brown*, ed. V. Surtees, 1981; citations by entry date.

Fraser 1972: *Essays on the Rossettis*, ed. R. S. Fraser, Princeton UP.

Freemantle 1901: *Some Poems by Alfred Lord Tennyson*, with illustrations by W. Holman Hunt, J. E. Millais and Dante Gabriel Rossetti printed from the original woodblocks; preface by Joseph Pennell, introduction by W. Holman Hunt, Freemantle & Co.

Friedrich 1992: Otto Friedrich, *Olympia: Paris in the Age of Manet*.

Friends of Llandaff Cathedral Annual Reports.

Friswell 1898: L. H. Friswell, *A Memoir of James Hain Friswell*.

Frith 1888: W. P. Frith, *Autobiography*, 2 vols.

Fry 1916: Roger Fry, 'Rossetti's Water Colours of 1857', *Burlington Magazine*, vol. 13, 100–109

Gaskell 1932: *Letters of Mrs Gaskell to Charles Eliot Norton*, ed. Jane Whitehill.

Gaunt 1943: William Gaunt, *The Pre-Raphaelite Dream*.

Gautier 1855: Theophile Gautier, *Les Beaux Arts en Europe*, Paris.

GBJ: Georgiana Burne-Jones, *Memorials of Sir Edward Burne-Jones*, 2 vols, 1904.

Germ 1901: *The Germ: a reprint of the literary organ of the Pre-Raphaelite Brotherhood published in 1850*, with introduction by W. M. Rossetti.

Gilchrist 1863: Alexander Gilchrist, *Life of William Blake*, 2 vols., 1863, reissued 1880.

Gilchrist 1887: *Anne Gilchrist: Her Life and Writings*, ed. H. H. Gilchrist.

Gillett 1990: Paula Gillett, *The Victorian Painter's World*, Rutgers UP.

Girouard 1981: Mark Girouard, *The Return to Camelot: Chivalry and the English Gentleman*.

Goldman 1994: Paul Goldman, *Victorian Illustrated Books 1850–1870*.

GPB: *The Diaries of George Price Boyce*, ed. V. Surtees, Norwich, 1980; citations by entry date.

Grieve 1971: Alastair Grieve, 'Whistler and the Pre-Raphaelites', *The Art Quarterly*, vol. 34.

Grieve 1973(a): A. I. Grieve, 'Rossetti's Illustrations to Poe', *Apollo*, vol. 97.

Grieve 1973(b): A. I. Grieve, *The Art of Dante Gabriel Rossetti*, Part I: *The Pre-Raphaelite Period 1848–50*, Hingham, Norfolk.

Grieve 1976: A. I. Grieve, *The Art of Dante Gabriel Rossetti*, Part II: *'Found' and the Pre-Raphaelite Modern Life Subject*, Norwich.

Grieve 1978: A. I. Grieve, *The Art of Dante Gabriel Rossetti*, Part III: *The Watercolours and Drawings of 1850–1855*, Norwich.

Grylls 1964: Rosalie Glynn Grylls, *Portrait of Rossetti*.

GUL: Whistler Study Centre, Glasgow University Library.

Hake 1892: T. G. Hake, *Memories of Eighty Years*.

Hake and Ricketts 1918: *The Life and Letters of Theodore Watts-Dunton*, ed. T. Hake and C. Compton Ricketts, 2 vols.

Hancock 1882: Thomas Hancock, 'Dante G. Rossetti', *Academy*, 6 May 1882.

Harding 1996: *Re-framing the Pre-Raphaelites: Historical and Theoretical Essays*, ed. Ellen Harding.

Hardinge 1890: W. H. Hardinge, 'A Reminiscence of Rossetti', *The Universal Review*, March 1890.

Harrison and Waters: Martin Harrison and Bill Waters, *Burne-Jones*, 1989.

Harrison: *The Letters of Christina Rossetti*, ed. Antony H. Harrison, UP of Virginia, 2 vols, 1997, 1999.

Harvard: Harvard University Library, MSS Dept.

Harvey and Press 1991: Charles Harvey and Jon Press, *William Morris: Design and Enterprise in Victorian Britain*, Manchester UP.

Harvey and Press 1996: Charles Harvey and Jon Press, *Art, Enterprise and Ethics: the Life and Works of William Morris*.

Henderson 1973: Philip Henderson, *Swinburne: Portrait of a Poet*.

Hirsch 1998: Pam Hirsch, *Barbara Leigh Smith Bodichon: Feminist, Artist and Rebel.*

Holiday 1914: Henry Holiday, *Reminiscences of My Life.*

Horner 1933: Frances Horner, *Time Remembered.*

Howitt 1889: *Mary Howitt: An Autobiography*, ed. Margaret Howitt.

HRA 1949: Helen Rossetti Angeli, *Dante Gabriel Rossetti: His Friends and His Enemies.*

HRA 1954: Helen Rossetti Angeli, *Pre-Raphaelite Twilight: the Story of Charles A. Howell.*

Hudson 1972: *Munby: Man of Two Worlds. The Life and Diaries of Arthur J. Munby*, ed. Derek Hudson.

Hueffer 1902: F. M. Hueffer, *Rossetti.*

Hueffer 1911: F. M. Hueffer, *Ancient Lights.*

Hunt 1932: Violet Hunt, *Wife of Rossetti.*

Ingram 1883: J. H. Ingram, *Oliver Madox Brown.*

Ionides 1927: A. C. Ionides, Jnr, *A Grandfather's Tale.*

Ionides 1996: Luke Ionides, *Memories*, 1925; reprinted 1996.

Ironside and Gere: Robin Ironside and John Gere, *Pre-Raphaelite Painters*, 1948.

James 1920: *The Letters of Henry James*, ed. Percy Lubbock, 2 vols.

James 1974: *The Letters of Henry James*, ed. Leon Edel.

James 1947: William James, *The Order of Release.*

Jameson 1845: Anna Jameson, *Memoirs of the Early Italian Painters*, 2 vols.

Jameson 1848: Anna Jameson, *Sacred and Legendary Art*; 3rd edn 1857.

Jay 1903: Harriet Jay, *Robert Buchanan.*

JGM: *The Life and Letters of Sir John Everett Millais*, ed. J. G. Millais, 2 vols, 1899.

Jones 1981: John Brandon Jones, 'The Importance of Philip Webb', *William Morris and Kelmscott*, Design Council.

JPM: J. Pierpont Morgan Library, New York.

JPRS and *JPRAS*: *Journal of Pre-Raphaelite [and Aesthetic] Studies*, under its different titles.

Keats 1848: *Life, Letters and Literary Remains of John Keats*, ed. Richard Monckton Milnes, 2 vols.

Kelvin: *Collected Letters of William Morris*, ed. Norman Kelvin, 4 vols, Princeton UP, 1984–96.

Knight 1887: Joseph Knight, *The Life of Dante Gabriel Rossetti.*

Lago 1982: *Burne-Jones Talking: His Conversations 1895–1898*, ed. Mary Lago.

Lamont 1912: *Thomas Armstrong CB A Memoir*, ed. L. M. Lamont.

Landow 1974–5: George P. Landow, 'Holman Hunt's Letters to Ernest Chesneau', *Huntington Library Quarterly*, vol. 38.

Landow 1976–7: George P. Landow, 'The Correspondence of John Ruskin and William Holman Hunt', *Bulletin of the John Rylands Library*, Manchester, vol. 59.

Landow 1983–4: George P. Landow, 'William Holman Hunt's Letters to Thomas Seddon,' *Bulletin of the John Rylands Library*, Manchester, vol. 66.

Lang 1959: *The Swinburne Letters*, ed. C. Y. Lang, 5 vols.

Lasner 1990: Mark Samuels Lasner, 'William Allingham', *The Book Collector*.

Layard 1894: G. S. Layard, *Tennyson and his Pre-Raphaelite Illustrators*.

LC: Library of Congress MS Division.

Lee 1955: Amice Lee, *Laurels and Rosemary: the Life of William and Mary Howitt*.

Lethève 1959: Jacques Lethève, 'Connaissance des peintres pré-raphaélites en France 1855–1900', *Gazette des Beaux Arts*, vol. 53.

Letters to Charles Eliot Norton, 1905.

Letters to WA 1911: *Letters to William Allingham*, ed. H. Allingham and E. B. Williams.

Lewis 1982: Roger C. Lewis, 'The Making of Rossetti's *Ballads and Sonnets* and *Poems* (1881)', *Victorian Poetry*.

Lewis 1995: Roger C. Lewis, *T. J. Wise and The Trial Book Fallacy*.

Life 1982: A. L. Life, 'Rossetti's Illustration for the Maids of Elfen-mere', *Victorian Poetry*, 65ff.

Lightbown 1978: Ronald Lightbown, *Sandro Botticelli*, 2 vols.

Lindsay 1956: J. Lindsay, *George Meredith*.

Llandaff MSS: Glamorgan CRO.

Lorimer 1978: Douglas Lorimer, *Colour, Class and the Victorians*.

Ludley 1991–2: D. A. Ludley, 'Anna Jameson and D. G. Rossetti', *Woman's Art Journal*.

Lutyens 1967(a): Mary Lutyens, *Millais and the Ruskins*.

Lutyens 1967(b): Mary Lutyens, 'Selling the Missionary', *Apollo* vol. 86.

Lutyens 1975: Mary Lutyens, introduction to reprint of *Parables of Our Lord*, New York.

Maas 1975: Jeremy Maas, *Gambart: Prince of the Victorian Art World*.

MacCarthy 1995: Fiona MacCarthy: *William Morris: A Man for Our Time*.

Macdonald 1919: Fred Macdonald, *As a Tale that is Told*.

Macdonald 1991: D. L. Macdonald, *Poor Polidori*, Toronto.

Mackail 1899: J. W. Mackail, *The Life of William Morris*, 2 vols.

Macleod 1982: Dianne S. Macleod, 'Rossetti's Two *Ligeias*: their Relationship to Visual Art, Music and Poetry', *Victorian Poetry*.

Macleod 1996: Dianne S. Macleod, *Art and the Victorian Middle Class*, Cambridge UP.

Macmillan 1908: *Letters of Alexander Macmillan*, privately printed.

Maneglier 1990: Hervé Maneglier, *Paris Impérial: la vie quotidienne sous le Second Empire*, Paris.

Marillier 1899: H. C. Marillier, *Dante Gabriel Rossetti: an Illustrated Memorial of his Art and Life*, 1899; 3rd edn 1904.

Marsh 1985: Jan Marsh, *Pre-Raphaelite Sisterhood*.

Marsh 1986: Jan Marsh, *Jane and May Morris*.

Marsh 1989(a): 'Pre-Raphaelite Artists and the Moxon Tennyson', *JPRAS*, ii–i, Spring 1989.

Marsh 1989(b): Jan Marsh, *The Legend of Elizabeth Siddal*.

Marsh 1998: Jan Marsh, '*Rupes Topseia*: a New Suggestion', *WMSJ*, 4–6.

Maurice 1913: C. E. Maurice, *Life of Octavia Hill*.

McGann 1999: Jerome McGann, *Rossetti and the Game that Must be Lost*.

McGann 2000: *The Complete Writings and Pictures of Dante Gabriel Rossetti: A Hypermedia Research Archive*, http://jefferson.village.edu/rossetti/rossetti.ht.

Meredith 1910: George Meredith, 'A Note on Cheyne Walk', *English Review*, vol. 1.

Meredith 1970: *Letters of George Meredith*, ed. C. L. Cline, 3 vols, Oxford.

Merimée 1857: Prosper Merimée, 'Les Beaux Arts en Angleterre', *Revue des deux mondes*, 15 October 1857.

Metzdorf 1953: R. F. Metzdorf, 'Rossetti's Sonnet on *Sordello*', *Harvard Library Bulletin*, 239ff.

Miles 1979: Frank Miles, *History of King's College School*.

Millais 1979: Geoffroy Millais, *Sir John Everett Millais*.

Miller 1920: Joaquin Miller, 'Recollections of the Rossetti Dinner', *Overland Monthly*, Feb. 1920.

Mills 1912: *Life and Letters of Frederic Shields*, ed. Ernestine Mills.

Mills College MSS archive.

Morris 1913: *Prose and Poetry by William Morris*, OUP.

Morris 1973: May Morris, *Introductions to the Collected Works of William Morris*, 2 vols, New York.

Muller 1856: Max Muller, *Oxford Essays*.

Murray 1982–3: C. D. Murray, 'The Fleshly School Revisited', *Bulletin of the John Rylands Library*, 207–9.

N&Q: *Notes and Queries*.

NAL: National Art Library, Victoria & Albert Museum, London.

National Portrait Gallery 1999: *Millais: Portraits*, exhibition catalogue by Peter Funnell and Malcolm Warner.

Newman and Watkinson 1991: Teresa Newman and Ray Watkinson, *Ford Madox Brown*.

NMM: National Museums on Merseyside MSS Archive.

Northwestern University Library MSS.

NSW: Mitchell Library MSS., New South Wales State Library.

NYPL: New York Public Library.

NYU: Fales Library, New York University.

O&C: Oxford & Cambridge Magazine, 1856.

OD: Oswald Doughty, A Victorian Romantic: Dante Gabriel Rossetti, Oxford 1949, reissued 1960.

Ogden MSS, University College, London.

Ormond 1967: Richard Ormond, 'Portraits to Australia: a group of Pre-Raphaelite drawings', Apollo, vol. 85, 1967, 25–7.

Ormond 1975: Leonee and Richard Ormond, Lord Leighton.

Packer 1965: The Rossetti-Macmillan Letters, ed. Lona M. Packer, Cambridge UP.

Parris 1984: Pre-Raphaelite Papers, ed. Leslie Parris.

Pater 1868: Walter Pater, 'The Poems of William Morris', Westminster Review, 1868, 300–12.

Pater 1877: Walter Pater, 'The School of Giorgione', Fortnightly Review.

Pater 1889: Walter Pater, Appreciations.

PDL 1900: Pre-Raphaelite Letters and Diaries 1854–1860, ed. W. M. Rossetti.

Peattie 1990: The Selected Letters of William Michael Rossetti, ed. Robert Peattie, Pennsylvania State UP.

Pedrick 1964: Gale Pedrick, Dante Gabriel Rossetti and His Circle.

Pennell 1911: E. R. and J. Pennell, The Life of James MacNeil Whistler, Philadelphia.

Pennell 1930: E. R. Pennell, Whistler the Friend.

Peters 1991: Catherine Peters, Wilkie Collins.

PMG: Pall Mall Gazette.

Pointon 1979: Marcia Pointon, William Dyce.

Pollen 1912: Anne Pollen, John Hungerford Pollen 1820–1902.

Postgate 1955: Raymond Postgate, Story of a Year: 1848.

Poulson 1999: Christine Poulson, The Quest for the Grail: Arthurian Legend in British Art 1840–1920.

PRBJ: The PRB Journal, ed. W. E. Fredeman, 1975; citations either by page number or entry date.

Preston 1953: The Letters of W. Graham Robertson, ed. Kerrison Preston.

Prinsep 1892: Val Prinsep, 'A Collector's Correspondence', Art Journal, August 1892.

Prinsep 1902: Val Prinsep, 'Chapter from a Painter's Reminiscences', Magazine of Art, 1902.

PRO: Public Record Office, Kew.

PUL: Princeton University Library MSS.

Purves 1931: John Purves, 'Dante Rossetti and his Godfather Charles Lyell of Kinnordy', *University of Edinburgh Journal*, vol. 4, 1931.

PWs 1891: *Dante Gabriel Rossetti Poetical Works*, ed. W. M. Rossetti.

RA Register: Register of Students Admitted to the Royal Academy from 1830, Royal Academy Archive.

Rees: Joan Rees, *The Poetry of Dante Gabriel Rossetti: modes of self-expression*, Cambridge UP, 1981.

Reynolds: Joshua Reynolds, *Discourses*, 1975 edn.

Riede 1983: David G. Riede, *Dante Gabriel Rossetti and the Limits of Victorian Vision*.

Riede 1992: David G. Riede, *Dante Gabriel Rossetti Revisited*, New York.

Roberson's Archive: University of Cambridge.

Robertson 1978: David Robertson, *Sir Charles Eastlake and the Victorian Art World*, Princeton UP.

Robinson 1882: Mary Robinson, 'DGR', *Harpers New Monthly Magazine*, European edn, vol. IV, 1882.

Rooksby 1997: Rikky Rooksby, *Algernon Charles Swinburne*.

Rose 1981: Andrea Rose, *Pre-Raphaelite Portraits*.

Rosenbaum 1961: R. A. Rosenbaum, *Earnest Victorians*.

Rota 1973: *Books from the Libraries of Christina, Dante Gabriel and William Michael Rossetti*, Bertram Rota.

Rothenstein 1931: William Rothenstein, *Men and Memories*, 2 vols.

Rothenstein 1965: John Rothenstein, *Summer's Lease*.

RP: *Rossetti Papers 1862–1870*, ed. W. M. Rossetti, 1903.

RRP: *Ruskin, Rossetti, Pre-Raphaelitism: Papers 1854–1862*, ed. W. M. Rossetti, 1899.

Ruskin 1855: John Ruskin, *Academy Notes* (1855), in *Pre-Raphaelitism: Lectures on Architecture and Painting by John Ruskin*, Everyman's Library, 1906.

Ruskin 1856: John Ruskin, *Modern Painters*, III and IV, in Ruskin CW.

Ruskin 1857: John Ruskin, *Academy Notes* (1857), in *Pre-Raphaelitism: Lectures on Architecture and Painting by John Ruskin*, Everyman's Library, 1906.

Ruskin 1958: *Ruskin's Diaries 1848–73*, ed. Joan Evans and J. H. Whitehouse, Oxford, vol. 2.

Ruskin CW: *The Works of John Ruskin*, ed. E. T. Cook and Alexander Wedderburn, 37 vols, 1903–12.

Sala 1895: G. A. Sala, *Life and Adventures*, 2 vols.

Sandys 1974: *Frederick Sandys 1829–1904*, exhibition catalogue, Brighton Museum and Art Gallery.

Sencourt 1929: R. A. Sencourt, *The Life of George Meredith*.

Sewter 1975: A. C. Sewter, *The Stained Glass of William Morris and His Circle*, 2 vols.

Sharp 1882: William Sharp, *Dante Gabriel Rossetti: A Record and a Study*.

Sharp 1910: E. A. Sharp, *Memoir of William Sharp*.

Sharp 1912: William Sharp, *Papers Critical and Reminiscent*.

Shonfield 1987: Zuzanna Shonfield, *Precariously Privileged*.

Skelton 1895: John Skelton, *The Table-Talk of Shirley: Reminiscences and Letters*, Edinburgh.

Smetham and Davies 1892: *Letters of James Smetham*, ed. S. Smetham and W. Davies.

Smith 1996: Alison Smith, *The Victorian Nude*, Manchester UP.

Speight 1962: Robert Speight, *William Rothenstein*.

Spencer 1989: *Whistler: A Retrospective*, ed. Robin Spencer.

Spencer 1991: Robin Spencer, 'Manet, Rossetti, London and Derby Day', *Burlington Magazine*, vol. 133.

SR: William Michael Rossetti, *Some Reminiscences*, 2 vols, 1906.

Stanford 1931: J. A. Stanford, *SP*, 35.

Stanford 1984: *The Letters of Robert Bridges*, ed. Donald Stanford, 2 vols.

Stephens 1894: F. G. Stephens, *Dante Gabriel Rossetti*.

Stillman 1901: W. J. Stillman, *Autobiography of a Journalist*.

Stirling 1926: *The Richmond Papers*, ed. A. M. W. Stirling.

Stratton 1996: *The Rossettis: Brothers and the Brotherhood*, ed. Mary C. Stratton, Bucknell UP.

Street 1858: G. E. Street, 'The Future of Art in England', *The Ecclesiologist*, vol. 19, 239.

Sulman 1897: Thomas Sulman, 'A Memorable Art Class', *Good Words*, 547ff.

Surtees 1972: *Sublime and Instructive: Letters from John Ruskin to Louisa Waterford, Anna Blunden and Ellen Heaton*, ed. V. Surtees.

Surtees 1979: *Reflections of a Friendship*, ed. Virginia Surtees.

Surtees 1984: Virginia Surtees, *The Ludovisi Goddess*, Wilton, Wilts.

Surtees 1997: Virginia Surtees, *The Actress and the Brewer's Wife*, Norwich.

TG 1984: *The Pre-Raphaelites*, exhibition catalogue, Tate Gallery London, citations by exhibit number.

TG 1997: *The Age of Rossetti, Burne-Jones and Watts: Symbolism in Britain 1860–1910*, exhibition catalogue, Tate Gallery, London, citations by exhibit number.

Tokyo 1990: *Dante Gabriel Rossetti*, exhibition catalogue, Tokyo Shimbun.

Trevelyan 1978: Raleigh Trevelyan, *A Pre-Raphaelite Circle*.

Troxell 1937: Janet Camp Troxell, *Three Rossettis: Unpublished Letters to and from Dante Gabriel, Christina, William*, Cambridge MA.

Turner 1927: A. M. Turner, 'Dante Gabriel Rossetti's Reading', *PMLA*, vol. 42, 465.

TW: *Thomas Woolner RA, Sculptor and Poet: His Life in Letters*, ed. Amy Woolner, 1917.

UBC: Rossetti-Angeli Collection, University of British Columbia.

UCL: University College London

UT: Humanities Research Center, University of Texas at Austin.

V&A 1996: *William Morris Centenary Exhibition* catalogue, ed. Linda Parry, Victoria & Albert Museum.

Vanderbilt 1959: Kermit Vanderbilt, *Charles Eliot Norton*, Harvard UP.

VP: *Victorian Poetry*.

VP 20, 1982: special DGR centenary issue of *VP*, edited by WEF.

VS: Virginia Surtees, *Dante Gabriel Rossetti: Paintings and Drawings, a Catalogue Raisonné*, 2 vols, 1971; citations by item number from vol. 1.

WA Diary: *William Allingham, A Diary*, ed. H. Allingham and D. Radford, 1907; Penguin edn 1985; citations by entry date.

Waagen 1854: Gustav Waagen, *Treasures of Art in Great Britain*, 2 vols.

Waagen 1857: Gustav Waagen, *Galleries and Cabinets of Art in Great Britain*.

Wahl 1954: *The Kelmscott Love Sonnets*, ed. J. R. Wahl, Cape Town.

Waller 1932: R. D. Waller, *The Rossetti Family 1824–1854*, Manchester UP.

Walpole Society 1972–74: 'Letters from Sir J. E. Millais and William Holman Hunt in the Henry E. Huntington Library', ed. Mary Lutyens, vol. 44.

Warner 1992: Malcolm Warner, 'The Pre-Raphaelites and London's National Gallery', *Huntington Library Quarterly*, vol. 55.

Watkinson 1983: Ray Watkinson, 'A Meeting with Mr Rossetti', *JPRS*.

Watson 1997: *Collecting the Pre-Raphaelites*, ed. M. F. Watson.

Watts-Dunton, 1916: Theodore Watts Dunton, *Old Familiar Faces*.

Waugh 1928: Evelyn Waugh, *Rossetti: His Life and Works*.

WBS: *Autobiographical Notes of William Bell Scott*, ed. W. Minto, 2 vols, 1892.

WEF 1961: W. E. Fredeman, "D. G. Rossetti's *Early Italian Poets*', *The Book Collector*, Vol I, 193–8.

WEF 1965(a): W. E. Fredeman, *Pre-Raphaelitism, A Bibliocritical Study*.

WEF 1965(b): W. E. Fredeman, 'Rossetti's "In Memoriam": an Elegiac Reading of *The House of Life*', *Bulletin of the John Rylands Library*, Manchester, vol. 47

WEF 1971: W. E. Fredeman, 'Prelude to the Last Decade: DGR in the summer of 1872', *Bulletin of the John Rylands Library*, Manchester, vol. 53.

WEF 1976: W. E. Fredeman, 'The Letters of Pictor Ignotus: William Bell Scott's Correspondence with Alice Boyd 1859–1884', *Bulletin of the John Rylands Library*, Manchester, vol. 58.

WEF 1982: W. E. Fredeman, 'A Shadow of Dante: Rossetti in the Final Years', plus editorial commentary in *Victorian Poetry*, 20, 1982.

WEF 1991: W. E. Fredeman, 'A Rossetti Cabinet', *JPRAS* special issue.

WEF 1996: W. E. Fredeman, 'Woodman, Spare that Block!', *JPRS*, new series 5, Spring 1996.

WEF forthcoming: *The Collected Letters of Dante Gabriel Rossetti*, ed. W. E. Fredeman, vols 1 and 2.

Weintraub 1978: Stanley Weintraub, *Four Rossettis*.

Wells 1891: Charles Wells, *Stories after Nature*, 1822, reprinted 1891 with preface by W. J. Linton.

Westwater 1984: Martha Westwater, *The Wilson Sisters*, Ohio UP.

Wharton and Martin sale catalogue, 5 July 1882, 'Contents of 16 Cheyne Walk, Chelsea'.

WHH 1886: William Holman Hunt, 'Pre-Raphaelitism: A Fight for Art', *Contemporary Review*, April, May, June 1886.

WHH 1890: William Holman Hunt, 'Memories of Rossetti', *Musical World*, vol. 70.

WHH 1905: William Holman Hunt, *Pre-Raphaelitism and the Pre-Raphaelite Brotherhood*, 2 vols; revised 2nd edn 1913.

Whistler 1878: J. M. W. Whistler, *The Red Rag*.

Whitehill 1932: *Letters of Mrs Gaskell to Charles Eliot Norton*, ed. Jane Whitehill.

Whitworth 1986: *William Morris and the Middle Ages*, exhibition catalogue, Whitworth Art Gallery, Manchester.

Wildman 1995: Stephen Wildman, *Visions of Love and Life: Pre-Raphaelite Art from the Birmingham Collection England*, Alexandria, VA.

Wilkinson 1857: Anon [J. Garth Wilkinson], *Improvisations from the Spirit*.

Williamson 1909: G. C. Williamson, *Murray Marks and his Friends*.

WMG: William Morris Gallery, London.

WMR 1867: W. M. Rossetti, *Fine Art, Chiefly Contemporary*.

WMR 1868: W. M. Rossetti, 'Notes on the Royal Academy Exhibition of 1868.'

WMR 1884: W. M. Rossetti, 'Notes on Rossetti and his Works', *Art Journal*.

WMR 1886: *The Collected Works of Dante Gabriel Rossetti*, ed. W. M. Rossetti, 2 vols.

WMR 1889: W. M. Rossetti, *D. G. Rossetti as Designer and Writer*.

WMR 1905: W. M. Rossetti, *A Bibliography of Dante Gabriel Rossetti*.

WMR Diary 1880: *Victorian Poetry*, 1982.

Wood 1904: Esther Wood, *Dante Gabriel Rossetti and the Pre-Raphaelite Movement.*

Woodring 1952: C. R. Woodring, *Victorian Samplers.*

Works 1911: *The Works of Dante Gabriel Rossetti,* ed. W. M. Rossetti.

Worth 1964: G. J. Worth, *James Hannay: his Life and Work.*

Wright 1919: Thomas Wright, *Life of John Payne.*

Yale: Beinecke Rare Books and MSS Library, Yale University.

Index